WONDERS OF THE SOLAR SYSTEM AND THE UNIVERSE

PROFESSOR BRIAN COX
& ANDREW COHEN

PART I

WONDERS OF THE SOLAR SYSTEM

WILLIAM
COLLINS

CHAPTER 1

THE WONDER

CHAPTER 2

EMPIRE OF THE SUN

CHAPTER 3

ORDER OUT OF CHAOS

CHAPTER 4

THE THIN BLUE LINE

CHAPTER 5

DEAD OR ALIVE

CHAPTER 6

ALIENS

CHAPTER 1

THE WONDER

There are worlds of searing heat and intense cold; planets with winds beyond the harshest of terrestrial hurricanes and moons with great sub-surface oceans of water.

On a frosty winter's afternoon the day after New Year 1959, a tiny metal sphere named *First Cosmic Ship* ascended, gently at first but with increasing ferocity, into a January sky above the Baikonur Cosmodrome a hundred miles east of the Aral Sea. Just a few minutes into her flight the little spacecraft separated from the third stage of her rocket and became the first man-made object to escape the gravitational grasp of planet Earth. On 4 January she passed by the Moon and entered a 450-day long orbit around the Sun somewhere between Earth and Mars, where she remains today. *First Cosmic Ship*, subsequently renamed *Luna 1,* is the oldest artificial planet and mankind's first explorer of the Solar System.

Half a century later, we have launched an armada of robot emissaries and twenty-one human explorers beyond Earth's gravitational grip and onwards to our neighbouring worlds. Five of our little craft have even escaped the gravitational embrace of the Sun on journeys that will ultimately take them to the stars. No longer confined to Earth, we now roam freely throughout the Empire of the Sun.

Our spacecraft have returned travellers' tales and gifts beyond value; an explorer's bounty that easily rivals the treasures, both material and intellectual, from the voyages of Magellan, Drake, Cook and their fellow navigators of Earth's oceans. As with all exploration, the journeys have been costly and difficult, but the rewards are priceless.

Our first half-century of space exploration – less than a human lifetime – has revealed that our Solar System is truly a place of wonders. There are worlds beset with violence and dappled with oases of calm; worlds of fire and ice, searing heat and intense cold; planets with winds beyond the harshest of terrestrial hurricanes and moons with great sub-surface oceans of water. In one corner of the Sun's empire there are planets where lead would flow molten across the surface, in another there are potential habitats for life beyond Earth. There are fountains of ice, volcanic plumes of sulphurous gases rising high into skies bathed in radiation and giant gas worlds ringed with pristine frozen water. A billion tiny worlds of rock and ice orbit our middle-aged yellowing Sun, stretching a quarter of the way to our nearest stellar neighbour, Proxima Centauri. What an empire of riches, and what a subject for a television series.

When we first began discussing making *Wonders of the Solar System,* we quickly realised that there is much

BELOW LEFT: A false colour close-up of the Great Red Spot, originally taken by the *Voyager 1* probe. The spot is a gigantic, stable weather system above the surface of Jupiter.

OVERLEAF: The barred spiral galaxy NGC 1672 in the constellation Dorado, seen by the Hubble Space Telescope.

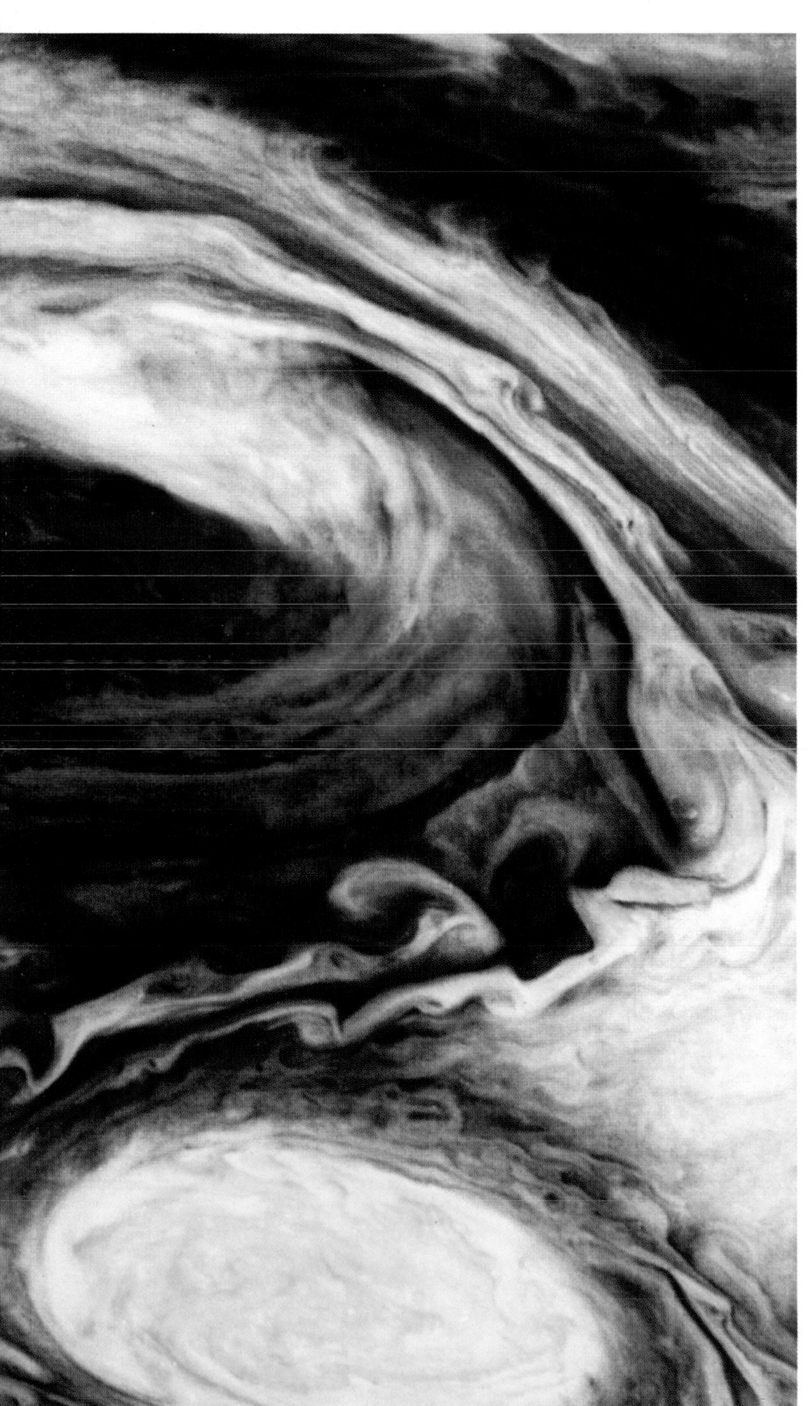

more to the exploration of space than the spectacular imagery and surprising facts and figures returned by our robot spacefarers. Each mission has contributed new pieces to a subtle and complex jigsaw, and as the voyages have multiplied, a greatly expanded picture of the majestic arena within which we live our lives has been revealed. Mission by mission, piece by piece, we have learnt that our environment does not stop at the top of our atmosphere. The subtle and complex gravitational interactions of the planets with our Sun and the billions of lumps of rock and ice in orbit around it have directly influenced the evolution of the Earth over the 4.5 billion years since its formation, and that influence continues today.

Our moon, unusually large for a satellite in relation to its parent planet, is thought to stabilise our seasons and therefore may have played an important role in allowing complex life on Earth to develop; we probably need our moon.

It is thought that comets from the far reaches of the outer Solar System delivered much of the water in Earth's oceans in a violent bombardment only half a billion years after our home planet formed. This event, known as the Late Heavy Bombardment, is thought to have been the result of an intense gravitational dance between the giant planets of our Solar System, Jupiter, Saturn and Neptune. Without this chance, violent intervention, there may have been little or no water on our planet; we probably need the comets, Jupiter, Saturn and Neptune.

More worryingly for us today, we have no reason to assume that this often-violent interaction with the other inhabitants of the Solar System has ceased; colossal lumps of rock and ice will visit us again from the distant vaults of the outer Solar System, and if undetected and unprepared for, we may not survive. It is thought that this very real threat is diminished by the gravitational influence of Jupiter on passing comets and asteroids, deflecting many of them out of our way; we probably need Jupiter.

This picture of the Solar System as a complex, interwoven and interacting environment stretching way beyond the top of our atmosphere is one of the central stories running throughout the series. In order to understand our place in space we must lift our eyes upwards from Earth's horizon and gaze outwards across a vast sphere extending perhaps for a light year beyond the Kuiper belt of comets and onwards to the edge of the Oort cloud of ice-worlds surrounding the Sun.

Our exploration of the Solar System has also given us very valuable insights into some of the most pressing and urgent problems we face today. Understanding the Earth's complex weather and climate system, and how it responds to changes such as the increase of greenhouse gases in the atmosphere, is perhaps the greatest challenge for early twenty-first century science. This is a planetary science challenge: Earth is one example of a planet with an atmosphere of a particular chemical composition, orbiting the Sun at a particular distance. For a scientist, having only one example of such a vast and interdependent system is less than ideal, and makes the task of understanding its subtle and complex behaviour tremendously difficult. Fortunately, we do have more than one example. Our Solar System is a cosmic laboratory, a diverse collection of hundreds of worlds, large and small, hot and cold. Some orbit closer to our star than we do, most are vastly further away. Some have atmospheres rich in greenhouse gases, far denser than our own, others have lost all but faint traces of their atmospheres to the vacuum of space. Our two planetary neighbours, Venus and Mars, are salient examples of what can happen to worlds very similar to Earth if conditions are slightly different. Venus experienced a runaway greenhouse effect that raised its surface temperature to over 400 degrees Celsius and atmospheric pressure to ninety times that of Earth. Because the laws of physics that control the evolution of planetary atmospheres are the same on Earth and Venus, our understanding of the Greenhouse Effect on Earth can be transferred to and tested on Venus. This provides valuable additional information that can be used to tune and improve those models. The discovery that this benign, blue planet which shimmers brightly and with such beauty in the twilight skies of Earth was transformed long ago into a hellish world of searing temperatures, acid rain and crushing pressure has had a genuine and profound psychological effect because it demonstrates in stark terms that runaway greenhouse effects can happen to planets not too dissimilar from our own.

Similar salutary insights have accrued from our studies of Mars. In the early days of Mars exploration, observations of the evolution of dust storms on the red planet provided support for the nuclear winter hypothesis on Earth. Storms that began in small local areas were observed to throw large amounts of dust into the Martian atmosphere. Over a period of a few weeks, the dust encircled the entire planet, exactly matching the models of the evolution of the dust and smoke clouds that would be created by a large-scale nuclear exchange. When a planet is shrouded in dust, the warmth of the Sun is reflected back into space and temperatures quickly fall, leading to a so-called nuclear winter that could last many decades. On Earth, this could lead to the extinction of many species, including perhaps our own.

Reaching for worlds beyond our grasp is an essential driver of progress and necessary sustenance for the human spirit. Curiosity is the rocket fuel that powers our civilization.

The observation of a mini-nuclear winter periodically playing itself out on Mars was a major factor in the acceptance of the theory, and this in turn profoundly influenced the thinking of major players at the end of the cold war. As former Russian president Mikhail Gorbachev said in 2000, 'Models made by Russian and American scientists showed that a nuclear war would result in a nuclear winter that would be extremely destructive to all life on Earth; the knowledge of that was a great stimulus to us, to people of honor and morality, to act in that situation'.

Wonders is also a story of human ingenuity and engineering excellence. Russia's *First Cosmic Ship* began its voyage beyond Earth just fifty-five years after the first powered flight by Orville and Wilbur Wright in December 1903. *Wright Flyer 1* was constructed from spruce and muslin, and powered by a twelve-horsepower petrol engine assembled in a bicycle repair shop. By 1969, less than one human lifetime away, Armstrong and Aldrin set foot on another world, launched by a Saturn V rocket whose giant

BELOW: Astronaut Ed White made the first American spacewalk during the *Gemini 4* mission on 3 June 1965, over the Pacific Ocean for twenty-three minutes.

OVERLEAF: Lift-off of the *Apollo 17 Saturn V Moon Rocket* from Kennedy Space Centre, Florida on 17 December 1972.

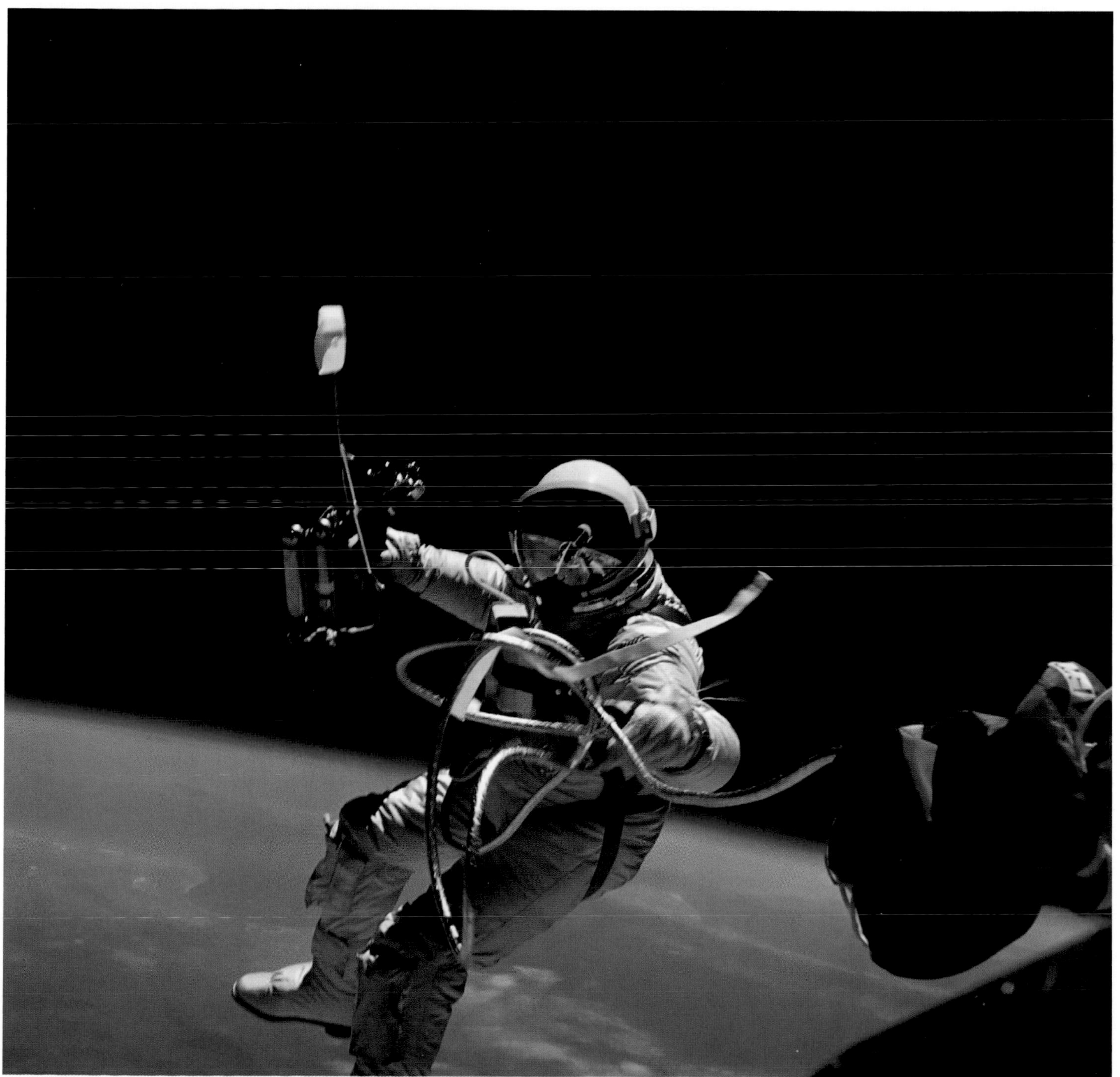

first-stage engines generated around 180 million horsepower between them. The most powerful and evocative flying machine ever built, the Moon rocket stood 111 metres (364 feet) high, just thirty centimetres (twelve inches) short of the dome of Wren's magisterial St Paul's Cathedral. Fully fuelled for a lunar voyage, it weighed 3,000 tonnes. Sixty-six years before *Apollo 11*'s half-a-million mile round trip to the Moon, *Wright Flyer 1* reached an altitude of three metres (ten feet) on its maiden voyage. This rate of technological advancement, culminating with our first journeys into the deep Solar System, is surely unparalleled in human history, and the benefits are practically incalculable.

Most importantly of all, *Wonders* is a celebration of the spirit of exploration. This is desperately relevant, an idea so important that celebration is perhaps too weak a word. It is a plea for the spirit of the navigators of the seas and the pioneers of aviation and spaceflight to be restored and cherished; a case made to the viewer and reader that reaching for worlds beyond our grasp is an essential driver of progress and necessary sustenance for the human spirit. Curiosity is the rocket fuel that powers our civilization. If we deny this innate and powerful urge, perhaps because earthly concerns seem more worthy or pressing, then the borders of our intellectual and physical domain will shrink with our ambitions. We are part of a much wider ecosystem, and our prosperity and even long-term survival are contingent on our understanding of it.

In 1962, John F. Kennedy made one of the great political speeches at Rice University in Houston, Texas. In the speech, he argued the case for America's costly and wildly ambitious conquest of the Moon. Imagine the bravado, the sheer power and confidence of vision in committing to a journey across a quarter of a million miles of space, landing on another world and returning safely to Earth. It might have been perceived as hubris at the time, but it worked. America achieved this most audacious feat of human ingenuity within nine years of launching their first manned sub-orbital flight. Next time you glance up at our shimmering satellite, give a thought to the human beings just like you who decided to go there and plant their flag for all mankind.

At the turn of the twenty-first century, the Solar System is our civilization's frontier. Our first steps into the unexplored lands above our heads have been wildly successful, revealing a treasure chest of new worlds and giving us priceless insights into our planet's unique beauty and fragility. As a species, we are constantly balanced on a knife-edge, prone to parochial disputes and unable to harness our powerful curiosity and boundless ingenuity. The exploration of the Solar System has brought out the best in us, and this is a precious gift. It rips away our worst instincts and forcibly thrusts us into a face-to-face encounter with the best. We are compelled to understand that we are one species amongst millions, living on one planet around one star amongst billions, inside one galaxy amongst trillions. The beauty of our planet is made manifest, enhanced immeasurably by the juxtaposition with other worlds. Ultimately, the value of young, curious and wonderful humanity as we take our first steps outwards from our home world is brought into such startling relief that all who share in the wonder must surely be filled with optimism and a powerful desire to continue this most valuable of journeys ◉

'Many years ago the great British explorer George Mallory, who was to die on Mount Everest, was asked why did he want to climb it. He said, "Because it is there." Well, space is there, and we're going to climb it, and the Moon and the planets are there, and new hopes for knowledge and peace are there. And, therefore, as we set sail we ask God's blessing on the most hazardous and dangerous and greatest adventure on which man has ever embarked.'

— John F. Kennedy, Rice University 1962

RIGHT: The first manned lunar landing mission, *Apollo 11*, launched from the Kennedy Space Centre on 16 July 1969. Aboard the spacecraft were astronauts Neil Armstrong, Michael Collins and Edwin E. (Buzz) Aldrin. In this photograph, Aldrin walks past some rocks, easily carrying scientific equipment which would have been too heavy to carry on Earth.

CHAPTER 3
COMET
CHAPTER 3
URANUS
CHAPTER 4
THE MAGELLAN SPACE PROBE
CHAPTER 5
MARS
CHAPTER 2
CHAPTER 3
MOON
CHAPTER 4
THE 'ENGLISH ELECTRIC LIGHTNING'
CHAPTER 6
ASTEROID 951 GASPRA
CHAPTER 5
MERCURY
CHAPTER 6
EARTH
CHAPTER 2
SUN
CHAPTER 5
VENUS
CHAPTER 2
HUBBLE TELESCOPE
CHAPTER 6
JUPITER

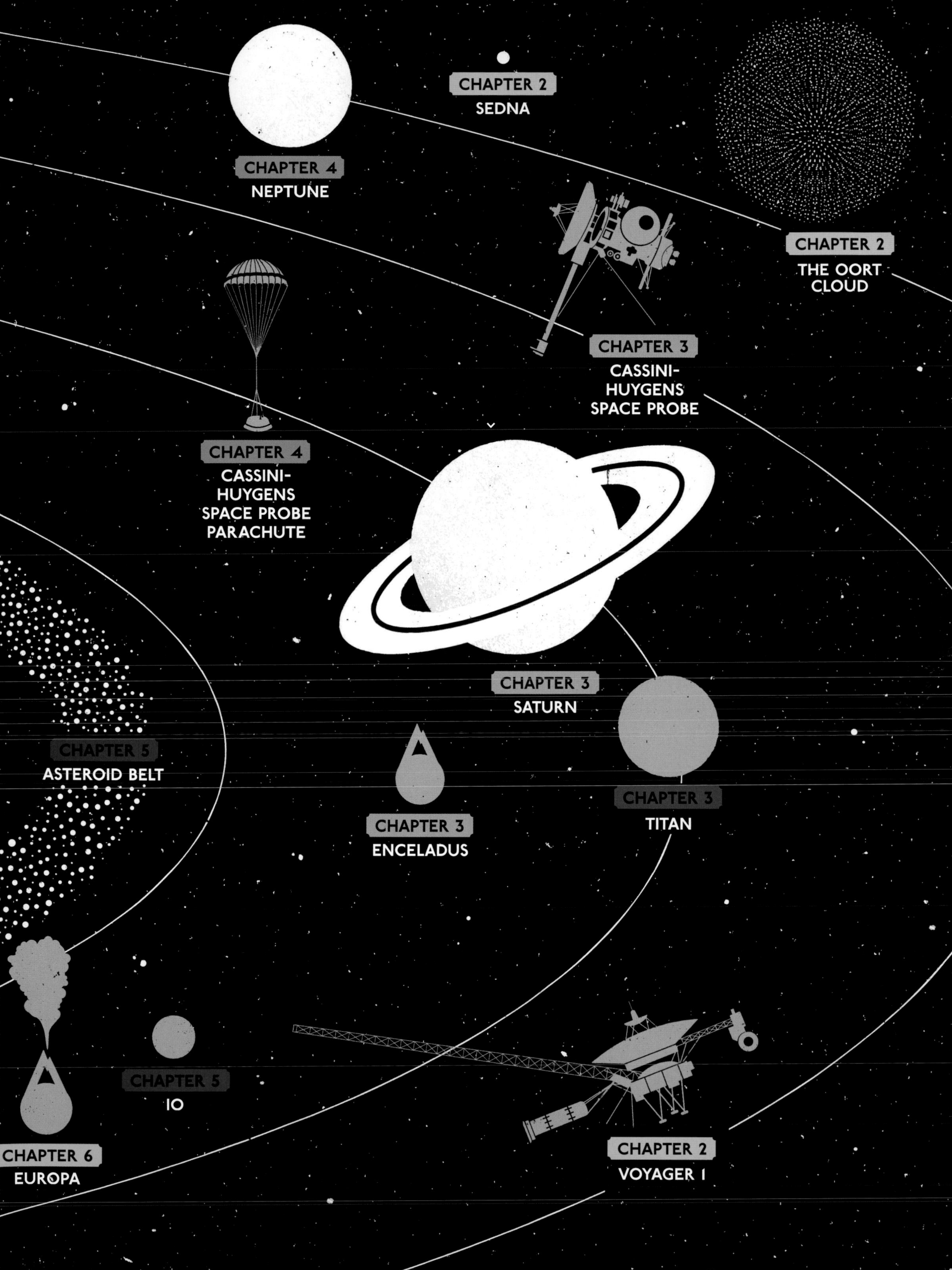
CHAPTER 2
SEDNA
CHAPTER 4
NEPTUNE
CHAPTER 2
THE OORT CLOUD
CHAPTER 3
CASSINI-HUYGENS SPACE PROBE
CHAPTER 4
CASSINI-HUYGENS SPACE PROBE PARACHUTE
CHAPTER 3
SATURN
CHAPTER 5
ASTEROID BELT
CHAPTER 3
TITAN
CHAPTER 3
ENCELADUS
CHAPTER 5
IO
CHAPTER 6
EUROPA
CHAPTER 2
VOYAGER 1

प्रदूषण नियन्त्रण खण्ड
प्रदेश जल निगम
AKTion
And World
paint you Not
Wear
IS
MINE

CHAPTER 2

EMPIRE OF THE SUN

AN ORDINARY STAR

At the heart of our complex and fascinating Solar System sits its powerhouse. For us it is everything, and yet it is just one ordinary star amongst 200 billion stars within our galaxy. It is a large wonder that greets us every morning; a star that controls each and every world that it holds in its thrall – the Sun. The Sun reigns over a vast empire of worlds and without it we would be nothing; life on Earth would not exist. Although we live in the wonderous empire of the Sun, it is a place we can never hope to visit. However, thanks to the continual advances in technology and space exploration, and through observation from here on Earth, each spectacular detail we see leads us closer to understanding the enigma that is the Sun.

BELOW: In July 2009, pilgrims flocked to Varanasi, on the sacred river Ganges, not just to bathe in the holy waters but also to watch the longest total eclipse of the Sun of the twenty-first century.

In the north of India, on the banks of the river Ganges, lies the holy city of Varanasi. It is one of the oldest continuously inhabited cities in the world, and for Hindus it is one of the holiest sites in all of India.

Varanasi, or Benares, to give the city its old name, is a city suffused with the colours, sounds and smells of a more ancient India. Mark Twain famously wrote: 'Benares is older than history, older than tradition, older even than legend, and looks twice as old as all of them put together'.

Each year a million pilgrims visit Varanasi to bathe in the holy river and pray in the hundreds of temples that cover the city. Part of what makes the city so special is the orientation of its sacred river as it flows past; it's the only place where the Ganges turns around to the north, making it the one spot on the river where you can bathe while watching the Sun rise on the eastern shore. And sunrise over Varanasi is certainly one of Earth's great sights. The humid, tropical air adds a soporific quality to the light, which in turn lends a fairy-tale quality to the brightly coloured buildings and palaces that line the holy river. It is a misty, pastel-shaded, dream-like experience, as though the city is materialising not from the dawn but from the past.

But on 22 July 2009, at precisely 6.24am, a different type of pilgrim was to be found waiting beside the Ganges to witness one of the true wonders of the Solar System.

At this time, across a small strip of the Earth's surface, the longest total eclipse of the Sun since June 1991 was about to be visible to a lucky few. For three and a half minutes the Moon would cover the face of the Sun and plunge this ancient city into darkness ◉

SOLAR ECLIPSES

A total solar eclipse is possibly the most visual and visceral example of the structure and rhythm of our solar system. It is a very human experience, and one that lays bare the mechanics of this system.

At the centre is the Sun, reigning over an empire of worlds that move like clockwork. Everything within its realm obeys the laws of celestial mechanics discovered by Sir Isaac Newton in the late seventeenth century. These laws allow us to predict exactly where every world will be for centuries to come. And wherever you happen to be, if there's a moon between you and the Sun, there will be a solar eclipse at some point in time.

Eclipses occur all over the Solar System; Jupiter, Saturn, Uranus and Neptune all have moons and so eclipses around these planets are a frequent occurrence. On Saturn, the moon Titan passes between the Sun and the ringed planet every fifteen years, while on the dwarf planet Pluto, eclipses with its large moon, Charon, occur in bursts every 120 years. But the king of eclipses is the gas giant Jupiter; with four large moons orbiting the planet, it's common to see the shadow of moons such as Io, Ganymede and Europa moving across the Jovian cloud tops. Occasionally the eclipses can be even more spectacular. In spring 2004, the Hubble telescope took a rare picture (opposite top) in which you can see the shadows of three moons on Jupiter's surface; three eclipses occurring simultaneously. Although this kind of event happens only once every few decades, the timing of Jupiter's eclipses is as predictable as every other celestial event. For hundreds of years we've been able to look up at the night sky and know exactly what will happen when. Historically, this precise understanding of the motion of the Solar System provided the foundation upon which a much deeper understanding of the structure and workings of our universe rests. A wonderful example is the extraordinary calculation performed by the little-known Dutch astronomer Ole Romer in the 1670s. Romer was one of many astronomers who attempted to solve a puzzle that seemed to make no sense.

The eclipses of the Galilean moons, Io, Europa, Ganymede and Callisto, by Jupiter were accurately predicted once their orbits had been plotted and understood. But it was soon observed that the moons vanished and reappeared behind Jupiter's disc about twenty minutes later than expected when Jupiter was on the far side of the Sun (the accurate modern figure is seventeen minutes). When the predictions of a scientific theory disagree with evidence the theory must be modified or even rejected, unless an explanation can be found. Newton's beautiful clockwork Solar System was on trail.

Romer was the first to realise that this delay was not a glitch in the clockwork Solar System. Instead, it was caused because light takes time to travel from Jupiter to Earth. The eclipses of the Galilean moons happen just as Newton predicts, but we don't see the eclipses on earth until slightly later than predicted when Jupiter moves further away from the Earth, simply because it takes more time for light to travel a greater distance.

From this beautifully simple observation of the eclipses of Jupiter, fellow Dutch astronomer Christiaan Huygens was able to make the first calculation of the speed of light. The speed of light, we now know, is a fundamental property of our universe. It is one of the universal numbers that is unchanging and fixed throughout the cosmos. Ultimately, an understanding of its true significance had to wait until Einstein's theory of space and time, Special Relativity, in 1905, but the long and winding road of discovery can be traced back to Romer and his eclipses.

Closer to home, eclipses become even more familiar. In 2004, the Mars Exploration Rover Opportunity looked up from the surface of Mars and took possibly the most beautiful picture of any extraterrestrial eclipse (opposite bottom). In this remarkable image you can see Mars' moon Phobos as it makes its way across the Sun – an image of a partial solar eclipse from the surface of another world.

Eclipses on Mars are not only possible but commonplace, with hundreds occurring each year, but one event we will never see on Mars is a total solar eclipse.

A TOTAL SOLAR ECLIPSE
This natural phenomenon occurs when the moon passes between the Earth and the Sun, completely obscuring the view of the Sun from Earth.

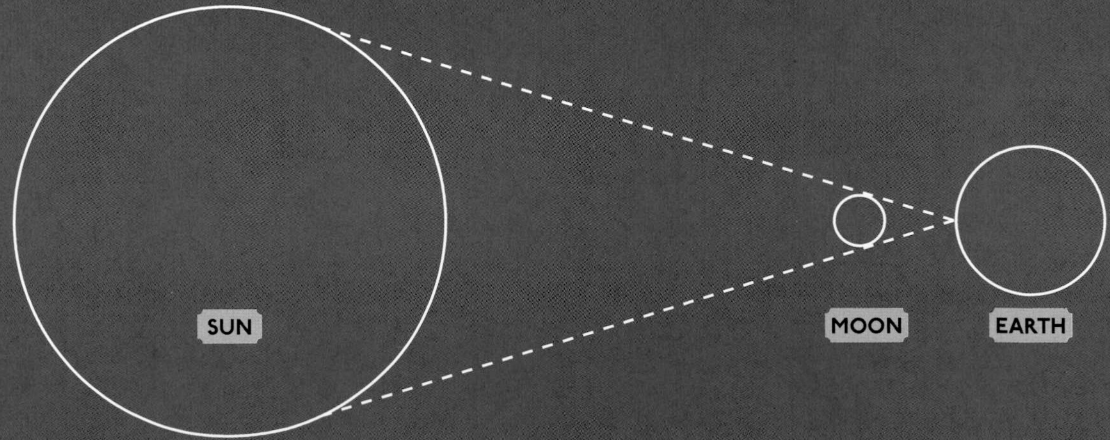

Here on Earth, though, humans have the best seat in the Solar System from which to enjoy the spectacle of a total eclipse of the Sun – all thanks to a wonderful quirk of fate.

For a perfect total solar eclipse to occur, a moon must appear to be exactly the same size in the sky as the Sun. On every other planet in the Solar System the moons are the wrong size and the wrong distance from the Sun to create the perfect perspective of a total solar eclipse. However, here on Earth the heavens have arranged themselves in perfect order. The Sun is 400 times the diameter of the Moon and, by sheer coincidence, it's also 400 times further away from the Earth. So when our moon passes in front of the Sun it can completely obscure it.

With over 150 moons in the Solar System you might expect to find other total solar eclipses, but none produce such perfect eclipses as the Earth's moon. It won't last forever, though; The clockwork of the Solar System is such that the raising of the tides on Earth caused by the Moon has consequences. As the Earth spins beneath tidal bulges raised by the Moon, its rate of rotation is gradually, almost imperceptibly, reduced by friction, and this has the effect of causing the Moon to gradually drift further and further away from Earth. This complex dance, in precise accord with Newton's laws, is also responsible for the fact that we only see one side of the Moon from the Earth – a phenomenon called spin-orbit locking.

The drift is tiny, only around 4 centimetres (1.6 inches) per year, but over the vast expanses of geological time it all adds up. Around 65 million years ago the Moon was much closer to Earth and the dinosaurs would not have been able to see the perfect eclipses we see today. The Moon would have been closer to Earth and would therefore have completely blotted out the Sun with room to spare. In the future, as the Moon moves away from the Earth, the unique alignment will slowly begin to degrade; while drifting away from our planet the Moon will become smaller in the sky and eventually too small to cover the Sun. This accidental arrangement of the Solar System means that we are now living in exactly the right place and at exactly the right time to enjoy the most precious of astronomical events ◉

BELOW: The king of eclipses. This image from NASA's Hubble space telescope clearly shows three black circles on Jupiter's surface, which are the shadows cast by three of the largest moons that circle the planet.

BOTTOM: The three images from left to right are taken by the Mars Exploration Rover Opportunity and show the journey of Mars's moon Phobos as it passes over the disk of the Sun in a partial solar eclipse.

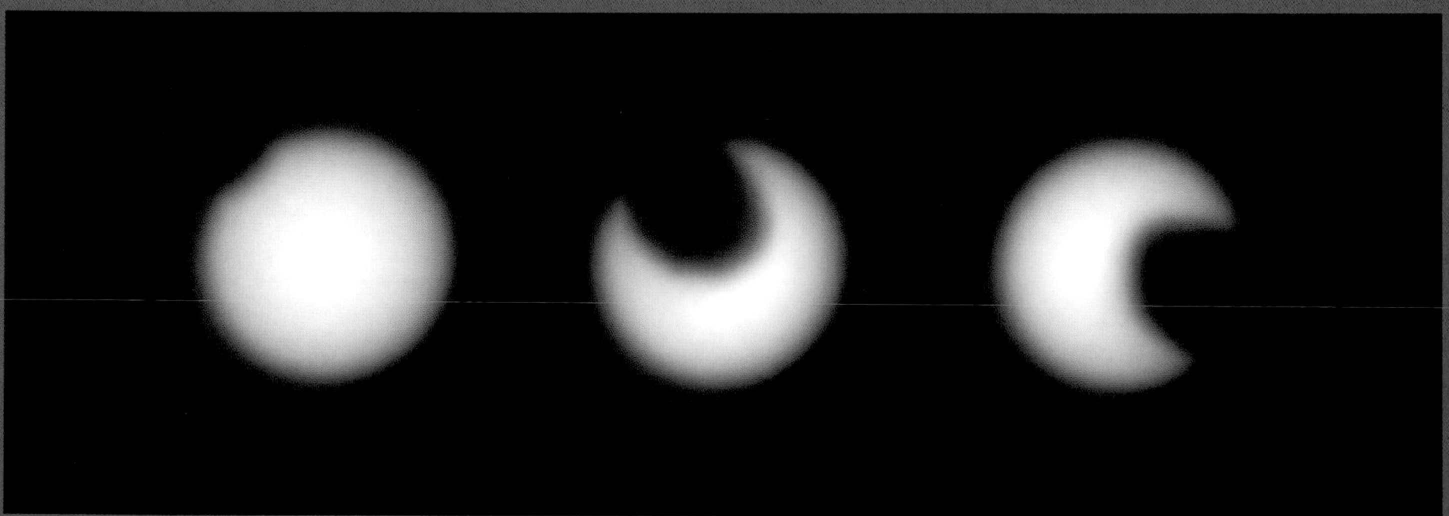

IN THE REALM OF THE SUN

Our closest star is the strangest, most alien place in the Solar System. It's a place we can never hope to visit, but through space exploration and a few chance discoveries our generation is getting to know the Sun in exquisite new detail. For us it's everything, and yet it's just one ordinary star among 200 billion starry wonders that make up our galaxy. To explore the realm of our sun requires a journey of over thirteen billion kilometres; a journey that takes us from temperatures reaching fifteen million degrees Celsius, in the heart of our star, to the frozen edge of the Solar System where the Sun's warmth has long disappeared.

On 14 November 2003, three American scientists discovered a dwarf planet at the remotest frontier of the Solar System. Sedna is a planetoid three times more distant from the Sun than Neptune. Around 1,600 kilometres (1,000 miles) in diameter, Sedna is barely touched by the Sun's warmth; its surface temperature never rises above -240 degrees Celsius. For most of its orbit Sedna is further from our star than any other known planetoid. On its slow journey around the Sun, one complete orbit – Sedna's year – takes 12,000 Earth years. From its frozen surface at least thirteen billion kilometres from Earth, a view of the Sun rising on Sedna would give a very different perspective on our solar system and a clear depiction of how far the Sun's realm stretches. Sunrise on Sedna is no more than the rising of a star in the night sky: from this frozen place, our blazing sun is just another star.

To travel from the outer reaches of Sedna's orbit to one of the first true planets of the Solar System we would need to cover over ten billion kilometres. Uranus was the first planet to be discovered with the use of a telescope, in 1781, by Sir William Herschel, and like all the giant planets (except Neptune) it is visible with the naked eye. Even so, sunrise on Uranus is barely perceptible; the Sun hangs in the sky 300

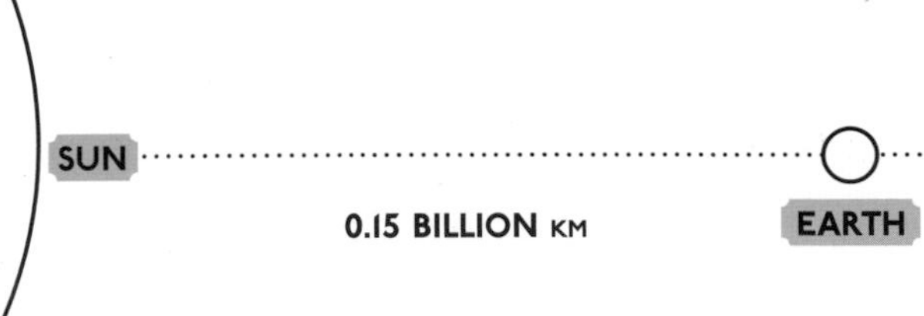

LEFT: Minor planet Sedna, discovered in 2003, is located at the most remote frontier of the Solar System. From the frozen planetoid, the Sun would appear merely as a remote star.

BELOW: This atmospheric shot of the Sun setting behind the Gusev crater on Mars was captured by the Exploration Rover Spirit. On Mars, twilight can last two hours.

times smaller than it appears on Earth. Only when we have travelled the two and a half billion kilometres past Jupiter and Saturn do we arrive at the first world with a more familiar view of the Sun. Over 200 million kilometres out, sunset on Mars is a strangely familiar sight. On 19 May 2005, the Mars Exploration Rover Spirit captured this eerie view as the Sun sank below the rim of the Gusev crater. The panoramic mosaic image was taken by the rover at 6.07pm, on the rover's 489th day of residency on the red planet. This sunset shot is not only beautiful, but it also tells us something fundamental about the Martian sky. Repeated observations have revealed that twilight on Mars is a rather long affair, lasting for up to two hours before sunrise and two hours after sunset. The reason for this long slow progression to and from darkness is the fine dust that is whipped up off the surface of Mars and lifted to incredibly high altitudes. At this height the Sun's rays are scattered by the dust from the sunlit side of Mars around to the dark side, producing the long, leisurely and beautiful journey between day and night. Here on Earth, some of the longest and most spectacular sunrises and sunsets are produced by a similar mechanism, when tiny dust grains are catapulted high into the atmosphere by powerful volcanoes, scattering light into extra-colourful moments on our planet.

Moving past Earth, which is 150 million kilometres out, we head to the heart of the Solar System. Mercury is the closest planet to the Sun, just forty-six million kilometres (twenty-nine million miles) away. It spins so slowly that sunrise to sunrise lasts for 176 Earth days. Beyond it there is nothing but the naked Sun, a colossal fiery sphere of tortured matter burning with a core temperature of about fifteen million degrees Celsius. The sheer scale of the Sun is difficult to conceive; at 1,400,000 kilometres (865,000 miles) across it is over 100 times the diameter of Earth, which means you could fill it with over a million Earths. Its mass is 2×10^{30} kilograms – 330,000 times that of our planet. If you add up the masses of all the planets, dwarf planets, moons and asteroids, you would find they contribute less than half a per cent of the total mass of the Solar System. The Sun is dominant – the rest is an afterthought ◉

Throughout human history, this majestic wonder has been a constant source of comfort, awe and worship, but our understanding of the Sun has developed slowly. For centuries, the finest minds in science struggled to understand how it created such a seemingly endless source of heat and energy. As recently as the nineteenth century science had little knowledge of what the Sun was made of, where it had come from, or the secret of its phenomenal power.

LEFT: Our brightest star. The Sun is just one of billions of stars, but to all living things on Earth it is of crucial importance – without it no life could exist.

THE ENERGY OF THE SUN

BELOW LEFT: Using just an umbrella, a tin of water and a thermometer, we measured the energy given off by the Sun in Death Valley, California – regularly the hottest place on the planet.

RIGHT: What appears to be a hole in the night sky is actually Molecular Cloud Barnard 68. This cloud of dust and molecular gas will eventually form a bright new star system.

In 1833, John Herschel, the most famous astronomer of his generation, travelled to the Cape of Good Hope in South Africa on an ambitious astronomical adventure to map the stars of the southern skies. This voyage was the end of an extraordinary odyssey for the Herschel family; he completed the work his father, William Herschel, had begun in the northern skies 50 years earlier.

In 1838, Herschel attempted to answer one of the most fundamental questions we can ask about the Sun – how much energy does it produce? It may seem an incredibly ambitious calculation, but Herschel knew that to measure this 'solar constant' he would need nothing more than a thermometer, a tin of water, an umbrella and the predictable blue skies of Cape Town.

When you want to measure the Sun's radiation across billions of miles of space you need to start small. So Herschel began by asking how much energy the Sun delivers onto a small part of the Earth's surface – in this case, onto a tin full of water. Herschel waited until December to conduct this experiment, when the Sun would be directly overhead, then placed his tin under the shade of the umbrella in the midday Sun. Once the water had heated up to ambient temperature he removed the shade to allow the Sun to shine directly onto the water. In direct sunlight, the water temperature begins to rise and by timing how long it takes the Sun to raise the water temperature by one degree Celsius, Herschel could calculate exactly how much energy the Sun delivered into the can of water.

The calculation was simple because Herschel already knew something called the specific heat capacity of water – in modern units it is the amount of energy required to raise the temperature of 1 kilogramme of water by one Kelvin. Kelvin is a temperature scale usually favoured in science: 1 Kelvin = 1 degree Celsius, and 0 Kelvin = -273 Celsius. (For the record, the specific heat capacity of water is 4187 Joules per kilogramme per Kelvin.) From this calculation it's a small step to scale the number up and work out how much energy is delivered to a square metre of the surface of the Earth in one second. It turns out that on a clear day, when the Sun is vertically overhead, that number is about a kilowatt. That equates to ten 100-watt bulbs being powered by the Sun's energy for every metre squared of the Earth's surface.

With this number Herschel could now take a leap of imagination and calculate the entire energy output of the Sun. He knew that the Earth is 150 million kilometres (93 million miles) away from the Sun, so he created an imaginary giant sphere around the Sun with a radius of 150 million kilometres.

Every second the Sun produces 400 million million million million watts of power – that is a million times the power consumption of the United States every year – radiated in one second.

By adding up each of those kilowatts for every square metre of this entirely imaginary sphere, he was able to estimate the total energy output of the Sun per second. It's a number that begins to reveal the sheer magnitude of our star. Every second the Sun produces 400 million million million million watts of power – that is a million times the power consumption of the United States every year – radiated in one second. It's an ungraspable power, but a power that we have calculated using the very simplest of experiments and some water, a thermometer, a tin and an umbrella.

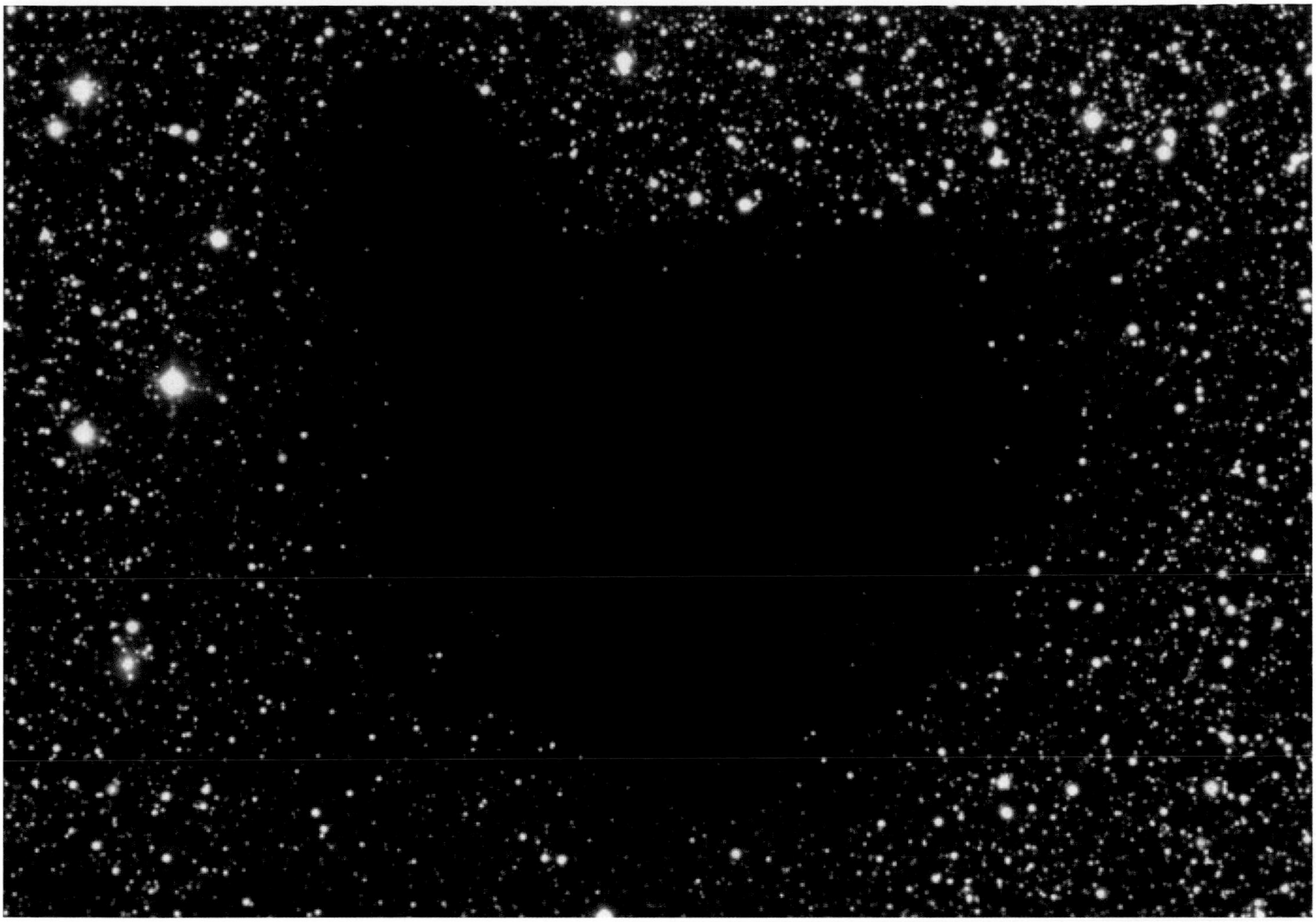

A STAR IS BORN

It's a wonder of the Sun that it has managed to keep up this phenomenal rate of energy production for millennia. Stars like the Sun are incredibly long-lived and stable – our best estimate for the age of the Universe is 13.7 billion years, and the Sun has been around for nearly five billion years of that, making it about a third of the age of the Universe itself. So what possible power source could allow the Sun to shine with such intensity day after day for five billion years? The best way to find the answer is to go back to the beginning, to a time when this corner of the galaxy was without light, and the Sun had yet to begin.

The picture above shows the Milky Way. The dark areas with an absence of stars are called molecular clouds; clouds of molecular hydrogen and dust that are lying between us and the stars of the Milky Way galaxy. Taken by the Very Large Telescope (VLT) at Paranal Observatory, in Chile, this image is of Barnard 68, a molecular cloud well within our galaxy at a distance of about 410 light years. Take a close look, because you are looking at a future star, a cloud of dust and gas that in the next 100,000 years or so will collapse and begin its journey to becoming a new light in the heavens.

Barnard 68, like all molecular clouds, contains the raw material from which stars are made, vast stellar nurseries that are among the coldest, most isolated places in the galaxy. This particular cloud is around half a light year across, or twenty million million kilometres, and has a mass that is about twice that of our sun. Most importantly, it is incredibly cold; in the heart of this cloud the temperature is no more than 4 Kelvin, that's -269 degrees Celsius. That matters because temperature is a measure of how fast things are moving, so in these clouds the clumps of hydrogen and dust are moving very slowly.

The stability of a cloud like Barnard 68 is in a fine balance. On one hand, the clumps of hygrogen and dust are moving around, which leads to an outward pressure that acts to expand the cloud. Counteracting this is the force of gravity – an attractive force between all the particles in the cloud that tries to collapse it inwards. In order for the cloud to become a star, gravity must gain the upper hand long enough to cause a dramatic collapse of the cloud. This can only happen if the particles are moving very slowly, i.e., if the temperature is low.

Over millennia gravity's weak influence dominates and the molecular clouds begin to collapse, forcing the hydrogen and dust together in ever-denser clumps. We have a name for clumps of gas and dust collapsing under their own gravity: protostars. As the clouds collapse further and further they begin to heat up and eventually in their cores they become hot enough for the hydrogen to begin to fuse into helium. The stars ignite, the clouds are no longer black and the life cycle of a new star has begun

Five billion years ago a star was born that would come to be known as the Sun. Its birth reveals the secret of our star's extraordinary resources of energy, because the Sun, like every other star, was set alight by the most powerful known force in the Universe.

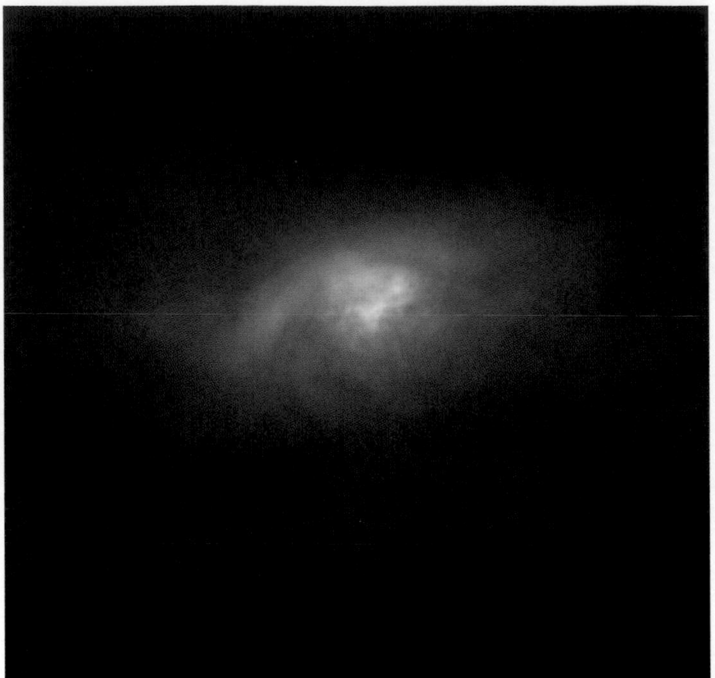

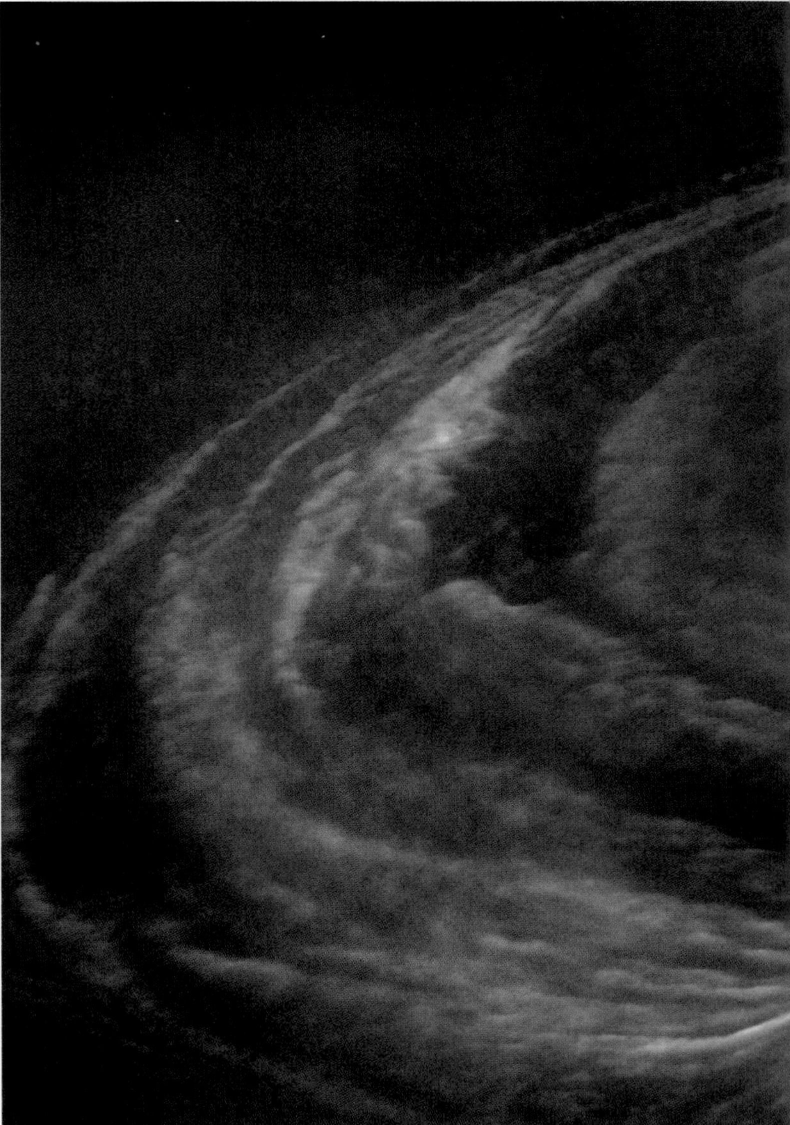

RIGHT: The Sun, as with any other star, was born from giant clouds of molecular dust and gas; it developed into a spinning ball of hot gas that is heated by a thermonuclear reaction at its core.

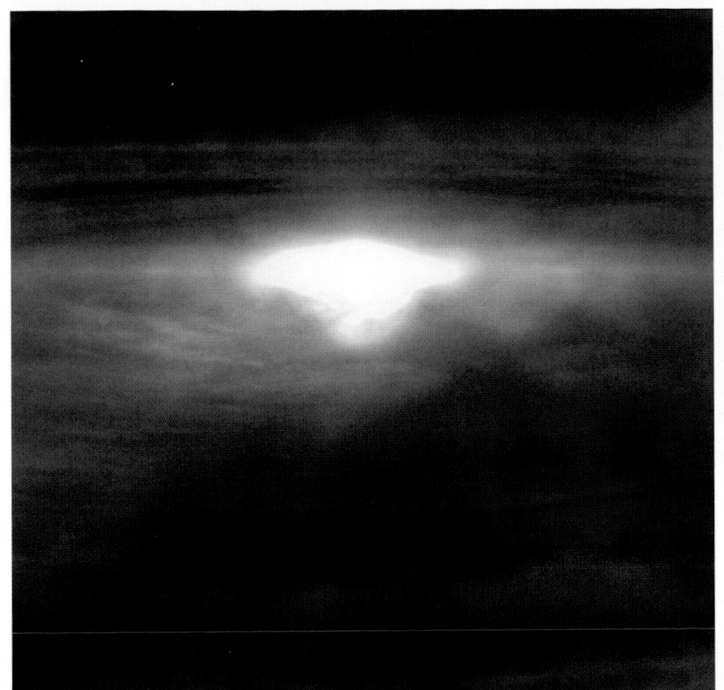

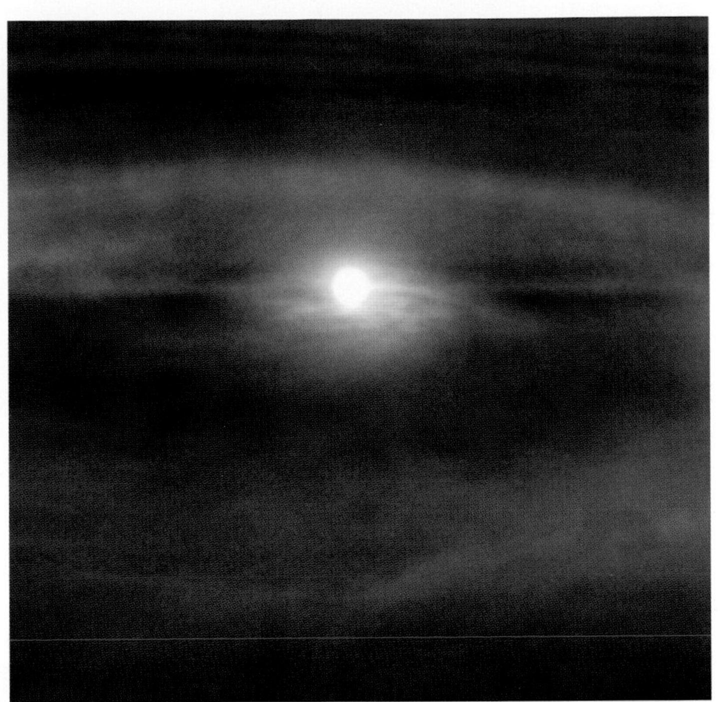

THE FORCES BEHIND THE SUN

RIGHT: The burning handle on the bottom right of the Sun shown here is known as the February 12 'prominence'. Prominences are loops of gas that are suspended above the surface of the Sun, which are anchored in place by opposing magnetic fields.

Nuclear fusion is the process by which all the chemical elements in the Universe, other than hydrogen, were produced. There are just three fundamental building blocks of matter required to make up everything we can see – from the most distant stars to the smallest piece of dust in our Solar System. Two kinds, the Up and Down quarks, make up the protons and neutrons in the atomic nuclei, and a third, the electrons, orbit around the nuclei to make atoms. These particles make up literally everything, including the book you are reading, the hand holding the book and the eyes reading the print. We live in a universe that is simple at heart!

The Universe today is, of course, far from simple. It is a complex, beautiful and diverse place with stars, planets and humans. Nuclear fusion is one of the primary processes that built that complexity.

The Universe began 13.7 billion years ago in the Big Bang. In the first instant it was unimaginably hot and dense, but it expanded and cooled very quickly. After just one second it was cold enough for the Up and Down quarks to stick together into protons and neutrons. The hydrogen nucleus is the simplest in nature, consisting of a single proton. Helium is the next simplest, built of two protons and one or two neutrons. Then comes lithium, beryllium, boron, carbon, nitrogen, oxygen and so on, each with one more proton and accompanying neutrons. This process of sticking more and more protons and neutrons together to form the chemical elements is known as nuclear fusion.

The process of fusion is not easy. Protons carry positive electric charge, which means that they feel a powerful repulsive force when they get close to one another. The force that drives them apart is one of the four fundamental forces of nature: electromagnetism. If the protons can get close enough, another force – called the strong nuclear force – takes over. The strong force is aptly named (it is the strongest in the Universe) and can easily overcome the weaker electromagnetic repulsion. We don't notice the strong force in everyday life because its effects are felt over a very short range and it stays trapped and hidden within the atomic nucleus.

The way to get protons close enough for fusion to occur is to heat them up to very high temperatures. As I've explained before, this is because temperature is a measure of how fast things are moving around; if the protons approach each other at high speed they can overcome the electromagnetic repulsion and get close enough for the strong force to take over and bind them together.

For the first few moments in the life of the Universe, all of space was filled with particles that were hot enough to smash together and fuse, but this only lasted a few brief minutes. Around ten minutes after the Big Bang, the Universe had cooled down enough for fusion to cease. At that time, our Cosmos was approximately 75 per cent hydrogen and 25 per cent helium, with very small traces of lithium. Fusion did not reappear in the Universe until the first stars were born, a few hundred million years later.

The high temperatures inside stars like our Sun mean that the hydrogen nuclei in their cores are moving fast enough for the electromagnetic repulsion to be overcome and the strong nuclear force to take over, initiating nuclear fusion. The process is quite complex and involved, and very, very slow. First, two protons must approach each

NUCLEAR FUSION
Naturally occurring in stars, this is the process by which several atomic nuclei fuse together to create one single heavier nucleus.

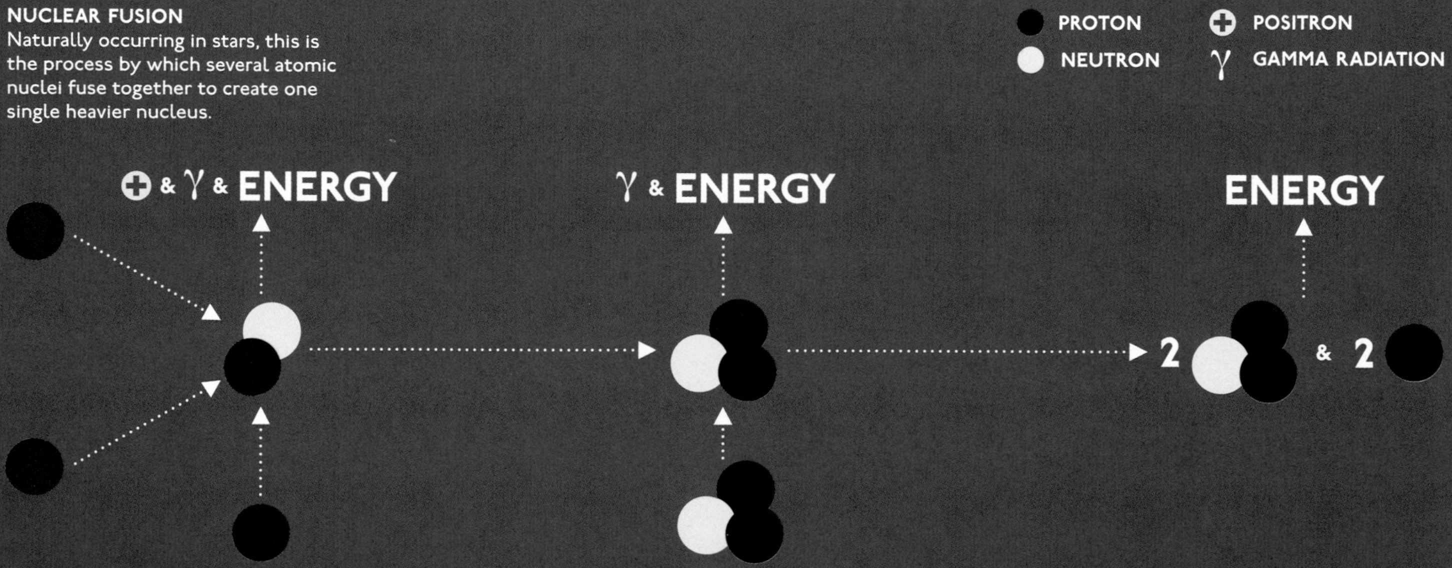

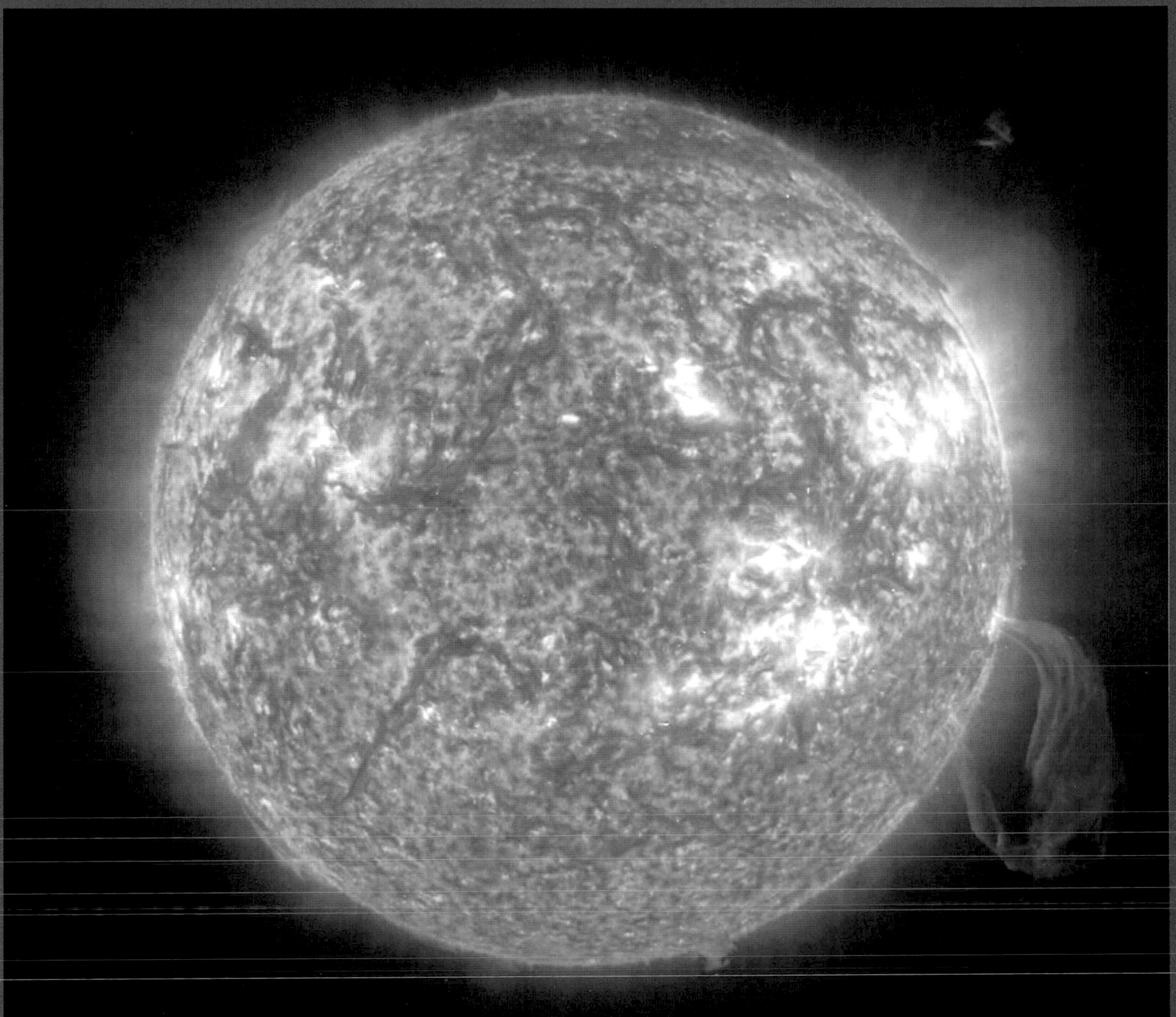

other to within a thousand million millionth's of a metre (written as 10^{-15} m). Then something very rare must happen – a proton must change into a neutron. This happens through the action of the third of the four forces of nature: the Weak Nuclear Force. The Weak Force is, as its name suggests, unlikely to act: an average proton will live for billions of years in the Sun's core before fusion begins.

When this first step towards fusion finally occurs, a closely bound proton and neutron are formed. This nucleus is known as Deuterium. In the process, an anti-matter electron (known as a positron) and a sub-atomic particle called a neutrino are released. There is also an important extra ingredient, which is the key to understanding why stars shine. If you add up the mass of the Deuterium, the electron and the little neutrino, you find that it is slightly less than the mass of the original two protons. Mass is lost in the fusion process and turned into energy. This is an application of Einstein's most famous equation: $E=mc^2$. This energy emerges from the Sun as sunshine – it is the primary power source for all life on Earth.

The fusion process then proceeds much more quickly because the action of the Weak Nuclear Force is no longer required. The positron bumps into an electron and disappears in another flash of energy. A proton fuses with the Deuterium nucleus to make a form of helium known as helium 3 (two protons and one neutron), and then two helium 3 nuclei fuse together to form helium 4 – the end product of fusion in the Sun – releasing two protons. At each stage mass is converted to energy, keeping the Sun hot and shining brightly.

At the end of their life, stars run out of hydrogen fuel in their cores and more complex fusion reactions occur. Heavier elements are produced – oxygen, carbon, nitrogen – the elements of life. Every element in the Universe today was fused together from the primordial hydrogen and helium left over from the Big Bang ◉

THE POWER OF SUNLIGHT

Once photons leave the Sun, the journey to Earth is a relatively short one. Light, like all forms of electromagnetic waves, travels at the same speed – almost 300 thousand kilometres a second, and so a photon leaving the surface of the Sun will reach the Earth in about eight minutes. Having travelled almost 150 million kilometres across space, each and every photon has a remarkable ability to shape and transform our planet.

ABOVE: The Iguaçu Falls, located on the border of Brazil and Argentina, is another example of how the power of the Sun shapes the contours of the Earth.

On the border of the Brazilian state of Paraná and the Argentine province of Misiones is the Iguaçu river. Stretching for over one thousand kilometres, the Iguaçu eventually flows into the Parana, one of the great rivers of the world. It's these river systems that eventually drain all the rainfall from the southern Amazonian basin into the Atlantic. Billions of gallons of water flow through this river system each day and all of it, every molecule in the river, every molecule in every raindrop in every cloud, has been transported from the Pacific over the Andes and into the continental interior here by the energy carried in single photons from our sun. The Sun is the power that lifts all the water on the Blue Planet, shaping and carving our landscape and creating some of the most breathtaking sights on Earth.

The Iguaçu Falls are one of the most spectacular natural wonders on our planet. Almost three kilometres (two miles) long, comprising over 275 individual falls and reaching heights of over 76 metres (250 feet), a quarter of a million gallons of water flow through the Falls every second.

The spectacular energy of these waterfalls is a wonderful example of how this planet is hardwired to the seemingly constant and unfailing power of the Sun. For centuries it was assumed that the Sun, like all the heavens, was perfect and unchanging, but gradually we've come to realise that the Sun is far more dynamic then just a perfect beautiful orb in the sky. Even tiny fluctuations in its brightness can have huge effects here on Earth ◉

SUNSPOTS: THE SEASONS OF THE SUN

BOTTOM: This cross-section of a sunspot visualises the temperatures around it. The red areas show where the temperature is higher than average; the blue where it is lower than average.

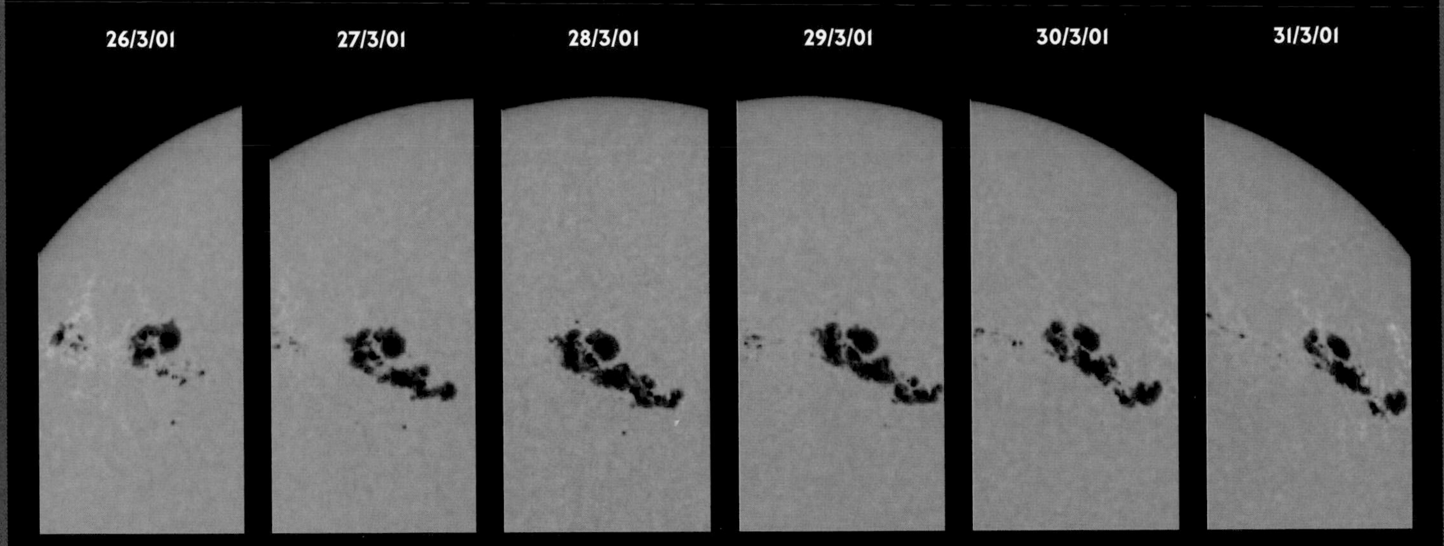

As long ago as 28 BC, Chinese astronomers in the Central Asian deserts had observed dark spots on the surface of the Sun. When the wind blew enough sand into the air to filter the Sun's glare they could see these strange spots and recorded them in the Chinese history book, *The Book of Han*. Over the next 1,500 years many other people recorded these strange dark spots on the surface of the Sun, but it wasn't until the invention of the telescope that Galileo was able to correctly explain the phenomena of sunspots.

The picture on the opposite page was taken by the SOHO spacecraft – the Solar and Heliospheric Observatory that was launched in December 1995. SOHO is giving us unprecedented detail on the life of our Sun and delivering the most beautiful and intricate images of our star that we've ever seen. In the picture above (also taken by SOHO) you can see a beautiful example of the birth, life and death of a sunspot. It may look small compared to the size of the Sun, but the sunspot you are looking at is in fact bigger than the Earth. Sunspots are transient events on the surface of the Sun that are caused by intense magnetic activity that inhibits the flow of heat from deep within the Sun up to the surface. These spots appear dark because they are dramatically cooler than the surrounding area – often 2,000 degrees Celsius cooler. In the eighteenth century it was thought they might even be cool enough to allow humans to land on the surface of a sunspot, but at a toasty 3,000–4,500 degrees Celsius even these cool spots on the Sun would melt a spaceship instantaneously.

Sunspots expand and contract as they move across the surface of the Sun, and they can be as large as

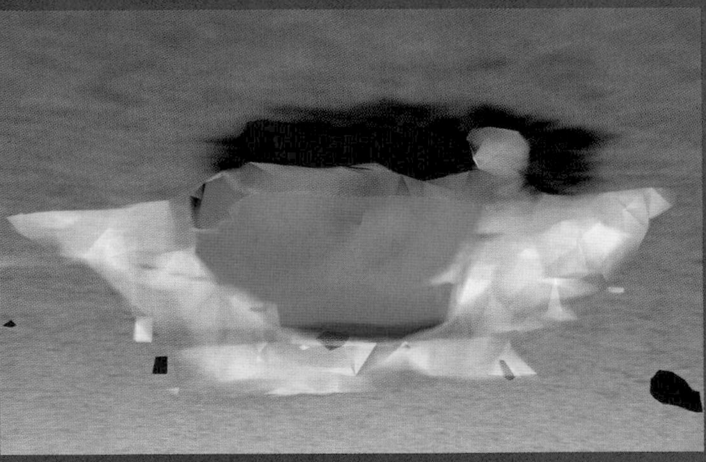

80,000 kilometres (50,000 miles) in diameter, making larger ones visible from Earth without a telescope. Advanced technology and space observation now allows us to track their numbers as they ebb and flow across the face of the Sun.

Since sunspots are cooler areas than on the rest of the Sun, we might have expected to find that the power of the Sun dimmed when the sunspot activity was at its height. In fact, we've found the opposite to be true: the greater the number of sunspots, the more powerful our star becomes. This variation is not just random, as we have studied the Sun in greater and greater detail we have begun to observe patterns emerging; patterns that seem to have direct links to our climate back here on Earth. We've discovered that the Sun has seasons

BELOW AND TOP OPPOSITE: The dark spots that appear on the surface of the Sun are fleeting blemishes. Sunspots expand and contract as they move across the Sun's surface; these photos were taken using the SOHO observatory, but some sunspots are so large that they are visible from Earth without the aid of a telescope.

THE SUN AND EARTH: SHARING A RHYTHM?

For decades scientists have sought to understand how these subtle changes in the Sun's power might be affecting the Earth. It's a puzzle that led one man to look away from the Sun and focus instead on the rivers around the Iguaçu Falls. Argentinean astrophysicist Pablo Mauas has spent the last decade analysing data that details every aspect of this river system – from water levels to flow rates – from 1904 all the way through the twentieth century. Unlike many of the world's great rivers, the Parana is so large that it can be navigated by very big ships – and where there are ships there are records. These records enabled Pablo to uncover an extraordinary history and to reveal that, just like sunspots, the river too has a rhythm.

Pablo and his team found that the stream flow of the river fluctuated dramatically three times during the last century, but the records gave no indication as to what was behind these fluctuations. The amount of water in the river Parana seems to follow a pattern, and Pablo had a hunch that this rhythm might be connected to the rhythms of the Sun. To try to link events on the Sun, 150 million kilometres away, to the flow of the great Parana, Pablo looked first at the most obvious rhythm of our star.

We've known for over 150 years (since the German astronomer Heinrich Schwabe collated the data that stemmed back to Galileo's earliest observations of sunspots) that the Sun follows a cycle that is repeated approximately every eleven years. This cycle reflects a rhythmic variation in the number of sunspots, which gives us a very clear indication of the amount of radiation given off by the Sun: the greater the number of sunspots, the greater the energy that is reaching the Earth. But when Pablo Mauas looked for a link between the Paranas rhythm and the eleven-year cycle, at first he found nothing. So instead he turned to calculations that described the Sun's underlying brightness during the last century. We already know that climate change and events such as El Niño can boost the flow of the river, but when Pablo removed both of these effects from the data there appeared to be a strong relationship between the solar data and the stream flow. Superimpose the solar data on the water levels in the river (see below) and you see that when solar activity rises, the volume of water in the river goes up. There is a beautiful correlation between the flow in these rivers and the solar output. Pablo has revealed an amazing link across 150 million kilometres of space that may one day help us to not only better understand the impact of the Sun on our climate, but also to predict the likelihood of floods in the heavily populated waterways of one of South America's greatest rivers.

Changes in the Sun seem to move weather systems elsewhere, too. In India, the monsoon appears to follow a similar pattern to the river Parana, boosting precipitation when solar activity is at its greatest, whereas in the Sahara desert the opposite seems to occur: more solar activity means less rain. The exact mechanisms by which our star may affect Earth's weather remain, for now, a mystery. We know that the energy production rate of the Sun – the power released in the fusion reactions at the core – is very constant, indeed. It doesn't change, as far as we can tell, and so the changes that we see must be to do with the way in which the energy exits the Sun. And while the amount of radiation that falls onto the surface of the Earth is only at the tenths of a per cent level, it really does reveal the intimacy and delicacy of the connection between the Sun and the Earth ◉

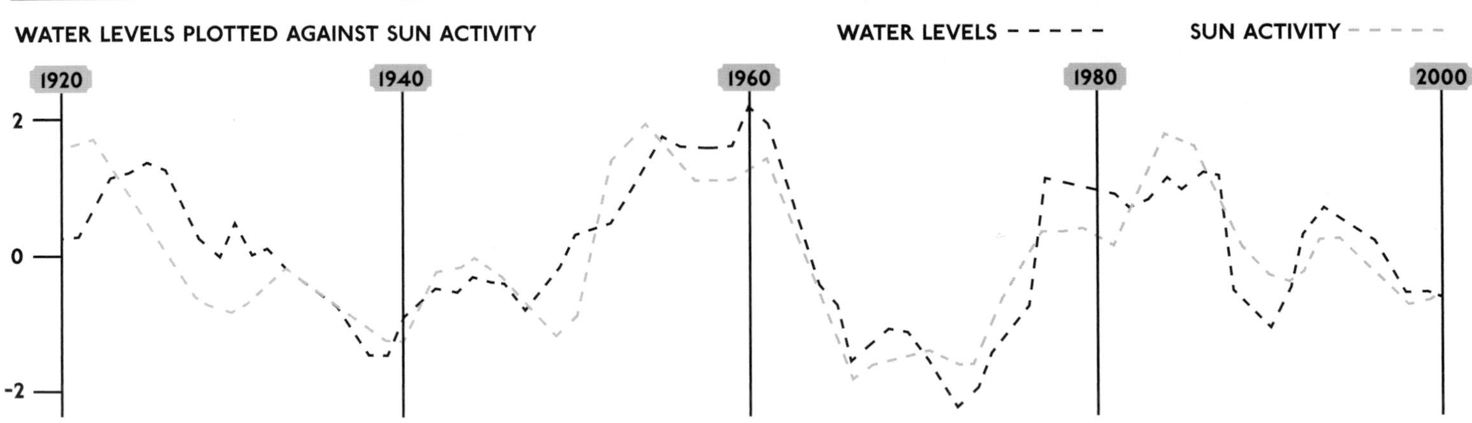

LEFT AND BELOW: Argentinean physicist Pablo Mauas's research suggested that there may be a direct correlation between the activity of the Sun and the flow of the Parana River.

HOW TO CATCH A SUNBEAM

We are tied to our star in the most intimate of ways. All the planets in our solar system are bathed in varying levels of sunlight, but only on one do we know of a phenomenon that does more than just passively receive the warmth of the Sun. Here on Earth, we actually feed on starlight. The Sun is the source of energy for almost all life on Earth; every plant, algae and many species of bacteria rely on the process of photosynthesis to create their own food using the power of the Sun. This in turn creates the foundations for the complex web of life here on Earth; not only does the process of photosynthesis maintain the normal level of oxygen in the atmosphere, but it is also the basis on which almost all life depends for its source of energy.

We are only just beginning to understand the complex mechanisms by which plants capture sunlight; some of this explanation may take us off into the quantum world, but at its most basic chemical level photosynthesis is a simple process. Inside every leaf are millions of organelles called chloroplasts, and it's these little units that do something magical when they capture a photon that has taken the eight-minute, 150-million-kilometre (93,000-million-mile) journey from the Sun. The chloroplasts take in carbon dioxide and water, and by capturing the energy from a sunbeam they convert this into oxygen and complex sugars. It's these complex sugars, or carbohydrates, that are the basis of all the food we eat – whether directly through the consumption of photosynthetic plants or indirectly through the consumption of animals that feed on them. The amount of energy trapped by photosynthesis is immense – around 100 terawatt-years, which is six times larger than the power consumption of human civilisation.

This intimate link between our planet and the Sun is all around us. Yet although we are surrounded by vast swathes of wonderful green machines that are all feeding on the Sun, the leaves and plants that cover so much of the planet do not just rely on any sunlight. In fact, plants are fussy eaters and have evolved to use just a fraction of the sunlight that makes its way through Earth's atmosphere.

On the surface of Earth sunlight may appear white, but when you pass it through a prism, you can see that it is made up of all the colours of the rainbow. Different wavelengths of light have different colours – from the blues with the shortest wavelength to the reds with the longest – but it's not just their colour that distinguishes them. The prism reveals the recipe of light that is specific to our star; we see the red, green and blue photons that make up the sunlight all around us and each of these photons has very specific characteristics. The red photons don't carry much energy but there are lots of them, whereas the blue photons, although there are fewer, carry a little more energy. Plants have evolved to gain the maximum energy most efficiently out of the recipe of light our star throws at us, so they don't just use any photons for photosynthesis but only the ones from the red and blue bit of the spectrum.

This intricate relationship between the evolution of plants and our star has had a profound effect on one of the defining features of our planet. When a red or blue photon hits a plant it is absorbed and so those wavelengths of light can no longer bounce back into your eye. Whereas when a green photon hits a plant it is not absorbed but reflected, so this wavelength of light bounces off a leaf and into your eye to create a living world that is defined by one colour more than any other: green. So the verdancy of the forests and jungles that cover our planet is all down to how plants have adapted to the quality of our star's light

LEFT AND BELOW: Plants rely on sunlight for survival, and have evolved to gain maximum energy from whatever level of sunlight they receive.

HOW A PRISM WORKS
As sunlight passes at an angle through a transparent material such as glass or plastic, the light bends (refracts) and breaks down into a rainbow of colours.

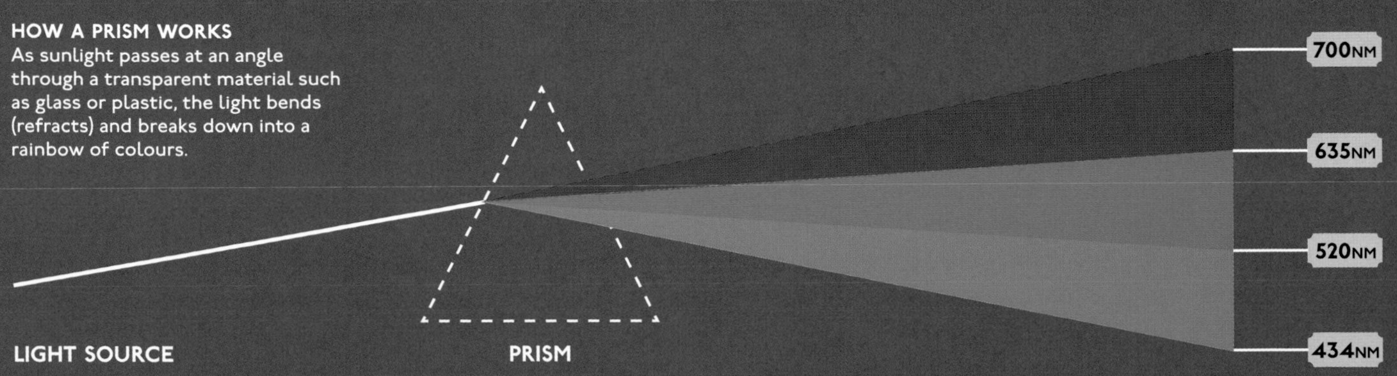

SOLAR ECLIPSE IN VARANASI

Nothing prepares you for a total solar eclipse, and nothing prepares you for Varanasi. The old Solar City is never quiet and deserted; it is a little slice of ancient India and feels more hectic and vibrant even than the twenty-first-century version. But on the morning of 22 July 2009, the banks of the holy river were packed with people. There was no room, not a square centimetre of space, amongst a million sandaled feet crammed onto the Ghats. Green, yellow, red and orange saris and bronzed torsos bared to the early morning

LEFT: On the banks of the Ganges, armed with protective glasses, the solar eclipse of July 2009 was a spectacular sight, and one of the most exciting events I've ever experienced.

summer Sun formed a continuous bridge between the stepped shore and the heavily silted Himalayan waters of the Ganges. The ritualistic instinct to wash in the holy river powered a continuous convective flow of bodies down the concrete steps of the Ghats to the water's edge – a circulating and impenetrable wall of humanity, simultaneously frenzied and calm. As I stood with them I marvelled at the patience of the Indian people – something British film crews dripping with tripods and flight cases will never be able to emulate.

With immense difficulty, we had found a place to stand in a miraculously under-populated Ghat. We subsequently discovered why it wasn't crowded – it was the public toilet. However, we decided that the unrivalled view of the rising Sun compensated for the smell and we settled down to drink water and wait.

The moment of first contact came at 5.28am, when the limb of the Moon touched the solar disc. The Sun hovered over the river, partially obscured by low cloud, which dimmed the light and made the first moments of the eclipse easier to see. There was little change in the mood of the crowd because, unless you had special cardboard solar sunglasses, there was no perceptible reduction in the Sun's power.

Over the next thirty minutes the Moon's disc quickly slipped across the face of the Sun and I became aware of a strange and unexpected feeling. The Moon moved quickly, and quite unlike the countless other nights I had stared up at its face, it was obviously in orbit – an inhabitant of space rather than a bright disc in the terrestrial sky. I developed a kind of vertigo, because the reality of the Moon as a ball of rock spinning quickly through space transferred to my own situation. I realised that I too was standing on a ball of rock.

By 6.20am, almost an hour after first contact, totality approached. Very, very quickly, the morning light seemed to ebb away, as if time was flowing backwards. But this dimming was not like a sunset because it was so fast. It was not a fading of light; more of a removal. The sound of a million voices dimmed, too, but the Sun still hung as a fainter disc, seemingly unobscured to unshielded eyes. Then at 6.24am, instantly and with Newtonian precision, the Moon slotted into place in front of our star like a perfect Rolexian cog. And quite spontaneously, an enormous cheer erupted from the Ghats.

I then had longer than any TV presenter will have this century to speak to camera about the eclipse. We had worked on words back in London, of course, because we knew this event would be one of the centrepieces of the series, but when the moment came all I could think of was the surprising vertiginous feeling. The red-blue sky of dawn had quickly faded to black as a dark rock swept across a glowing sphere of plasma on its orbital path, leaving me and a million other souls exposed on our own rock to the void. I glimpsed Pascal's terror at the silence of the infinite spaces, turned to camera and said what I felt: 'If you ever needed convincing that we live in a solar system, that we are on a ball of rock orbiting around the Sun with other balls of rock, then look at that. That's the Solar System coming down and grabbing you by the throat.' ◉

THE INVISIBLE SUN

From 150 million kilometres away the Sun in our sky looks like a perfect disc. It is in fact closer to a near-perfect sphere than any planet or moon in the Solar System; it measures half a million kilometres across, but the variation in its breadth from top to bottom and side to side is little more than ten kilometres. However, this near perfection belies the incredible complexity of the structure. Its constituents are simple enough – to a very good approximation, our Sun is composed of the two simplest elements in the Universe – hydrogen and helium.

RIGHT: Here, the solar eclipse of 22 July 2009 reaches the point of totality as the Moon blocks the Sun entirely. As it does so, the solar corona, invisible at all other times, is clearly on show.

THE STRUCTURE OF THE SUN'S ATMOSPHERE

Hydrogen makes up about three-quarters of the mass of the Sun, with helium making up about a quarter. Less than 2 per cent consists of heavier elements such as iron, oxygen, carbon and neon. This spinning ball of the simplest elements is almost 330,000 times as massive as Earth. It is neither gas, liquid or solid, but a fourth state of matter known as a plasma. A plasma is a gas in which a large proportion of the atoms have had their orbiting electrons removed. This happens because the temperature is high enough to literally strip the atomic nuclei of their electrons. Plasmas are the most common state of matter in the Universe, and in fact we encounter them every day on Earth – fluorescent light bulbs are filled with glowing plasma when they are illuminated. Because plasmas contain a high proportion of naked, positively charged atomic nuclei and free negatively charged electrons, they are electrically conductive and so hugely responsive to magnetic fields.

This gives the Sun a whole host of strange characteristics that are not found on any other body in the Solar System. It rotates faster at its equator than at its poles, with one rotation taking twenty-five days at the equator and over thirty days at the poles.

One hundred and fifty times denser than water and reaching temperatures of up to fifteen million degrees Celsius, the core of the Sun is a baffling and bewildering structure. It is where the Sun's fusion reactions occur, generating 99 per cent of its energy output. Around 600 million tonnes of hydrogen are fused together every second, creating 596 million tonnes of helium. The missing four million tonnes is converted into energy – as much as ninety billion megatons of exploding TNT – and this energy is transported to the surface by the high-energy photons or gamma rays released in the fusion reactions.

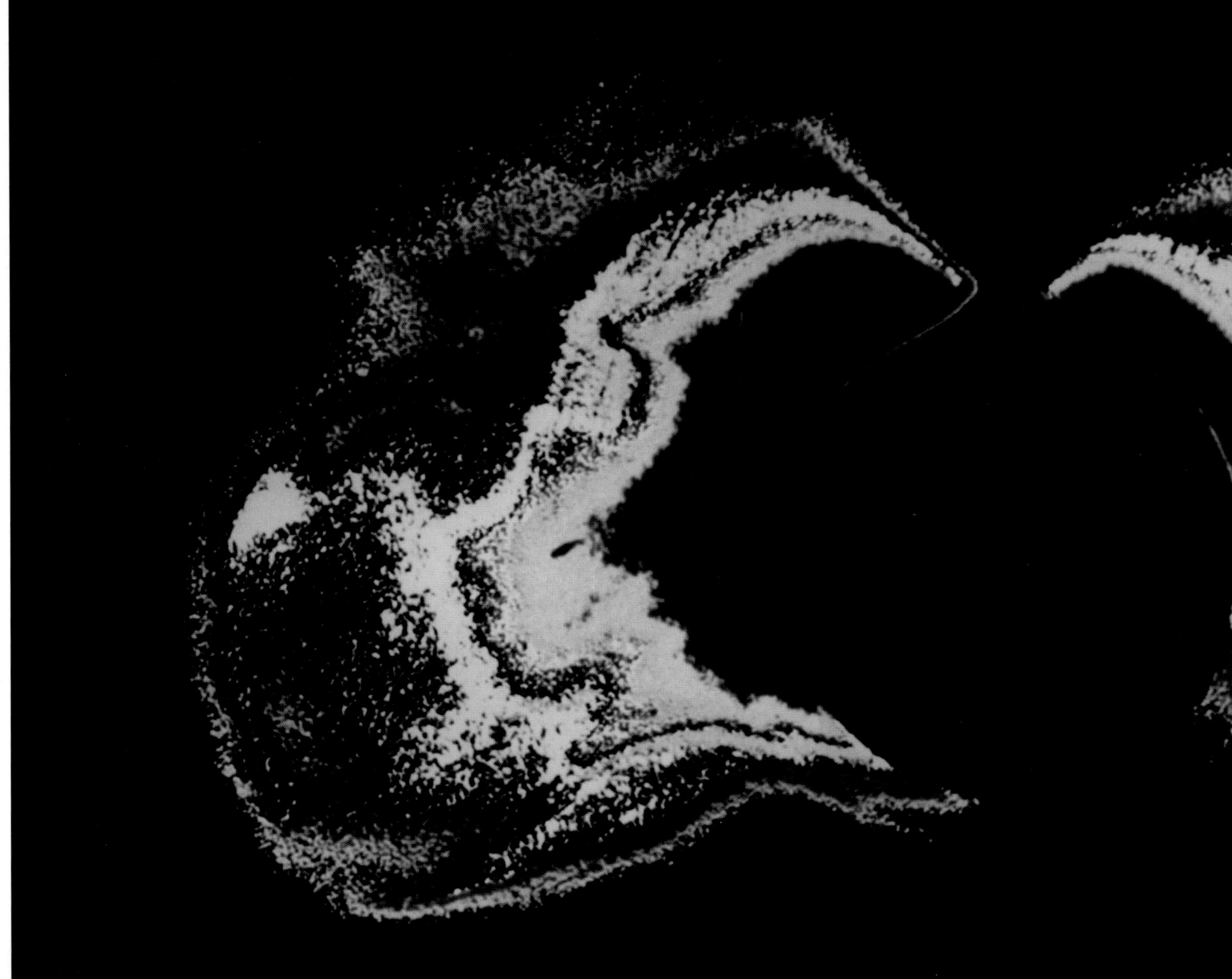

The life of a newly created photon in the core of the Sun is a not a simple one, though. Most are quickly absorbed within a few millimetres of their point of creation by the dense plasma of the core, then they are re-emitted in random directions. In this way the journey of a gamma ray from the core of the Sun to its surface is like a very hot, very long and very unpredictable game of pinball; one that results in the release of millions of lower-energy photons at the Sun's surface. All the light that reaches us here on Earth is incredibly ancient; it is estimated that a single photon can take anywhere from 10,000 to 170,000 years to make the journey from the Sun's core to surface before it can make the eight-minute journey into our eyes.

By the time a photon reaches the surface, or photosphere, the Sun's temperature has dropped from thirteen million degrees Celsius to about 6,000 degrees. It's this massive change in temperature that causes the vast convection currents that swirl through the Sun, creating thermal columns that carry hot material to the surface and create its characteristic granular appearance we see from Earth.

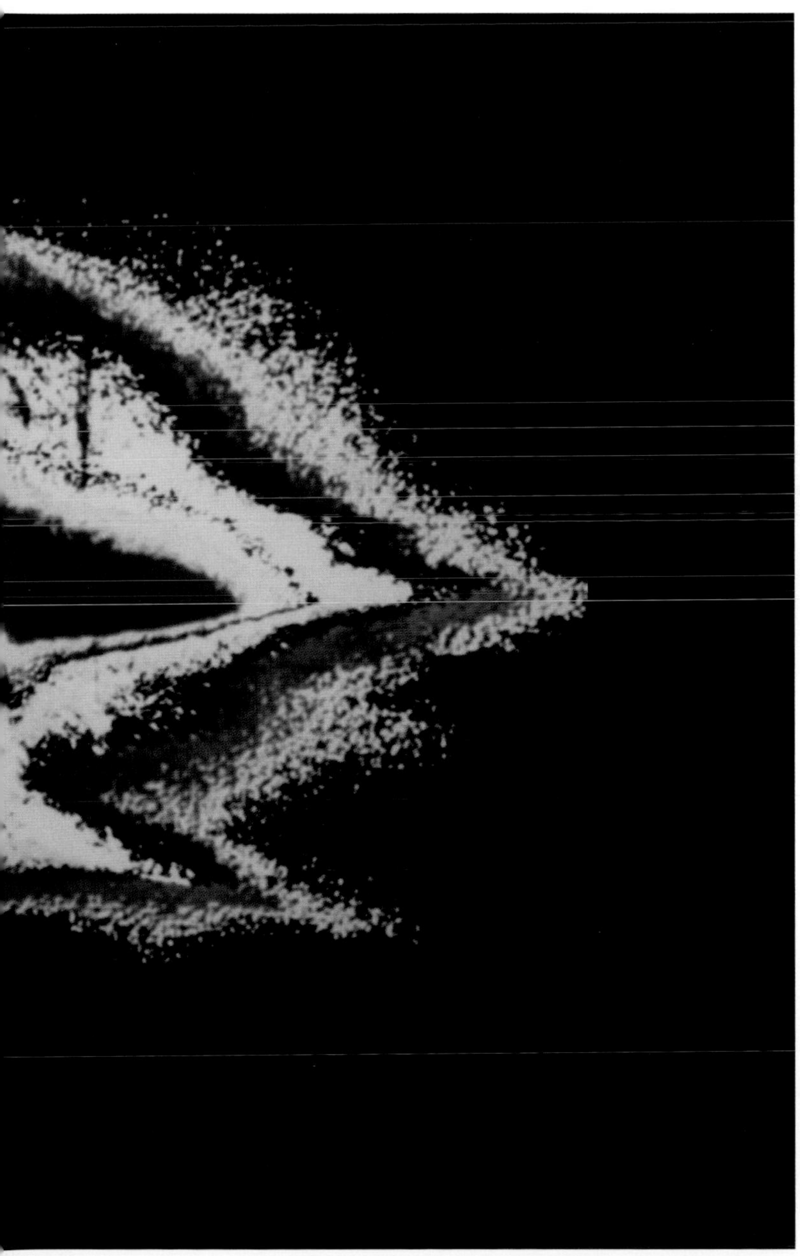

This is only just the beginning of the story of our sun's mighty physical presence. Beyond the surface of the Sun is the strange and invisible layer known as the solar atmosphere. Only visible to the naked eye on Earth during a total solar eclipse, the Sun's atmosphere is made up of a thin collection of electrically charged particles, protons and electrons. Unsurprisingly, the atmosphere of the Sun cools as you get further away from the surface. At a distance of 500 kilometres (310 miles) is an area known as the Temperature Minimum, which has a temperature of around 4,400 degrees Celsius. This location, as the name implies, is the coolest area of our star and the first place in which we can find simple molecules like water and carbon dioxide surviving in close proximity to the Sun. Beyond this region something odd happens. As you move further away from the Sun into space, the atmosphere doesn't get cooler, it gets dramatically hotter. This outer region of the Sun's atmosphere is known as the corona. This mysterious layer of the Sun only becomes visible to the naked eye during a total solar eclipse but when it is revealed

One hundred and fifty times denser than water and reaching temperatures of over 13 million degrees Celsius, the core of the Sun is a baffling and bewildering structure.

you are seeing a structure that is larger and hotter than the Sun itself. With an average temperature of a million degrees Celsius and some areas reaching colossal temperatures of up to twenty million degrees Celsius, this vast cloud is, in places, hotter than the core of the Sun. The mechanisms that drive the corona to these high temperatures are not yet fully understood, but this effect is certainly due to the complex magnetic interactions that occur between the surface and the corona. What is known is that each and every day, at the very top of the atmosphere, some of the most energetic coronal particles are escaping. The Sun leaks nearly seven billion tonnes of corona every hour into space; a vast superheated supersonic collection of smashed atoms that en masse are known as the solar wind. This is the beginning of an epic journey that will see the Sun's breath reach the furthest parts of the Solar System, creating the final vast structure of our star – the heliosphere ◉

LEFT: The solar corona is the outer atmosphere of the Sun, which stretches out more than one million kilometres from its surface. It is visible to us on Earth as a halo around the Sun, but only during a total solar eclipse when the Sun's surface is obscured.

THE HELIOSPHERE

The heliosphere is a gigantic magnetic bubble in space that contains our solar system, the solar wind and the entire solar magnetic field. This bubble extends far into the Solar System, possibly even forty to fifty times further from the Sun than the Earth, and is shaped by the solar winds coming from the Sun.

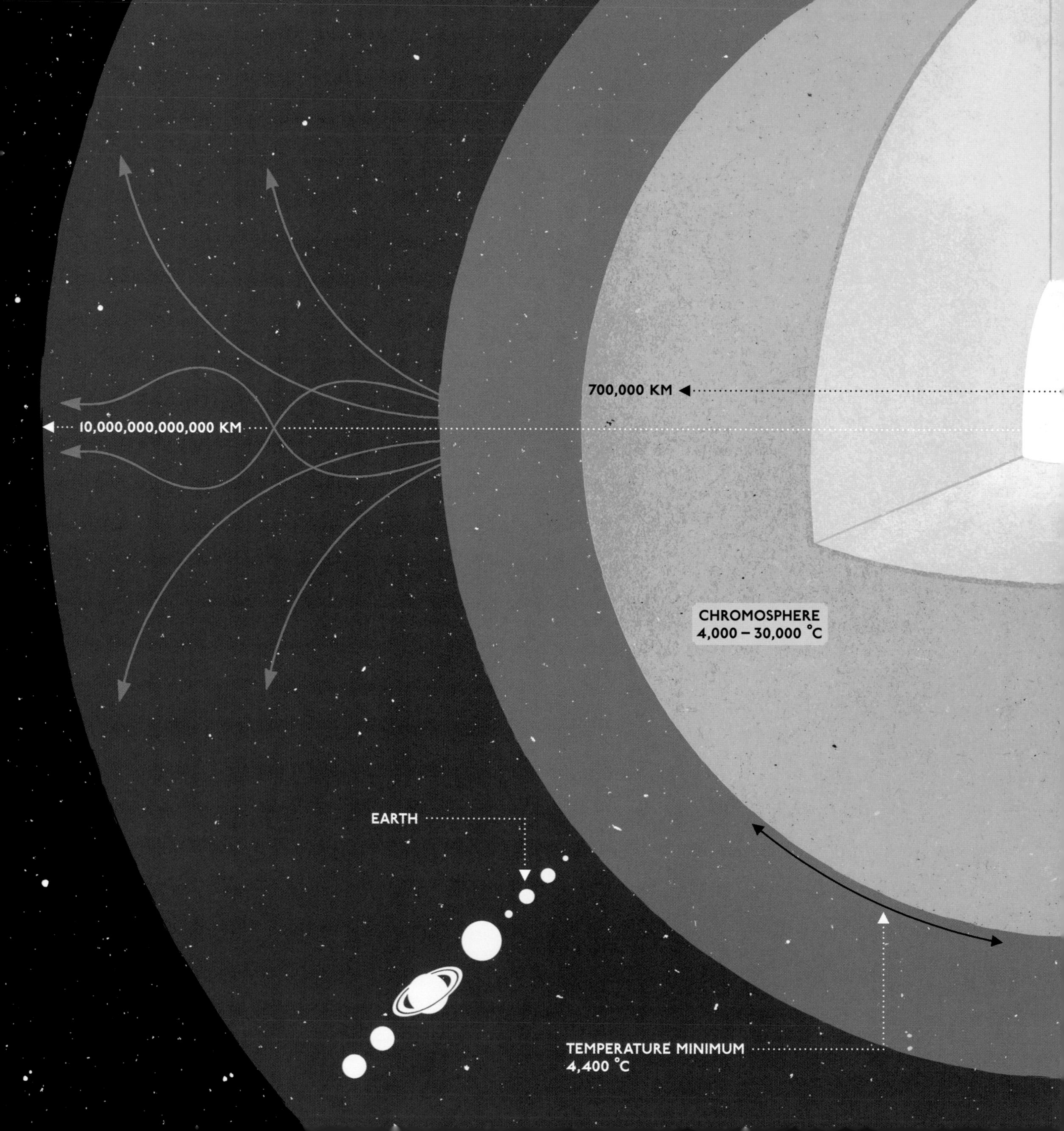

700,000 KM

10,000,000,000,000 KM

CHROMOSPHERE
4,000 – 30,000 °C

EARTH

TEMPERATURE MINIMUM
4,400 °C

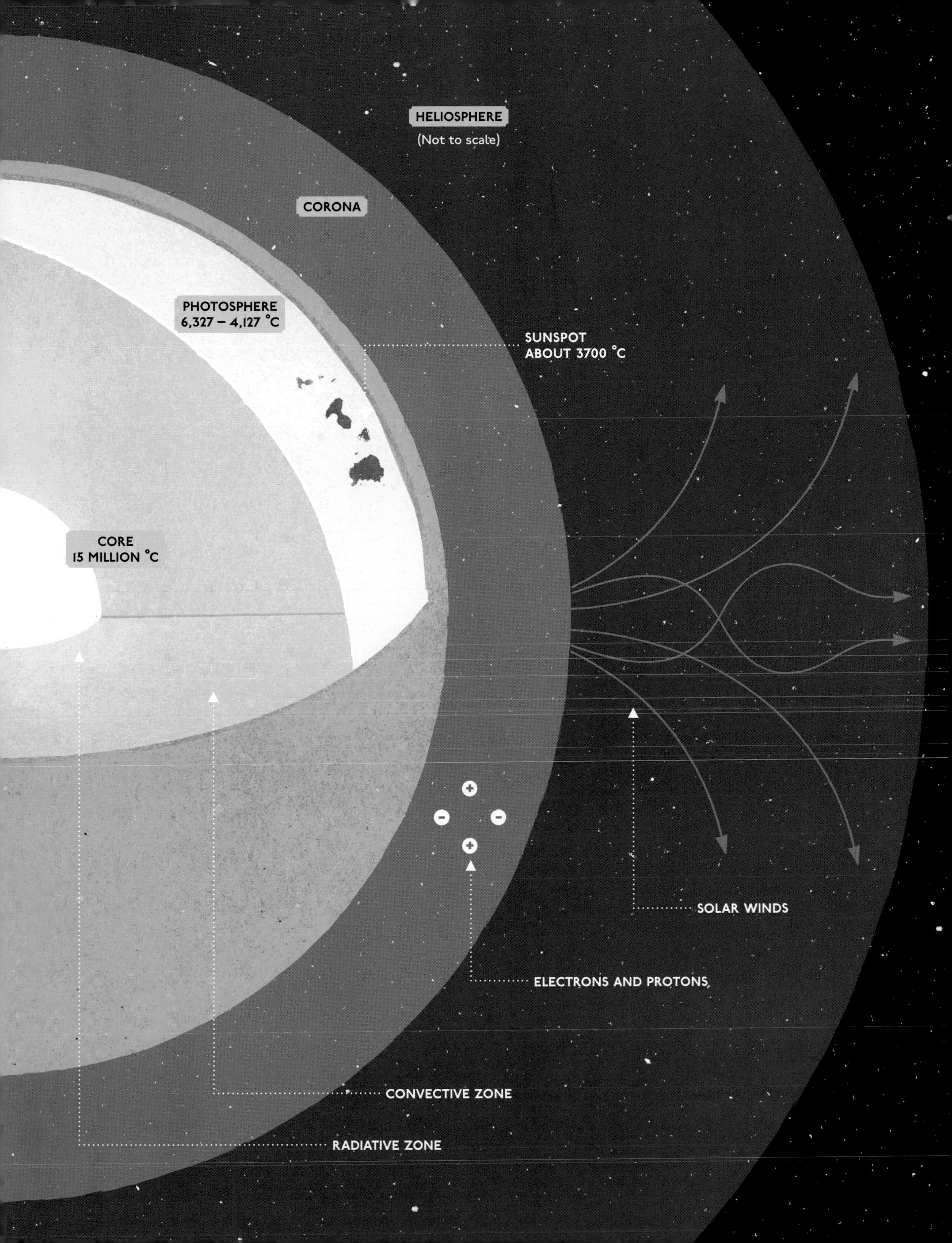

HELIOSPHERE

(Not to scale)

CORONA

PHOTOSPHERE
6,327 – 4,127 °C

SUNSPOT
ABOUT 3700 °C

CORE
15 MILLION °C

SOLAR WINDS

ELECTRONS AND PROTONS

CONVECTIVE ZONE

RADIATIVE ZONE

RIGHT: This image of a solar flare was captured by the TRACE spacecraft on 21 April 2002. Solar flares are explosive bursts of gas that release huge amounts of energy. In the geomagnetic storm that follows each flare, particles and radiation are hurled out into space.

On a beautiful sunny winter's day in the Arctic, it's hard to imagine that our star could be a threat. Yet, high above us deadly solar particles stream our way at speeds topping a million kilometres an hour and bombard the Earth.

DEFENCE AGAINST THE FORCE OF THE SUN

Astronomy has a long history of discoveries by amateurs. From Clyde Tombaugh, the man who discovered Pluto, to David Levy, the co-discoverer of the Shoemaker-Levy comet, the freedom of the skies has always tempted non-professionals to bypass the experts and break new ground. Amateur British astronomer Richard C. Carrington is a worthy member of this list. In 1858, Carrington made the first observation of an event that would eventually become known as a solar flare.

This massive explosion in the Sun's atmosphere releases a huge amount of energy and Carrington noticed that this event was followed by a geomagnetic storm, a massive disruption in the Earth's magnetic field, the day after the eruption. Carrington was the first to suspect the two events may be connected. Beyond the weather in our swirling atmosphere, the solar wind creates another more tenuous atmosphere and weather system that surrounds our planet. We rarely notice this ethereal weather high above us, because by the time the solar wind reaches Earth it's pretty diluted. If you went into space close to the Earth and held up your hand, you wouldn't feel a thing. In fact, there are about five protons and five electrons for every sugar cube's worth of space, but they're travelling very fast, carrying a lot of energy – enough to severely damage our planet's atmosphere, were it not for a defence system generated deep within the Earth's core.

On a beautiful sunny winter's day in the Arctic, it's hard to imagine that our star could be a threat. Yet, high above us deadly solar particles stream our way at speeds topping a million kilometres an hour and bombard the Earth. Down here on the surface we're protected from that intense solar wind by a natural shield that deflects most of it around us. To see that shield, you need nothing more than a compass. That's because the Earth's force field is magnetic, an invisible shell that surrounds the planet in a protective cocoon.

The magnetic field emanates from deep within our planet's spinning iron-rich core. It's this gigantic force field, known as the magnetosphere, that deflects most of the lethal solar wind harmlessly away into space. However, the planet doesn't escape completely; when the solar wind hits the Earth's magnetic field, it distorts it. It stretches the field out on the night side of the planet and in some ways it's like stretching a piece of elastic. More and more energy goes into the field and over time this energy builds up, stretching the tail until it can no longer hold on to it all. Eventually the energy is released, accelerating a stream of electrically charged particles down the magnetic field lines towards the poles. When these particles, energized by the solar wind, hit the Earth's atmosphere, they create one of the most beautiful sights in nature: the aurora borealis, or Northern Lights ●

LIGHT FANTASTIC – THE AURORA BOREALIS

The northern Norwegian city of Tromso is known as the gateway to the Arctic. At latitude seventy degrees North, deep inside the Arctic Circle, it has permanent sunlight from mid-May until the end of July, and permanent darkness from late November to mid-January. In late March the Arctic Ocean is a dark frosty blue, the white-crested waves matching the layers of snow and ice packed solid onto the wooden jetties and the well-weathered decks of the fishing boats. It was an utterly magical place to begin filming on 22 March 2009.

We had gone to see the aurora borealis. Tromso is perfectly positioned on the auroral arc – the thin circle around the North Pole along which the elusive light show usually appears. March and September are the best months to see it, due to the alignment of the Earth's magnetic field relative to the Sun, and we were told that, given clear skies, we would have a strong chance of glimpsing the Northern Lights.

Our guide told me of a Sami legend about the aurora. (The Sami are the people of the North, whose domain stretches from Tromso in the west, across northern Sweden

The Northern Lights reveal in exquisite beauty our planet's connection with the rest of the Solar System. The Earth's environment does not end at the edge of our atmosphere; it stretches at least to the Sun.

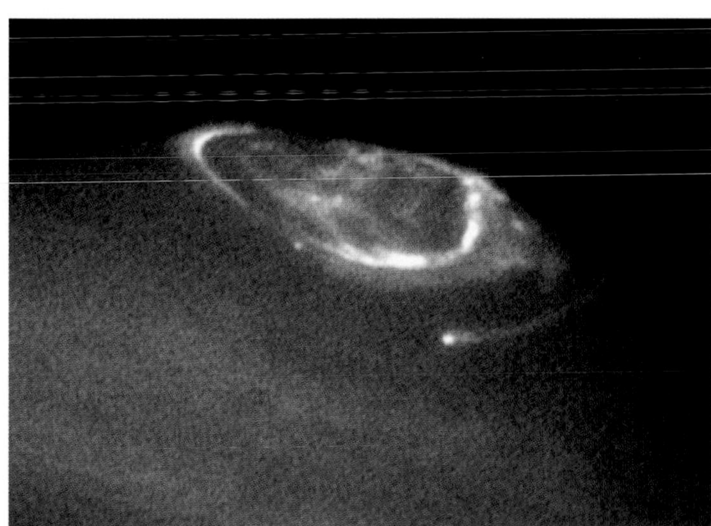

LEFT: Waiting for the Northern Lights in Norway – we travelled well out of the city in the hope of witnessing this fantastic natural light show.

LEFT, TOP: The Northern Lights were a spectacular sight that were well worth the wait. The crystal-clear skies were punctuated by green shafts of light that seemed to rise up from the mountain range.

ABOVE: Jupiter has the largest and most powerful magnetic field in the Solar System, so aurorae are a permanent fixture around the planet's poles and have also been seen around its moons.

and Finland and into Russia.) The legend has it that the aurorae are the spirits of women who died before they had children. Trapped between the frozen land and heaven, they are condemned to dance forever in the dark Arctic skies. As dusk fell, we rode snowmobiles out into the dense forests by the Fjord to get away from the city lights and settled down in the Sami camp with hot reindeer stew to wait.

Just after midnight, the aurora came. I walked out into the frigid night air, enjoying the crunch of footsteps in fresh snow, and looked up. They came gently, a vague hint of green, but built quickly; sheets of colour drifted slowly then suddenly broke off and danced impossibly fast, a three-dimensional rain of light rising and falling between land and sky. They were mostly green, with hints of orange and red close to the horizon. They were like nothing I have ever seen, and as I turned to camera I realised that I didn't care about the physics of what I was seeing. My reaction, composed whilst sitting at my desk in Manchester, was worthless in the face of Nature at its most magnificent. The Sami had it right – an aurora isn't the light shaken out of atoms of nitrogen and oxygen as they are bombarded by high-energy particles from Earth's ionosphere accelerated down magnetic field lines towards the poles, it is made of majestic, mournful, dancing spirits, trapped in the Arctic night.

The Northern Lights reveal in exquisite beauty our planet's connection with the rest of the Solar System. The Earth's environment does not end at the edge of our atmosphere; it stretches at least to the Sun. We are bound to our star by the visible light that creates and nurtures life on Earth and the unseen, constant solar wind that only appears to us at night in special circumstances. Each and every planet in the Solar System shares this connection, and the same laws of physics apply. As the solar wind races out into the Solar System, wherever it meets a planet with a magnetosphere aurorae spring up. Jupiter's magnetic field is the largest and most powerful in the Solar System, and the Hubble space telescope reveals that there are permanent aurorae over the Jovian poles. Jupiter's moons, Io, Europa and Ganymede also have aurorae, created by Jupiter's atmospheric wind interacting with the moons' atmospheres. Saturn too puts on an impressive display, with aurorae at both its poles, but because Saturn's magnetic field is uneven, the aurorae are smaller and more intense in the north.

As the solar wind reaches the edge of the heliosphere it begins to run out of steam. Incredibly, there is a probe out there that will discover where these solar winds end ◉

BELOW: Aurora Borealis, natural light displays which are only visible from the northern hemisphere, are on show here over Lake Thorisvatn in Iceland.

VOYAGERS' GRAND TOUR

BELOW: Voyager 1 has been of vital importance to space exploration for over thirty years. The craft was responsible for this picture of the Moon and the Earth, which was the first of its kind taken by a spacecraft, recorded on 18 September 1977.

RIGHT: On 5 September 1977, Voyager 1 was launched from Kennedy Space Center at Cape Canaveral, Florida. Although its twin spacecraft, Voyager 2, was launched sixteen days earlier, Voyager 1 followed a faster flight path, which meant it reached Jupiter first.

In the autumn of 1977, a pair of identical 722-kilogramme (1,592-pound) spacecraft were launched from Cape Canaveral, Florida. Voyagers 1 and 2 were about to embark on a very special mission: to visit all four of the Solar System's gas giants – Jupiter, Saturn, Uranus and Neptune. Normally such a journey would take thirty years to complete, but by a stroke of good fortune these spacecraft were designed at a time when the planets were uniquely aligned, allowing the probes to complete their grand tour in less than twelve years. Today, over thirty years after their launch, both spacecraft are alive and well, and remarkably Voyager 1 is still reporting back to Earth – the ultimate and most wonderful example of mission creep in the history of space exploration.

Voyager 1 is currently the furthest man-made object from Earth. Travelling at seventeen kilometres (eleven miles) per second, this extraordinary spacecraft is just over seventeen billion kilometres (eleven billion miles) from home and delivering knowledge that it was never designed or expected to uncover. Listening to Voyager 1 is the sensitive ear of the Goldstone Mars station in the Mojave desert, California; one of the few telescopes in the world that is capable of communicating over such vast distances. Voyager is so far away that it takes the signal around fifteen hours to arrive, travelling at the speed of light. It may appear as little more than a blip on a screen, but the information Voyager is sending is providing the first data from the frontier of our solar system, from the edge of the heliosphere, and constantly measuring the solar wind as it fades away. Voyager 1 has now reached the point where this wind that emanated so powerfully from the surface of the Sun has literally run out of steam. The heliopause is the boundary at which the solar wind is no longer strong enough to push against the stellar winds of the surrounding stars. Beyond this point Voyager will leave its home and head off into interstellar space. With the batteries expected to struggle on until 2025, this spacecraft will continue to feed us data as it becomes the first man-made object to leave our solar system ◉

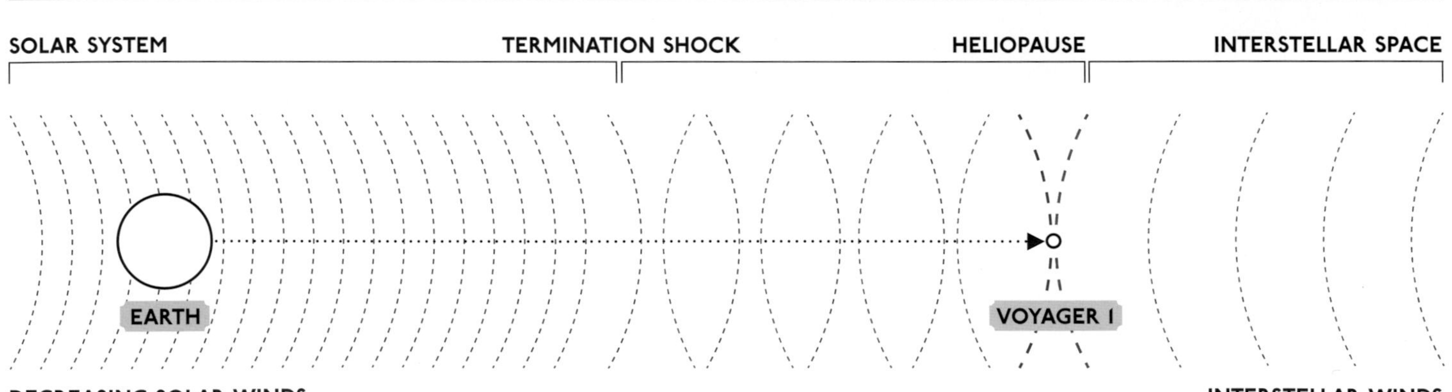

FROM EARTH TO THE OORT CLOUD

BELOW: You could be forgiven for missing the small red star in the middle of this image. Its light is so faint that this dwarf star, Proxima Centauri, the nearest star to the Sun, was only discovered in 1915.

BOTTOM: The Oort cloud is an almost spherical collection of icy objects that is believed to lie approximately one light year away from the Sun. Gravitational pull from other stars can cause these icy objects to enter the Solar System as comets.

Our journey through the Sun's Empire doesn't end at this distant frontier, seventeen billion kilometres (eleven billion miles) away, where the solar wind meets the interstellar wind. The Sun has a final, invisible force that reaches out much further. Our star is by far the largest wonder in the Solar System. In fact, it alone makes up 99 per cent of the Solar System's mass. It is this immensity that gives the Sun its furthest reaching influence – gravity.

This is the full extent of the Sun's empire; the lightest gravitational touch that retains a cloud of ice that encloses the Sun in a colossal sphere. Beyond this Oort cloud there is nothing. Only sunlight escapes; light that will take four years to reach even the Sun's closest neighbour, Proxima Centauri – a red dwarf star among the 200 billion others that make up the Milky Way. And it's by looking here, deep into our local galactic neighbourhood, that we're learning to read the story of our own star's ultimate fate ◉

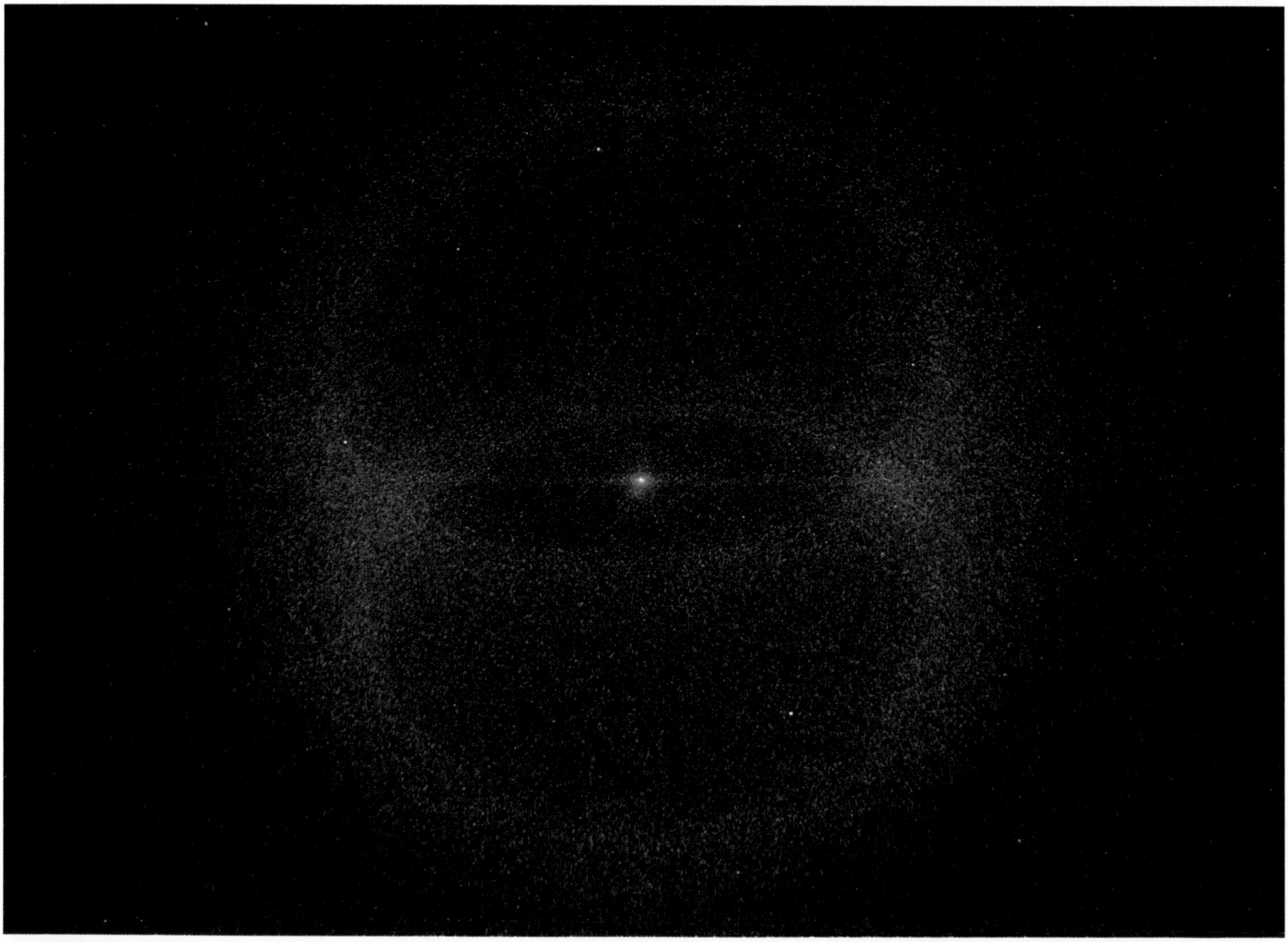

INVESTIGATING THE FUTURE OF OUR SUN

The Sun's empire is so vast and so ancient, and its power so immense, that it seems an audacious thought to imagine that we could even begin to comprehend its end – the death of our sun. However, that is exactly what astronomers are trying to do, and many of them head to the most arid and barren desert on Earth, the Atacama, in Chile, looking for answers.

There, high up on an the sides of an extinct volcano at an altitude of 2,635 metres (8,643 feet), sits Paranal Observatory, home to the world's most powerful array of telescopes. On arrival we were given 'important information for a safe stay on Paranal'. As the observatory is about two and a half kilometres (one and a half miles) in the air, we were advised that if we experienced any of the following, we should consult a paramedic immediately: headache and dizziness, breathing problems, ringing or blocking of the ears, or seeing stars. It honestly said that if you saw stars at the Paranal Observatory you should consult a paramedic immediately!

Perched high above the clouds is the reason why so many astronomers venture to this desert. Here, four colossal instruments make up the European Southern Observatory's 'Very Large Telescope', or VLT. If you look up at the sky with these mighty machines you quickly notice that the stars are not just white points of light against the blackness of the sky, but are actually coloured. Through these lenses, orangey-red, yellow and bluey-white stars fill the clear Chilean sky.

However, this beauty is not just one of the wonders of our night sky, it has also revealed something much deeper. To gaze upon the galaxy full of stars is to observe them at all the stages of their lives – from youthful bright stars to middle-aged yellow stars very similar to the Sun. Contained within the night sky we can see a colour code that allows us to plot the life cycle of every star, including our own ◉

If you look up at the sky with these mighty machines you quickly notice that the stars are not just white points of light against the blackness of the sky, but are actually coloured. Through these lenses, orangey-red, yellow and bluey-white stars fill the clear Chilean sky.

ABOVE LEFT: The European Southern Observatory's Very Large Telescope consists of four 8-metre (26-foot) aperture telescopes that work independently or combined as one of the world's most powerful telescopes.

ABOVE: The Very Large Telescope is famous for its high level of observation and its spectroscopic resolution. This spectacular image of the Orion Nebula demonstrates the exceptional work of this machine.

THE HERTZSPRUNG-RUSSELL DIAGRAM

For the last 100 years astronomers have meticulously charted the nearest ten thousand stars to Earth and arranged each according to its colour and brightness. From this was born the Hertzsprung-Russell diagram; a powerful and elegant tool that allows astronomers to predict the history and evolution of stars, and in particular the future life of our sun. Most of the stars, including our own, are found in the 'main sequence' – the band of stars that runs from the top left to the bottom right. The Sun will spend most of its life there, steadily burning its vast reserves of hydrogen fuel, which will last for another five billion years. After which, it will pass through a Red Giant phase.

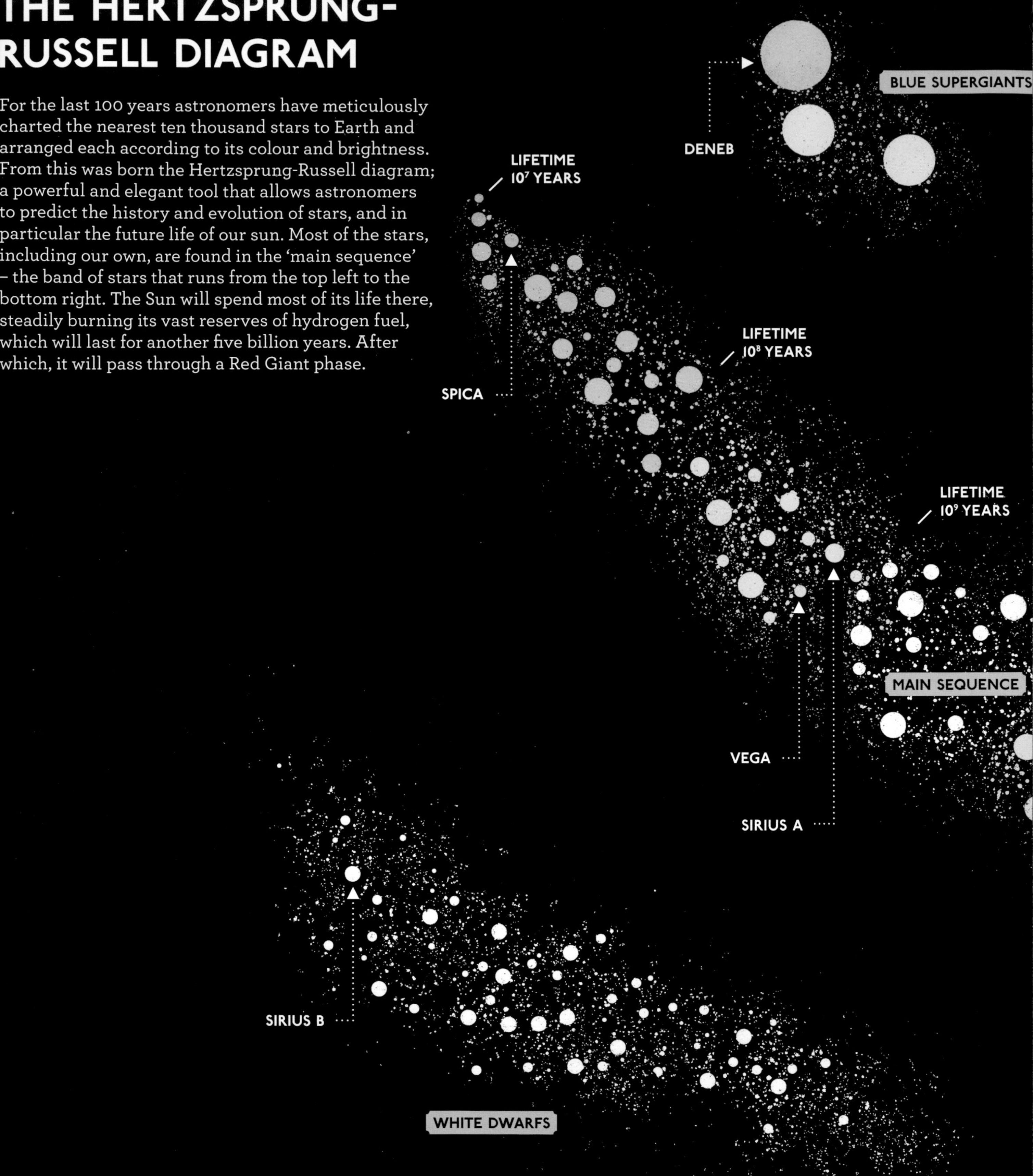

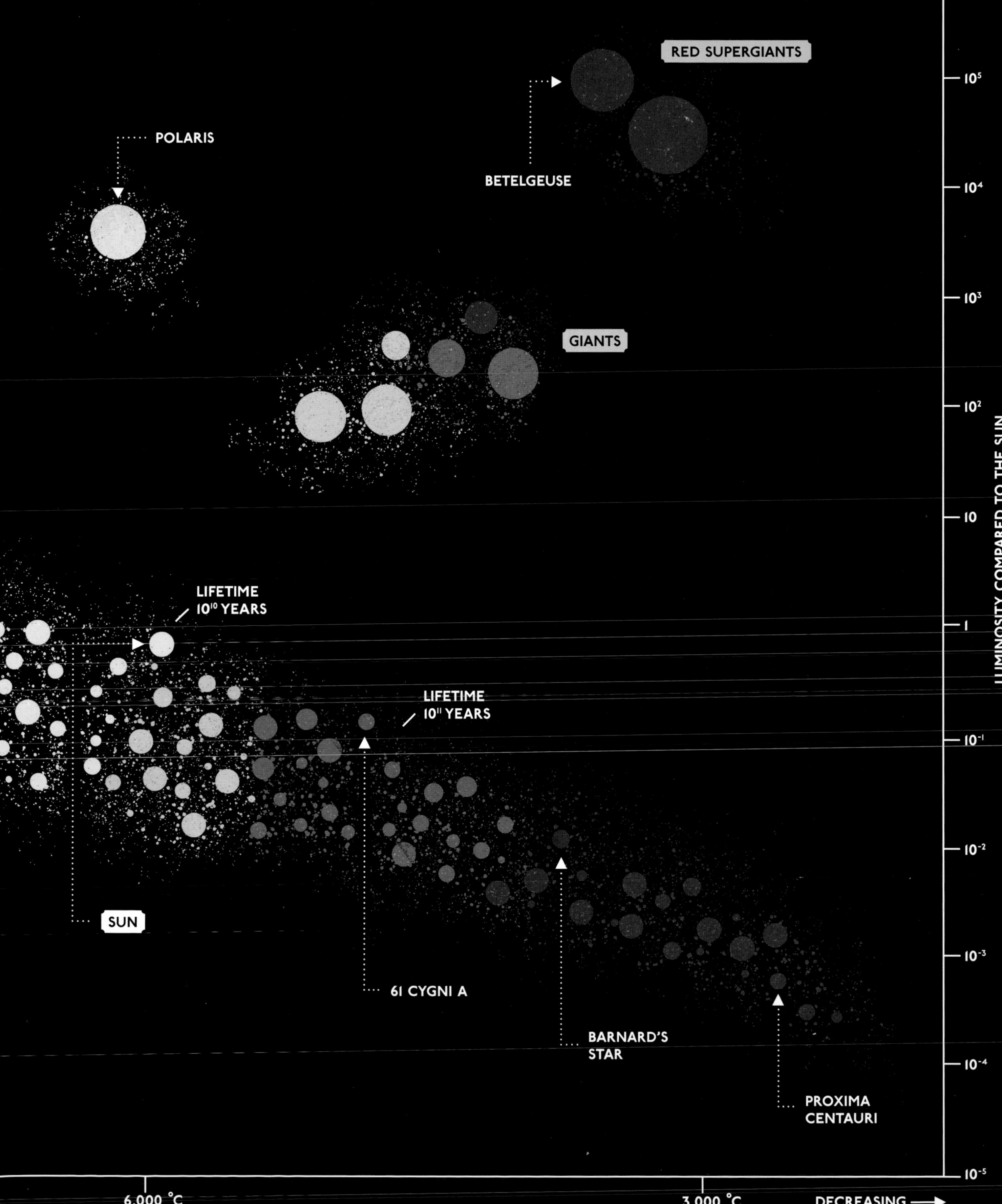
RED SUPERGIANTS
BETELGEUSE
POLARIS
GIANTS
LIFETIME
10¹⁰ YEARS
LIFETIME
10¹¹ YEARS
SUN
61 CYGNI A
BARNARD'S
STAR
PROXIMA
CENTAURI
LUMINOSITY COMPARED TO THE SUN
10⁵
10⁴
10³
10²
10
1
10⁻¹
10⁻²
10⁻³
10⁻⁴
10⁻⁵
6,000 °C
3,000 °C
DECREASING

THE DEATH OF THE SUN

Eventually, like all stars, the Sun's fuel will run out, its core will collapse and our star will begin its final journey. At this stage you may expect it to slowly burn out and splutter its way into oblivion, but there is a final, remarkable twist to our Sun's ten-billion-year story.

When the fuel does finally run out, the nuclear fusion reactions in the Sun's core will grind to a halt and gravity will be master of our star's fate once more. The Sun will no longer be able to support its own weight and it will begin to collapse. Just as in its formation, this collapse will start to heat the Sun once more, until the layers of plasma outside the core become hot enough for fusion to begin again – but this time on a much bigger scale. Our star's brightness will increase by a factor of a thousand or more, causing it to swell to many times its current size. The Sun will then drift off the main sequence and into the top right-hand side of the Hertzsprung-Russell diagram, into the area known as the Giant Branch.

As the outer layers expand, the temperature of the surface will fall and its colour will shift towards red. Mercury will be little more than a memory as it is engulfed by the expanding red sun, which will grow to two hundred times its size today. As it swells the Sun will stretch all the way out to the Earth's orbit, where our own planet's prospects are dim.

So it seems that the wonder that has remained so constant throughout all of its ten billion years of life will end its days as a giant red star. For a few brief instants the Sun will be two thousand times as bright as it is now, but that won't last long. Eventually our star will shed its outer layers and all that will be left will be its cooling core – a faint cinder, or White Dwarf, that will glow pretty much to the end of time, fading slowly into the interstellar night. As it does so, all its wonders – the aurorae that danced through the atmospheres of planets of the Solar System, and its light that sustains all the life here on Earth – will be gone.

The gas and dust of the dying Sun will drift off into space, and in time they will form a vast dark cloud primed and full of possibilities. Then, one day, another star will be born, perhaps with a similar story to tell, the greatest story of the cosmos ◉

CHAPTER 3

ORDER OUT OF CHAOS

THE CLOCKWORK SOLAR SYSTEM

The story of the Solar System is the story of the emergence of order out of chaos, guided by the simplest law of physics: gravity. The planets and their moons exist in relatively stable orbits because of a delicate interplay between gravity and angular momentum, and this beautiful natural balance is written before our eyes in the spinning patterns and rhythms of the heavens.

In the small ancient city of Kairouan on the north-eastern plains of Tunisia lies the fourth most holy site in the Islamic world. Founded by Arabs in 670 CE, this city of just 150,000 people is home to the oldest place of Muslim worship in the Western world. The great mosque of Kairouan is both impressive in its beauty and also in its scale. Covering over 9,000 square metres (97,000 square feet), the Mosque resembles a great fortress as well as a place of worship. At its heart is a vast courtyard and near the centre is a beautiful piece of astronomical engineering – an ancient sundial. Humans have used sundials like this one to follow the brightest star in the heavens for over 5,500 years.

For the last fourteen centuries, the sundial at the centre of this great mosque has measured the relentless passing of the days, marking out the passage of time as the Sun travels across the sky, plotting the call to prayers before dawn, at sunrise, at noon, at sunset and in the evening.

The sundial is a beautifully simple piece of technology. Originally nothing more complicated than a stick in the ground or the length of a human shadow, sundials have enabled us to measure time by following the movement of the Sun across our sky. For thousands of years this movement appeared to confirm the Earth's position at the centre of the Universe. From the most simple of observations it seemed to make perfect sense that the Sun orbits the Earth every 23 hours and 56 minutes. Yet the simple, regular rhythm that each one of us witnesses every day is nothing more than an illusion. It is not the Sun that's moving, what we are observing is the rotation of the Earth as it travels through space.

BELOW: The great mosque at Kairouan is the oldest in Africa, and at the heart of its spectacular central courtyard is a beautiful piece of astronomical engineering – an ancient sundial.

It's wonderful to think that across the planet the rhythms of our lives are governed by our journey through space. From waking up to going to bed, eating strawberries in July or a tangerine in December.

BELOW: The powerful effect of the Solar System on our climate is seen at this french market. The stall is laden with seasonal strawberries and mushrooms.

Travelling at 108,000 kilometres an hour, on a 900-million-kilometre journey around the Sun, our planet completes this epic journey once every 365.25 days. The year in the life of our planet is just one of the endless rhythms by which we live our life – and all of these are governed by the seemingly clockwork motion of our planet. It carries us through cycles of night and day as it turns on its axis, rotating at 1,700 kilometres an hour every twenty-four hours. The length of the day at a particular place on the Earth's surface is dictated by the precise angle of our planet in relation to the Sun.

We have seasons here, too, due to the fact that the Earth's axis is tilted by twenty-three degrees. As we journey around the Sun this angle creates the changing dynamic that defines the cycles of many of the creatures that live both on the land and in the oceans. In the Northern Hemisphere the summer months coincide with the North Pole leaning towards the Sun; when, at this time of year, the angle favours the northern half of our planet with extra energy from our star. By winter the dynamic has changed; the North Pole is pointing away from the Sun and the Southern Hemisphere is bathed in additional sunlight.

It's wonderful to think that across the planet the rhythms of our lives are governed by our journey through space. From waking up to going to bed, wearing a jumper one month and a T-shirt the next, eating strawberries in July or a tangerine in December, each of these everyday events is intimately connected to a journey through space that catapults us at 108,000 kilometres (67,000 miles) per hour around a star, but leaves most of us completely unaware of this rollercoaster ride through the cosmos.

It's not only Earth that is subject to these rhythms – the whole Solar System is full of these cycles, with each planet orbiting the Sun at its own distinct tempo. Mercury is the fastest; closest to the Sun, it reaches speeds of 200,000 kilometres (124,000 miles) per hour, completing its orbit in just eighty-eight days. Venus rotates so slowly that it takes longer to spin on its axis (225 days) than it does to go around the Sun, so that on Venus (and also on Mercury) a day is longer than a year. Further out, the planets orbit more and more slowly. Mars completes one orbit of the Sun every 687 days, just a couple of months short of two Earth years. Jupiter, the largest planet, takes twelve Earth years to complete each orbit, Saturn almost thirty years, Uranus eighty-four years and at the very furthest reaches of the Solar System, four and a half billion kilometres from the Sun, Neptune travels so slowly that by 2009 it hadn't completed a single orbit since it was discovered in 1846.

The Solar System is driven by these rhythms, so regular that the whole thing could be run by clockwork. It seems extraordinary that such a well-ordered system could have come into being spontaneously, but this little island of order that we call our solar system is in fact a wonderful example of the beauty and symmetry that emerges as a result of the action of the simple physical laws that govern the Universe. Studying these laws has lead us not only to understand how that order emerged from the chaos of space, but has also helped us to understand the origins and formation of the Solar System itself. Understanding our position in the Solar System is one of the great journeys of science and is a story that is as old as human civilisation ●

RHYTHMS OF THE SOLAR SYSTEM

All the planets in the Solar System are subject to specific rhythms and cycles and they are all as regular as clockwork. Each planet orbits the Sun at its own distinct tempo; however, the closer the planet is to the Sun, the faster it completes its orbit.

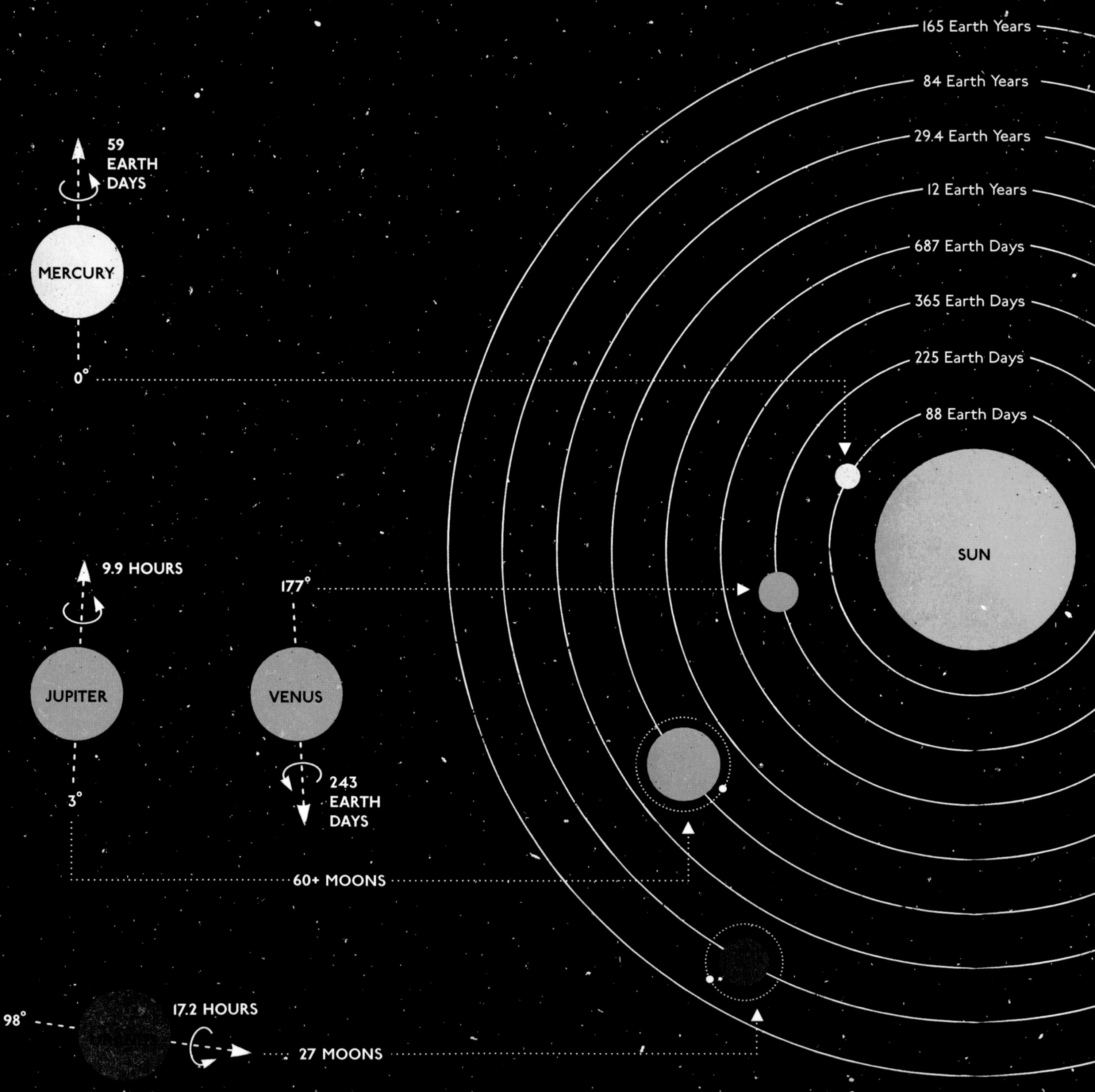

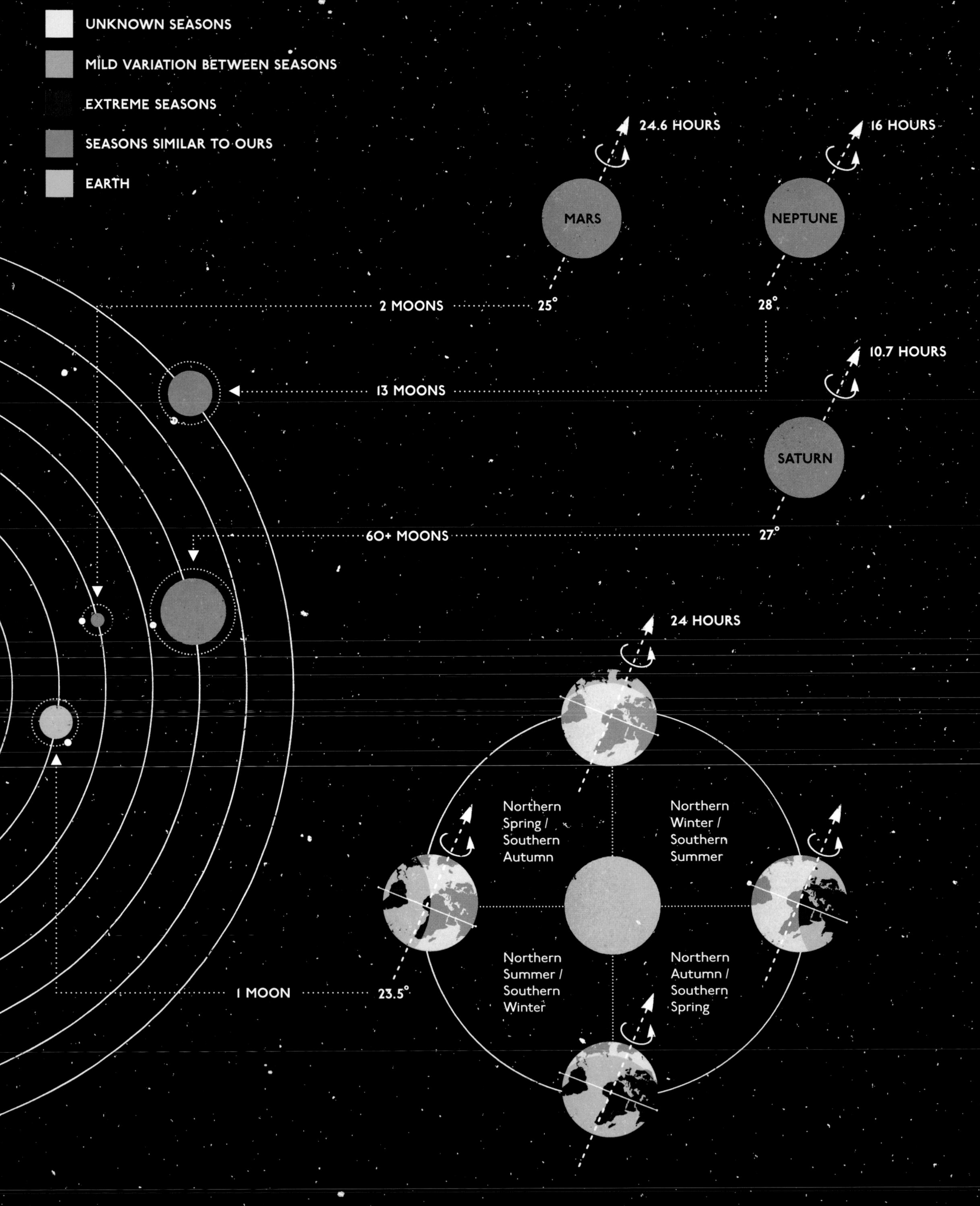

UNKNOWN SEASONS
MILD VARIATION BETWEEN SEASONS
EXTREME SEASONS
SEASONS SIMILAR TO OURS
EARTH
24.6 HOURS
MARS
25°
2 MOONS
16 HOURS
NEPTUNE
28°
13 MOONS
10.7 HOURS
SATURN
27°
60+ MOONS
24 HOURS
Northern Spring / Southern Autumn
Northern Winter / Southern Summer
Northern Summer / Southern Winter
Northern Autumn / Southern Spring
1 MOON
23.5°

THE CENTRE OF THE UNIVERSE

According to Greek mythology, Atlas was the powerful God who carried the Earth on his shoulders, supporting the heavens from the Atlas mountains in North Africa. Today these mountains are still one of the finest places to view the stars. City life may have robbed us of our connection to the night sky, but from the inky black of the Atlas mountains it's easy to appreciate the profound effect it would have had on our ancestors. They looked into the sky to understand their place in creation, and the movement of the stars told them one thing: they were at the centre of the Universe.

Watch the night sky for any length of time and it's no surprise they came to this conclusion. The North Star, Polaris, almost exactly aligned with the Earth's spin axis, adds to the illusion that all the stars are rotating through the sky at that point. It's what the ancients thought for thousands of years, but even though it appears obvious, it is, of course, wrong.

To understand the Earth's real position in the Solar System we need to look at the one set of bodies that doesn't behave as predictably as the stars. The Greeks named them planets, or wandering stars, and we have kept the name planet to describe them.

ABOVE: Star trails in the night sky over Tunisia. The movement of the stars traces spectacular concentric arcs.

RIGHT: In this combination of images taken over a few months, we can trace the movement of Mars in the Earth's sky. Generally it travels in a straight line, but once every two years Mars is passed by Earth and the planet appears to be moving backwards – a phenomenon known as retrograde motion.

The picture of Mars opposite shows how, rather than travelling in a straight line across the background of the stars, the planet occasionally changes direction and loops back on itself. The Greeks had observed this strange movement as long ago as 1534 BCE but could not explain it. Why would this planet create such strange patterns in the sky if it was orbiting around the Earth at the centre of the Universe? Explaining this retrograde motion of Mars didn't come easy; in fact, it took over 3,000 years to reach the right answer.

For half that time the work of one man, Claudius Ptolemaeus, dominated our view of the Universe. In around 150 CE Ptolemaeus published his great work, *The Almagest* – a complete explanation of the complex movement of the planets and stars. For well over a thousand years the Ptolemic view of the Solar System was set in stone, with the Earth at the centre and everything else revolving around it. This was science and religion working hand in hand. With man as the most important of God's creations, it was only right that the Earth should be at the centre of a perfect and uniform universe. Something seemingly as inexplicable as the retrograde motion of Mars was explained by the presence of smaller orbits known as epicycles, which perfectly matched the observed data.

This tendency, perhaps innate in humans, to accept the word of authority in earthly and heavenly matters, has been one of the great obstacles to progress throughout history. The Royal Society in London, the oldest scientific society in the world, was formed in 1660 and took on the motto '*Nullius in verba*', which translates as 'Take nobody's word for it'. In other words, a true and deep understanding of the Universe is gained not by reading the authoritative words of the ancients, but by careful observation of Nature and original thinking.

To drag the Earth away from the centre of the Solar System was the life's work of a Polish astronomer, Nicolaus Copernicus, one of the founding fathers of modern science. Copernicus quite literally turned our view of the Solar System inside out. Using the most basic of instruments, he collected the data that would lead him to create an entirely new view of the heavens, the heliocentric view – one that placed the Sun very firmly at its centre ●

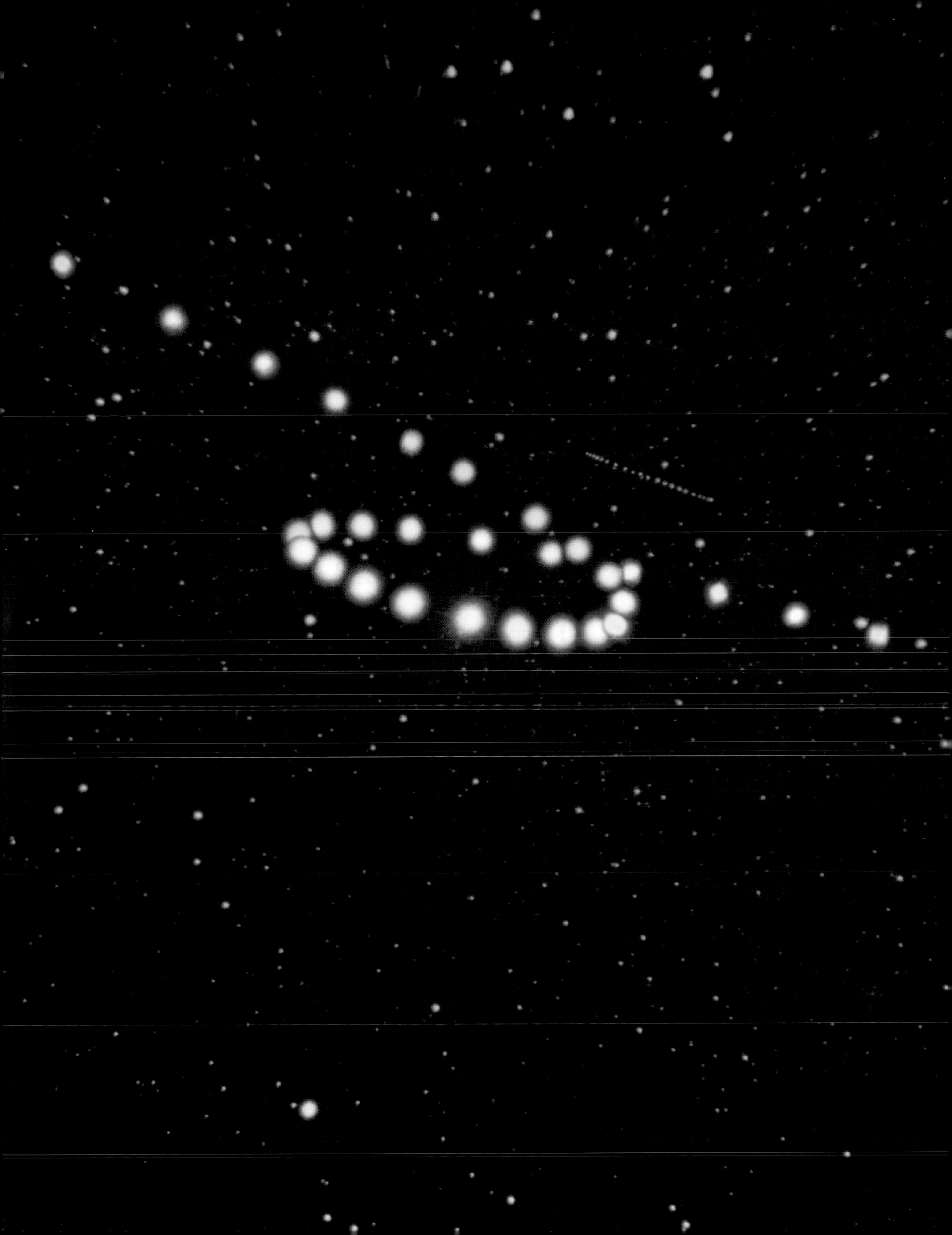

THE HELIOCENTRIC VIEW

Although completed over a decade earlier, Copernicus' theory was only published shortly before his death in 1543. *On the Revolutions of the Celestial Spheres* took apart 1,500 years of astronomical thought, replacing it with a new way of thinking. At its heart was an explanation for the mysterious retrograde motion of a planet like Mars.

The diagram opposite explains his theory. With the Sun at the centre of the Solar System and the planets going around it in almost circular orbits, you suddenly find we are sitting in a very different seat here on Earth to watch the celestial clockwork. As we speed around the Sun together, Mars appears to move in a straight line across the sky. It makes sense that as Mars and Earth move we appear as two speeding cars next to each other on a motorway. Remember that Mars is travelling slower than Earth, twenty-four kilometres (fifteen miles) per second to Earth's thirty kilometres (nineteen miles) per second, and so Earth catches then overtakes Mars and suddenly our perspective is shifted. Earth then pulls away from Mars, which appears to move backwards against the fixed stars – it seems to reverse its direction. Just like a car overtaking on the inside, the slower planet appears to move in reverse.

Mars continues to appear to move backwards across the sky until Earth has sped so far in front that the perspective changes once again and Mars regains its usual direction of travel across the night sky. So Mars seems to have executed a strange looping motion in the sky because Earth overtook it on the inside, which is why we see retrograde motion. It's simple when explained, but it took millennia to work out!

Understanding the retrograde loops was one of the major achievements of early astronomy. It created the concept of the Solar System and allowed us to build the first accurate maps of the planets and their orbits around the Sun. Once we had this picture, many new questions arose. Building on the work of Copernicus, generations of scientists have explored the fundamental workings of our solar system. In doing so they were forced to ask profound questions about its origins, such as: why is it so ordered, and how did that order emerge from the chaos of the heavens?

To find answers we must search for clues in what we see. A good place to start is the circular motions of the planets. The explanation for this astronomical clockwork lies beyond our solar system, because it requires an understanding of the physical principles that govern the whole Universe. To understand the origins of our solar system, we need to look around us ◉

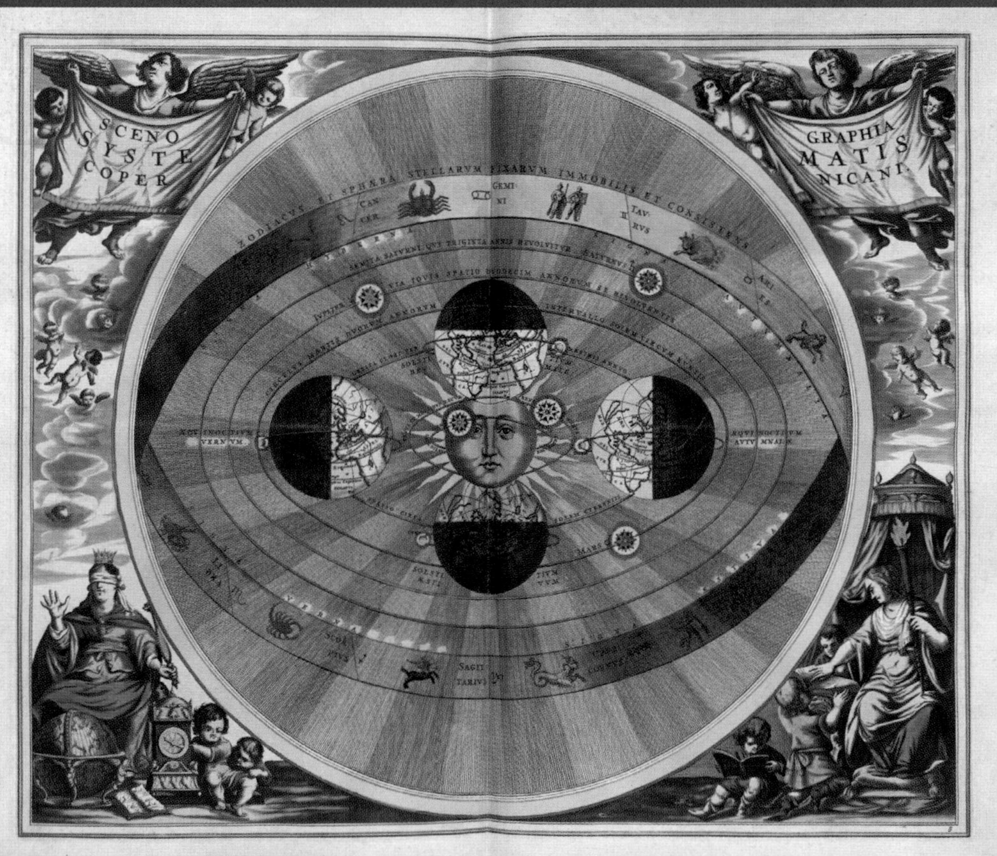

LEFT: This engraving by Andreas Cellarius in 1660 illustrates the theory of Nicolaus Copernicus' world system. This essentially suggests that the Sun is at the centre of the Universe, around which the Earth and other planets move in a circular, uniform motion.

MARS IN RETROGRADE

When in retrograde, Mars moves backwards with respect to the fixed star positions behind it. It seems to travel in a loop as Earth overtakes it from the inside.

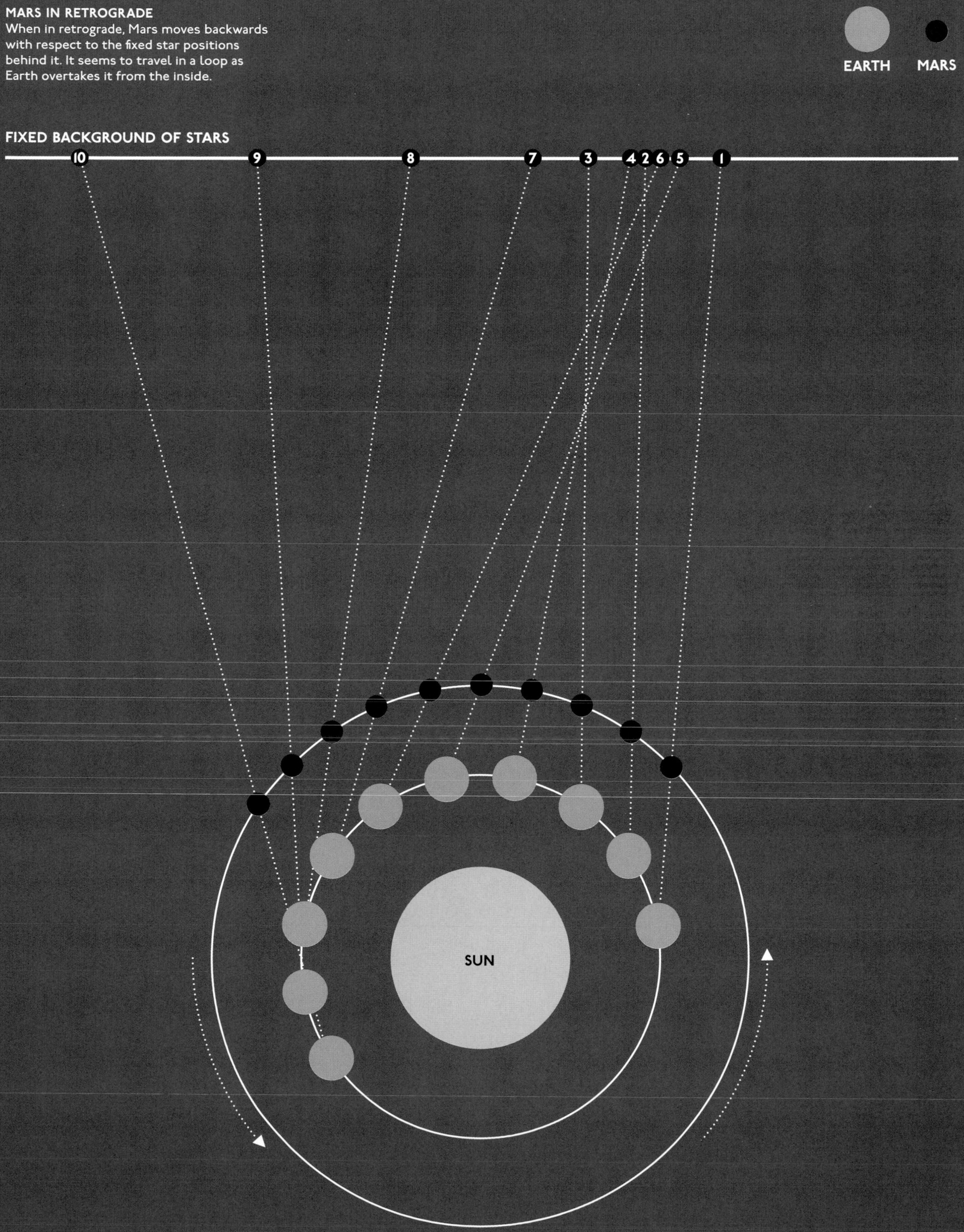

THE BIRTH OF THE SOLAR SYSTEM

BELOW AND BOTTOM: Lying in the middle of what is known as Tornado Alley, the US state of Oklahoma experiences hundreds of tornadoes between April and June every year. These giant rotating storms tear across the ground, leaving chaos and destruction in their wake.

One of the remarkable things about the laws of Nature is that they are universal. In other words, the same laws that describe the formation of the Solar System must also describe the most mundane things on Earth. The majestic spinning motions of the planets as they journey around the Sun must therefore be described by the same laws as other things that spin – like the seemingly ordinary motion of water as it spirals down out of a sink. Spinning spirals are seen all over the Earth and all across the Universe. We see them everywhere because the laws of physics are the same everywhere.

Each year in Oklahoma these universal laws unleash forces that drive some of the most powerful and destructive phenomena on our planet. Oklahoma lies in the middle of a part of the United States known as Tornado Alley, where between April and July hundreds of twisters tear across the landscape. They are incredibly dangerous and destructive, and their key feature is a violent, spinning column of air.

For professional storm chasers, the challenge is to get as close to a tornado as possible. However, playing with the most intense of all atmospheric phenomenon does come loaded with risk. A tornado can pick up a car and throw it half a kilometre through the air, crushing it into a ball. This immense destructive power is generated by intense low pressure, which seeds the high wind speeds and rapid rotation that characterise a twister.

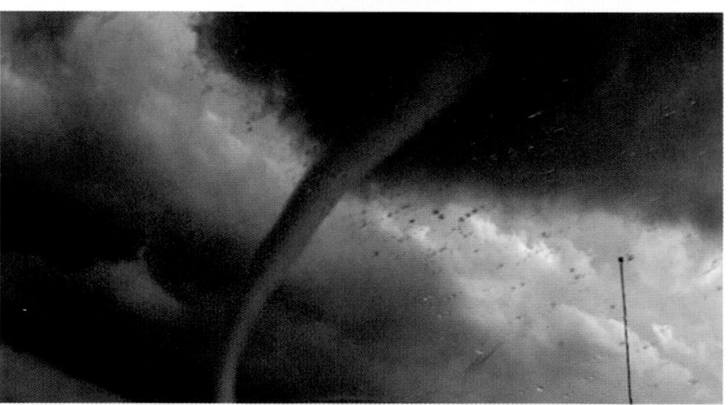

Tornadoes are most often born from a type of thunderstorm known as a supercell. These giant rotating storms start high in the atmosphere, but as they develop they descend towards the ground, sucking up hot air and contracting into a tightly spinning funnel. The wind speed increases as the storm contracts, in order to obey one of the most fundamental of universal principles, known as the conservation of angular momentum. On Earth, if the conditions are right, the conservation of angular momentum in these colossal collapsing storm systems can rapidly generate wind speeds of at least 300, sometimes 400, and in exceptional cases 500, kilometres an hour.

ANGULAR MOMENTUM

To a physicist, quantities that are conserved are of overwhelming importance. A conserved quantity is something that never changes – something that can be neither created nor destroyed. Energy is an example of such a conserved quantity, but there are others. One with which we are probably all familiar, although it may have an unfamiliar name, is linear momentum.

Momentum to a physicist is the speed of something (or, more accurately, its velocity, which is its speed in a particular direction) multiplied by its mass – 'mv'. Imagine a cannon sat waiting to be fired. Both the cannon and the cannon ball are still. This means the momentum of both is zero because nothing has a speed. Now fire the cannon. The cannon ball flies out at high speed and therefore has a momentum equal to its velocity times its mass. But momentum is a conserved quantity, which means it cannot be created or destroyed. This means that even as the cannon ball is flying through the air, the combined momentum of the cannon and the ball must still be zero. It is, because the cannon recoils in the opposite direction to the ball, and the sum of its and the ball's momentum will be zero. The cannon doesn't fly backwards at the same speed as the ball because its mass is bigger, and it is only the product of its mass and speed that must balance – bigger mass, smaller speed, same momentum. You might ask what happens to all the momentum when the cannon ball hits the ground or the cannon stops recoiling. It isn't destroyed – the ball transfers its momentum to the Earth as it ploughs into the ground, and transfers a bit to molecules of air that it hits as it flies through the air. The cannon will transfer its momentum to the molecules in the ground through friction. If we were sufficiently clever we could track the movements of all the molecules jiggled around by the cannon and ball, and the momentum of everything combined would always add up to zero.

Linear momentum has a counterpart called angular momentum. Instead of measuring the speed with which something flies in a straight line, angular momentum deals with the speed at which something spins. For mathematicians: if something of mass 'm' is flying in a circle at a distance 'r' from the centre with a (tangential) velocity 'v', the angular momentum about the centre of the circle is 'mvr' (see below).

Like linear momentum, angular momentum is conserved – it too can be neither created nor destroyed. A classic example of the conservation of angular momentum in action is a spinning ice-skater. If the skater starts to spin then pulls her arms inwards, she will spin faster. This is because the angular momentum of her hands is bigger the further they are from the centre of her spin – in this case, her body. If she pulls her arms in, therefore, angular momentum from her hands is lost, and this must be compensated for by an increase in the spin rate of the rest of her body – she speeds up.

Again, the observant reader may have noticed a subtlety here. How did the skater start to spin if angular momentum can't be created? The answer is that the skater pushed against the ice to start spinning, and the ice is connected firmly to the Earth. Just as the cannon recoiled against the cannon ball to conserve angular momentum, the entire Earth recoils against the spinning skater to conserve angular momentum and the Earth's spin rate changes. This is a miniscule effect, of course, because the Earth is many millions of times bigger than the skater. As the skater slows down through friction with the ice, just as for the cannon, the angular momentum is redistributed back to the Earth by friction. The total spin of everything never changes, though; angular momentum is always conserved.

MOMENTUM = M_1V_1

MOMENTUM = M_2V_2

ONE PRINCIPLE OF GENERAL RELATIVITY
(i) Linear momentum is conserved. (ii) Momentum before =0. Therefore (iii) m1v1 + m2v2 =0. (iv) Heavy cannon recoils slowly against fast moving cannon ball.

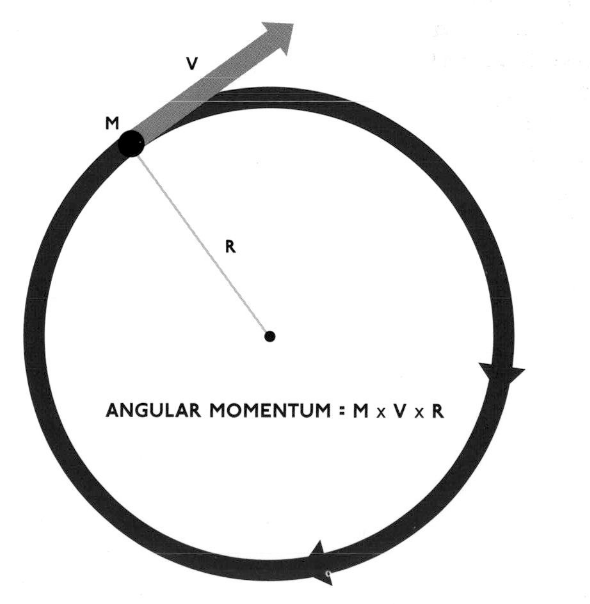

CONSERVATION OF ANGULAR MOMENTUM
If the mass (M) is constant, any decrease in the length (R) results in an increase in the velocity (V) – hence why a skater spins faster when she pulls her arms in, effectively reducing her R.

BELOW: In 1995, NASA's Hubble space telescope captured the image of three space pillars, dubbed 'The Pillars of Creation'. These dramatic pillars in the Eagle Nebula were formed over millions of years from radiation and dust from around twenty or more huge stars.

OPPOSITE: The dark spots in this picture reveal a type of interstellar cloud known as a Bok globule. Bok globules are the least understood objects in the Universe, despite extensive studies by the astronomer Bart Bok, from whom they get their name. These small, cold, gas and dust clouds condense to form stars.

Bizarre as it sounds, the universal processes that shape these vast storm systems are the same as those that sculpted the early Solar System, because the laws of physics are universal and apply equally to everything. The Eagle Nebula, an interstellar cloud of dust, hygrogen and helium and a sprinkling of heavier elements, is about 6,500 light years away from Earth. It is almost 100 trillion kilometres (60 trillion miles) tall and within its towering pillars, stars are made. This famous photograph (below), known as 'The Pillars of Creation', was taken by the Hubble space telescope in 1995. As well as being stunningly beautiful, it also gives us a glimpse of where we came from. Five billion years ago everything we know and see around us was formed from a nebula just like

this – a giant cloud of gas and dust. Drifting across light years of space, that cloud remained unchanged for millions of years, until something happened that caused it to coalesce into the Solar System we have today. It is thought that a supernova, the explosive death of a nearby star, sent shockwaves through the nebula and caused a clump to form in the heart of the cloud.

Ths clump would have been denser than the surrounding cloud, so its gravitational pull would have been stronger. Very slowly, over millions of years, it would have pulled in more and more gas and dust. Eventually the whole cloud would have collapsed in on itself faster and faster, but crucially, as it collapsed it was doing something that would establish a series of events that we all experience today: the cloud was spinning.

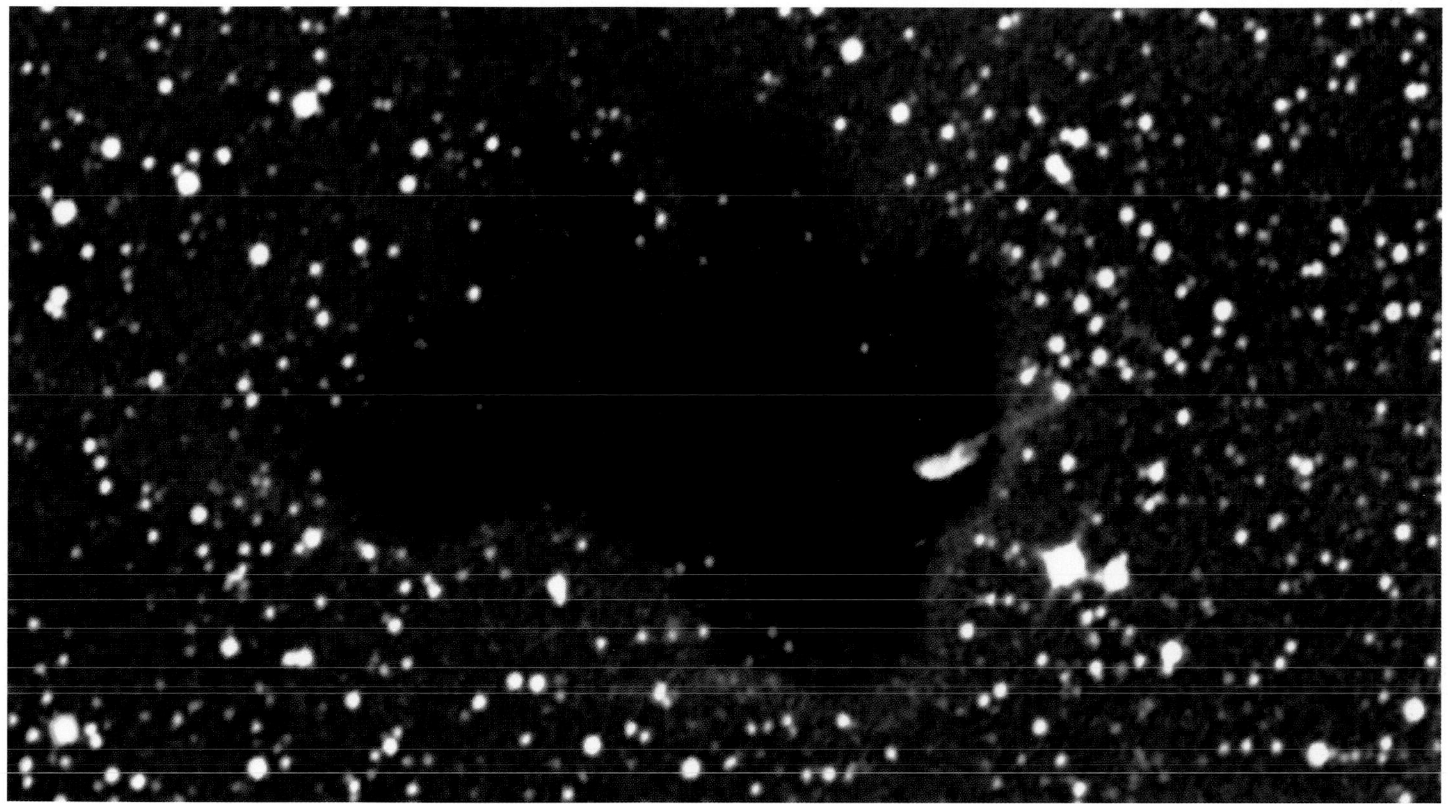

The initial spin would probably have come from the glancing blow dealt by the supernova shockwave. Just like the spinning vortex of a tornado, this spinning cloud of cosmic dust from which all of us emerged had to follow the universal laws of the cosmos. It doesn't matter if you are a tiny molecule of air on a minuscule planet, or a vast cloud of gas containing all the ingredients of a solar system, if something spinning contracts then the universal principle of conservation of angular momentum dictates that it must rotate faster.

In the case of a tornado this contraction unleashes incredibly destructive forces. The core rotates faster and faster and a column of violently rotating air descends from the cloud, wreaking havoc on any man-made structures that it encounters. Strangely and wonderfully, the universal principle responsible for this violence is also responsible for creating the stability of the Solar System, because it is angular momentum that stops the Solar System collapsing completely.

As the cloud collapsed, one of the strangest and least understood objects in the Universe was formed. A Bok globule is one of the coldest known objects in the natural universe. Its low temperature is critically important, because it means that the gas and dust molecules are moving very slowly and are therefore more easily captured by the weak force of gravity, and pulled together. As the collapse continued, one particularly dense area dominated and the gas slowly formed a more familiar shape. Out of the cold a new star was born.

While gravity caused one part of our early solar system to contract further and further, until nuclear fusion reactions halted the collapse, the rest of the spinning disc was stabilised by a different mechanism. It was the conserved spin that balanced the inward pull of gravity. Imagine you throw a tennis ball through the air. It forms an arc in a curved path called a parabola, upwards at first, but then back downwards to the ground, where it lands some distance away from you. Unless you throw it vertically upwards, the tennis ball has angular momentum relative to the Earth. This angular momentum would be conserved were it not for the fact that the ball bumps into the ground. But imagine that you could throw the ball very fast – so fast that by the time it moved downwards to the ground the Earth had curved away beneath it. The tennis ball would then be in orbit around the Earth, and if there were no air resistance, no forces would act upon it other than gravity because it would never bump into the ground. It would be constantly falling towards the Earth, and be constantly missing! Because angular momentum, or spin, is conserved, this is a completely stable situation – gravity ensures that the ball keeps falling, and as long as no other forces act, the ball keeps missing the ground and stays in orbit. In exactly the same way, a planet doesn't fall into the Sun even though it is only feeling the attractive force of gravity; it is constantly falling towards the Sun but constantly missing ◉

This is how our Solar System was born: rather than the whole system collapsing into the Sun, a disc of dust and gas extending billions of kilometres into space formed around the newly shining star. In just a few hundred million years, pieces of the cloud collapsed to form planets and moons, and so a star system, our Solar System, was formed. The journey from chaos into order had begun.

LEFT: This image of the Eagle Nebula – so-called because it looks like an eagle from afar – gives us a remarkable insight into the birth of a solar system. The tall pillars and round balls of dust and gas signify where new stars are being formed.

SATURN:
THE INFANT SOLAR SYSTEM

Of all the Solar System's wonders, there is a place we can go to where the processes that built the Solar System are still in action today. It is a place of outstanding beauty and complexity; a place that has entranced astronomers for centuries. It is the planet Saturn.

SATURN

1.4 billion kilometres away from the Sun, Saturn sits six planets away from the centre of the Solar System. It takes almost thirty years to orbit the Sun, and a day on Saturn is only around ten and a half hours long, although it is believed to fluctuate more than our stable days on Earth. Saturn is the second largest planet after Jupiter, but while it dwarfs the Earth in volume, it is only ninety-five times the mass of our home planet. This is because of its surprisingly low density. One of the more amusing facts about our solar system is that Saturn would float in water, if you could find an ocean big enough. Saturn's low density is a result of its composition; it is mainly composed of hydrogen and helium, with small amounts of other trace elements. Along with the other three outer planets – Jupiter, Uranus and Neptune – Saturn is a gas giant.

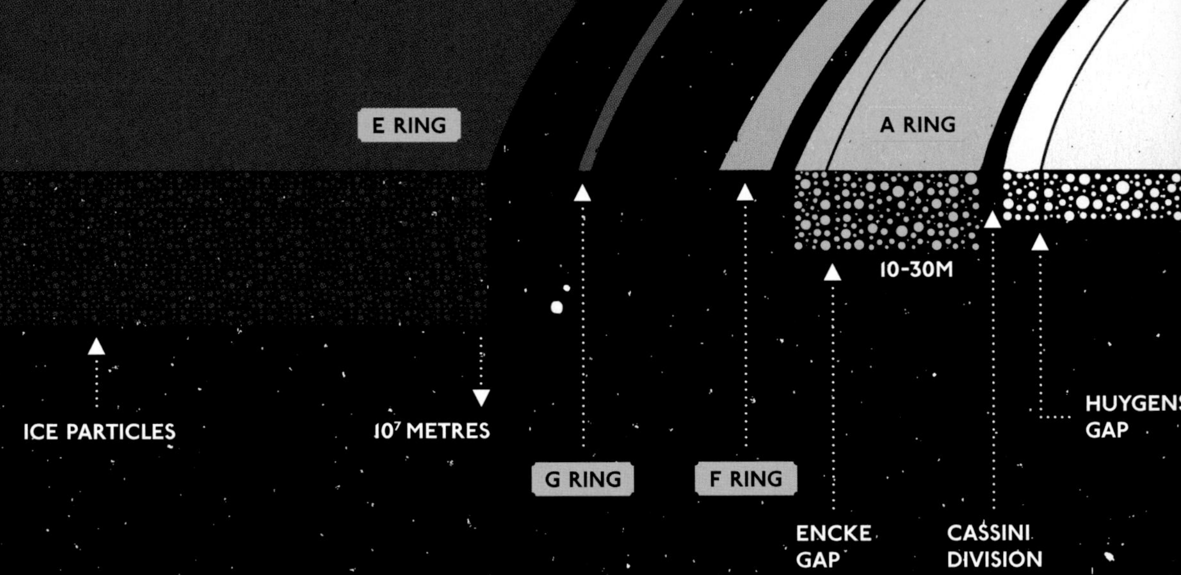

SATURN'S MOONS

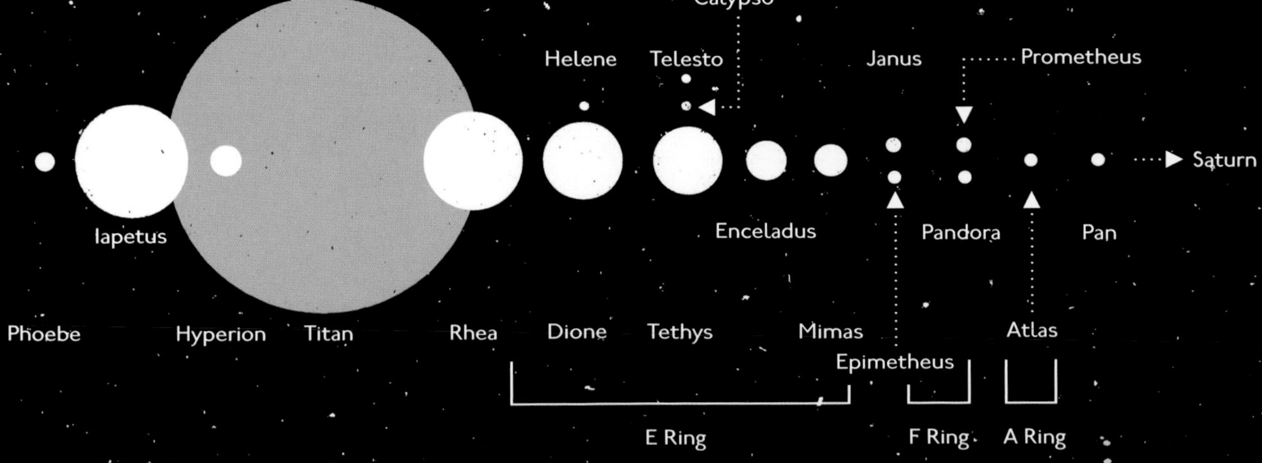

B RING
C RING
5-10M
5M
MAXWELL
GAP
COLOMBO
GAP
D RING

SATURN'S RINGS

Humans have known about Saturn since they first stared up at the sky, because it appears as a bright and beautiful, wandering yellow star. 1.3 billion kilometres (800 million miles) from Earth, it is the furthest planet visible with the naked eye and has had a special place in ancient mythology for millennia. For all that time and for all the eyes that were trained on this wandering yellow star, though, not a single person was aware of the one characteristic that today draws us to Saturn more than to any other planet. Not until Galileo first trained his telescope on Saturn in 1610 did humans see one of the true wonders of the Solar System: Saturn's rings.

Galileo thought the rings were two moons nestling on either side of the giant planet, and it was forty-five years before the Dutch astronomer Christiaan Huygens, using a more powerful telescope that magnified the planet fifty times, distinguished 'a thin flat ring' for the first time. Huygens was also the first to discover Saturn's largest moon, Titan, but it was the great Italian astronomer Giovanni Cassini who unravelled the first details of the rings' intimate structure. In 1675, having already discovered four more of Saturn's smaller moons – Iapetus, Rhea, Tethys and Dione – Cassini discovered a gap in the rings, now known as the Cassini division.

For the last 350 years, Huygens and Cassini have had their names intimately linked with Saturn. In 1997, this legacy came to a fitting climax with the launch of one of the most extraordinary and ambitious missions ever sent into the outer solar system. The launch of the robotic spacecraft mission, Cassini-Huygens, was controlled from NASA's laboratory in Pasadena, California.

On 1 July 2004, after a 3.5-billion-kilometre (2-billion-mile) journey that included slingshots around Venus and flybys past Earth and Jupiter, Cassini became our one, and to date only, spacecraft in orbit around Saturn. Its purpose is to study Saturn and its rings in such detail that Giovanni Cassini could only have dreamt of. It may take eighty minutes for one of the Cassini spacecraft's images to be sent by radio waves across space to us here on Earth, but again and again the wait has been worth it. For over six years the spacecraft has been sending back the most amazing pictures. They have revealed that the rings are impossibly intricate, made up of thousands upon thousands of individual bands and gaps and surrounded by a network of moons. Part of Cassini's mission is to discover how the rings came to be like this; how all this incredible structure was created. This is interesting in itself, of course, but there is a deeper reason for studying Saturn and her rings: their intricate structure is as

LEFT AND BELOW: Saturn is well known for its distinctive appearance. However, it took early astronomers years to identify Saturn's rings, believing them to be moons. The picture opposite was taken by the Cassini spacecraft, launched in 1997; this and the Cassini division were named after Giovanni Cassini, who discovered the rings in 1675.

The more we can understand the forces at work in the rings, the more we can piece together the origins of our own existence.

close as we can get to the disc of dust, rock and ice that surrounds the primordial Sun, and out of which the planets formed. That is why the Saturnian system has so much to teach us.

Professor Carl Murray is part of the Cassini mission's imaging team and has spent a lifetime studying Saturn's rings. For him the rings are far more than just one of the most beautiful sights in our cosmic backyard, they are a unique opportunity to understand the origins of our solar system through direct observation. 'They are like a miniature solar system because the moons are the equivalent of the planets and Saturn is the equivalent of the Sun', he told me when we met and stood in the gallery above the control room of Cassini. 'The physical processes that go on in the rings and their interaction with the small moons that are around them are probably similar to what went on in the early solar system after the planets formed.' In Murray's eyes, looking at the rings of Saturn is like looking at the Solar System four and a half billion years ago, with the Sun at the centre surrounded by a disc of dust not unlike Saturn's rings.

It is this similarity, the history of our solar system contained within the rings, that convinces Murray of the importance of studying them. 'If we can't understand a disc of material that's in our own backyard, what chance do we have of understanding a disc that's long since disappeared?'

The more we can understand the forces at work in the rings, the more we can piece together the origins of our own existence – and that means understanding the structure of the rings in intricate detail. Now, for the first time, by using the data from Cassini we are able to recreate almost every aspect of the rings. We can journey from the vast scale of the disc to the minute structure of individual ringlets. We can measure the immense speeds of the individual rings as they orbit Saturn. Like the planets orbiting the Sun, the rings nearest Saturn are the fastest, travelling at over eighty thousand kilometres an hour. While the rings appear solid, casting shadows onto the planet, they are also incredibly delicate; the main disc of the rings is over a hundred thousand kilometres across, and less than one kilometre thick.

Saturn's rings are undoubtedly beautiful, and when you see the magnificent pictures sent back from Cassini, it's almost impossible to imagine that that level of intricacy, beauty and symmetry could have emerged spontaneously, but emerge spontaneously it did. For that reason alone, Saturn's rings are a wonder of the Solar System, but there is more to it than that, because in studying the origin and evolution of Saturn's rings, we have at last begun to gain valuable and unprecendented insights into the origins and evolutions of our own solar system ◉

SATURN'S RINGS ON EARTH

There were two things the boat driver told me about these icebergs when we visited Iceland: one was that they can come up from the bottom of the seabed without any warning, fly up to the surface, tip the boat over and then you die. The other was that if you collect some ice and take it home, it's absolutely brilliant in whisky because the water is pure, a thousand years old, with no pollutants in it and it makes whisky taste superb. So it's either death or whisky. That's my kind of pond!

It's difficult to imagine the scale, beauty and intricacy of Saturn's rings here on Earth, but the glacial lagoons in Iceland can transport our minds across millions of kilometres of space and help us to understand the true nature of the rings. There, as the ancient glacier tumbles off the mountain, huge chunks of ice break off and fill the lagoon below with icebergs as far as the eye can see. At first sight, the lagoon appears to be a solid sheet of pristine ice, but that is an illusion. The surface is constantly shifting, an almost organic, ever-changing raft of thousands of individual icebergs floating on the water. The structure of Saturn's rings is similar, because despite appearances the rings aren't solid. Each ring is made up of hundreds of ringlets and each ringlet is made up of billions of separate pieces. Captured by Saturn's gravity, the ring particles independently orbit the planet in an impossibly thin layer.

But the similarity doesn't end with the layout. The reason Saturn's rings are so incredibly bright from Earth is because they are predominantly made of glacially pure water ice, sparkling as they reflect the faint sunlight; billions of pieces of frozen water, a billion kilometres away from Earth. Most of the pieces are smaller than a centimetre, many are micron-size ice crystals, but some are as big as an iceberg, some are as big as houses and some can be over a kilometre across.

What a wonderful thing it would be to stand on one of the larger pieces of Saturn's rings and gaze out over thousands of kilometres of glistening ice. The lagoon is perhaps as close as a human being will get for hundreds of years, but its beauty allows the imagination to fly. I hope that, one day, we will follow.

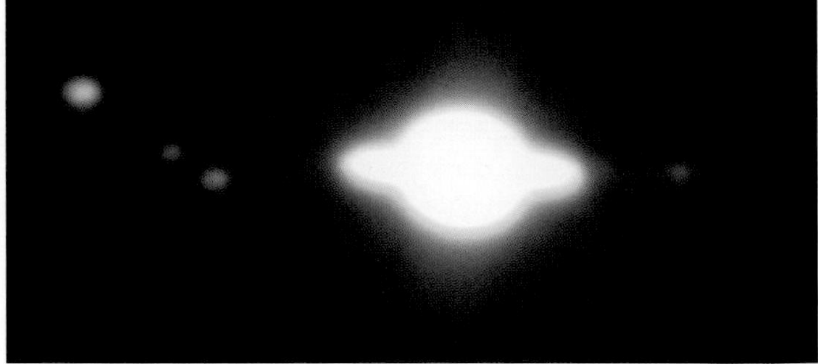

TOP: The structure of Saturn's rings is remarkably similar to the way these beautiful, shifting icebergs float in this Icelandic lagoon.

ABOVE: A truly incredible sight; Saturn and its rings viewed through a telescope – you can even make out several moons around the planet.

YOUNG OR OLD

The brightness of the ice in Saturn's rings is a puzzle because our solar system is a very dirty place. It is full of dust, and until recently it was thought that Saturn's rings must be relatively newly formed, because otherwise their magnificence would have been dimmed as the surfaces of the ice crystals became coated in this interplanetary debris. It is now thought that they are much older – hundreds of millions or even billions of years old. The reason the rings shine so brightly is that, like the icebergs in the lagoon, the rings are constantly changing. Paradoxically, despite their intricate, almost eternally beautiful structure, we now know that the rings are a chaotic place, at least in the small scale of individual ice particles. As the ring particles orbit Saturn, they crash into each other and collect into giant clusters that are endlessly forming and breaking apart. As they collide, the particles shatter, exposing bright new faces of ice that catch the sunlight. It is because of this constant recycling that the rings are able to stay as bright and shiny as they were when they formed.

This dynamism is one of the most remarkable and surprising things about Saturn's rings. Their constant renewal is why they are clean enough to reflect sunlight and allow us to see them at all. If they were static, their magnificence would have long ago been dimmed by dust. They are different today than they were a thousand years ago; they'll be different in a hundred or a thousand years' time, too, but that structure and that beauty, that magnificence, will remain, possibly for as long as there is a solar system ◉

Each ring is made up of hundreds of ringlets and each ringlet is made up of billions of separate pieces. Caught within the grasp of Saturn's gravity, the ring particles independently orbit around the planet in an impossibly thin layer.

The reason Saturn's rings are so incredibly bright from Earth is because they are made of almost pure water ice, sparkling in the sunlight, billions of these pieces, a billion kilometres away from Earth.

As the ring particles orbit Saturn, they're continually crashing into each other and collecting into giant clusters that are endlessly forming and breaking apart. As they collide, the particles shatter exposing bright new faces of ice that catch the sunlight. It's because of this constant recycling that the rings are able to stay as bright and shiny as they were when they formed.

Most of the pieces are smaller than a centimetre, many are micron-size ice crystals, but some are as big as an iceberg, some are as big as houses and some can be over a kilometre across.

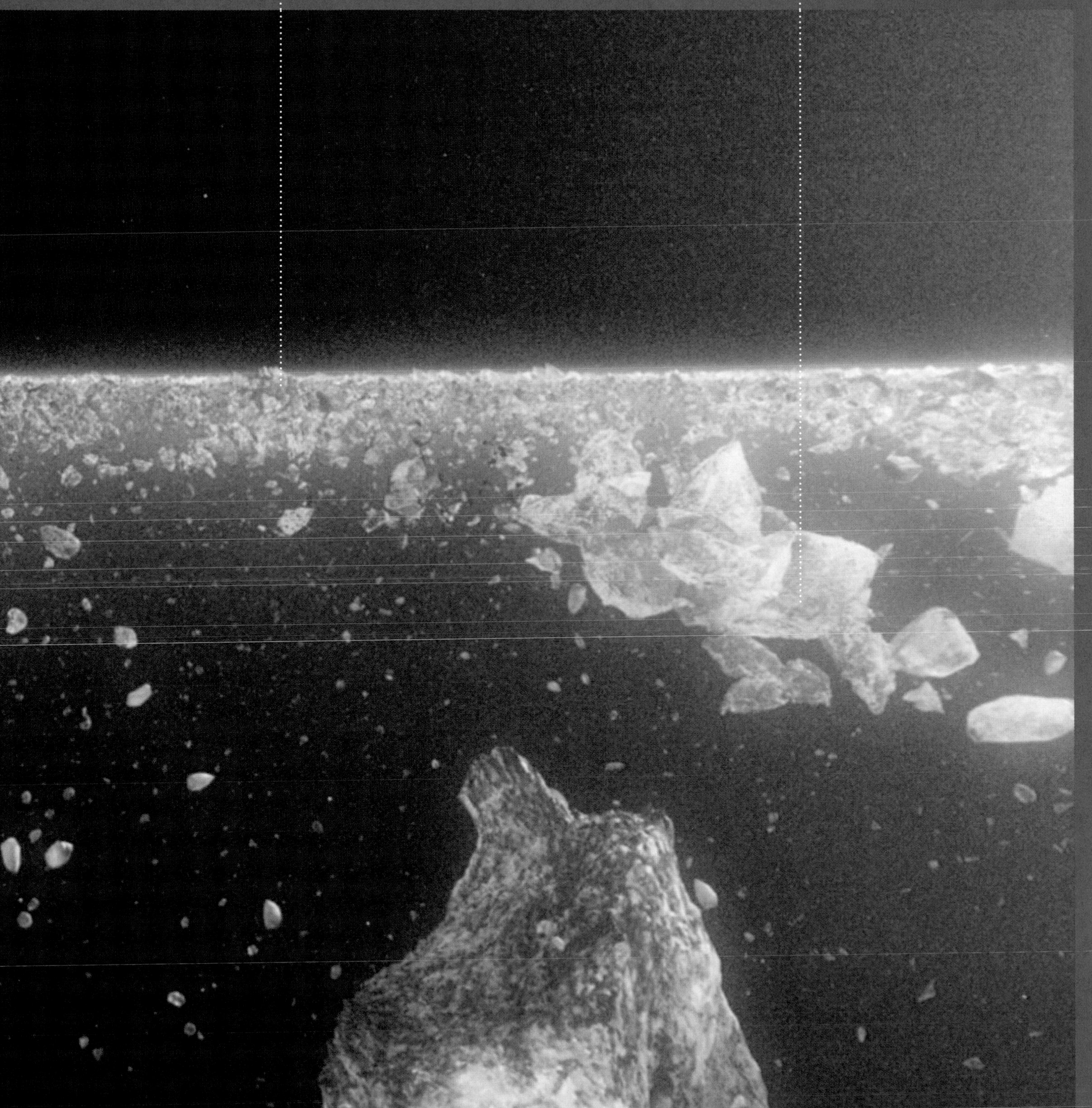

THE MOONS OF SATURN

When Galileo first looked up at Saturn through his primitive telescope in 1610, he thought the planet had ears. With a telescope no more powerful than a pair of modern binoculars, Galileo could only guess at what he was seeing. Having recently discovered four moons orbiting Jupiter he came to the obvious conclusion – Saturn had two giant moons orbiting the planet and the 'lobes' he could see were simply an illusion. To his dismay, as the celestial dance between Earth and Saturn progressed under his watchful eye, these 'moons' seemed to disappear; Saturn, it seemed, had 'swallowed' its children. What Galileo was actually seeing were the rings of Saturn disappearing as Saturn and Earth danced around the Sun, shifting our perspective so that the rings were edge-on to us.

Although his first observation was wrong, Galileo's guess that Saturn, like Jupiter, has a phalanx of moons was right. We have discovered sixty-two moons orbiting the planet to date, and they hold the key to understanding why the rings have such an intricate structure. Saturn is like a mini solar system, with the moons orbiting like planets around the Sun. From Earth we can only see the larger moons, but as Pioneer, Voyager and Cassini explored the system in more detail, it has become clear that these sixty-two satellites are a weird and wonderful bunch.

Dione is typical of Saturn's icy moons. Discovered by Cassini in 1684, it looks similar to our own moon but its composition is very different. It's about two-thirds water but the surface temperature is -190 degrees Celsius, and at those temperatures, the surface behaves like solid rock. It is a world covered in craters and ice cliffs and, just like our moon, it's tidally locked to Saturn, which means the same side of Dione always faces towards its master.

Iapetus is the third largest moon of Saturn and also one of the most mysterious. It has a strange ridge running around its equator and is so far away from Saturn that if you were to stand on its surface, you would be able to see Saturn's entire ring system dominating the night sky. When Cassini discovered this moon in 1671, he couldn't understand why he could only observe it when it was on the western side of Saturn. When it should have been on the east, it simply disappeared from view. Cassini concluded, correctly, that the reason for this mysterious observation was the great contrast between the two sides of the moon: one half is clean ice and the other is coated in black dusty deposits. The strange split personality of Iapetus' surface has led to it being nicknamed the Yin and Yang moon. The Cassini spacecraft has explored Iapetus in intricate detail, and it is now believed that half of the surface is covered in a layer of carbon. These dark deposits are thought to have come from an initial meteorite impact, but since that impact another characteristic of Iapetus has made the dark and light contrast of the two sides even more pronounced. Iapetus has a very slow rotation rate; one day on this moon lasts seventy-nine Earth days. This means that each side of the moon spends a long time being warmed by the dim light of the distant Sun, and this in turn leads to the highest daytime temperatures and the lowest nighttime temperatures of any of Saturn's satellites. Like all dark surfaces, the carbon-covered ice on the dark side absorbs more heat than the bright, reflective ice on the light side. This extra heat causes the ice to evaporate, leaving behind a carbon residue that makes the dark side even darker (and as the evaporated water moves to the cooler side, it makes the light side lighter, too). The darker the surface gets, the more heat it absorbs, increasing the temperature further and so creating a runaway effect that over millions of years has divided the surface of Iapetus neatly in two.

Saturn's largest moon is Titan. This giant moon is bigger than the planet Mercury, almost as big as Mars and is the second largest moon in the Solar System. The unique thing about Titan is its atmosphere: it is the only moon that we know of that has a fully developed atmosphere. And what an atmosphere it is! Four times as dense as our atmosphere here on Earth, it is rich in organic molecules and may have a chemistry very similar to that of the primordial Earth, before life began. Titan is without doubt one of the most fascinating places in the Solar System, and we'll return to it in detail in Chapter 4.

Hyperion is a moon unlike any other. It is not round, and its battered surface has the texture of a sponge. One theory is that Hyperion is a comet that drifted in from the distant icy reaches of the Solar System and was captured by Saturn's gravity.

Saturn's moons are a truly breathtaking collection of diverse and fascinating objects, but they aren't just a celestial freak show – they are the driving force behind the beauty and structure of the rings ◉

DIONE

DISCOVERED: 1684
APPEARANCE: Similar to the Moon – it is covered in craters and made of one-third rock; two-thirds ice
DIAMETER: 1,123 kilometres (698 miles)

TITAN

DISCOVERED: 1655
APPEARANCE: Formed by Earth-like processes, it is craterless with probable areas of liquid methane
DIAMETER: 5,150 kilometres (3,200 miles)

IAPETUS

DISCOVERED: 1671
APPEARANCE: One-half is clean ice and the other coated in black dusty deposits
DIAMETER: Saturn's third largest moon; 1,471 kilometres (917 miles)

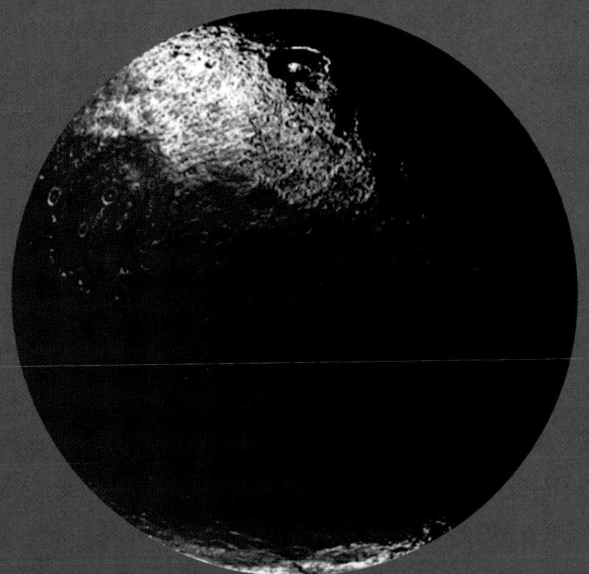

HYPERION

DISCOVERED: 1848
UNIQUE FEATURE: Potato-shaped
DIMENSIONS: 328 km x 260 km x 214 km (204 miles x 162 miles x 134 miles)

Perhaps the most remarkable of Saturn's moons is buried in the heart of the E ring. This moon, Enceladus, is rapidly becoming one of the most intriguing places in the Solar System.

RIGHT: Enceladus, Saturn's sixth largest moon, is an astronomical mystery. It has defied geological theory; somehow this tiny icy moon has survived when it should have long since died.

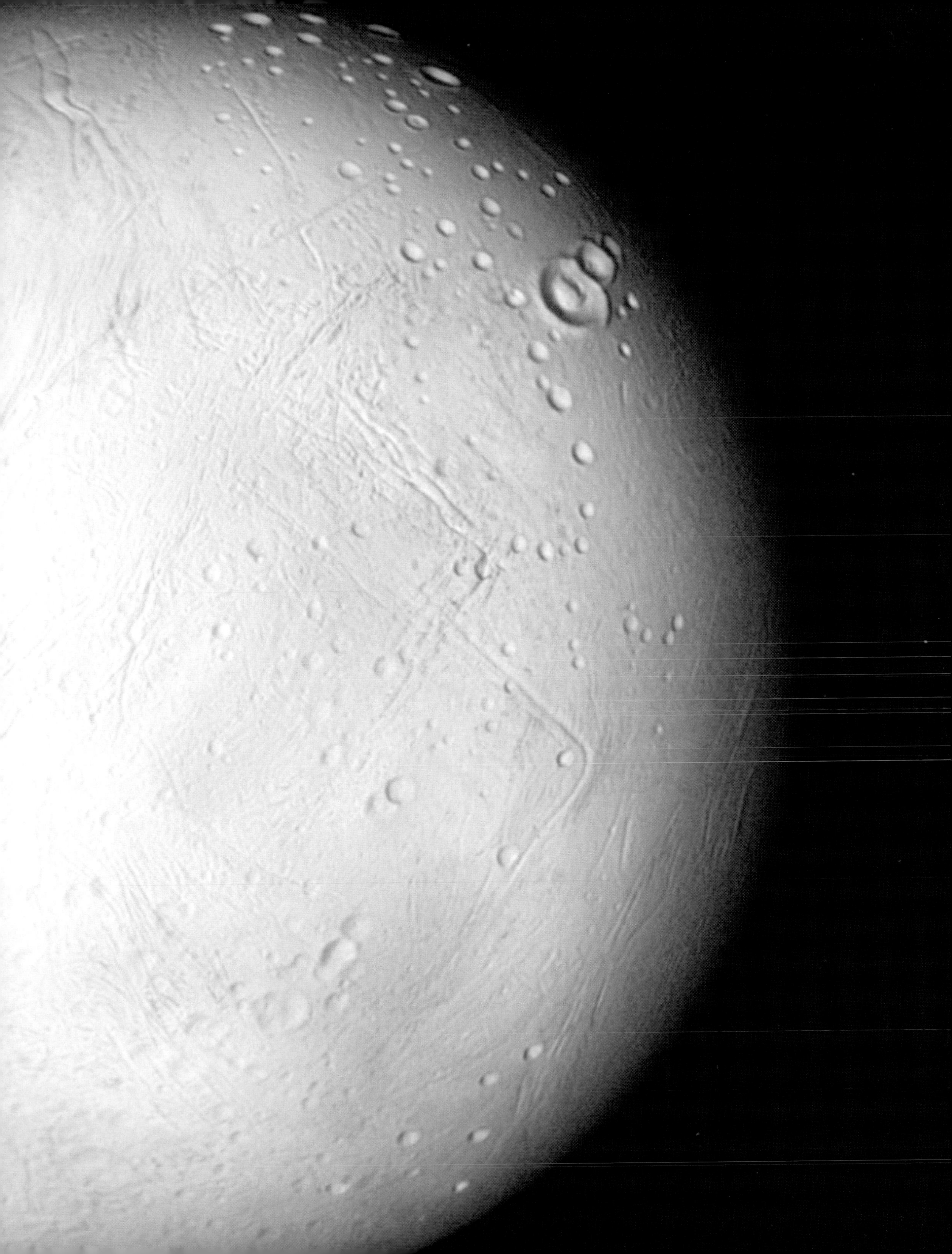

ENCELADUS: THE BRIGHTEST MOON

The icy moon of Enceladus was first discovered by Sir Frederick William Herschel on 28 August 1789. Herschel was trained as a musician and composed twenty-four symphonies in his lifetime, but it was his inventiveness as an astronomer that ultimately assured his place in history. Herschel's crowning achievement was the discovery of Uranus in 1781, which he originally named Georgium Sidus in honour of King George III, who was passionately interested in astronomy. Despite believing that every planet was inhabited, including the Sun, Herschel was a brilliant telescope builder, innovator and observer of the night sky. He founded something of an astronomical dynasty. His sister Caroline was also a brilliant observer, discovering several comets and nebulae, and his son, John, became a famous astronomer, too (see page 30). William Herschel lived to the ripe old age of eighty-four, a number that links him to Uranus in the most fitting of ways, as Uranus takes eighty-four years to complete its orbit of the Sun.

In 1789, Herschel built the largest and most famous of all his telescopes in the garden of his home in Slough. This twelve-metre (forty-foot) telescope was then the largest telescope in the world, and on the very first night Herschel used it he became the first person to see Saturn's sixth largest moon.

Enceladus is tiny in comparison to our own moon, and in diameter it is smaller than the length of United Kingdom. For 200 years after its discovery we learnt little more about Enceladus beyond Herschel's initial observations. Besides knowing that it was made of water ice, we knew only its orbit and had estimations for its mass and volume. There was one other intriguing property of Enceladus that marked out the tiny moon as an astronomical curiosity: Enceladus is the most reflective object in the Solar System; its icy surface reflects almost all the sunlight that strikes it. Over a billion kilometres

BELOW LEFT: The dramatic landscape of Iceland owes much to the separation of two major tectonic plates. As the continents slowly drift apart they tear apart the surface of the Earth.

RIGHT: The southern side of Enceladus is in direct contrast to the smooth surface elsewhere; here, four parallel trenches – the 'Tiger Stripes' – are carved into the ice.

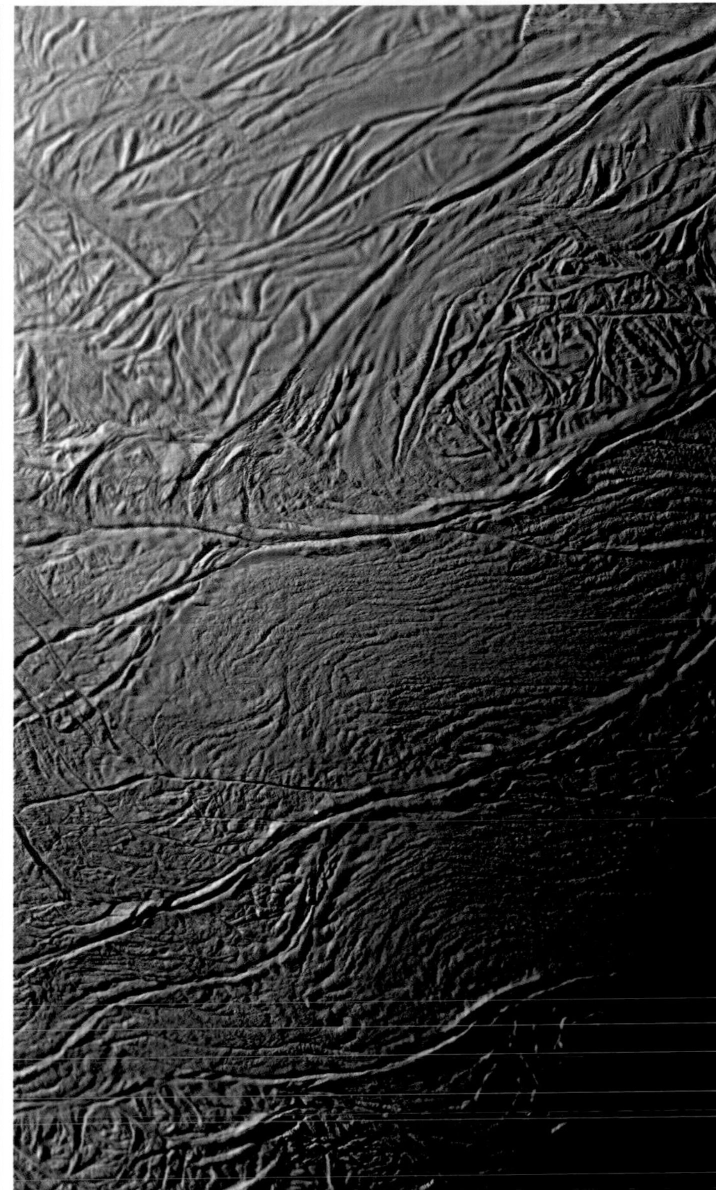

away from Earth and only 500 kilometres (310 miles) across, however, the extraordinary secrets of Enceladus remained a mystery for over two centuries since there was no telescope large enough to uncover them. To do that, we had to fly there.

Our first proper glimpse of Enceladus came in 1981 when the Voyager spacecraft passed within 87,000 kilometres (54,000 miles) of the moon. Buried deep within the E ring of Saturn's intricate system, the images it took of Enceladus revealed something that no one was expecting. This ancient moon was not covered with impact craters as had been assumed, instead vast swathes of its surface were smooth. Virtually every moon in the Solar System is riddled with impacts from asteroids, so if the evidence of these destructive collisions has disappeared, then this demands an explanation. It is impossible for any place in the Solar System to have escaped the heavy bombardment of debris from space over billions of years, so the surface of Enceladus must be young. Its terrain must be constantly regenerating, erasing the record of countless thousands of collisions, so this frozen moon must be geologically active.

Only now that we have the images from Cassini have we begun to understand the strange and wonderful truth behind the smooth surface of Enceladus. Its heavily cratered northern hemisphere looks like any other icy moon, but the southern hemisphere tells a very different story. Its smooth, crater-free surface is scarred by canyons and riven by cracks and it looks remarkably similar to the geology of Earth, but carved in ice rather than rock. Right over the South Pole are the most extraordinary features we have found on Enceladus. An image photographed in incredibly high resolution by Cassini in July 2005 (right) shows four parallel trenches over 130 kilometres (80 miles) long, 40 kilometres (25 miles) apart and possibly hundreds of metres deep. Nicknamed the 'Tiger Stripes', these features look like tectonic fault lines found on our home planet, but Earth's geology is powered by the powerful heat source of its molten core. This heat is partly left over from Earth's formation 4.5 billion years ago, and partly due to the slow decay of heavy radioactive elements in the core. But a tiny world like Enceladus should have lost its meagre supplies of heat long ago to the cold of space, and should surely be geologically dead.

Iceland is home to some of the most dramatic landscapes on Earth. Sat on the dividing line between two continents, this great divide is one of the best places on the planet to explore the geological origin of Enceladus' mysterious Tiger Stripes. In this dramatic landscape you can see the inner workings of our planet exposed. The North American plate, the land mass that forms the western half of the North Atlantic and the United States, Canada and parts of Siberia, is moving slowly west, whilst the Eurasian plate, comprising Europe and Northern Asia, is drifting east. Standing at the boundary, you can see the result of the inexorable drift of the continents, ripping apart the surface of the Earth and creating a plain of new crust between two towering cliff tops, formed from molten lava pushing up from deep beneath the surface. Carolyn Porco, head of the Cassini imaging team, believes something similar may be happening on Enceladus. Standing on the edge of the continental cliffs, she explained to me how such a rift valley could be created on tiny Enceladus, sculpted not from molten rock but from ice.

On 14 July 2005, Cassini flew directly over Enceladus' South Pole at a distance of just 175 kilometres (109 miles) from the surface. Using the infrared spectrometer built into the spacecraft, Porco and her team discovered the first direct evidence of geological activity beneath the surface of this moon. The thermal readings taken showed hot spots under the Tiger Stripes; the average surface temperature of Enceladus is around 75 Kelvin, but around the stripes the temperatures reached at least 130 Kelvin. This was a startling

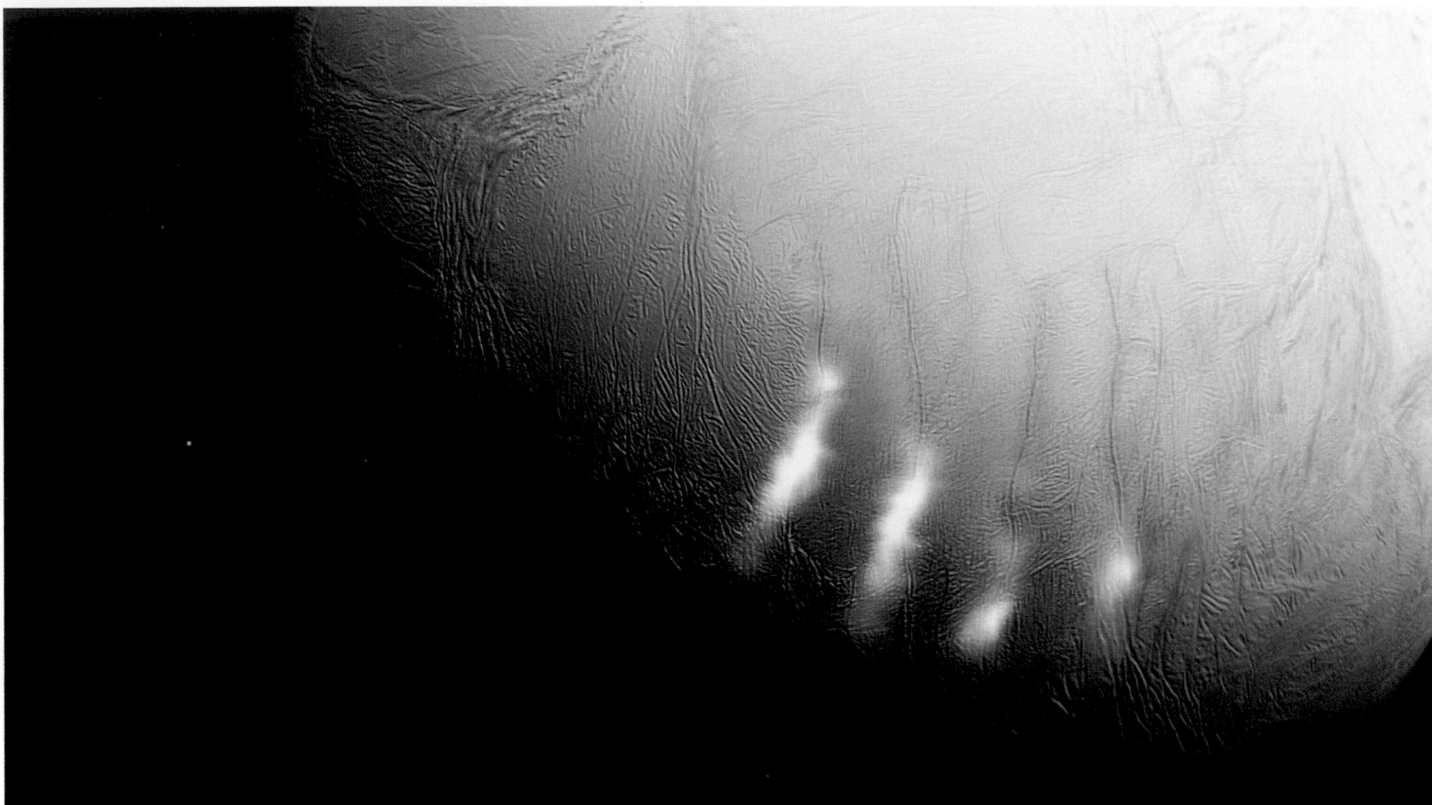

discovery. There is more heat coming out of the southern polar cap of Enceladus than is coming out of the equatorial regions. As Porco commented, it would be like finding that there's more heat coming out of Antarctica than the Equator here on Earth.

The greatest revelation, however, was yet to come. During November 2005, Cassini photographed Enceladus just as the sun was setting behind it (see right). What it showed has become one of the most remarkable discoveries ever made in the outer solar system. The backlit images revealed giant fountains erupting from the Tiger Stripes, volcanoes blasting out ice instead of rock. For Carolyn Porco these images were the culmination of a journey that began with her first work on the Voyager probe a quarter of a century before. 'Those images blew everybody away. I mean, that was like game over, you know? Here you have these dozen or more narrow jets and they just look ghostly and fantastic.'

Until a few years ago, Enceladus was thought to be an unremarkable world, a small, frozen, barren lump of rock and ice. But those fountains of ice erupting thousands of kilometres out into space reveal that there's something incredibly interesting going on beneath its surface. To understand exactly what's going on requires a journey to another one of Iceland's geological wonders: the Great Geysir in the Haukadalur Valley, Iceland. First documented in the Middle Ages, this regular towering fountain of boiling water and steam gave its name to the phenomena wherever it is found on Earth. The Great Geysir is currently dormant – it was last revived by an earthquake in 2000 – but just a few metres away is the Strokkur Geyser, which erupts every few minutes. Geysers are the earthly phenomena most like the ice fountains of Enceladus.

TOP: Fine ice particles and vapour spew out of the 'Tiger Stripes', which are believed to be the hottest part of Enceladus. This geological activity ensures the moon's survival.

ABOVE: This dramatic image, captured by Cassini, shows fountains of ice shooting out of Enceladus from the location of the Tiger Stripes.

BELOW: Geysers, towering fountains of boiling water and steam that erupt from below the Earth's surface, are the closest phenomena we have to the ice fountains of Enceladus.

'Those images blew everybody away. I mean, that was like game over, you know! Here you have these dozen or more narrow jets and they just look ghostly and fantastic.'

Geysers on Earth require three things: a ready source of water, an intense source of heat just below the surface and just the right geological plumbing. If the geysers on Enceladus are based on a similar mechanism, this raises an intriguing possibility. There must be a source of liquid water beneath the surface of the moon; small lakes or perhaps even an ocean that feeds the explosive volcanoes of ice. Yet Enceladus is a billion kilometres away from the Sun, in the cold outer reaches of the Solar System, and it is far too small to have retained any meaningful source of heat in its core. So where does that heat come from? On Earth, the geysers are driven by the same primordial heat source that powers the drift of the continents, but Enceladus is so tiny that its core should be frozen solid.

Enceladus must therefore be getting its heat from somewhere else. The source in all probability comes from its peculiar orbit around Saturn. Enceladus moves around Saturn in an elliptical orbit – in other words, its orbit is not a circle. This means that during each orbit Enceladus moves closer and then further away from Saturn. This eccentric orbit has a profound effect on Enceladus, changing the gravitational force exerted on the moon during every turn. As the difference in forces between the near and far sides of the moon changes, it literally flexes the moon as it travels around Saturn, distorting its shape and creating vast amounts of friction deep within. Friction causes heat,

Bursting through the surface at thirteen hundred kilometres an hour, they rise thousands of kilometres into space. They must be one of the most impressive sights in the Solar System.

and it is thought that the interior of Enceladus is heated just enough to melt a small underground ocean of water. As this water meets the vacuum of space, it immediately vaporises and explodes out of the surface, creating a true wonder of the Solar System.

Geysers on Earth are incredibly impressive natural phenomena, but they pale into insignificance when compared to the ice fountains of Enceladus. While on planets geysers erupt every few minutes at most, blasting boiling water twenty metres (sixty-five feet) into the air, on Enceladus the plumes are thought to be erupting constantly, and for them, the sky is the limit. Bursting through the surface at thirteen hundred kilometres (eight hundred miles) an hour, they rise thousands of kilometres into space. They must be one of the most impressive sights in the Solar System.

The water vapour in the plumes then freezes into tiny ice crystals. Some of it falls back onto Enceladus' surface, giving the moon its reflective icy sheen, but the rest keeps going all the way round Saturn. The ice fountains are creating one of Saturn's rings as we watch; the whole E ring is made from pieces of Enceladus.

Enceladus is not the only moon that shapes the rings, though; Saturn's other moons also play a crucial role in creating these beautiful patterns but they do so indirectly ◉

SATURN'S ICE RINGS
The constantly erupting ice fountains on Enceladus send out plumes of ice, which in turn replenish Saturn's E ring.

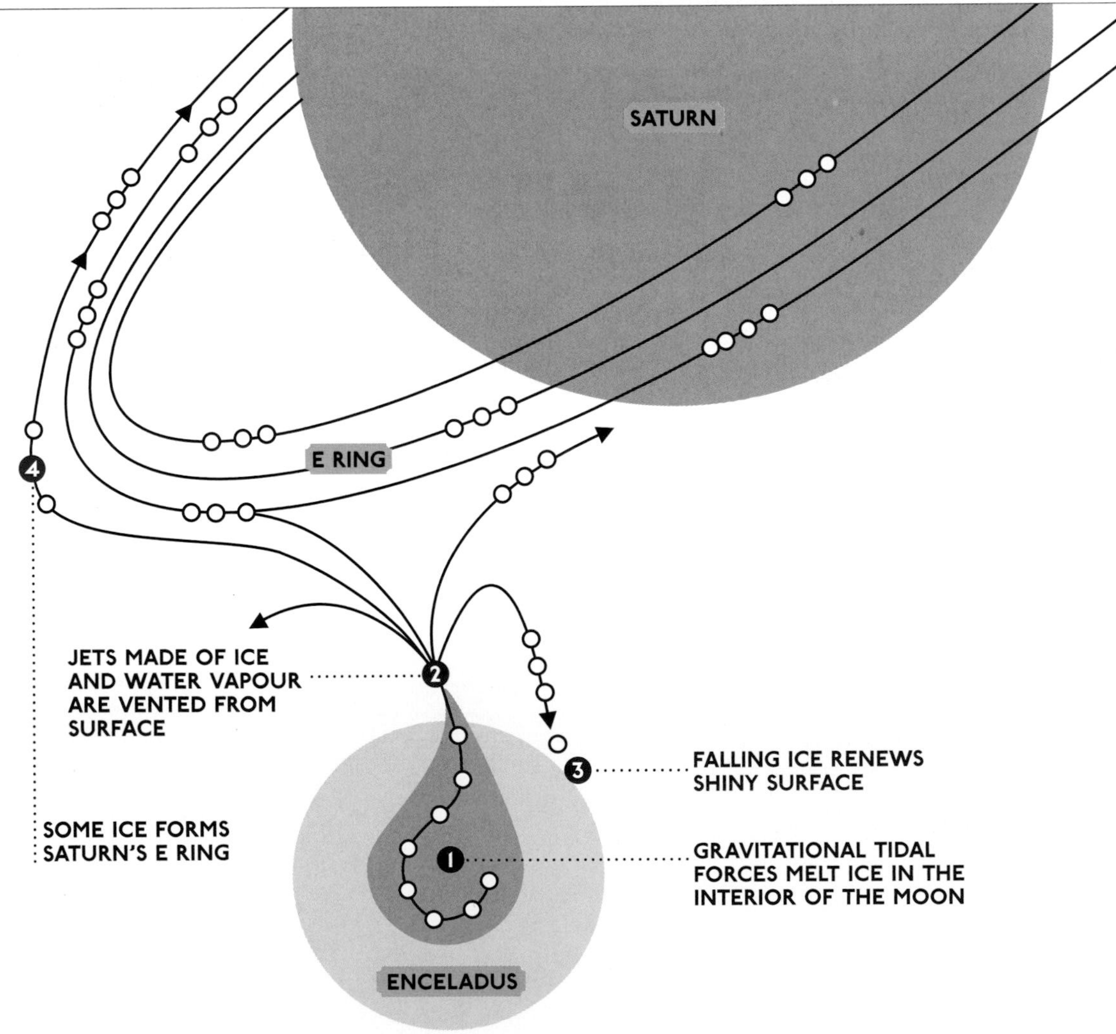

GRAVITY: THE GREATEST SCULPTURE

BELOW: The behaviour of the shifting sands in the Sahara desert provide an excellent model for explaining how moons form in Saturn's rings.

The Sahara desert may seem an unlikely place in which to explain Saturn's rings, but the behaviour of the sand in the desert can help us to understand how the moons form the patterns in their planet's rings.

At first sight the Sahara desert seems an immensely chaotic place; billions of grains of sand being blown randomly around by the desert winds. But look a little bit closer and you start to see order amidst the chaos. There are sand dunes as far as the eye can see, and remarkably the angles of the front of all the sand dunes are exactly the same – never exceeding thirty-four degrees. In the Sahara the emergence of that order is driven by the desert winds that always blow in the same direction, day after day, year after year, moving the sand around. The angle of the dunes is related to the physics of tumbling grains, and is a property not only of sand but of all small grains – salt would behave in a similar way. Try pouring some salt into piles on the table at home – you'll see that the little pyramidal heaps all have the same angled sides. In nature, simple physical processes can create ordered structures that look for all the world as if they have been sculpted by a great artist. In the Saturnian system, the order, beauty and intricacy of the rings is created not by the desert winds roaring across the sand, but by the force of gravity.

ORBITAL RESONANCE

Gravity is a simple force to describe. For the purposes of understanding Saturn's rings, we need only use Isaac Newton's description of gravity first published in 1687. Albert Einstein completely rewrote our understanding of gravity in his theory of General Relativity, published in 1915, but his superior and more accurate theory is

ORBITAL RESONANCE FORMING THE CASSINI DIVISION

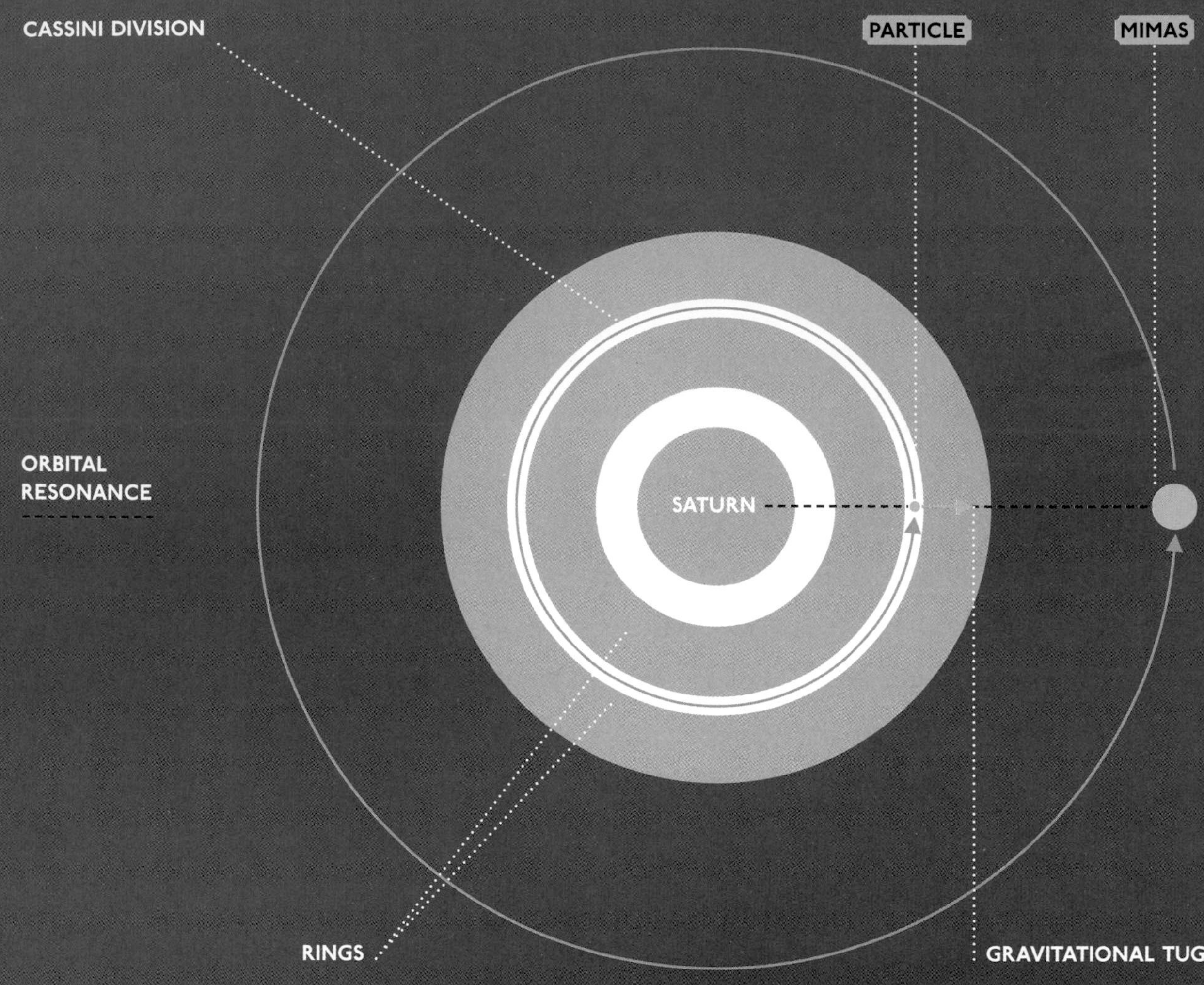

not necessary for understanding the clockwork of the Solar System, with the exception of the orbit of the planet Mercury, which is so close to the massive Sun that relativistic effects are important.

Gravity acts between all objects that have mass, providing an attractive force that is proportional to their masses and falls away with the square of the distance between them. (If we were using Einstein's theory, we should say energy as well, but we don't need such subtleties here!) So Saturn's moons gravitationally attract the tiny particles of ice in the rings towards them, and if you double the distance between the ice particle and the moon, the force of gravity drops by a factor of four. Imagine the complexity of the gravitational tugs on the ice particles in the rings as they orbit the giant planet, constantly being pulled by Saturn's vast phalanx of orbiting moons in an intricate complex dance. It is this complex gravitational field created by Saturn and its moons that gives rise to the structure in the rings.

This gravitational mishmash is present around any planet that has moons, but Saturn is special because there is a sheet of orbiting dust and ice sprinkled throughout the system, allowing us to see gravity in action. You may have sprinkled iron fillings on a sheet of paper over a bar magnet and watched them line up into a beautiful pattern that reveals the hidden magnetic field. This is exactly what is happening around Saturn, except it is the gravitational field that is being revealed before our eyes by billions of tiny sprinkles of ice.

The easiest structure in the rings to explain is the biggest: that is the vast gap in the rings between the A and B rings, known as the Cassini division. This huge swathe of the rings is devoid of ice particles because of the influence of the moon Mimas – the Death Star moon – which orbits well outside the rings. It is a general feature of orbits that the further away from the planet the orbit is, the longer it takes to complete a single orbit. All the rings are inside the orbit of Mimas, and so all the particles orbit Saturn faster and constantly overtake Mimas. When they get to their closest approach to Mimas, the gravitational force exerted by the Moon on the particles will be at its greatest, disturbing their orbit a little. For most of the ring particles, this extra little kick happens at quite random points during the orbit, and the overall effect cancels out.

But there are particles in the rings whose orbits have an interesting relationship with Mimas. They go round

BELOW: One of Saturn's outer rings, the F ring, is twisted into a spiral as two moons, Pandora and Prometheus, pass close by and distort it by their gravitational pull.

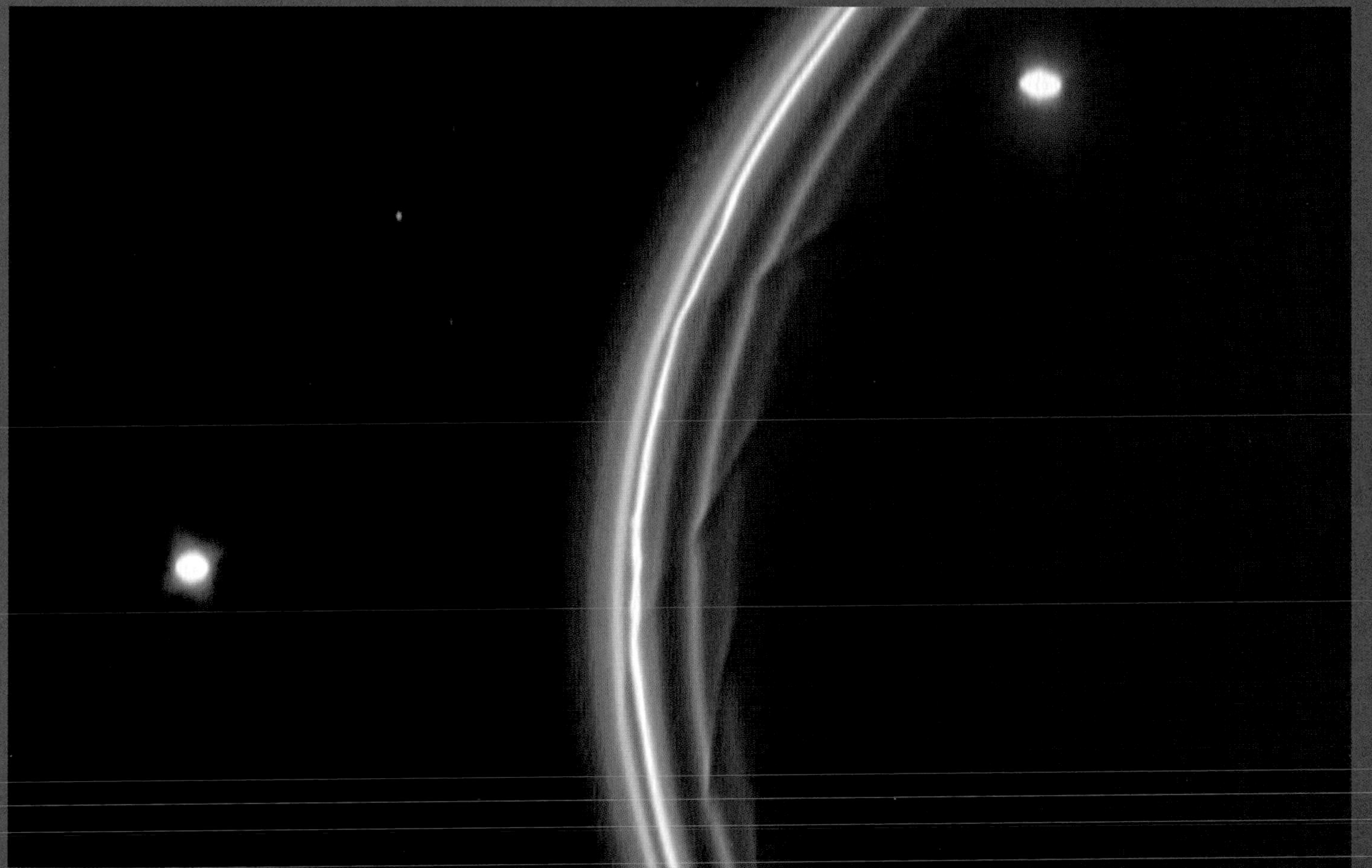

Saturn twice for every single orbit of Mimas. This means that on a regular basis they will meet Mimas – they get close to the moon on one out of every two of their orbits, because by the time they have gone around Saturn twice, Mimas will have returned to the same position. This special relationship has a name – we say that the particle and Mimas are in an orbital resonance. In other words, the particles in resonance with Mimas are the ones at just the right distance from Saturn to keep meeting it periodically as they orbit around it. This means that they get periodic gravitational kicks on a regular basis, and their orbits are disturbed.

Perhaps you can guess what the effect will be: if a particle has an orbit around Saturn that is resonant with the orbit of Mimas, then its orbit will be changed by the regular gravitational kick and it will move out of that orbit, leaving a gap. This is the case for any particle that wanders into the Cassini division. The gap is the place in a space where ring particle orbits would be resonant with Mimas.

It is thought that much of the structure in Saturn's rings is down to resonances, some more complex than others, between the ring particles and one or more of the planet's moons.

There are other, more subtle but beautiful effects. As the moons orbit Saturn, we can see their gravitational effects sweeping through the rings. A series of images taken by Cassini reveal the moons as they work and show gravity in action. As the moons pass close to the rings, their gravitational pull tugs the ring particles towards them, distorting their shape. The F ring, one of the outer rings, is twisted into a spiral shape by two moons, Prometheus and Pandora. In the image above you can see how Prometheus drags plumes of material away as it passes close to Saturn's rings.

This exquisite structure, so delicately sculpted by the action of gravity, is an immense part of the wonder of Saturn's rings, because it is such a vivid illustration of how a simple force of Nature can carve order out of chaos.

But perhaps more than that, understanding how Saturn's moons shape the rings can shed light on the events that shaped the early Solar System; events that helped to create the world we live in; events that remained unknown to us until the greatest series of human expeditions in history opened our eyes to the chaotic origins of our solar system ◉

VIOLENT BEGINNINGS

It seems that between 4.1 and 3.8 billion years ago the Moon came under an extraordinary attack, bombarded in a meteorite storm that transformed and shaped the surface we see today. This showering of debris should also have affected the Earth and other inner planets. Many scientists now believe that this is evidence of an incredibly violent period in our solar system's history, known as the Late Heavy Bombardment. But what could have caused this colossal bombardment and turned the Solar System into a shooting gallery?

RIGHT: The Barringer Crater in Arizona, USA, was named after Daniel Barringer who was the first to suggest that it was produced by meteorite impact.

THE LATE HEAVY BOMBARDMENT

On 26 July 1971, the Apollo 15 mission blasted off from the Kennedy Space Center in Florida with astronauts Scott, Worden and Irwin on board. This was the fourth Apollo team to land on the Moon and the first 'J-class mission' designed to put scientific investigation at the heart of the endeavour. On board the lunar module was an audacious piece of kit that transformed the capability of the astronauts to gather data. The Lunar Roving Vehicle, or 'moon buggy' as it became known, was a battery-powered car designed to allow astronauts to roam across the lunar surface and gather large samples of the rocks, allowing the geology of the Moon to be studied in much greater detail than ever before.

Landing in an area known as Mare Imbrium (Sea of Rains), the crew used the buggy to collect over 77 kilogrammes (170 pounds) of lunar rock samples. Mare Imbrium is a vast basin on the Moon's northwesterly surface that was created by a colossal impact early in its history. Its smooth surface was created when the then volcanically active moon flooded the impact crater with lava, creating the flat surface we see today. The moon buggy never returned to Earth and sits in Mare Imbrium to this day, but the samples it helped to collect did return and analysis of them has given us a unique and valuable glimpse into the violent early history of our solar system.

Many of the rock samples collected on the Apollo 15, 16 and 17 missions were impact melt rocks, created by the extreme conditions of direct meteorite impacts. Samples like this collected from all over the Moon have been dated using radioactive dating techniques and the results throw up a surprising pattern. A significant number of the rocks seem to have been created by impacts that took place in a relatively short timeframe during the Late Heavy Bombardment.

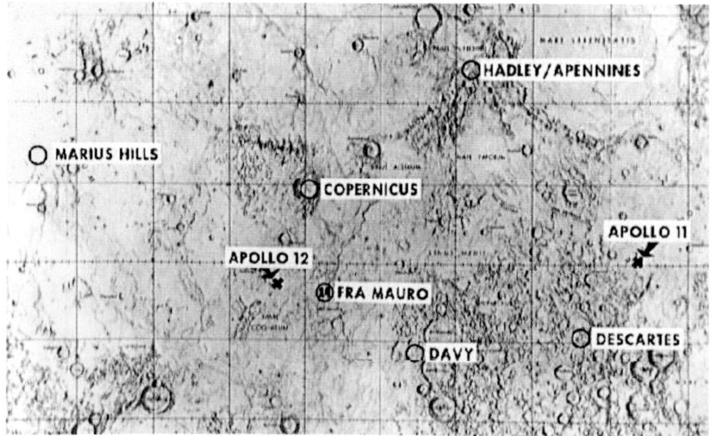

ABOVE: It is thanks to technology such as the moon buggy that astronauts and scientists can now navigate around the Moon and select landing areas in previously unexplored areas.

The Late Heavy Bombardment didn't only affect the lunar surface. If the Moon was showered in cosmic debris, the Earth and other inner planets should have suffered the same fate. Current estimates suggest that during this period Earth would have been peppered with thousands of impacts, with many creating impact craters over 1,000 kilometres (620 miles) across and some up to 5,000 kilometres (3,100 miles) in diameter. The cause of this bombardment may lie in exactly the same phenomenon that shaped the structure and complexity of Saturn's rings – orbital resonance.

Resonance can be much more than a delicate sculptor because it is not only small moons and particles of ice that can enter orbital resonance with each other. It is now thought that billions of years ago the two giants of the Solar System, Jupiter and Saturn, entered a resonance. In the case of Saturn's rings, resonances between ice particles in the Cassini division and the moon Mimas change the orbit of the particles, throwing them out of the gap. Likewise, if planets enter a resonance, the orbits of the planets are changed; and when planets start to fly around, the Solar System becomes an incredibly turbulent and violent place.

Using detailed simulations of the early Solar System, it is now thought that Saturn, Uranus and Neptune formed much closer to the Sun than they are today. Their orbits drifted slowly for hundreds of millions of years until Jupiter and Saturn entered a resonance. Once every cycle, the two planets aligned in exactly the same spot, creating a gravitational surge that played havoc with the orbits of all the other planets. Saturn, Uranus and Neptune all migrated outwards and plunged the Solar System into a violently unstable era, triggering the Late Heavy Bombardment. In particular, Neptune was catapulted outwards and smashed into the ring of icy material in the outer solar system, randomly scattering them into orbits that crisscrossed it.

For a hundred million years, the Solar System turned into a shooting gallery as a rain of comets ploughed through it, peppering the planets and creating many of the craters we see on the planets and moons today. It's remarkable to think that this Late Heavy Bombardment, 3.6 billion years ago, was triggered by the same subtle phenomena, orbital resonance, which delicately sculpts Saturn's rings today ◉

BELOW: The Apollo Lunar Roving Vehicle (more affectionately and simply known as the moon buggy) revolutionised explorations of the Moon. This electric vehicle enabled astronauts to venture further across the Moon's surface to collect a wider range of samples.

A GIFT TO EARTH

Today, it's almost impossible to find any direct evidence on our planet of the Late Heavy Bombardment, the impact craters long ago became shrouded by the ever-changing surface of the Earth. However, one defining characteristic of our planet that we can observe may be a direct result of the thousands of comet impacts that battered the Earth around 3.6 billion years ago.

Comets have a different composition to asteroids. This becomes visible when they venture into the inner solar system, close enough to be warmed by the Sun. As they absorb the Sun's heat they display a tail and an atmosphere as the ingredient they have in abundance evaporates away into space: water.

It is thought that the intense onslaught of comets during this turbulent time changed the Earth's environment radically and dramatically, but those changes weren't necessarily catastrophic. As the Solar System descended into chaos it seems that that a significant amount of the water in the Earth's oceans today was delivered by the impacts of water-rich comets and other objects during the Late Heavy Bombardment, which means that impacts could have played a key role in the development of life on Earth.

Before the Late Heavy Bombardment the Earth may have been a relatively barren rock, starved of water; afterwards it supported the oceans that would become the crucible for life. Without this water delivered in the Late Heavy Bombardment, life on Earth may never have evolved. It's quite a thought that this water-rich world we see today may have been shaped by violent resonances generated by the orbiting gas giants Jupiter and Saturn.

It is one of the most wonderful gifts to the astronomer that the finest example of the remarkable journey from chaotic collapsing dust cloud to delicately sculpted beauty is also the most stunning laboratory for studying how the Solar System works: Saturn's rings.

It's often the case in science that answers to the most profound questions can come from the most unexpected of places. Saturn's rings were initially studied because of their beauty, but understanding their formation and evolution has led to a deep understanding of how form, beauty and order can emerge from violence and chaos.

It is also worth remembering that life on Earth is a part of the Solar System. We are ordered structures, formed from the chaos of the primordial dust cloud 4.5 billion years ago. We are just as much a product of gravitational collapse as the rocky inner planets, the majestic gas giants and the impossibly delicate artistry of Saturn's rings. We were formed by the same laws of Nature, and important steps in our formation are written in the sky for us to read. We are part of the heavens and intimately connected to them. And that is truly one of the wonders of the Solar System ◉

BELOW: Comet Hale–Bopp and observatories. These observatories are on the summit of Mauna Kea, Hawaii, USA. From left to right they are: Subaru Telescope, Keck 1 and Keck 2 telescopes, and NASA Infrared Telescope Facility. Hale–Bopp was discovered on 23 July 1995. It was visible to the naked eye for over 18 months between May 1996 and December 1997.

AeroShell
ExecuJet
BEFORE FLIGHT

CHAPTER 4

THE THIN BLUE LINE

EXPLORING EARTH'S ATMOSPHERE

The Solar System is a violent, inhospitable place. On every planet and moon we've explored, from our nearest neighbours to the most distant corners of the Sun's realm, we have encountered extremes. We've discovered worlds defined by the fiercest heat and the bitterest cold; seen landscapes sculpted by overwhelming pressure, and witnessed storms the size of planets. Amongst all these hostile wonders sits our Earth, an oasis of calm amidst the violence of the Solar System. Yet all that separates us from what's out there, from the extremes that sit above our heads, is a thin, flimsy envelope of gas. Our atmosphere may be an invisible presence in our daily lives but it's thanks to this thin blue line that we have the air that we breathe, the water that we drink and the landscape that surrounds us.

JOURNEY TO THE EDGE OF THE EARTH

BELOW AND RIGHT: In Cape Town I achieved a lifelong dream – to witness the thin blue line of the Earth's atmosphere at close quarters. Thanks to the phenomenal engineering of the English Electric Lightning plane, after a vertical ascent I was taken eighteen kilometres (eleven miles) up into the sky; where the only people above me were those on the space station.

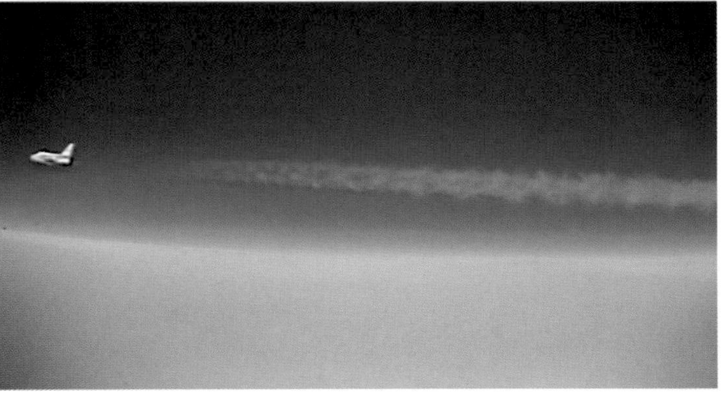

Hidden away on the outskirts of Cape Town International Airport is an aeronautical toy box like no other. From Blackburn Buccaneers to Hawker Hunters, this place is home to the finest and largest collection of classic military aircraft in the world – and they are all still flying. One aircraft in the collection, however, stands out as a truly wondrous piece of engineering. The English Electric Lightning is a supersonic jetfighter that was designed and built in the 1950s. Capable of flying at over twice the speed of sound (Mach 2.27, 2,400 kilometres or 1,500 miles per hour), this beautiful machine was used by the Royal Air Force for almost thirty years as an interceptor aircraft – designed to hunt down and destroy enemy bombers at great speed.

As well as its swiftness, the Lightning is also renowned for another characteristic: it can fly incredibly high. Although it was officially a military secret, it's now well documented that the Lightning can fly way beyond its designated operating height of over 18,000 metres (60,000 feet). In 1984, during a NATO exercise, an RAF pilot took the craft to 27,000 metres (88,000 feet) to test its ability to intercept the supposedly untouchable U2 spy plane. It not only succeeded in carrying out its mission but it also carried the pilot to a height that took him above 99 per cent of the Earth's precious atmosphere.

In the 1970s the Lightning was the aircraft every plane-spotting kid loved – a piece of science fiction that would not have looked out of place in Star Wars.

I grew up with Lightnings. In the 1970s the Lightning was the aircraft every plane-spotting kid loved – a piece of science fiction that would not have looked out of place in *Star Wars*. It was the fastest, sleekest and most powerful interceptor on the planet. Up close it isn't a delicate or balletic aircraft. Anything that flies at twice the speed of sound has to be solid; no rattles or creaks. The cockpit is small and surprisingly high off the ground. You feel perched out on a limb, bolted securely

but precariously onto two Rolls-Royce Avon engines and tanks of combustible gases and fluids. White instrumented dials in grey boxes and toggle switches labelled with a cold-war-era font are randomly slotted around the ejector seats. Between your legs (which are attached by seat-belt fabric to the automatic leg retraction system to preserve your knees, should you decide to kick out), is the control stick, barnacle-encrusted with gun-triggers and missile launch controls. It is, in short, a place that any kid with a bit of bottle would want to be.

Engine start-up in a jet fighter is always a careful affair. The pilot watches the dials, looking for any abnormality in temperature. This is analogue, and the information about the health of the Avons is in the nuances of the needles. It is also surprisingly quiet and vibration-free from the inside – more airliner than war machine. When the pilot is happy, ex-RAF Lightning XS 451 gently taxis to the end of the runway at Cape Town International Airport, behind a South African Airways Airbus A340.

I was waiting for a brutal start to the take-off roll, but the pilot accelerates the Lightning quite gently along the runway. It feels no faster than a passenger jet – until we get airborne. I am then treated quite unexpectedly to the Lightning's party trick; a rotation take-off. The afterburners are kicked in as soon as the undercarriage is retracted, and the aircraft enters a near-vertical climb, rolling to one side as it goes to reduce the stress on the airframe. It is a rocket launch.

Only fifteen minutes after take-off I am reminded why we came here to film with the silver machine. We reach 17,700 metres (58,000 feet), inverted to reduce airframe stress in the climb, then flip over into level flight 6,000 metres (20,000 feet) higher than a passenger jet. In an instant, an expansive and powerfully moving vista materialises. I see the Earth, but not as the geometrically flat expanse of land I'm used to gazing across from an airliner window. It is curved. Very curved. Overwhelmingly small, because there is enough curvature to allow the mind to recreate the rest and construct a tiny planet. It is at once majestic and diminutive.

I'm seeing the land, the air and the beginnings of the vacuum of infinite space in a single field of view, and the word to describe it is 'fragile'.

Stretching upwards from the horizon is a graduated wash of fading colour; bright sky blue where the land meets the air, but quickly darkening towards a deeper, twilight azure. I'm seeing the land, the air and the beginnings of the vacuum of infinite space in a single field of view, and the word to describe it is 'fragile'. Most excellent canopy, indeed, but a surprisingly delicate majestical roof. This is the thin blue line that shields us from infinity, and strangely you have to climb above ninety per cent of it to be able to see and understand it.

We touch down forty minutes after take-off, having journeyed to the edge of planet Earth and back. For me the Lightning has changed its character. The *Star Wars* interceptor has become an enabler; a necessary tool to deliver a vital experience. It would not be possible to see our planet and atmosphere wandering delicate and precious through the emptiness without the brutal power of the cold-war interceptor. Engineering is the route to enlightenment because it transports us to the places where our terrestrial perspective is shaken to breaking point and forcibly replaced. We are a complacent and parochial bunch, scuttling around on our rock beneath our foul and pestilent congregation of vapours, and if it takes a pair of afterburning Rolls-Royce Avons to free our minds, then so be it.

THE THIN BLUE LINE

The Earth would not be the wonderfully diverse place that it is without the thin blue line. It acts as a soothing blanket that traps the warmth of the Sun, yet protects us from the harshness of its radiation. Its movements can be traced in the gentlest breeze and the most devastating hurricane. The oxygen, water and carbon dioxide the atmosphere holds plays a fundamental role in the ongoing survival of millions of different species living on the planet. In this chapter we'll explore how the laws of physics that created our unique atmosphere are the same laws that created many diverse and different atmospheres across the Solar System.

When perfectly balanced, a world as familiar and beautiful as the Earth can evolve beneath the clouds, but the slightest changes can lead to alien and violent worlds. There are planets in our solar system that have been transformed into hellish worlds by nothing more than the gases in their atmosphere. Just as atmospheres can choke a planet to death, they're also powerful enough to shape their surfaces. There are even worlds out there that are all atmosphere – giant balls of churning gas where storms three times the size of the Earth have raged for hundreds of years. All atmospheres in the Solar System are unique, but the ingredients and forces that shape them are universal. At the heart of each is a fundamental force of nature that holds the Solar System together: gravity ◉

LEFT: The Hubble space telescope was launched by NASA in 1990. As the Earth's atmosphere blocks some light from space, by placing this telescope above it, we can receive clearer images of space.

THE BINDING FORCE OF GRAVITY

Gravity is by far the weakest known force in the Universe. You can see that because it's really easy for me to pick a rock up off the ground, even though there's a whole planet – Earth – pulling the rock down. I can just lift it up; incredibly weak, but important because it's the only force there is to hold an atmosphere to the surface of a planet.

Gravity is one of the four fundamental forces of Nature. Isaac Newton first explained it in 1687, describing it as the force by which objects with mass are attracted to one another. We now know that this is an approximation: Albert Einstein provided us with a more sophisticated picture of gravity in his General Theory of Relativity in 1915. Gravity exists because space and time are curved by the presence of mass and energy, and we feel the results of this curvature as an attractive force between all objects. For our purposes, and indeed for most purposes, Newton's simpler view is sufficient.

Compared to the other three fundamental forces of Nature – the strong nuclear force, the weak nuclear force and the electromagnetism – gravity is the weakest, and yet when combined with these forces, it creates the conditions for stars to ignite, holds planets and moons in their orbits and binds the galaxies together.

According to Newton, the force of gravity between two objects can be described by the simplest of equations. (see diagram opposite). With the help of G – the universal gravitational constant – the force between two objects is calculated by multiplying the mass of each and then dividing that by the square of the distance that separates them. This beautifully simple equation allows us to explain and predict so much about our universe and solar system. There is possibly no greater example of the power of simple mathematics than the story behind the discovery of the most distant planet from the Sun in our solar system – a planet whose existence was predicted by Newton's law of gravitation long before it was directly observed by the human eye.

Over four billion kilometres (three billion miles) away from Earth, the beautiful blue planet of Neptune is one of the coldest places in the Solar System and the only planet entirely invisible to the naked eye. Impossible to detect before the invention of the telescope, Neptune was probably first observed by Galileo in 1612, but it was mistaken for a fixed blue star in the night sky. This is because what Galileo didn't know as he observed it was that Neptune only appeared to be stationary, as on that evening this giant ice planet was beginning a retrograde loop (see page 76) and so was just changing direction in the night sky. The real clue to Neptune's existence, however, came not from the observation of this planet but from the observation of its nearest neighbour, Uranus.

NEWTON'S LAW OF UNIVERSAL GRAVITATION

The gravitational force exerted by one mass on another is proportional to the product of the masses and inversely proportional to the square of the distance, r, between them. The magnitudes of the forces exerted by each object on the other, F1 and F2, will always be equal in magnitude and opposite in direction. G is the gravitational constant.

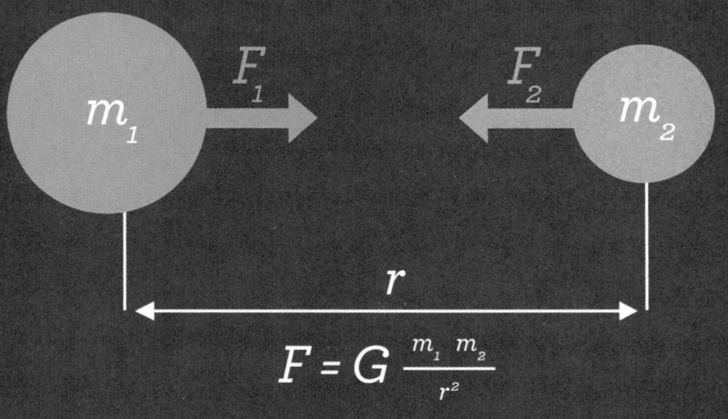

$$F = G\frac{m_1 m_2}{r^2}$$

Discovered in 1781 by William Herschel, Uranus was the first planet to be discovered since ancient times, so its passage through the night sky was plotted by hundreds of astronomers keen to follow this newest addition to the Solar System. In 1821, the first astronomical tables of Uranus' orbit were published by French astronomer Alexis Bouvard. Using Newton's Law of Gravitation, the tables provided accurate predictions for the future position of the planet as it travelled around the Sun. It soon became clear, however, that Uranus was not behaving exactly as predicted. The path it took on its orbit did not agree with the path that Newton's Law predicted. At times on its orbit Uranus was either forward or behind its predicted position. Something seemed to be wrong. Astronomers of the time were baffled by the discrepancy and struggled for an explanation. Could Newton's Law be wrong? Or was the quality of the observed data at fault? The only other option seemed to be that something was disturbing the journey of this giant planet around the Sun. Many of these scientists thought the last of these reasons was the most likely, and that the disturbance to the orbit was due to a gravitational perturbation caused by an as yet undiscovered planet. If

BOTTOM: The farthest planet in our solar system, Neptune is also one of the coldest. It was probably discovered in 1612, but it was in 1989 that Voyager 2 became the first spacecraft to observe the planet. Neptune owes its distinctive blue colour to the methane in its upper atmosphere.

GRAVITATIONAL PERTURBATION
Here two planets are orbiting a common star. When the planets are at A, the gravitational force exerted by the outer planet on the inner planet causes the inner planet to accelerate, moving ahead of the position calculated by considering the Sun's gravity alone. When the planets are at B, the reverse is true and the inner planet is decelerated. This slight deviation in the path taken by the inner planet is said to be due to a gravitational perturbation. This led to the prediction and discovery of the planet Neptune.

there was an unknown planet orbiting outside Uranus, then according to Newton there would be an additional gravitational force between this mystery planet and Uranus. This would alter Uranus' orbit, and explain the discrepancy between the theoretical predictions and the experimental observations.

In 1845–46, the French astronomer Urbain le Verrier and English astronomer John Adams independently calculated the mass and position of such a new planet. By using the observed data from Uranus, they could employ Newton's equation to calculate the mass and distance of this planet from the Sun and Uranus, according to the gravitational force it appeared to exert. Although it is uncertain who actually reached the end of the calculations first, their collective work led to the precise prediction of the existence of a giant planet orbiting outside Uranus. This prediction was rapidly confirmed when German astronomer Johann Galle made the first telescopic observation of Neptune in September 1846.

The story of the discovery of Neptune is a beautiful example of the predictive power of the Laws of Physics and the universal influence of gravity. In this case, it described the massive force between two giant planets orbiting the Sun, but it can also predict far more subtle interactions and explain the tenuous connection that joins a planet with its most nebulous characteristic – the atmosphere ◉

LOBSTERS ON THE OCEAN FLOOR

Our atmosphere – the thin, fragile layer of gas that surrounds Earth – is held to our planet by nothing more than gravity. Just as two planets exert a force on one another, so there is a force between each atom in our atmosphere and the Earth. This incredibly weak force binds these life-giving atoms to our planet. Whether it's oxygen, nitrogen, argon, carbon dioxide or any of the other gases that fill our sky, each atom is tenuously bound to Earth by the gravitational force between its tiny mass and the enormous bulk of our planet. This is all there is to prevent Earth's atmosphere disappearing into space. The more massive the planet, the greater the gravitational force binding the atoms in the atmosphere to the surface. Fortunately for us, the Earth has enough mass to keep a tight grip on the heavier gas molecules that make up our atmosphere. It holds them against the surface and allows almost every living thing to survive.

In the case of our planet, gravity has glued a cocktail of gases to the Earth; the main constituent being nitrogen. Almost seventy-eight per cent of the air around us contains this invisible, odourless and tasteless gas. One of the main reasons for this is that nitrogen gas is extremely stable and so reacts with very little, making it an incredibly long-lived gas in the atmosphere. Almost all of the rest of our atmosphere is made up of oxygen. At just twenty-one per cent of the total volume, it is by far the most abundant component after nitrogen. The inert gas argon is the third most abundant gas, at just under 1 per cent. The rest of the atmosphere consists of trace gases, such as carbon dioxide, neon, nitrous oxide and methane. These trace gases are so sparse that when added together they comprise just 0.039 per cent of the Earth's atmosphere.

We don't normally notice the presence of this vast mass of gas that surrounds us, but in fact we have evolved to live under a massive weight of air. There are five million billion tonnes of air surrounding the Earth, and at any one moment that huge mass of air is pressing on each and every one of us. Without even realising it, we all live our lives under pressure. On every square centimetre of our bodies there is a force that is equivalent to the weight of a one-kilogramme object pressing down. To put it another way, if the average person is about a metre square in area, the atmospheric pressure is the equivalent of a ten-tonne object pushing us.

Life on the surface of this planet survives surrounded by this enormous mass of gas, and just like lobsters scuttling around on the ocean floor, we have evolved to deal with the

This thin blue line makes the Earth the wonderfully diverse place that it is. It acts as a soothing blanket that traps the warmth of the Sun, yet protects us from the harshness of its radiation.

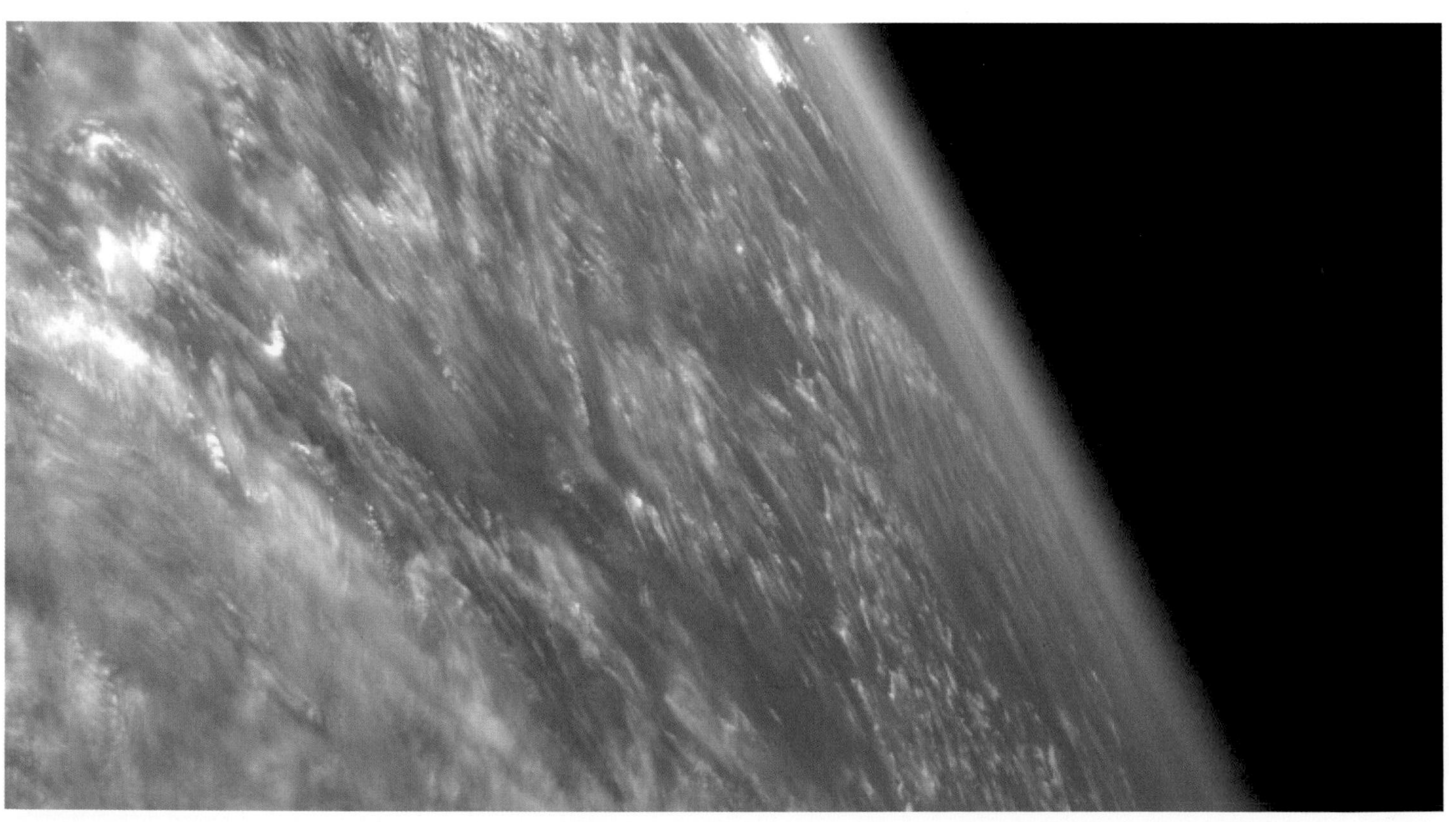

OPPOSITE: Here, over north-western Africa, we can clearly see the thin blue line that represents the Earth's atmosphere. This fine, fragile layer of gas follows the curvature of the Earth's surface, ensuring our survival on this planet. Composed of 78 per cent nitrogen, 21 per cent oxygen and 1 per cent other constituents, the Earth's atmosphere acts as a shield against nearly all harmful radiation coming from the Sun and other stars, while trapping their warmth at a beneficial level.

BELOW: This spectacular picture was taken by the STS-125 crew of Atlantis as they returned home from Hubble in May 2009. Beyond the payload bay of the shuttle, the thin blue line of the Earth's atmosphere cuts through the blackness of space.

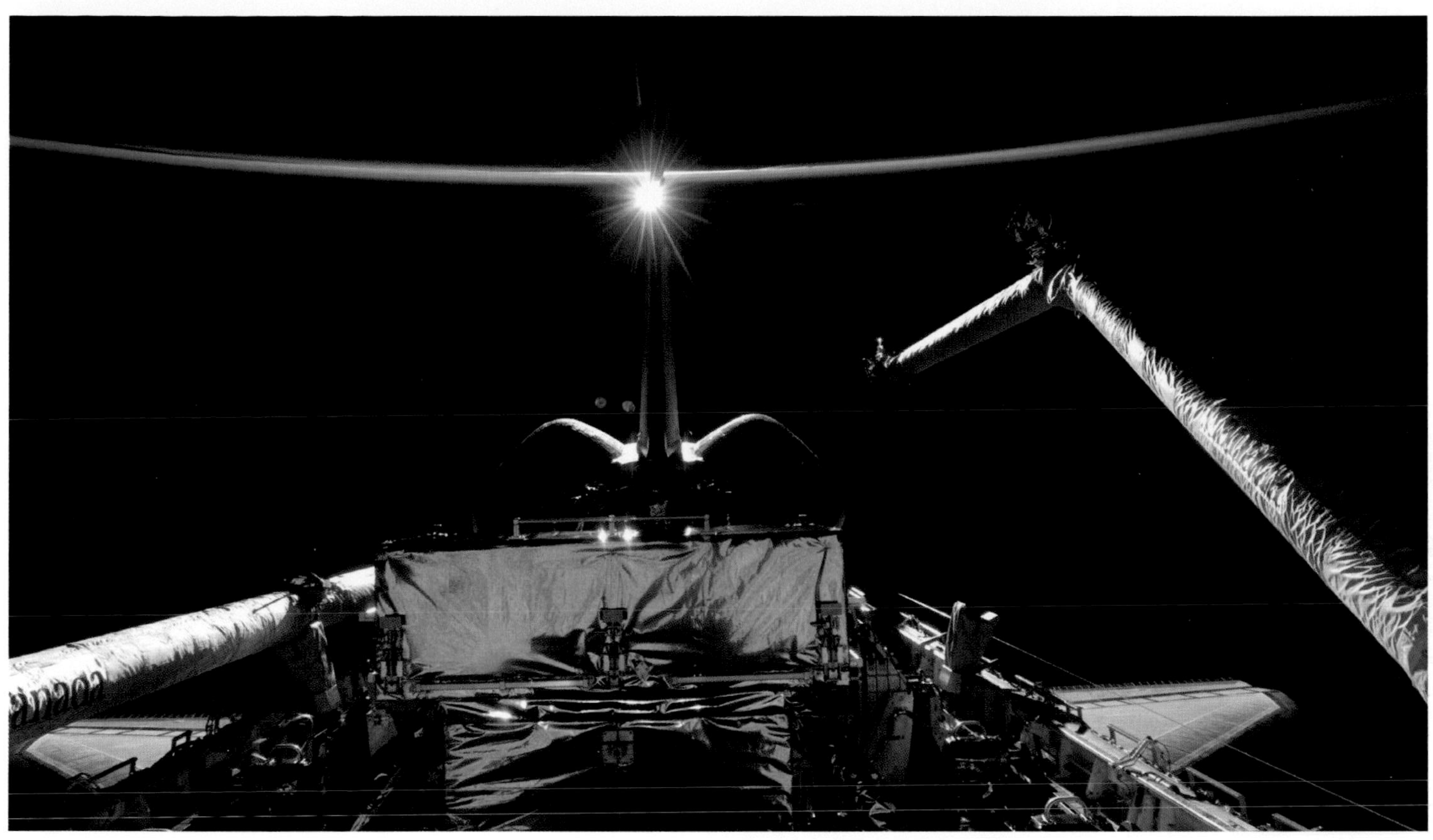

pressure so effectively, we don't even notice it's there. We just breathe it in and use the oxygen to allow our bodies to function. But that's not the end of our intimate relationship with the air around us; our atmosphere does more than just allow us to breathe, it protects us from the most powerful force in the Solar System: our sun.

UNDERSTANDING AIR PRESSURE

Air pressure is a slightly counter-intuitive concept. It's an easy linguistic mistake to make to say that all that vast mass of air above our heads is pressing down on us, crushing us onto the surface of the Earth. But that's not how air pressure works. It presses on us in every direction at once – otherwise how could we possibly be strong enough to support the equivalent of a ten-tonne object pressing 'down' on our bodies?

The air pressure is due to the billions of molecules in the atmosphere bouncing off us as they jiggle around. Imagine someone smashing a tennis ball into your face. As the ball bounces off, it hurts because the change in direction of the ball requires a force to act. Your nose provides that force, and since to every action there is an equal and opposite reaction, you'll feel that force on your nose! The molecules in the atmosphere are exactly the same as little tennis balls, only much smaller, so as they continually bounce off your body they exert a force on you. Pressure is defined as the force per unit area – in other words, it is the net effect of all the molecules of air bouncing off every square centimetre of your body. Thinking of it in these terms, it's easier to see that it doesn't matter whether the square centimetre of your body in question is pointing up, down or sideways – the number of air molecules that bounce off it will be the same and so the air pressure will act equally in all directions.

If you still don't believe this explanation, you can do this simple experiment. Half-fill a glass with water and carefully place a piece of paper over the top of the glass. Holding the paper in place, you can turn the glass over and then let go of the paper, and the pressure of the atmosphere pushing upwards on the paper will hold the water in the glass.

Our bodies are actually completely open to the air – there are no sealed air pockets inside us. This means that we can exist quite happily at much higher or lower pressures than atmospheric pressure. A scuba diver can happily descend to twenty, thirty or even forty metres below the surface of the ocean without any special equipment. At a depth of forty metres the pressure is five times the atmospheric pressure – that's equivalent to a fifty-tonne object pressing on every square metre of the diver's body! As long as the diver keeps breathing and popping her ears, the pressure inside and outside her body will remain in perfect balance and therefore she will feel no ill effects ◉

EARTH'S AMBIENT TEMPERATURES

The average temperature on Earth is a balmy thirteen degrees Celsius, but of course it varies enormously across the planet. The highest recorded temperature on our planet is 56.7 degrees Celsius in the Libyan deserts; the coldest is -89 degrees Celsius in the depths of Antarctica, but compared to other places in the Solar System our temperature swings are fairly gentle. The cause of this stability and the reason for our average temperature may appear to be straightforward. We are 150 million kilometres (93 million miles) away from the Sun and the distance from this heat source sets the amount of energy being received, which determines the temperature. Just as we expect to be warmer when we are closer to a fire, so it would be reasonable to expect that every planet gets warmer the closer it is to the Sun. But things aren't quite that simple.

RIGHT: Namib Desert, Namibia.

A TALE OF TWO ATMOSPHERES

As the Sun sinks below the horizon in the Namib desert in Namibia, south-western Africa, the temperature change from day to night can be as much as thirty degrees Celsius. That's an immense amount in just a few hours; one of the biggest day-to-night swings on the planet. The reason for this dramatic change is that the Namib desert is also one of the driest places on Earth.

The levels of water vapour in the Earth's atmosphere vary across the planet, but wherever there are small amounts of water vapour in the atmosphere there are large day-to-night temperature swings. This is because the ability of the atmosphere to trap heat is directly related to the insulating effect of the water vapour. In the dry environment of the desert the level of insulation is low, and so when the Sun disappears, the heat disappears quickly into space. There are many other gases in the atmosphere as well as water that act as insulators, turning our atmosphere into a warming blanket. These greenhouse gases, such as carbon dioxide, methane and nitrous oxide, trap the heat of the Sun, ironing out the difference between day and night so effectively that we think a change of thirty degrees is significant!

Difficult to see from Earth, Mercury suffers the biggest temperature swings of all the planets. This is because it has been stripped of the one thing that could protect it: its atmosphere.

BOTTOM LEFT: Here in the Namib desert, the change in temperature from day to night can be up to thirty degrees Celsius. This feels immense, but it is nothing compared to the extreme temperature change that occurs on planets such as Mercury.

BELOW: Mercury, the smallest planet in our solar system, has been stripped of its atmosphere since its inception. Left unprotected in this way and without insulation, Mercury experiences the largest temperature swings of all the planets.

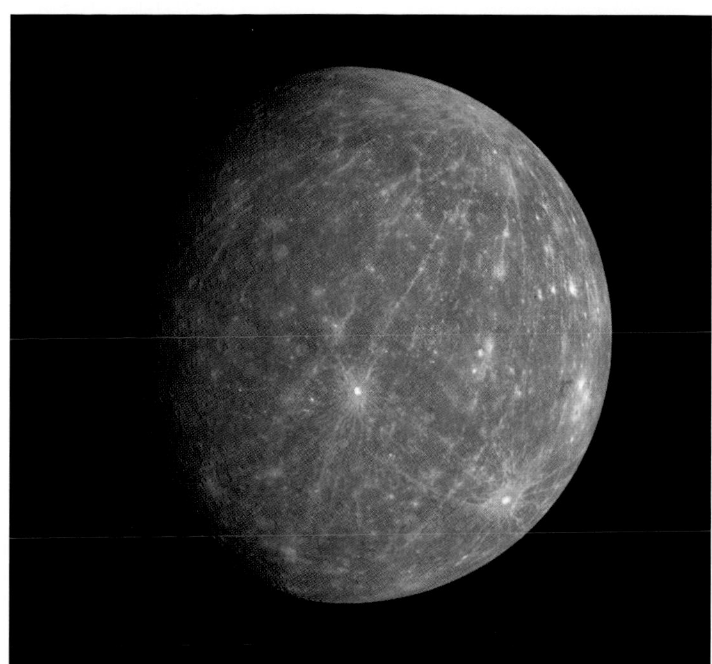

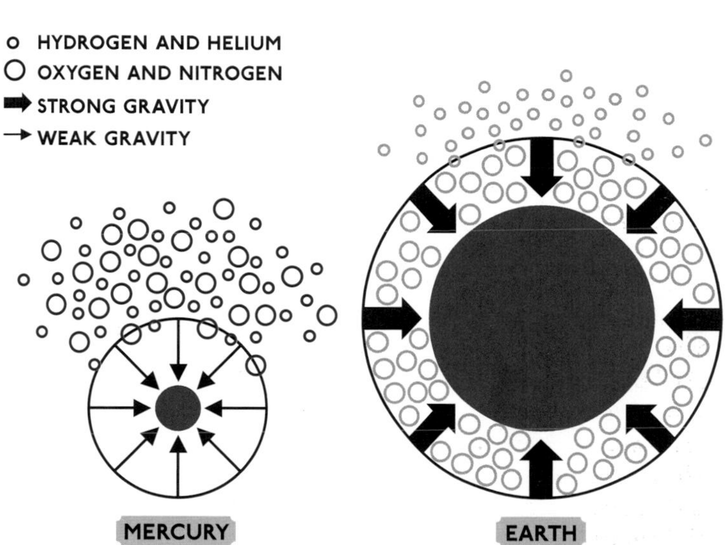

THE GREENHOUSE EFFECT

Almost 100 million kilometres (60 million miles) closer to the Sun than the Earth is a planet where the temperature shift from day to night is immense. Mercury, the smallest of all the planets, is roughly fifty-eight million kilometres (thirty-six million miles) from the burning heart of our solar system. Difficult to see from Earth because of its proximity to the Sun, this tortured piece of rock suffers the biggest temperature swings of all the planets, from 427 degrees Celsius in the day to -173 degrees Celsius at night. This is all because Mercury has been stripped of the one thing that could protect it: its atmosphere.

Like all the rocky inner planets of the Solar System, Mercury had an atmosphere at formation. In fact it's thought all eight of the Sun's planets had similar atmospheres when they formed over four billion years ago, composed of lighter gases like hydrogen and helium, with smaller amounts of heavier gases like oxygen and nitrogen.

Planets hang on to their atmosphere by the force of gravity – it's the only way they can stop the fragile line of gas disappearing off into space – so the more massive the planet, the stronger the gravitational pull and the easier it is for the planet to keep hold of its atmosphere. The temperature of the atmosphere also affects this balance, because the hotter the atmosphere, the faster the molecules are whizzing around and the harder it is for the gravitational force to hang on to them.

The giant planets of the outer solar system, Jupiter Saturn, Uranus and Neptune, were large enough and cold enough to exert the massive gravitational force needed to hold on to the lighter gases such as hydrogen and helium, but on the inner, warmer and smaller rocky planets the story was very different. The lightest gases would have gradually escaped into space from Mercury, Venus, Earth and Mars, leaving behind atmospheres rich in heavier gases such as oxygen and nitrogen. Fortunately for us, the Earth is big enough and far enough away from the Sun to exert a force of gravity that can tightly hold on to these gases, and our atmosphere has been able to evolve with them in place over billions of years. On Mercury, the story is very different. Mercury is tiny compared to Earth; with a trip around its equator of 15,329 kilometres (9,504 miles), the surface area of Mercury is one-seventh of Earth's surface, and its mass is just five per cent of that of our planet. Coupled with its high surface temperature, that means the gravitational force is not strong enough to hold on to the heavier gases, so Mercury rapidly lost almost its entire atmosphere.

The impact of this on the two planets today is striking. Here on Earth, at sea level, in a volume about the size of a sugar cube there are twenty-five billion billion molecules of gas. On Mercury, in the same volume, there would be around a hundred thousand – over 100 million million times less. So Mercury was just too small and too hot to hang on to its atmosphere and the consequences for the planet were devastating. Atmospheres may be just a thin strip of molecules but they're a planet's first line of defence. Without them, a planet like Mercury is at the mercy of our violent solar system ◉

SURFACE TEMPERATURE

Although you would expect the surface temperature of a planet to decrease the further away it is from the Sun, the interaction between the Sun and the atmosphere means that some planets are warmer than they should be, such as Venus, whilst others are colder, such as the Earth.

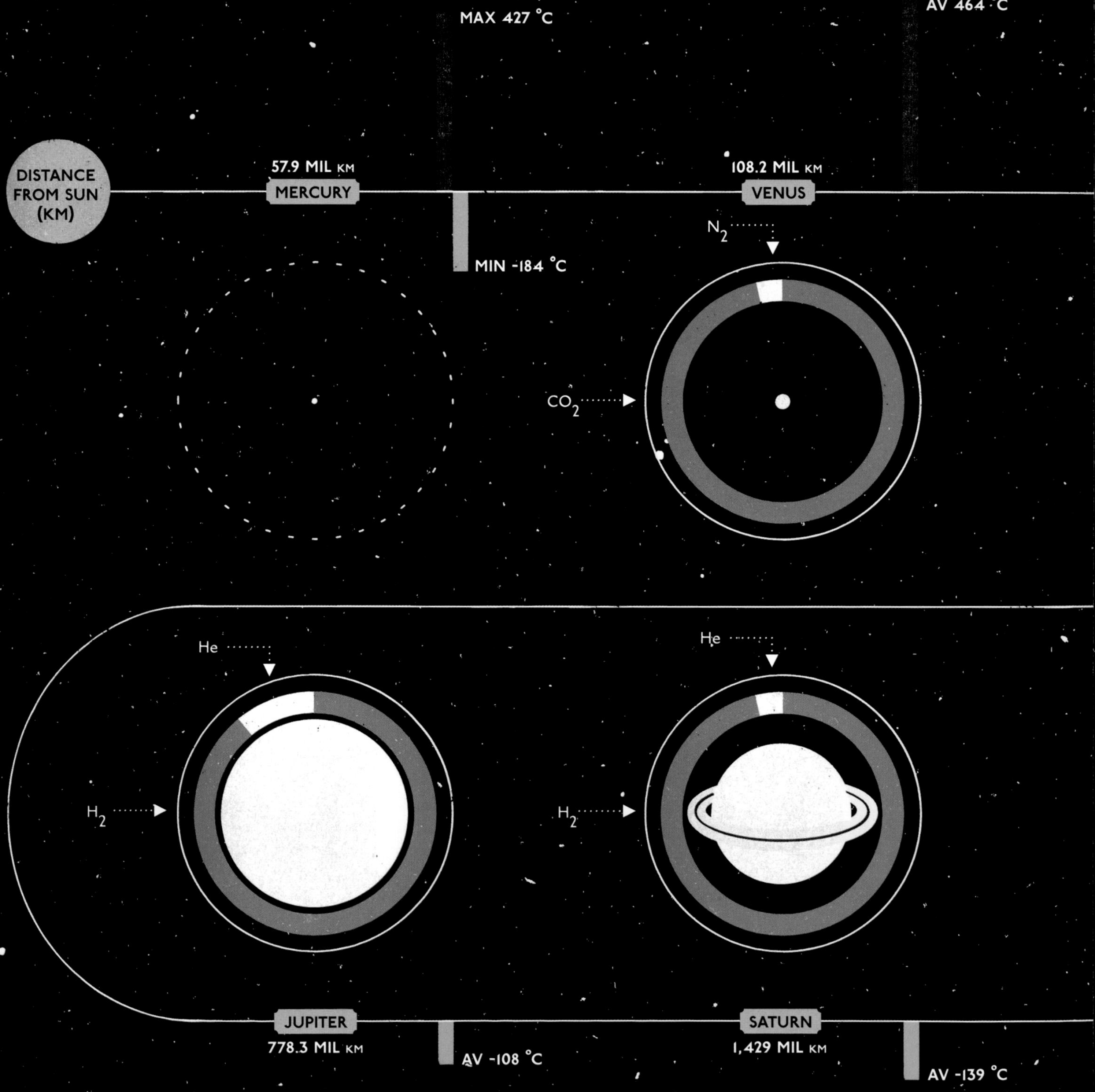

MAX 427 °C
AV 464 °C
DISTANCE FROM SUN (KM)
57.9 MIL KM
MERCURY
108.2 MIL KM
VENUS
MIN -184 °C
N_2
CO_2
He
He
H_2
H_2
JUPITER
778.3 MIL KM
AV -108 °C
SATURN
1,429 MIL KM
AV -139 °C

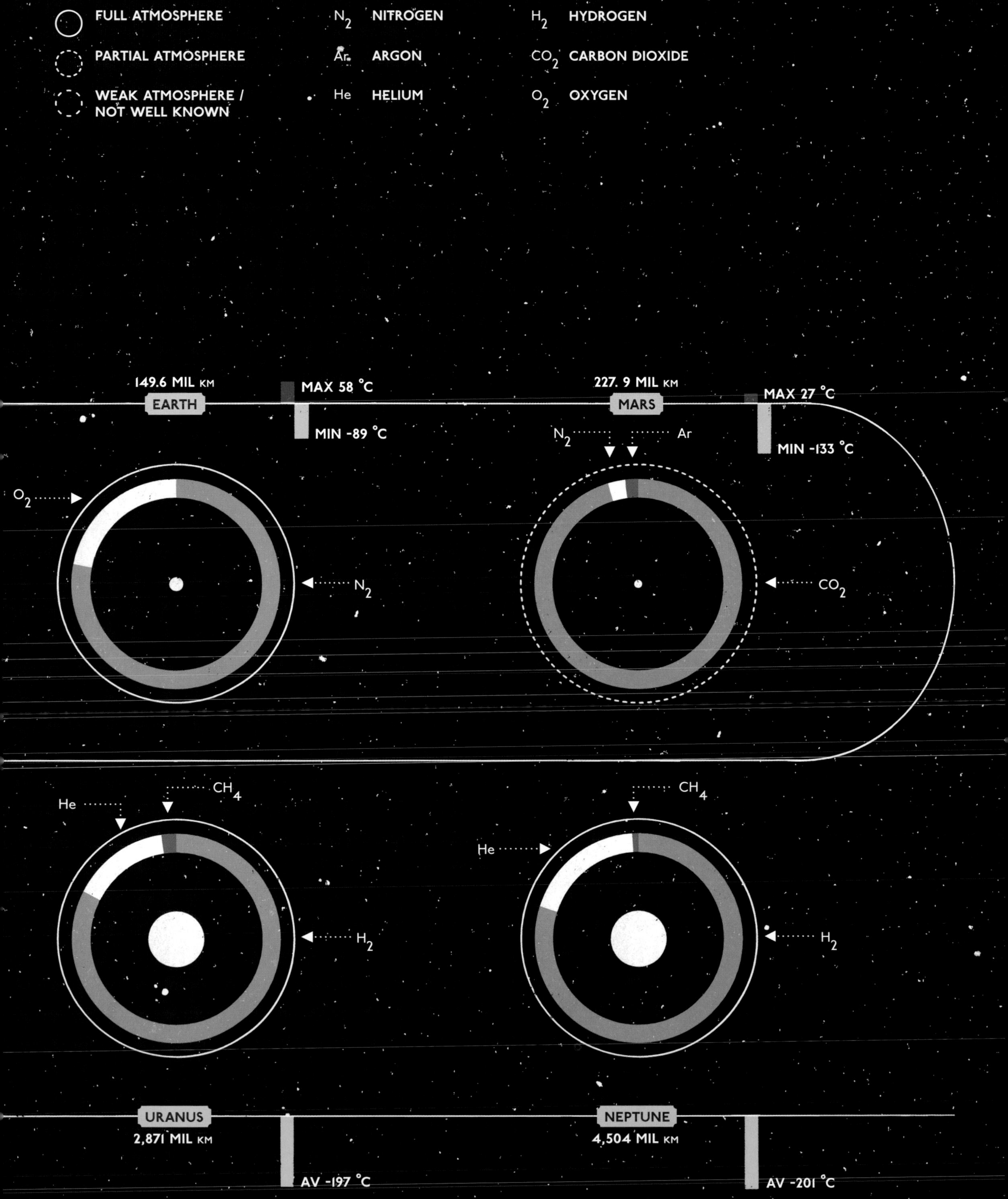

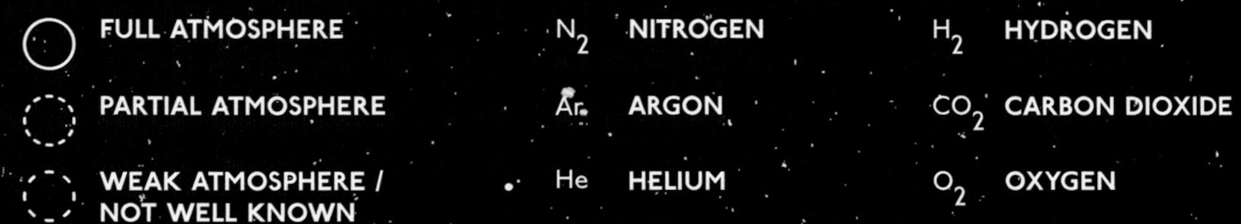

FULL ATMOSPHERE
PARTIAL ATMOSPHERE
WEAK ATMOSPHERE / NOT WELL KNOWN
N_2 NITROGEN
Ar ARGON
He HELIUM
H_2 HYDROGEN
CO_2 CARBON DIOXIDE
O_2 OXYGEN
149.6 MIL KM
EARTH
MAX 58 °C
MIN -89 °C
O_2
N_2
227. 9 MIL KM
MARS
MAX 27 °C
MIN -133 °C
N_2
Ar
CO_2
He
CH_4
H_2
CH_4
He
H_2
URANUS
2,871 MIL KM
AV -197 °C
NEPTUNE
4,504 MIL KM
AV -201 °C

FIRST LINE OF DEFENCE

BELOW AND BOTTOM: On 20 November 2008, the dark winter skies of western Canada were unexpectedly illuminated by a fireball five times as bright as the Moon. Saskatchewan was bathed in an eerie blue light as an asteroid entered the Earth's atmosphere.

The province of Saskatchewan in western Canada is a cold dark place to be in winter, but on 20 November 2008 the night sky was lit up by a fireball five times as bright as a full moon. The light show witnessed that night was the result of an asteroid – a space rock weighing about ten tonnes – entering Earth's atmosphere and landing in a place called Buzzard Coulee. It's certainly not unusual for rocks this size to hit the Earth (on average, it happens about once a month), but what was unusual about the Buzzard Coulee meteorite was that its trajectory took it over quite densely populated areas so that tens of thousands, if not hundreds of thousands, of people saw and heard it. Most spectacularly, it was also captured by a lot of CCTV cameras charting its journey across hundreds of kilometres of sky. These images created a remarkable record of the meteorite as it streaked across the night sky at twenty kilometres (twelve miles) per second, turning it blue.

These remarkable images enabled a group of scientists to triangulate the impact site of the meteorite with far greater accuracy than is normally possible. Thus a team of meteorite hunters could search for the debris from the explosion in a precise location, a field just outside the city of Lloydminster.

Leading the team is University of Calgary professor Dr Alan Hildebrand, one of the world's leading meteorite experts and a member of the team behind the discovery of the ancient Chicxulub Crater in the Yucatan peninsula of Mexico. This

BELOW: Dr Alan Hildebrand, professor at the University of Calgary, leads the hunt for fragments of the meteorite that hit Buzzard Coulee. The landscape is peppered with this debris – if you know what to look for. The moment you find a dark, smooth-sculpted rock, you feel the painstaking search is worth it.

vast crater, over 180 kilometres (112 miles) in diameter, is thought to date back to the end of the Cretaceous period 65 million years ago, and it remains the prime candidate for the catastrophic event that wiped out the dinosaurs.

Fortunately for the people of Canada, Dr Hildebrand's latest search is on a far smaller scale; however, there is still a huge amount of information to be gleaned from this lightweight impact. A ten-tonne rock travelling at fifty times the speed of sound has an extremely large amount of energy. 'It would be like stocking up 400 tonnes of TNT to explode,' explains Hildebrand. 'It's really quite dramatic.'

There is only one thing that can possibly protect the Earth's surface from a projectile with that amount of energy on a direct collision course with our planet; just one thing that can cause it to slow down and break up and so prevent all of the energy slamming into the Earth's surface in one place. Night after night our atmosphere slows down and breaks up meteorites just like this one. Entering the atmosphere at twenty kilometres a second and heading directly towards Buzzard Coulee from the depths of space, this lump of rock and iron that was originally about the size of a desk, would have immediately begun to compress the thickening atmospheric gases in front of it. When air is compressed, it heats up, and this in turn heats the meteorite until it is white-hot. For a brief time, this billion-watt bulb shone high in the sky; then, after just five seconds, its billion-year journey suddenly and dramatically comes to an end as it disintegrated in a series of explosions, peppering the fields below with lumps of rock the size of golf balls.

In just a few seconds, this survivor from the distant past became just another part of planet Earth. It must have been quite incredible to be standing in Saskatchewan on that night as the sky turned blue, watching these heavy rocks raining down.

Hunting for meteorite fragments requires a certain kind of talent. These rocks have streamed through the

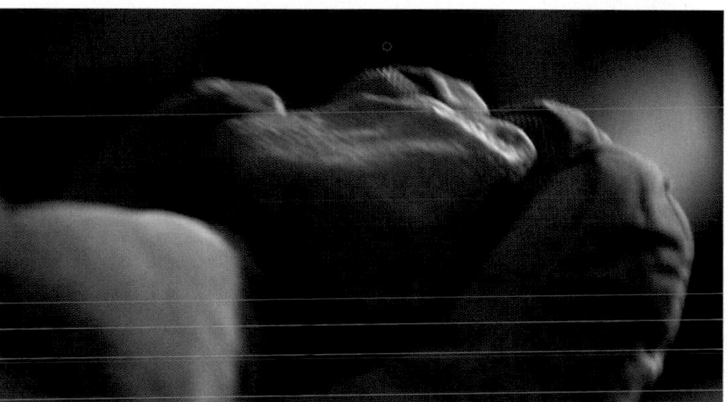

atmosphere with such intensity that their surface melts as it reaches temperatures of 6,000 degrees Celsius – the surface temperature of the Sun. This searing heat creates a tell-tale dark crust over the meteorite, so I was told we were looking for an oddly sculpted dark rock on the ground. (A rock that Hildebrand helpfully points out looks remarkably like the cow pats that litter this landscape.) However, the mind-numbing, slow search feels well worth it when I did find one of these astonishing rocks.

Each of these little rocks scattered across the frozen fields has had an amazing history. They would have approached the Earth as part of a meteorite known as a Chondrite. Chondrites are very old, having formed at the very beginning of the Solar System over 4.5 billion years ago. They have never been a part of a larger planet or moon; they are pure, wandering fossils of an earlier age.

If the meteorite had hit the ground intact, the explosion would have left a crater twenty metres (sixty-five feet) wide. Our planet was only spared this colossal impact because of the tenuous strip of gases that surrounds us, a strip of gas that we hardly notice. Nowhere is the crucial role of this protective blanket demonstrated more starkly than on the battered surface of our smallest neighbour – Mercury ◉

MERCURY'S CRATERS

On 30 January 2008, the NASA Messenger space probe took images of Mercury's surface. This was the first time humans had seen these parts of Mercury's scorched surface and it confirmed what had long been known about this tortured planet: it is a battered, barren piece of rock.

Until Messenger swept past Mercury, we knew little about the precise surface details of the planet. The only spacecraft to previously visit was the Mariner 10, which completed its mission in 1975, having mapped only 45 per cent of the planet's surface with what was, by today's standards, low-resolution equipment. Messenger is planning to fill in the gaps.

Launched on 3 August 2004, the spacecraft is designed to deal with the very specific problems of travelling to the inner solar system. Probes travelling to the outer planets have to accelerate to high speeds to travel across the vast distances in a reasonable time. They do this by a complex series of gravitational slingshots around the inner planets of the Solar System to speed them up. They must also carry enough fuel to slow them down when they reach their destination or, like Voyager, sweep past on a fleeting visit before vanishing off into interstellar space. Messenger has the opposite problem; because of Mercury's proximity to the Sun, the force of gravity causes Messenger to accelerate faster and faster as it approaches Mercury. It is rather like dropping a ball down a deep well. But unlike Mariner 10, Messenger is designed to go into orbit around the scorched planet. This requires Messenger to slow down enough to be captured by Mercury's weak gravitational field – an immensely tall order. It's like having to stop the falling ball halfway down the well.

To achieve this feat of spacecraft navigation, Messenger has been on an extended and complex journey, flying by Mercury three times over the first five years of its mission, each time using Mercury's gravity and orbital speed to slow down enough to enter orbit around Mercury in March 2011. Once in place, the probe is tasked with answering many of Mercury's mysteries; from the suspicion that there may be ice on the poles of this sun-drenched planet, to the theory that Mercury may be shrinking in size. Perhaps most important of all will be the completion of the work started by the Mariner probe in mapping the whole surface of Mercury and filling in the gaps that exist in our understanding of its geological history. As we capture more and more new images from the surface of the planet, it is becoming abundantly clear that one kind of geological feature dominates the surface.

For the last 4.6 billion years, Mercury has been bombarded with countless asteroids and comets. Unlike our planet's protective blanket, Mercury had nothing to shield it from the onslaught. When a meteorite hits naked Mercury, there is no atmosphere to break it up or slow it down; it strikes the ground at full speed and intact. As Messenger's images are revealing in beautiful vivid detail, the whole history of the planet's violent past is laid out on its surface, a world pitted with hundreds of thousands of craters inside craters, inside craters.

Mercury was damned from the start. It's too small and too hot to have retained any meaningful traces of atmosphere. Earth, though, is big and cold enough to have retained this envelope of gases that allows living things to evolve and to use that atmosphere to breathe and to live.

That's not where our luck ends, though. There is a place out there in the Solar System whose atmosphere began with the same ingredients as our own. A planet roughly the same size as Earth, and not much nearer the Sun. On this planet the characteristics of its atmosphere and place in the Solar System have been only slightly remixed, and yet it is a world that couldn't be more different from our own ◉

DEFENCELESS PLANET
Mercury is constantly being hit by comets and asteroids. It suffers these onslaughts because it has no atmosphere, so there is nothing to heat up the asteroid and break it into smaller pieces.

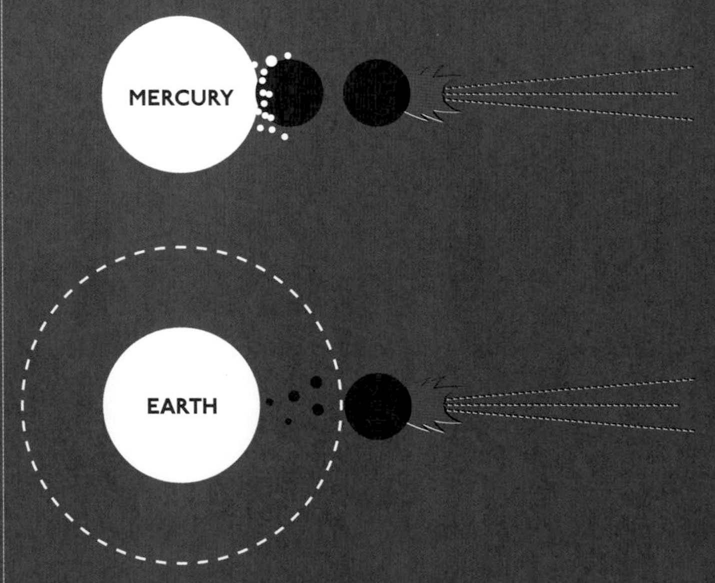

BELOW: The first visitor to Mercury was the Mariner Venus/Mercury spacecraft, also known as Mariner 10. It was launched on 3 November 1973 from NASA's Kennedy Space Center, and the following year it flew past Mercury, managing to map only 45 per cent of the planet's surface with what modern technology now views as low-resolution equipment.

BELOW AND BOTTOM: The Messenger space probe has relayed spectacular and informative images of Mercury in its three fly pasts so far. The image below shows the Brahms Crater, with a diameter of ninety-eight kilometres (sixty miles).

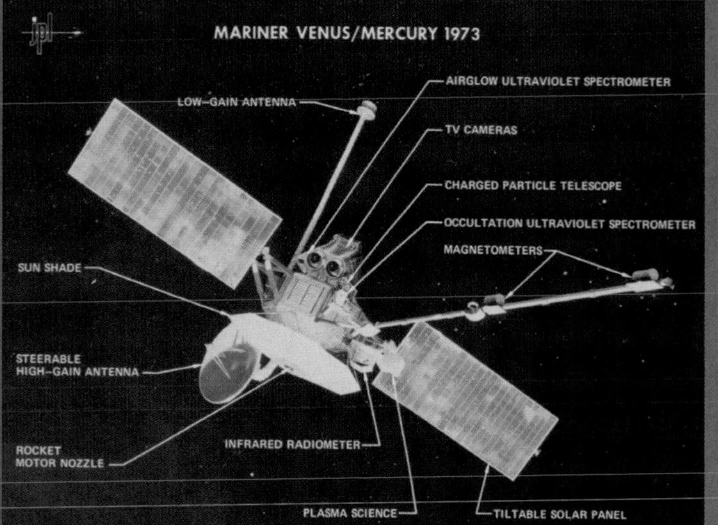

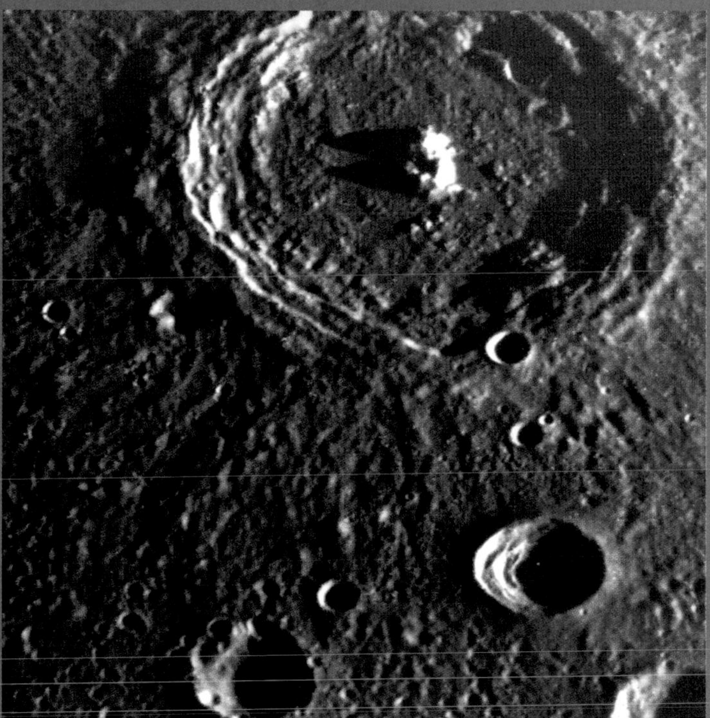

GOLDILOCKS ATMOSPHERES

Roughly 108 million kilometres (67 million miles) from the Sun sits Venus, the brightest planet in our night sky. Completing its orbit every 225 days, Venus is luminous enough to cast shadows on Earth as it reaches its maximum brightness just before sunrise or just after sunset. Venus and Earth share many similarities. We sit next to each other in space, we were formed from the same material, we are roughly the same size and we also share a similar mass and therefore gravitational field. But that's where any similarities end.

Venus is a tortured world where thick clouds of sulphuric acid are driven by high-speed winds and temperatures at the surface are hot enough to melt lead. It's not surprising that Venus is often known as Earth's evil twin. The reason for this hellish difference between these two superficially similar worlds is primarily down Venus's atmosphere, which evolved along a very different path to our own.

On 10 August 1990, the Magellan space probe began a four-year mission in orbit around Venus. Its aim was to give us the first images from beneath the shroud of cloud that had hidden our view of Venus for centuries. The images that Magellan sent back revealed a tortured landscape of volcanoes and impact craters. Beneath the clouds of sulphuric acid the landscape bore little resemblance to anything we can see here on Earth.

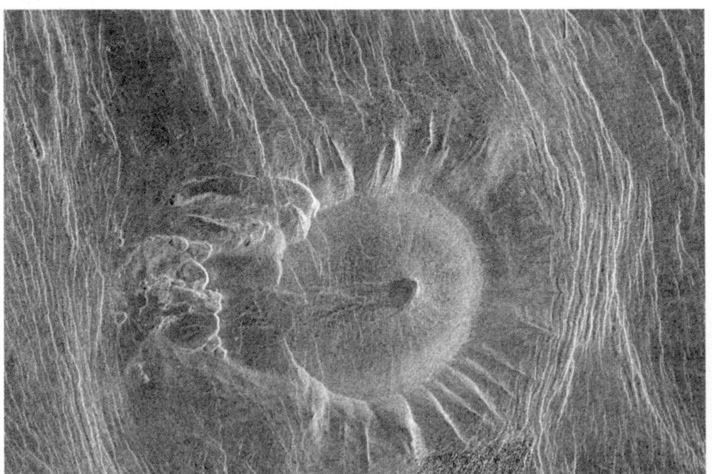

ABOVE: This picture, taken by the Magellan space probe on its mission in the early 1990s, shows our neighbouring planet Venus. During its four-year voyage, Magellan captured images of the Face of Venus, which clearly show the presence of volcanoes. Here is an example of a fairly common type of Venusian volcanic feature, known as a 'tick'. It is a volcano that is probably about thirty kilometres (twenty miles) wide at its peak, encircled by ridges and valleys that radiate down its sides and give it the insect-like appearance from which it gets it name.

Despite almost fifty years of interplanetary travel, sending images like this across forty-two million kilometres (twenty-six million miles) of space still remains an extraordinary feat of engineering. Venus was the destination for the first interplanetary mission when Mariner 2 reached the planet in December 1962. The hardware on Magellan may have been light years ahead of Mariner's (the very best that the late twentieth century could offer), but the mathematics needed to carry these detailed images back to Earth was the same and much, much older.

Almost every image that NASA has ever sent across space has relied on the work of the French mathematician and physicist Joseph Fourier in the early nineteenth century. The Fourier transform is a beautiful piece of mathematics

Beneath the clouds of sulphuric acid the landscape bore little resemblance to anything we can see here on Earth.

that was originally developed with no practical application in mind, and yet today Fourier's work can be found in virtually every electronic image we see; from our family photographs stored as JPEGs to the images we gather from the far reaches of the Solar System. It is the mathematics that drives our ability to compress huge amounts of information into files that are small enough to send around the world, or even around the Solar System.

However, when the Magellan space probe went to work, Fourier's contribution to our understanding of Venus wasn't just limited to the technology required to send images flooding back to Earth. In 1824, Fourier became the first scientist to describe an effect that is both crucial to our understanding of Venus and vital for the future health of our own planet.

The greenhouse effect has become a well-known contemporary phrase, one that is now synonymous with global warming; but in fact the idea originally came from the notebooks of Fourier in the nineteenth century. He was the first scientist to suggest that gases in the Earth's atmosphere might cause the planet to heat up. In doing so, Fourier paved the way not only towards an understanding of our climate, but also the extreme effects of the greenhouse effect on our sister planet Venus ◉

BELOW: This computer-simulated image shows the northern hemisphere of Venus. The planet is known as the evil twin of Earth; they are similar in size but Venus is closer to the Sun, which means temperatures on the planet soar to above 370 degrees Celsius. Earth is known as the Goldilocks planet because, unlike its neighbours Venus and Mars, which both experience extreme temperatures, the temperature on our planet is 'just right' for life.

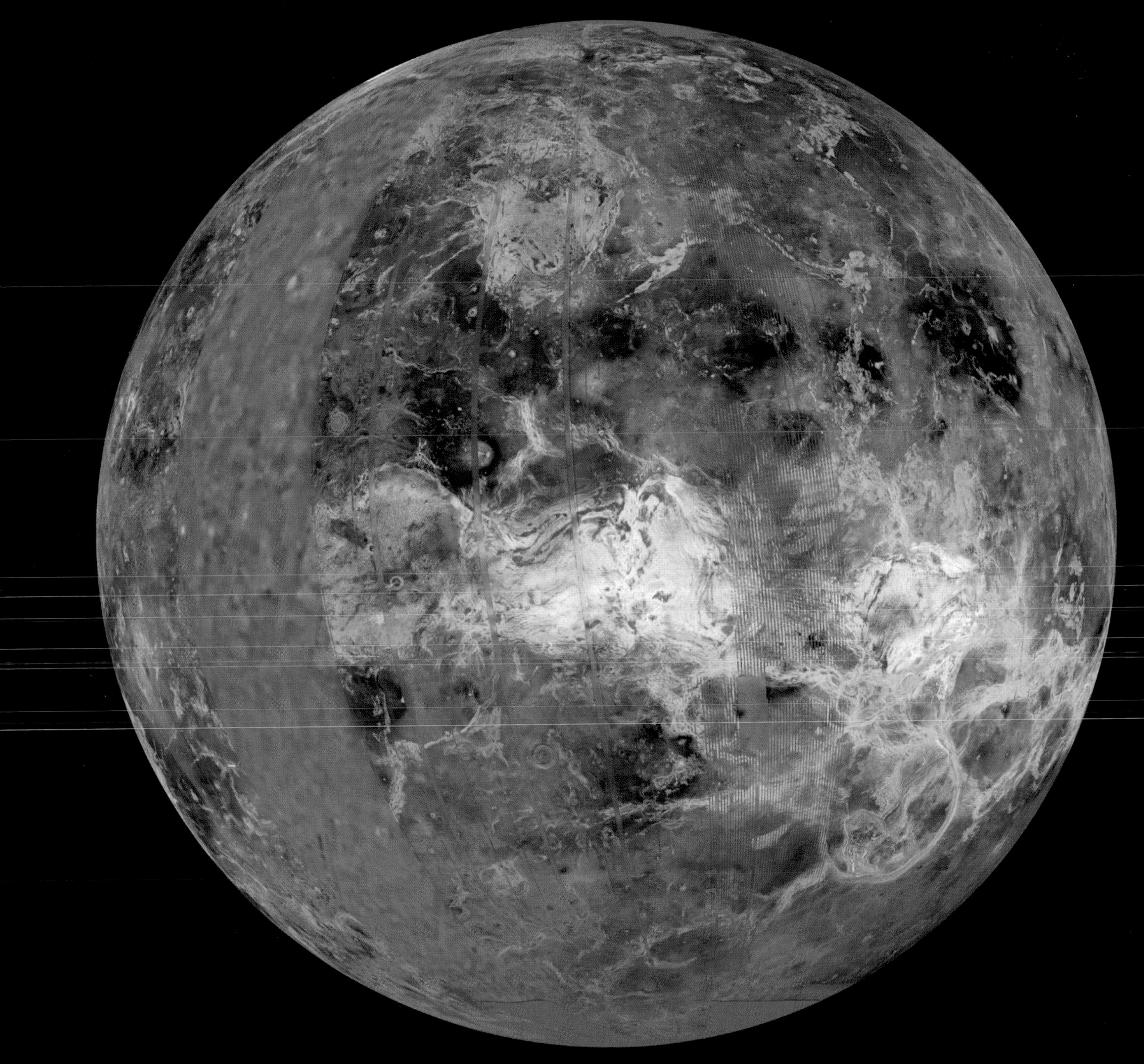

THE GREENHOUSE EFFECT

The greenhouse effect is basically a very simple piece of physics. The gases in a planetary atmosphere absorb the light of some wavelengths and allow others to pass through to the ground unimpeded. Earth's atmosphere is mostly transparent to visible light, which is obvious because we can see the Sun in the sky! Fortunately for life on Earth, much of the damaging, shorter wavelength, UV light is absorbed in the upper atmosphere by ozone. The sunlight allowed through by our atmosphere warms the Earth's surface, which then re-radiates this energy as infrared radiation. Infrared light has a longer wavelength than visible and UV light, and atmospheric gases such as carbon dioxide and water vapour are very good at absorbing it. In other words, some of the heat radiation from the ground is prevented from escaping back into space by so-called greenhouse gases. This means that the atmosphere gradually heats up, raising the temperature of our planet.

On Earth, the greenhouse effect is essential to our survival. Without the concentrations of greenhouse gases in our atmosphere we have today, our planet would be on average thirty degrees Celsius colder; far too cold to support life as we know it. A little greenhouse effect is a good thing, but if the concentrations of gases such as carbon dioxide are raised too much, we only have to look to our nearest neighbour to see the devastating consequences.

Venus' atmosphere is flooded with greenhouse gases. The rising temperatures would have long ago boiled away its oceans, pumping water vapour into the atmosphere. Carbon dioxide from thousands of erupting volcanoes added to the stifling mix. Venus grew hotter and hotter – far hotter than its position closer to the Sun than Earth would merit. The planet slowly choked to death ◉

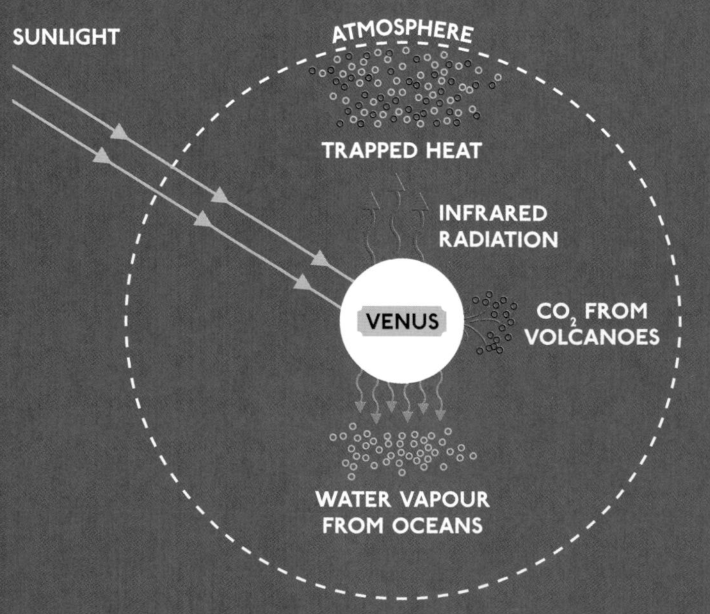

BELOW: On Earth, greenhouse gases are essential; without them our planet would be thirty degrees Celsius colder, which would make life unsupportable. Venus, however, suffered at the hands of excess greenhouse gases, choking to death on them.

THE RED PLANET

LEFT: On the rover's 2,052nd Martian day, here is a view of NASA's Mars Exploration Rover Spirit's robotic arm.

The Namib desert in Namibia is not the hottest desert in the world, nor is it the driest, but its ancient sand dunes form part of the oldest desert anywhere on the face of the Earth. Stretching over 1,900 kilometres (1,200 miles) along the south-western Atlantic coast of Africa, this vast expanse has been starved of rain for over fifty-five million years. It is a spectacular landscape, made even more fascinating for planetary astronomers because it is an extraordinarily accurate analogue for the surface of Mars. If you want to experience the sensation of standing on Mars here on Earth, at least visually, there is no better location to place your feet than in the crescent-shaped Barchan dunes of the Namib. Your eyes will be transported fifty-five million kilometres (thirty-four million miles) across space to the surface of another world.

ABOVE: In January 2005, NASA's Mars Exploration Rover Opportunity found an iron meteorite on Mars, the first meteorite of any type ever discovered on another planet. The Rover got close enough to the pitted meteorite, which is the size of a tennis ball and now called 'Heat Shield Rock', to determine that it is mostly made of iron and nickel.

The reason we understand the landscape of Mars in such beautiful detail is because we have first-hand evidence. The first successful landing on Mars was made, very briefly, by the Russian Mars 3 probe in 1971, but it only managed to transmit data back to Earth for fifteen seconds. The first truly important and revelatory landings were made by NASA's Viking probes in 1976. Viking searched unsuccessfully for signs of life on the red planet, although some of its results remain controversial to this day, and there are those who believe that Viking may have seen such evidence for life. Until the next biology-focused missions land on the Martian surface, we will probably never know.

In January 2004, the Opportunity Rover and the Spirit Rover touched down on the red planet and began the most intense and direct exploration of any landscape other than our own. Designed to roam Mars for ninety days, these little rovers are undoubtedly two of the most successful spacecraft ever launched. At the time of writing this book, in summer 2010, both rovers are still in contact with Earth, although Spirit appears to be stuck in the sands of Mars. For spacecraft that were not expected to see out 2004, this is nothing short of astonishing and one of the great feats of human exploration. Day after day, year after year, Spirit and Opportunity have driven across the surface of Mars and sent back exquisitely detailed images. Again and again the images reveal landscapes that have an eerie familiarity. Mars has vast sand dunes, enormous volcanoes, giant ice sheets, canyons and river valleys. It is a dry, frozen version of our home, covered in red dust and sand, entirely familiar and yet entirely inhospitable to human life. The barren landscape is due to the fact that today Mars has virtually no atmosphere. Yet as the rovers have searched the planet they have found compelling evidence to suggest that Mars hasn't always been this way.

In January 2005, the rover found a rock that turned out to be a nickel iron meteorite; four years later, in August 2009, it found another, which was estimated to be ten times bigger than the first. This makes it the biggest meteorite ever discovered on a planet other than our own, and its very existence makes no sense given what we know of the Martian atmosphere today.

Mars' atmosphere is incredibly thin. It consists of 95 per cent carbon dioxide, 3 per cent nitrogen and 1.6 per cent argon, with only traces of water and oxygen. In comparison to Earth, the mass of the atmosphere is tiny; 25 million million tonnes compared to the Earth's 5,000 million million tonnes.

BELOW: This picture is one of the first captured by the camera attached to the Pathfinder lander not long after it touched down on Mars on 4 July 1997. In the foreground you can see multiple images of the same little space rover, named Sojourner. On the horizon are two hills beyond the dusty rocky landscape of the planet's surface.

If you want to experience the sensation of standing on Mars here on Earth ... there is no better location to place your feet than in the crescent-shaped barchan dunes of the Namib.

Standing on Mars you would be exposed to less than 1 per cent of the Earth's surface atmospheric pressure – equal to the pressure we'd experience at an altitude of thirty-five kilometres (twenty-two miles). If the meteorite found by Opportunity had hit the planet today there would have been nothing to slow it down. The Martian atmosphere is too thin to provide any significant braking force to a meteorite of this size, and so it would have been travelling so fast when it hit the surface that it would have disintegrated on impact. It simply shouldn't be there!

The most likely explanation for this seeming paradox is that at some point in the past when this meteorite hit Mars, the atmosphere was significantly denser; dense enough to slow it down so that it could land on the surface intact.

If this is correct, then why did Mars lose its thick atmosphere and become the barren planet we see today? Atmospheres are fragile ghosts around a planet and there are many ways for them to be disrupted and lost to outer space. When you realise how fragile they are it begins to feel like a miracle that we've still got ours at all. It is thought that the reason Mars lost its atmosphere is down to the red planet's interaction with the powerful and far-reaching influence of our sun.

The solar wind is a stream of super-heated, electrically charged particles that constantly flow away from the Sun at over a million kilometres per hour. This wave of smashed atoms may be invisible and appear innocuous to us here on Earth, but it has the power to strip a planet of its atmosphere. We are protected by an invisible shield that completely surrounds our planet, known as the Earth's magnetic field. The origin of the Earth's magnetic field is in its molten iron core. This magnetic shield is strong enough to deflect most of the solar wind that comes our way (see page 52), in stark contrast to Mars ◉

HOW MARS LOST ITS ATMOSPHERE

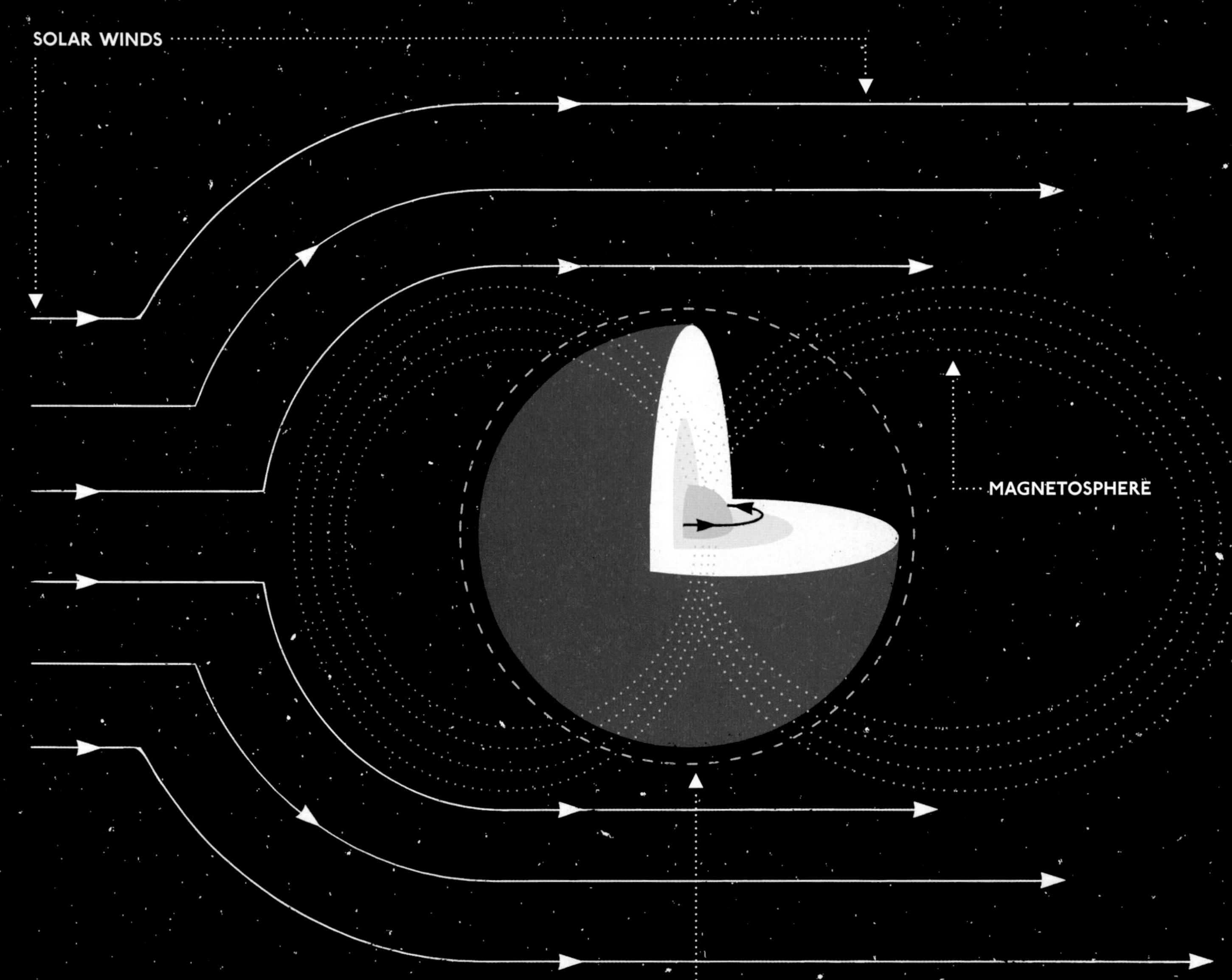

About four billion years ago, Mars had a molten core. Mars, after all, was formed by the same processes as Earth, from the same material around the same star and its molten core would have generated a protective magnetic field. There is, however, one crucial difference between the planets; Earth is nine times bigger, with Mars' total surface area being the size of the area of the dry land on Earth. This size difference is crucial because the larger the ratio of the surface area to the volume of an object, the quicker it will lose its heat.

Early in Mars' history the planet lost its internal heat through its surface and out into space, its core solidified, electric currents could no longer flow and its magnetic field vanished. Without these defences, the solar wind would have blasted Mars and stripped its atmosphere, and with no atmosphere to insulate it, this once Earth-like world was transformed into the frozen desert we see today, a shadow of its former self. Although Mars has lost most of its atmosphere, those few molecules of atmosphere that remain still have the power to sculpt its surface.

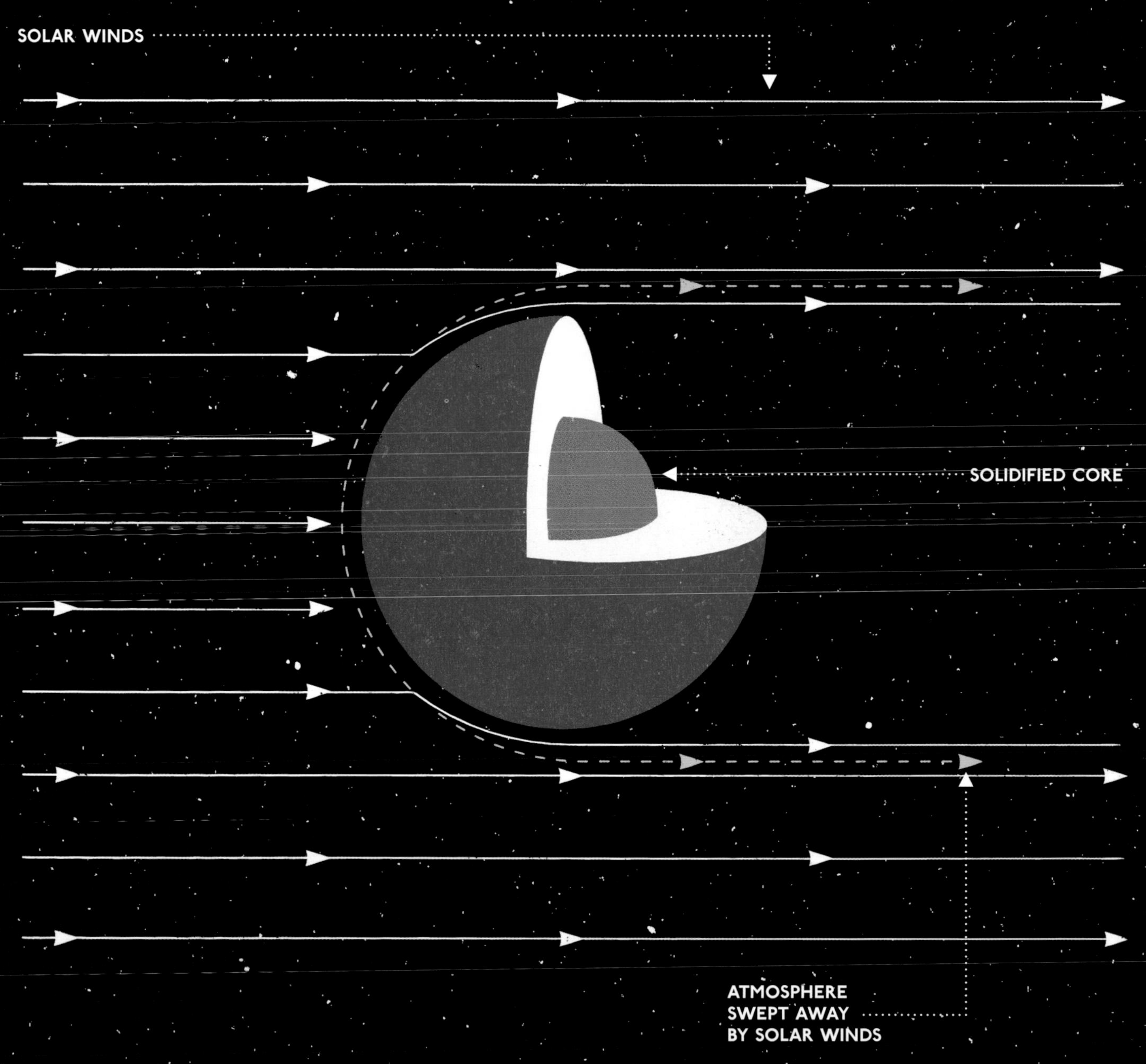

MARS AFTER

THE STORMY SOLAR SYSTEM

Weather is a feature of every planet with an atmosphere – however tenuous and diffuse it might be. Wind, storms, clouds and even rain can be found on worlds beyond our own. Wherever there is an atmosphere there is a delicate and complex interaction between the heat of the Sun, the surface of the planet and the swirling mass of gas that surrounds it. It is easy to see and understand how our world is transformed as the huge mass of air moves across the Earth's surface. But as we look out into the Solar System, we have discovered that it only takes the slightest trace of an atmosphere to produce extraordinary weather.

RIGHT: A deadly windstorm strikes central Kansas, USA.

JUPITER

EARTH

Jupiter's atmosphere is mostly made up of molecular hydrogen and helium and is many thousands of kilometres thick. It is divided into four layers (subject to altitude) and is in a constant state of seething motion and experiences cyclones, anticyclones, storms and lightning.

THE GREAT RED SPOT
Large enough to swallow our planet three times over and to be visible from telescopes on Earth, this is an anticyclonic storm that has persisted for at least 180 years, and possibly as many as 350.

BELOW: The largest planet in our solar system, Jupiter is a giant ball of gas and liquid. Its surface is made up of dense red, yellow, brown and white clouds and boils with storms that are far more powerful than anything we experience on Earth.

JUPITER: A PLANET OF WEATHER

Weather is a feature of every planet with an atmosphere, however tenuous and diffuse it might be. Wherever there is an atmosphere there is a delicate and complex interaction between the heat of the Sun, the surface of the planet and the swirling mass of gas that surrounds it. To experience the most extreme and violent weather in the Solar System, we need to visit Jupiter, the largest planet around our star. This giant is over 140 thousand kilometres (87 thousand miles) in diameter, dwarfing the Earth in volume. Over thirteen hundred Earths could comfortably fit inside Jupiter. Primarily made of hydrogen and helium, Jupiter is almost all atmosphere. There is no thin blue line; instead the Jovian atmosphere is many thousands of kilometres thick and in a constant state of seething motion, boiling with gigantic storms.

Yet this most alien world shares a feature with our own planet. Jupiter crackles to the sound of electrical storms. Bolts of lightning thousands of times brighter than lightning here on Earth illuminate the Jovian sky. These gigantic storms may look alien through the eyepiece of a telescope, but the forces that drive them are identical to the forces that drive storms here on Earth.

If there is warm moist air deep in an atmosphere it will start to rise, and as it rises it cools and the moisture condenses out to form clouds. That rising air leaves a gap beneath it, a low-pressure area, and so more warm moist air is sucked in, which this fuels the beginnings of a storm.

Here on Earth, the storm systems are driven by the power of the Sun. It is the Sun heating the Earth that creates the convection currents that churn our atmosphere into action. Without the Sun's energy, our planet would be a much calmer place. Jupiter, by contrast, is five times further away from the Sun, which means it receives twenty-five times less solar energy per square metre. This means that you might expect its storms to be considerably weaker. Intriguingly, we have discovered that the opposite is true; the storm systems on Jupiter are far more powerful than anything we have experienced on Earth. So what mechanism could possibly power these intensely violent storms?

The secret to Jupiter's storm-tossed atmosphere lies hidden deep within the gas giant. On Earth we have clear boundaries between the gaseous sky, the liquid oceans and the solid ground. On Jupiter there are no such boundaries; Jupiter is a giant ball of hydrogen and helium – a planet built almost entirely of atmosphere. But as you go deep down into Jupiter's atmosphere, something very strange and interesting happens to those gases.

Jupiter's atmosphere is so dense that 20,000 kilometres (12,000 miles) beneath the cloud tops the pressure is two million times greater than the surface pressure on Earth. Under these immense pressures the hydrogen gas in the atmosphere is transformed into a strange metallic liquid. When gases turn into liquids on this colossal scale, vast amounts of energy are released. Think of it this way: you have to put energy into a pan of liquid for it to boil and turn into steam. So if you do the opposite and condense steam back into liquid water, energy must be released. The same is true for gaseous and liquid hydrogen. It is this energy source that creates the convection currents that fuel some of the biggest storms in the Solar System.

The biggest of all the Jovian storms raging at the moment is the Great Red Spot, a gigantic storm 40,000 kilometres (25,000 miles) from east to west and 14,000 kilometres (9,000 miles) from north to south. This giant anticyclone has been raging for hundreds of years and is three times larger than the Earth. It is thought that the wind speeds reach over 400 kilometres (250 miles) per hour as this violent atmospheric feature circles the great planet every ten hours. We do not know why the storm has raged for so long or what makes it so red. It is thought that complex organic molecules formed from methane in Jupiter's upper atmosphere as it reacts with the Sun's ultraviolet radiation could be one factor behind its vivid colour.

The Great Red Spot is an extraordinary example of the violent alien weather that exists around the Solar System, but if we want to experience the most Earth-like atmosphere outside of our planet, then we need to look at a much smaller world. Orbiting the gas giant Saturn, one and a half billion kilometres from Earth, there is a magical frozen world that until recently hid its wonderful secrets beneath a thick impenetrable veil of cloud ◉

TITAN: THE MYSTERY MOON

LEFT: The mysterious moon, Titan, is captured in this false-colour composite created from images taken by the Cassini spacecraft on 16 April 2005. The green areas are where Cassini could see down to the surface; red are areas high in Titan's stratosphere where atmospheric methane is absorbing sunlight; and the blue illustrates the thick, Earth-like atmosphere that surrounds it.

Of all the 170 known moons in the Solar System, we have only been aware of one for any length of time. Our moon has been a source of wonder for millennia; the Moon is the fifth biggest natural satellite in the Solar System, and it dominates our night sky because it is by far the biggest moon in the Solar System in relation to the size of its parent planet. Our moon has a profound effect on the life of our planet, driving the ocean tides that are intimately linked to the cycles of Nature. It may even have been the case that tidal pools were the cradle for the origin of life on our planet.

It is also the only world beyond Earth on which humans have stood, and we discovered a dead, dusty world. Buzz Aldrin's famous description of the Lunar surface as 'magnificent desolation' is a savage yet romantic and perfectly apt description of the Moon's harsh beauty. Our only satellite is riddled with craters, the ancient remains of volcanoes and an atmosphere so tenuous that it is virtually indistinguishable from a vacuum. The very word 'moon' conjures a sense of a lifeless, inert world, a world as different to our dynamic planet as could be.

We have long thought of our moon as the archetypal moon of the Solar System, perhaps because we know it so well. This has meant that when we began our journeys into space many scientists expected the planets to be the stars of the show. The majority of those moons out there were thought to be dead, uninteresting worlds, but this could not be further from the truth. As is always the case with exploration, you genuinely don't know what you'll find until you actually go there. This is as true for the frozen outer solar system as it is for the most distant and isolated places on Earth. However, as we have begun to visit these worlds and fly spacecraft to within a few kilometres of their surfaces, we've found that the moons are an astonishingly interesting, varied and fascinating bunch of worlds.

One such place is Titan – Saturn's largest moon and the second largest moon in the Solar System. Bigger than the planet Mercury, this giant moon remained a virtual mystery until the Cassini spacecraft and its tiny sister, Huygens, arrived in the Saturnian system in 2004. The picture opposite, taken by Cassini in April 2005, illustrates why this world has always remained an intriguing but mysterious place, unique amongst the moons of the Solar System.

Surrounding Titan is an atmosphere that is 600 kilometres (370 miles) deep and four times as dense as that of the Earth. Titan is a magical place – a moon circling around a distant planet in the outer reaches of the Solar System, with an atmosphere that is more substantial than our own. It is the most Earth-like atmosphere we know of anywhere out there in space; a thick blue line rich in nitrogen and containing methane.

It seems almost beyond imagination that a world this small should be able to hold on to such a dense atmosphere. Mercury is too small and hot to have the gravitational grip needed to hold on to its atmosphere and Titan, although larger in volume, is half the mass of Mercury and so has an

BELOW: As the sunlight glows and scatters through the periphery of Titan's atmosphere, it produces a circle of light around the planet.

Chinese lanterns explain a simple bit of physics; high temperatures mean fast-moving molecules. By lighting the fuel beneath the lantern, the air inside heats up, making the molecules inside whizz around, increasing the pressure in the lantern.

even weaker grasp on the atoms of gas surrounding it. The reason that Titan has its wonderful atmosphere is because it lies in a much colder region of the Solar System – and that makes all the difference.

HOW TITAN KEEPS ITS ATMOSPHERE

The temperature of a gas is essentially a measure of how fast molecules are moving around – the higher the temperature, the faster they are moving. The speed of the molecules is also related to the pressure the gas exerts, because pressure is simply the effect of the molecules smashing against something, and the faster they are moving, the harder they smash into things and the higher the pressure. School chemisty lessons will have left you with an equation imprinted in your brain that summarises all of this – it's called the ideal gas law. It says that the pressure times the volume is proportional to the temperature – $PV = nRT$ – where P is the pressure, V is the volume, n is the number of molecules (measured in an obscure quantity called 'moles'), T is the temperature and R is a number known as the ideal gas constant. What this says in words is that if you keep the volume of a container fixed and raise the temperature, you have to raise the pressure or lower the number of molecules to keep everything in balance.

You can demonstrate what all this means beautifully with a Chinese lantern. If you light the fuel beneath the lantern, the air inside the lantern heats up. This means that the molecules inside start whizzing around faster and the pressure inside the lantern begins to increase. But the lantern is open at the bottom, and therefore the pressure inside the lantern must remain the same as the pressure outside. The pressures equalise by molecules of air rushing out of the bottom of the lantern and disappearing off into the atmosphere. If you look at our equation, n is decreasing in order to allow T to increase and keep everything else the same. Because molecules are constantly rushing out of the lantern, it weighs less and less as time goes by and eventually it is light enough to float gently off into the sky. Thus Chinese lanterns explain a simple bit of physics; high temperatures mean fast-moving molecules.

BELOW: Chinese lanterns are a beautiful example of the ideal gas law in action.

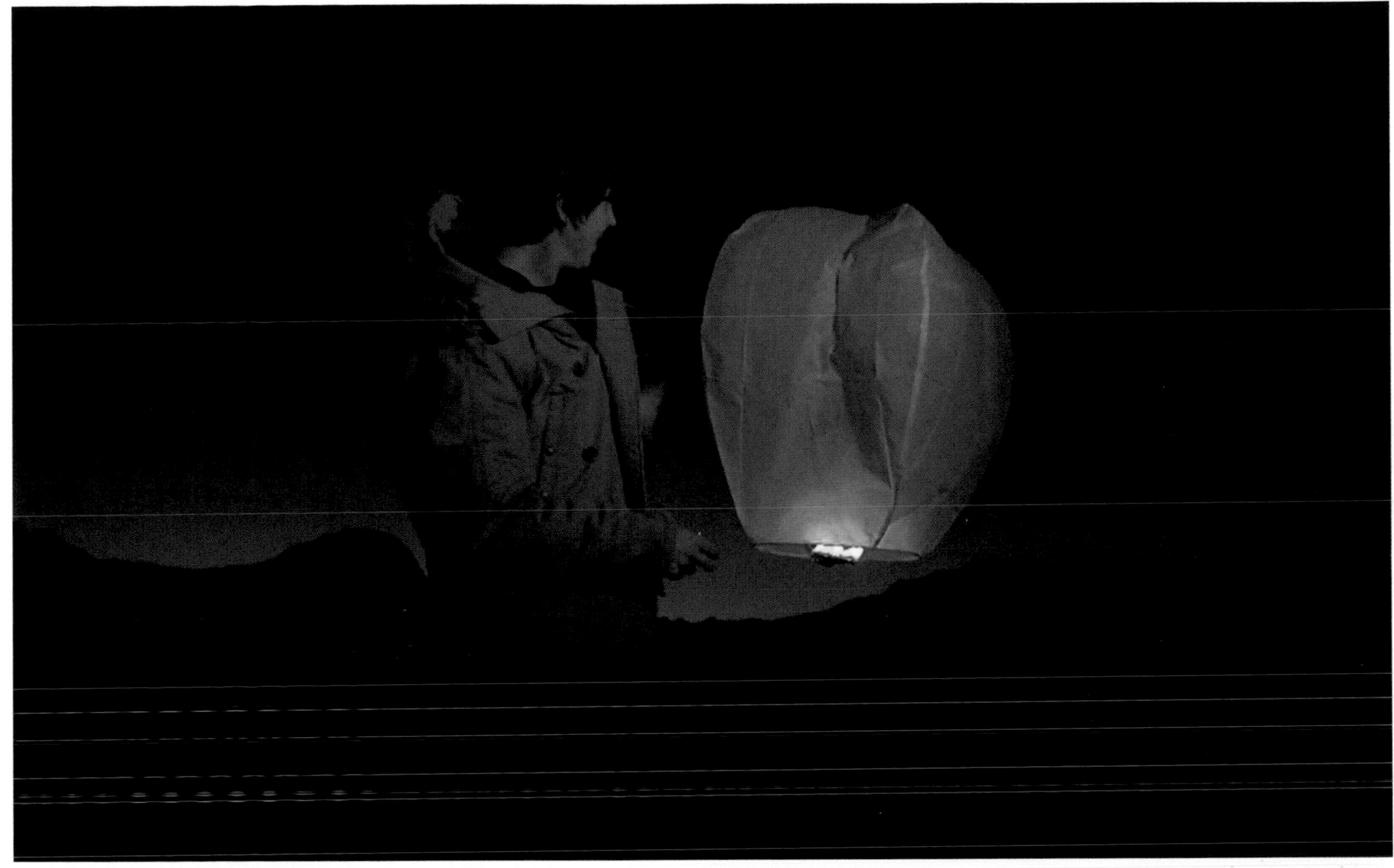

One and a half billion kilometres away from the Sun, Titan barely feels the warm glow of our star. Out here, the Sun is barely more than another star in the sky, making Titan a very cold place indeed. This means its atmospheric molecules are moving very slowly relative to ours. If Titan were in the same region of the Solar System as we are it would not be able to hold on to its atmosphere. It is a much less massive body than Earth, and so it has a much weaker gravitational pull. If the Sun heated Titan to Earth-like temperatures its atmosphere would soon vanish into space because it could not hang on to the fast-moving molecules. Move fourteen hundred million kilometres further out into the darkness to Titan's current position, however, and the weakness of Titan's gravitational pull is offset by the fact that its atmospheric molecules are moving around much more slowly than ours, allowing Titan to hang on to its dense atmosphere.

It was first suspected Titan had an atmosphere over 100 years ago. The Spanish astronomer José Comas Solá noticed a phenomenon known as the 'limb darkening' of Titan in 1903. He suspected that the transition in the intensity of the light he observed from the centre of Titan to its edge indicated that there was a layer of gas surrounding it. It took the work of an extraordinary astronomer with extraordinary eyesight to provide the first direct evidence of Titan's atmosphere, though. Gerard Kuiper was famed for his ability to see things that no one else could see. His incredibly acute eyesight allowed him to see stars with his naked eye that were four times fainter than those visible to virtually anybody else.

As well as having the Kuiper Belt, the region of planetoids and asteroids beyond Neptune, named after him, Kuiper was also the first to gather the spectroscopic data that confirmed the presence of an atmosphere on Titan. He was even able to estimate the pressure on the surface of the moon. With the thick cloud of gas shrouding Titan, it was difficult to explore the secrets of this intriguing moon any further using telescopes based on Earth. Nobody could see through the clouds. The Voyager space probe made the first detailed observations, but even from nearby, only the cloud tops were visible. It took a mission of even greater audacity to reveal the world beneath the haze ◉

JOURNEY TO TITAN

BELOW AND BOTTOM: The man behind the mission: Ralph Lorenz was one of the team who designed the Huygens probe that was launched in 1997. The probe sent back unique images of the planet from a distance as it flew through its atmosphere, and close-ups upon landing on its surface.

RIGHT: This set of images was taken by the Huygens probe on 14 January 2005. The pictures show angles north, south, east and west at five different altitudes above Titan's surface, revealing the frozen body to have lakes and dunes and a landscape not unfamiliar to us on Earth.

In 1997, the Cassini space probe began its journey to Titan. It carried with it the Huygens probe, a lander designed to set down on the surface of the enigmatic frozen moon. Huygens remained dormant aboard Cassini throughout the six-and-a-half-year journey to its release point above Titan, but on Christmas Day 2004, Huygens separated from Cassini and began the bumpy ride through the most intriguing atmosphere in the Solar System. For the next twenty-two days Huygens gently coasted towards the moon, with nothing switched on except for a 'wake-up' timer, programmed to awake Huygens fifteen minutes before it hit the atmosphere.

As the tiny probe approached the end of its billion-kilometre journey, it deployed a parachute to slow its descent and switched on systems designed to have power for just 153 minutes. Huygens gently swayed down, the thick clouds parted and the surface of Titan was revealed for the first time.

Huygens took two and half hours to reach the surface, but aerospace engineers are masters at building machines that exceed their design specifications, so while Huygens should have sent data from the ground for only the remaining precious few minutes, it actually delivered a unique view of our solar system for over an hour and a half. On the opposite page are some of the images taken by Huygens on its descent. The world it revealed was more familiar than we could have imagined.

One of the first scientists to see these incredible images was a man who helped to design the probe, Ralph Lorenz. I was lucky enough to hear first-hand from Ralph his extraordinary account of how it felt to be the explorer of another world as those first images came through. He told me, 'It was amazing because we ... we had no idea what to expect. We didn't know whether it would be cratered like the moon or just a flat expanse of sand, and then these first pictures came back and it was just astonishingly familiar.'

In the Huygens images you can clearly see rounded stones dotting the landscape. They're smooth and look like they have been eroded by tumbling water, similar to pebbles and stones found on river beds on Earth. It seemed for all the world as if Huygens had landed on a river channel, but this interpretation was initially disputed. Surely there could be no rivers on this frozen moon? Science is not a matter of opinion, however, and the evidence was so overwhelming that it was quickly accepted. This was an extraordinary discovery; evidence of flowing rivers had never been found before on a moon, but this wasn't the only surprise Titan held in store ◉

150 KM
100 MI
30 KM
20 MI
8 KM
5 MI
1.5 KM
1 MI
0.3 KM
0.2 MI
ALTITUDE

The Matanuska glacier in Alaska is one of the most beautiful places on our planet; a whole landscape that stands testament to the erosive power of ice and rock rolling down a valley over hundreds of thousands of years. The reason that glaciers can exist and sculpt our planet's surface is down to the delicate balance of the Earth's atmosphere.

THE MYSTERY OF TITAN'S LAKES

Our planet is just at the right temperature and pressure to allow water to exist at the surface as a solid, a liquid and as a vapour in the clouds. This happy accident of temperature and pressure allows the Sun to heat up the oceans, raise the water vapour high above the surface as clouds, move it over the tops of the highest mountains and return it to the landlocked ground as rain. The falling rain can then turn to solid ice, become a glacier and sweep down the valley to sculpt astonishing landscapes like the Alaskan Matanuska glacier.

There is a narrow range of temperatures and atmospheric pressures around which substances can exist as solid, liquid and gas simultaneously on the surface of a planet or moon. Because of this delicate balance, worlds that have just the right combination of temperature and pressure to allow water or some other substance to exist as solid, liquid and gas at their

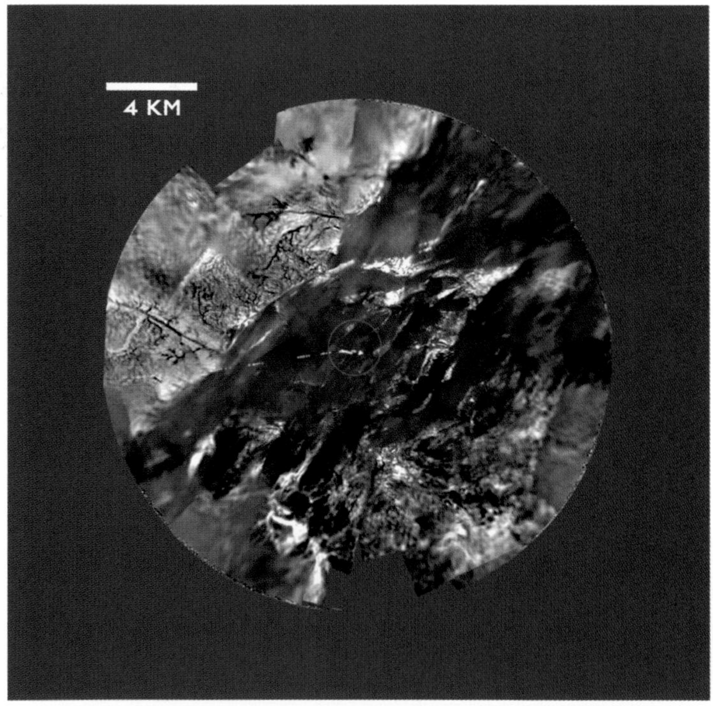

surface are extremely rare and precious places. Titan is just such a place – it has the perfect temperature and pressure to allow something to exist that has never been seen before on a world beyond Earth.

The picture above was taken by Cassini in June 2005. The images taken by it at this time have become some of the most important and fascinating in the history of space exploration. The interesting thing on the one above are the black blobs. Immediately, the Cassini scientists were hooked

ABOVE LEFT: The white tracks on this image of Titan's surface show the path of the Huygens probe. The dark, narrow, linear markings on the image have been interpreted as channels cut through the brighter terrain. The complexity of this network of channels across the moon's surface suggests the presence of methane 'rain' and possibly springs.

ABOVE: On Titan the atmospheric pressure of the moon means that methane exists as a solid entity there. So the gigantic lakes on Titan are not filled with water, but liquid methane.

and asked many questions, but an explanation as to what these dark patches were had to wait just over a year until July 2006, when Cassini passed over the same area again and took more images. These radar images showed the north pole of Titan, and the huge black areas are once more visible. In this case the black denotes where radar waves bounced on to Titan's surface from Cassini were not reflected back to the spacecraft, and there is only one really good explanation for that. These features are incredibly flat, so any surface detail at all would cause radar signals to be bounced back. What Cassini saw were surfaces of liquid – the first observation of lakes on the surface of a body other than the Earth in the Solar System (see pages 158–159).

These lakes cannot, of course, be lakes of liquid water, because the surface temperature on Titan is -180 degrees Celsius. At these temperatures, water is frozen as hard as rock. So if these expanses of black in the pictures of Titan's surface are not lakes of water, what are they?

BELOW: Methane is everywhere throughout the Solar System, but on Earth it is an unstable, highly flammable gas. Put a match to methane gas and watch it go up in flames.

RIGHT: These two radar images were recorded by the Cassini radar on 21 July 2006 and are believed to show very strong evidence for hydrocarbon lakes on Titan. The dark patches are scattered all over the high latitudes around Titan's north pole. Some scientists believe that these may have been formed by liquid methane or ethane, particularly near the colder polar regions.

Lake Eyak in Alaska on Prince William Sound is a tranquil place to be in the early morning. The pine-covered foreground hills rising up from the lake occasionally part to reveal higher jagged peaks dappled with snow, even in early autumn, with an Alaskan chill over the waters.

Beyond the picturesque, Lake Eyak is a great place to come to collect a substance that we know is very abundant on Titan. Methane is common throughout the Solar System, and here on Earth it exists as a gas that bubbles up from the depths of Lake Eyak. The floor of the lake is covered in rotting vegetation. The dead leaves, broken trees and twigs are broken down by bacteria, whose metabolic processes produce large quantities of this volatile gas. It's easy to collect the methane that bubbles up – simply tip a boat upside down and leave it overnight in the lake. In the morning, the boat will be filled with methane gas.

It's even easier to show just how unstable methane is here on Earth. Put a match to a bag of methane and in the presence of oxygen you get what chemists call an exothermic reaction. Methane plus oxygen goes to water plus carbon dioxide, and some energy. In other words, it burns.

The Earth's temperature and atmospheric pressure mean that methane can only exist as a highly flammable gas, but on Titan the characteristics of methane are very different indeed. Titan's combination of atmospheric pressure and temperature is perfect to allow methane to exist as a solid, a gas and a liquid. The images Cassini captured are gigantic lakes of liquid methane, the first-ever discovery of a liquid pooling on the surface of another world in the Solar System.

The largest body of liquid on Titan is a lake known as Kraken Mare. At over 400,000 square kilometres (154,400 square miles), it is almost five times the size of Lake Superior, North America's greatest lake. It is a true wonder of the Solar System; a vast expanse of liquid on a world almost a billion kilometres from home.

On Titan, methane plays exactly the same role that water does here on Earth. Where we have clouds of water, Titan has clouds of methane with methane rain; where we have lakes and oceans of water, Titan has lakes of liquid methane; and whereas here on Earth the Sun warms the water in the lakes and oceans and fills our atmosphere with water vapour, on Titan the Sun lifts the methane from the lakes and saturates the atmosphere with methane. On Earth we have a hydrological cycle, whereas on Titan there is a methanological cycle.

There is no doubt that rain would be an absolutely magical sight on Titan. The atmosphere is so dense and the gravity of the moon is so weak that the drops of methane rain would grow to about a centimetre in size and would fall to the ground as slowly as snowflakes fall onto the surface of our own planet. Thousands and thousands of gallons of liquid

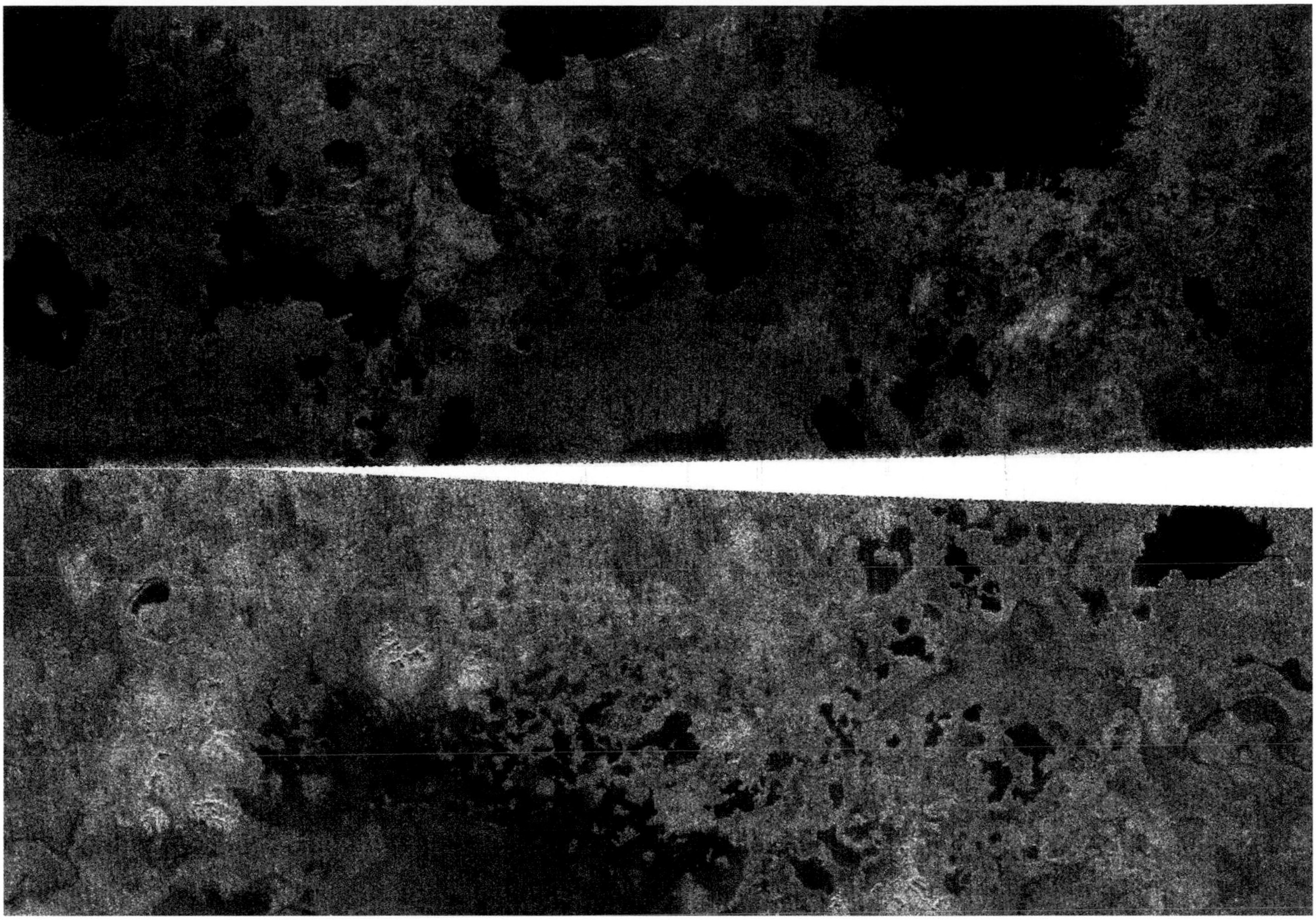

TITAN'S METHANE CYCLE
Titan's methanological cycle follows the same pattern as our hydrological one.

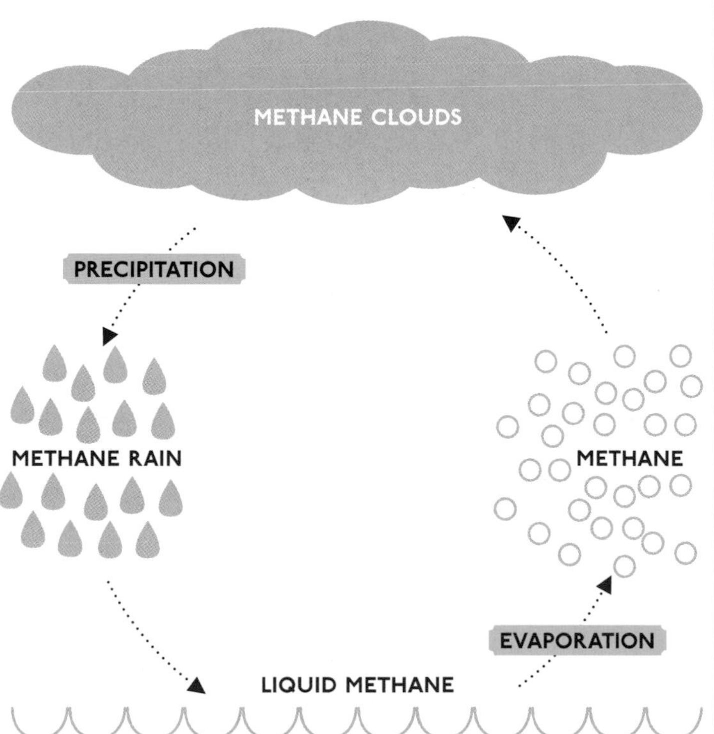

methane must have slowly rained down on to the surface, making rivers and streams swell and burst, cutting deep gullies into the frozen water landscape.

It all looks and seems so familiar because it is familiar. We are gazing from space on to a landscape sculpted by the same forces of nature and the same cycles that we see here on Earth. The atmosphere of Titan shapes the surface in exactly the same way that our atmosphere shapes the surface of our home planet.

Titan is like a primordial Earth caught in a deep freeze. It's a place with rivers and lakes and clouds and rain. It's a place with water, albeit frozen as hard as steel, and a place of methane, albeit so cold that the methane is a liquid that flows and shapes the landscape just like water does here on Earth. It's almost like looking back in time over four billion years and observing our planet before life began; before our atmosphere was changed by the delicate processes of life into the oxygen-rich canopy of vapours we see today.

Perhaps the most important thing of all about Titan is that we now have two Earth-like worlds in our solar system. One in a warm region, 150 million kilometres away from the Sun, and the other in deep freeze, a billion kilometres away from our star and in orbit around another planet. Surely that must greatly increase the probability that there are other Earth-like planets in orbit around the hundreds of billions of stars out there in the Universe? ◉

CHAPTER 5

DEAD OR ALIVE

THE HEAT WITHIN

Since the dawn of human history we've been able to gaze up into the night sky, but we're lucky because we're the first generation that's been able to build machines to actually go to those planets and moons. We've found that they're more beautiful, more violent, more magnificent and more fascinating than we could have possibly imagined. The more worlds we study, the more we realise that our solar system is a cosmic laboratory. Even the slightest differences in size or position can create a world radically different from its neighbours.

BELOW: Our knowledge of natural wonders, such as the Grand Canyon in Arizona, was once limited to our own planet, but now space exploration has brought new, equally spectacular worlds into view.

In 1540, the Spanish explorer García López de Cárdenas was stationed in the tiny outpost of Cibola, in Arizona, when he was asked to conduct a reconnaissance mission. Reports had suggested that there was a large river somewhere north of the camp and so Cardenas set off to try and establish the whereabouts of this precious source of water and food. After twenty days of walking northwards, Cardenas found what he was looking for. Ahead of him lay the waterway they named the river Tzion. The river, which would one day become known as the Colorado river, was within his sights, but despite days of trying he could not find a way down to the water. The precious waters of the river eluded him by the sheer scale of the drop. Although the mission was a failure, Cardenas had become the first European to see one of the greatest wonders on our planet. In his search for water, Cardenas found himself standing on the South Rim of the Grand Canyon.

Almost 500 years later, the Grand Canyon has lost none of its ability to awe and inspire. Over five million people a year make the pilgrimage to view this epic landscape and to gaze out across what is undoubtedly one of the most stunning views on Earth.

As well its beauty, a visitor to the Grand Canyon is also looking at an extraordinary example of planetary engineering. Estimates suggest the origins of this valley date back approximately seventeen million years, when the Colorado river began to carve its way through the rock. It is amazing to think that in this short space of time a valley 466 kilometres (277 miles) long, 29 kilometres (18 miles) wide and 1.6 kilometres (1 mile) deep has been etched and carved by nothing more than the action of running water.

Perhaps most remarkable of all the stories the Grand Canyon has to tell is the extraordinary history of our planet etched into the walls of the ravine. From top to bottom, the layers of rock reveal a journey through two billion years of the Earth's history; evidence of rising sea levels and ice ages, ancient swamps and extinct volcanoes, chronicle the ever-changing life of our planet. The walls of the canyon provide us with one of the most complete geological columns on Earth, and despite the wonderful variety of tales it has to tell, one thing connects them all: our planet is alive. It remains today as it has been for billions of years – dynamic, changing and vibrant – a world driven by intense heat at its core and shaped by the journey this heat takes to the surface and beyond.

The great forces that shape our world are universal – all planets and moons share the same basic laws of physics. The level of geological activity, or inactivity, is the very essence of a planet's character. As we've explored the Solar System we have seen how these forces can manifest themselves in many different ways; creating worlds that are more alien than we could ever have imagined and worlds more familiar than we could have guessed. Again and again the wonders of our planet are eclipsed in size and scale by the new wonders we are discovering through our exploration of the Solar System ◉

This is the first image of the largest-known canyon in the Solar System, compiled from a series of pictures taken by NASA's Viking spacecraft in the 1970s. Eight kilometres (five miles) deep, up to 600 kilometres (372 miles) wide and over 3,000 kilometres (1,860 miles) long, on Earth it would run all the way from Los Angeles to New York. The Valles Marineris is a canyon so vast that you could fit our own Grand Canyon into one of its side channels.

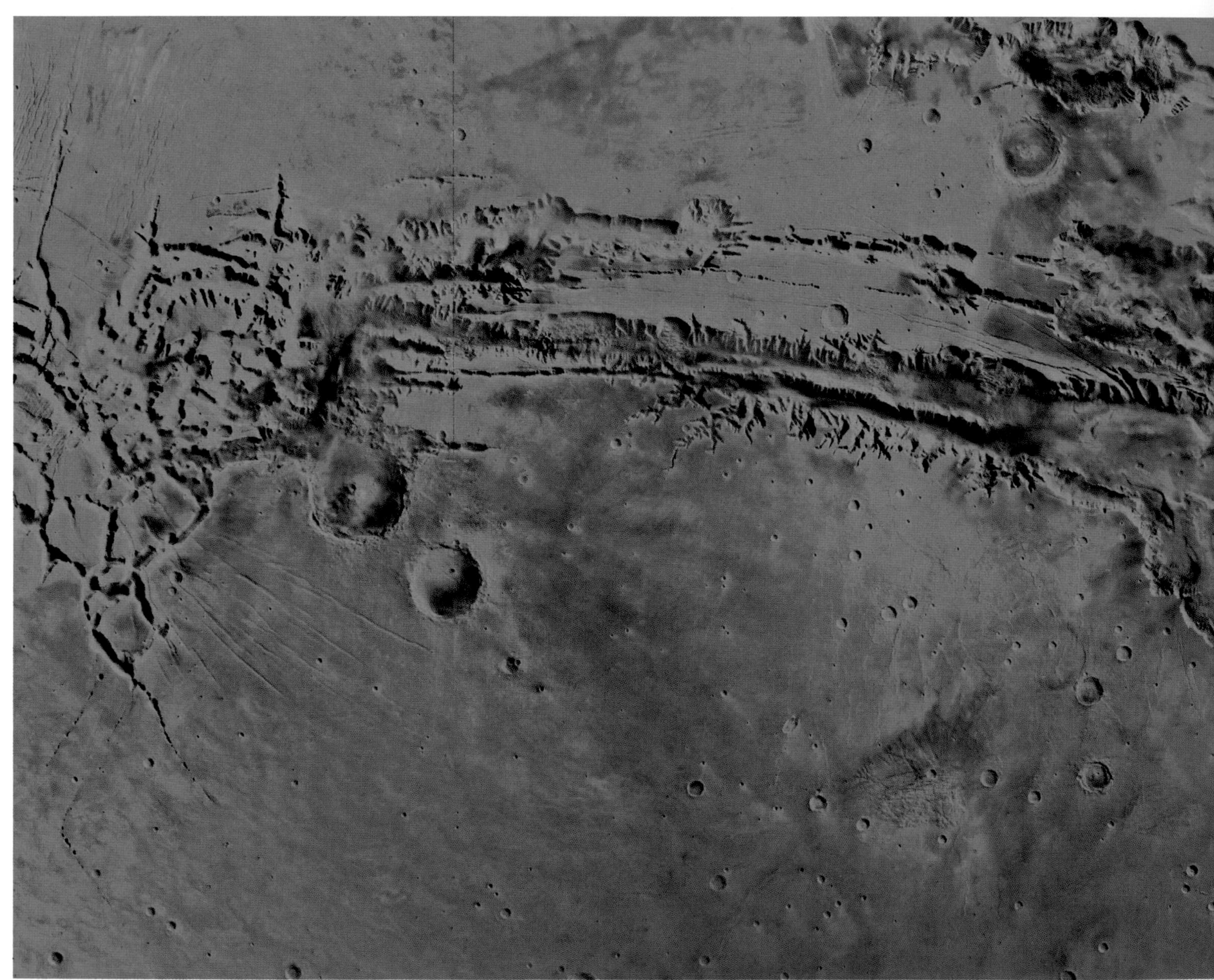

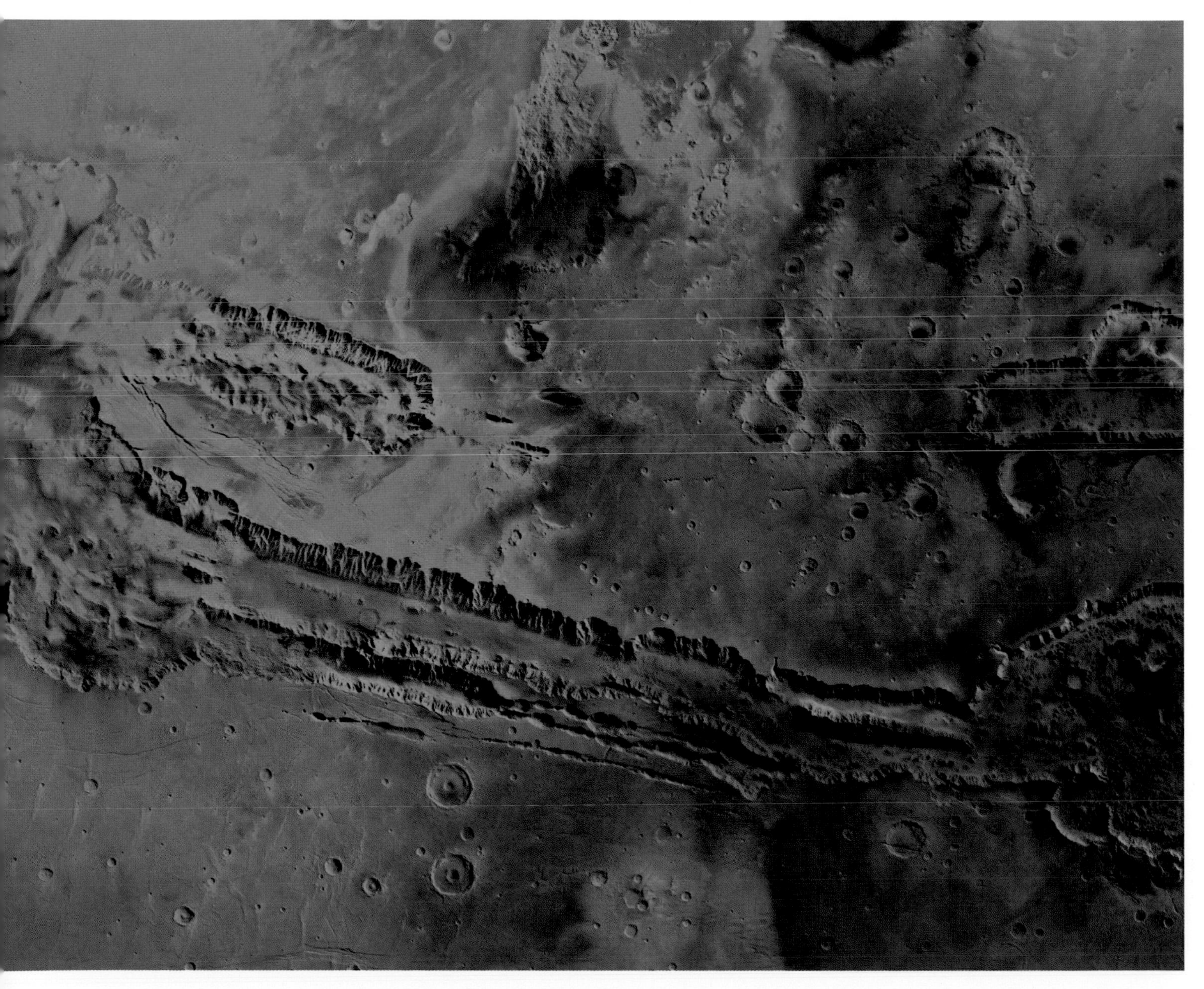

MARS: A FAMILIAR WORLD

The Valles Marinieris is named after the space probe that first discovered it, Mariner 9. Launched in 1971 at the height of the Cold War, Mariner 9 was the first spacecraft to orbit another planet, and the images it sent back revealed the many landscapes and features that we share with Mars. Today, we have three functioning spacecraft orbiting Mars and two rovers, Spirit and Opportunity, on the Martian surface. Together, these are helping us to build a deep and quite profound understanding of the geological evolution of the planet. Unlike any other planet in the Solar System, we have eyes and ears on the surface of Mars and the success of these missions has demonstrated that there really is no substitute for proper exploration on the actual planet. We have sent robotic explorers across millions of miles of space to touch the soil and taste the air. The images they have sent back have allowed us to look up, and gain a new perspective on our solar system.

From the view of our sun setting on the horizon of an alien world to the movement of clouds across the Martian sky, these images reveal the deep similarities between Mars and Earth. These clouds are believed to be composed entirely of water-ice particles, in sizes of several micrometres, formed as part of a band of cloud that occurs near the Equator when Mars is at the coldest, most distant part of its orbit around the Sun. During this cooler part of the Martian year, atmospheric temperatures and the amount of water vapour in the atmosphere allow the formation of large-scale clouds that would not be out of place in the skies of Earth.

Everywhere we look on Mars we are confronted with scenes that remind us of home. It is a landscape that echoes Earth from the very smallest detail to the grandest features, such as the Valles Marinieris. Most scientists now agree that the Valles Marinieris is a tectonic crack that was created in the same way that the plate tectonics here on Earth created the East African Rift Valley. And it is not just tectonic activity that appears to have left its mark on the surface of Mars; we have also found evidence of landscapes formed by water courses and the permanent polar ice caps that ebb and flow with the seasons.

Despite all the similarities between Mars and Earth, it is the differences between these two planets that are most telling. Mars is a cold planet, with an average temperature of minus sixty-five degrees Celsius. It is also a planet with a tenuous atmosphere, compared to Earth.

Mars is now a desolate and dead wasteland, a world where the processes that sculpted its now familiar landscapes seized up long ago. There are no waters to flow, no active volcanoes to erupt, and we have so far found no evidence of life either on the planet's surface or beneath it. Mars appears to be a dead world, a sobering example of how the laws of Nature can play out across our solar system in radically different ways.

BELOW: Mars is currently orbited by three active satellites: Odyssey and Reconnaissance are in normal orbits and Express is in a very elliptical orbit, travelling up to 6,200 miles (10,000 kilometres) away from the surface of Mars.

BOTTOM: Even the skies on Mars are reminiscent of those on Earth, as atmospheric temperatures and water vapour combine to create clouds.

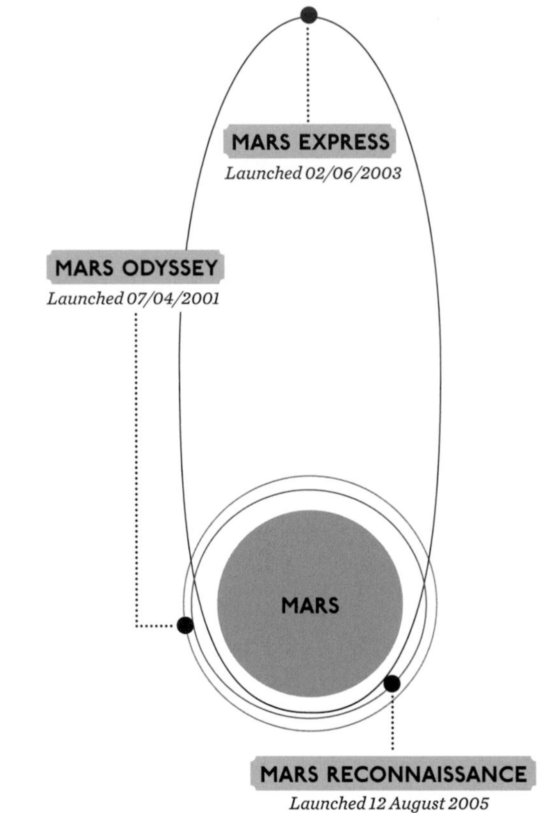

BELOW: This picture of the surface of Mars looks like it could have been taken at Arizona's Grand Canyon; except there we can see the river below that carved this formation, while on Mars we have no explanation for this dramatic rocky landscape.

BOTTOM: The origin of the vast canyon on Mars is unclear, but some scientists believe it began as a tectonic crack billions of years ago.

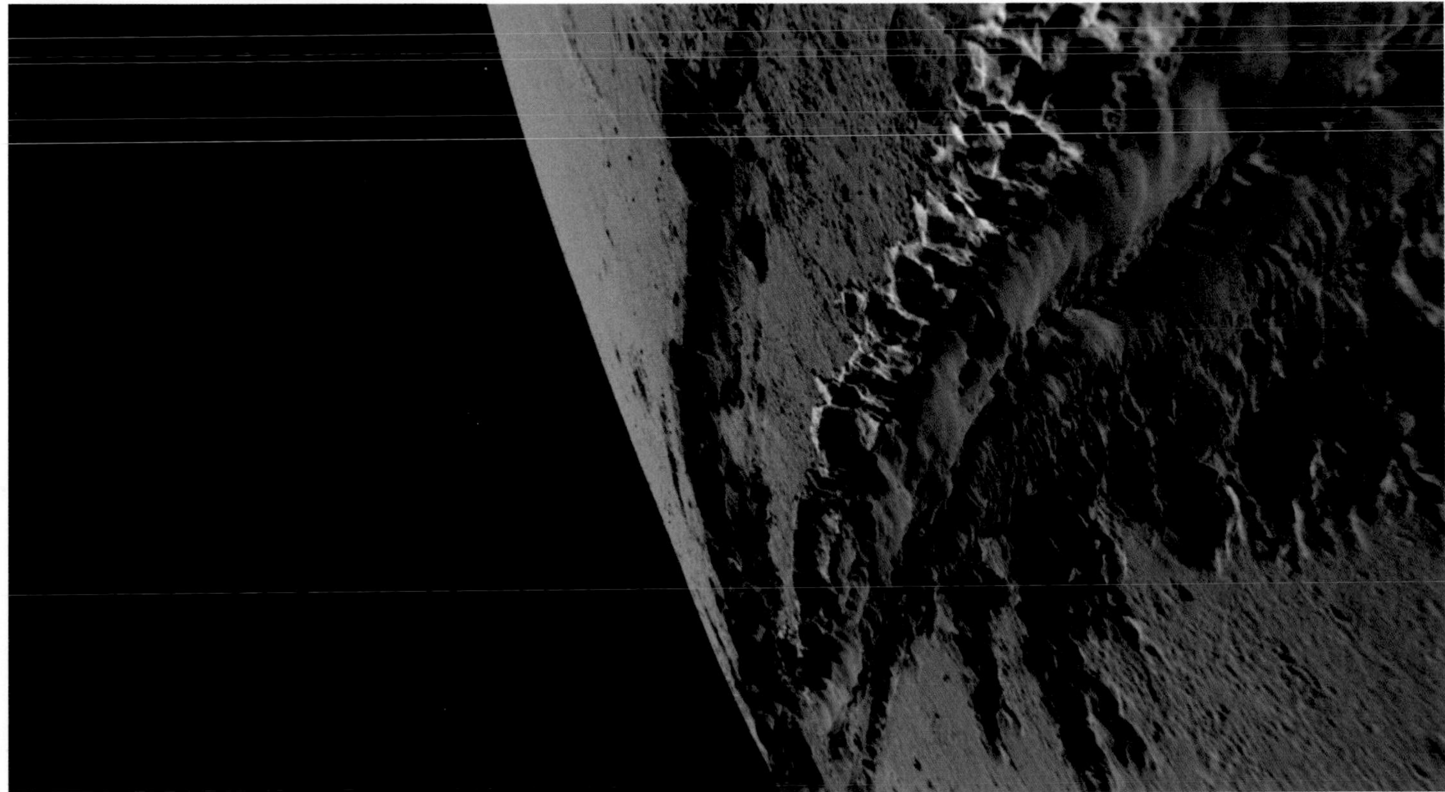

BELOW AND RIGHT: The molten lava spewing out of the volcano Kilauea on Hawaii's Big Island may look destructive, but such eruptions are part of Earth's geological heartbeat. Here is the perfect demonstration of how a planet can be kept alive by nothing more than a flow of heat.

To understand the forces that keep a planet alive, there is no better place on Earth to study than the Big Island of Hawaii. Set amongst the most remote group of islands on the planet, Big Island is part of an undersea mountain range that breaks through the Pacific Ocean to create a chain that runs for over 2,400 kilometres (1,500 miles). This is the perfect place in which to witness how a planet survives by nothing more than the simple flow of heat, because everything on this magnificent island range is created by the intense heat that sits within the Earth's core.

Although the Hawaiian Islands are far from any tectonic plate boundary, they are above a geological hotspot, a narrow stream of lava that is thought to link it all the way to the boundary between the Earth's mantle and its core. As the Pacific Plate drifts over this hotspot, it creates some of the most intense volcanic activity in the world; the magma pushes through, it builds up over time to create the island volcano. As the plate drift moves the volcano away from the hotspot, the magma source is removed and eruptions cease.

The Big Island is built from five shield volcanoes, and by far the most active of these is Kilauea, which means 'spewing'. It's been erupting almost continuously since 1983 and is thought to be one of the most active volcanoes in the world.

Every day you can see molten rock flowing down the side of the mountain, destroying everything in its path. Forests are turned to ash and the Pacific Ocean boils as the lava hits the water and explodes. This might look like widespread destruction, but volcanic eruptions are Earth's geological heartbeat. The surface of our planet has been created and shaped by active volcanoes that make our planet a vibrant living world.

A few kilometres north of Kilauea you can see just what volcanic action can produce, given enough time. Mauna Kea lies dormant today, but its scale is testament to the enormous power that exists within the Earth. Although this mountain is four kilometres (two miles) above the surface of the Pacific, it's ten kilometres (six miles) above the surface of the Pacific floor, making it the highest mountain on Earth, but tiny compared to the biggest volcano in the Solar System ◉

THE VOLCANOES OF MARS

BELOW: This colour mosaic taken by the Viking I Orbiter shows Olympus Mons, named after Mount Olympus – the mythical home of the Greek gods. It is the highest volcano on Mars, with a footprint the size of Arizona.

BOTTOM: Olympus Mons is a staggering 550 kilometres (340 miles) in diameter and its 80-kilometre (50-mile) -wide summit caldera is positioned 25 kilometres (16 miles) above the surrounding plains.

MOUNT EVEREST: 9KM
OLYMPUS MONS: 25KM
MAUNA KEA: 10KM
SEA LEVEL

ARIZONA

Located near the Martian equator is a region known as Tharis. This vast volcanic plateau, found at the western end of the Valles Marineris, is home to some of the biggest volcanoes in the Solar System, but one volcano dwarfs them all. Its vast outpouring of lava stretches over 600 kilometres (370 miles) wide, but it is the height of Olympus Mons that is truly breathtaking.

It soars twenty-five kilometres (sixteen miles) into the Martian sky, two and a half times the full height of Mauna Kea, making it the highest mountain we have ever seen. Astronomers have peered at the greatest mountain in the Solar System since the late nineteenth century, but it wasn't until 1971, when the Mariner 9 space probe took the first images of it, that its true scale was revealed. Just like Mauna Kea, Olympus Mons is a shield volcano. Over millions of years, layer upon layer of lava has built up during long periods of continuous eruptions, slowly raising the mountain to truly gargantuan heights. With a footprint roughly the size of the state of Arizona and gentle slopes leading kilometre after kilometre up to its summit, Olympus Mons is so vast that if you were standing on its foothills it would be impossible to see to the top. It grew so tall because of the specific geology of Mars. In Hawaii, a string of volcanoes is being produced as the Pacific Plate moves over a static hotspot. As the plate drifts northwards over the hotspot, new volcanoes are formed and existing ones become extinct as they are carried away from their source of heat. On Mars, the lack of plate movement over the hotspot beneath Olympus Mons has meant the lava has simply piled up.

Apart from its sheer size, almost everything else about Olympus Mons is familiar. It shares many of the features and qualities we find in shield volcanoes on Earth because the geological processes that built them are identical. Mars and Earth share more than geological similarities, however. The origins of all the rocky inner planets – Mercury, Venus, Earth and Mars – are very similar. The story of their formation can be traced back billions of years to the fiery birth of the Solar System and the planet we call home

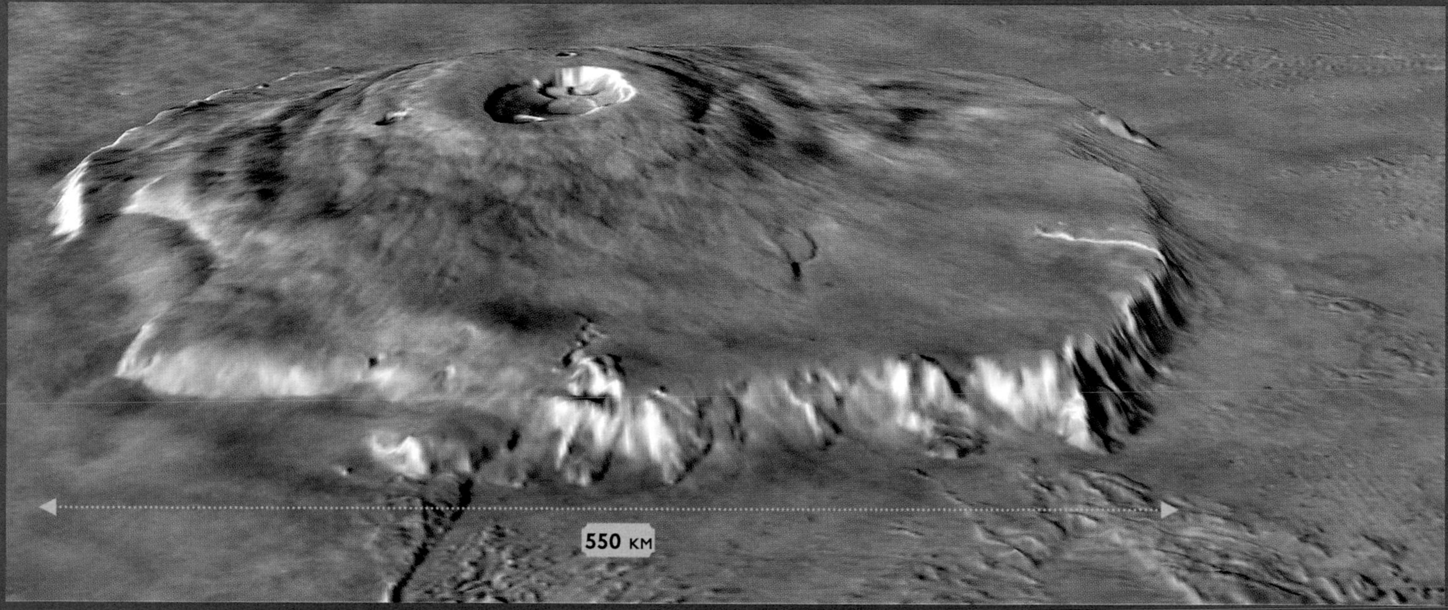

LEFT: This artist's animation shows the swirling disc of dust that will build a new planet. It is believed that planets are born small, developing into larger planets as they slowly accumulate dust and gas in bigger clumps. As they grow they collide with proto-planets, until eventually they form a few Earth-sized rocky planets.

THE FORMATION OF ROCKY PLANETS

Around 4.6 billion years ago, the Sun had just ignited and the infant Solar System was nothing more than a disc of gas and dust orbiting around a newly formed star. This proto-planetary disc contained all the matter that would later form the planets and moons of our solar system, a process that would take millions of years of slow construction.

The processes by which solar systems form out of discs of dust and gas surrounding young stars are not fully understood, but the most widely accepted explanation is known as the 'planetesimal' theory. Planets are born small, growing through a gradual accumulation of dust and gas into larger and larger clumps. Dust particles in the disc form small clumps as they collide together randomly over millions of years, and some accumulate more and more mass through these collisions until they reach a critical size of about one kilometre (0.6 miles). These solid, ill-defined objects are known as planetesimals. After reaching this critical size, it is thought that mini-planet-sized objects grow very quickly, because their growth rate increases as their mass increases. This process is known as runaway accretion and lasts only a few tens of thousands of years. There are frequent collisions between the many proto-planets orbiting around the young Sun, but eventually, through a process of continual collisions and mergers, a few Earth-sized rocky planets will be left.

Slowly, these newly formed balls of rock are transformed. A combination of heat from multiple collisions, plus the heat generated by the decay of radioactive elements that were present in the proto-planetary disc, can melt whole areas deep inside the planets. This allows gravity to take over, and so the heavy elements, such as iron and many of the heavier radioactive nuclei, sink to the planet's core ◉

PLANET FORMATION

The Solar System consists of three major types of planet: ice giant, gas giant and terrestrial. These are produced because the protoplanetary disc has different proportions of rock and ice depending on its distance from the Sun. Terrestrial planets develop closer to the Sun where the protoplanetary disc is mainly rock, whilst ice giants develop furthest away from the Sun where the protoplanetary disc is mainly ice.

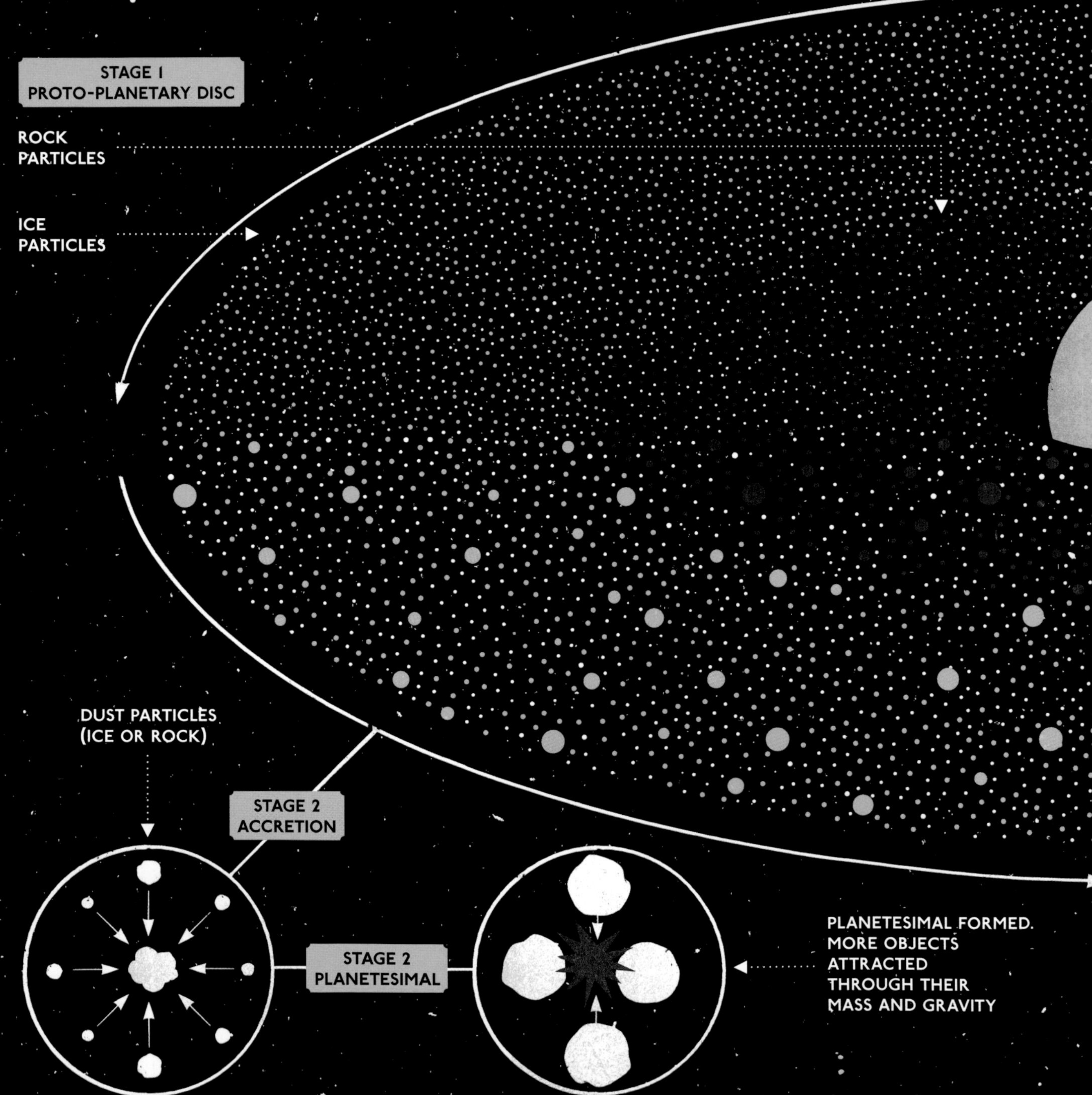

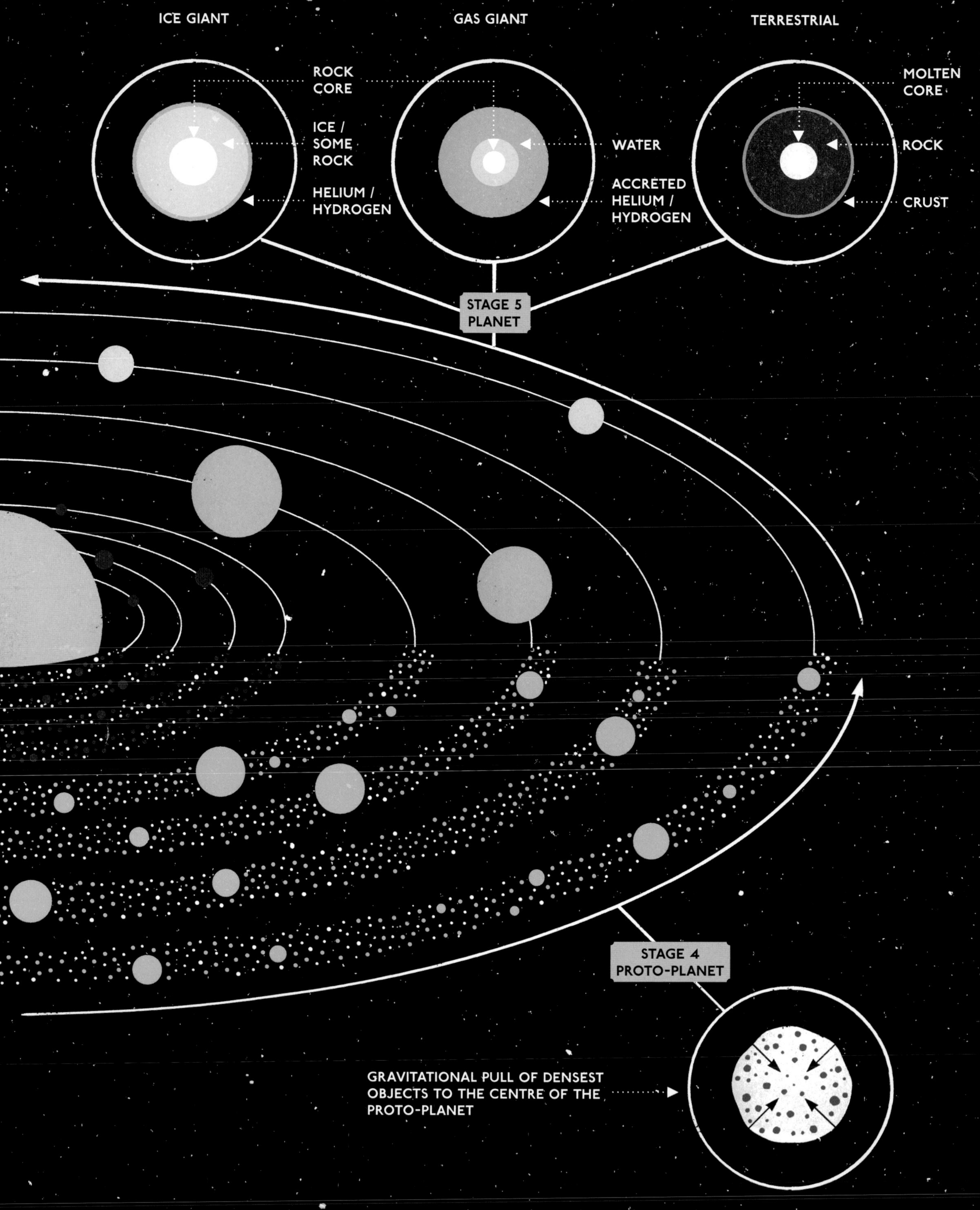
ICE GIANT
GAS GIANT
TERRESTRIAL
ROCK CORE
ICE / SOME ROCK
HELIUM / HYDROGEN
WATER
ACCRETED HELIUM / HYDROGEN
MOLTEN CORE
ROCK
CRUST
STAGE 5 PLANET
STAGE 4 PROTO-PLANET
GRAVITATIONAL PULL OF DENSEST OBJECTS TO THE CENTRE OF THE PROTO-PLANET

Today on Earth, we can still see the remains of this primordial source of heat that has been trapped for billions of years inside our planet's core. It is released in the most spectacular fashion through the eruption of volcanoes. All of the Earth's volcanoes are driven by this ancient source of power, as are the shifts in our tectonic plates that move whole continents and raise great mountain ranges towards the sky. However, elsewhere in the Solar System this powerful source of energy ran out long ago.

The volcanoes on Mars are little more than a petrified memory of a distant, more active past. For all its grandeur, Olympus Mons stands cold and extinct, and when we look down across the rest of the surface of Mars, we see no evidence of any kind of geological activity. As far as we can tell, Mars is now a dead world; its geological heartbeat has been extinguished. Despite having the biggest volcanoes in the Solar System, the primordial heat that formed them is no longer beneath the Martian surface. Something has stopped the red planet in its tracks.

LEFT: Eruption of Pu'u O'o Crater, Hawaii, 1985.

NEWTON'S LAW OF COOLING

Space is cold, very cold. The temperature of the Universe is on average just over 2.72 Kelvin – around -270 degrees Celsius. This is very close to absolute zero. The fact that the Universe isn't at 0 Kelvin is significant, because this precisely known number is the background radiation left over from the beginning of the Universe; a fading echo of the Big Bang 13.7 billion years ago.

In this freezing heat bath hotter objects, including planets, lose heat to space. This is not lost by convection or conduction, since space is almost a vacuum, instead planets lose their heat through radiation – the emission of infrared light. The overwhelming majority of this energy radiated into space is simply the energy a planet receives from the Sun. If Earth didn't re-radiate the Sun's energy away at the same rate at which it received it, it would rapidly heat up.

Earth's internal heat source plays an important role; the primordial heat left over from its formation and the radioactive decay of elements deep within its core. The rate of loss of this heat is determined by the ratio of a planet's surface area to its volume, because the internal heat must be radiated out into space from its surface.

This is the key to understanding why Mars is now geologically dead. Mars is about half the diameter of Earth and just one-eighth of its volume. A bit of maths explains this: volume is proportional to the cube of the diameter (volume is measured in cubic metres, the diameter of a sphere in metres), so Mars would have stored less internal heat initially because it is smaller. The critical factor is the surface area available to radiate the heat away. Surface area is proportional to the square of the diameter (measured in square metres), so Mars has one-quarter of the surface area of Earth but only one-eighth of the volume. This means it has more surface area in relation to its original heat store and so lost its inner heat much faster.

The combination of these two factors defines the life of a planet. Millions of years ago when the interior of Mars grew cold, the volcanoes lost their life blood, the geological heart of the planet died and its surface ground to a halt. The fate of a whole planet was destined by the simplest of laws of physics and the unstoppable flow of heat ◉

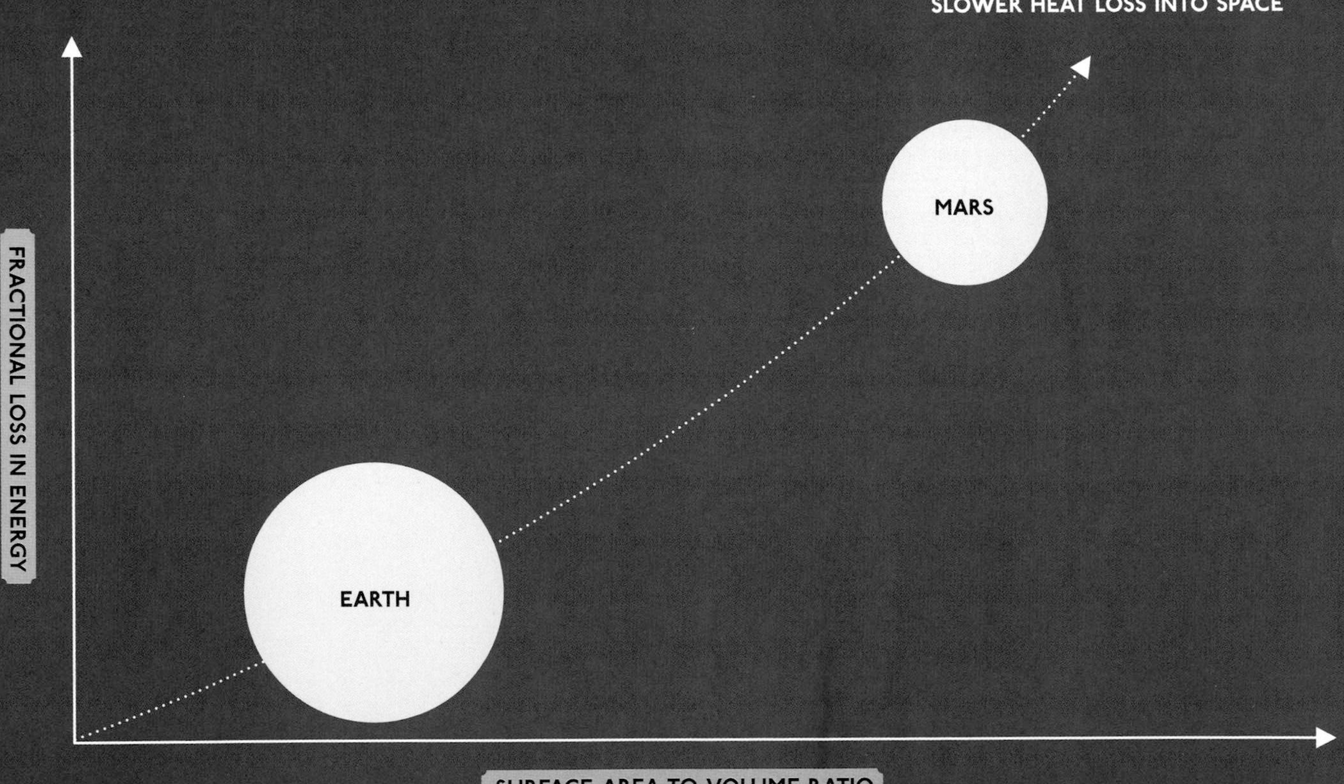

PLANETARY HEAT LOSS IN SPACE
As the Earth is eight times the volume of Mars, it has more primordial heat. It also has four times the surface area, thus loses heat more slowly. The combination of these two factors results in a warm Earth and a geologically dead Mars.

VENUS: A TORTURED HISTORY

Here on Earth, we have seen one beautiful manifestation of how simple laws of nature play out and build a planet. On Mars, we have another example of what happens when you take a planet smaller than Earth: it loses its heat more quickly and becomes geologically inactive. In the cosmic laboratory of our solar system these are just two examples of the delicately balanced processes that decide a planet's fate, but we also have another nearby planetary experiment to explore. There is a planet just like Earth, but that is positioned a little closer to the Sun; it is the brightest point of light in our night sky, so similar in size to our own world that it has been called Earth's twin.

However, Venus is a tortured world. With an average surface temperature of 464 degrees Celsius, it has the hottest surface of any place in the Solar System other than the Sun. Standing on Venus, you would not only be roasted but also crushed by an atmospheric pressure of over ninety times that of the Earth. The clouds of sulphuric acid above your head would threaten you with rain that would never fall on you because the heat of the planet would evaporate it before it reached the ground. No human could ever stand on the surface of Venus today, but wind back a couple of billion years and the hellish planet may not have been so inhospitable. In its early history, Venus was probably not such a foreboding place.

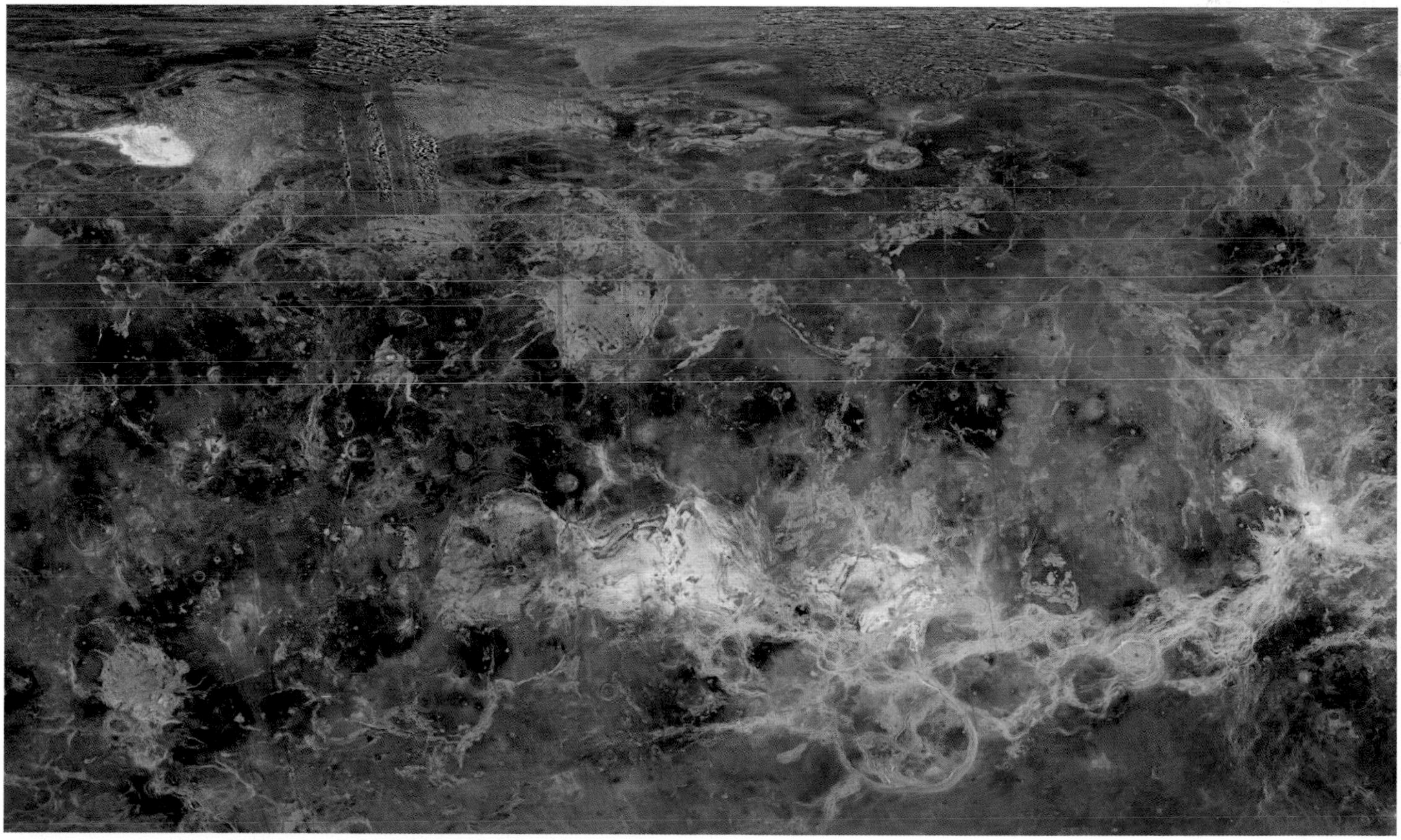

ABOVE: This is a composite image of the complete radar image collection obtained by the Magellan mission. Launched aboard the space shuttle Atlantis in May 1989, the Magellan spacecraft began mapping the surface of Venus in September 1990.

TOP: Venus is an inhospitable world whose surface temperature prevents the existence of life. It is a planet of volcanoes, with over 1,600 located on its surface, including Sif Mons, seen in the background here.

BELOW: The distinctive stepped shape gives this Indian hill its name – the Deccan Traps. One of the largest volcanic features on Earth, it provides a clue to understanding how Venus choked to death.

The Deccan Traps in India is a lush green expanse of hills, many with a particular stepped shape (hence the name 'deccan', Dutch for stairs). Today this rich landscape extends for over 500,000 square kilometres (193,000 square miles), but hidden beneath the green is a secret that holds a tantalising clue to understanding how Venus choked to death.

The Deccan Traps are one of the largest volcanic features on Earth. Sixty-five million years ago this area of central-west India witnessed a series of colossal eruptions that lasted for at least thirty thousand years. At one point an area the size of half of modern India was covered by lava, a staggering 1.5 million square kilometres (600,000 square miles). The impact on the Earth's climate was equally enormous; millions of tonnes of volcanic ash and gases were hurled into the atmosphere with a devastating effect on life. These eruptions affected the climate so profoundly that it is possible they played a role in the mass extinction events at the end of the cretaceous period that wiped out over two-thirds of the species on Earth.

It's almost impossible to imagine how these colossal eruptions must have looked when you visit the Deccan Traps today, but despite the tranquil appearance of the verdant-stepped hills, this place was created from one of the most sustained and violent events our planet has ever known, and the formation of this landscape is echoed on the surface of our nearest planetary neighbour.

Until the Magellan probe arrived in 1990, the thick layer of opaque cloud that surrounds Venus severely limited our knowledge of the planet's surface. With the radar-mapping equipment aboard this pioneering probe, we could peer through the cloud and create the first, and to date, best images of the hidden landscape below. Magellan saw a world of volcanic destruction way beyond anything seen on Earth. It is a landscape built on exactly the same geological foundations as the Deccan Traps, but on a far larger scale.

We have discovered over 1,600 volcanoes on Venus' surface, far more than on any other planet in the Solar System. At least 85 per cent of the planet is covered in basalt lava plains that have poured across the surface. It is not know for certain if Venus is still volcanically active, but because it is a similar size to Earth it might be expected still to have a hot geological heart powering its volcanoes. As yet we haven't directly witnessed any eruptions, but there are clues that suggest volcanoes have been active in the relatively recent past. The Magellan probe spotted ash flows near the summit and north flank of Venus' tallest volcano, the eight-kilometre (five-mile) -high Maat Mons, and more recently, in 2010, the ESA spacecraft Venus Express provided evidence of volcanic activity occurring as recently (in geological terms) as 2.5 million years ago, and maybe even much later.

Many of the volcanoes on Venus are identical to the ones found on Earth. Shield volcanoes like Maat Mons litter the surface, but although the underlying geology is the same, the character of these volcanoes can be very different. On Earth, shield volcanoes like Mauna Kea and the Hawaiian volcanoes can be up to ten kilometres (six miles) high but much wider, but on Venus some volcanoes have footprints of hundreds of square kilometres but average heights of only 1.5 kilometres (1 mile). The Venusian volcano Sif Mons is a massive 300 kilometres (186 miles) across but only 2 kilometres (1.2

BELOW: These three circles signify volcanoes located in the Guinevere Planitia lowland on Venus. The central volcano appears to be very round with steep slides and a flat top.

BOTTOM: This aerial view clearly shows approximately 200 small volcanoes scattered over the surface of Venus. The volcanoes range in diameter from two to twelve kilometres (one to seven miles).

miles) high. Venus also has a type of volcano that doesn't exist on Earth. The 'tick' volcanoes were so-called because of their resemblance to the insect and are thought to be the remains of volcanic domes that have collapsed. Another of Venus' oddities are the thousands of strange flat volcanoes called pancake domes that are clustered in groups across the Venusian surface and are much wider than any similar structures on Earth. Venus truly is a world dominated by volcanoes, but unlike on Earth, this intense geological activity pushed our cosmic twin down a path of no return.

Four billions years ago it is thought that Venus was a world much like our own. The climate was cooler and the surface may have been covered in vast oceans of water. Just like our own planet, this wet warm environment may have been the perfect place to harbour life. How long these conditions lasted for is still unknown, but there is evidence suggesting that Venus was a more welcoming place for up to two billion years. If this was the case, then many scientists believe Venus could have been the most likely place for life to evolve beyond our own planet. If the conditions were stable enough for a few hundred million years, then life may even have flourished before the character of the planet turned ugly.

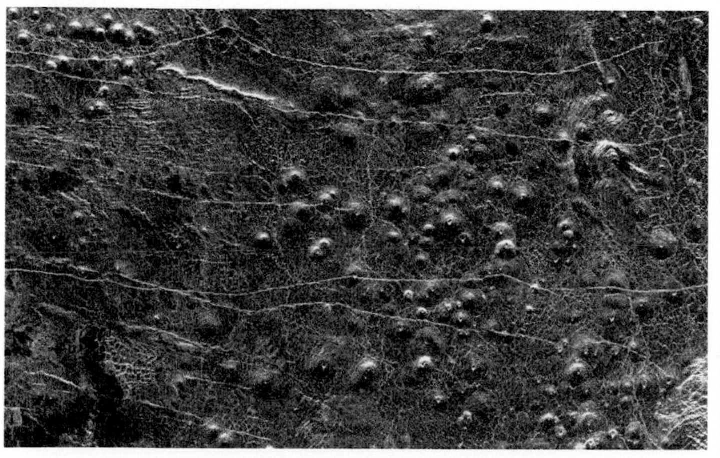

This is one reason why understanding the history of Venus is so important. This hellish world provides the most telling example our solar system has to offer of the potential fragility of planetary environments.

Explaining why Venus and Earth reacted so differently to the same kind of volcanic cataclysm requires an understanding of a matrix of different factors. Volcanoes don't just produce heat and lava, they also produce vast amounts of greenhouse gases like carbon dioxide. Every planet, including Earth, absorbs energy from the Sun as visible light. This light streams through our atmosphere almost untouched and is absorbed by the ground, heating it up day after day. The ground then re-radiates this energy as infrared radiation. Atmospheric gases, particularly carbon dioxide, are very good at absorbing infrared light, and so they trap the heat and the planet heats up. The more greenhouse gases in the atmosphere, the more a planet will heat up.

On Earth, we are beginning to see the effect that an increase in greenhouse gases created from the burning of fossil fuels has on our climate. Global warming is a phrase that has only recently entered popular vocabulary, but it would have wreaked havoc on our planet long ago if it hadn't have been for a familiar characteristic of our weather.

One of the most important reasons we have taken such a different path to Venus is something that happens so often on Earth that we take it for granted. Rain plays a significant role in keeping our planet a pleasant place to live. It acts as part of a global recycling system, keeping our atmosphere in balance by washing out potent greenhouse gases like carbon dioxide and locking them away in rocks and oceans. On Venus, the planet's position in the Solar System, combined with the laws of physics, have conspired to make it impossible for rainfall to cleanse its atmosphere. Because it is slightly closer to the Sun, and so a little hotter than Earth, Venus lost all its liquid water. The oceans of Venus would have gradually evaporated into the atmosphere. The potentially life-giving water would have simply escaped off into space.

With no water, there is no rain on Venus, and so for billions of years there has been nothing to temper the build-up of volcanic gases in its atmosphere. Venus ended up cocooned in a thick, dense, high-pressure blanket of greenhouse gases, making the temperature inexorably rise and turning Venus into the hell-like world we see today.

Compared to scorched Venus and frozen Mars, our planet is a very special ball of rock. Although governed by the same universal set of rules, the Earth is not too big, not too small, not too hot and not too cold. This is why Earth has been called the 'Goldilocks planet', because everything seems just right, but the life and death of our planet is influenced by more than just the forces emanating from the depths of our own world. Our fate is intimately connected with our cosmic neighbours in ways that are subtle and complicated but extremely powerful ◉

JUPITER: KING OF THE GIANTS

Jupiter, King of the Gods, the fifth planet from the Sun, has been revered since ancient times. Visible to the naked eye in the night sky, it can also be seen during the day when the Sun is low on the horizon. For millennia, humans have looked to Jupiter and imbued it with power. From the Romans to the Greeks, the Chinese to the Hindus, almost every civilisation on Earth has gazed at its light without realising the true influence that it exerts over our solar system.

RIGHT: An artist's concept of *Pioneer* over Jupiter's Red Spot.

JUPITER: THE ETHEREAL PLANET

JUPITER NORTH POLE – DEC 2000

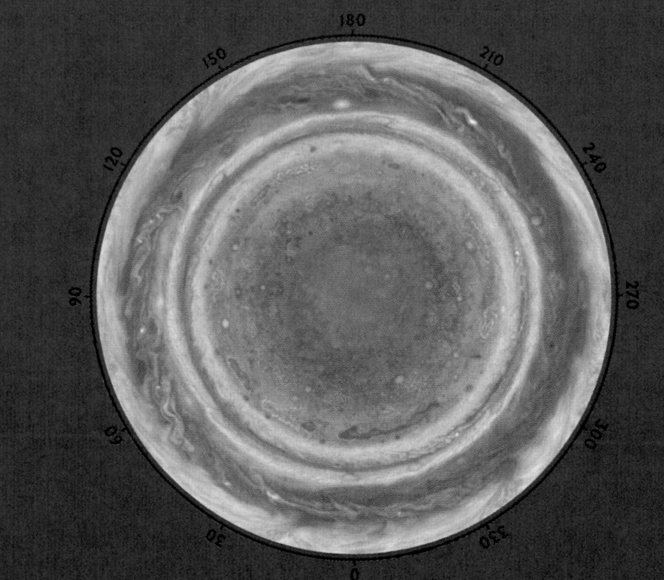

JUPITER SOUTH POLE – DEC 2000

ABOVE: These maps were constructed using images produced by NASA's Cassini spacecraft. They are the most detailed global colour maps of Jupiter ever produced and use colours that would be close to those that the human eye would see when viewing Jupiter. The maps show views of both poles of the planet, featuring colourful clouds, parallel reddish-brown and white bands, the Great Red Spot and blue-grey areas that denote 'hotspots'.

OPPOSITE: This sequence of nine images shows Jupiter as it rotates through more than a complete 360-degree turn. This massive planet rotates more than twice as fast as Earth, completing a single rotation in around ten hours. Its powerful gravitational force directly influences every other object in the Solar System.

Jupiter is by far the largest planet, so big you could fit the Earth inside it over 1,000 times, and it is of a completely different character to the inner rocky worlds. It's one of the four gas giants that circle the Sun, and along with Saturn, Uranus and Neptune, it is made up of the same stuff as a star – hydrogen and helium, the most common elements in the Universe. Although it may have a solid core made up of heavier elements, Jupiter, like all the gas giants, is an ethereal planet, a planet with no real boundaries between its skies and no substance further down. It is a vast atmosphere that gets denser and denser as you travel deeper. Despite its seemingly insubstantial nature, though, Jupiter is truly a massive planet. It has a mass that is two and a half times that of all the other planets put together. It is so big, theoretical models suggest that if it were any more massive, it would begin to collapse further under its own gravity, transforming into a sub-star-like object called a Brown Dwarf. Jupiter is probably about as big as a planet of its composition and construction can be, and that means it dominates the rest of our solar system.

Astrologers have long claimed that Jupiter can influence our lives, but we now have scientific evidence that this mighty planet does indeed have a significant connection with our own small world, although not in the way that the ancients thought. Despite the fact that, as Sir Patrick Moore famously said, astrology proves only that there is one born every minute, Jupiter influences our planet across more than half a billion kilometres of space through the force of nature that binds the galaxy together.

Gravity is one of the four fundamental forces of Nature. It shapes so much of our universe and yet it is by far the weakest force, a force that we can resist with ease. As stated previously, pick a rock up off the ground and you are defying the force of an entire planet. Despite its weakness, gravity does have two properties that allow

it to shape our universe. Everything that has mass (or energy) attracts everything else, and if you add more mass to something the gravitational force between it and other objects increases. It also has an infinite range, which means that its influence can stretch across the entire Solar System and beyond. Gravity never quite goes away, so you can be a long way from its source and still feel its effects.

As the force of gravity is directly related to the mass of an object, because it is the most massive planet Jupiter has the most powerful gravitational field in the Solar System other than that of the Sun. It is this gravitational force that directly influences every other object in the Solar System. Jupiter's gravitational pull is strong enough to profoundly influence the orbits of passing interplanetary asteroids and other wandering space debris, even at large distances away.

This effect on the wandering stuff of our solar system can play out in three different ways. Firstly, Jupiter can capture it, literally pulling it inwards on a collision course and ultimately merging it with the gas giant itself. Secondly, it can change its orbit around the Sun in such a way that it throws it out of the Solar System forever. The third of Jupiter's options as it marshals the solar traffic is perhaps the most worrying one for us today. If the angles are just right, the planet can deflect an orbiting asteroid into a new orbit, and occasionally place it on a direct collision course with the rocky inner planets, including our own ◉

ARMAGEDDON WATCH

BELOW: At the top of the mountain of Heleakala, Hawaii, is the technological solution to the problem of detecting dangerous asteroids on course to Earth. The telescope contains one of the largest digital cameras ever built, designed to capture images of 1,400 megapixels.

RIGHT: This meteorite is a sample of the crust of the asteroid Vesta. This is only the third object collected from the Solar System beyond Earth (the other two are Mars and the Moon). This unique meteorite is almost entirely made of the mineral pyroxene, which is common in lava flows.

This telescope, known as the PS-1 Observatory, sits on top of the mountain of Heleakala on the Hawaiian honeymoon island of Maui, and it could one day save your life. It contains some of the largest digital cameras ever built, designed to capture images with a staggering 1,400 megapixels (1.4 billion pixels) on an area about forty square centimetres (six square inches). To put that into context, a good domestic digital camera contains about ten megapixels on a chip just a few millimetres across. The telescope is designed with one purpose in mind – to hunt down killer asteroids. The threat is easy to state: if anything bigger than a kilometre in size hits the Earth, it would probably kill almost everyone on the planet. This is the reason that on most nights, as you sleep soundly in your bed, this revolutionary camera is scanning vast swathes of the sky looking for signs of an approaching apocalypse.

Most of the known asteroids within our solar system orbit in the asteroid belt that sits between Mars and Jupiter. We don't know for certain how many objects sit in this belt, but over 200 are known to be larger than 100 kilometres (60 miles) across and a few million bigger than a kilometre. That sounds like a lot, but in fact the asteroid belt is mostly empty and no spacecraft we have sent through it has ever encountered a problem.

If anything bigger than a kilometre in size hits the Earth, it would probably kill almost everyone on the planet.

One of the objects in this region, named Ceres, is so big that it was classified as the eighth known planet when it was

BELOW: This spectacular image of asteroid 951 Gaspra was captured by the Galileo spacecraft in 1991 when it made the first close flyby of an asteroid. The blue patches are believed to be fresher rock than the older, reddish areas . The asteroid is about 19 by 12 by 11 kilometres (12 by 7 by 7 miles) in size.

PLANET OR ASTEROID? Until 2006, Ceres was considered the largest asteroid in the main asteroid belt. However, it has now been reclassified as a dwarf planet because, unlike the other asteroids, it can become spherical under its own gravity.

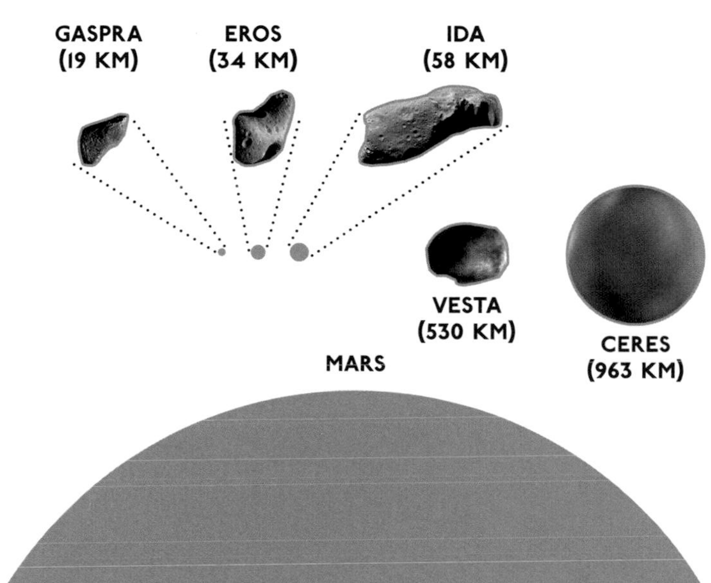

discovered in 1801. When other rocky bodies were found in the same area scientists realised Ceres was just one of many, and so by the middle of the century it was relegated to the new status of asteroid (meaning star-like) coined by William Herschel. It wasn't until 1991 that we got close enough to the asteroid belt with the Galileo spacecraft to take an intimate look at one of these mini-worlds.

The orbit of most of these millions of asteroids takes them around the Sun without any threat to Earth. But as well as these predictable asteroids, there is another type that poses a far greater risk. We currently know of over seven thousand Near-Earth Asteroids, with nearly a thousand of these being bigger than one kilometre (0.6 miles). These are asteroids with orbits distorted from the harmless majority that stay away from the inner solar system, bringing them near enough to Earth for concern. We have catalogued thousands of these, but nobody can be sure how many are out there, or what effect a subtle change in the orbit of one we know about would be. Thus, the work of the PS-1 Observatory and other lookouts across the planet are crucial for our future safety.

Each night the observatory team are looking for any unidentified objects that might be heading our way. Any point of light could be an asteroid in an orbit that brings it perilously close to Earth, but spotting the rocks from the stars is not an easy process. To help them to make as accurate an analysis as possible, the camera at the PS-1 Observatory captures several images of the same patch of sky, taken minutes apart. The team can then see if anything has moved, relative to the backdrop of stars. By literally subtracting the images from each other, anything that stands still – i.e. stars – will disappear, but anything that has moved in the time between the two photographs will still be there. Fast-moving bright objects are all that will remain in the photographs.

In the whole night sky we may well be able to detect hundreds of objects that we have never known existed. Many of these menacing lumps of rock are in eccentric orbits that bring them close to Earth – and all because at some point in their lives they came under the influence of Jupiter's gravity ◉

If you ever needed a demonstration of how congested space is near the Earth, just look at the picture opposite. Every one of those points of light is an asteroid that we know of, and Earth is swimming right through the centre of them. So when you look up into a nice clear night sky for reassurance that we are safe, remember this picture, remember that our planet always has been and always will be trapped in a deadly game of dodge ball – in a game where the gravitational stranglehold of Jupiter regularly throws asteroids our way.

RIGHT: The sky is now being methodically scanned for asteroids that might cross Earth's orbit (the blue streak in the time-lapse photograph right). The complex interaction between the gravitational pull of the Sun and the other planets (particularly Jupiter) and these near Earth objects means it is very difficult to calculate precisely their final trajectories and, as some of them pass between the Earth and the Moon, the margin for error is quite small.

COLLISION

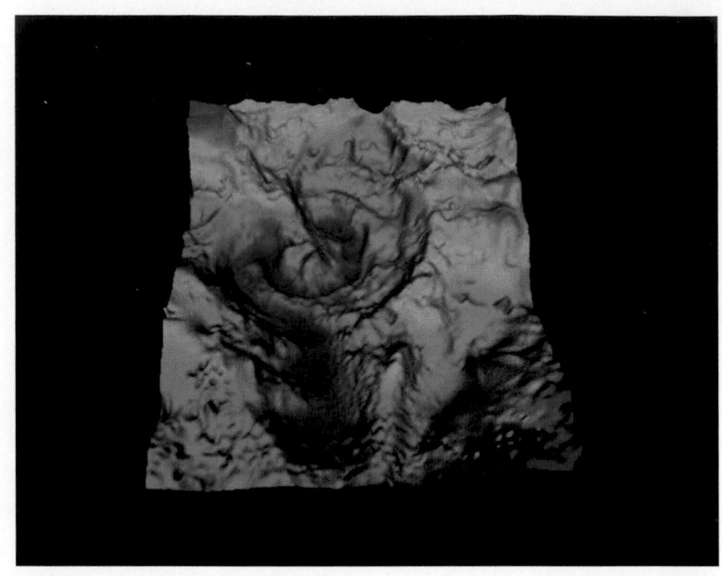

BELOW: One of the world's most famous impact sites is the Barringer Crater in Arizona. Around 50,000 years ago, a 300,000-tonne, 50-metre (30-feet) in diameter lump of iron and nickel entered the Earth's atmosphere, making this crater.

RIGHT: This computer-generated image is a gravity map of the Chicxulub Crater discovered on Mexico's Yucatan peninsula, which shows the crater is made of many rings, including an outer one of 300 kilometres (186 miles) in diameter.

When geophysicist Glen Penfied began searching for oil in the Yucatan peninsula of Mexico in the late 1970s, he had no idea of the discovery that was lurking beneath his feet. Penfield was surveying this area in order to pinpoint new locations to begin drilling in, but his interest was quickly diverted to a different kind of geological treasure. The geophysical data Penfield began to unearth suggested that hidden within this area was an impact crater of vast proportions. The evidence suggested that a catastrophic impact had taken place here that created a crater that is over 180 kilometres (112 miles) wide.

Today, this extraordinary feature is known as the Chicxulub Crater. Named after the town at its centre, the crater has been studied for over twenty years by hordes of experts. It is one of the largest-known impact craters on the planet and it is estimated that the object that struck here was at least ten kilometres (six miles) across. The scale of this impact alone makes it an extraordinary location, but the timing of the impact is what has elevated Chicxulub into the A-list of asteroid sites.

The asteroid that struck here is thought to have slammed into the Earth 65 million years ago at the end of the Cretaceous period. It coincides perfectly with the most famous extinction event in the history of the planet – the mass extinction event that caused the disappearance of the dinosaurs. Although there is no complete agreement amongst the scientific community about this link, the overwhelming consensus is that the Chicxulub impact was the trigger for the extinction of the largest creatures ever to walk the Earth.

We may never know for certain where this enormous asteroid came from or what set it on its course to Earth, but we are pretty sure it originated in the heart of the asteroid belt between Mars and Jupiter. Some scientists have suggested that the dinosaurs' fate was sealed by a collision in the asteroid belt that created a family of asteroids, with one in particular that headed for Earth. What is certain is that wherever the asteroid came from, its journey to Earth was influenced by the mighty presence of Jupiter. Jupiter's gravitational influence on passing space debris has made our planet a world under constant bombardment. Earth is littered with impact sites, from the most visually stunning and famous, such as the Barringer Crater in Arizona, to the hidden craters that have dissolved from our view over billions of years ◉

JUPITER'S GRAVITATIONAL KICK

The asteroid belt is a vast expanse of space extending over 240 million kilometres (150 million miles) between Mars and Jupiter, further than the distance from the Earth to the Sun.

Now and again, because of collisions in the asteroid belt, a stray asteroid will get thrown into a position where it periodically aligns with Jupiter over and over again and settles into a rhythm known as orbital resonance. Jupiter is such a massive planet that it will give such an asteroid a gravitational kick, changing its orbit. Over time these orbits can become elongated or elliptical rather than circular, which means that they can get thrown into the inner solar system and cross the orbits of the inner planets, including that of the Earth.

Jupiter was once thought to be our protector, its enormous gravity swallowing up dangerous asteroids, but we now realise its gravitational influence can actually propel some of those asteroids in our direction, creating the huge craters we see in places like Chicxulub. Although the idea of these impacts appears to be purely destructive, the surprising thing is that these catastrophic events may actually have been instrumental in shaping our planet and the life that has flourished on it since. Impacts have been one of the driving forces of evolution on Earth, changing the climate and triggering extinctions – when huge swathes of life on Earth are wiped out, it creates the ecological niches into which other species like ourselves evolve.

It is incredible to think that a planet located more than half a billion kilometres away could dictate our fate and define the life and death of a whole world ◉

AN ASTEROID'S UNSTABLE ORBIT

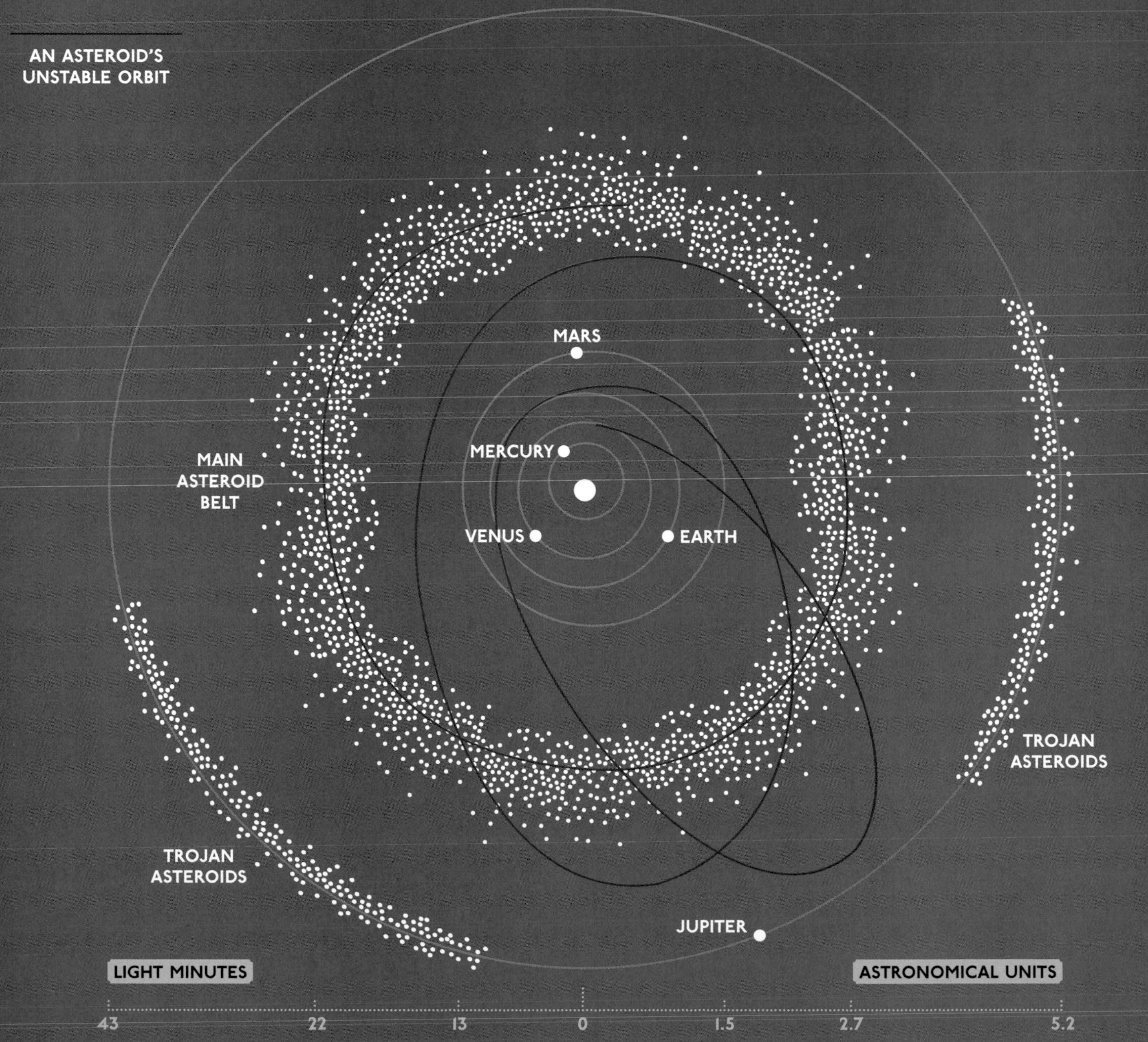

POWERFUL CONNECTIONS: THE MOON AND TIDES

BELOW AND OPPOSITE: The Minas Basin, in the Bay of Fundy, Nova Scotia, Canada, experiences the most dramatic differences between low and high tides on Earth. Typically the high tide (shown opposite) at the head of the Bay of Fundy can be as much as seventeen metres (fifty-six feet) higher than at low tide (shown below). These large tides are the result of tidal resonance, which can become synchronised with the lunar tides, amplifying its effect.

Our understanding of the Solar System began much closer to home. Gazing down at us, it was our moon, with its regularly changing face, that first fired our interest in worlds beyond our own. When we could look further out, we discovered the Solar System was full of moons, each invisibly connected to their parent planets by gravity.

Every year on 18 August, thousands of people trek to the Quiantang river in south-eastern China to witness one of the great spectacles of the natural world. The river and bay are famed as the location of the world's largest tidal bore, a phenomenon that creates a wall of water up to fifty metres (thirty feet) feet high, travelling at forty kilometres (twenty-five miles) per hour. This true tidalwave crashing along the Quiantang river is a spectacular reminder of one of the most powerful effects on Earth. Tidal bores occur in only a handful of places as they need both a particular shape of river system and a large tidal range, but these rare events are just one extreme example of something that many of us witness every day without giving it a second thought.

Across our planet tides rise and fall every twelve hours

THE EFFECT OF THE MOON ON EARTH'S TIDES

High tides occur at the point where the gravitational pull on Earth's oceans is strongest, pulling the water towards it and raising the level of water. Spring tides occur when the Sun and Moon are aligned.

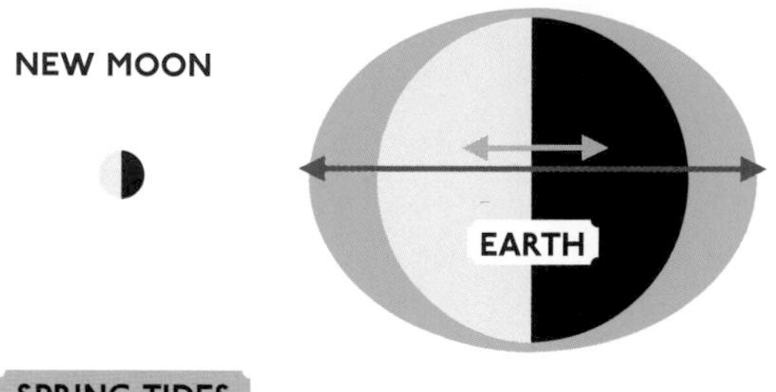

SPRING TIDES

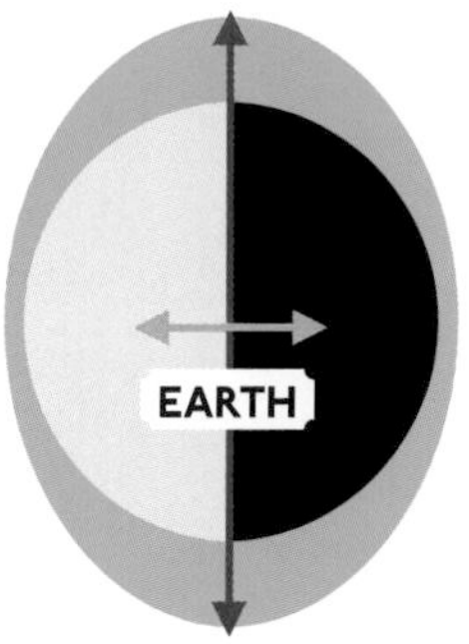

NEAP TIDES

and twenty-five minutes. They are the most visible mark of the most intimate interaction we have with any celestial body. Stand on a beach and watch the tide ebb and flow and you are witnessing the direct effect of the Moon on the body of water that covers our planet. On one side of the planet the high tide occurs at the point on Earth where the ocean is closest to the Moon, and so the gravitational force is at its strongest, pulling the water towards it. Twelve hours later and this same location will be at the furthest point from the Moon and so the gravitational pull on the water in the ocean is at its weakest. At this point the Earth is pulled towards the Moon slightly more than the water, and there is a high tide at that point. The Sun can also affect the tides on Earth through the same differential gravitational effect, but even though the Sun is significantly more massive than the Moon, it is further away and so the effect is much weaker. It is our lunar companion that most powerfully drives this bi-daily rise and fall of the oceans. We've been studying the tides and plotting their rhythms for thousands of years, unaware that elsewhere in the Solar System an identical relationship between a moon and a planet has created a much more extreme tidal phenomenon ◉

JUPITER'S MOONS

BELOW: Ganymede is one of Jupiter's four largest moons, completing an orbit of the planet every seven days. It is also the largest moon in the Solar System – even larger than the planet Mercury and just over three-quarters of the size of Mars.

OPPOSITE: In this image of Europa taken by NASA's Galileo spacecraft, the colours have been enhanced to show the differences in materials that cover the moon's icy surface. The red lines show cracks and ridges, thousands of kilometres long, which are caused by the tides raised by the gravitational pull of Jupiter.

Gravity is a two-way street. Isaac Newton put it in more scientific terms; to every action there is an equal and opposite reaction. So not only does the Moon exert a force on the Earth, but the Earth exerts an equal and opposite force on the Moon. Over hundreds of millions of years, this gravitational embrace between Earth and Moon has had a profound effect. We only see one side of the Moon facing Earth because the Moon is 'tidally locked'; its rotation rate matches its orbital period around the Earth. This is no coincidence but a consequence of the gravitational interaction between the two bodies. However, on a daily basis the impact of Earth's gravity is minimal. There is no liquid water on our moon and so there are no ocean tides, and Earth's gravity is too weak to have a significant effect on the Moon's rocky constitution.

Half a billion kilometres away, we've discovered a very different story. The powerful gravitational bond that exists between one moon and its parent planet, Jupiter, has done something astonishing; it has brought the moon to life, making it the most violent place in the Solar System.

Four hundred years ago, Galileo was the first human to turn his telescope to the night sky and look at Jupiter. He immediately noticed that the giant planet was not alone. On 7 January 1610, Galileo observed three points of light around Jupiter. He described them at first as 'three little stars', but over the next few nights he quickly realised that they moved in relation to the planet, disappearing from view and reappearing. He correctly surmised they could not be stars; they must be objects orbiting in the Jovian system. By 13 January, Galileo had observed and catalogued the four largest moons of Jupiter, and in doing so confirmed Copernicus' revolutionary view of the Solar System. No longer did our view of the Universe adhere to the Aristotlean one that all heavenly bodies must orbit the Earth. Here was direct evidence of other worlds orbiting another planet, unequivocally breaking the divine symmetry of the Earth-centred cosmos for good and challenging what for many was a deeply held belief.

Jupiter's four largest moons are named after the lovers of the Greek god Zeus. Furthest out is Callisto, a ball of rock and ice the size of Mercury and the third-largest moon in the Solar System. Next is Ganymede, the largest moon in the Solar System, which is the only moon known to have its own internally generated magnetic field, and which may harbour a saltwater ocean deep below its surface. Next is icy Europa, the smoothest, most tantalising moon. Its surface is crisscrossed by dark streaks and gathered evidence suggests there is a vast ocean below its surface. For many scientists, Europa is now the most likely candidate to harbour extraterrestrial life. Finally, closest to Jupiter is the small yellow-tinged moon, Io. Modern space probes have revealed that Io is an incredibly tormented world; somewhere we can glimpse by visiting one of the most inhospitable places on Earth ◉

JUPITER

(Not to scale)

	IO	EUROPA	GANYMEDE	CALLISTO
Discovered	1610	1610	1610	1610
Mass (Earth = 1)	1.4960e-02	8.0321e-03	2.4766e-02	1.8072e-02
Equatorial radius (Earth = 1)	2.8457e-01	2.4600e-01	4.1251e-01	3.7629e-01
Distance from Jupiter (km)	421,600	670,900	1,070,000	1,883,000
Orbital period (days)	1.77	3.55	7.15	16.69
Orbital velocity (km/sec)	17.34	13.74	10.88	8.21

ERTA ALE, NORTH-EASTERN ETHIOPIA

In the Afar region of north-eastern Ethiopia stands one of the rarest geological phenomena on our planet. Erta Ale is the most active volcano in Ethiopia, and at just 610 metres (2,000 feet) high it is one of the lowest volcanoes in the world. But what makes this volcano special are the lava lakes that have continuously dominated its summit for over a century. Lava lakes are incredibly rare; there are currently only five sites on Earth where they can be seen, but none have existed as long as those on the 'smoking mountain' of Ethiopia.

Erta Ale was by far the most challenging place we visited during the filming of *Wonders of the Solar System*. It sits in the Danakil Depression, the remote and hostile region of north-east Africa where the Great Rift Valley meets the Red Sea. The region is intensely geologically active because it is situated at the Afar Triple Junction, a delicate place in the Earth's crust where the Red Sea and Gulf of Aden meet the East African Rift. The Earth's crust is literally being ripped apart, leading to intense earthquakes and volcanic activity. Even as I write these words from the vantage point of a year, I find recalling this adventure both evocative and exciting. The Great Rift Valley is our birthplace – we are all related to someone who lived in the place we now call Ethiopia. In a remarkable piece of research based on the human genome project, it has been shown that human genetic diversity declines steadily with distance from Addis Ababa, Ethiopia's capital city. In other words, we began the long march across the globe from the region around Addis. Ethiopia itself as a geopolitical entity is Africa's oldest independent nation, with a rich history stretching back well over 2,000 years, but a great civilisation existed in this region many hundreds if not thousands of years before that. You cannot visit Ethiopia without glimpsing in your peripheral vision a line of ghosts standing by your shoulder, winding back through the ages to the birthplace of our species.

We began the intrepid part of our journey from a military airfield in the northern city of Mek'ele. The machine charged with ferrying our film crew to Erta Ale was an ageing but reassuringly rugged-looking Russian Mi8 transport helicopter; a reliable workhorse, I was told – there are more Mi8s flying than any other type of helicopter in the world.

The approach to Erta Ale from the air was unusually bleak and quite daunting. The landscape is lunar – although more desolation than magnificent desolation. It is an unremitting expanse of slate-grey basalt and baked brown rock, drained of colour by the brutal Sun. To protect us from the 'smoking mountain' were a dozen Afar tribesmen, the nomadic people whose permission and protection are essential for a visit to Erta Ale. To the locals, the volcanoes largest lava lake is known as the Gateway to Hell.

ALL IMAGES: We were flown out by military helicopter to the farthest, most inhospitable reaches of north-east Africa. There we saw one of the rarest geological phenomena on our planet – a volcano with a lake of molten lava. The volcano has been named Erta Ale by local people, which means 'smoking mountain'.

LEFT: Erta Ale, in the Afar region of Ethiopia, is surrounded completely by an area below sea level. Volcanoes with lava lakes are very rare.

Erta Ale's lake of lava is a mesmerising sight, especially at night. The vertical edge of its crater is illuminated by the bright red glow of liquid rock. The surface of the lake itself is mostly dark, because the lava quickly cools as it meets the air, but it is crisscrossed by a series of almost perfectly drawn, jagged red lines. The reason for these strangely shaped lines is unknown. Staring at the lake is addictive, because every now and then a violent mini-eruption occurs somewhere on the surface of the lava, throwing molten rock vertically upwards into the night sky and clearing a hole in the darker crust to reveal the bright red lava beneath. This burst of activity is accompanied by a bubbling, sloshing sound, a rapid increase in brightness and occasionally a caustic wave of gases that instantly burn the throat. This is the signal to grab a gas mask rather than turn and run, because it is virtually impossible to avert your gaze from the mountain when its anger rises. I think anger is the correct word; we developed a respect, already possessed by our Afar companions, for Erte Ale. It has a presence that is very difficult to put into words; alive would be too strong, but its unpredictable power lies somewhere in the shadowed spaces between animate and inanimate. I understand absolutely why the Afar believe that demons emerge from the depths to drag unwary travellers to the Ethiopian equivalent of Hyades. And we had to camp beside it for three nights.

Erta Ale is a window into our planet's history – a portal not only into its depths, but backwards in time – a slopping and gasping reminder of our Earth's formation.

The magma rises up from many kilometres below the Earth's crust, circulating to the surface and sinking back down again. It is a native and vital anachronism left over from the birth of a large rocky planet close to the Sun, yet we have seen something similar in the far reaches of the Solar System ◉

THE MOST VIOLENT PLACE IN THE SOLAR SYSTEM

BOTTOM: Jupiter's moon, Io, is the most geologically active body in the Solar System today and provides the most extreme example of the effect of tidal forces. Here we see Pele erupting.

In 1979, the Voyager spacecraft became the first mission to study and photograph the moons of Jupiter close up, including innermost Io. Io is approximately the same size as our own moon, and for 400 years we'd assumed it was a cold dead world, although the Voyager mission scientists knew that expectations are often dashed in a spectacular way when new worlds are visited.

How exciting, then, must it have been to stand in mission control when the first close-up pictures of Io arrived back at Voyager's home planet.

Not everyone was quite so in the dark about what Io might have in store, however. Just weeks before Voyager arrived at Jupiter, three scientists made a prediction that appeared to many planetary scientists as nothing more than fantasy. Using the same physics that underpins our understanding of tides on Earth, they predicted that Io should have an intense internal heat source because of its unique position in the Solar System. Io orbits very close to massive Jupiter – about the same distance from its parent planet as our own moon orbits Earth. It is also surrounded by its large sister moons, Europa and Ganymede, which are orbiting further out. This configuration of moons and planets means Io is under the influence not just of the massive gravitational pull of Jupiter but also the additional pull of its neighbouring moons. This gravitational tug of war has a miraculous effect on Io, transforming it from a dead world into one of the most dynamic geological bodies in the Solar System.

Io circles Jupiter every 1.77 days but crucially, for every orbit of Io, Ganymede goes around almost exactly four times and Europa goes around just twice. This beautiful symmetry is no coincidence – it is a consequence of the same complex gravitational dynamics that locked our moon's face forever towards Earth. The technical term for this relationship is 'orbital resonance'. Whilst the mathematics and terminology might be complicated, the effect is simple to explain. Periodically, Io, Europa and Ganymede line up together, and when they do Io gets a powerful gravitational kick on a regular basis. This has the effect of forcing Io out of a nice circular orbit into an elliptical or eccentric one. This means

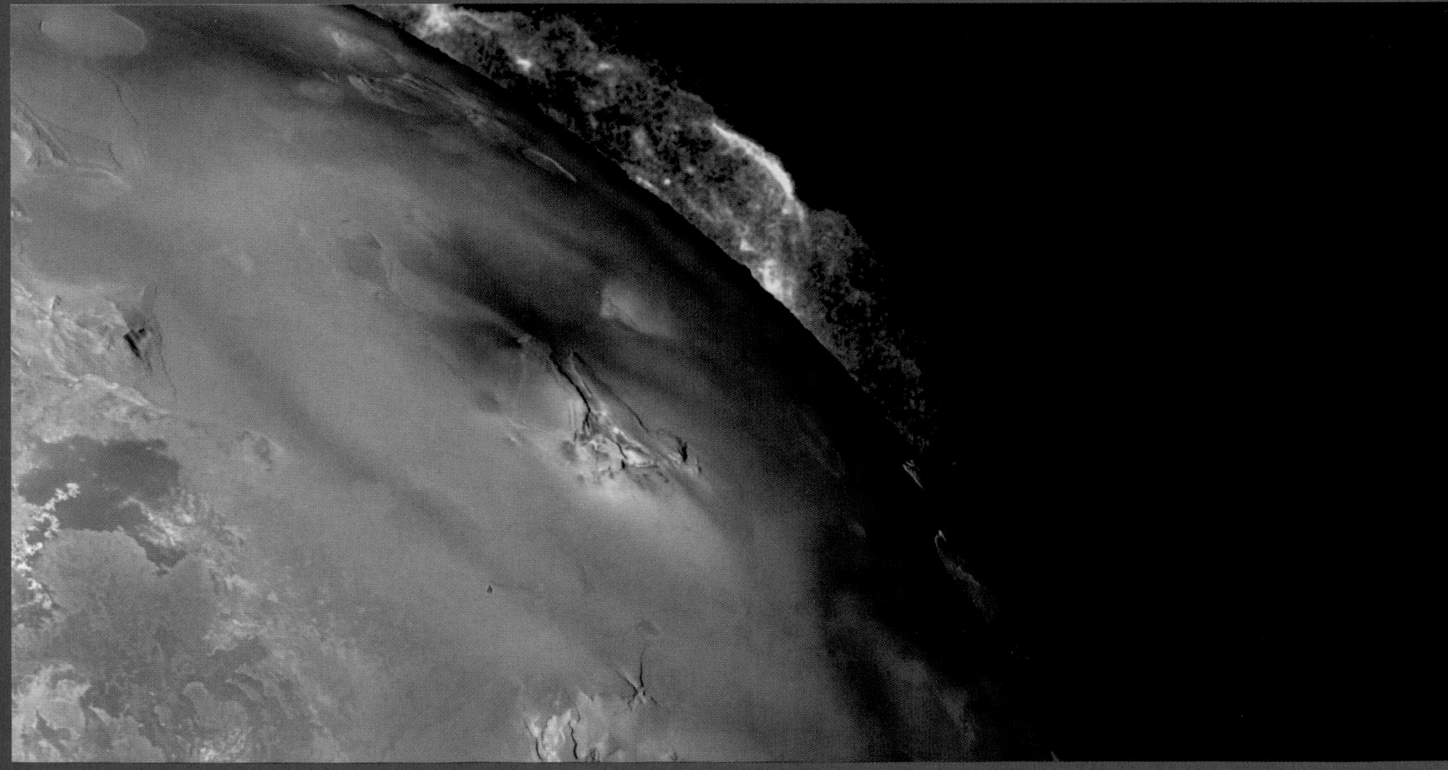

BOTTOM: Two different images showing a volcano erupting on Io. Hundreds of such volcanic systems cover the moon's surface.

that Io moves closer and farther away from Jupiter in every orbit as it orbits in an ellipse with the gas giant at one focus. Because Jupiter's gravitational field is so great, that has the effect of continually stretching and squashing Io as it sails periodically closer to and farther from the planet. This is exactly the same effect that creates Earth's ocean tides, but on Io it is not water that is pulled and pushed, but the solid rock of the moon itself.

Just like a squash ball, as Io is stretched and squashed repeatedly it heats up by the friction, transferring vast amounts of energy from its orbit to the rocky interior of the moon itself. Over time, this vast energy transfer would cause Io's orbit to become more circular, but the elegant relationship between its orbit and its sister moons Europa and Ganymede ensures that it must continue its eccentric elliptical path around Jupiter. This relentless gravitational tug of war keeps Io literally boiling hot, moving rock as if it were nothing more than water and transforming it into a world seething with heat, alive with volcanic activity. As the images came back from Voyager, it was immediately clear that the three scientists were right: Io was anything but a dead dusty moon.

We have since sent a probe even closer to Io. At the end of the last century, the Galileo spacecraft took the best images we have to date of Io, helping to create a detailed picture of the geological life of the volcanic bubbling moon. We now know that just one of the many lava lakes on Io releases more heat than all Earth's volcanoes put together. The lava lakes on Io are vast; the largest is 180 kilometres (112 miles) in diameter, dwarfing magnificent Erta Ale. Io's surface is covered with hundreds such volcanic centres, making it by far the most volcanic place in the Solar System, endlessly pumping out heat into the cold vacuum of space.

Io is a surprising and bizarre world. Being so far from the Sun, its surface is about -155 degrees Celsius. It is covered in frozen sulphur, giving it a rich yellow colour. Yet amidst the frigid yellow planes, Io is scarred by cauldrons of molten lava; thousands of tons of flowing rock melted by energy extracted from Jupiter's powerful gravitational field as it traces its eccentric orbital path ◉

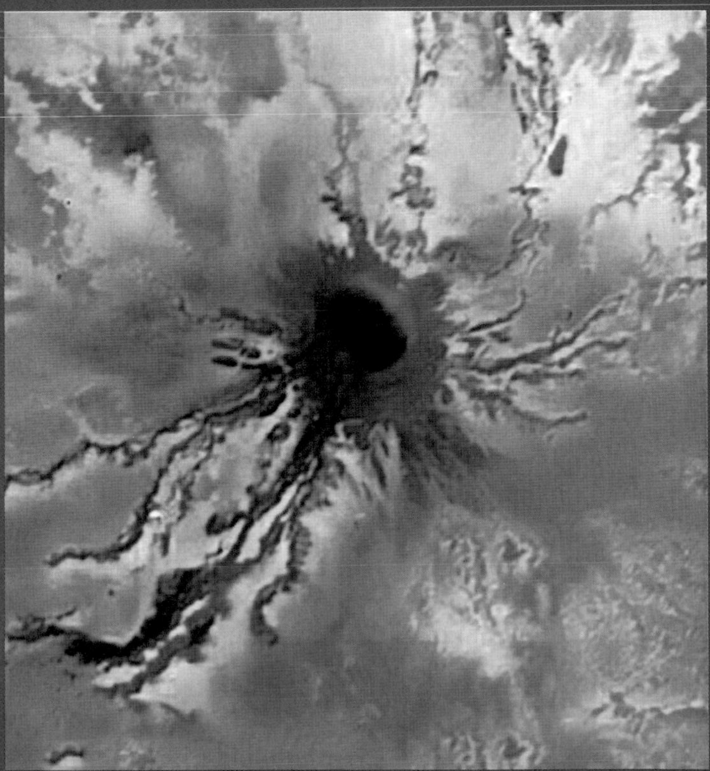

VOLCANISM ACROSS THE SOLAR SYSTEM

Volcanism is found throughout the Solar System. It is generally produced by either internal heat, as found on Venus, Earth and Mars, or by tidal heating caused by gravitational pull, as found on Io and Enceladus.

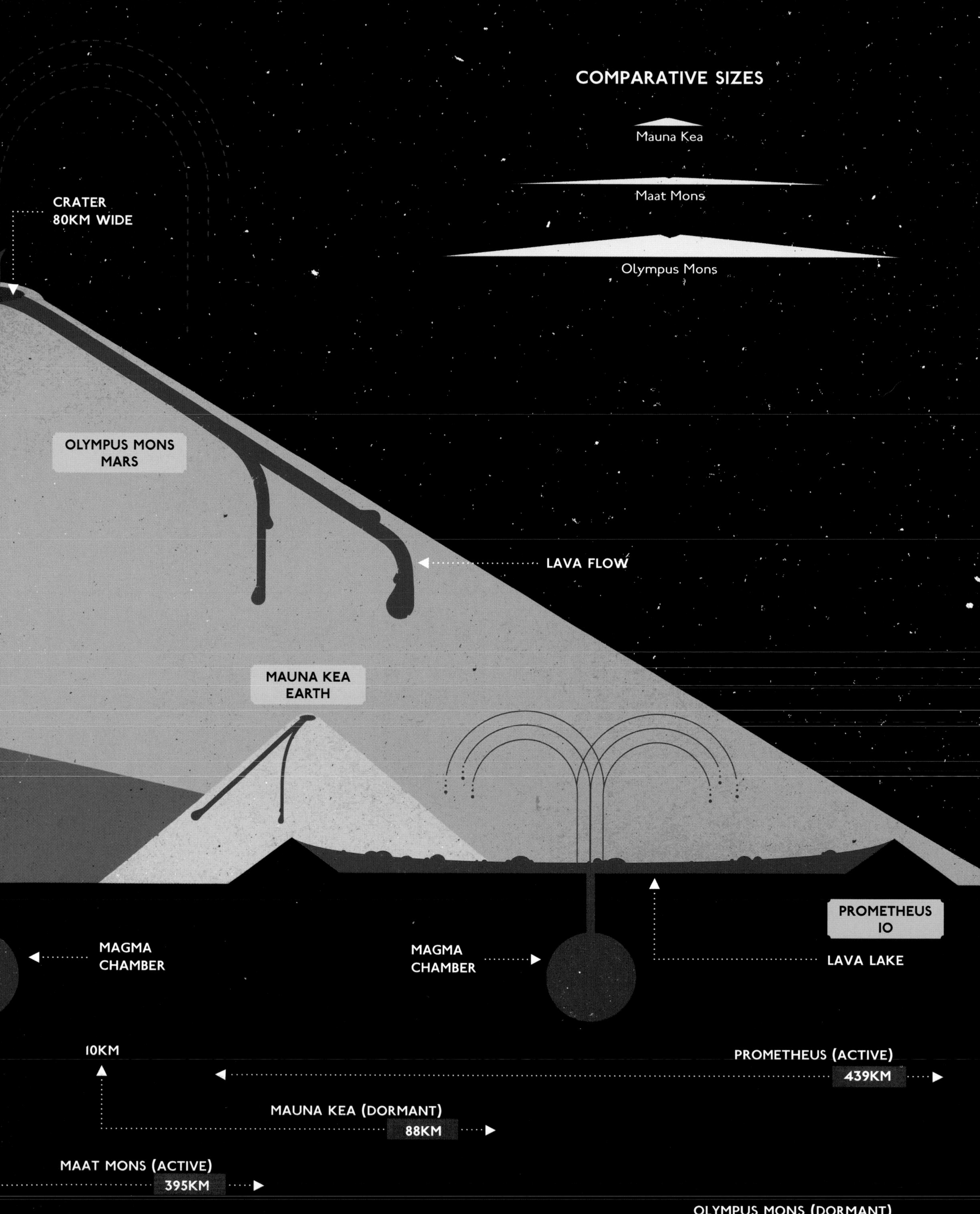
COMPARATIVE SIZES
Mauna Kea
Maat Mons
Olympus Mons
CRATER
80KM WIDE
OLYMPUS MONS
MARS
LAVA FLOW
MAUNA KEA
EARTH
PROMETHEUS
IO
MAGMA
CHAMBER
MAGMA
CHAMBER
LAVA LAKE
10KM
PROMETHEUS (ACTIVE)
439KM
MAUNA KEA (DORMANT)
88KM
MAAT MONS (ACTIVE)
395KM
OLYMPUS MONS (DORMANT)
624KM

THE ECHOES OF THE SOLAR SYSTEM

Io is a world beyond our imagination. Its unique gravitational connection to its parent planet provides a seemingly inexhaustible supply of heat. As well as its huge lava lakes, the heat also powers the largest volcanic eruptions in the Solar System. Molten rock and gas blast out from the frigid surface; the gas expands, shattering lava into giant fountains of fine particles. With weak gravity and a sparse atmosphere, Io's volcanic plumes tower over 300 kilometres (186 miles) above the moon's surface.

This incredible phenomenon, volcanism, comes from the simplest of laws of physics; the heat contained within a planet will eventually find a way to escape into the coldness of space. But what a spectacular way for the laws of physics to play out!

In the most unexpected of places, in the coldest reaches of the Solar System, the simple flow of heat has created a fiery world of wonder. And as we have seen, Io is not alone. We have discovered that many of the moons in the Solar System are far from dead, barren and uninteresting worlds; they are active, sometimes violent and always beautiful.

Io is fascinating. It doesn't derive its energy from an internal heart source in the same way that the Earth does; it extracts energy from its orbit around its parent planet, Jupiter. Having lived for three nights beside the magnificent, brooding pretence of Erta Ale, I can barely begin to imagine what an astonishing sight the vast lava lakes on Io must be. Io is indeed a true wonder of the Solar System.

Our exploration of the planets and moons orbiting our star has given us valuable insights into the nature of our own world, and changed our view of our planet's place in space. Out there are many truly violent and hostile worlds, but they are driven by the same laws that shape and control our own world. The laws of Nature can create vastly different worlds, given the tiniest of changes in temperature and composition. Worlds can also be profoundly changed by the influence of neighbouring planets and moons. Their very life and death is governed by delicate gravitational interconnections that span the Solar System. In fact, we might not be here if it weren't for these subtle connections.

Perhaps the most profound lesson of all is that we don't live on a planet isolated from the rest of the Solar System; there are echoes of other planets on Earth. We live in a place that is intimately connected to our sister worlds, orbiting around the star we all share ◉

CHAPTER 6

ALIENS

LIFE ON EARTH

I think we're living through the greatest age of discovery our civilisation has known. We've voyaged to the farthest reaches of the Solar System; we've photographed strange new worlds, stood in unfamiliar landscapes and tasted alien air. The one thing we haven't found on those worlds is the thing that makes our planet unique: life.

But is that really true? Is the Earth the only place in the Solar System that could support life, or are there other worlds that also harbour the conditions to do so? What we find on these worlds may help us to answer the question: Are we alone in the Universe? It's not only one of the great fundamental questions for science, it's also one of the great unanswered questions in human history.

BELOW: The research vessel Atlantis cruises the Sea of Cortez, Mexico. It is the mother ship for the submarine Alvin, which is built like a spacecraft for exploring the deepest depths of the ocean.

The Sea of Cortez, off the coast of Mexico, is one of the most diverse ecosystems on the planet. Visitors to this narrow strip of water include manta rays, leatherback sea turtles and many species of whales, particularly the world's largest animal – the blue whale. All of these animals, and thousands of others, combine to make it one of the most unique locations on Earth. It is the perfect place to explore the one characteristic that defines our planet more than any other. There are so many rich and diverse forms of life on Earth that, amongst the millions of species that flourish here, our interest is often only drawn to the grandest of animals. But some of the most remarkable and interesting wonders of life on Earth are hidden much further from our view.

One visitor that regularly makes the migration back to the Sea of Cortez is the research vessel Atlantis. This 92-metre (300-foot) floating laboratory is operated by the Woods Hole Oceanographic Institution and on board is a legendary intrepid explorer of our deep oceans. Alvin is a seventeen-tonne, deep ocean submersible. Built like a spacecraft, it is designed to take three lucky humans on a nine-hour journey 4,600 metres (15,000 feet) below the ocean waves. It is one of the world's most rugged submarines, and since its launch in 1964, it has explored some of the most extreme environments on Earth, including the wreck of the Titanic. Alvin is an explorer of some of the most alien environments we know.

On the morning of our Alvin dive, I confess to having been irrationally apprehensive. Irrational, because Alvin has a perfect safety record stretching back almost fifty years; apprehensive, because on the ocean floor beneath the Sea of Cortez, this little 4.9-centimetre (1.8-inch) -thick titanium sphere will be subjected to a pressure 200 times Earth's atmospheric pressure and will be utterly isolated from the

LIFE UNDER PRESSURE
At 900 m below the surface of the sea, the pressure is the same as found at the surface of Venus. Alvin has discovered life that lives under pressures that are more than twice that found on the surface of Venus.

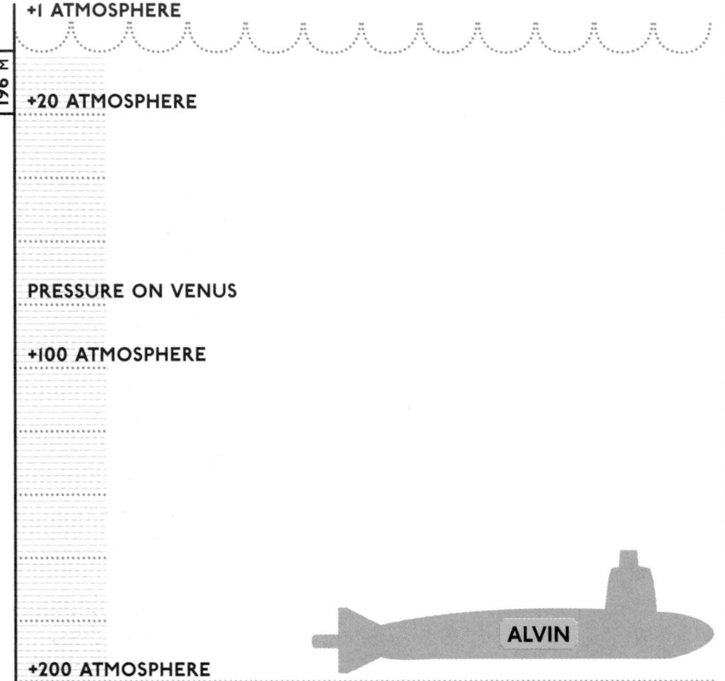

BELOW: Alvin, named after the engineer Allyn Vine who was instrumental in its development, has been in operation since 1964. Deployed from an A-frame gantry on the tender ship *R/V Atlantis* (bottom), it can then submerge to over 4,267 metres (14,000 feet). It completes nearly 200 dives per year and since its first launch has found over 300 species new to science.

BELOW RIGHT: 2,000 metres (6,600 feet) below the ocean's surface, these tube worms thrive in the most extreme living conditions. From the white tubes these animals extend feathery red plumes that take in chemicals and release waste. The colonies of symbiotic bacteria that live inside the worm then convert these chemicals into nutrients on which the worm will feed.

rest of the world. It takes a space shuttle around one hour from the firing of its retro rockets in orbit to return safely to Earth; it takes Alvin two hours to return from 2 kilometres (1.2 miles) below the surface of the ocean.

Alvin is not large or luxurious; its living quarters are 208 centimetres (81 inches) in diameter, which is just big enough to allow three people to sprawl inside with legs partially intertwined – unless you can sit cross-legged for eight hours, I can't. The curved polished-titanium sides of the sphere are exposed where racks of equipment and oxygen cylinders do not obscure them – Alvin carries enough air for a three-day stay under the ocean, should rescue become necessary. The most exciting features of the vessel are three thick portholes that become beautifully and unnervingly transparent once submerged. Through these windows, generations of undersea explorers have gazed out across the ocean's most exotic and alien vistas.

Launch would be unpleasant were it not for the adrenalin of the virgin aquanaut. Alvin is swung out over a choppy Sea of Cortez on a crane and dumped into the waves, where it bobs, uncontrolled, until the final pre-dive checks are completed. The sea conditions on our dive are marginal, which makes the experience rather like I would imagine it would be sitting in a detergent ball in a washing machine. I am told it will be much worse when we re-surface, because in these conditions recovery can take up to an hour.

Within moments of being cleared to dive, however, the Alvin becomes a serene and calm place to be as it begins its

It takes a space shuttle around one hour from the firing of its retro rockets in orbit to return safely to Earth; it takes Alvin two hours to return from two kilometres below the surface of the ocean.

long journey to the seabed. Through the portholes, darkness rapidly descends, and the only sound is the hum of the air conditioning and the occasional beep from the electronics. All sounds, including speech, have an unnatural lack of reverberation inside Alvin. It's like those first few seconds outside your house after a deep snowfall, when the world loses its echoes along with its colours. 'Beeping is never good', I say to the pilot. 'It's my pre-set depth alarms', he replies calmly.

After an hour of gentle descent, illuminated only by the magnificent flicker of bioluminescent organisms drifting past the portholes, we arrive at the ocean floor. Alvin's lights are switched on and a new world appears.

Hidden 2,000 metres (6,600 feet) below the surface of the ocean is one of the most bizarre environments on our planet. Clustered around a hydrothermal vent – a volcanic opening in the Earth's crust through which clouds of sulphurous chemicals pour into the ocean, suspended in water heated to nearly 300 degrees Celsius – is an underwater city. This miniature skyline, with fantastically complex spires reaching only a few metres into the blackness, but with an intricacy that tricks the eye and removes the sense of scale, is created by energy released through the ever-moving San Andreas Fault. Above the surface this fault is connected with death and destruction (most famously in the Great 1906 San Francisco Earthquake that devastated the city), however, below the waves the fault does not take life, but creates it.

The vast majority of the known life forms on our planet rely on energy from the Sun to fuel their existence, but deep down on the ocean floor there is no sunlight to power them. Some of the Sun's energy does make it slowly down in the form of decaying plant and animal debris from the higher levels of the ocean. This biological material has captured the Sun's energy via photosynthesis, and so delivers a slither of solar power to the ocean floor. Yet it cannot meet the energy needs of the vast density of life we see living in the dark cold depths of the ocean.

Spanning the floor of the city around the vents are carpets of yellow bacteria, forming the foundation of the ecosystem that flourishes here. Tiny shrimp-like creatures called amphipods feed directly on the bacteria. Larger organisms visit the city from the shallows, creating a complex food chain that supports a web of animals from snails and crabs to tube worms and octopuses.

Tube worms play a particularly important role in the ecology of these environments. These strange creatures can grow up to 2.5 metres (8 feet) long and spend their entire lives miles beneath the ocean. They have a well-developed nervous system, and their circulatory system uses complex haemoglobin molecules that are similar to those found in our blood to transport oxygen around their bodies. This creates the striking red plume that extends from the tip of the worms to their base, but for all their vascular complexity these animals have no mouth or digestive tract. Instead they absorb nutrients directly into their tissues through a symbiotic relationship with the bacteria that live inside them. Over half the body weight of a tube worm is bacteria, and this biological marriage is consummated by the exchange of molecules that are essential for each of these organisms to survive.

RIGHT: Mars Antenna, at NASA's Deep Space Network in Goldstone in the Mojave Desert, California. We have been searching for extraterrestrial life for thousands of years, but since the invention of the telescope 400 years ago our obsession with other worlds has only increased.

It is a relationship dependent on a chemical that is abundant around all hydrothermal vents and is essential to allow this ecosystem to survive. Hydrogen sulphide, which smells of rotten eggs, is produced when seawater comes into contact with sulphate in the rocks below the ocean floor. The bacteria living around the vents have evolved to use this molecule instead of sunlight as their energy source in a process known as chemosynthesis. Reacting hydrogen sulphide with carbon dioxide and oxygen, these unique bacteria create organic molecules that all the other organisms around them can feed off. They also produce solid globules of sulphur that give the ocean floor its vivid yellow colour. The oxygen, carbon dioxide and hydrogen sulphide are delivered to the bacteria by way of the tube worms' extraordinary circulatory systems. The red plume filters these chemicals from the seawater, then the blood transports them to the mass of bacteria in the worms' bodies. The bacteria then provide the organic compounds; the food for the worms.

This extraordinary relationship reveals the sheer adaptability of life as it evolves in the most unlikely of environments. Without the one vital ingredient associated with almost all life on the surface – sunlight – these biological renegades have found a completely novel way of bioforming.

The fascinating thing about finding life in this alien environment is that the conditions on the deep ocean floor are more similar in many ways to the conditions on worlds hundreds of millions of kilometres away in the Solar System than they are to the conditions just two kilometres above on the Earth's surface. It is incredibly dark; there is no sunlight and a brutal mixture of hot and cold water is in contact with rock and minerals. If life can not only survive but even flourish in these conditions, then it is not unreasonable to speculate that life might also survive and flourish out there in the Solar System if similar conditions are present. And as we have found again and again throughout our scientific journey to the edges of the Solar System, the way to search for the conditions necessary for life on other worlds is to actually go there and explore.

The search for extraterrestrial life stretches back thousands of years and has played a central role in both Eastern and Western thought. The Greek philosopher Thales is believed to be the first Western philosopher to introduce the idea of life outside our planet. He suggested that the stars were not just lights in the sky but other worlds, opening up the possibility of other life existing within them. Jewish, Hindu and Islamic thinkers also hinted at the idea of other worlds in their ancient literature. With the spread of Christianity in the West and its central tenet of a geocentric universe, however, speculation about the existence of extraterrestrial life became unfashionable and even opposed to Christian doctrine for many centuries.

It wasn't until the invention of the telescope 400 years ago that astronomers were able to start looking for direct signs of life on our neighbouring worlds. As technology has improved, we have been able to search the planets in more and more detail, but an increase in acuity has not always led to an increase in accuracy.

William Herschel, the discoverer of Uranus and one of the forefathers of modern astronomy, believed that every planet was inhabited; he even produced calculations to prove that the Sun was populated by a race of giant-headed beings

who could only survive in such conditions because of the size of their heads. At the turn of the twentieth century, Mars became the centre of our attention in the search for direct evidence of cosmic neighbours. American astronomer Percival Lowell convinced much of the world that Mars was covered in intricately constructed canals that were direct evidence of a complex Martian civilisation. His romantic vision of a civilisation channelling scarce Martian water from the poles to the great cities at the equator wasn't entirely dismissed until Mariner 4 arrived for a close-up look in 1965.

As our exploratory ambitions and technical prowess have increased throughout the twentieth century, the evidence for any form of living companions in the Universe has diminished. Again and again we've searched more and more carefully and found nothing. This doesn't mean the rest of the Solar System is dead; we have, after all, only scratched the surface of what's beyond us. There are literally hundreds of other worlds out there – a vast and diverse collection of planets and their moons of the Solar System that we have barely explored. Amongst them may be worlds that hold the conditions to support life, and the most accessible way to understand what the limits of those conditions might be is to look at the one place where we know life flourishes: the Earth ◉

WHAT IS LIFE?

Life is a difficult thing to define. Scientists still struggle to come up with a description that is specific enough to cover all the life forms that we already know of and broad enough to encompass the new life forms that we continue to discover here, and perhaps one day on other worlds. Many definitions have been put forward over the years that encompass the essential elements of life – metabolism, reproduction, growth, adaptation and organisation. One of the simplest definitions, the idea that life is 'a self-sustained chemical system capable of undergoing Darwinian evolution', is perhaps one of the most accurate.

Reduced to its most basic building blocks, life is nothing more than chemistry. It is an emergent property; a consequence of the many and varied reactions between a wonderfully intricate and ordered system of both simple and complex molecules. Given this, for life to exist you only need three things. First, you need the right chemistry set. A human is made up of approximately forty elements, almost half of the known elements. This is complicated, and many of them are essential to our biological function, although 96 per cent of our bodies are made of only four: carbon, nitrogen, oxygen and hydrogen. Secondly, you need an energy source; a battery that generates a flow of electrons to power the processes of life. Here on Earth, most of the life we know of uses the power of the Sun, but as we've seen around the hydrothermal vents on the ocean floor, this is not essential. As long as energy can be harvested – whether through photosynthesis capturing the power of the Sun or the chemosynthesis of hydrogen sulphide liberating the binding energy stored within molecules – life can potentially flourish. Thirdly, and seemingly universally, you need a medium through which the chemical processes of life can play themselves out. On Earth, you don't have to look far to find that medium; the solvent of life is everywhere, because it's water

OUR HUMAN MAKE-UP

Around 96 per cent of our human bodies are made up of just four elements; the other 4 per cent is made up of around 36 other elements.

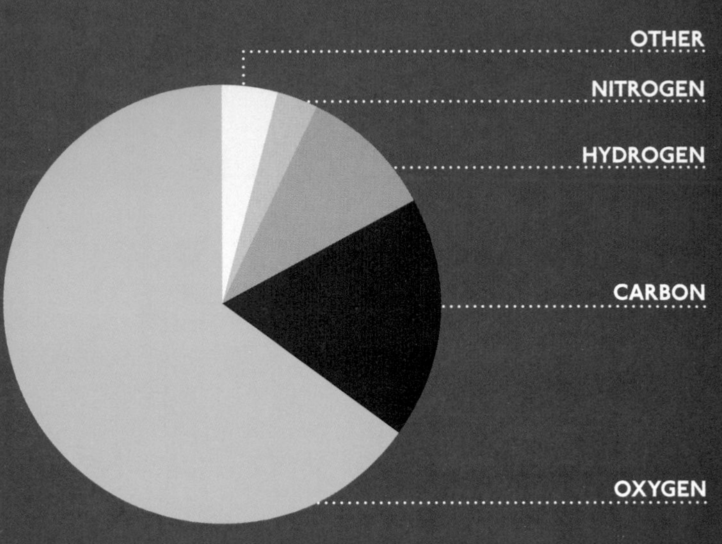

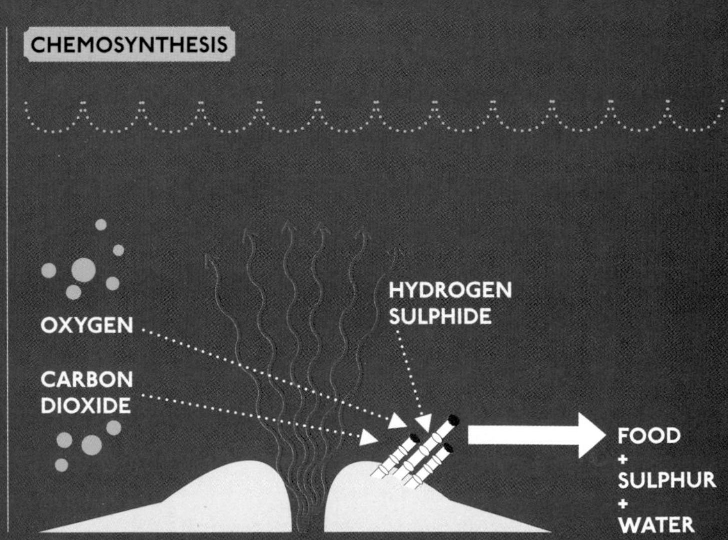

HOW LIVING OBJECTS CREATE ENERGY FOR LIFE

On Earth's surface, most life forms use the power of the Sun to create food and oxygen through photosynthesis. But where sunlight is absent, such as in the depths of the dark oceans, they have adapted to use other means to create essential elements for life, such as chemosynthesis.

WATER: AN ESSENTIAL LIFE FORCE

BELOW: The Atacama Desert in Chile is considered the driest place in the world. In its almost complete absence of rain, no life forms can be sustained here – not even bacteria.

If you want to see how important water is to life, there's no better place to come than the Atacama Desert in Chile. The Atacama is widely considered to be the driest desert in the world. This 1,000-kilometre (600-mile) -long rainless plateau in northern Chile is sandwiched between the Andes and the Chilean coastal range of mountains. This unusual geological position creates a rain shadow, a meteorological phenomenon that prevents this thin strip of land receiving even the smallest amounts of precipitation.

All deserts are characterised by a lack of moisture, but the Atacama takes that to the extreme. Some weather stations here have never received rain; others have measured just one millimetre of rainfall in ten years. There are river valleys that have been dry for 120,000 years and there are rocks that haven't seen rainfall for twenty million years. Evidence suggests that there was no significant rainfall for 400 years in the Atacama from 1570 to 1971. It is so dry, it makes the Sahara Desert look wet – even the great African wilderness receives fifty times more rainfall than the Atacama.

Scientists have searched for bacteria, the most basic form of life, in the Atacama and in some places they have found absolutely nothing. The land is so dead that in places the soil is more sterile than a hospital operating theatre. It's the starkest evidence we have to suggest that every life form, even the most primitive, needs water to survive. On Earth, we have found no exceptions to this rule.

This seemingly fundamental link between water and life is driving the search for life in the Solar System, because wherever we find water the evidence shows that these will be the best places to look for life beyond Earth. We are certain that Earth is currently the only planet that has standing liquid water on its surface. The other planets are either too close to the Sun and too hot – like Venus, where any water evaporated long ago – or too far away – like Mars, where the only surface water we know of is locked away in the polar caps. Further out in the Solar System, there is plenty of water. Many of the moons around the gas giants and even the rings of Saturn are made of large quantities of water, but in the depths of space it is frozen into solid ice.

However, this emphatically does not signal the end of the search. Water may be hiding below the surface of a moon or planet, and it is also very possible that liquid water once flowed across the surfaces of other planets at some point in the Solar System's history. If it did, we should be able to find the evidence, because the one thing our study of the Earth's landscape tells us is that wherever water goes, it always leaves its footprint ◉

THE SIGNATURE OF WATER

ALL IMAGES: For the ultimate demonstration in how water sculpts our landscape, there is no better place to visit than the spectacular Scablands in the northwestern United States.

Nowhere on Earth is the faded presence of once-flowing water more obviously imprinted on the land than in the extraordinary landscape found in a remote part of the northwestern United States. The Scablands are a unique geological formation that stretch across a vast area of the state of Washington, demonstrating on a spectacular scale how water can carve its signature into rock.

First studied in the 1920s, the origin of the Scablands was a mystery that defied any conventional geological explanation. A normal river valley leaves behind a characteristic V-shaped cross section that is replicated in river systems across the globe. The other commonly observed effect of water are the U-shaped valleys carved by glaciers. The valleys of the Scablands have a rectangular cross section, however, and when first studied this could not be explained by any known geological phenomenon. It is obviously not a normal river system, because all the valleys are carved in straight lines through the rock. There is no gentle meandering of a river; instead these valleys simply look like great big rectangular holes.

J. Harlen Bretz was the first geologist to study this area. He concluded that the unique geometric erosion patterns, potholes and ripple marks of the Scablands were caused by a vast quantity of water, hundreds of cubic kilometres in

volume, passing though the area in a very short period of time. Without any explanation for where the water came from, his theory was ridiculed and dismissed. It was only when he began collaborating with another geologist, J. T. Pardee, that they were able to offer a full explanation for this extraordinary site. After decades of careful research, Bretz and Pardee arrived at a theory that not only explained the observed features of the Scablands, but subsequently helped geologists to understand similar formations on another planet millions of kilometres away.

Today, the Scablands are an area of intense interest for astro-geologists such as Jim Rice from the Arizona State University. Rice believes that understanding the events that created this landscape can help in the search for water on other planets. As our helicopter flew through the geometric canyons of a landscape unlike anything I've ever seen on Earth, Rice explained to me that investigating the origin of places like the Scablands feels more like the study of a crime scene than a geological expedition. All this detective work has revealed that these unique scars in the landscape bear witness to the largest flood the Earth has ever seen.

Between 13,000 and 15,000 years ago, at the end of the last ice age, a huge glacial lake known as Lake Missoula lay 320 kilometres (200 miles) to the east of the Scablands. It

'If you took every river in the world, put them in the same location, had them flowing at the same time, these floods were ten times larger than that.'

was held in place by a vast wall of ice – a dam that held back millions of cubic kilometres of water for thousands of years during the ice age. As the water levels increased behind the dam, the ice wall was put under more and more strain until eventually, inevitably, it failed. When it ruptured, over 2,000 cubic kilometres (480 cubic miles) of water swept out in a single catastrophic event. The floodwaters were at least a kilometre deep, travelling at 130 kilometres (80 miles) per hour. The energy released was equivalent to 4,500 megatonnes of TNT. Imagine what a terrifying sight this massive wave must have been, perhaps the largest and most devastating wave in history, rumbling across the landscape loaded with huge chunks of ice from the dam and vast boulders of basal rock ripped from the ground.

As the floodwaters tore across the landscape, they carved out a thirty-kilometre (twenty-mile) -long canyon, and at its head they left giant horseshoes. At over 122 metres (400 feet) high and 8 kilometres (5 miles) across, this was the largest waterfall the world has ever known. As we stood looking across this landscape, it was virtually impossible to imagine the scale of the wave of water that had flowed through here. Jim Rice, though, had a simple way of putting the event into perspective: 'If you took every river in the world, put them in the same location, had them flowing at the same time, these floods were ten times larger than that.'

What's perhaps even more astounding, though, is the speed with which this landscape was formed. Current estimates suggest that this vast and complex landscape was created in no more than a week, perhaps even as little as forty-eight hours. As Jim Rice put it: 'It's instantaneous geology' on an epic scale.

The Scablands reveal one of the characteristic signatures that water can carve into the landscape. It is a signature so bold and vivid that it can even be seen from Earth's orbit, and if we can see these features on our own planet, then when we turn our telescopes outwards we must therefore be able to look for similar evidence of water's mighty work on the surface of other worlds ●

LIFE ON MARS?

For over a century, Mars has been held up as a prime candidate for a location on which alien life might be found. For a brief moment the astronomical imagination of Percival Lowell convinced us of the existence of a network of canals on the red planet, and popular culture became suffused with tales of Martians, such as in H. G. Wells' science fiction classic, *The War of the Worlds*. The enduring legacy and romance of the Victorians' imaginary Martians persisted throughout the twentieth century, and in many ways it is still with us. However, today the evidence we are looking for is not the handy work of extraterrestrial builders, although just like Lowell we are still searching diligently for the tell-tale signs of waterways on the red planet.

OPPOSITE: This image of an impact crater called Victoria, about 800 metres (2,600 feet) across, with scalloped edges eroded by winds and fretted sand dunes on its floor, was taken by NASA's Mars Reconnaissance Orbiter in October 2006.

SCARS ON MARS

Images taken by the Mars Exploration rover Opportunity, which landed on the red planet in 2004, reveal that our next-door neighbour has features cut into its surface that are almost identical to those in the Scablands. Mars is covered in outflow channels – straight wide canyons exactly like those of Washington – filled with identical geological features. This all suggests that similar huge floods might have torn across the surface of the planet.

The pictures here reveal just how similar the landscapes appear to be. Viewed from the air, we can see that the horseshoe shapes of the dry falls in Washington state are replicated on the surface of Mars. And there are other striking similarities. Upstream of the falls on Earth and Mars, we can see grooves cut into the landscape as the water cascaded down and flowed over the falls. This collection of similar geological characteristics suggests that the same story played out in these gigantic valleys, and that vast amounts of water rapidly flowed over the surface of Mars at some point in the past.

These images and their interpretation, combined with the many other geological features we have studied on Mars, make a compelling case that very large volumes of liquid water once flowed across the surface of the red planet. This is an important step in the search for Martian life, because it shows us that one of the non-negotiable prerequisites for life – water – must have been present. But on their own, Scabland-like erosion features do not point to the existence of the conditions that we believe life requires. If the same processes that formed the Scablands on Earth formed the Martian landscapes, the floods that created them may only have lasted a matter of days, and for life to get a foothold you need more than that; you need areas of standing water, lakes and rivers that persist for many millions of years. In order to look for evidence of that standing water, we've done the only thing that we can. We've sent an army of robotic explorers to the surface of the planet

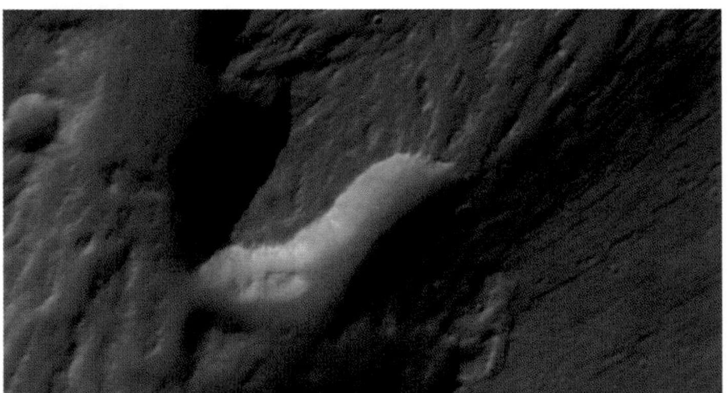

BELOW LEFT: The horseshoe shapes present at the dry falls in the Scablands (bottom) are also present in this image of Mars' surface (top).

BELOW: These two images (Scablands bottom, Mars top) demonstrate again the similar characteristics shared by both landscapes.

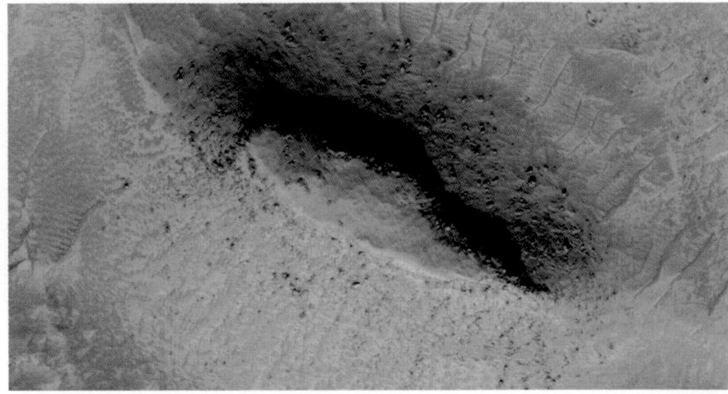

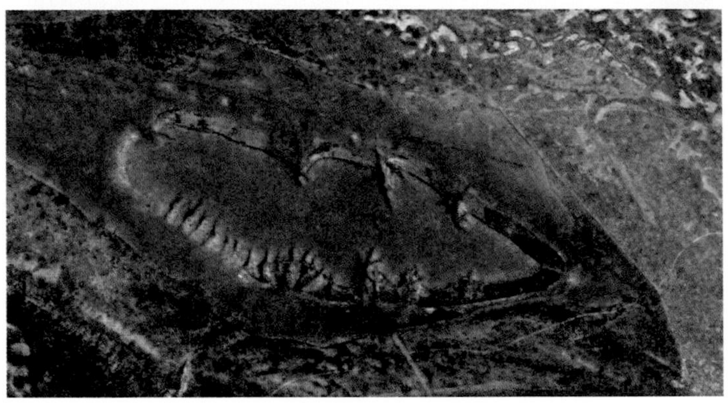

These images ... combined with the many other geological features we have studied on Mars, make a compelling case that very large volumes of liquid water once flowed across the surface of the planet.

BELOW: These outflow channels that cover the surface of Mars appear to have exactly the same formation as those in the Scablands and are filled with identical geological features.

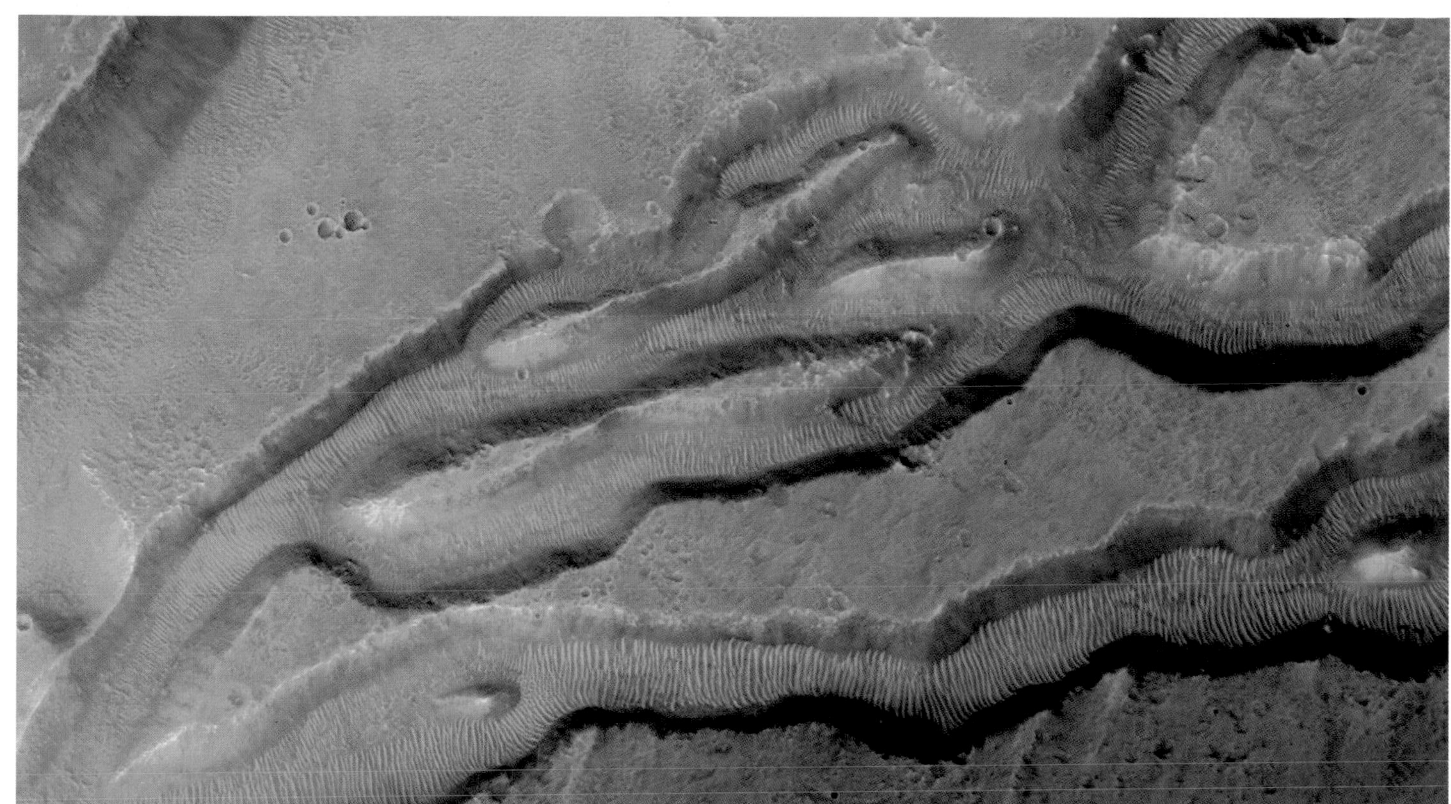

MARS' MINERALS

Over the last thirty-five years, we've landed six robot probes on Mars, and one of them, Opportunity, is still rolling across the surface in 2010, investigating today's Martian geology. Opportunity and her sister craft, Spirit, have captured many people's imaginations, not least amongst the school-age space enthusiasts who will form the next, vitally important, generation of explorers, scientists and engineers. The rovers genuinely are explorers in the old-fashioned sense; they are the direct extension of our senses to the surface of another world. They have also been of priceless scientific importance because you can't really get to know another planet from orbit. You've got to get down to the surface; you've got to touch it, and you've got to dig down and examine it microscopically. By doing just that, the rovers have made some extremely important scientific discoveries.

One of the most significant of those discoveries was made in November 2004. The Opportunity rover was examining an impact feature called the Endurance Crater,

LEFT: The world's largest salt works are on the Baja peninsula, Mexico. There, lagoons are pumped full of seawater, which then evaporates, leaving behind its precious residue: salt.

BELOW AND BOTTOM: These images from the rover Opportunity show just some of the gypsum crystals found in the Endurance Crater and networks of sand dunes on Mars, which suggest that large areas of the planet were once covered in water.

Mars was once a much warmer and wetter planet. A planet with oceans and floods, vast areas of standing water and a hydrological cycle.

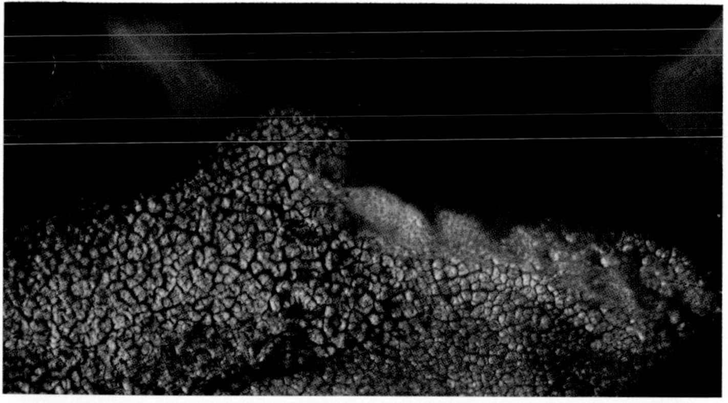

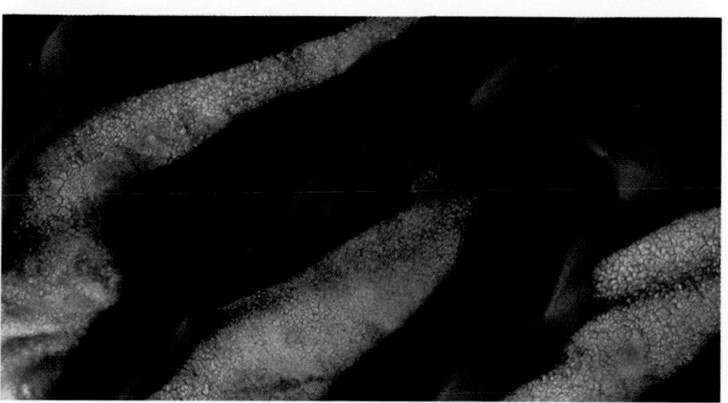

when it detected deposits of a remarkable mineral: gypsum. This is a very soft mineral that has been discovered in large deposits on the surface of Mars, and although we can't yet bring any Martian gypsum mineral back to Earth to test it further, its very existence provides another crucial piece of evidence in our search for life on Mars.

On the Baja peninsula in Mexico, the largest salt works in the world stretch across a vast landscape. It's a lucrative but simple industry that requires seawater to be pumped into lagoons where it evaporates, leaving behind a residue of sodium chloride, or table salt, that eventually finds its way to millions of dinner tables across the world. It's not just table salt that appears from the seawater; other salts and minerals crystallise out and emerge at different stages of the process. In one of the lagoons, pond number 9, the seawater is at exactly the right concentration to precipitate out a very beautiful crystal that covers the entire floor of the lagoon.

These crystals are gypsum; exactly the same stuff that the Opportunity rover found on the surface of Mars. What's interesting about Opportunity's discovery is that it tells us something fundamental about the story of water on the red planet. The chemical formula of gypsum is $CaSO_4$ $2H_2O$ – calcium sulphate dihydrate. The dihydrate is the bit that's important for our story, because that refers to the two molecules of water bonded loosely to the calcium sulphate. We know of only one way in which calcium sulphate can combine with water like this here on Earth; it simply requires calcium and sulphate ions to be in the presence of liquid water that is stationary for long periods of time.

With large deposits of gypsum found at multiple locations across the surface of Mars, it seems the only conclusion to draw is that there must have been standing water on the planet's surface at some point. If this interpretation of the discovery of gypsum is correct, then it is another crucial piece of evidence to suggest that all the factors needed for life to occur have existed at some point in Martian history.

Everywhere we look on Mars, from the microscopic evidence left in the rocks to the subsequent discoveries of gypsum in amongst the networks of sand dunes and the vast geological structures that are so suggestive of flowing water that cover the planet's surface, it is difficult to escape the conclusion that Mars was once a much warmer and wetter planet. A planet with oceans and floods, vast areas of standing water and a hydrological cycle that created the ghosts of a familiar Earth-like landscape that we glimpse today through the arid dust.

Although Mars may once have been a more hospitable place, any liquid water has long since disappeared from its surface. About three billion years ago, Mars died as a planet. Its core froze and the volcanoes that had produced its atmosphere seized up. The solar winds then stripped away the remains of that atmosphere. Any liquid water left on the planet's surface would have evaporated or soaked into the soil, where it froze. This left the surface of Mars too cold, too exposed and too dry to support life, but that is not to say that life couldn't exist somewhere on the red planet today. Maybe we're just looking in the wrong place; maybe there are other potential habitats for life on Mars ◉

MARS' UNEXPLORED SUBTERRANEA

In September 2007, the NASA Mars Odyssey spacecraft discovered seven strange circles high up on the slopes of a Martian volcano known as Arsia Mons. These very dark circular shapes varied in size from 100 to 250 metres (330 to 820 feet) in diameter and they completely puzzled the scientists who found them. To try and solve the mystery, the team deployed the Odyssey craft's infrared cameras to record the temperature swing of the holes across a series of Martian days. The results that came back were surprising. The temperature change from day to night in these holes was much less than the change in the surrounding area; about a third of the temperature swing seen outside of the circles. Such stable temperatures that seem to iron out the change from day to night are seen all over the Earth. Caves on Earth maintain a constant temperature; the deeper they are, the more they can resist the effect of the passing Sun outside. It's why so many life forms use caves across our planet as shelter and it's why the NASA scientists realised that they were looking through seven mysterious doorways into the unexplored world of subterranean Mars.

The scientists at NASA called these holes the Seven Sisters and named them Dena, Chloe, Wendy, Annie, Abby, Nikki and Jeanne. Three images of 'Annie' taken by the spacecraft show how its opening, the size of two football pitches, is colder than the adjacent area in the afternoon and warmer than the immediate surface at night. Nobody can be sure whether these circles are deep openings into an expansive cave system or narrow vertical shafts, but what is certain is that they open up another front in our search for life on Mars.

These caves are almost certainly at too high an altitude to have supported any form of microbial life in the past or present, but their very existence opens up the possibility that somewhere on Mars there may be a cave system that could have protected life from the hostile environment outside. We know there may be water down there, too: satellite data shows permafrost, ice frozen in the soil. Deep below the surface, that ice may melt to form liquid water. These are tantalising glimpses into a hidden world that may be harbouring Martian life, concealed behind the darkness of these cave entrances. These may not appear to be the perfect conditions for life as we know it on our own world, but our exploration of life on Earth also suggests that not all living things are always so fussy ◉

ABOVE: (i) Images are from Odyssey's neutron and gamma ray detectors (ii) blue colour demonstrates water-ice (iii) in winter, the water-ice is hidden by a layer of dry-ice (frozen carbon dioxide) (iv) in spring/summer, the carbon dioxide is heated and dissipates, revealing large quantities of water-ice across the north pole of the planet.

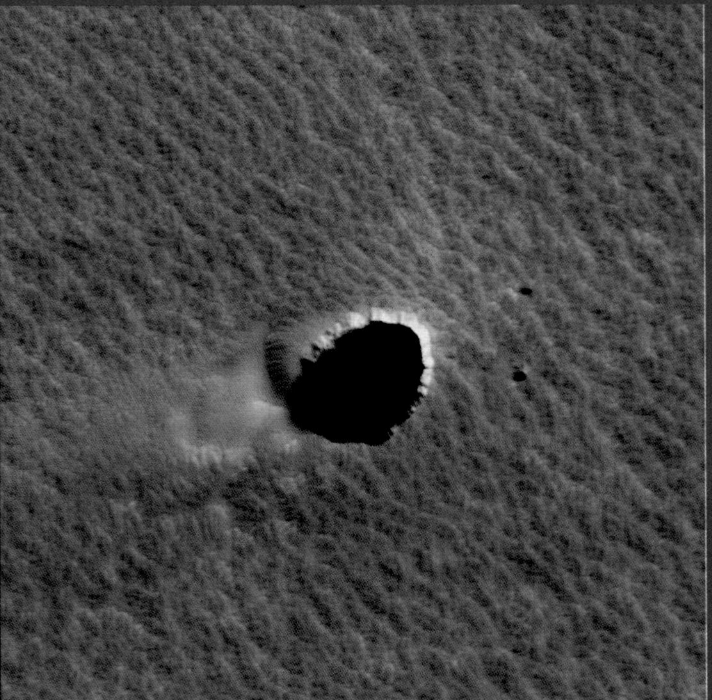

ABOVE: Tharsis Montes is the largest volcanic region on Mars. It is approximately 4,000 kilometres (2,500 miles) across, 10 kilometres (6 miles) high and contains twelve large volcanoes. The largest volcanoes in the Tharsis region are four shield volcanoes named Ascraeus Mons, Pavonis Mons, Arsia Mons and Olympus Mons.

LIFE UNDERGROUND

BELOW: The Cueva de Villa Luz in Tabasco, Mexico, is a subterranean maze filled with toxic gases – not a place you'd expect to be teeming with life.

The Cueva de Villa Luz in Tabasco, Mexico, the 'cave of the lighted house', is the very definition of a hostile environment to a human being.

Here on Earth, it is easy to jump to the conclusion that the perfect habitat for life would look like the green, lush landscapes around the jungle river of southern Mexico. This is the very definition of biodiversity: a warm climate, lots of liquid water, a beautiful dense atmosphere and an abundance of living things in both number and variation.

All life in the jungle, and indeed most of the life forms we meet every day and are familiar with, thrive in pretty much the same conditions that we do, driven by the heat and light of the Sun. The more sunlight and the more water present, the more life appears to like it, but just a few kilometres away from here is a form of life hidden deep beneath the surface of our planet, one that flourishes in a completely different environment and may hint at the forms of life that could be hidden away on Mars.

The Cueva de Villa Luz in Tabasco, Mexico, the 'cave of the lighted house', is the very definition of a hostile environment to a human being. This subterranean maze, over 2 kilometres (1.2 miles) in length, is full of hydrogen sulphide gas, pumped into the cavern by a spring rich in this corrosive gas. The gas dissolves in the water to produce sulphuric acid that has eaten its way through the limestone rock to create the cave system. It not only pungently smells of rotten eggs,

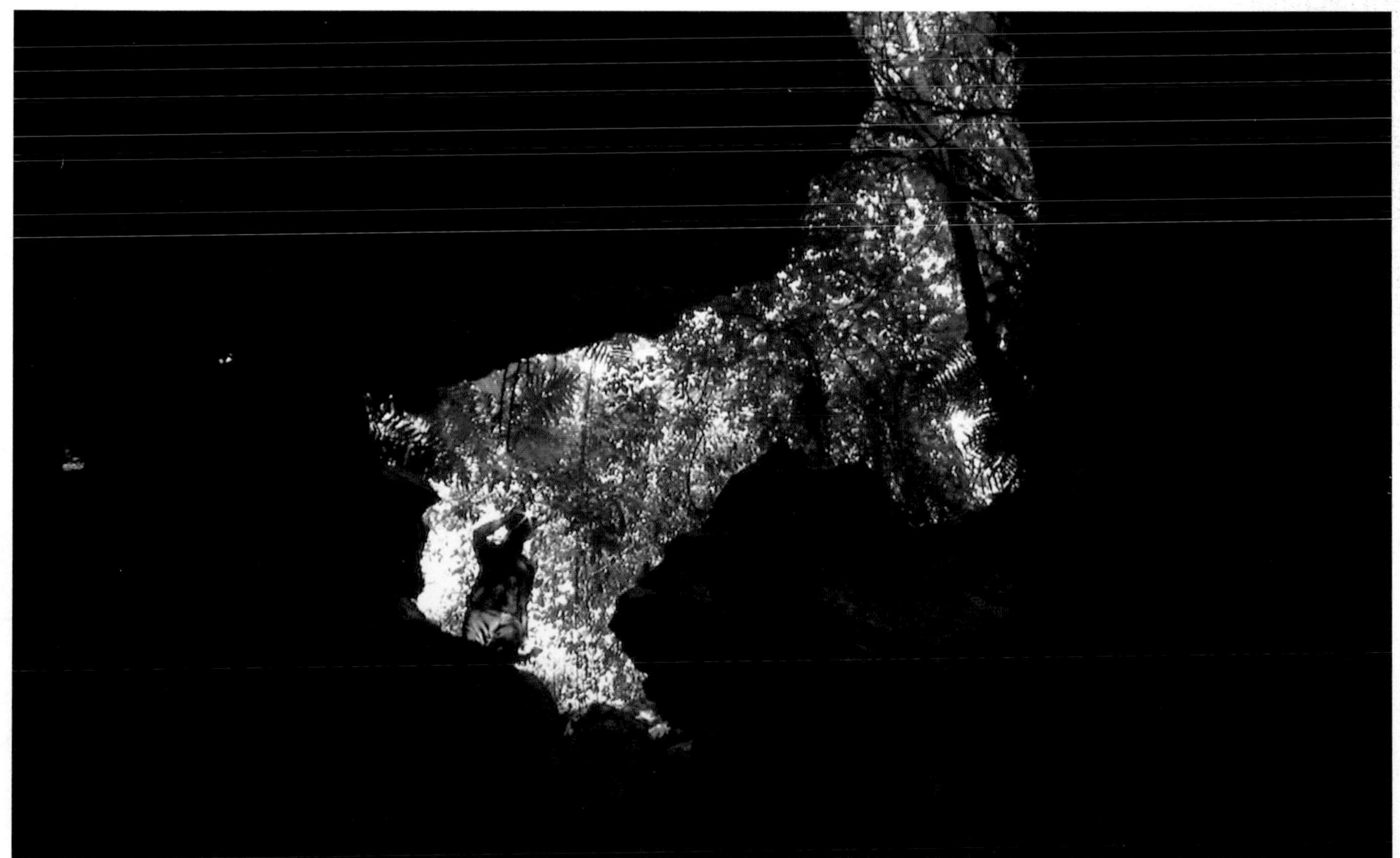

BELOW: The tiny snottites use the hydrogen sulphide gas around them to drive their metabolism, producing a secretion so acidic that it would have burnt my skin if I'd touched it while taking a test sample. It has a pH level of almost zero – making it a highly concentrated and dangerous acid.

it is also incredibly toxic to humans, even in small quantities. To step inside, you need to be kitted out with a gas monitor and a gas mask in case it all gets too much. It's a place where, at first sight, you would not expect a great many life forms to survive and flourish. Although the cave is a potential death trap for us, that doesn't mean that nothing lives here. In fact, it's teeming with life.

Everywhere in the cave water swim strange fish called *Poecilia sulphuraria*, which are beautifully adapted to tolerate these conditions. If you look at them closely, they're quite pink, and this is thought to be because they have large quantities of haemoglobin in their blood that allows them to move around using the sparse quantities of available oxygen in the water surrounding their bodies. They are a beautiful example of how life adapts to the most inhospitable of environments, adjusting the parameters of biology to suit their external environment.

Delve deeper into this toxic cave and things become even more intriguing. In the depths of the caves, where the concentration of poisonous gas sets off every alarm, is a profoundly interesting organism. Down here, far from the light of the Sun, is a life form that derives its energy not from the Sun but from the noxious gases around it. These tiny creatures use the hydrogen sulphide gas bubbling up through the springs to drive their metabolism. The very same gas that would squeeze the life out of a human is the breath of life for these creatures.

These are the snottites. They are surely one of the most alien life forms on Earth because they metabolise hydrogen sulphide. They react this nasty gas with oxygen to produce sulphuric acid, a totally exotic form of respiration. Whereas we breathe in oxygen and react it with sugars to produce carbon dioxide and energy, these little things breathe in hydrogen sulphide and oxygen and produce sulphuric acid.

It's a form of life so corrosive to us that we can't even touch it safely. The secretion dripping off the snottites has a pH of almost zero – it's a highly concentrated sulphuric acid that is as brutal as battery acid. By every definition of the word, these organisms are alien life forms, with the one discrepancy being that they are living just below the surface of our planet.

Surprisingly, the snottites are not alone. Organisms that can extract energy from the minerals around them are found under the ground all over the world. In fact, this way of life is so successful that it's thought there may be more life mass living beneath the Earth's surface than there is on it, and that raises an intriguing possibility. If life can thrive below the Earth's surface, why couldn't organisms like snottites survive and flourish beneath the surface of Mars? Living below the surface of Mars might in fact be quite a good idea, because the surface is incredibly hostile. Any life form on the Martian surface would be subjected to intense ultraviolet radiation from the Sun. Mars is also a very cold place, and the atmospheric pressure doesn't allow liquid water to exist on the surface.

If there is life below the surface of Mars, however, then obviously we would appear to have a problem detecting it. Interestingly, there is one last tantalising clue for us that suggests there might be something going on below the Martian surface ◉

THE FINAL PIECE OF THE JIGSAW

In 1768, the Italian physicist Alexander Volta was still thirty years away from making his most famous contribution to science: the development of the first battery. As a totally unconnected preamble to his great invention, save for a demonstration of his intense curiosity about Nature, he spent his time collecting gases from the marshes around his home in the north of Italy. One of the gases he collected and studied was methane, a simple molecule with the chemical formula CH_4. Volta demonstrated with great flair that methane could be ignited from an electric spark. Today, we use this combustible gas as one of our main sources of fuel, because methane is the main component of natural gas and its abundance makes it widely available and relatively cheap. The deposits of methane under the Earth's surface are generated by the decay of organic material and are often linked to sites containing other fossil fuels, but methane is also present in our atmosphere.

Termites, or white ants, are very unusual animals because they eat dead organic matter; their primary diet is wood. There are many species of these insects, billions of individuals across the planet, and in the process of digesting wood they produce vast quantities of methane, pumping an estimated fifty million tonnes of it into the Earth's atmosphere every year.

Termites aren't the only methane producers on the planet, though. There is lots of methane occurring naturally in our atmosphere, produced either biologically or by active geological processes such as mud volcanoes. That makes it all the more surprising that methane has been detected in the atmosphere of Mars, a planet we have thought of as both geologically and biologically dead. As far as we know, there is no non-biological or geological process that could produce and sustain the levels of methane we observe in the Martian atmosphere.

In January 2009, researchers at the Keck Observatory in Hawaii announced that they had discovered substantial pockets of methane on the surface of Mars. Using the infrared telescope facility on top of this famous volcano, the NASA-led team had previously detected only tiny amounts of methane in the Martian atmosphere. Closer observations subsequently revealed that the gas was being produced in far greater quantities than had been suspected, although

LEFT AND BELOW RIGHT:
Termites, or white ants, are very unusual animals because they feed on decaying wood. As they eat the wood across the globe, they produce methane, contributing fifty million tonnes of the gas into the Earth's atmosphere every year.

NATURAL SOURCES OF ATMOSPHERIC METHANE
Well over half the methane production on Earth stems from human activity, but it is also produced by natural sources in significant quantities, which could explain methane's presence on Mars.

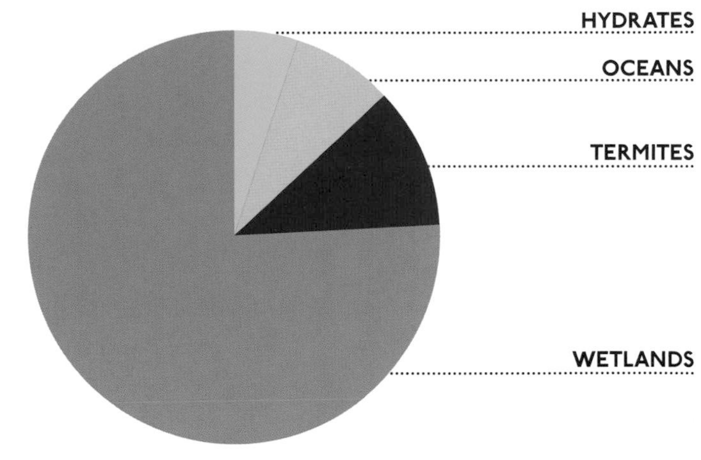

it is concentrated in a handful of plumes that vary with the seasons. In the warmer summer months, thousands of tonnes of the gas are released from vents in the surface. As far as we know, this can mean only one of two tantalising things. The simplest explanation is that, just as here on Earth, the methane plumes are emanating from previously unknown geological processes. This would be a great discovery in itself, because it would mean that far from being dead, Mars is still a geologically active planet. The other option is that the methane is being produced from a biological source; living organisms on Mars that are producing methane just like the termites on Earth.

No one is seriously suggesting that there are termites running around beneath the surface of Mars, but it's not actually the termites that are particularly interesting about this story – it's the way they digest the wood. They use symbiotic micro-organisms called *Archaea*, which live in their guts, to do the methane-producing work for them.

Archaea used to be thought of as an unusual group of bacteria, but we now know that these basic living units are in fact a completely distinct branch of life. Along with bacteria and the more complex cellular units known as *Eukaryotes, Archaea* are one of the three separate branches of life on Earth. They are found all over our planet; filling the soil, the oceans and the guts of humans, cows and termites. They are also the most common organisms found beneath the surface of the Earth.

Archaea thrive in many of the Earth's most extreme environments. The snottites, as seen in Cueva de Villa Luz, are members of the *Archaea*, as are many of the micro-organisms found living around deep-sea hydrothermal vents, producing millions of tonnes of methane that is pumped into the atmosphere. As we learn more about the *Archaea* on Earth, it raises the tantalising prospect that the methane we see in Mars' atmosphere might just be produced by organisms like these living below the Martian surface.

Going the extra vital step to proving this incredible hypothesis for the origin of the Martian methane will almost certainly involve a manned mission to Mars, or at the very least the development of another advanced generation of robotic explorers. With so much evidence calling us back to explore, it seems impossible not to imagine that we will take this final step in our long search for companions in the cosmos. The idea that we are potentially just one mission away from the most profound discovery in human history must surely be reason enough to embark on at least one more journey to the red planet of Lowell and Wells ◉

The idea that we are potentially just one mission away from the most profound discovery in human history must surely be reason enough to embark on at least one more journey to the red planet.

EUROPA:
LIFE IN THE FREEZER

While Mars remains one of the prime candidates in the search for extraterrestrials, it is no longer the only place in the Solar System that we think could harbour alien life. As we leave behind the familiarity of the rocky planets and travel further from the Sun, the Solar System becomes a very different place. In our search for water, the far-flung reaches of the outer solar system provide a plentiful source of H_2O, but half a billion kilometres away from the Sun, any water might be expected to be frozen as hard as steel.

OPPOSITE: At first sight, Jupiter's frozen moon, Europa, seems to harbour conditions too hostile to support any form of life.

Jupiter, the vast gas giant, is surrounded by a network of sixty-three moons, with many containing vast amounts of ice. The largest four are the moons discovered by Galileo in January 1610. Out here, where the Sun is little more than a bright star in a dark sky, you might imagine these moons to be cold, desolate places, and that's how they appear at first sight.

Callisto is the most distant of the Galilean moons from Jupiter. Orbiting not far short of 2 million kilometres (1.2 million miles) away from its mother planet, Callisto takes 16.7 days to complete an orbit and the same amount of time to turn on its axis and complete a Calliston day. A giant moon, it's the third-largest satellite in the Solar System, and analysis suggest that it is made up of approximately half water ice. In this foreboding part of the Solar System, the ice is frozen as hard as steel on its surface, at a temperature of -155 degrees Celsius.

Travelling 800,000 kilometres (500,000 miles) towards Jupiter, the next Galilean moon is the largest moon in the Solar System – Ganymede. With a diameter of over 5,200 kilometres (3,200 miles) this moon is bigger than the planet Mercury. Composed of silicate rock and ice, Ganymede has an uninviting surface temperature of -160 degrees Celsius.

Callisto and Ganymede don't seem likely places on which to find life. Despite an abundance of water, the freezing temperatures on their surfaces mean the solvent of life is locked up in kilometres of thick ice, making these moons seemingly far too hostile to support life of any kind.

Looks can be deceiving, though, and among these frozen wastes we have found one world that is of particular interest in our search for life beyond the planet Earth; a world that seems to defy its freezing position in the outer reaches of the Solar System.

BELOW: These images, taken by NASA's Galileo spacecraft in June 1996, show the cracked surface of Jupiter's moon Europa. The top image shows Europa from a distance of 5,340 kilometres (3,310 miles), which reveals crustal plates on the surface, and the bottom one from about 2 kilometres (1.2 miles), which clearly shows the parallel ridges on its surface.

Beyond Callisto and Ganymede, as we journey towards Jupiter, is the ice moon Europa. It's about the same size as our moon and is the smallest of the four Galilean satellites. It orbits Jupiter in just over 3.5 days at an average distance of 671,000 kilometres (417,000 miles) from the planet. It has a tenuous atmosphere, composed of oxygen, but this sliver of gas is not the reason for our fascination with this moon.

When we look closely at the moon's surface, it becomes truly intriguing. Europa is the smoothest body in the Solar System; its surface is made of an unbroken shell of ice at a temperature of a chilly -160 Celsius. Etched into this ice is a network of mysterious red markings. This seems an incredibly unlikely home for life, and the photographs taken by the Galileo spaceprobe seem at first sight to confirm that suspicion. Just like Callisto and Ganymede, Europa appears to be a vast icy wilderness, but if you look more closely you start to see features that hint at a very different story. Beneath its thick layer of ice, Europa holds an astonishing secret.

Images taken by the Galileo spacecraft in 1998 revealed something quite remarkable about Europa's icy surface. One image of the Conamara region (named after a district in the west of Ireland), reveals deep cracks that crisscross the surface of Europa. At higher magnification, we see even more

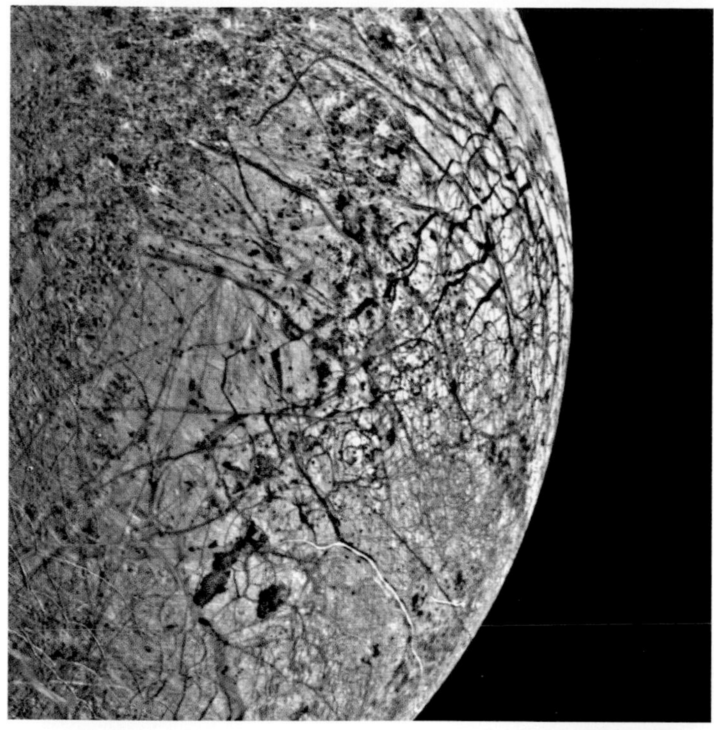

LEFT: This early image of Europa was taken by Voyager in 1979, from a distance of 241,600 kilometres (149,800 miles). The visible complex patterns suggested there were cracks over the moon's surface.

BELOW: This photograph of the Getz Ice Shelf along Antarctica's Amundsen Coast, taken by NASA scientists, reveals the similarity between Earth's icebergs and the surface of Europa.

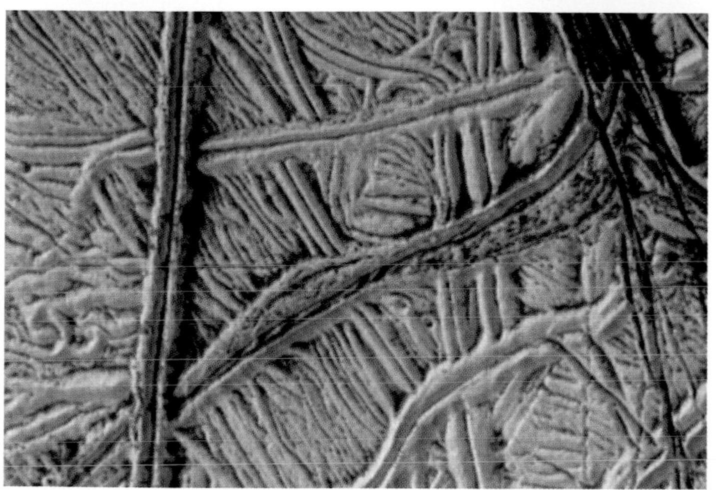

Deep cracks crisscross the surface of Europa, where ice has been broken into icebergs and jumbled up before freezing.

complexity on the surface – areas where the ice has been broken into icebergs and jumbled up before refreezing.

Compare this to an image of sea ice on Earth and the similarity is immediately apparent. These formations on our planet that resemble so closely the Conamara region of Europa are caused by the movements of the ocean under the ice that make it bend and crack. This is highly suggestive that something similar may be happening on Europa, and therefore there must be liquid water, an ocean, under Europa's icy shell.

Since the Voyager spacecraft first photographed these cracks in the late 1970s, we have been studying them to try to understand the exact forces that created them. Almost twenty years after Voyager, the Galileo probe arrived and began taking images of much higher quality that allowed detailed geological maps to be made of the surface. Studying these maps and trying to understand the origin and evolution of the cracks has provided powerful additional evidence for the theory of a subterranean ocean on Europa ◉

EUROPA'S ECCENTRIC ORBIT

As Europa orbits around Jupiter, it doesn't quite follow a circle. This slight eccentricity of the orbit is maintained by the gravitational interaction with its neighbouring moons Io and Ganymede. Just as for the volcanic moon Io, the effect of the eccentric orbit on Europa is profound. Europa is stretched and squashed as it sweeps close to and then further away from Jupiter on every orbit. This causes the interior of the moon to heat up by friction, which melts the frozen ice to produce a subterranean ocean.

The effects of the tidal stretching are not just confined to heating, however. As the surface of Europa is constantly stressed, the ice fractures and cracks, but the position of those cracks is not quite where you'd expect them to be. Europa, as with many moons in the Solar System, including our own, is tidally locked to its parent planet and so always keeps the same face pointing towards it. With this knowledge, planetary geologists can calculate exactly how and where these cracks in the ice should form, but they find that only the youngest cracks are where they are expected to be, the older cracks appear to have drifted across the surface of the moon over time. The preferred explanation for this is that the moon's surface is rotating at a different rate to its interior. The icy surface of Europa has shifted since the formation of the cracks. The only way this could have happened over a short period of time is if Europa has an ocean of liquid water surrounding the entire moon, between the rocky core and the icy shell, that allows the surface to slip around freely. The cracks could then have formed and literally slipped around the moon over time.

ORBITAL RESONANCE, FORCED ECCENTRICITY
Orbital resonance occurs when the orbital period of two satellites are related by an integer ratio, causing them to periodically align. Every time the satellites are aligned, the inner satellite S2 experiences a gravitational kick from the outer satellite S1. The effect is to pull S2 away from the planet. The net effect over a long period of time is to force S2 into an elliptical orbit. Note that, at the same time, S1 feels a gravitational kick from S1, also moving into an elliptical orbit.

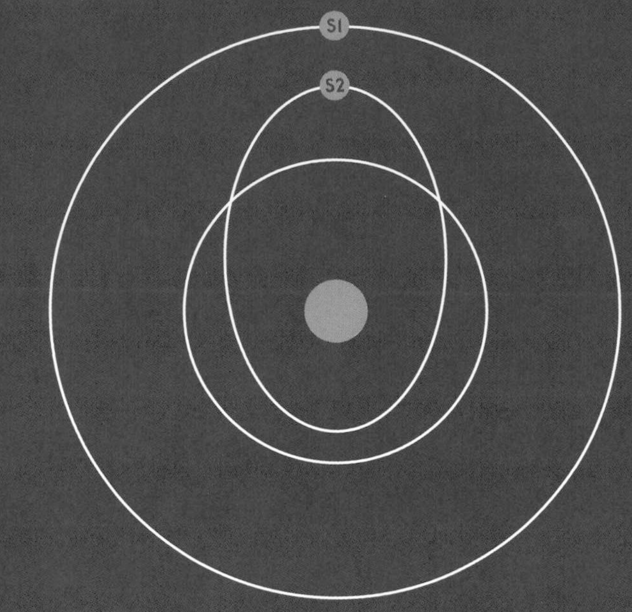

GALILEAN RESONANCE
The Galilean resonance system is made up of three satellites: Io, Europa and Ganymede in a 1:2:4 orbital resonance. For every two orbits Io makes, Europa makes one; for every two orbits Europa makes, Ganymede makes one. The satellites do not align at one common conjunction point: Io and Europa align as shown in the diagram. Europa and Ganymede have a conjunction point 180 degrees around the orbital plane.

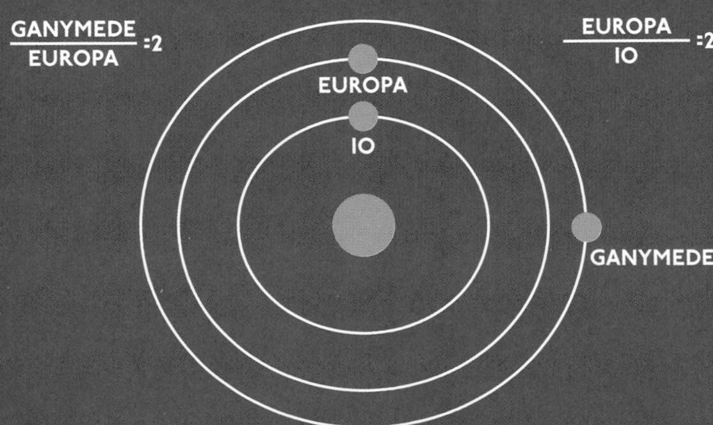

EUROPA'S INTERIOR
Beneath Europa's icy exterior is believed to lie an ocean 100 kilometres (60 miles) deep, and beneath that a rocky interior at the heart of which is a metallic core.

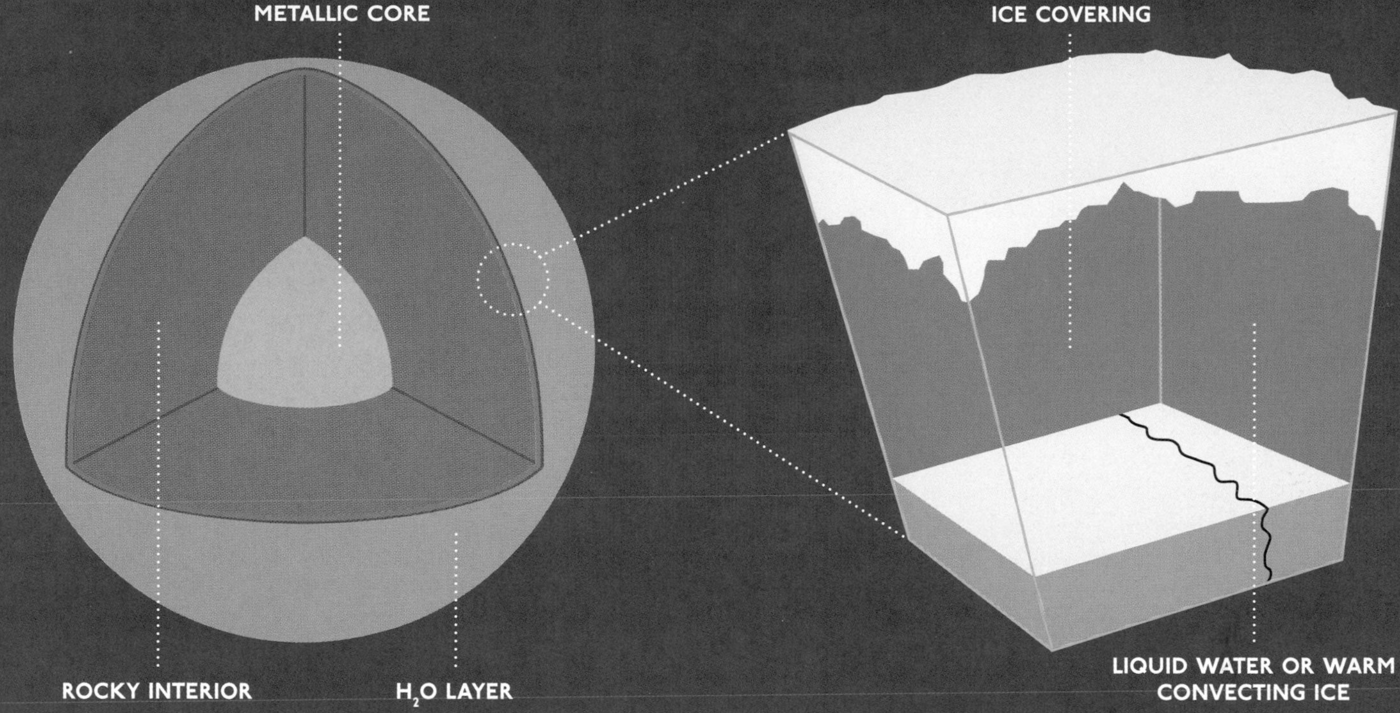

CRACKS ON EUROPA'S SURFACE
Europa is repeatedly squeezed and stretched during its elliptical orbit, due to Jupiter's strong gravitational field. Jupiter's gravity also causes the underground ocean to be raised and lowered, just like the tides on Earth. This puts pressure on the moon's icy surface, causing it to crack. The crack is then opened and closed by tidal flexing, causing the ridge-like structures seen across the surface.

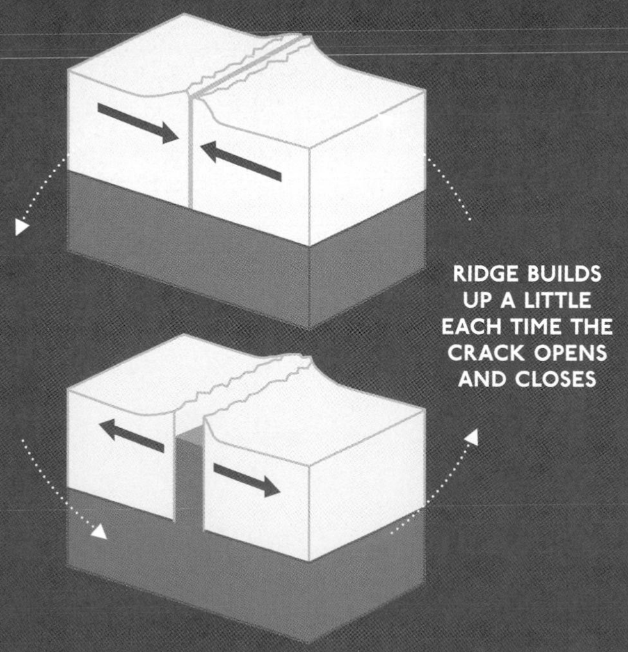

There is one final piece of evidence that completes the compelling case for the existence of liquid water beneath the surface of this frozen moon. Measurements of Europa's magnetic field and its interaction with the powerful magnetic field of its parent planet have suggested its ocean may be salt water and may be a staggering 100 kilometres (60 miles) deep. That means there is more than twice as much life-giving liquid water on this tiny moon than in all of Earth's oceans combined. This is a remarkable conclusion, especially when you consider that we've never landed on Europa, let alone burrowed through its icy shell to see what lies beneath. Fortunately and wonderfully, plans are now afoot for a joint NASA/ESA mission to launch a robotic explorer in 2020, which is being designed to land on the surface of this potential paradise moon and unlock its secrets.

If the conclusions from these various measurements of Europa are correct, and her vast salty ocean does exist, then we already know how life could, in principle, thrive there. Hidden below the ice and unable to capture the energy of the Sun, life on Europa may well mimic the ecosystems we see clustered around the hydrothermal vents in the deep oceans of our own planet; dependent on chemosynthesis rather than on photosynthesis. We don't know if Europa's ocean is too salty or too cold to support life, or if its ecosystem has remained stable for long enough for life to develop, but the discoveries we have made two-thirds of a billion kilometres away, combined with the discoveries we have made by exploring our own oceans, have created a tantalising case for this being the most likely habitable environment in our solar system

VATNAJOKULL GLACIER, ICELAND

BELOW: Here at the Vatnajokull Glacier in Iceland, it seems implausible that any life form could exist in these frozen conditions, but scientists are using just such locations to disprove this theory. The ice core taken from this ice cave revealed bacteria living in the frozen sample.

It is not just the evidence for a hidden ocean that has catapulted Europa to the forefront of our search for alien life. Scientists here on Earth are beginning to rewrite our understanding of how life can withstand not just the extremes of the deep ocean but also the extreme environments on the surface of our planet. The spectacular ice caves in the Vatnajokull Glacier are a beautiful demonstration of how the laws of physics can conspire to create an awe-inspiring cathedral of ice.

This cave tunnels into the heart of the glacier, where the ice has been frozen for 1,000 years. The walls are the deepest, purest crystal blue, cut through by lines of fine silt that tell the story of the eruptions of Iceland's many volcanoes over the millennia it took for the glacier to form. But there is more to be found in these ice caves than mere beauty; they may also tell us something about what we could expect to find within the frozen ice fields of Europa.

This is what brings astro-biologists like NASA scientist Richard Hoover to locations such as these, and us alongside him. He has spent his career looking for life in the most unlikely places, and in this particular location he is interested in taking samples of the ancient ice to explore what might be lurking inside. Conventional thinking would suggest that any organisms found in ice of this age would not be living, but recent work is beginning to challenge our understanding of the boundaries of life. Once he had taken an ice core, we headed back to our freezing base in a small and isolated wooden building at the foot of the glacier. Of all the places I filmed for *Wonders of the Solar System*, our little base in the snow in the middle of Iceland in November was undoubtedly the coldest.

Richard Hoover explained the thinking behind his research ideas. 'For a long time it was thought that micro-organisms in ice were present only in the state of what is called deep antibiosis – suspended animation. It's now becoming quite clear that that isn't necessarily the case for all the micro-organisms. There may be others that are actually actively living in the ice.'

It's an incredible thought, to think that this beautiful cave could be alive, populated by living things, not frozen but truly living, dividing and reproducing. It's this prospect of finding things living in solid ice that has had an enormous impact on our ideas of where life could survive in the Solar

If life can exist here, trapped in the deep glaciers of Iceland, then is it such a leap to imagine a similar life form existing in the icy crust of Europa?

System. Under a microscope you can clearly see living bacteria in Hoover's sample, organisms that, it might be inferred, have been trapped in the glacier for thousands of years. You're seeing life in ice; a form of organism that Hoover believes is actually adapted to live in this frozen environment. 'We now know that some micro-organisms are capable of actually causing the ice to melt because they generate essentially anti-freeze proteins,' he explains. 'They change the temperature at which ice goes from a solid state to a liquid state, forming little tiny pockets, maybe only a few microns in diameter. If they can make a two- or three-micron diameter ball of liquid water and they have the ability to move, then that bacterium is now not in a glacier, he's in an ocean.'

If life can exist here, trapped in the deep glaciers of Iceland, then is it such a leap to imagine a similar life form existing in the icy crust of Europa? This also raises the intriguing possibility of an organic explanation for the mysterious red stains that cover the moon. The Lineae are the most striking of all of Europa's features, creating a network of colour across the entire surface of the moon. The larger formations are more than twenty kilometres (twelve miles) across, interwoven with patterns of dark and light material. This wide variety of colour could suggest the presence of microbial life, since these tell-tale colours are very reminiscent of the cyanobacteria we find on Earth. Could it really be that the ice of Europa contains viable living micro-organisms? It's a controversial idea, but it is a dizzying thought that the mysterious red stains on the surface of Europa may be the visible signs of alien life.

The question is as evocative as it is ancient. Are we alone in the Universe? Is our pale blue world the only planet amongst the billions of planets in our galaxy, amongst the billions of galaxies in the Universe, to harbour life? This is surely one of the most important and profound questions, perhaps the most important question, that we can ask. Think about what it would mean for us to have an answer. If the answer is that there is no other life in the Solar System, in our nearby star systems, perhaps throughout vast swathes of the Milky Way or even across the Universe, then how valuable would that make planet Earth? How valuable would that make us? A single island of beauty and meaning in a meaningless void. But imagine the alternative answer. What if it transpires that on every moon of every planet, where the conditions are right, life does survive and flourish. What if we discover that the Universe is teeming with life and that we are part of a vast and vital cosmic community. How might that change our behaviour? What would that tell us about the way we respond to our differences, with other species and with each other? We should then see the Earth as one village amidst a billion continents – our own local community adrift in a sea of alien life.

If knowing the answer to the question is so profoundly important, then surely striving to find the answer should be of overwhelming importance. I believe it's the most important of the great and timeless existential questions that we as a civilisation can possibly ask, because we have a chance of answering it. It would be a gross and unforgivable dereliction of our duty as civilised beings to sit tight and wonder rather than to stand up and explore.

BELOW: People crowd the streets of the Shibuya area of Japan, going about their busy lives. Few of us have time to stop and think that Earth is the only place in the Solar System where life is complex and stable enough to build a civilisation – this is what makes our planet so precious.

What we've learned from exploring such extreme places on Earth is that if there is life out there in the Solar System, it will almost certainly be simple: single-celled organisms like bacteria eking out an existence in the most hostile of environments.

One thing seems certain: the only place in the Solar System where there is life complex enough to build a civilisation is here on planet Earth. But how did that happen? What is it that makes our world so special, because, after all, everything in the Solar System shares the same genesis?

Our little corner of the galaxy was created out of nothing more than a spinning cloud of gas and dust 4.5 billion years ago. Solid worlds condensed out of the swirling mists, but each world was radically different. Across the Solar System there are worlds that erupt with volcanoes of sulphur and others with geysers of ice; there are worlds with rich atmospheres and swirling storms, and there are moons with surfaces sculpted from ice that conceal oceans of liquid water. But amidst all the wonders, there's only one world where the laws of physics have conspired to combine all these features in one place.

Only on Earth are the temperatures and atmospheric pressure just right to allow oceans of liquid water to exist on the surface of the planet. Earth is big enough to have retained its molten core that not only powers geysers and volcanoes, but also produces our magnetic field that fends off the solar wind and protects our thick, nurturing atmosphere.

It is the combination of all these wonders in one place that allowed life to begin and to get a foothold here on Earth. Yet to allow that life to evolve into such complex creatures as ourselves requires one more ingredient, and that is time, deep time – the vast and sweeping vistas of time over which mountains rise and fall, planets are formed and stars live and die. When all is said and done, it is perhaps this that makes the Earth so rare and so precious in the cosmos, because it has been stable enough for long enough for life to evolve into such magnificent complexity.

Life on Earth today is the result of hundreds of millions of years of stability, and the most remarkable, complex and wonderful component in this priceless and possibly uniquely sophisticated and interconnected ecosystem is us, humankind, a species that has developed to the point where we can bend and shape and change the world around us. We have even left our home planet behind to begin exploring our cosmic surroundings. We are powerful, and with that power comes great responsibility, for we are now the custodians of Earth. Through our evolved intelligence, we have the capability to protect, damage or destroy it as we chose. And it is a choice – a choice that is best informed by perspective ●

You could take the view that our exploration of the Universe has made us somehow insignificant; one tiny planet around one star amongst hundreds of billions. But I don't take that view, because we've discovered that it takes the rarest combination of chance and the laws of Nature to produce a planet that can support a civilisation, that most magnificent structure that allows us to explore and understand the Universe. That's why, for me, our civilisation is the wonder of the Solar System, and if you were to be looking at the Earth from outside the Solar System that much would be obvious. We have written the evidence of our existence onto the surface of our planet. Our civilisation has become a beacon that identifies our planet as home to life.

'We shall not cease from exploration.
And the end of all our exploring
Will be to arrive where we started
And know the place for the first time.'

– T. S. Eliot

RIGHT: Having begun to explore our cosmic surroundings, we are more aware than ever before of our fragility and our responsibility to protect planet Earth in the future.

INDEX

Entries in *italics* denote photographs and diagrams

E

I

J

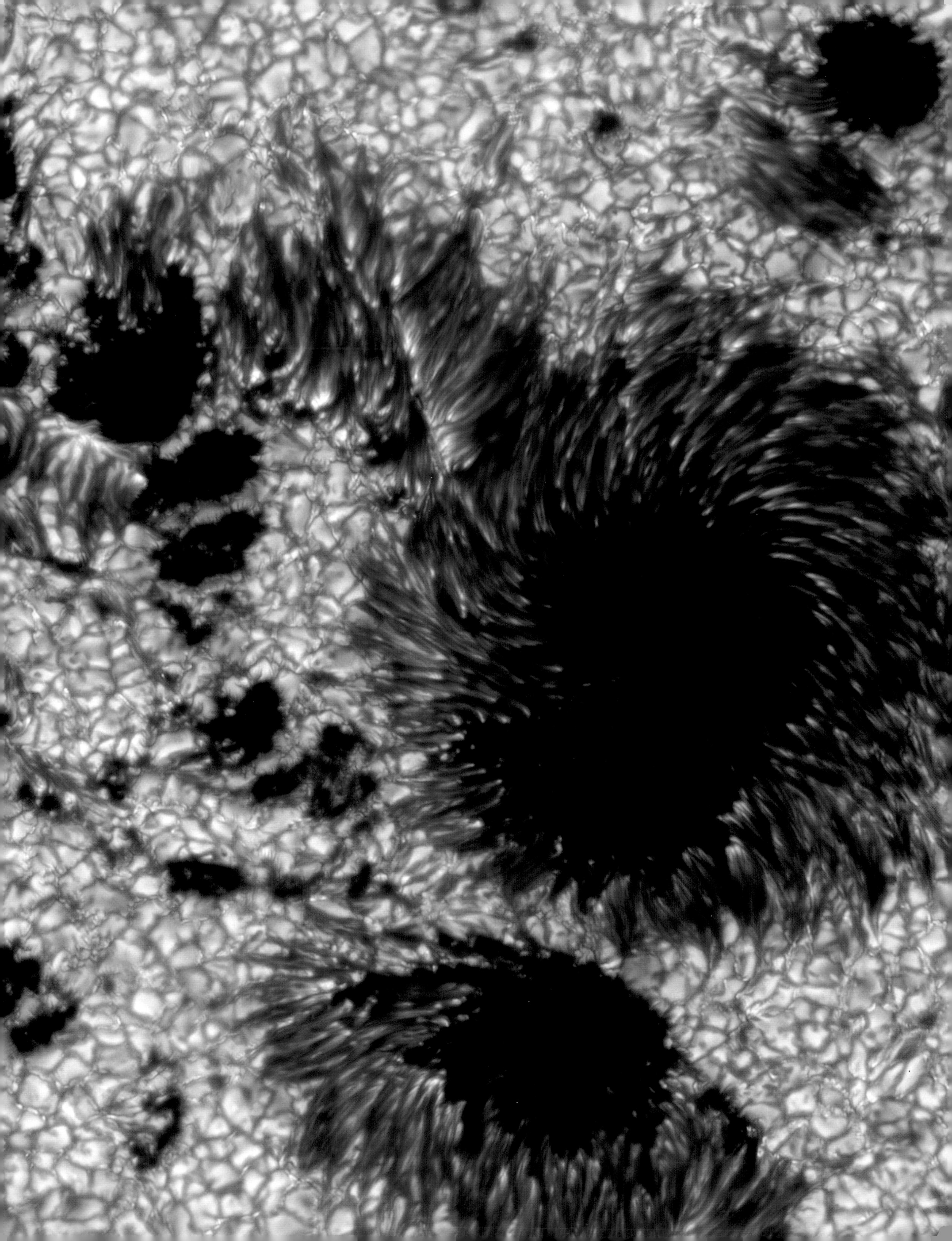

M

N

O

P

R

S

T

Z

डा. के. एल. गांगुली

PICTURE CREDITS

All pictures are copyright the BBC except:

18, 50, 62, 72, 86, 128, 142, 172, 200 Nathalie Lees © HarperCollins; 8–9 Corbis; 10–11 NASA-Hubble Heritage/digital/Science Faction/Corbis; 13 NASA/digital/Science Faction/Corbis; 28 Diego Giudice/Corbis; 47 Roger Ressmeyer with Jay Pasachoff/Williams College/Science Faction/Corbis; 56–57 Arctic-Images/Corbis; 70 Peter Richardson/Robert Harding World Imagery/Corbis; 110 David Nunuk/Science Photo Library; 138 HO/Reuters/Corbis; 145 Jim Reed/Corbis; 174 Corbis; 181 Bettmann/Corbis; 209 National Undersea Research Program/NOAA/Science Photo Library; 228 Sinclair Stammers/Science Photo Library; 240 TWPhoto/Corbis; 248 Scharmer et al, Royal Swedish Academy of Sciences/Science Photo Library; 253 NASA/JPL/SSI/Science Photo Library; 14, 17, 25 (both), 31, 35, 38 (both), 48, 53, 58, 59, 60 (top), 61 (top), 75, 80, 81, 82, 89 (left), 95 (top 2), 100 (bottom), 108, 109, 118, 121, 122, 123, 133 (all), 134, 135, 139, 140 (top), 146, 147, 148, 150, 153, 156, 159, 164, 169 (both), 170, 177 (both), 179 (both), 182, 183, 185 (both), 188 (top), 190, 191, 192, 193, 198, 219, 224 (left), 231, 232, 233 (all), 243 NASA; 32-33 (bottom), 39, 60 (bottom), 69 (both), 85, 92, 97, 100 (top), 157 Prime Focus/BBC; 41, 42, 54 (bottom), 90 (top), 107, 125, 136, 154, 236 Brian Cox

P248: Sunspots are cooler regions of the Sun's surface that appear dark against their brighter, hotter surroundings.

P253: Saturn and its rings, as seen by the wide-angled camera on NASA's Cassini spacecraft.

ACKNOWLEDGEMENTS

In writing this book we are indebted to the hard work and creativity of all those who were involved in the BBC television production of *Wonders of the Solar System*. Danielle Peck who lead the team with great passion and drive, Gideon Bradshaw, Michael Lachmann, Chris Holt and Paul Olding who produced and directed such beautiful films.

We'd also like to thank, Rebecca Edwards, Diana Ellis-Hill, Tom Ranson, Ben Finney, Laura Mulholland, Kevin White, George McMillan, Paul Jenkins, Simon Farmer, Chris Titus King, Freddie Claire, Darren Jonusas, Gerard Evans, Martin Johnson, Louise Salkow, Lee Sutton, Laura Davey, Rebecca Lavender, Alison Castle and David Pembrey, Sheridan Tongue, Donna Dixon, Julie Wilkinson, Sara Revell, Anna Charlton, Louise Farley, Nicola Kingham and the team at Prime Focus London.

We'd also like to thank Dr Andy Pilkington for his work on the book and Professor Jeff Forshaw and Professor John Zarnecki for the generous time and thought they gave to the project.

Brian would also like to thank The University of Manchester and The Royal Society for allowing him the time to make *Wonders*. He is also particularly indebted to Professor Alan Gilbert (11 September 1944 – 27 July 2010), the Inaugural President and Vice Chancellor of The University of Manchester, who knew the true value of universities and encouraged his institution and academics to make a difference to society far beyond the ivory towers.

PART 2

WONDERS OF THE UNIVERSE

WILLIAM COLLINS

CHAPTER 1

MESSENGERS

CHAPTER 2

STARDUST

CHAPTER 3

FALLING

CHAPTER 4

DESTINY

G-STAR

INTRODUCTION

THE UNIVERSE

At 13.7 billion years old, 93 billion light years across and filled with 100 billion galaxies – each containing hundreds of billions of stars – the Universe as revealed by modern science is humbling in scale and dazzling in beauty. But, paradoxically, as our knowledge of the Universe has expanded, so the division between us and the cosmos has melted away. The Universe may turn out to be infinite in extent and full of alien worlds beyond imagination, but current scientific thinking suggests that we need it all in order to exist. Without the stars, there would be no ingredients to build us; without the Universe's great age, there would be no time for the stars to perform their alchemy. The Universe cannot be old without being vast; there may be no waste or redundancy in this potentially infinite arena if there are to be observers present to gaze upon its wonders.

The story of the Universe is therefore our story; tracing our origins back beyond the dawn of man, beyond the origin of life on Earth, and even beyond the formation of Earth itself; back to events – perhaps inevitable, perhaps chance ones – that occurred less than a billionth of a second after the Universe began.

AN ANCIENT WONDER

On Christmas Eve 1968, Apollo 8 passed into the darkness behind the Moon, and Frank Borman, Jim Lovell and William Anders became the first humans in history to lose sight of Earth. When they emerged from the Lunar shadow, they saw a crescent Earth rising against the blackness of space and chose to broadcast a creation story to the people of their home planet. A quarter of a million miles from home, lunar module pilot William Anders began:

'We are now approaching lunar sunrise and, for all the people back on Earth, the crew of Apollo 8 has a message that we would like to send to you.
In the beginning God created the heaven and the Earth.
And the Earth was without form, and void; and darkness was upon the face of the deep.
And the Spirit of God moved upon the face of the waters. And God said, Let there be light: and there was light.
And God saw the light, that it was good: and God divided the light from the darkness.'

The emergence of light from darkness is central to the creation mythologies of many cultures. The Universe begins as a void; the Maori called it *Te Kore*, the Greeks *Chaos*. The Egyptians saw the time before creation as an infinite, fathomless ocean out of which the land and the gods emerged. In some cultures, God is eternal: He created the Universe out of nothing and will outlast it. In others, such as some Hindu traditions, a vast primordial ocean predates the heavens and Earth. Lord Vishnu floated, asleep, on the ocean, entwined in the coils of a giant cobra, and only when light appeared and the darkness was banished did he awake and command the creation of the world.

We still don't know how the Universe began, but we do have very strong evidence that something interesting happened 13.75 billion years ago that can be interpreted as the beginning of our universe. We call it the Big Bang. (We must

The cosmos is about the smallest hole that a man can hide his head in.

— G.K. Chesterton

be careful with our choice of words here, because this is a book about science, and the key to good science is the separation of the known from the unknown.) This interesting thing that happened corresponds to the origin of everything we can now see in the skies. All the ingredients required to build the hundreds of billions of galaxies and thousands of trillions of suns were once contained in a volume far smaller than a single atom. Unimaginably dense and hot beyond comprehension, this tiny seed has been expanding and cooling for the last 13.75 billion years, which has been sufficient time for the laws of nature to assemble all the complexity and beauty we observe in the night skies. These natural processes have also given rise to Earth, life, and also consciousness, which in many ways is harder to comprehend than the mere emergence of the seemingly infinite stars.

Care is in order, because the very beginning – by which we mean the events that happened during the Planck epoch – the time period before a million million million million million million millionths of a second after the Big Bang, is currently beyond our understanding. This is because we lack a theory of space and time before this point, and consequently have very little to say about it. Such a theory, known as quantum gravity, is the holy grail of modern theoretical physics and is being energetically searched for by hundreds of scientists across the world. (Albert Einstein spent the last decades of his life searching in vain for it.) Conventional

When you set sail for Ithaca, wish for the road to be long, full of adventures, full of knowledge.

— C. P. Cavafy

thinking holds that both time and space began at time zero, the beginning of the Planck era. The Big Bang can therefore be regarded as the beginning of time itself, and as such it was the beginning of the Universe.

There are alternatives, however. In one theory, what we see as the Big Bang and the beginning of the Universe was caused by the collision of two pieces of space and time, known as 'branes', that had been floating forever in an infinite, pre-existing space. What we have labelled the beginning was therefore nothing more significant than a cosmic collision of two sheets of space and time.

It may be that the question 'Why is there a Universe?' will remain forever beyond us; it may also be that we will have an answer within our lifetimes, but the quest has to date proved more valuable than the answer because the ancient search for origins lies at the very heart of science. Indeed, it lies at the heart of much of human cultural development. The desire to understand events beyond the terrestrial seems to be innate, because all the great civilisations of antiquity have shared it, developing stories of beginnings, origins and endings. It is only recently that we have discovered that this quest is also profoundly useful in a practical sense. When coupled with the scientific method, this quest has allowed us not only to better understand nature, but to manipulate and control it for the enrichment of our lives through technology. The well-spring of all that we take for granted, from medical science to intercontinental air travel, is our curiosity.

THE VALUE OF WONDER

The idea that a journey to the edge of the Universe is deeply relevant to our everyday lives lies at the heart of *Wonders of the Universe*. I cannot emphasize enough my strong conviction that exploration, both intellectual and physical, is the foundation of civilisation. So whilst building rockets to the Moon and telescopes to capture the light from the most distant stars may seem like an interesting luxury, such a view would be superficial, incorrect and downright daft – to borrow a phrase from my native Oldham. We are part of the Universe; its fate is our fate; we live in it and it lives in us. How can anything be more important, relevant and useful than understanding its workings?

When we began to think about the series, we wanted to make programmes that were more than a simple tour of the wonders of the Universe. Of course black holes, colliding galaxies and stars at the edge of time are fascinating, and we see them all, but to characterise the ancient science of

PREVIOUS SPREAD AND LEFT: The work of the space programmes across the world cannot be viewed as a luxury, but rather as a necessity. It is through the missions of space shuttles such as Atlantis (left) and Endeavour (previous page) that we can truly begin to understand the origins and the workings of the Universe and use this information to plan for our future on Earth.

astronomy as a spectator sport would be to miss the point. The wonders we see through our telescopes are laboratories where we can test our understanding of the natural world in conditions so extreme that we will never be able to recreate them here on Earth. With this in mind, we decided to base the programmes around scientific themes rather than the wonders themselves.

'Messengers' is about light – our only connection with the distant Universe that may lie forever beyond our reach. But it is also about the information stored within light itself, and how that information got there; the fingerprints of the chemical elements are to be found in the most distant starlight, enabling us to know with certainty the composition of the most distant star.

'Stardust' asks an ancient question: what are the building blocks of the Universe? And also, how was the raw material of a human being assembled from the debris of the Big Bang? – a searingly hot, yet beautifully ordered fireball with no discernable structure.

'Falling' tells the story of the great sculptor of the Universe: gravity. For some reason that we do not understand, gravity is by far the weakest of the four fundamental forces in the Universe, but because it has an infinite range and acts between everything that exists, its influence is all-pervasive. Our most precise theory of gravity, Einstein's General Theory of Relativity, dates from 1915, which makes it the oldest of the modern theories of the forces. The theory of the electromagnetic force, Quantum Electrodynamics, dates from the 1950s, while the theory of the Strong Nuclear Force from the 1960s and 70s. Our description of last of the four, the Weak Nuclear Force, resides in the Standard Model of particle physics. This theory, a product of the 1970s, unifies the description of the Weak Nuclear Force with Quantum Electrodynamics, although there is a missing piece of the theory known as the Higgs Boson that is currently being searched for at the Large Hadron Collider at CERN in Geneva. Until the Higgs Boson, or whatever does its job, is found, we cannot claim to have a working description of the Weak Nuclear Force and its relationship with electromagnetism.

However despite the long pedigree and beautiful accuracy and elegance of Einstein's theory of gravity, it is known to be incomplete. Our description of the Universe breaks down in the heart of its most evocatively named wonders. Black holes are known to exist at the centre of galaxies such as the Milky Way, and are dotted throughout the cosmos; the carcasses of the most massive stars in the

RIGHT: Armed with a greater knowledge and understanding of our universe, and also with new technology and modern approaches to science, we can discover wonders of the Universe that would have remained hidden to us centuries ago. Galaxies such as the spiral-shaped Dwingeloo 1 have recently been found hidden behind the Milky Way. This discovery supports what we already know: that there are many more wonders out there in the Universe that we have yet to discover.

Universe. We see them by their influence on passing stars and by detecting the intense radiation emitted by gas and dust that has the misfortune to venture too close to their event horizons. We have even seen their formation in the most violent cosmic events – supernova explosions. These events mark the destruction of stars that once burned brightly for millennia, completed in a matter of minutes.

The final chapter, 'Destiny', delves into the distant past and the far future; following the inevitable ticking of the universal clock. It is also the chapter that most directly touches on the great contribution of engineering to our story. The science of thermodynamics, which has become our guide to the ultimate fate of the Universe, arose from considerations of the efficiency of steam engines in the nineteenth century and not a desire to peer out towards a possibly infinite future. In 'Destiny' we describe thermodynamics in detail, and show how this quintessentially nineteenth-century science allows us to speculate with some grounding in reality about events that will happen 10,000,000,000,000,000,000,000,000,000 ,000,000,000,000,000,000,000,000,000,000,000,000,000, 000,000,000,000,000,000,000,000,000,000,000,000 years from now. Not bad for the pioneers of the age of steam.

So as we look to the future and survey the wonders of our universe, we discover that Einstein's theory of gravity, our best description of the fabric of the Universe, predicts its demise inside black holes. The collapsing remnants of the most luminous stars represent the edge of our understanding of the laws of physics and therefore the edge of our understanding of the wonders of the Universe. This is exactly where every scientist wants to be. Science is a word that has many meanings; one might say science is the sum total of our knowledge of the Universe, the great library of the known, but the practice of science happens at the border between the known and the unknown. Standing on the shoulders of giants, we peer into the darkness with eyes opened not in fear but in wonder. The fervent hope of every scientist is that they glimpse something that not only requires a new scientific theory, but that requires the old theory to be replaced. Our great library is constantly being rewritten; there are no sacred tomes; there are no untouchable truths; there is no certainty; there is simply the best description we have of the Universe, based purely on our observations of its wonders.

The scientific project is ultimately modest: it doesn't seek universal truths and it doesn't seek absolutes, it simply seeks to understand – and therein lies its power and value. Science has given us the modern world, of that there can be no doubt. It has improved our lives beyond measure; increased life expectancy, decreased child mortality, eradicated many diseases and rendered many more impotent. It has given many of us the gift of time, freed us from the drudgery of mere survival and allowed us to open our minds and explore. Science is therefore a virtuous circle; its discoveries creating more time and wealth that we can, if we are wise, invest in further voyages of exploration and discovery. But for all its undoubted usefulness, I maintain that science is fuelled not by utilitarian desire but by curiosity. The exploration of the Universe and its wonders is as important as the search for new medical treatments, new energy sources or new technologies, because ultimately all these valuable advances rest on an understanding of the basic laws that govern everything in nature, from atoms to black holes and everything in between. This is why curiosity-driven science is the most valuable of pursuits, and this is why we must continue our journey into the darkness ◉

CHAPTER 1

MESSENGERS

THE STORY OF LIGHT

Throughout recorded history humans have looked up to the sky and searched for meaning in the heavens. The science of astronomy may now conjure thoughts of telescopes and planetary missions, but every modern moment of discovery has a heritage that stretches back thousands of years to the simplest of questions: what is out there? Light is the only connection we have with the Universe beyond our solar system, and the only connection our ancestors had with anything beyond Earth. Follow the light and we can journey from the confines of our planet to other worlds that orbit the Sun without ever dreaming of spacecraft. To look up is to look back in time, because the ancient beams of light are messengers from the Universe's distant past. Now, in the twentieth century, we have learnt to read the story contained in this ancient light, and it tells of the origin of the Universe.

Karnak Temple, home of Amun-Re, universal god, stands facing the Valley of the Kings across the Nile in the city of Luxor. In ancient times Luxor was known as Thebes and was the capital of Egypt during the opulent and powerful New Kingdom. At 3,500 years old, Karnak Temple is a wonder of engineering, with thousands of perfectly proportioned hieroglyphs, and an architectural masterpiece of ancient Egypt's golden age; it is a place of profound power and beauty. Ten European cathedrals would fit within its walls; the Hypostyle Hall alone, an overwhelming valley of towering pillars that once held aloft a giant roof, could comfortably contain Notre Dame Cathedral.

Religious and ceremonial architecture has had many functions throughout human history. There is undoubtedly a political aspect – these monumental edifices serve to cement the power of those who control them – but to think of the great achievements of human civilisation in these terms alone would be to miss an important point. Karnak Temple is a reaction to something far more magnificent and ancient. The scale of the architecture forcibly wrenches the mind away from human concerns and towards a place beyond the merely terrestrial. Places like this can only be built by people who have an appropriate reverence for the Universe. Karnak is both a chronicle in stone and a bridge to the answer to the eternal question: what is out there? It is an observatory, a library and an expression carved out of the desert of cosmological curiosity and the desire to explore.

Egyptian religious mythology is rich and complex. With almost 1,500 known deities, countless temples and tombs and a detailed surviving literature, the mythology of the great civilisation of the Nile is considered the most sophisticated religious system ever devised. There is no such thing as a single story or tradition, partly because the dynastic period of Egyptian civilisation waxed and waned for over 3,000 years. However, central to both life and mythology are the waters of the Nile, the great provider for this desert civilisation. The annual floods created a fertile strip along the river that is strikingly visible when flying into Luxor from Cairo, although since 1970 the Aswan Dam has halted the ancient cycle of rising and falling waters and today the verdant banks are maintained by modern irrigation techniques. The rains still fall on the mountains south of Egypt during the summer, and before the dam they caused the waters of the Nile to rise and flood low-lying land until they cease in September and the waters recede, leaving life-giving fertile soils behind.

The dominance of the great river in Egyptian life, unsurprisingly, found its way into the heart of their religious tradition. The sky was seen as a vast ocean across which the gods journeyed in boats. Egyptian creation stories speak of an infinite primordial ocean out of which a single mound

PREVIOUS PAGE: The spectacular remains and towering pillars of Karnak Temple are a testament to the Egyptian belief in the power and importance of the Amun-Re, the Sun God, in their daily life, and of the Sun itself.

LEFT: The power of the supreme god Amun-Re is felt everywhere at Karnak. Representations of him cover the walls; the carvings mostly depict him as human with a double-plumed crown of feathers alongside the Pharoah, but also in animal form as a ram.

BELOW AND RIGHT: The location and alignment of this impressive building, like everything else about it, has meaning. Egyptologists have evidence to support their belief that it was constructed as a sort of calendar; two columns frame the light of the sun as it rises on the winter solstice.

of earth arose. A lotus blossom emerged from this mound and gave birth to the Sun. In this tradition, each of the primordial elements is associated with a god. The original mound of earth is the god Tatenen, meaning 'risen land' (he also represented the fertile land that emerged from the Nile floods), while the lotus flower is the god Nefertem, the god of perfumes. Most important is the Sun God, born of the lotus blossom, who took on many forms but remained central to Egyptian religious thought for over 3,000 years. It was the Sun God who brought light to the cosmos, and with light came all of creation.

At Karnak, the Sun God reigns supreme as Amun-Re, a merger between the god Amun, the local deity of Thebes, and the ancient Sun God, Re. This tendency to merge gods is widespread in Egyptian mythology, and with the mergers comes increasing theological complexity. Amun can be seen as the hidden aspect of the Sun, sometimes associated with his voyage through the Underworld during the night. In the Egyptian *Book of the Dead*, Amun is referred to as the 'eldest of the gods of the eastern sky', symbolising his emergence as the solar deity at sunrise. As Amun-Re, he became the King of the Gods, and as Zeus-Ammon he survived into Greek and Roman times. Worship of Amun-Re as the supreme god became so widespread that the Egyptian religion became almost monotheistic during the New Kingdom. Amun-Re was said to exist in all things, and it was believed that he transcended the boundaries of space and time to be all-seeing and eternal. In this sense, he could be seen as a precursor to the gods of the Judeo-Christian and Islamic traditions.

The walls of Karnak Temple are literally covered with representations of Amun-Re, usually depicted in human form with a double-plumed crown of feathers – the precise meaning of which is unknown. He is most often seen with the Pharaoh, but he also appears at Karnak in animal form, as a ram.

The most spectacular tribute of all to Amun-Re, though, lies in Karnak's orientation to the wider Universe. The Great Hypostyle Hall, the dominant feature of the temple, is aligned such that on 21 December, the winter solstice and shortest day in the Northern Hemisphere, the disc of the Sun rises between the great pillars and floods the space with light, which comes from a position directly over a small building inside which Amun-Re himself was thought to reside. Standing beside the towering stone columns watching the solstice sunrise is a powerful experience. It connects you directly with the names of the great pharaohs of ancient Egypt, because Amenophis III, Tutankhamen and Rameses II would have stood there to greet the rising December sun over three millennia ago.

The Sun rises at a different place on the horizon each morning because the Earth's axis is tilted at 23.5 degrees to the plane of its orbit. This means that in winter in the Northern Hemisphere the Earth's North Pole is tilted away from the Sun and the Sun stays low in the sky. As Earth moves around the Sun, the North Pole gradually tilts towards the Sun and the Sun takes a higher daily arc across the sky until midsummer, when it reaches its highest point. This gradual tilting back and forth throughout the year means that the point at which the Sun rises on the eastern horizon also moves each day. If you stand facing east, the most southerly rising

point occurs at the winter solstice. The sunrise then gradually drifts northwards until it reaches its most northerly point at the summer solstice. The ancients wouldn't have known the reason for this, of course, but they would have observed that at the solstices the sunrise point stops along the horizon for a few days, then reverses its path and drifts in the other direction. The solstices would have been unique times of year and important for a civilisation that revered the Sun as a god.

Standing in Karnak Temple watching the sunrise on this special midwinter day the alignment is obvious, but proving that ancient sites are aligned with events in the sky is difficult and controversial. This is because a temple the size of Karnak will always be aligned with something in the sky, simply because it has buildings that point in all directions! However, a key piece of evidence that convinced most Egyptologists that Karnak's solstice alignment was intentional concerns the two columns on either side of the building in which Amun-Re resides – one to the left and one to the right when facing the rising Sun. These columns are delicately carved, and it is the inscriptions that suggest the sunrise alignment is deliberate. The left-hand column has an image of the Pharaoh embracing Amun-Re, and on one face are three carved papyrus stems – a plant that only grows along the northern reaches of the Nile. The right-hand column is similar in design, except the Pharaoh embraces Amun-Re wearing the crown of upper Egypt, which is south of Karnak. The three carved stems on this column are lotus blossoms, which only grow to the south.

It seems clear therefore that the columns are positioned and decorated to mark the compass directions around the temple, which is persuasive evidence that the heart of this building is aligned to capture the light from an important celestial event – the rising of the Sun in midwinter. It is a colossal representation of the details of our planet's orientation and orbit around our nearby star.

The temple represents the fascination of the ancient Egyptians with the movement of the lights they saw in the sky. Their instinct to venerate them was pre-scientific, but the building also appears to enshrine a deepening awareness of the geometry of the cosmos. By observing the varying position of sunrise, an understanding of the Earth's cycles and seasons developed, which provided essential information for planting and harvesting crops at optimum times. The development of more advanced agricultural techniques made civilisations more prosperous, ultimately giving them more time for thought, philosophy, mathematics and science. So astronomy began a virtuous cycle through which the quest to understand the heavens and their meaning lead to practical and intellectual riches beyond the imagination of the ancients.

The step from observing the regularity in the movement of the heavenly lights to modern science took much of recorded human history. The ancient Greeks began the work, but the correct description of the motion of the Sun, Moon and planets across the sky was discovered in the seventeenth century by Johannes Kepler. Removing the veil of the divine to reveal the true beauty of the cosmos was a difficult process, but the rewards that stem from that innate human fascination with the lights in the sky have proved to be incalculable ◉

By following the light we have mapped our place among the hundreds of billions of stars that make up the Milky Way Galaxy. We have visited our nearest star, Proxima Centauri, and measured its chemical compositions, and those of thousands of other stars in the sky. We have even journeyed deep into the Milky Way and stared into the black hole that lies at the centre of our galactic home. But this is just the beginning...

RIGHT: The Universe is an awe-inspiring place, full of wonder and demanding the answers to so many questions. We have so much to learn and so many places to explore.

OUR PLACE IN THE UNIVERSE

The scale of the Universe is almost impossible to comprehend and yet that's exactly what we've been able to do from the vantage point of the small rock we call Earth. As we have discovered the grand cycles that play out above our heads we have come to realise that we are part of a structure that extends way beyond our solar system and the 200 billion stars that make up our galaxy.

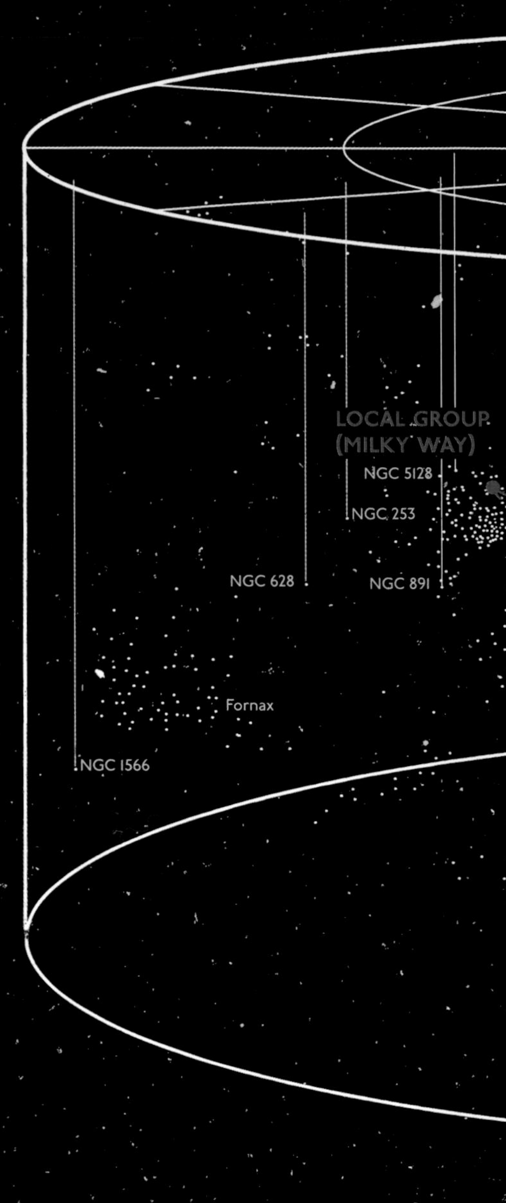

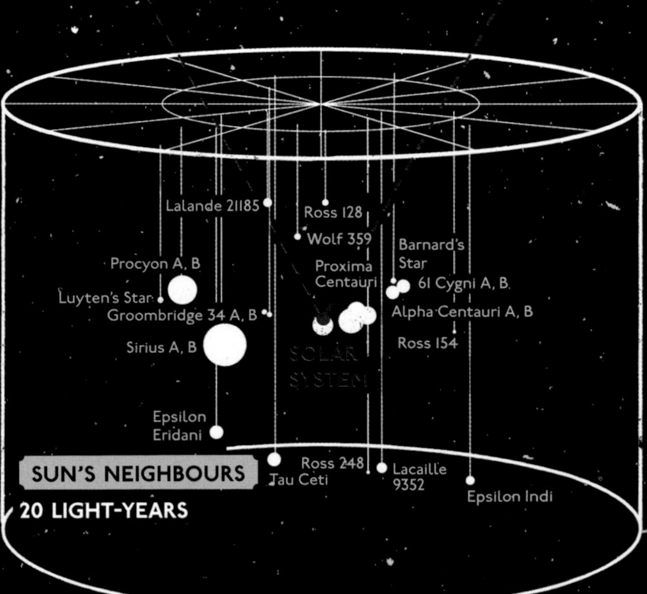

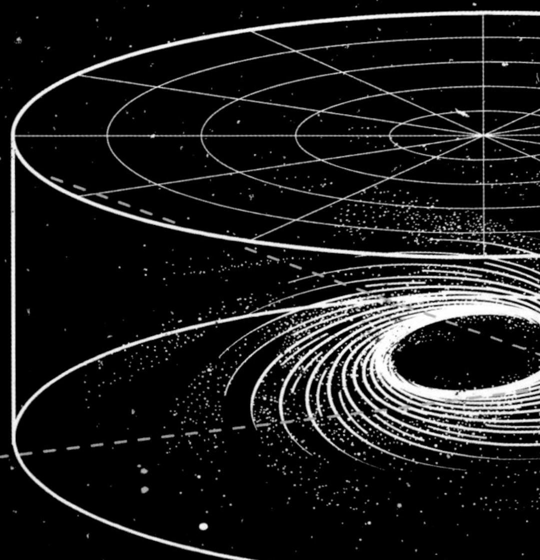

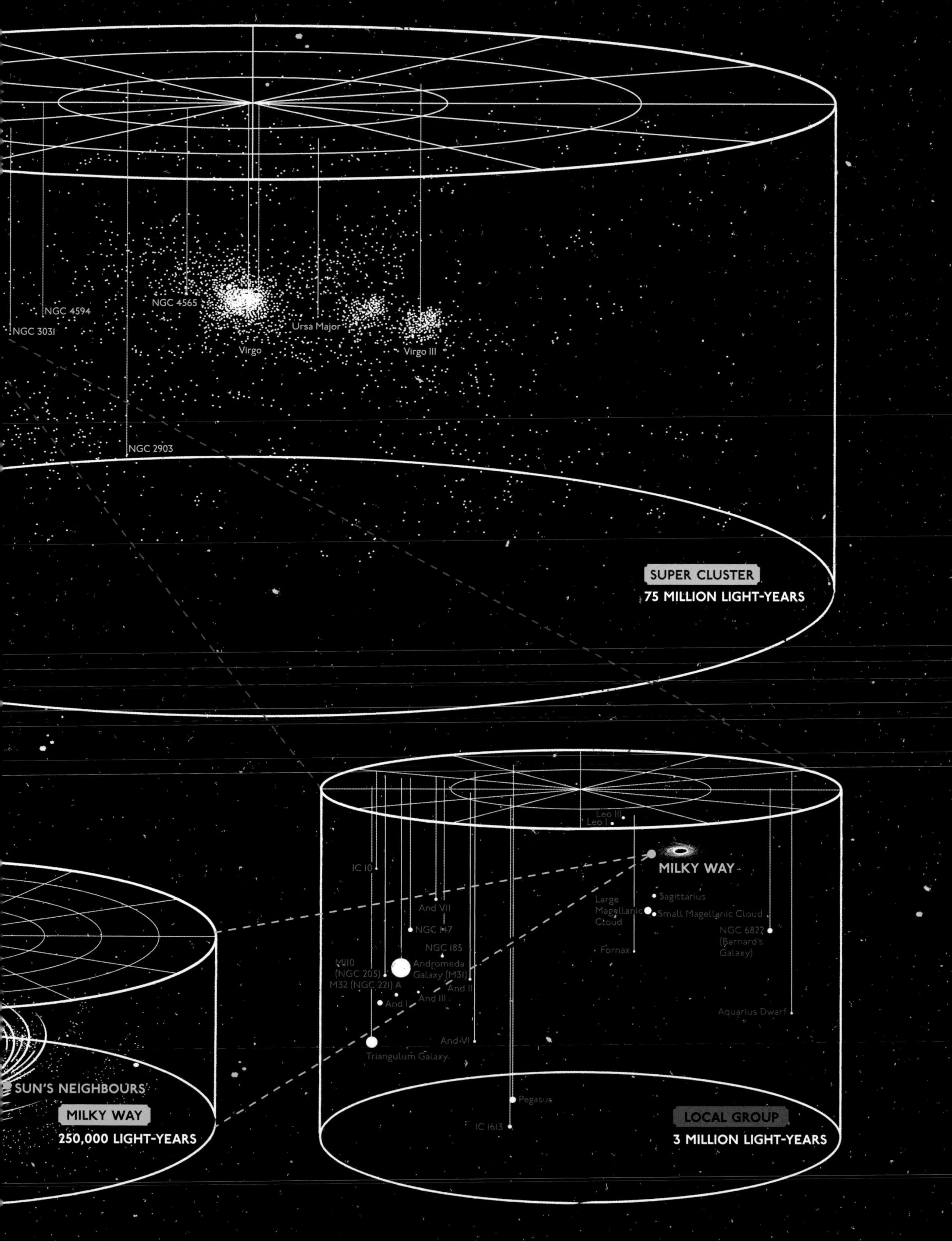
NGC 4594
NGC 3031
NGC 4565
Ursa Major
Virgo
Virgo III
NGC 2903
SUPER CLUSTER
75 MILLION LIGHT-YEARS
Leo III
Leo I
MILKY WAY
IC 10
Sagittarius
Large Magellanic Cloud
Small Magellanic Cloud
And VII
NGC 147
NGC 6822 (Barnard's Galaxy)
NGC 185
Fornax
M110 (NGC 205)
Andromeda Galaxy (M31)
M32 (NGC 221) A
And II
And III
And I
Aquarius Dwarf
And VI
Triangulum Galaxy
SUN'S NEIGHBOURS
MILKY WAY
250,000 LIGHT-YEARS
Pegasus
IC 1613
LOCAL GROUP
3 MILLION LIGHT-YEARS

OUR GALACTIC NEIGHBOURHOOD

From our small rock, we have a grandstand seat to explore our local galactic neighbourhood. Our nearest star, the Sun, is 150 million kilometres (93 million miles) away, but each night when this star disappears from view, thousands more fill the night sky. In the most privileged places on Earth, up to 10,000 stars can be seen with the naked eye, and all of them are part of the galaxy we call home.

A galaxy is a massive collection of stars, gas and dust bound together by gravity. It is a place where stars live and die, where the life cycles of our universe are played out on a gargantuan scale. We think there are around 100 billion galaxies in the observable universe, each containing many millions of stars. The smallest galaxies, known as dwarf galaxies, have as few as ten million stars. The biggest, the giants, have been estimated to contain in the region of 100 trillion. It is now widely accepted that galaxies also contain much more than just the matter we can see using our telescopes. They are thought to have giant halos of dark matter, a new form of matter unlike anything we have discovered on Earth and which interacts only weakly with normal matter. Despite this, its gravitational effect dominates the behaviour of galaxies today and most likely dominated the formation of the galaxies in the early Universe. This is because we now think that around 95 per cent of the mass of galaxies such as our own Milky Way is made up of dark matter. In some sense this makes the luminous stars, planets, gas and dust an after-thought, although because it is highly unlikely that dark matter can form into complex and beautiful structures like stars, planets and people, one might legitimately claim that it's rather less interesting. The search for the nature of dark matter is one of the great challenges for twenty-first-century physics. We shall return to the fascinating subject of dark matter later in the book.

The word 'galaxy' comes from the Greek word *galaxias*, meaning milky circle. It was first used to describe the galaxy that dominates our night skies, even though the Greeks could have had no concept of its true scale. Watching the core of our galaxy rise in the night sky is one of nature's greatest spectacles, although regrettably the light of our cities has robbed us of this majestic nightly display. For many people it looks like the rising of storm clouds on the horizon, but as the Earth turns nightly towards the centre of our galaxy, the hazy band of light reveals itself as clouds of stars – billions of them stretching thousands of light years inwards towards the galactic centre. In Greek mythology this ethereal light was described as the spilt milk from the breast of Zeus's wife, Hera, creating a faint band across the night sky. This story is the origin of the modern name for our galaxy – the Milky Way. The name entered the English language not from a scientist, but from the pen of the Medieval poet, Geoffrey Chaucer: 'See yonder, lo, the Galaxyë, Which men clepeth the Milky Wey, For hit is whyt.'

M87
Virgo A

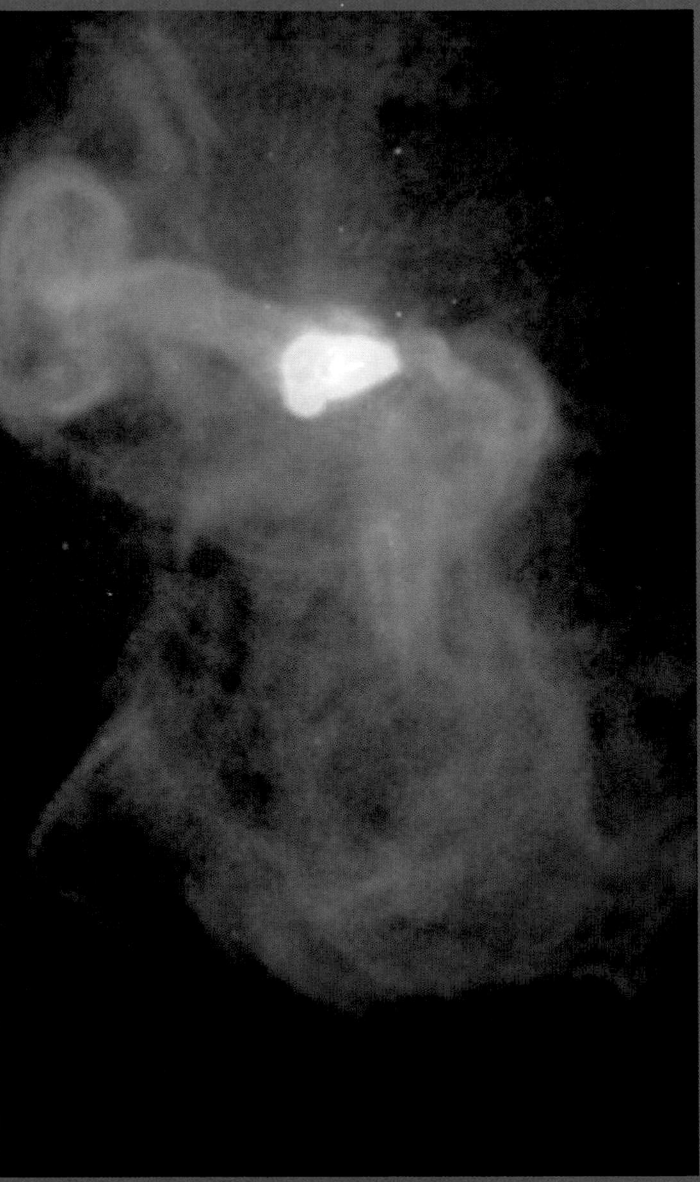

ABOVE: M87, also known as Virgo A and Messier 87, is a giant elliptical galaxy located 54 million light years away from Earth in the Virgo Cluster. In this image the central jet is visible, which is a powerful beam of hot gas produced by a massive black hole in the core of the galaxy.

M31
Andromeda Galaxy

Milky Way Galaxy

M51
Whirlpool Galaxy

M33
Triangulum Galaxy

NUBECULA MINOR
Small Magellanic cloud

DWARF GALAXY
Zwicky 18

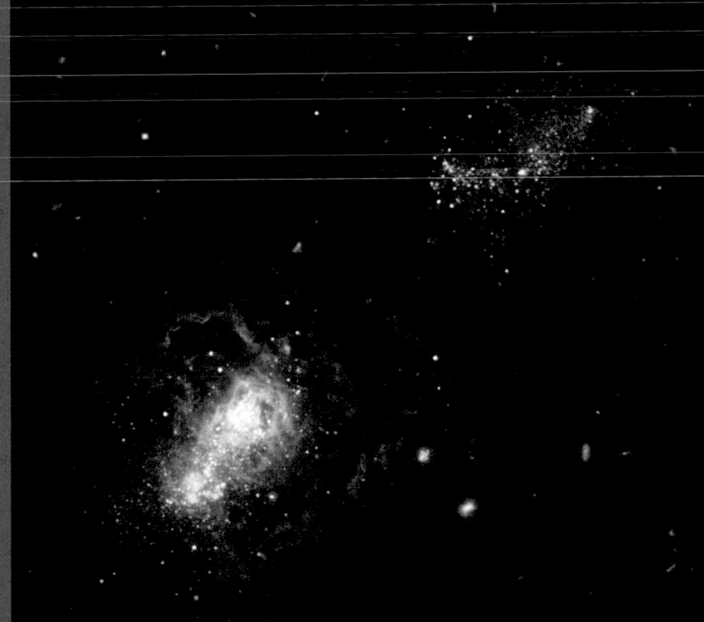

ABOVE: Taken in December 2010, this is the most detailed picture of the Andromeda Galaxy, or M31, taken so far. It is our largest and closest spiral galaxy, and in this picture we can clearly see rings of new star formations developing.

TOP: This image of the galaxy M51 clearly shows how it got its other name: the Whirlpool Galaxy. The spiral shape of the galaxy is immediately obvious, with curving arms of pinky-red, star-forming regions and blue star clusters.

ABOVE: Zwicky 18 was once thought to be the youngest galaxy, as its bright stars suggested it was only 500 million years old. However, recent Hubble Space Telescope images have identified older stars within it, making the galaxy as old as others but with new star formations.

TOP: M33, also known as the Triangulum, or Pinwheel, Galaxy is the third-largest in the Local Group of galaxies after the Milky Way and Andromeda Galaxies, of which it is thought to be a satellite.

MAPPING THE MILKY WAY GALAXY

Our galaxy, the Milky Way, contains somewhere between 200 and 400 billion stars, depending on the number of faint dwarf stars that are difficult for us to detect. The majority of stars lie in a disc around 100,000 light years in diameter and, on average, around 1,000 light years thick. These vast distances are very difficult to visualise. A distance of 100,000 light years means that light itself, travelling at 300,000 kilometres (186,000 miles) per second, would take 100,000 years to make a journey across our galaxy. Or, to put it another way, the distance between the Sun and the outermost planet of our solar system, Neptune, is around four light hours – that's one-sixth of a light day. You would have to lay around 220 million solar systems end to end to cross our galaxy.

At the centre of our galaxy, and possibly every galaxy in the Universe, there is believed to be a super-massive black hole. Astronomers believe this because of precise measurements of the orbit of a star known as S2. This star orbits around the intense source of radio waves known as Sagittarius A* (pronounced 'Sagittarius A-star') that sits at the galactic centre. S2's orbital period is just over fifteen years, which makes it the fastest-known orbiting object, reaching speeds of up to 2 per cent of the speed of light. If the precise orbital path of an object is known, the mass of the thing it is orbiting around can be calculated, and the mass of Sagittarius A* is enormous, at 4.1 million times the mass of our sun. Since the star S2 has a closest approach to the object of only seventeen light hours, it is known that Saggitarus A* must be smaller than this, otherwise S2 would literally bump into it. The only known way of cramming 4.1 million times the mass of the Sun into a space less than 17 light hours across is as a black hole, which is why astronomers are so confident that a giant black hole sits at the centre of the Milky Way. These observations have recently been confirmed and refined by studying a further twenty-seven stars, known as the S-stars, all with orbits taking them very close to Sagittarius A*.

Beyond the S-stars, the galactic centre is a melting pot of celestial activity, filled with all sorts of different systems that interact and influence each other. The Arches Cluster

The distance between the Sun and the outermost planet of our solar system, Neptune, is around four light hours – that's one-sixth of a light day. You would have to lay around 220 million solar systems end to end to cross our galaxy.

LEFT: This artist's impression shows the Arches Cluster, the densest known cluster of young stars in the Milky Way Galaxy.

ABOVE LEFT: Along with the Arches Cluster, the Quintuplet Cluster is located near the centre of the Milky Way Galaxy.

ABOVE RIGHT: The bright white dot in the centre of this image is the Pistol Star, one of the brightest stars in our galaxy.

is the densest known star cluster in the galaxy. Formed from about 150 young, intensely hot stars that dwarf our sun in size, these stars burn brightly and are consequently very short-lived, exhausting their supply of hydrogen in just a couple of million years. The Quintuplet Cluster contains one of the most luminous stars in our galaxy, the Pistol Star, which is thought to be near the end of its life and on the verge of becoming a supernova (see pages 130–1). It is in central clusters like the Arches and the Quintuplet that the greatest density of stars in our galaxy can be found. As we move out from the crowded galactic centre, the number of stars drops with distance, until we reach the sparse cloud of gas in the outer reaches of the Milky Way known as the Galactic Halo.

In 2007, scientists using the Very Large Telescope (VLT) at the Paranal Observatory in Chile were able to observe a star in the Galactic Halo that is thought to be the oldest object in the Milky Way. HE 1523-0901 is a star in the last stages of its life; known as a red giant, it is a vast structure far bigger than our sun, but much cooler at its surface. HE 1523-0901 is interesting because astronomers have been able to measure the precise quantities of five radioactive elements – uranium, thorium, europium, osmium and iridium – in the star. Using a technique very similar to carbon dating (a method archaeologists use to measure the age of organic material on Earth), astronomers have been able to get a precise age for this ancient star. Radioactive dating is an extremely precise and reliable technique when there are multiple 'radioactive clocks' ticking away at once. This is why the detection of five radioactive elements in the light from HE 1523-0901 was so important. This dying star turns out to be 13.2 billion years old – that's almost as old as the Universe itself, which began just over 13.7 billion years ago. The radioactive elements in this star would have been created in the death throes of the first generation of stars, which ended their lives in supernova explosions in the first half a billion years of the life of the Universe (see Chapter 2) ◉

THE SHAPE OF OUR GALAXY

As well as being vast and very, very old, our galaxy is also beautifully structured. Known as a barred spiral galaxy, it consists of a bar-shaped core surrounded by a disc of gas, dust and stars that creates individual spiral arms twisting out from the centre. Until very recently, it was thought that our galaxy contained only four spiral arms – Perseus, Norma, Scutum–Centaurus and Carina–Sagittarius, with our sun in an offshoot of the latter called the Orion spur – but there is now thought to be an additional arm, called the Outer arm, an extension to the Norma arm.

Close to the inner rim of the Orion spur is the most familiar star in our galaxy. The Sun was once thought to be an average star, but we now know that it shines brighter than 95 per cent of all other stars in the Milky Way. It's known as a main sequence star because it gets all its energy and produces all its light through the fusion of hydrogen into helium. Every second, the Sun burns 600 million tonnes of hydrogen in its core, producing 596 million tonnes of helium in the fusion reaction. The missing four million tonnes of mass emerges as energy, which slowly travels to the Sun's photosphere, where it is released into the galaxy and across the Universe as light ◉

THREE MAIN TYPES OF GALAXY: ELLIPTICAL, SPIRAL AND BARRED SPIRAL

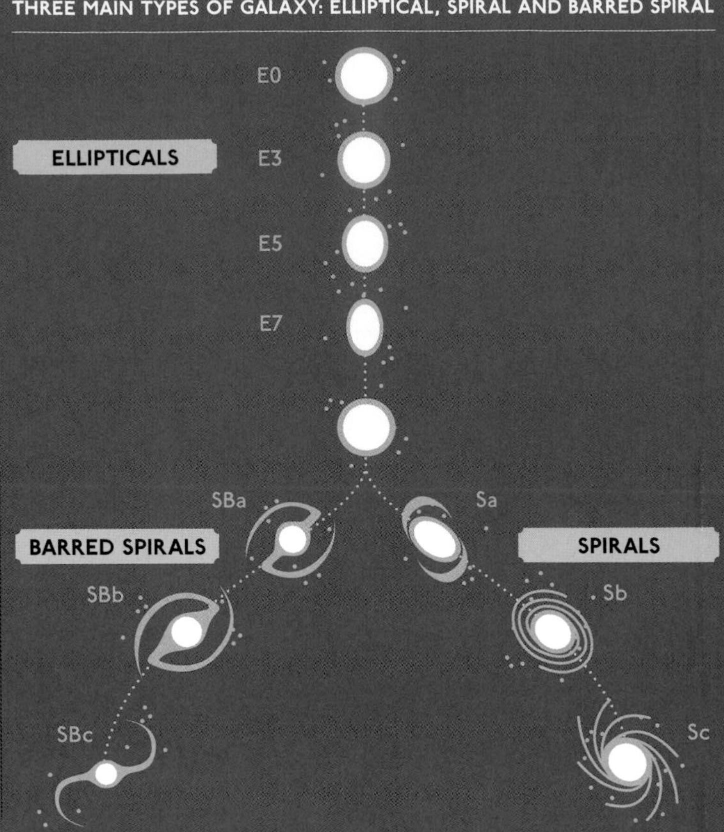

THE SPIRALLING ARMS OF THE MILKY WAY GALAXY

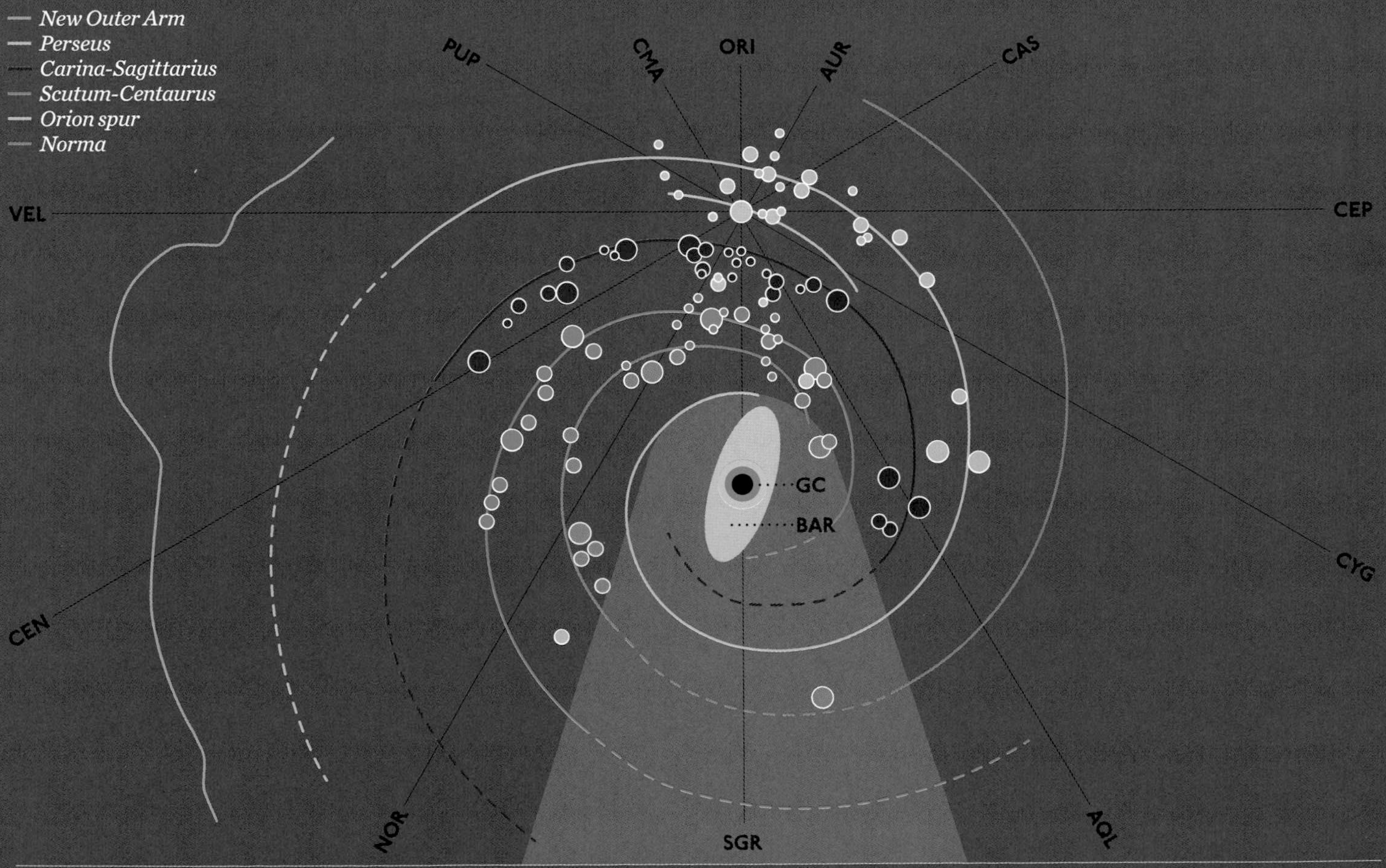

— *New Outer Arm*
— *Perseus*
— *Carina-Sagittarius*
— *Scutum-Centaurus*
— *Orion spur*
— *Norma*

A STAR IS BORN

Our sun is in the middle of its life cycle, but look out into the Milky Way and we can see the whole cycle of stellar life playing out. Roughly once a year a new light appears in our galaxy, as somewhere in the Milky Way a new star is born.

The Lagoon Nebula is one such star nursery; within this giant interstellar cloud of gas and dust, new stars are created. Discovered by French astronomer Guillaume Le Gentil in 1747, this is one of a handful of active star-forming regions in our galaxy that are visible with the naked eye. This huge cloud is slowly collapsing under its own gravity, but slightly denser regions gradually accrete more and more matter, and over time these clumps grow massive enough to turn into stars.

The centre of this vast stellar nursery, known as the Hourglass, is illuminated by an intriguing object known as Herschel 36. This star is thought to be a 'ZAMS' star (zero ago main sequence) because it has just begun to produce the dominant part of its energy from hydrogen fusion in its core. Recent measurements suggest that Herschel 36 may actually be three large young stars orbiting around each other, with the entire system having a combined mass of over fifty times that of our sun. This makes Herschel 36 a true system of giants.

BELOW: The Andromeda Galaxy is our nearest galactic neighbour, and our own Milky Way Galaxy is believed to look very much like it.

BOTTOM: Located 5,000 light years away, the Lagoon Nebula is one of a handful of active star-forming regions in our galaxy that are visible from Earth with the naked eye.

Eventually Herschel 36 and all the stars in the Milky Way will die, and when they do, many will go out in a blaze of glory.

Eta Carinae is a pair of billowing gas and dust clouds that are the remnants of a stellar explosion from an unstable star system. The system consists of at least two giant stars, and shines with a brightness four million times that of our sun. One of these stars is thought to be a Wolf-Rayet star. These stars are immense, over twenty times the mass of our sun, and are engaged in a constant struggle to hang onto their outer layers, losing vast amounts of mass every second in a powerful solar wind. In 1843, Eta Carinae became one of the brightest stars in the Universe when it exploded. The blast spat matter out at nearly 2.5 million kilometres (1.5 million miles) an hour, and was so bright that it was thought to be a supernova explosion. Eta Carinae survived intact and remains buried deep inside these clouds, but its days are numbered. Because of its immense mass, the Wolf-Rayet star is using up its hydrogen fuel at a ferocious rate. Within a few hundred thousand years, it is expected that the star will

Out in the Milky Way we can see the whole cycle of stellar life playing out. Roughly once a year a new light appears, as somewhere in the Milky Way a new star is born.

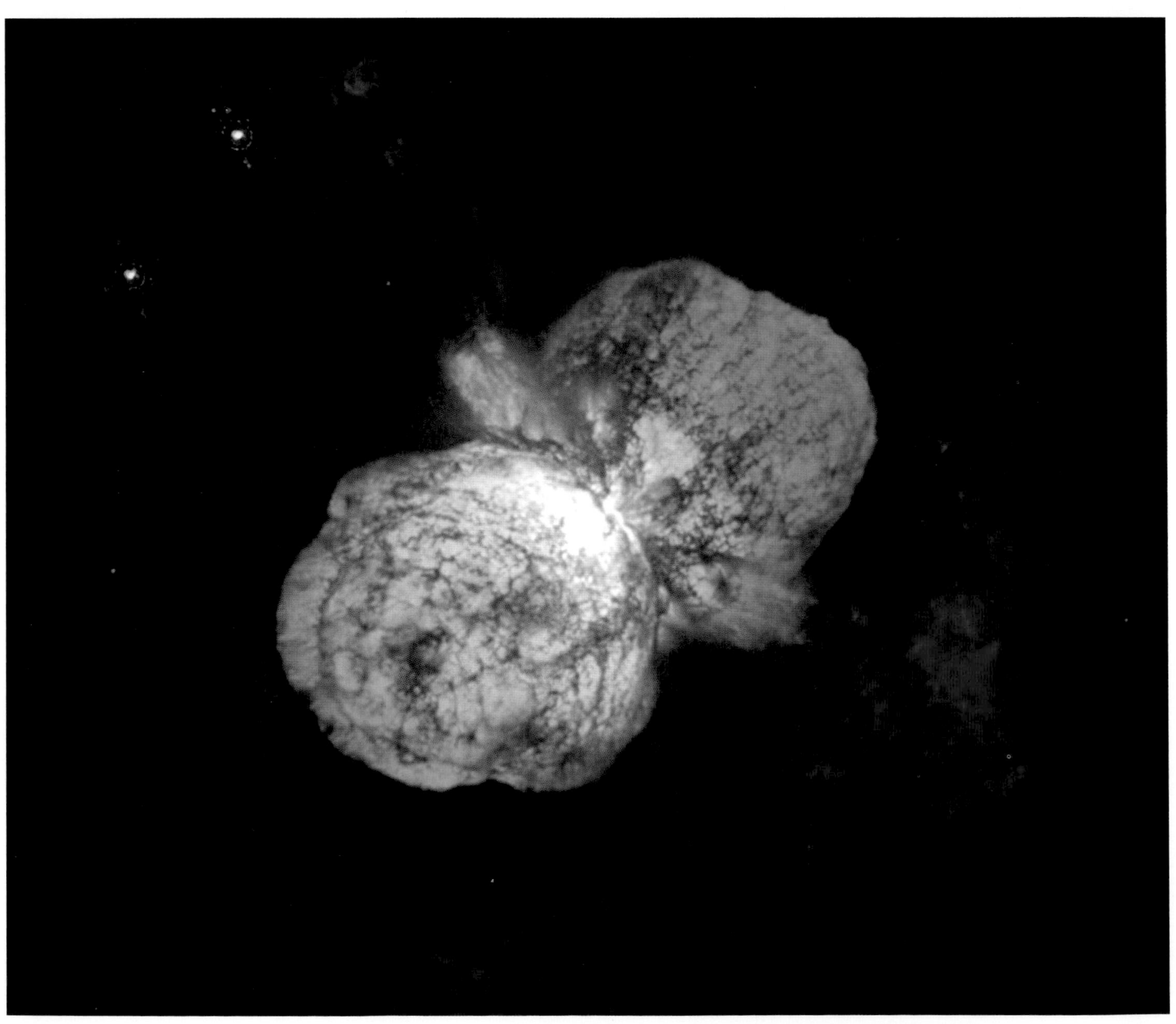

explode in a supernova or even a hypernova (the biggest explosion in the known Universe), although its fate may be sealed a lot sooner. In 2004, an explosion thought to be similar to the 1843 Eta Carinae event was seen in a galaxy over seventy million light years from the Milky Way. Just two years later, the star exploded as a supernova. Eta Carinae is very much closer – at a distance of only 7,500 light years – so as a supernova it may shine so brightly that it will be visible from Earth even in daylight.

Seeing the light from these distant worlds and watching the life cycle of the Universe unfold is a breathtaking reminder that light is the ultimate messenger; carrying information about the wonders of the Universe to us across interstellar and intergalactic distances. But light does much more than just allow us to see these distant worlds; it allows us to journey back through time, providing a direct and real connection with our past. This seemingly impossible state of affairs is made possible not only because of the information carried by the light, but by the properties of light itself ◉

LEFT: Eta Carinae is one of the most massive and visible stars in the night sky, but because of its mass it is also the most volatile and most likely to explode in the near future.

BELOW: Eventually all the stars in the Milky Way will die, many in spectacular explosions. Herschel 36 was formed from just such a stellar explosion, which occurred within the Eta Carinae system.

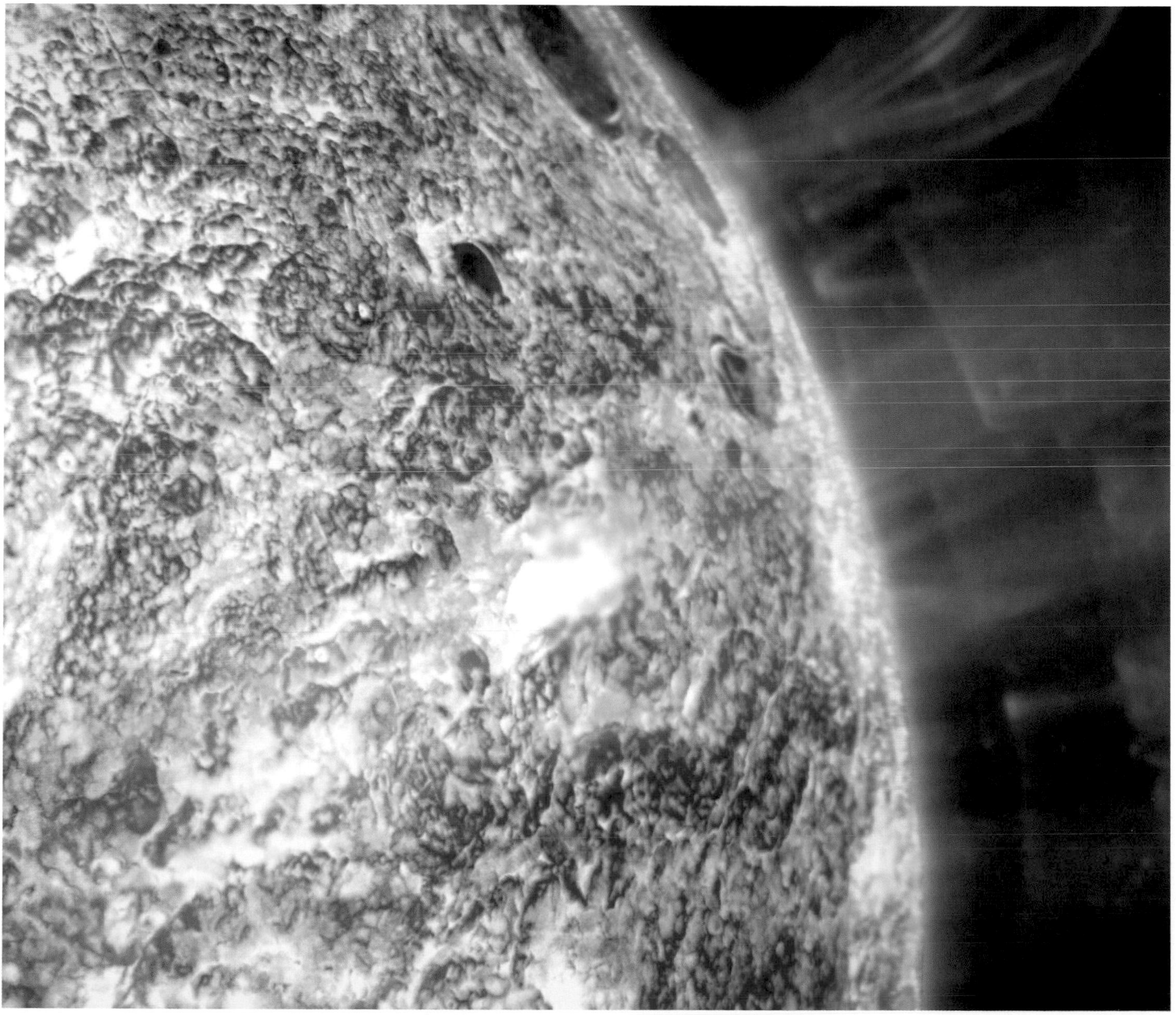

WHAT IS LIGHT?

If we aspire to understand the world around us, one of the most basic questions we must ask is about the nature of light. It is the primary way in which we observe our own planet, and the only way we will ever be able to explore the Universe beyond our galaxy. For now, even the stars are far beyond our reach, and we rely on their light alone for information about them. By the seventeenth century, many renowned scientists were studying the properties of light in detail, and parallel advances in engineering and science both provided deep insights and catalysed each other. The studies of Kepler, Galileo and Descartes, and some of the later true greats of physics – Huygens, Hooke and Newton – were all fuelled by the desire to build better lenses for microscopes and telescopes to enable them to explore the Universe on every scale, and to make great scientific discoveries and advances in the basic science itself.

YOUNG'S DOUBLE-SLIT EXPERIMENT

BELOW: The results of Young's double-slit experiment are revealed in this detailed, wide pattern. The experiment demonstrates the inseparability of the wave and particle natures of light and other quantum particles.

By the end of the seventeenth century, two competing theories for light had emerged – both of which are correct. On one side was Sir Isaac Newton, who believed that light was composed of particles – or 'corpuscles', as he called them in his *Hypothesis of Light*, published in 1675. On the other were Newton's great scientific adversary, Robert Hooke, and the Dutch physicist and astronomer, Christiaan Huygens. The particle/wave debate rumbled on until the turn of the nineteenth century, with most physicists siding with Newton. There were some notable exceptions, including the great mathematician Leonhard Euler, who felt that the phenomena of diffraction could only be explained by a wave theory. In 1801, the English doctor Thomas Young appeared to settle the matter once and for all when he reported the results from his famous double-slit experiment, which clearly showed that light diffracted, and therefore must travel in the form of a wave.

Diffraction is a fascinating and beautiful phenomena that is very difficult to explain without waves. If you shine light onto a screen through a barrier with a very thin slit cut into it, you don't see a bright light on the screen opposite the slit, but instead you see a complex but regular pattern of light and dark areas.

The explanation for this is that when you mix lots of waves together they don't only have to add up. Imagine two waves on top of each other with exactly the same wavelength and wave height (technically known as the amplitude), but aligned precisely so that the peak of one wave lies directly on the trough of the other (in more technical language, we say that the waves are 180 degrees out of phase), and so the waves cancel each other out. If these waves were light waves you would get darkness! This is exactly what is seen in diffraction experiments through small slits. The slits act like lots of little sources of light, all slightly displaced from one another. This means that there will be places beyond the slits where the waves cancel each other out, and places where they will add up, leading to the light and dark areas seen by experimenters like Young. This was taken as clear evidence that light was some kind of wave – but waves of what?

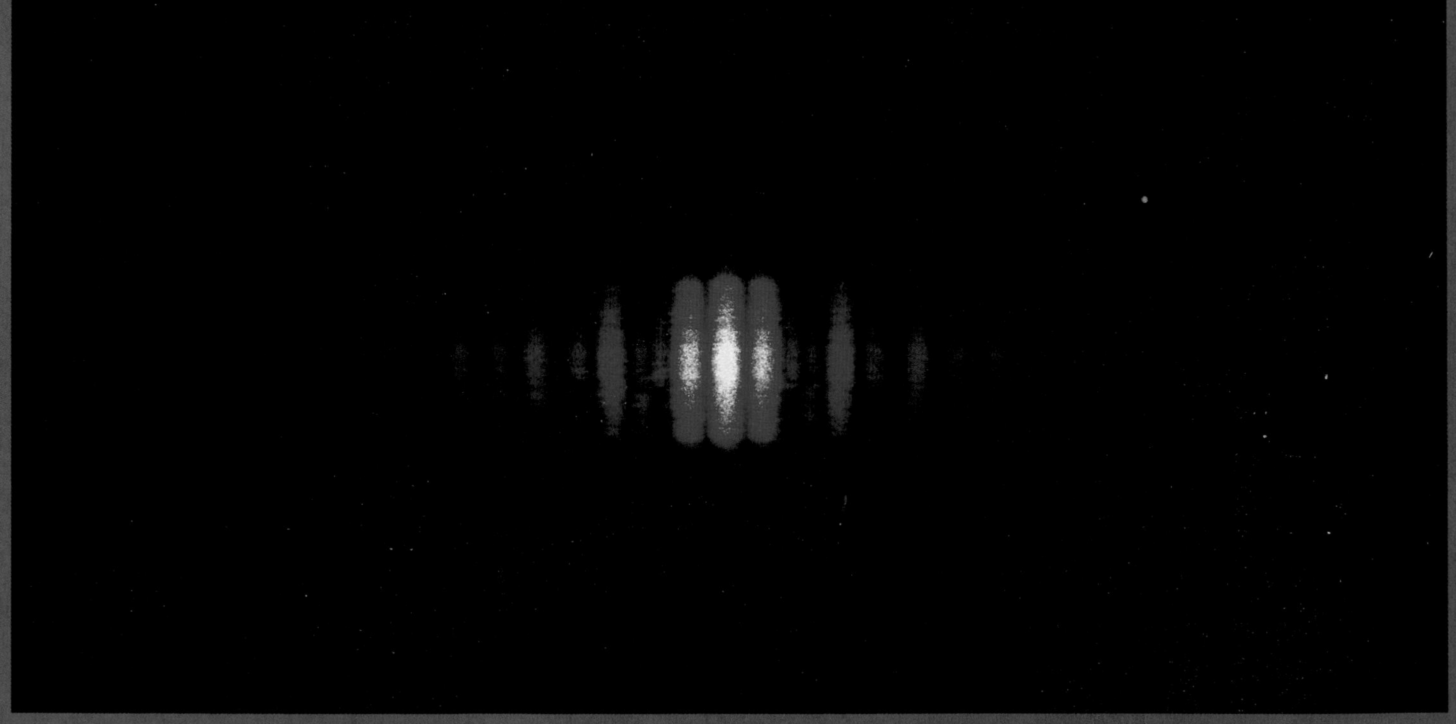

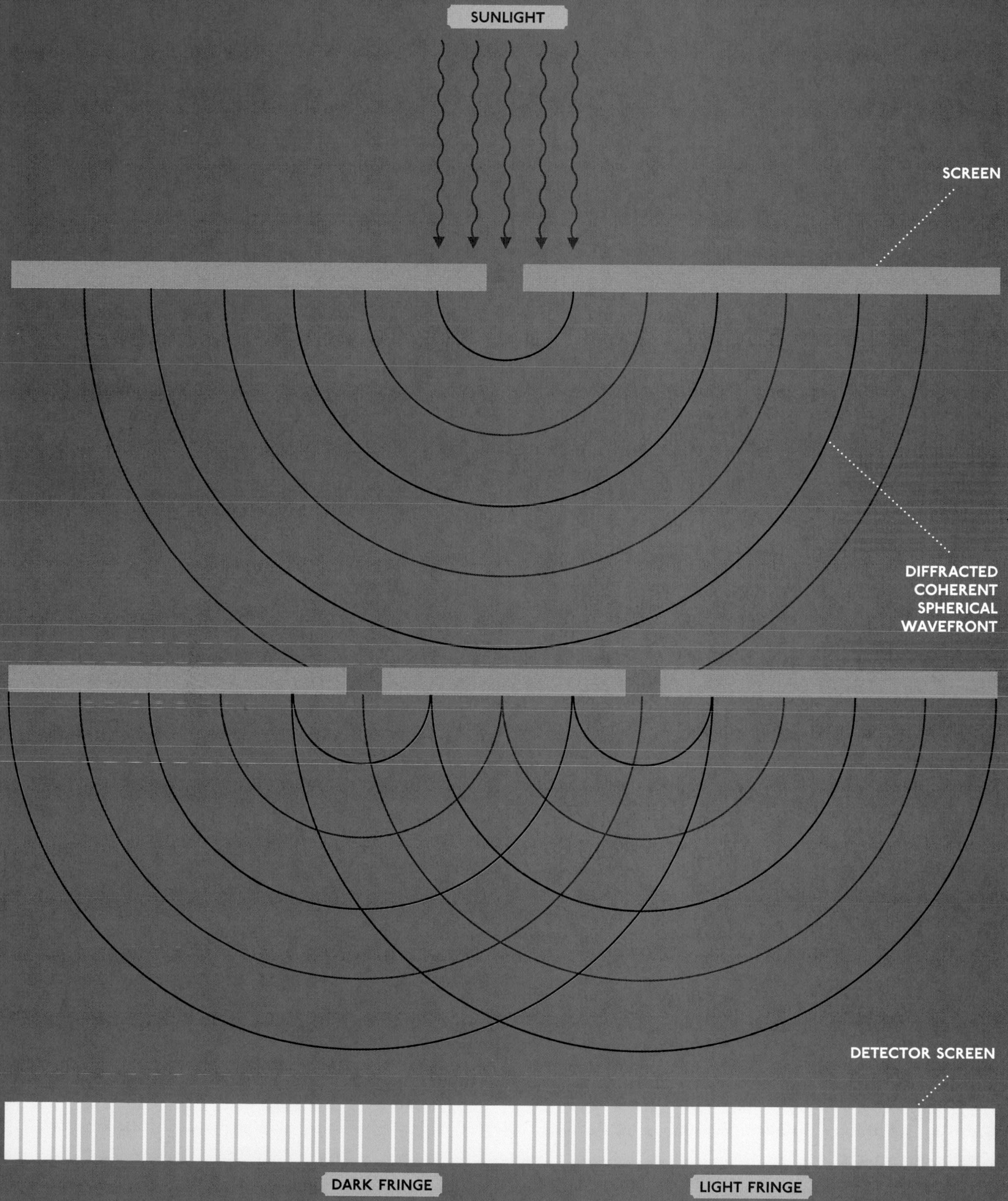

SUNLIGHT
SCREEN
DIFFRACTED COHERENT SPHERICAL WAVEFRONT
DETECTOR SCREEN
DARK FRINGE
LIGHT FRINGE

MESSENGERS FROM ACROSS THE OCEAN OF SPACE

As is often the way in science, the correct explanation for the nature of light came from an unlikely source. In the mid-nineteenth century, the study of electricity and magnetism engaged many great scientific minds. At the Royal Institution in London, Michael Faraday was busy doing what scientists do best – playing around with wire and magnets. He discovered that if you push a magnet through a coil of wire, an electric current flows through the wire while the magnet is moving. This is a generator; the thing that sits in all power stations around the world today, providing us with electricity. Faraday wasn't interested in inventing the foundation of the modern world, he just wanted to learn about electricity and magnetism. He encoded his experimental findings in mathematical form – known today as Faraday's Law of Electromagnetic Induction. At around the same time, the French physicist and mathematician André-Marie Ampère discovered that two parallel wires carrying electric currents experience a force between them; this force is still used today to define the ampere, or amp – the unit of electric current. A single amp is defined as the current that must flow along two parallel wires of infinite length and negligible diameter to produce an attractive force of 0.0000007 Newtons between them. Next time you change a thirteen-amp fuse in your plug, you are paying a little tribute to the work of Ampère. Today, the mathematical form of this law is called Ampère's Law.

By 1860, a great deal was known about electricity and magnetism. Magnets could be used to make electric currents flow, and flowing electric currents could deflect compass needles in the same way that magnets could. There was clearly a link between these two phenomena, but nobody had come up with a unified description. The breakthrough was made by the Scottish physicist James Clerk Maxwell, who, in a series of papers in 1861 and 1862, developed a single theory of electricity and magnetism that was able to explain all of the experimental work of Faraday, Ampère and others. But Maxwell's crowning glory came in 1864, when he published a paper that is undoubtedly one of the greatest achievements in the history of science. Albert Einstein later described Maxwell's 1860s papers as 'the most profound and the most fruitful that physics has experienced since the time of Newton.' Maxwell discovered that by unifying electrical and magnetic phenomena together into a single mathematical theory, a startling prediction emerges.

Electricity and magnetism can be unified by introducing two new concepts: electric and magnetic fields. The idea of a field is central to modern physics; a simple example of something that can be represented by a field is the temperature in a room. If you could measure the temperature at each point in the room and note it down, eventually you would have a vast array of numbers that described how the temperature changes from the door to the windows and from the floor to the ceiling. This array of numbers is called the temperature field. In a similar way, you could introduce the concept of a magnetic field by holding a compass at places around a wire carrying an electric current and noting down how much the needle deflects, and in what direction. The numbers and directions are the magnetic field. This might

LEFT: The movement of waves across the ocean can be explained by a set of equations; Maxwell discovered a similar form of equation explained waves within magnetic fields.

BELOW: These picture strips illustrate maps of the Milky Way Galaxy as they appear in different wavelength regions.

RADIO

INFRARED

OPTICAL

X-RAY

GAMMA RAY

THE RELATIONSHIP BETWEEN ELECTRICITY, MAGNETISM AND THE SPEED OF LIGHT IS SUMMARIZED IN THE EQUATION:

Where c is the speed of light and the quantities μ_0 and ε_0 are related to the strengths of electric and magnetic fields. The fact that the velocity of light can be measured experimentally on a bench top with wires and magnets was the key piece of evidence that light is an electromagnetic wave.

$$C = \frac{1}{\sqrt{\mu_0 \varepsilon_0}}$$

Maxwell's equations had exactly the same form as the equations that describe how soundwaves move through air or how water waves move through the ocean.

seem rather abstract and not much of a simplification, but Maxwell found that by introducing the electric and magnetic fields and placing them centre stage, he was able to write down a single set of equations that described all the known electrical and magnetic phenomena.

At this point you may be wondering what all this has to do with the story of light. Well, here is something profound that provides a glimpse into the true power and beauty of modern physics. In writing down his laws of electricity and magnetism using fields, Maxwell noticed that by using a bit of simple mathematics, he could rearrange his equations into a more compact and magically revealing form. His new equations took the form of what are known as wave equations. In other words, they had exactly the same form as the equations that describe how soundwaves move through air or how water waves move through the ocean. But waves of what? The waves Maxwell discovered were waves in the electric and magnetic fields themselves. His equations showed that as an electric field changes, it creates a changing magnetic field. But in turn as the magnetic field changes, it creates a changing electric field, which creates a changing magnetic field, and so on. In other words, once you've wiggled a few electric charges around to create a changing electric and magnetic field, you can take the charges away and the fields will continue sloshing around – as one falls, the other will rise. And this will continue to happen forever, as long as you do nothing to them.

This is profound in itself, but there is an extra, more profound conclusion. Maxwell's equations also predict exactly how fast these waves must fly away from the electric charges that create them. The speed of the waves is the ratio of the strengths of the electric and magnetic fields – quantities that had been measured by Faraday, Ampère and others and were well known to Maxwell. When Maxwell did the sums, he must have fallen off his chair. He found that his equations predicted that the waves in the electric and magnetic fields travelled at the speed of light! In other words, Maxwell had discovered that light is nothing more than oscillating electric and magnetic fields, sloshing back and forth and propelling each other through space as they do so. How beautiful that the work of Faraday, Ampère and others with coils of wire and pieces of magnets could lead to such a profound conclusion through the use of a bit of mathematics and a sprinkling of Scottish genius! In modern language, we would say that light is an electromagnetic wave.

In order to have his epiphany, Maxwell needed to know exactly what the speed of light was. Remarkably, the fact that light travels very fast, but not infinitely so, had already been known for almost two hundred years. As we will discover now, it had first been measured by Ole Romer in 1676 ◉

CHASING THE SPEED OF LIGHT

BELOW: The question, how fast is the speed of light, has plagued scientists for thousands of years. Part of the answer came from observing how light travels between points: from the Sun to Earth.

Open your eyes and the world floods in; light seems to jump from object to retina, forming a picture of the world instantaneously. Light seems to travel infinitely fast, so it is no surprise that Aristotle and many other philosophers and scientists believed light travelled 'without movement'. However, as the Greek philosophers gave more thought to the nature of light, a debate about its speed of travel ensued that continued for thousands of years.

In one corner sat eminent names such as Euclid, Kepler and Descartes, who all sided with Aristotle in believing that light travelled infinitely fast. In the other, Empedocles and Galileo, separated by almost two millennia, felt that light must travel at a finite, if extremely high, velocity. Empedocles's reasoning was elegant, pre-dating Aristotle by a century. He considered light travelling across the vast distance from the Sun to Earth, and noted that everything that travels must move from one point to another. In other words, the light must be somewhere in the space between the Sun and the Earth after it leaves the Sun and before it reaches the Earth. This means it must travel with a finite velocity. Aristotle dismissed this argument by invoking his idea that light is simply a presence, not something that moves between things. Without experimental evidence, it is impossible to decide between these positions simply by thinking about it!

Galileo set out to measure the speed of light using two lamps. He held one and sent an assistant a large distance away with another. When they were in position, Galileo opened a shutter on his lamp, letting the light out. When his assistant saw the flash, he opened his shutter, and Galileo attempted to note down the time delay between the opening of his shutter and his observation of the flash from his assistant's lamp. His conclusion was that light must travel extremely rapidly, because he was unable to determine its speed. Galileo was, however, able to put a 'limit' on the speed of light, noting that it must be at least ten times faster than the speed of sound. He was able to do this because if it had been slower, he should have been able to measure a time delay. So, the inability to measure the speed of light was not deemed a 'no result', but in fact revealed that light travels faster than his experiment could quantify.

The first experimental determination that the speed of light was not infinite was made by the seventeenth-century

BELOW: These spectacular star trails are produced in the sky as a result of diurnal motion. This is the motion created as Earth spins on its axis at fifteen degrees per hour, rotating once over twenty-four hours.

Danish astronomer, Ole Romer. In 1676, Romer was attempting to solve one of the great scientific and engineering challenges of the age; telling the time at sea. Finding an accurate clock was essential to enable sailors to navigate safely across the oceans, but mechanical clocks based on pendulums or springs were not good at being bounced around on the ocean waves and soon drifted out of sync. In order to pinpoint your position on Earth you need the latitude and longitude. Latitude is easy; in the Northern Hemisphere, the angle of the North Star (Polaris) above the horizon is your latitude. In the Southern Hemisphere, things are more complicated because there is no star directly over the South Pole, but it is still possible with a little astronomical know-how and trigonometry to determine your latitude with sufficient accuracy for safe navigation.

Longitude is far more difficult because you can't just determine it by looking at the stars; you have to know which time zone you are in. Greenwich in London is defined as zero degrees longitude; as you travel west from Greenwich across the Atlantic, your time zone shifts so that in New York it's earlier in the day than in London. Conversely, as you travel east from Greenwich your time zone shifts so that in Moscow or Tokyo it's later in the day than in London.

Your precise time zone at any point on Earth's surface is defined by the point at which the Sun crosses an imaginary arc across the sky between the north and south points on your horizon, passing through the celestial pole (the point marked by the North Star in the Northern Hemisphere). Astronomers call this arc the Meridian. The point at which the Sun crosses the Meridian is also the point at which it reaches its highest position in the sky on any given day as it journeys from sunrise in the east to sunset in the west. We call this time noon, or midday. Earth rotates once on its axis every twenty-four hours – fifteen degrees every hour. This means two points on Earth's surface that are separated by fifteen degrees of longitude will measure noon exactly one hour apart. So to determine your longitude, set a clock to read 12 o'clock when the Sun reaches the highest point in the sky at Greenwich. If it reads 2pm when the Sun reaches its highest point in the sky where you are, you are thirty degrees to the west of Greenwich. Easy, except that you need a very accurate clock that keeps time for weeks or months on end ◉

THE SEARCH FOR A COSMIC CLOCK

RIGHT: Jupiter appears spotty in this false-colour picture from the Hubble Space Telescope's near-infrared camera. The three black spots are the shadows of the moons Ganymede (top left), Io (left) and Callisto. The white spot above centre is Io, while the blue spot (upper right) is Ganymede. Callisto is out of the image to the right.

In the early seventeenth century, King Philip III of Spain offered a prize to anyone who could devise a method for precisely calculating longitude when out of sight of land. The technological challenge of building sufficiently accurate clocks was too great, so scientists began to look for high-precision natural clocks, and it seemed sensible to look to the heavens. Galileo, having discovered the moons of Jupiter, was convinced he could use the orbits of these moons as a clock, as they regularly passed in and out of the shadow of the giant planet. The principle is beautifully simple; Jupiter has four bright moons that can be seen relatively easily from Earth, and the innermost moon, Io, goes around the planet every 1.769 days, precisely. One might say that Io's orbit is as regular as clockwork, therefore by watching for its daily disappearance and re-emergence from behind Jupiter's disc you have a very accurate and unchanging natural clock. Thus by using the Jovian system as a cosmic clock, Galileo devised an accurate system for keeping time. Observing the eclipses of these tiny pinpoints of light around three-quarters of a billion kilometres (half a billion miles) from Earth from a rolling ship was impractical, however, so although the logic was sound, Galileo failed to win the King's prize. Despite this, it was clear this technique could be used to measure longitude accurately on land, where stable conditions and high-quality telescopes were available. Thus observing and cataloguing the eclipses of Jupiter's moons, particularly Io, became a valuable astronomical endeavour.

By the mid-seventeenth century, Giovanni Cassini was leading the study of Jupiter's moons. He pioneered the use of Io's eclipses for the measurement of longitude and published tables detailing on what dates the eclipses should be visible from many locations on Earth, together with high-precision predictions of the times. In the process of further refining his longitude tables, he sent one of his astronomers, Jean Picard, to the Uraniborg Observatory near Copenhagen, where Picard employed the help of a young Danish astronomer, Ole Romer. Over some months

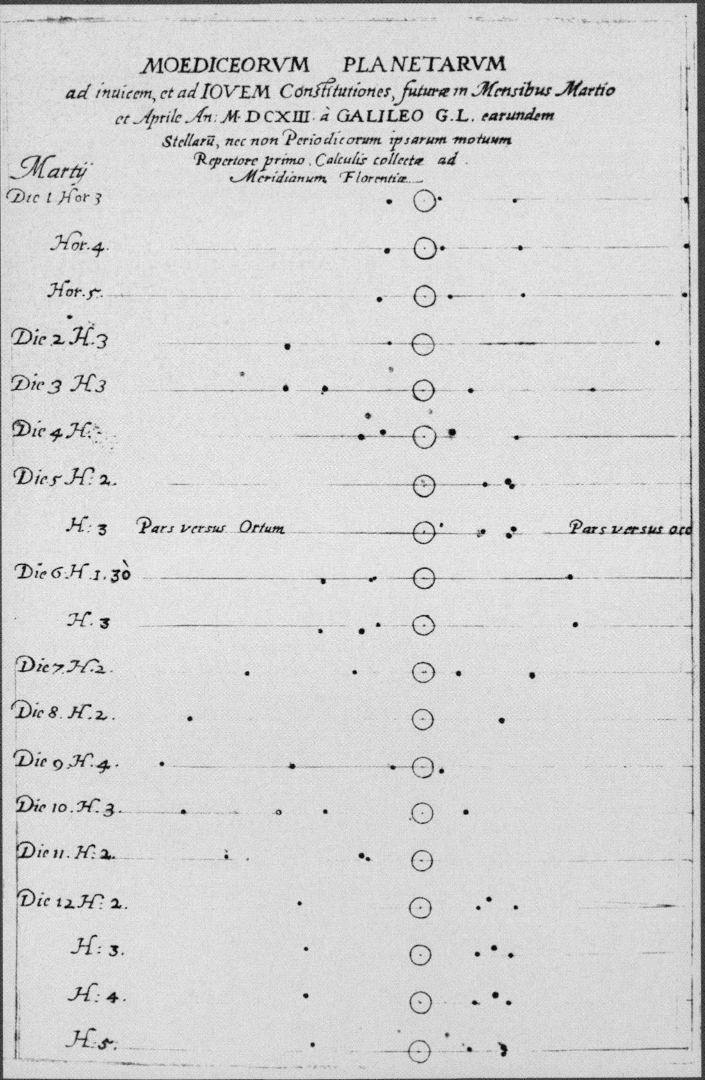

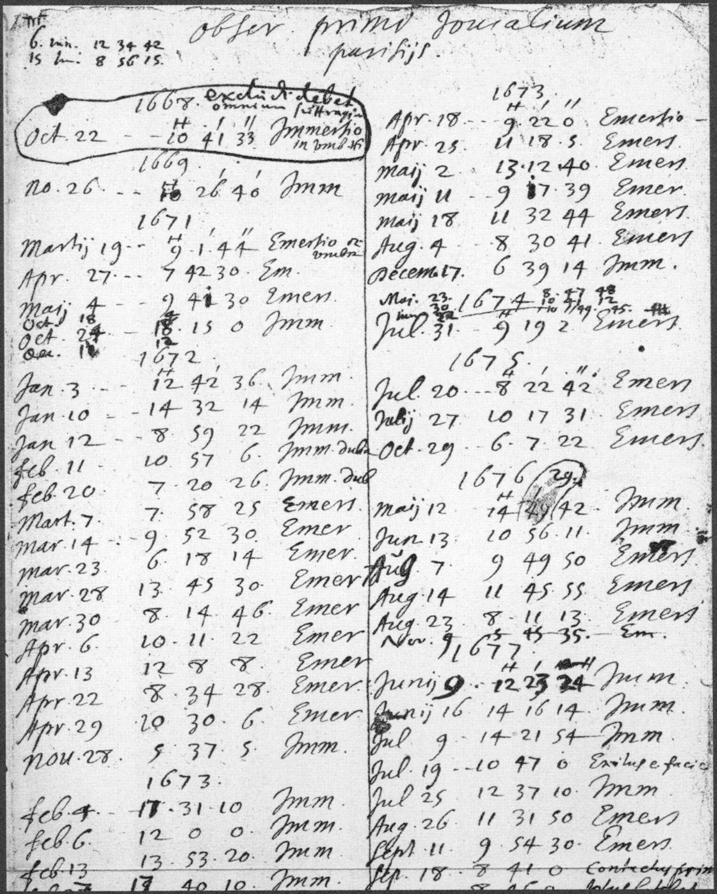

LEFT: These sketches (published in Istoria e Dimonstrazione in 1613) show the changing position of the moons of Jupiter over 12 days. Jupiter is represented by the large circle, with the four moons as dots on either side.

ABOVE: Ole Romer's recorded observations show his detailed research into the movement of Io.

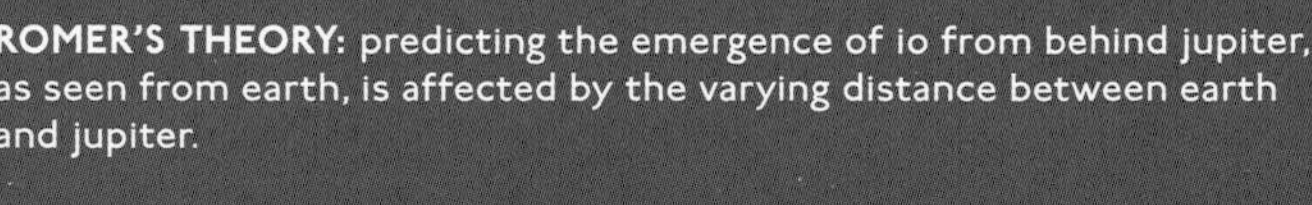

ROMER'S THEORY: predicting the emergence of io from behind jupiter, as seen from earth, is affected by the varying distance between earth and jupiter.

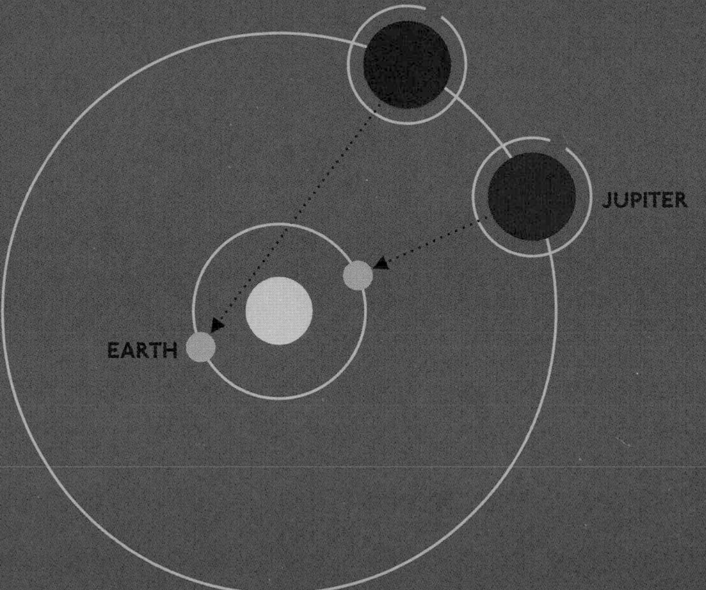

in 1671, Romer and Picard observed over one hundred of Io's eclipses, noting the times and intervals between each. He was quickly invited to work as Cassini's assistant at the Royal Observatory, where Romer made a crucial discovery. Combining the data from Uraniborg with Cassini's Paris observations, Romer noticed that the celestial precision of the Jovian clock wasn't as accurate as everyone had thought. Over the course of several months, the prediction for when Io would emerge from behind Jupiter drifted. At some times of the year there was a significant discrepancy of over twenty-two minutes between the predicted and the actual observed timings of the eclipses. This appeared to ruin the use of Io as a clock and end the idea of using it to calculate longitude. However, Romer came up with an ingenious and correct explanation of what was happening.

Romer noticed that the observed time of the eclipses drifted later relative to the predicted time as the distance between Jupiter and Earth increased as the planets orbited the Sun, then drifted back again when the distance between Jupiter and Earth began to decrease. Romer's genius was to realise that this pattern implied there was nothing wrong with the clockwork of Jupiter and Io, because the error depended on the distance between Earth and Jupiter and had nothing to do with Io itself. His explanation, which is correct, was simple. Imagine that light takes time to travel from Jupiter to Earth; as the distance between the two planets increases, so the light from Jupiter will take longer to travel between them. This means that Io will emerge from Jupiter's shadow later than predicted, simply because it takes longer for the light to reach you. Conversely, as the distance between Jupiter and Earth decreases, it takes the light less time to reach you and so you see Io emerge sooner than predicted. Factor in the time it takes light to travel between Jupiter and Earth and the theory works. Romer did this by trial and error, and was able to correctly account for the shifting times of the observed eclipses. The number that Romer actually calculated was the light travel time across the diameter of Earth's orbit around the Sun, which he found to be approximately twenty minutes. For some reason, perhaps because he felt the diameter of Earth's orbit was not known with sufficient precision, he never turned this number into the speed of light in any Earth-based units of measurement. He simply stated that it takes light twenty-two minutes to cross the diameter of Earth's orbit. The first published number for the speed of light was that obtained by the Dutch astronomer Christiaan Huygens, who had corresponded with Romer. In his 'Treatise sur la lumière' (1678), Huygens quotes a speed in strange units as 110 million toises per second. Since a toise is two metres (seven feet), this gives a speed of 220,000,000 metres per second, which is not far off the modern value of 299,792,458 metres (983,571,503 feet) per second. The error was primarily in the determination of the diameter of Earth's orbit around the Sun.

No consensus about the speed of light was reached until after Romer's death in 1710, but his correct interpretation of the wobbles in the Jovian clock still stands as a seminal achievement in the history of science. His measurement of the speed of light was the first determination of the value of what scientists call a constant of nature. These numbers, such as Newton's gravitational constant and Planck's constant, have remained fixed since the Big Bang, and are central to the properties of our universe. They are crucial in physics, and we would live (or not live, because we wouldn't exist) in a universe that was unrecognisable if their values were altered by even a tiny amount ◉

Everything in our universe has a speed limit, and for much of the twentieth century humans seemed obsessed with breaking one of them. In the 1940s and 1950s the sound barrier took on an almost mythical status as engineers worldwide tried to build aircraft that could exceed the 1236 kilometres per hour (768 miles per hour) at which sound travels in air at twenty degrees Celsius. But what is the meaning of this speed limit? What is the underlying physics, and how does it affect our engineering attempts to break it?

Sound in a gas such as air is a moving disturbance of the air molecules. Imagine dropping a saucepan lid onto the floor. As it lands, it rapidly compresses the air beneath it, pushing the molecules closer together. This increases the density of the air beneath the lid, which corresponds to an increase in air pressure. In a gas, molecules will fly around to try to equalise the pressure, which is why winds develop between high and low pressure areas in our atmosphere. With a falling lid, some of the molecules in the high-pressure area beneath it will rush out to the surrounding lower-pressure areas; these increase in pressure, causing molecules to rush into the neighbouring areas, and so on. So the disturbance in the air caused by the falling lid moves outwards as a wave of pressure. The air itself doesn't flow away from the lid (this would leave an area of lower pressure around it that would have to be equalised), it is only the pulse of pressure that moves through the air.

The speed of this pressure wave is set by the properties of the air. The speed of sound in air depends on the air's temperature, which is a measure of how fast the molecules in the air are moving on average, the mass of the air molecules (air is primarily a mixture of nitrogen and oxygen) and the details of how the air responds when it is compressed (known as the 'adiabatic index'). To a reasonable approximation, the speed of the sound wave depends mainly on the average speed of the air molecules at a particular temperature.

The speed of sound is therefore not a speed limit at all; it is simply the speed at which a wave of pressure moves through the air, and there is no reason why an object shouldn't exceed this. This was known long before aircraft were invented, but it did not satisfy those who wanted to propel a human faster than sound. Many attempts were made during World War II to produce a supersonic aircraft, but the sound barrier was not breached until 14 October 1947, when Chuck Yeager became the first human to pilot a supersonic flight. Flying in the Bell–XS1, Yeager was dropped out of the bomb bay of a modified B29 bomber, through the sound barrier and into the history books.

The speed of sound is not a speed limit at all; it is simply the speed at which a wave of pressure moves through the air, and there is no reason why an object shouldn't exceed this.

Today, aircraft routinely break the sound barrier, but the routine element hides the fascinating aerodynamic and engineering challenges that had to be overcome so that humans could travel faster than sound. Test pilot Dave Southwood demonstrated these to me in the making of the programme in a beautiful aircraft that was not designed to break the sound barrier in level flight – the Hawker Hunter.

Designed in the 1950s, the Hawker Hunter is a legendary British jet fighter of the post-war era. Designed to fly at Mach 0.94, this aircraft cannot fly supersonic in level flight, but in the right hands it can exceed the 1,200 kilometres (745 miles) per hour to take me through the sound barrier. We climbed to 12,800 metres (42,000 feet), flipped the Hunter into an inverted dive, then plunged full-throttle towards the Bristol

ABOVE AND RIGHT: Once we reached 12,800 metres, the pilot put the Hawker Hunter into the roll and we dived down through the clouds, upside down. Almost immediately, we broke through the sound barrier.

Channel. In just seconds the jet smashed through the sound barrier and the air flow surrounding the jet changed, which is heard on the ground as an explosion, or a sonic boom.

So the sound barrier is not a barrier at all; it is a speed limit only for sound itself, determined by the physics of the movement of air molecules. Is the light barrier the same? It would seem from our description of light as an electromagnetic wave that is so. Why shouldn't a sufficiently powerful aircraft or spacecraft be able to fly faster than a wave in electric and magnetic fields? The answer is that the 'light barrier' is of a totally different character and cannot be smashed through, even in principle. The reason for this is that light speed plays a much deeper role in the Universe than just being the speed at which light travels. A true understanding of the role of this speed, 299,792,458 metres (983,571,503 feet) per second, was achieved in 1905 by Albert Einstein in his special theory of relativity. Einstein, inspired by Maxwell's work, wrote down a theory in which space and time are merged into a single entity known as 'spacetime'. Einstein suggested we should not see our world as having only three directions – north/south, east/west and up/down, as he added a fourth direction – past/future. Hence spacetime is referred to as four-dimensional, with time being the fourth dimension.

A full explanation of this is beyond the scope of this book, suffice to say that Einstein was forced into this bold move primarily because Maxwell's equations for electricity and magnetism were incompatible with Newton's 200-year-old laws of motion. Einstein abandoned the Newtonian ideas of space and time as separate entities and merged them. In Einstein's theory there is a special speed built into the structure of spacetime itself that everyone must agree on, irrespective of how they are moving relative to each other. This special speed is a universal constant of nature that will always be measured as precisely 299,792,458 metres (983,571,503 feet) per second, at all times and all places in the Universe, no matter what they are doing. This is critical in Einstein's theory because it stops us doing something strange in spacetime; if past/future is simply another direction like north/south, why can't we wander backwards and forwards in it? Why can we only travel into the future, not the past?

In Einstein's theory of relativity it is the existence of this unanimously agreed special speed that makes time direction different to that of space and prevents time travel. In this sense, the special speed is built into the fabric of space and time itself and plays a deep role in the structure of our universe. What does it have to do with the speed of light? Nothing much! There is a reason why light goes at this speed, and it seems to be a complete coincidence. In Einstein's theory, anything that has no mass is compelled to travel at the special speed through space. Conversely, anything that has mass is compelled to travel slower than this speed. Particles of light, photons, have no mass, so they travel at the speed of light. There is no deep reason we know of why photons have to be massless particles, so no deep reason why light travels at the speed of light! We only call the special speed 'light speed' because it was discovered by measuring the speed of light.

The key point is that the speed of light is a fundamental property of the Universe because it is built into the fabric of space and time itself. Travelling faster than this speed is impossible, and even travelling at it is impossible if you have mass. It is this property of the Universe that protects the past from the future and prevents time travel into the past ◉

TIME TRAVEL

Without realising it, we are all travelling back in time by the most miniscule amount. The consequence of light travelling fast, but not infinitely fast, is that you see everything as it was in the past. In everyday life the consequences of this strange fact are intriguing but irrelevant. It may be strictly true that you are seeing your reflection in the mirror in the past, but since it takes light only one thousand millionths of a second to travel thirty centimetres (twelve inches), the delay is all but invisible. However, the further away we get from an object, the greater the delay becomes. Although over tiny distances the effect is always utterly negligible, it should be obvious that once we lift our eyes upwards to the skies and become astronomers, profound consequences await us.

RIGHT: A rare sight; in this picture Earth's crescent moon is visible above Venus (bottom) and Jupiter (right) in the night sky. As light takes longer to reach Earth from other planets and moons, depending on how far away they are, we see further into their respective pasts.

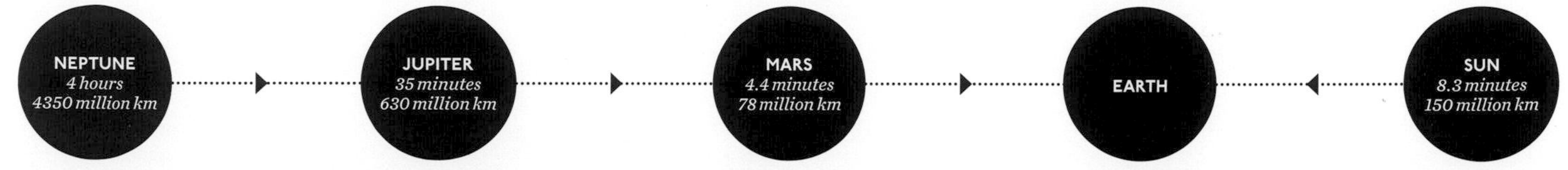

Look up at the Moon and you are looking at our closest neighbour a second in the past, because it is on average around 380,000 kilometres (236,120 miles) away; perceptible certainly, but not important. However, take a look at the Sun and you really are beginning to bathe in the past.

The Sun is 150 million kilometres away (93 million miles) – this is very close by cosmic standards, but at these distances the speed of light starts to feel rather pedestrian. We are seeing the Sun as it was eight minutes in the past. This has the strange consequence that if we were to magically remove the Sun, we would still feel its heat on our faces and still see its image shining brightly in the sky for eight minutes. And because the speed of light is actually the maximum speed at which any influence in the Universe can travel, this delay applies to gravity as well. So if the Sun magically disappeared, we would not only continue to see it for eight minutes, we would continue to orbit around it too. We are genuinely looking back in time every time we look at the Sun.

However, this is just the beginning of our time travelling. As we look up at the planets and moons in our solar system, we move further and further into the past. The light from Mars takes between four and twenty minutes to reach Earth, depending on the relative positions of Earth and Mars in their orbits around the Sun. This has a significant impact on the way we design and operate vehicles intended for driving on the surface of Mars. When Mars is at its furthest point from Earth it would take at least forty minutes to be told that a Mars Rover was driving over a cliff and then be able to tell it to stop, so Mars Rovers need to be able to make up their own minds in such situations or must do things very slowly. Jupiter, at its closest point to Earth, is around thirty-two minutes away, and by the time we journey to the outer reaches of our solar system, the light from the most distant planet, Neptune, takes around four hours to make the journey. At the very edge of the Solar System, the round-trip travel time for radio signals sent and received by Voyager 1 on its journey into interstellar space is currently thirty-one hours, fifty-two minutes and twenty-two seconds, as of September 2010.

But look beyond our solar system and the time it takes for light to travel from our nearest neighbouring stars is no longer measured in hours or days, but years. We see Alpha Centauri, the nearest star visible with the naked eye, as it was four years in the past, and as the cosmic distances mount, so the journey into the past becomes ever deeper ◉

TO THE DAWN OF TIME

When filming a series like *Wonders of the Universe,* the locations are chosen to be visually spectacular, but they must also have a narrative that enhances the explanation of the scientific ideas we want to convey. Occasionally, the locations deliver more. There is a resonance, a symbiosis between science and place that serves to amplify the facts and generates something deeper and more profound on screen. For me, the Great Rift Valley was such a place.

We arrived in Tanzania on 10 May 2010 for the first day of filming. After a brief overnight stay close to the airport at Kilimanjaro, we were driven out into the Serengeti in vintage dark green Toyota Land Cruisers, complete with exaggerated front cattle bars and shovels tied to the rear doors. The landscape is unmistakably African; the warm, damp light still wet from the rains illumines plains seemingly too vast to fit on

The Great Rift Valley is not just an extraordinary geological feature ... there is more to this place because the echoes of the history of humanity ring louder across these plains than anywhere else on the planet.

our planet. The horizon, darkened by scattered thunderclouds stark against the early summer skies, is simply more distant than it should be. The rains have brought with them journeys, and as you drive you experience first-hand the thousand-mile migration of the Serengeti wildebeest. The relentless advance of these herds creates ruts in the drying savannah along the precise and ancient roads that always seem to run at right angles to your direction of travel, shaking the Land Cruisers to the edge of their design tolerance. Zebras, giraffe and Grant's gazelles graze, unconcerned, as our intrepid film crew rattles by.

LEFT AND BELOW: The Great Rift Valley, Tanzania, is one of the most spectacular geological locations on Earth. The summer skies were darkened by rainclouds, but these soon departed to reveal dusty, unmistakably African landscapes and breathtaking vistas.

Our camp is idyllic by the strictest definition of the word. Khaki tents nestle beneath acacia trees in the shadow of a giant copper-striped rock populated by a tribe of itinerant baboons intent on stealing our tape stock. Fortunately, we are guarded by the Masai, who, all cliché aside, are as tough as hell and scare not only the baboons but also the Serengeti lions and the BBC in equal amount.

So much for the visuals; the reason for the resonance of this place lies in the deep past of this dramatic landscape of life. The Great Rift Valley is not just an extraordinary geological feature that stretches 6,000 kilometres (3,700 miles) from Syria to Mozambique; there is more to this place because the echoes of the history of humanity ring louder across these plains than anywhere else on the planet. To walk this earth is to walk in the footsteps of the true ancients. Ancestors like Lucy, one of the most important fossils ever discovered, a skeleton uncovered in the Ethiopian section of the valley in 1974 by Donald Johanson. Lucy is 3.2 million years old; the remains of an *Australopithecus,* an extinct hominid species many anthropologists believe links directly to our own heritage. Further down the rift, in Tanzania, more closely related human ancestors have been discovered. In the early 1960s, Mary and Louis Leakey unearthed the remains of the earliest known species of our genus, *Homo. Homo habilis* is thought to have been a direct descendant of *Australopithecus,* and may be the first of our ancestors to have made tools. It's all in the mind, I suppose, but sitting around a fire on a cool evening in the Serengeti I felt as if I had returned to the place where I had been born after many years away. There is something about geographic origins that resonates, over a lifetime or a hundred thousand lifetimes ◉

FINDING ANDROMEDA

BELOW LEFT: This Homo habilis skull was found in the Olduvai Gorge in Tanzania and is believed to be around 1.8 million years old.

The connection between the history of the Serengeti and the science of light is a dimly glowing jewel in the velvet Tanzanian sky. With no cities to pollute the darkness, the plains of the African night are bathed in the light of a billion suns. The glowing arc of the Milky Way Galaxy dominates the sky, a silver mist of stars so numerous, they are impossible to count. Every single point of light and every patch of magnificent mist visible to the unaided human eye have as their origin a star in our own galaxy, or the misty clouds known as the Magellanic clouds – two small dwarf galaxies in orbit around the Milky Way. All except for one…

To find it, you first need to recognise the distinctive 'W' shape of the constellation of Cassiopeia. It sits on the opposite side of Polaris, the North Star, to the constellation Ursa Major, otherwise known as The Great Bear or The Plough. Cassiopeia, being so close to Polaris, is a constant feature in the northern skies – it simply rotates around the pole once every twenty-four hours and never sets below the horizon at high latitudes. If in your mind's eye you put the 'W' of Cassiopeia upright, then just beneath the right-most 'V' you will be able to see quite a large, faint, misty patch in the sky. It is comparable in brightness to most of the stars surrounding it, although dimmer than the bright stars of Cassiopeia. This unremarkable little patch is, in my view, the most intellectually stunning object you can see with the naked eye, because it is an entire galaxy beyond the Milky Way. It is called Andromeda, and is our nearest galactic neighbour. It is home to a trillion suns, over twice as many stars as our galaxy. It is roughly twenty-five million million million kilometres (fifteen million million million miles) away, and here is the connection.

Two and a half million years ago, when our distant relative *Homo habilis* was foraging for food across the Tanzanian savannah, a beam of light left the Andromeda Galaxy and began its journey across the Universe. As that light beam raced across space at the speed of light, generations of pre-humans and humans lived and died; whole species evolved and became extinct, until one member of that unbroken lineage, me, happened to gaze up into the sky below the constellation we call Cassiopeia and focus that beam of light onto his retina. A two-and-a-half-billion-year journey ends by creating an electrical impulse in a nerve fibre, triggering a cascade of wonder in a complex organ called the human brain that didn't exist anywhere in the Universe when the journey began ◉

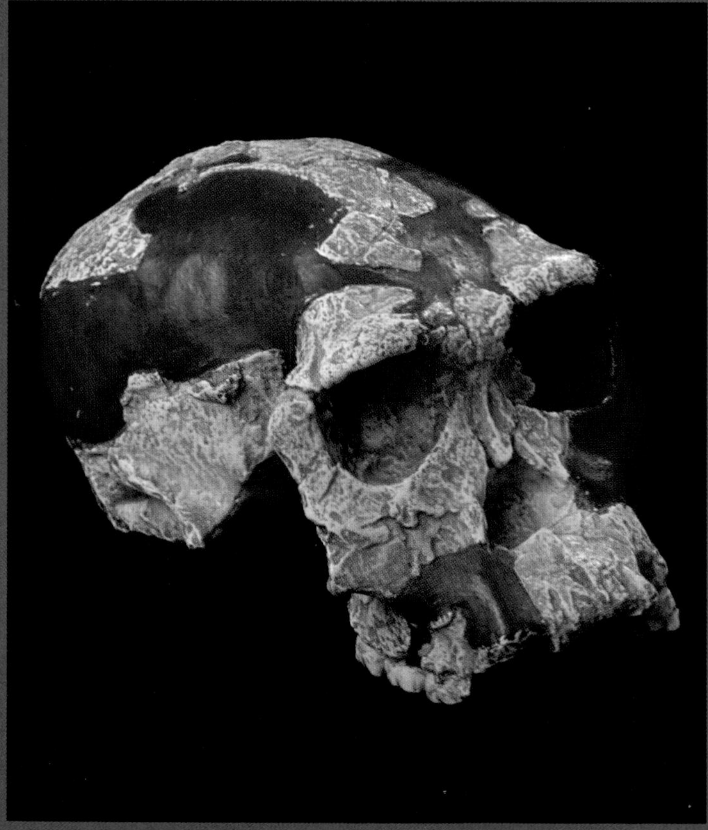

LEFT AND BELOW: On autumn and winter evenings, the spiral galaxy M31 (Andromeda) is visible to the naked eye in northern skies. To locate it, you first need to identify Cassiopeia, and its distinctive 'W' shape. Using the point of the 'V' on the right-hand side as an arrow, look beneath it for a large misty patch in the sky.

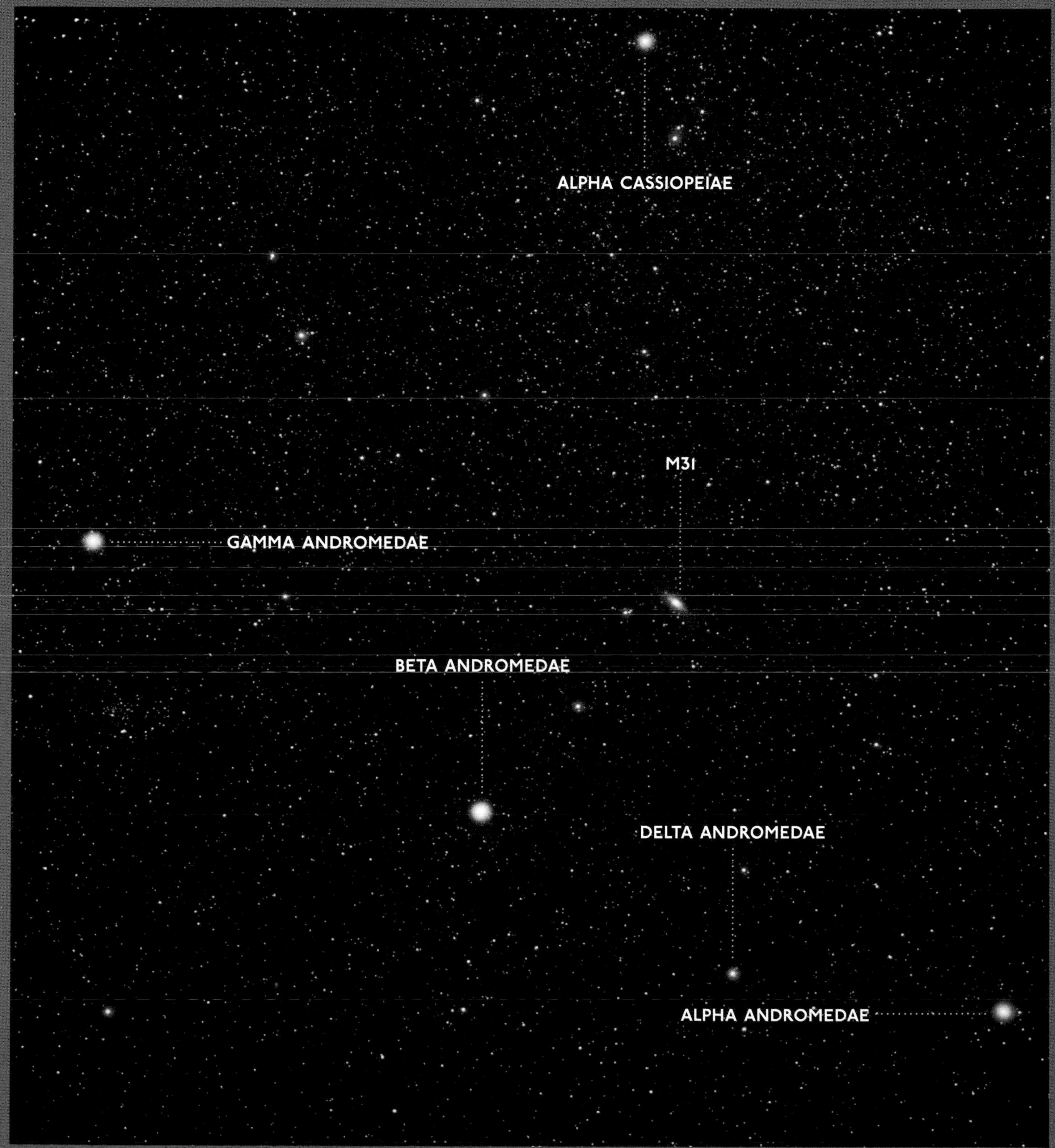

Observing the night skies with the naked eye can only take us so far on our journey to discover and understand the wonders of our universe. Advances in technology have brought us crafts that can take humans on expeditions beyond our planet, but also sophisticated equipment that has changed our view of the Universe entirely.

RIGHT: The Hubble Space Telescope being repaired by an astronaut from Endeavour. This eleven-tonne telescope has allowed astronomers and scientists to see further into our universe than ever before.

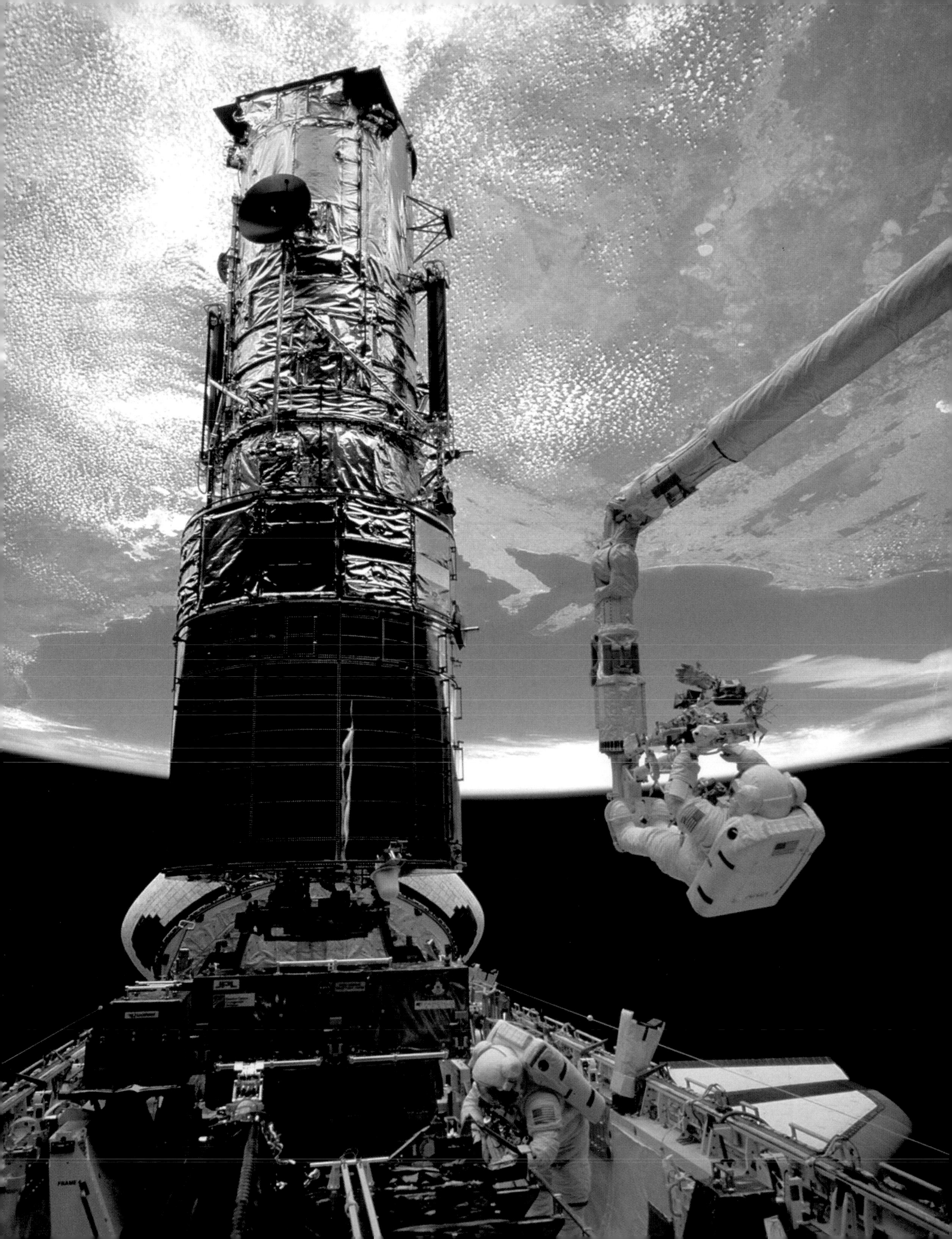

THE HUBBLE TELESCOPE

The naked eye can only allow us to travel back in time to the beginnings of our species; a mere 2.5 million light years away. Until recently, Andromeda was the furthest we could look back unaided, but modern, more powerful telescopes now enable us to peer deeper and deeper into space, so that we can travel way beyond Andromeda, capturing a bounty of messengers laden with information from the far distant past.

In the history of astronomy, no telescope since Galileo's original has a greater impact than the eleven-tonne machine called Hubble. The Hubble Space Telescope was conceived in the 1970s and given the go-ahead by Congress during the tenure of President Jimmy Carter, with a launch date originally set for 1983. Named after Edwin Hubble, the man who discovered that the Universe is expanding, this complex project was plagued with problems from the start. By 1986, the telescope was ready for lift off, three years later than planned, and the new launch date was set for October of that year. But when the Challenger Space Shuttle broke apart seventy-three seconds into its launch in January 1986, the shutters came down not only on Hubble, but on the whole US space programme. Locked away in a clean room for the next four years, the storage costs alone for keeping Hubble in an envelope of pure nitrogen came to $6 million dollars a month.

With the restart of the shuttle programme, the new launch date was set for 24 April 1990 and, seven years behind schedule, shuttle mission STS-31 launched Hubble into its planned orbit 600 kilometres (370 miles) above Earth. The promise of Hubble was simple: images from the depths of space unclouded by the distorting effects of Earth's atmosphere. A new eye was about to open and gaze at the pristine heavens, but within weeks it was clear that Hubble's vision was anything but 20:20. The returning images showed there was a significant optical flaw, and after preliminary investigations it slowly dawned on the Hubble team that after decades of planning and billions of dollars, the Hubble Space Telescope had been launched with a primary mirror that was minutely but disastrously misshapen. Designed to be the most perfect mirror ever constructed, Hubble's shining retina was 2.2 thousandths of a millimetre out of shape, and as a result its vision of the Universe was ruined.

Such was the value and promise of Hubble that an audacious mission was immediately conceived to fix it. This

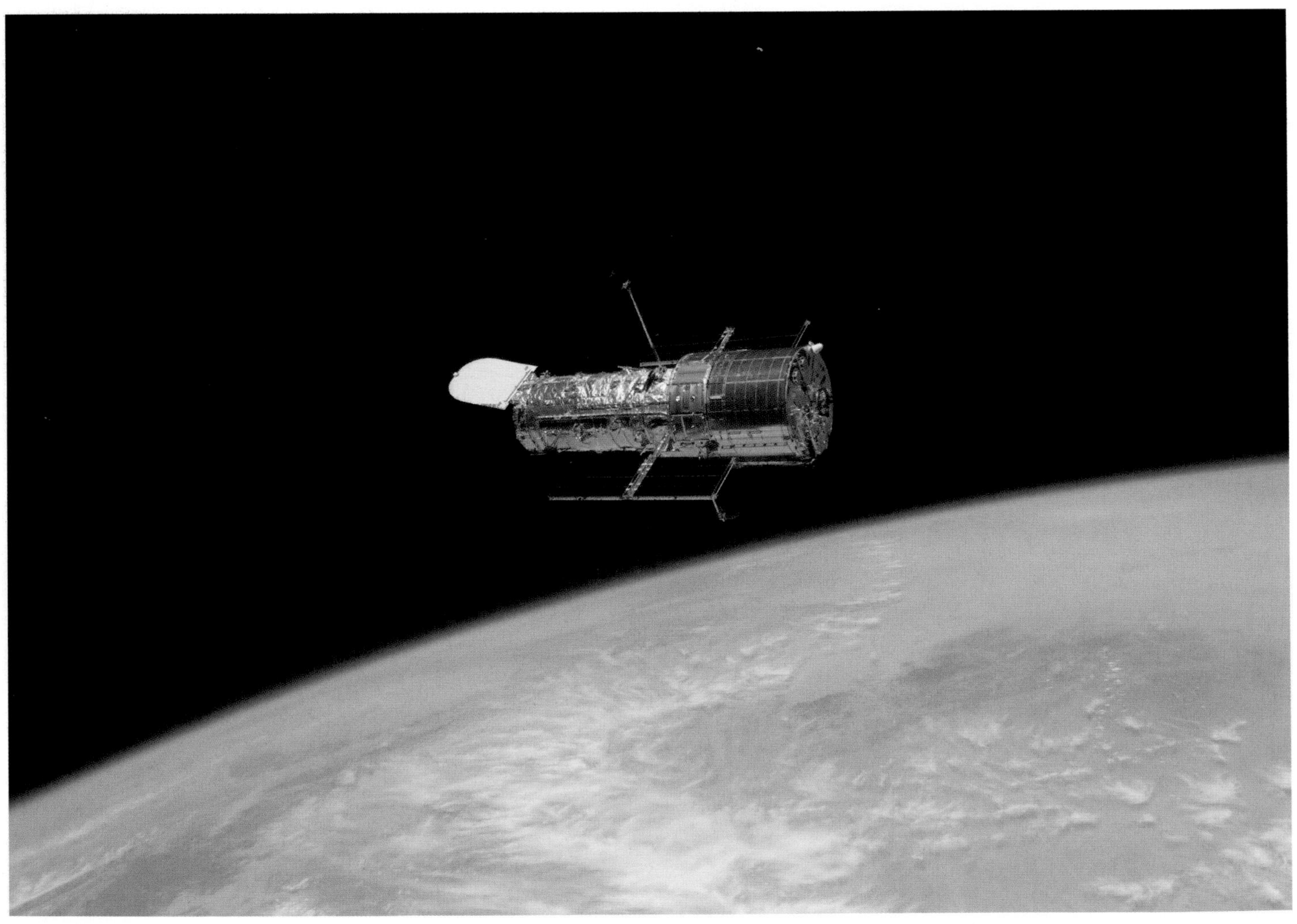

LEFT: The Hubble Space Telescope has had a greater impact on astronomy than any other telescope. This huge telescope orbits Earth, sending back images of parts of the Universe that would otherwise remain invisible to us. The telescope has been orbiting Earth since 1990, and its revolutionary and revelatory journey continues to this day.

BELOW: The Hubble Space Telescope has brought us incredible images of other galaxies that we might never have been able to see. This shot of the spiral galaxy NGC1300 is one of the largest images taken by the telescope.

Seven years behind schedule, shuttle mission STS-31 launched Hubble ... A new eye was about to open and gaze at the pristine heavens...

was possible because Hubble was designed to be the first, and to date only, telescope to be serviceable by astronauts in space. A new mirror could not be fitted, but by precisely calculating the disruptive effect of the faulty mirror, NASA engineers realised that they could correct the problem by fitting Hubble with spectacles.

In December 1993, astronauts from the Shuttle Endeavour spent ten days refitting the telescope with new corrective equipment. In charge of the repairs, by far the most complex task ever undertaken by humans in Earth orbit, was astronaut Story Musgrave. Already a veteran of four shuttle flights, a test pilot with 16,000 flying hours in 160 aircraft types, ex-US Marine and trauma surgeon with seven graduate degrees, Musgrave is quite an extraordinary example of what people can do if they put their minds to it. He is a metaphor for the space programme itself; in Musgrave's own words, this is what restoring sight to Hubble meant. 'Majesty and magnificence of Hubble as a starship, a spaceship. To work on something so beautiful, to give it life again, to restore it to its heritage, to its conceived power. The work was worth it – significant. The passion was in the work, the passion was in the potentiality of Hubble Space Telescope.'

On 13 January 1994, NASA opened Hubble's corrected eye to the Universe and opened the eyes of our planet to the extraordinary beauty of the cosmos. A decade late and costing around $6 billion dollars, it has proved to be worth every cent ◉

HUBBLE'S MOST IMPORTANT IMAGE

LEFT: The Hubble Ultra Deep Field is one of the most spectacular and important pictures taken by the Hubble Space Telescope. This image shows nearly 10,000 galaxies of various ages, sizes, shapes and colours. The nearest galaxies appear larger and brighter, but there are also around one hundred galaxies here that appear as small red objects. These are the most remarkable features in this image; these are among the most distant objects we have ever seen.

For almost two decades the Hubble Space Telescope has captured the faintest lights and enabled us to rebuild these spectacular images, providing a window onto places billions of light years away and events that happened billions of years ago. These are places forever beyond our reach. However, there is one Hubble image that has done more than any other to reveal the scale, depth and beauty of our universe. Known as the Hubble Ultra Deep Field, this shot was taken over a period of eleven days between 24 September 2003 and 16 January 2004. During this period Hubble focused two of its cameras – the Advanced Camera for Surveys (ACS) and Near Infrared Camera and Multi-object Spectrometer (NICMOS) – on a tiny piece of sky in the southern constellation, Fornax. This area of sky is so tiny that Hubble would have needed fifty such images to photograph the surface of the Moon.

From the surface of Earth this tiny piece of sky is almost completely black; there are virtually no visible stars within it, which is why it was chosen. By using its million-second shutter speed, though, Hubble was able to capture images of unimaginably faint, distant objects in the darkness. The dimmest objects in the image were formed by a single photon of light hitting Hubble's camera sensors every minute. Almost every one of these points of light is a galaxy; each an island of hundreds of billions of stars, with over 10,000 galaxies visible. If you extend that over the entire sky, it means there are over 100 billion galaxies in the observable Universe, each containing hundreds of billions of suns.

As we stare at Hubble's masterpiece we are looking back in time; deep time, time beyond human comprehension ... the Hubble Ultra Deep Field transports us back through the history of the Universe.

However, there is something more remarkable about this image than mere scale, due to the slovenly nature of the speed of light compared to the distances between the galaxies. The thousands of galaxies captured by Hubble are all at different distances from Earth, making this image 3D in a very real sense. But the third dimension is not spatial, it is temporal. As we stare at Hubble's masterpiece we are looking back in time; deep time, time beyond human comprehension. Just as an ice core leads us back through layer after layer of Earth's history, so the Hubble Ultra Deep Field transports us back through the history of the Universe.

The photograph contains images of galaxies of various ages, sizes, shapes and colours; some are relatively close to us, some incredibly far away. The nearest galaxies, which appear larger, brighter and have more well-defined spiral and elliptical shapes, are only a billion light years away. Since they would have formed soon after the Big Bang, they are around twelve billion years old. However, it is the small, red, irregular galaxies that are the main attraction here.

There are about 100 of these galaxies in the image, and they are among the most distant objects we have ever seen. Some of these faint red blobs are well over twelve billion light years away, which means that when their light reaches us it has been travelling for almost the entire 13.75-billion-year history of the Universe. The most distant galaxy in the Deep Field, identified in October 2010, is over thirteen billion light years away – so we see it as it was 600,000 years after the beginning of the Universe itself.

It is hard to grasp these vast expanses of space and time. So, consider that the image of this ancient galaxy was created by a handful of photons of light; when they began their journey, released from hot, primordial stars, there was no Earth, no Sun, and only an embryonic and chaotic mass of young stars and dust that would one day evolve into the Milky Way. When these little particles of light had completed almost two-thirds of their journey to Hubble's cameras, a swirling cloud of interstellar dust collapsed to form our solar system. They were almost here when the first complex life on Earth arose and within a cosmic heartbeat of their final destination when the species that built the Hubble first appeared.

The story hidden within the Hubble Ultra Deep Field image is ancient and detailed, but how can we infer so much from a photograph? The answer lies in our interpretation of the colours of those distant, irregular galaxies ◉

ALL THE COLOURS OF THE RAINBOW

The breathtaking Victoria Falls are one of the most famous and beautiful natural wonders on our planet. Fuelled by the mighty Zambezi River, the falls lie on the border between Zambia and Zimbabwe in southern Africa. The falls were named by David Livingstone in 1855, the first European to see them. He later wrote: 'No one can imagine the beauty of the view from anything witnessed in England. It had never been seen before by European eyes; but scenes so lovely must have been gazed upon by angels in their flight.' That's about right from where I stood. There are few better places on Earth from which you can experience the visceral power of flowing water, but there is an ethereal feature of the falls that is just as enchanting and far more instructive for our purposes, because it holds the key to interpreting the Hubble Deep Field Image.

Hovering in the skies above the falls are magnificent rainbows, a permanent feature in the Zambian skies when the Sun shines through the mist. Rainbows are natural phenomena that have enchanted humans for thousands of years; to see one is to marvel at a simple but beautiful property of light and, as is often the case in nature, they are made more beautiful when you understand the science behind them.

Scientists have attempted to understand rainbows since the time of Aristotle, trying to explain how white light is apparently transformed into colour. Our old friend Ibn al-Haytham was one of the first to attempt to explain the physical basis of a rainbow in the tenth century. He described them as being produced by the 'light from the Sun as it is reflected by a cloud before reaching the eye'. This isn't too far from the truth. The basis of our modern understanding was delivered by Isaac Newton, who observed that white light is split into its component colours when passed through a glass prism. He correctly surmised that white light is made up of light of all colours, mixed together. The physics behind the production of a rainbow is essentially the same as that of the prism. Light from the Sun is a mixture of all colours, and water droplets in the sky act like tiny prisms, splitting up the sunlight again. But why the characteristic arc of the rainbow?

The first scientific explanation, which pre-dated Newton by several decades, was given by René Descartes in 1637. Water droplets in the air are essentially little spheres of water, so Descartes considered what happens to a single ray of light from the Sun as it enters a single water droplet. As the diagram opposite illustrates, the light ray from the Sun (S) enters the face of the droplet and is bent slightly. This is known as refraction; light gets deflected when it crosses a boundary between two different substances (point A), then when the light ray gets to the back surface of the raindrop, it is reflected back into the raindrop (point B), finally emerging out of the front again, where it gets bent a little more (point C). The light ray then travels from the raindrop to your eye (E).

The key point is that there is a maximum angle (D) through which light that enters the raindrop gets bounced back. Descartes calculated this angle for red light and found it to be forty-two degrees. For blue light, the angle is forty degrees. Colours between blue and red in the spectrum have maximum angles of reflection of between forty-two and forty degrees. No light gets bounced back with angles greater than this, and it turns out that most of the light gets reflected back at this special, maximum angle. So, here is the explanation for the rainbow. When you look up at a rainbow, imagine drawing a line between the Sun, which must be behind you, through your head and onto the ground in front of you. At an angle of forty-two degrees to this line, you'll see the so-called rainbow, or Descartes' ray of red light. At an angle of forty degrees to this line, you'll see the Descartes' ray of blue light, and all the colours of the rainbow in between. There is some light reflected back to your eye through shallower angles, which is why the sky is brighter below the arc than above it. You don't see the colours below the arc because all the rays merge to form white light. On the picture on the previous page, you can see the sky brightening inside the rainbow over the Victoria Falls, and the relative darkness of the sky outside it.

So raindrops separate the white sunlight into a rainbow because each of the consituent colours gets reflected back to your eye at a slightly different maximum angle. But why the arc? In fact, rainbows are circular. Think of the imaginary line again between the Sun, your head and the ground. There isn't just one place at which the angle between this line and the sky is forty-two degrees, there is a whole circle of points surrounding the line. The reason you can't see a complete circle is that the horizon cuts it off, so you only see the arc. This is also why you tend to see rainbows in the early morning

THE ELECTROMAGNETIC SPECTRUM
The electromagnetic spectrum is composed of a range of wavelengths from radio waves at the very longest end to gamma rays at the shortest. Our eyes are sensitive to a limited range in the middle which we know as visible light.

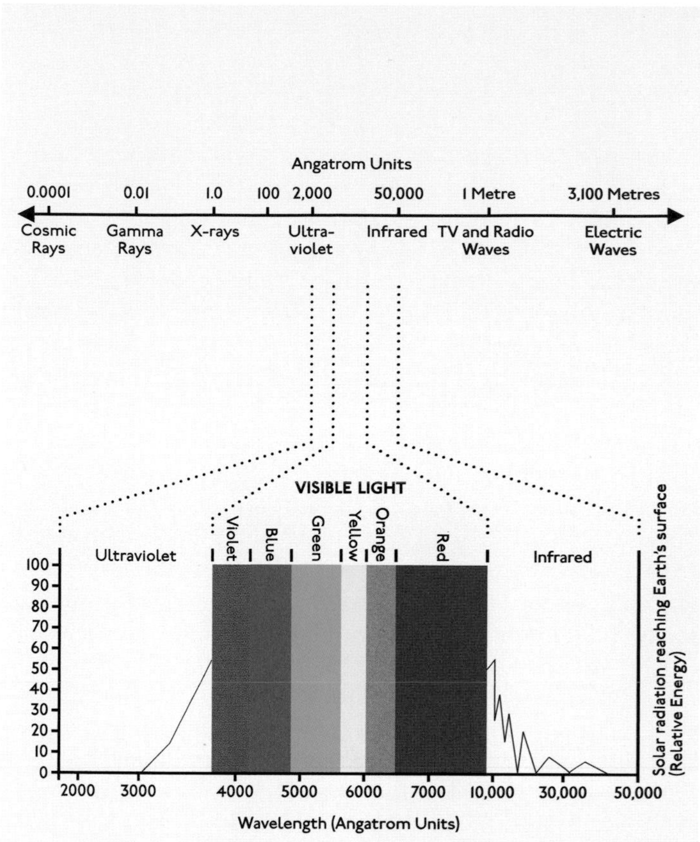

WHAT MAKES A RAINBOW AN ARC?
Decartes' theory was based on what happens to a single ray of light from the Sun as it enters a water droplet; he discovered that each colour that makes up this light is refracted, or bent, at slightly different angles to each other.

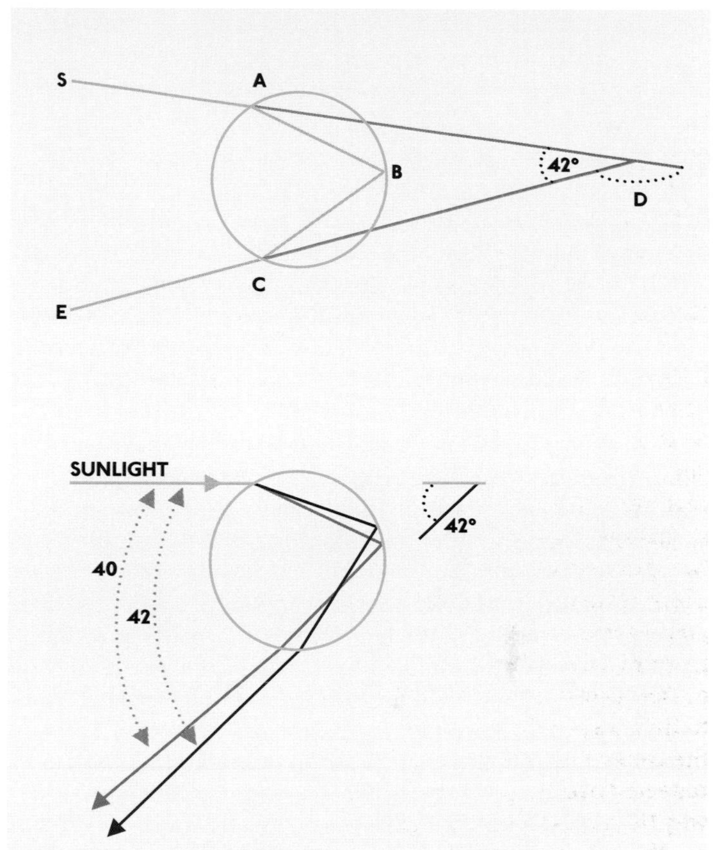

In fact, rainbows are circular. The reason you can't see a complete circle is that the horizon cuts it off, so you only see the arc. This is also why you tend to see rainbows in the early morning or late afternoon.

LEFT AND PREVIOUS SPREAD: All the way back to Aristotle, scientists have been trying to understand rainbows and how white light is transformed to colour through this medium. The Victoria Falls are perhaps one of the most spectacular places on Earth to see rainbows; here, these features hover in the sky above the cascading waters whenever the Sun shines through the mist.

or late afternoon. As the Sun climbs in the sky, the line between the Sun and your head steepens and the rainbow, which is centred on this line, drops closer and closer to the horizon until at some point it will vanish below the horizon.

These colours hidden in white light are not only revealed in rainbows; wherever sunlight strikes an object the different colours are bounced around or absorbed in different ways. The sky is blue because the blue components of sunlight are more likely to be scattered off air molecules than the other colours. As the Sun drops towards the horizon, and the sunlight has to pass through more of the atmosphere, the chance of scattering rays of yellow and red light increases, turning the evening skies redder. Leaves and grass are green because they absorb blue and red light from the Sun, which they use in photosynthesis, but reflect back the green light.

But what is the difference between the colours that makes them behave so differently? The answer goes back to our understanding of light as an electromagnetic wave. Waves have a wavelength – which is the distance between two peaks (or troughs) of the wave. Blue light has a shorter wavelength than green light, which has a shorter wavelength than red light. Our eye has evolved to discern about ten million different colours, which is to say that it can differentiate between ten million subtle variations in the wavelength of electromagnetic waves. This simple idea is all you need to read the story of the Hubble Ultra Deep Field image ●

HUBBLE EXPANSION

BELOW LEFT: This image shows some of the most distant galaxies that we have observed – and all appear in a bright, sharp, red colour.

So, how do we know that the irregular, messy galaxies in the Hubble image are billions of light years away? The picture below shows some of the most distant galaxies we have observed. The most obvious thing about them is that they are all red. Why is this so? To answer this question correctly, we need our friend Edwin Hubble, the astronomer, again.

During the 1920s, Edwin Hubble was using what was then the world's most powerful telescope at the Mount Wilson Observatory in Pasadena, California, to observe stars called Cepheid variables. These Cepheid variables are stars whose brightness varies regularly over a period of days or months, and they are astonishingly useful to astronomers because the period of their brightening and dimming is directly related to their intrinsic brightness. In other words, it is a simple matter to work out exactly how bright a Cepheid variable star actually is just by watching it brighten and dim for a few months. If you know how bright something really is, then measure how bright it looks to you, you can work out how far away it is. Edwin Hubble's research project was simply to search for Cepheid variables in the sky and measure their distance from Earth. During his observations, he discovered two remarkable things: firstly, he quickly determined that the Cepheid variables he found in the so-called spiral nebulae (which at the time were thought to be clouds of glowing gas within the Milky Way) were in fact well outside our galaxy. For the first time, Hubble showed that there are other galaxies in the Universe, millions of light years away.

Hubble's second observation was of even greater scientific importance. While he and others were also busy measuring the spectrum of the light from the stars in the spiral nebulae, which thanks to Hubble were now understood to be other galaxies beyond the Milky Way, they quickly observed that many of the galaxies appeared to be emitting light that was redder than it should be. Hubble quantified the amount of reddening in each galaxy as a number called redshift. Remember that red light has a longer wavelength than blue light, so seeing light redshifted simply means the wavelength is longer than expected. Hubble made his second great discovery by plotting a graph of the redshift of the light from the distant galaxies against their distance, which he had calculated from his observations of the Cepheid variables.

To his great surprise, Hubble noticed that his graph was approximately a straight line. This is because the further away a galaxy is, the greater its redshift – i.e. the more its light is stretched, and there is a very simple relationship between the distance and the redshift. Why is this? Well, the interpretation of Hubble's result is quite remarkable. The more distant the galaxy, the further the light has travelled across the Universe to reach us. Also, the further it has travelled, the more it has been stretched. This relationship

HUBBLE'S LAW: This diagram illustrates Hubble's Law; the redshift of the light from distant galaxies is plotted against their actual distance, resulting in a straight line on the graph.

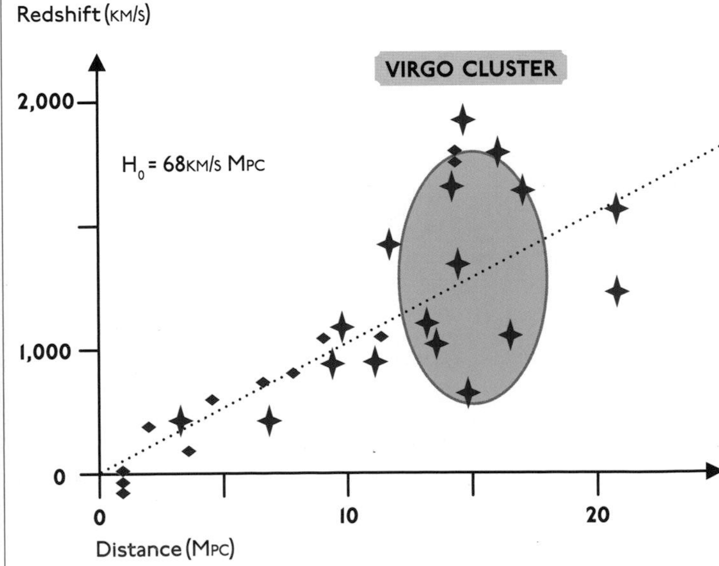

BELOW: Stephan's Quintet is a cluster of five galaxies in the constellation Pegasus, two of which, in the centre, appear to be intertwined. Studying the individual redshifts reveals that one of the galaxies is an interloper: the larger, bluer one at upper left is in fact a foreground galaxy seven times closer to us than the others. So redshifts allow us to create a three-dimensional model of the Universe.

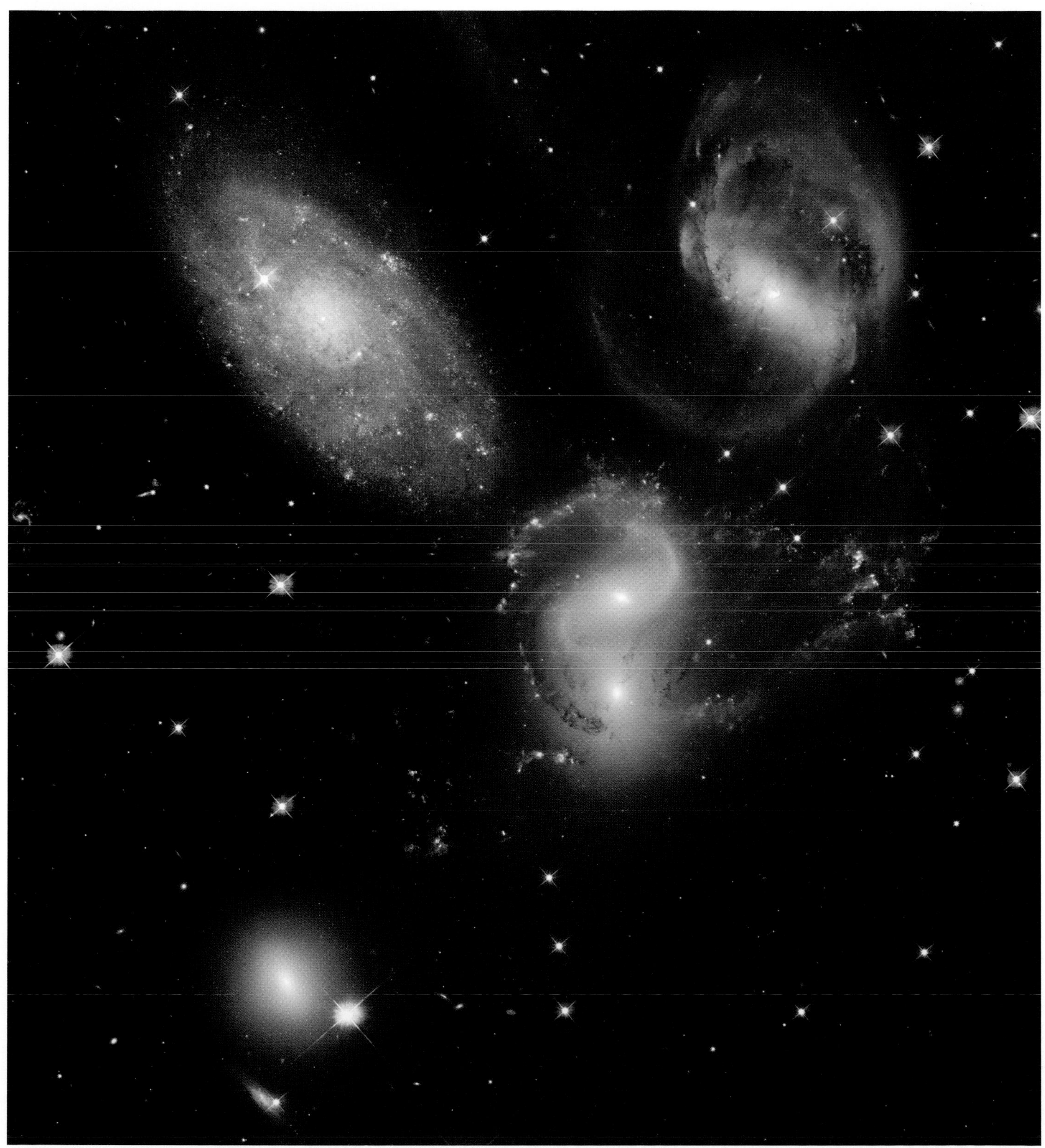

REDSHIFT

Although first discovered in the early twentieth century, redshifts were really put into their cosmological context through the work of Edwin Hubble. He discovered that there is a very simple relationship between the distance and the redshift of a galaxy – the further away a galaxy is, the greater its redshift. This is because the further light has had to travel, the more the travelling light is stretched, and this occurs when the Universe is expanding.

REDSHIFTED SPECTRUM LINE

Other galaxy moving in expanding space

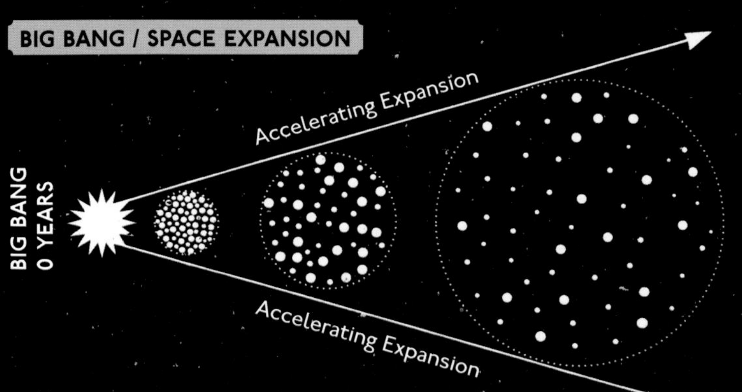

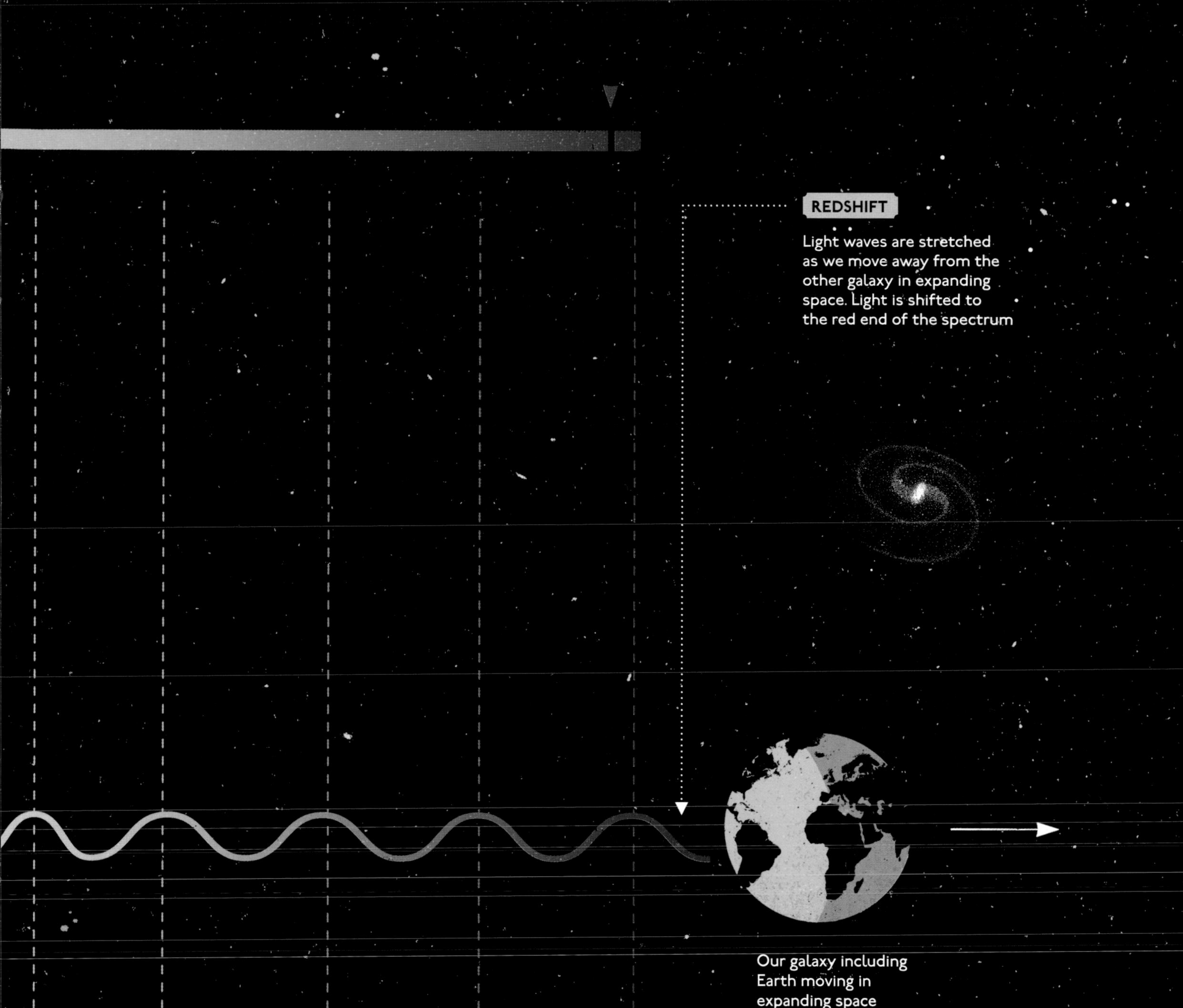
REDSHIFT
Light waves are stretched as we move away from the other galaxy in expanding space. Light is shifted to the red end of the spectrum
Our galaxy including Earth moving in expanding space

between distance travelled and amount of stretching occurs when something very simple but surprising is happening to the Universe. It is expanding! In other words, over the hundreds of millions of years during which the light has been travelling, space itself has been stretching at a relatively constant rate, and this has stretched the wavelength of the light in direct proportion to the distance it has had to travel. This is why the most distant galaxies have the largest redshift – their light has travelled through our expanding universe for longer and has therefore become more stretched. Hubble's discovery of this so-called 'cosmological redshift' was one of the great intellectual moments in twentieth-century science, because he discovered that we live in an expanding universe.

There is a vast amount of information contained within Hubble's simple graph. Redshift can be expressed as the amount of stretching you would see if something were flying away from you at a particular speed. The ratio of the redshift expressed in this way to the distance to the galaxy – which is the gradient of the line on Hubble's graph – is called the Hubble constant. Its value as measured today is 68 kilometres (42 miles) per second, per megaparsec. A megaparsec is a measure of distance commonly used by astronomers – 1 megaparsec is 3.3 million light years. So, another way to think of Hubble's law is that a galaxy that is 3.3 million light years away will be receding from us at a velocity of about 70 kilometres (45 miles) per second. That's pretty slow! A

BELOW: Hubble's discovery of the cosmological redshift brought about another important discovery: we are living in an expanding universe.

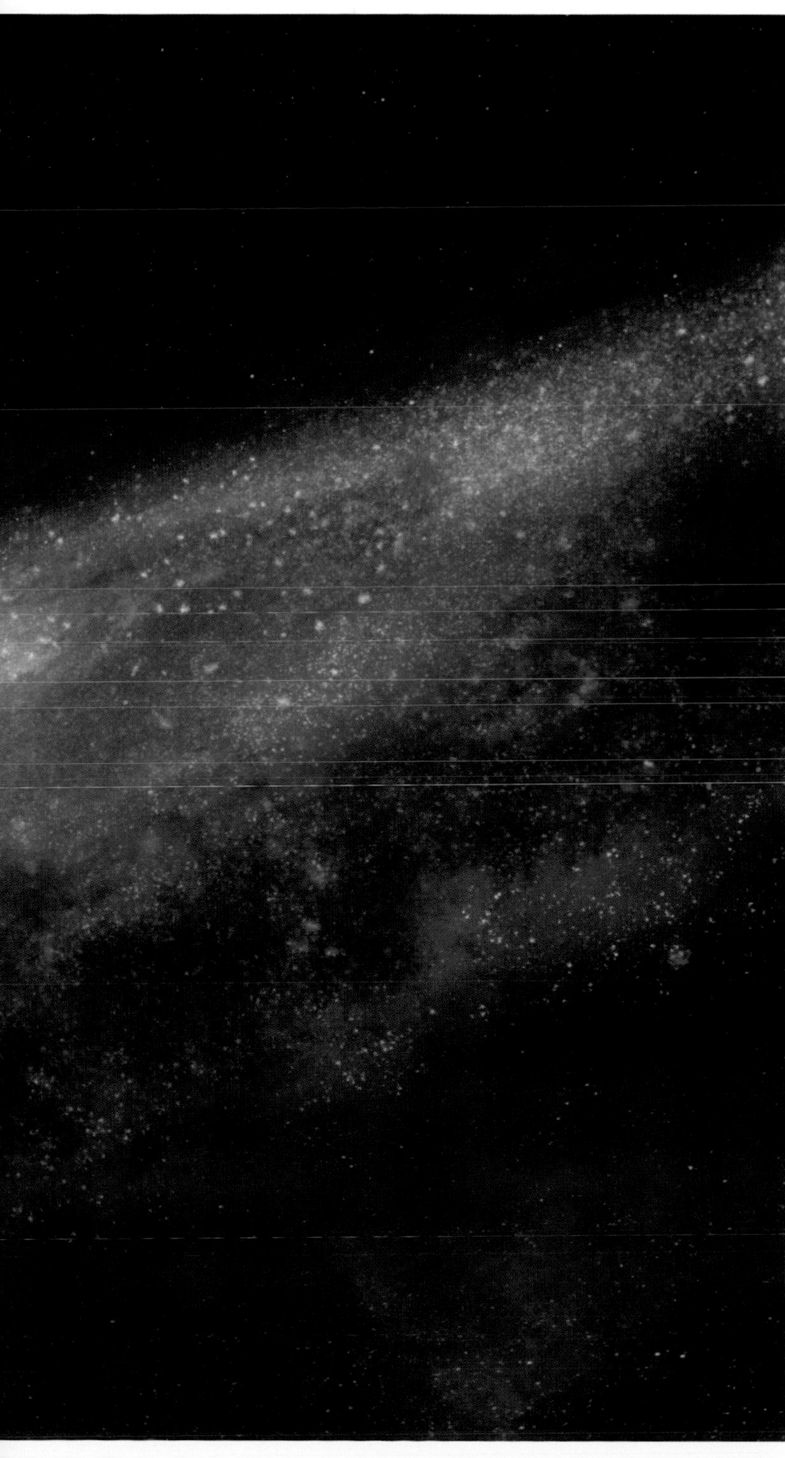

galaxy that is 6.6 million light years away will be receding at about 140 kilometres (90 miles) per second, and so on. And further, if you simply invert the Hubble constant, then you get a number with the units of time. For a Hubble constant of 70 kilometres (45 miles) per second per megaparsec, this corresponds to 14.3 billion years, which can be interpreted as the age of the Universe! (For the more mathematically inclined, you can calculate this number easily by converting megaparsecs to kilometres.) As an aside, the attentive reader might have noticed that our current best measurement for the age of the Universe is slightly lower than this, at 13.75 billion years; this is because precision measurements over the last few decades have shown us that the expansion of the Universe is not in strict accord with Hubble's simple law. The best data we have today tells us that the Universe is accelerating in its expansion due to the presence of something called dark energy.

This might seem complicated, but the conclusion is simple and profound. The reddening of the distant galaxies tells us that the Universe is expanding. This means that the galaxies we see in the sky today must have been closer together in the past. If, in your mind's eye, you keep winding back time and you watch the galaxies getting closer and closer together, then, at a time given by the inverse of the Hubble constant, you will find that they must have all been on top of each other. In other words, the Universe we see today must have been incredibly tiny. This all happened around fourteen billion years ago, and that event is what we call the Big Bang. So Hubble's remarkable observation is direct evidence that the Universe began with a big bang around fourteen billion years ago. All this was deduced in the 1920s simply by capturing the light from Cepheid variable stars and distant galaxies.

The Big Bang is difficult to visualise; it is easy to think of it as a vast explosion that flung matter out into a pre-existing void – a giant empty box, if you like – but this is completely wrong. The currently accepted picture is that all of space came into existence at the Big Bang. In fact, in the spirit of Einstein we should more correctly say that all of spacetime came into existence at the Big Bang. This means that the Big Bang didn't just happen out there somewhere in the Universe, it happened everywhere at once. So the Big Bang happened in the bit of space between you and this book; it happened inside your head, across the road, at every point in the Solar System and inside the most distant galaxies. In other words, it happened at every point in the Universe. All of space was there at the Big Bang, and all it has done is stretch ever since. This has the rather mind-bending consequence that if the Universe is infinite today, it was born infinite. Everywhere that is here now was there then, but just squashed a lot! Nobody said cosmology was easy. So when we look at the distant galaxies and we see them all flying away from us, this is not because they were flung out in some massive explosion at the beginning of time; it is because space itself is stretching, and it's been stretching since the Big Bang.

The Hubble expansion is one piece of evidence for the Big Bang, but there is another, perhaps more remarkable, fingerprint of the Universe's violent beginning, delivered to us by the most ancient light in the cosmos ◉

THE BIRTH OF THE UNIVERSE

Every second, light from the beginning of time is raining down on Earth's surface in a ceaseless torrent. Only a fraction of the light present in the Universe is visible to the naked eye, though; if we could see all of it, the sky would be ablaze with this primordial light both day and night. However, some of this hidden light is not quite a featureless glow; the long wavelength universal glow known as the Cosmic Microwave Background (CMB) in fact displays minute variations in its wavelength. The CMB carries with it an image of our universe as it was just after its birth, and this discovery has provided key evidence that the beginning really did start with the Big Bang.

RIGHT: It was at the Big Bang that all of spacetime came into existence. The stars and galaxies stretched away across an infinite universe and many are still to be found today. Space is stretching still; housing the old galaxies alongside numerous new star-forming regions, such as NGC 281 k.

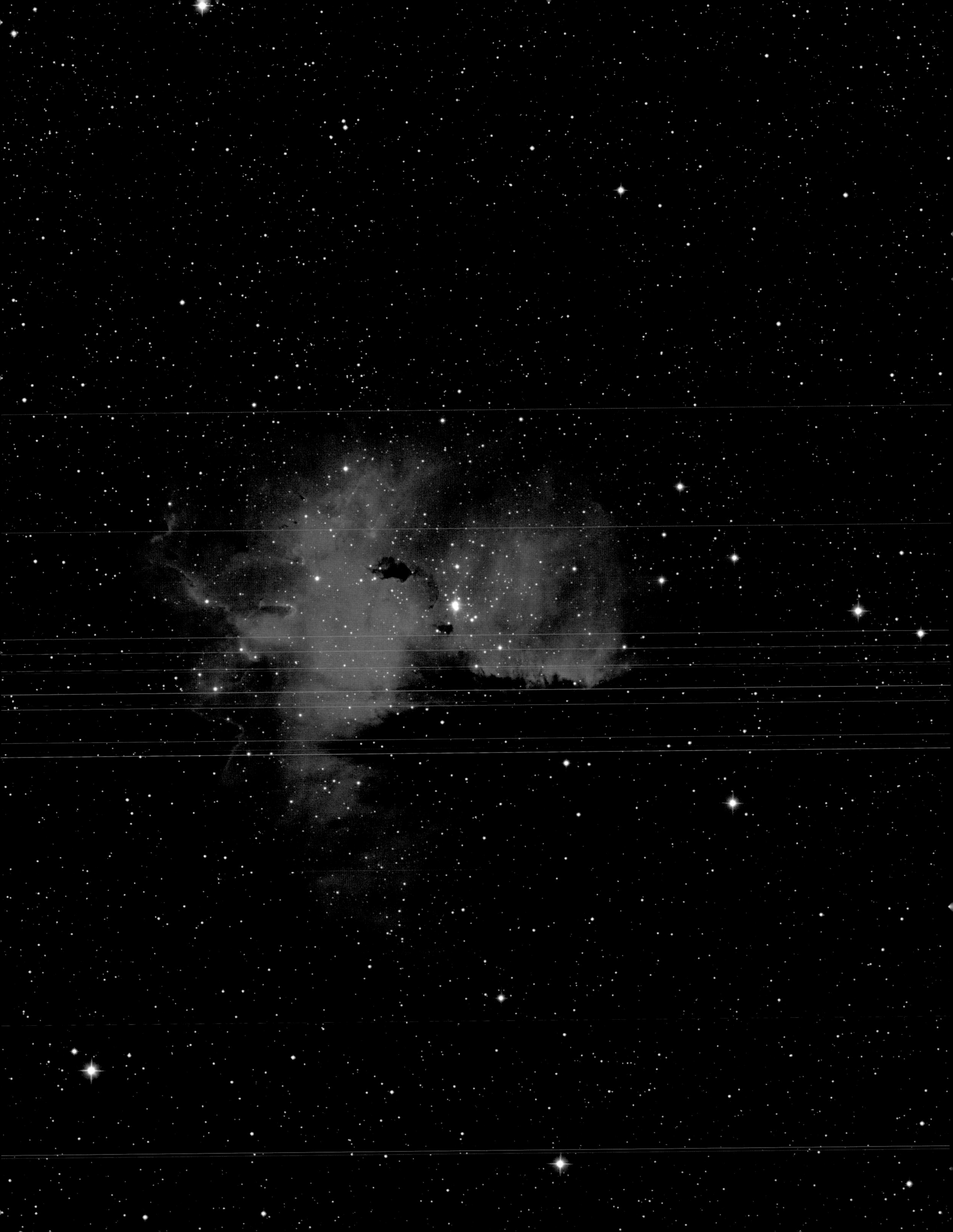

VISIBLE LIGHT

Stretching along the west coast of southern Africa is the Namib Desert. It is the oldest desert in the world; its landscape is a shifting sea of sand of over 77,700 square kilometres (30,000 square miles) which changes every minute, a consistently arid wilderness that has stubbornly avoided moisture for over fifty million years. This is a world sculpted by the Sun; its energy drives the wind that shapes the tiny grains of sand into magnificent dunes, and the colours hidden in its light paint the landscape deep orange. Yet even when the Sun has set, the desert remains awash with light and colour, but the human eye can't see it.

Visible light is a tiny fraction of the light in the Universe. Beyond the red, the electromagnetic spectrum extends to wavelengths too long for our eyes to detect. It's still light; still the sloshing back and forth of the electric and magnetic fields driving forwards through the void at the special universal speed, it's just we didn't evolve to see it. In the Namib Desert you can feel this light, though, if you hold your palms towards the sand. The dunes are warm long after sunset, and this residual heat is nothing more than long-wavelength light. A scientist would call it infrared light; the only difference between infrared and visible light is the wavelength – infrared has a longer wavelength than visible light. Travel further along the spectrum, past infrared, and we arrive at microwaves, with wavelengths unsurprisingly about the size of a microwave oven. The spectrum then seamlessly slides into the radio region, with wavelengths the size of mountains.

Throughout most of human history we have been blind to these more unfamiliar forms of light, but to detect them you don't need expensive, hi-tech kit, just a radio. When tuning a radio you are not tuning into a sound wave, you are picking up information encoded in a wave of light. Most of the radio waves we are familiar with are artificially created and used for communication and broadcasting, but just as there is plenty of visible light in the Universe that isn't manmade, so there are naturally occurring microwaves and radio waves too. And just like the visible photons from the most distant galaxies, the microwave and radio photons are messengers, carrying detailed information about distant places and times across the Universe and into our technologically created artificial eyes.

Next time you are tuning a radio and can hear static, you are actually listening to a deeply profound sound – you are listening to the Big Bang.

Next time you tune a radio, listen to the static between the stations. About 1 per cent of this is music to the ears of a physicist because it is stretched light that has travelled from the beginning of time. Deep in the static is the echo of the Big Bang. These radio waves were once visible light, but light that originated 400,000 years after the Big Bang. Prior to

LEFT: Standing among the dunes of the Namib Desert you become aware of the sheer scale of the landscape. It is a landscape sculpted by the Sun and coloured by it at all times.

BELOW: Forget state-of-the-art kit, all you need to use to detect hidden forms of light is a simple radio. As you tune, it you will pick up information encoded in a wave of light.

BOTTOM: Only a fraction of light is visible in the Universe. This infrared image shows the massive scale of the Universe and demonstrates how the electromagnetic spectrum extends to wavelengths that are too long for our eyes to detect. Here we can see hundreds of thousands of stars at the core of the Milky Way Galaxy, but so many are still hidden from our view.

that, the observable universe was far smaller and hotter than it is today. At 273 million degrees Celsius, this is an order of magnitude hotter than the centre of a star, so hot that the hydrogen and helium nuclei then present in the Universe couldn't hold onto their electrons to form atoms. The Universe was a super-heated ball of naked atomic nuclei and electrons known as a plasma. Light cannot travel far in dense plasma because it bounces off the electrically charged subatomic particles. It was only when the Universe had expanded and cooled down enough for the electrons to combine with the hydrogen and helium nuclei to form atoms that light was free to roam. This point in the evolution of the Universe, known as recombination, occurred around 400,000 years after the Big Bang, when the Universe had cooled to about 3,000 degrees Celsius and was around a thousandth of its present size. That is close to the surface temperature of red giant stars, so the whole Universe would have been glowing with visible light like a vast star. The Universe has become cooler and more diffuse since, so this ancient light has been free to fly through space, and it is some of these wandering messengers that we collect with a detuned radio today. However, as the Universe has expanded, space has stretched and so too has the light – so much so that the light is no longer in the visible part of the spectrum. It has moved beyond even the infrared, and is now visible to us only in the microwave and radio parts of the spectrum. This faint, long, wavelength universal glow is known as the Cosmic Microwave Background, or CMB, and its discovery in 1964 by Arno Penzias and Robert Wilson was key evidence in proving that the Universe began in a Big Bang ●

PICTURING THE PAST

BELOW: This detailed picture of the Universe in its infancy was pieced together from data collected over several years by the Wilkinson Microwave Anisotropy Probe (WMAP). The different colours reveal the 13.7-billion-year-old temperature fluctuations that correspond to the seeds from which the galaxies grew.

On 30 June 2001, the Wilkinson Microwave Anisotropy Probe, known as WMAP, was launched from the Kennedy Space Center in Florida. This highly specialised telescope was built with a single purpose: to capture the faint glow of the CMB and create the earliest possible photograph of the Universe. After nine years of service, WMAP has recently been retired, but its photograph is still the object of frenzied research because it contains so much rich detail about the early Universe and its expansion and evolution ever since.

This much-studied image is probably the most important picture of the sky ever taken. It may not look like much; it doesn't have the beauty of a spiral galaxy or nebula, but to a scientist it is the most beautiful picture ever taken because it contains a vast amount of information about the history of our Universe.

The raw image from WMAP shows the glow of our Milky Way Galaxy as it creates a hot bright band across the sky, but once this detail and other observational side-effects are removed, we are left with this simplified, but equally important and informative, picture below. This photograph of the night sky documents in extraordinary detail the structure of our universe at the time of recombination. Over the nine years in which WMAP was in service, the detail of this image has been repeatedly refined, which in turn reveals more and more detailed information encoded in the primordial light.

The WMAP data is presented as a temperature map of the sky. The wavelength of the detected light at any particular point corresponds to a temperature; shorter wavelengths are higher temperatures, longer wavelengths are lower ones. The red areas are hotter than the blue, but only by around 0.0002 degrees. The average temperature of the CMB is 2.725 degrees above absolute zero. On the Kelvin temperature scale, that's 2.725 K, or -270.425 Celsius.

Despite being incredibly tiny, these temperature differences are of overwhelming importance because they tell us that in the very first moments of our universe's life there were regions of space that were slightly denser than others. These virtually imperceptible differences might not seem much, but without them we would not exist. That's because these little blips in the CMB are the seeds of the galaxies. The red spots in the CMB correspond to parts of the Universe that were on average around half a per cent denser than the surrounding areas at the time of recombination. As the whole Universe expanded, these areas would have expanded slightly more slowly than their surroundings because of their higher density – effectively, their increased gravity due to their higher density would have slowed the expansion, causing their density to increase further relative to the space around them. By the time the Universe was one-fifth of its present size, just over a billion years after the Big Bang, these regions would have

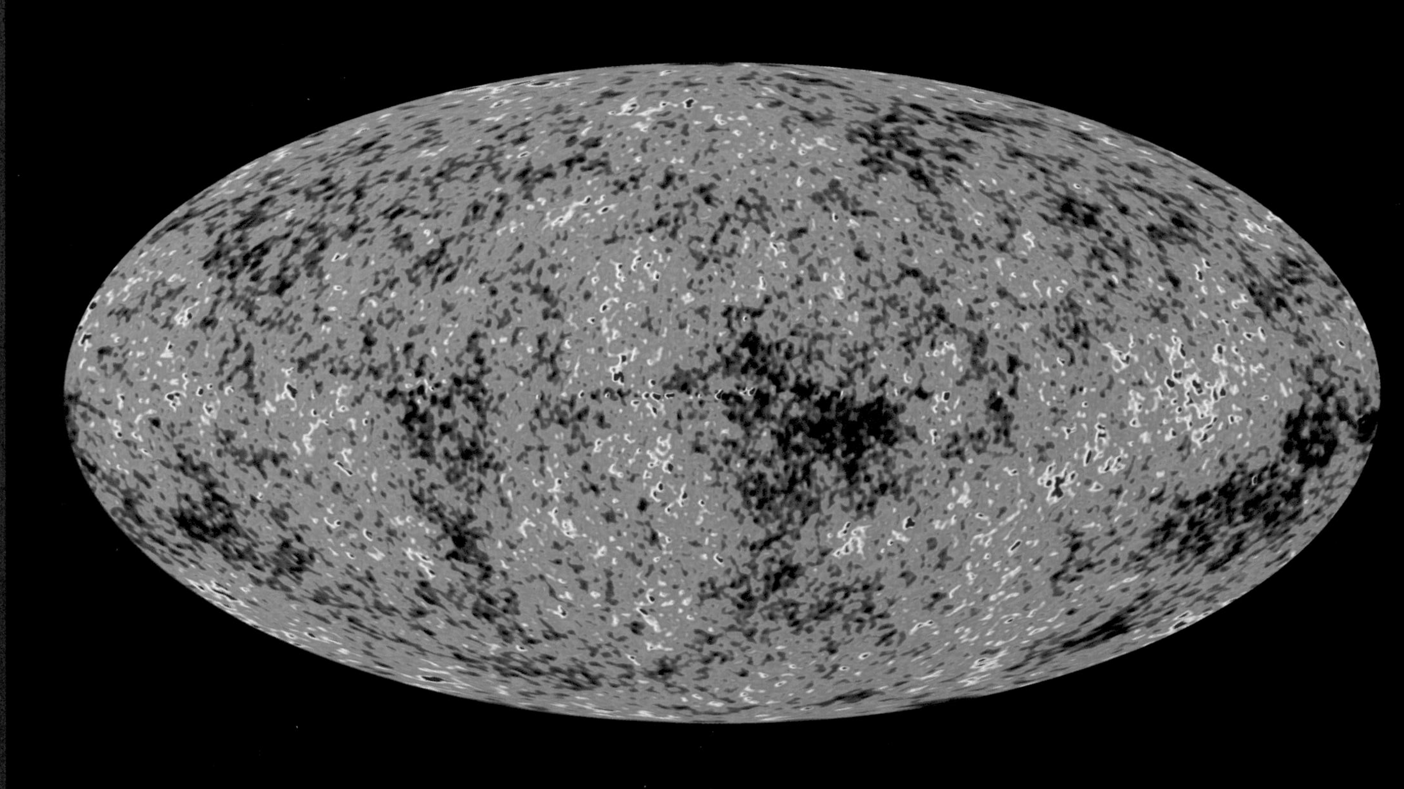

BELOW: As the Universe expanded, the denser areas within it expanded more slowly than others because of their increased gravity. By the time these areas were twice as dense as their surroundings, the matter within them was sufficiently cool and dense to collapse under their own gravity and form the first stars and cores of new galaxies.

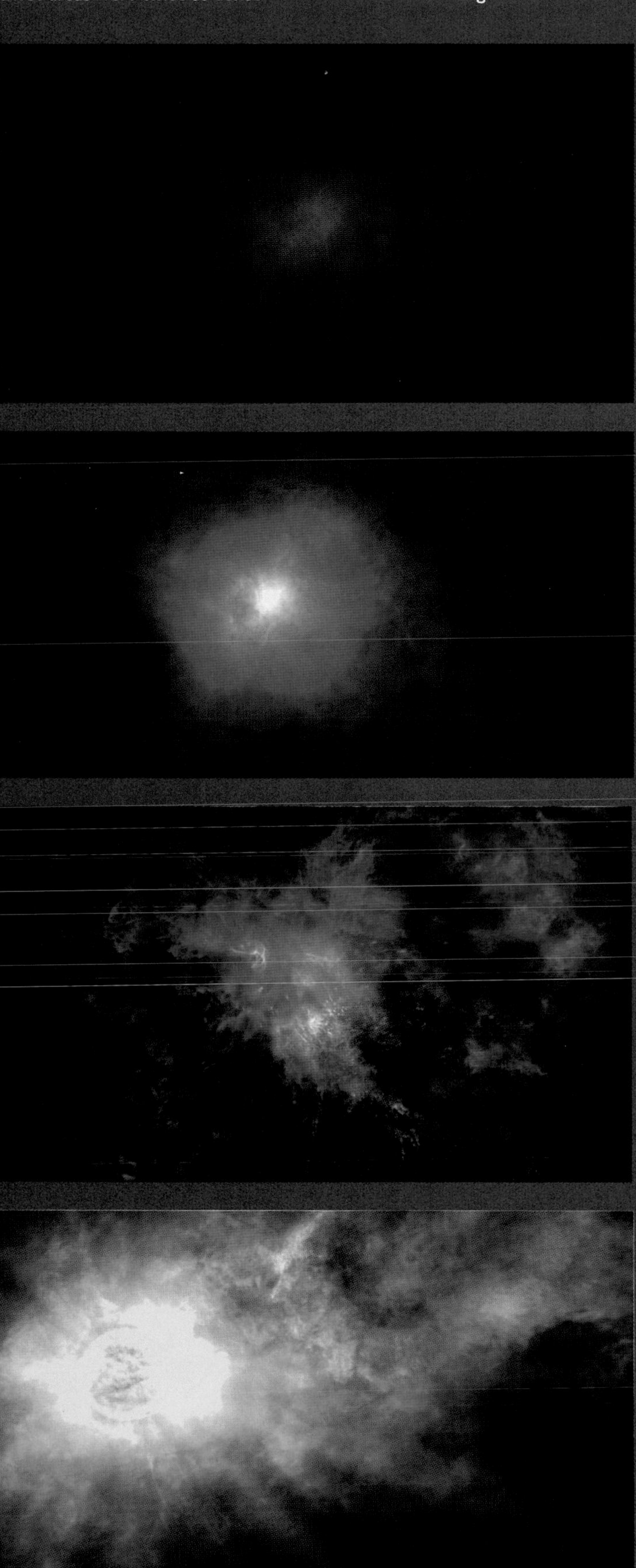

been twice as dense as their surroundings. By this time the matter in these regions was dense enough and cool enough to begin to collapse under its own gravity, leading to the first star formation and the emergence of the cores of the galaxies, including our own Milky Way. This is the cosmic epoch we see in the most redshifted Hubble Space Telescope data – the formation of the first galaxies – and their seeds are the minute fluctuations visible in the Cosmic Microwave Background Radiation.

The rest, as they say, is history. Across the cosmos, countless suns began to switch on and to fill the Universe with light. For billions of years, generations of stars lived and died until, 9 billion years after it all began, in an unremarkable piece of space known as the Orion Spur off the Perseus Arm of a galaxy called the Milky Way, a star was born that became known as the Sun. This is the story of how our solar system has its ultimate origin in those dense areas of space that appeared in the first moments of our Universe's life. But what is the origin of those tiny fluctuations in density that we see in the CMB?

This is perhaps the most remarkable piece of physics of all. The most popular current model for the very very early Universe is known as inflation. The idea is that around 10–36 seconds after the Big Bang, the Universe went through an astonishingly rapid phase of expansion in which it increased in volume by a factor of around 10^{78}! In less scientific notation, that's a million million million million million millionths of a second after the Big Bang, and an increase in volume by a factor of a million billion billion billion billion billion billion billion billion billion. This was all over by 10^{-32} seconds or so. Before inflation, the part of the Universe we now observe, all the hundreds of billions of galaxies in our night sky, would have been far, far smaller than a single subatomic particle. At these minute distance scales, quantum mechanics reigns supreme, and tiny quantum fluctuations before inflation would have been magnified by the rapid expansion to form the denser regions we observe in the Cosmic Microwave Background spectrum. If inflationary theory is correct, the CMB is therefore a window onto a time in the life of the Universe far earlier than 400,000 years after the Big Bang. We are seeing the imprint of events that happened in the truly mind-blowing first million million million million million millionths of a second after it all began. I find this the most astonishing idea in all of science. From a vantage point of 13.7 billion years, little beings like you and me scurrying around on the surface of a rock on the edge of one of the galaxies are able to understand the evolution of the Universe and speculate intelligently about the very beginning of time itself, just by decoding the messages carried to us across the cosmos on beams of light. The power of science is quite genuinely daunting, the richness of its stories unparalleled, the cosmos it reveals, beautiful beyond imagination.

There is one last twist to this story. Throughout our journey, light has been the messenger, carrying stories of far-flung places and the distant past to our shores. But there is evidence from one of the ancient sites on our home planet that light may have played a far more active role in our history than mere muse ◉

FIRST SIGHT

Hidden in the high Rocky Mountains in British Columbia, Canada, is one of the most important and evocative scientific sites on Earth, and it's where the story of light and our lives begins. Around 505 million years ago, when this whole area lay deep beneath the surface of a primordial ocean, it was hit by a huge mudflow. The mud buried everything in its path and created a snapshot of a remarkable time in the evolution of life on Earth. A whole ancient ecosystem was frozen and preserved intact in the mud; the lives of the primitive creatures documented by a chance geological event with the care and precision with which the Egyptians created their glorious tombs half a billion years later. For hundreds of millions of years, this ancient treasure trove was locked away, but in 1909 it was uncovered high on a mountainside. This is the Burgess Shale.

The Burgess Shale is one of the most important fossil sites in the world. It is not just the number and diversity of the animals found here, it's their immense age. Before around 540 million years ago, there are no fossils of complex life forms found anywhere on the surface of Earth. We know that there was life before this period, but the animals were very simple creatures that didn't possess skeletons of any kind. This means that they don't show up on the fossil record. In the geological blink of an eye in the period of time immortalised in the Burgess Shale, known as the Cambrian Era, it appears

One current theory for the origin of the Evolutionary Big Bang is that the emergence of the eye in animals such as the trilobite triggered the Cambrian Explosion. Once one predatory species develops eyes, there is a powerful selection mechanism in favour of others developing and refining eyes too.

that a vast range of complex multi-cellular life emerged on the planet. Biologists call it the Evolutionary Big Bang, or the Cambrian Explosion.

So what triggered the evolution of complex life? There is a clue in these fossil beds that lie high in the Canadian Rocky Mountains. The picture left shows one of the ancient animals found here; a complex organism called a trilobite. Trilobites, now long extinct, had external skeletons and jointed limbs, but most strikingly they had complex, compound eyes. These prehistoric predators could see shapes, detect movement and use their eyes very effectively to chase their prey. The ability to see made these trilobites very successful animals indeed; in fact they survived for a quarter of a billion years, only vanishing from Earth in the Permian mass extinction 250 million years ago.

One current theory for the origin of the Evolutionary Big Bang is that the emergence of the eye in animals such as the trilobite triggered the Cambrian Explosion. Once a predator possesses eyes which will help it chase its prey, a new force in natural selection is immediately introduced. The animals that survive this selection are those that are best adapted to this new threat; they may camouflage themselves, leading to an increasingly sophisticated visual appearance, or dodge the predators with enhanced sense organs. In other words, once one predatory species develops eyes, there is a powerful selection mechanism in favour of others developing and refining eyes too. In turn, this selects far more sophisticated predators, and so on. This is in a sense an evolutionary arms

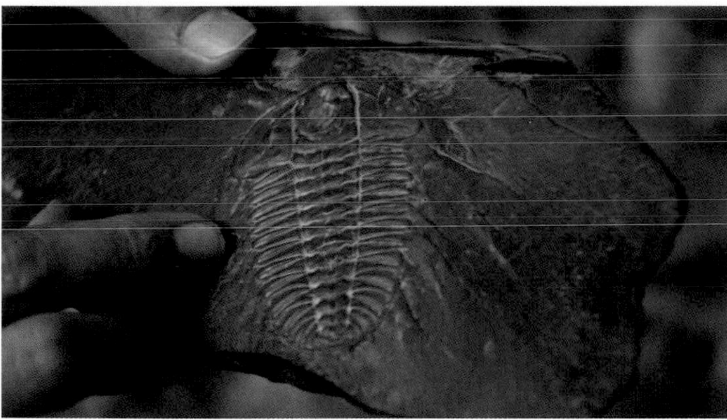

LEFT AND TOP: The Burgess Shale is one of the most important and exciting fossil sites in the world, where a staggering amount of diverse animals are to be found, dating back over 500 million years.

ABOVE: Numerous genera of trilobites have been found in the Burgess Shale. These fossils are so detailed and well preserved that they have enabled scientists to make important observations about the structure and behaviour of these now-extinct organisms.

race, as the pressure of natural selection leads more and more complex life forms to develop.

These early creatures, immortalised in the Burgess Shale, were among the very first to harness the light that filled the Universe. Before they emerged, the rise and fall of the Sun and the stars in the night sky went unnoticed. These creatures are our ancestors, and in fact there is also evidence at Burgess that we humans may only exist because of one particular adaptation in a strange, worm-like creature called a Pikaia. Although the Pikaia looks unimpressive, it may be one of the most important animals ever discovered. It is thought by some, although not all, evolutionary biologists that the Pikaia is the earliest known ancestor of modern vertebrates – the branch of life that we are categorised in – so it could be that this little worm-like creature is our earliest known ancestor. What is also fascinating about Pikaia is that it may have had light-sensitive cells that allowed it to evade predators and survive in the Cambrian seas – cells that may have evolved over many hundreds of millions of years into our eyes. This is all speculative, but it is possible that without Pikaia's primitive yet remarkable ability to detect the light from the Sun, we humans may never have appeared on planet Earth. Perhaps there would never have been a life form

We have even been able to capture the light from the beginning of time and we have glimpsed within it the seeds of our own origins.

here with the ability to do the one thing that has allowed us to understand our universe more than anything else: to look up.

Understanding the Universe is like reading a detective story, and the essential evidence we need to solve it has been carried to us across the vast expanses of space and time by light. We have even been able to capture the light from the beginning of time and we have glimpsed within it the seeds of our own origins. We've seen things our ancestors wouldn't believe: stars being born in distant realms, and galaxies lost in time at the very edge of the visible Universe and our cosmos just moments after it all began.

It's a wonderful thought that these primitive biological light detectors that emerged on Earth half a billion years ago in the Cambrian Explosion have evolved into those most human of things; our green, blue and brown eyes that are able to gaze up into the night sky, capture the light from distant stars and tell the story of the Universe ◉

LEFT: The Carina Nebula is a large bright nebula that surrounds several clusters of stars. It contains two of the most massive and luminous stars in our Milky Way galaxy, Eta Carinae and HD 93129A. Located 7500 light years away, the nebula itself spans some 260 light years across, about seven times the size of the Orion Nebula, and is shown in all its glory in this mosaic. It is based on images collected with the 1.5-metre Danish telescope at ESO's La Silla Observatory.

CHAPTER 2

STARDUST

THE ORIGINS OF BEING

What are we made of? This is an old question, maybe one of the oldest, and one that thinkers and scientists have been working hard to answer since ancient times. This work continues today, and it may be that by the time you read this book the story of the search for the building blocks of the Universe will have another chapter. Such is the power, excitement and rate of progress of modern science. This chapter is the story of how those building blocks were created in the very early Universe, fused into more complex structures over billions of years in the furnaces of space, and delicately assembled by the forces of nature into planets, mountains, rivers and human beings.

RIGHT: The Large Hadron Collider (LHC) is the highest energy particle accelerator at CERN (the European particle physics laboratory near Geneva, Switzerland). In this huge machine, 27km (17 miles)in circumference, proton beams are accelerated so that they collide head-on. The resultant particles can be detected and recorded so that scientists can then try to understand how they fit together.

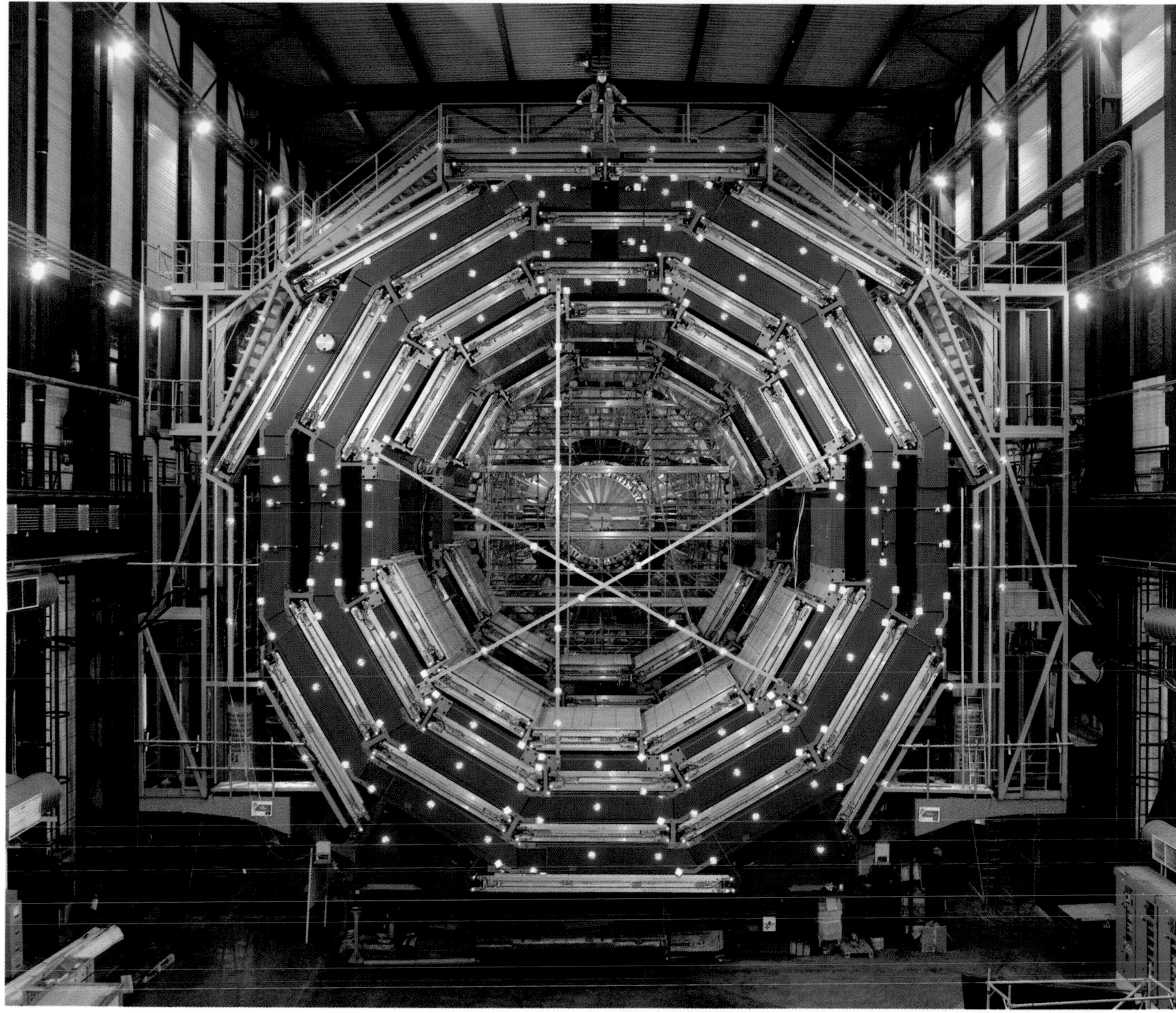

The ancient Greeks thought deeply about the question of what we are made of, although they lacked the scientific methodology and technology to arrive at a definitive answer. This led to many competing hypotheses, including some that got close to our modern view: we are all made out of smaller pieces. That there are the smallest building blocks of matter (indivisible basic units that can be fitted together to build the world) was termed the 'atomic hypothesis', a theory usually credited to two thinkers – Leucippus and Democritus – in around 400 BC. They held that the world was created from an infinite number of different types of indivisible and indestructible atoms. Each had a different shape, allowing them to fit together neatly to build large objects. So, iron was made of one type of atom, water of another, human flesh of another, and so on. They thought atoms possessed the properties of their real-world substances – water atoms were slippery, while metal ones were shaped so that they locked together to produce very hard substances. We now know that this is not only wrong, but a gross overcomplication. While their hypothesis correctly stated that the world is made from smaller pieces, you don't need an infinite number of atom types to build the complexity around us. A human is made of the same stuff as a rock; a fish of the same stuff as the Earth; the sky of the same stuff as the oceans. Enumerating the basic building blocks and understanding how they fit together is the province of the science of particle physics, and this quest continues at the Large Hadron Collider at CERN, in Geneva.

By early 2011, we had discovered that the Universe is composed of twelve basic building blocks, only three of which are required to build everything on our planet, including our bodies. These three components, known as the up and down quarks and the electron, can be assembled into the more familiar protons and neutrons – two up quarks and a down quark make a proton, and two down quarks and an up make up a neutron. In turn, the protons, neutrons and electrons make up the chemical elements – ninety-four of which are known to occur naturally – including the basic chemical elements hydrogen, carbon, oxygen, iron, gold and silver ●

THE CYCLE OF LIFE

BELOW: The Bagmati River is lined with funeral pyres burning the bodies of the deceased.

Fifteen miles northeast of the Nepalese capital city of Kathmandu, three small streams come together to mark the beginning of one of the holiest rivers in the world. At its source the Bagmati is a fast-running mountain stream, but by the time it winds through the Kathmandu valley and enters the great city of the Himalayas it has become a wide and majestic river.

In the eastern part of the city, where the river's mythical power is at its greatest, stands the fifth-century Pashupatinath Temple, one of the most sacred sites in the Hindu world. Pilgrims come from all over India and Nepal to worship there and pay their respects to the god Shiva.

I have always found the Hindu faith fascinating; it is rich and complex, a disorientating mix of mythology and philosophy, a continual and jagged juxtaposition of temples, holy sites, rituals and everyday life that produces a joyful assault on the senses. Pashupatinath is no exception. It is at once vibrant and ethereal, a place where the colours and noise of India meet the gentle philosophy of Tibet and the hybrid dissolves into the crystal-clear, high Himalayan air in the smoke of a thousand burning bodies on the funeral pyres lit at this holy place. The scent of burning flesh mixes with incense and tinkling bells, and the sound of chanting Monkey Gods continually interrupts the calls of market traders.

A central tenet of Hindu philosophy is the concept of the Trimurti – the triad of the three fundamental aspects of the Supreme Being, represented as the great gods Brahma, Vishnu and Shiva. Lord Brahma is the creator of the Universe, Lord Vishnu the preserver, and Lord Shiva the destroyer. Shiva represents darkness, as an angry god who will eventually bring an end to Earth, yet in Hinduism this destruction is seen as an essential part of the cycle of life, because in order for new things to be created, the old order must first be destroyed. Shiva is therefore also a regenerative

LEFT: For Hindus, the passing of a loved one is a stage in the endless cycle of death and rebirth that is central to their beliefs. Cremations are a familiar sight along the holy Bagmati River; the body is dipped in the river three times before cremation, and at the end of the ceremony the chief mourner must bathe in the river's water, often accompanied by the other attendant mourners.

or reproductive power, part of the endless cycle of death and rebirth that is central to the Hindu belief system. This is why the Pashupatinath Temple and the river it stands beside are revered as places to die.

Hindus believe that the purpose of a soul's time on Earth is to work through a cycle of rebirth and reincarnation until it becomes perfect. Only then can it be reunited with the Universal Soul and be freed from its material existence. The *Bhagavad Gita* says: 'Just as a man discards worn-out clothes and puts on new clothes, the soul discards worn-out bodies and wears new ones'. By having your body cremated on the riverbank beside Shiva's Pashupatinath Temple, it is believed that your soul will be released from the worn-out body as quickly and easily as possible.

According to the Nepalese Hindu tradition, the dead body must be dipped three times into the Bagmati River before cremation. The chief mourner, usually the first son of the deceased, lights the funeral pyre and must bathe in the waters of the holy river immediately after the cremation. Many of the relatives who join the funeral procession also bathe in the river or sprinkle the holy water on their bodies. This makes the river bank a strange and crowded place. To my British eyes it is somewhat shocking, because death is rarely, if ever, paraded like this; but here in Kathmandu it is not seen to be insensitive to wander between the pyres as the relatives and friends go through their rituals.

In Hindu tradition the human body consists of five elements: air, water, fire, earth and ether. Remarkably, according to modern science, this is overcomplicated, but their belief about what happens to these elements after death parallels our modern understanding of how the world works.

Underlying the cremation ceremony is the conviction that the elements of the body vacated by the soul are returned to Earth to be re-used and recycled. Death is therefore not an end for the immortal soul or the mortal flesh, it is simply the conclusion of one stage of existence and the beginning of another; part of a natural cycle of death and rebirth. As far as the atoms and molecules in our bodies are concerned, modern science is in complete agreement with that idea. When I die my constituents aren't going to be magically destroyed; they will be returned to Earth and, given enough time, they will become part of some other structure.

Of course, Hinduism isn't alone in having rich and lyrical stories about the origin and evolution of Man and the Universe. Virtually every society and every religion around the world has at its heart a creation story that explains where we come from, how we came to be here, and what will happen to us when we die. This suggests that curiosity about our origins is an innate, perhaps even a defining part, of the human condition.

Underlying the cremation ceremony is the conviction that the elements of the body vacated by the soul are returned to Earth to be re-used and recycled ... As far as the atoms and molecules in our bodies are concerned, modern science is in complete agreement with that idea.

In common with the great systems of thought throughout history, modern science has its own creation story to tell – one based on physics and cosmology. It can tell us what we're made of and where we came from – in fact, it can tell us what everything in the world is made of and where it came from. It also answers that most basic of human needs: to feel part of something much bigger, because to tell this story you have to understand the history of the Universe. It also teaches us that the path to enlightenment is not in understanding our own lives and deaths, but in understanding the lives and deaths of the stars ◉

BELOW: The Dunhuang star chart dates back to AD 700 and is the oldest existing star chart. It was named after the place where it was found along the Silk Road trade route in northern China (in the twentieth century) and is now owned by the British Library. It depicts the stars in the sky according to the Chinese constellation tradition.

RIGHT: This celestial map shows a more detailed, highly illustrated view of the constellations according to Dutch cartographer Frederik de Wit in the seventeenth century.

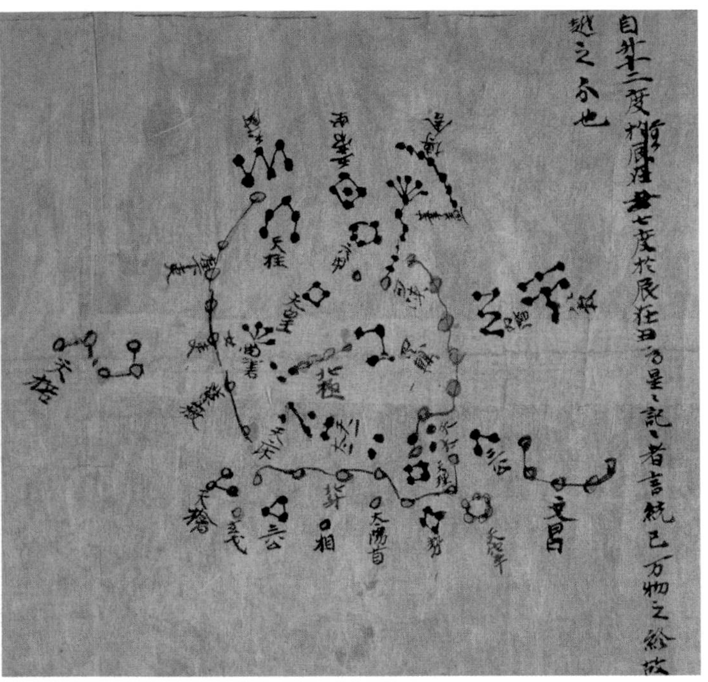

MAPPING THE NIGHT SKY

The moment you leave a city and experience a truly dark night sky, it becomes obvious why our ancestors spent a great deal of time looking up at the stars. They are a bewildering array; a patterned silver canopy self-evidently not devoid of meaning or purpose. For thousands of years ancient astronomers endeavoured to capture and catalogue every light; to observe, log and name as many of these distant suns (for we now know their true nature) as they could. The oldest-known record of a star chart may be over thirty thousand years old. A carved ivory mammoth's tusk, discovered in Germany in the late 1970s, appears to be imprinted with a pattern that resembles the constellation of stars we now call Orion. In France, cave paintings have been discovered which reveal that humans were mapping the night skies tens of

For thousands of years ancient astronomers endeavoured to capture and catalogue every light; to observe, log and name as many of these distant suns (for we now know their true nature) as they could.

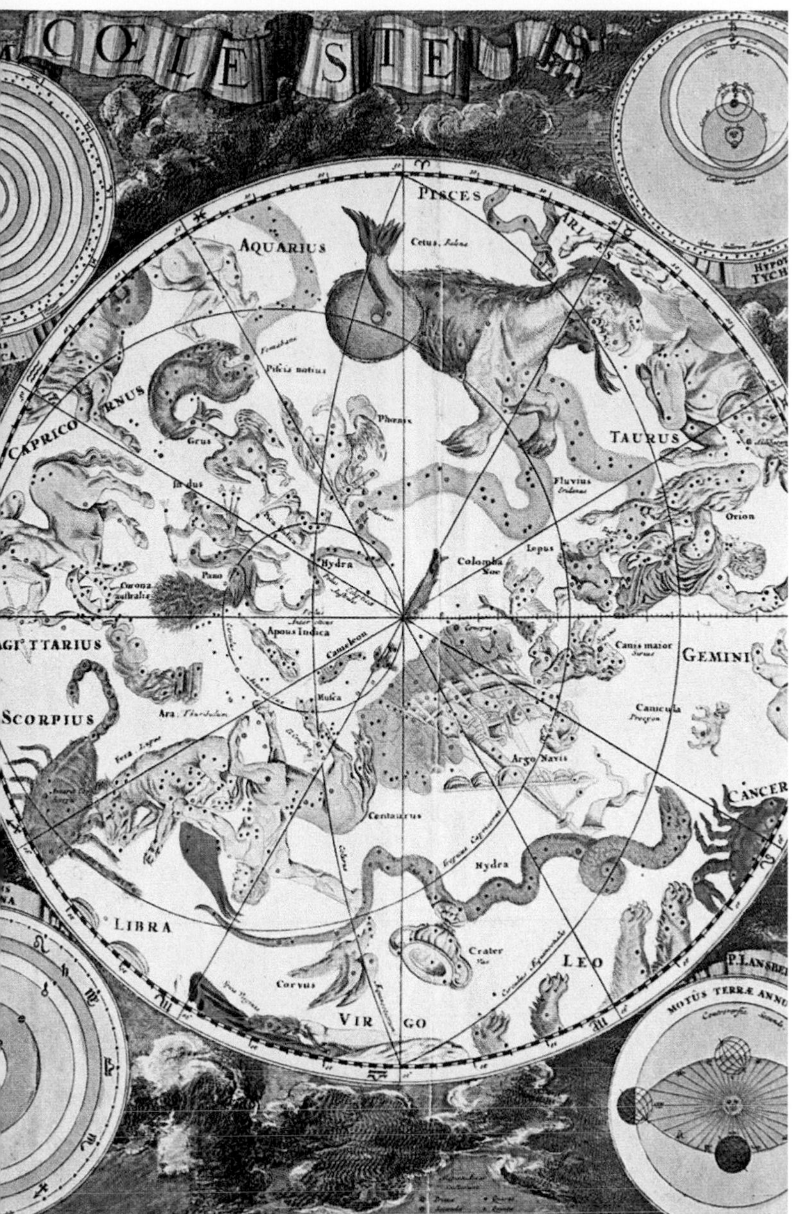

BELOW: In AD 185, Chinese astronomers witnessed a brightness in the sky comparable to that of Mars, and this remained for eight months. This phenomena was the first recorded occurrence of a supernova explosion, but it was not until late 2006 that the remains of this cosmic event were identified. This picture, taken by the Chandra X-ray Observatory, shows an object now known as RCW 86. The image shows low-, medium- and high-energy X-rays in red, green and blue respectively. It was the study of the distribution of X-rays with energy, combined with measuring the remnant's size, that enabled scientists to conclude that RCW 86 was created by the explosion of a massive star around 8,000 light years away.

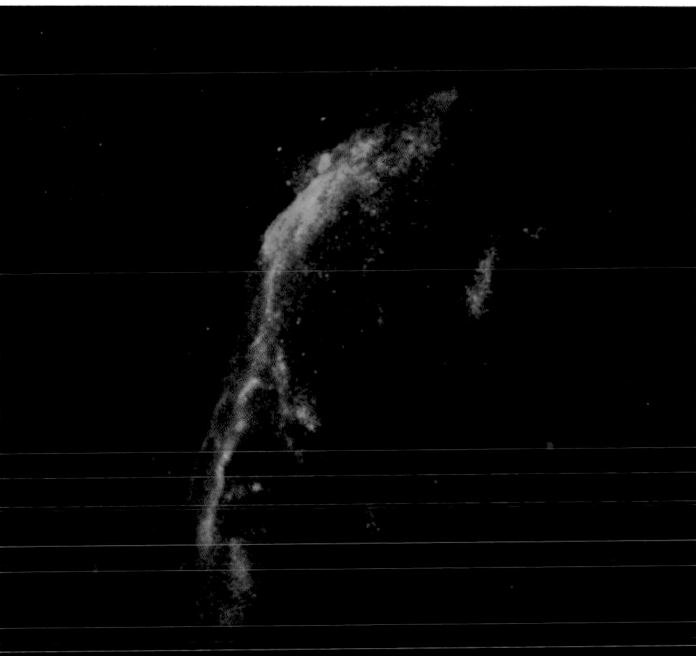

thousands of years before the great civilisations of antiquity began to slowly explore the Universe in more detail.

The Egyptians were one of the first ancient cultures to not only map the night sky but to name some of the stars they observed. They called the North Star the 'star that cannot perish', and they also recorded the names of constellations. The Sumerians and Babylonians went a step further by writing down these early names and patterns and creating astronomical catalogues that listed and grouped stars in ever-increasing complexity. Greek, Chinese and Islamic astronomers all continued to build ever more complex systems of classification, with many stars today still being referred to by their original Arabic names.

To the ancients, the stellar backdrop had a deceptive permanence that no doubt motivated them to record and mythologise the patterns they saw. But in AD 185, for the first time in recorded history, a particular type of fleeting addition to the lights in the night sky was observed and documented. Understanding the nature of this rare and spectacular phenomenon eventually led us beyond merely naming the stars and enabled us to tell the story of their births and deaths.

In late 2006, the remains of the cosmic event of AD 185 that illuminated the skies and minds of Chinese astronomers almost two thousand years ago was identified. The picture above, taken by the Chandra X-ray Observatory, is that of the object known as RCW 86. This object is thought to be the still-glowing remains of one of the most powerful events in our universe – a supernova explosion.

Supernovae are the final act in the lives of massive stars, colossal explosions in which a single star can shine as brightly as a billion suns. If RCW 86 is the remains of the AD 185 supernova, then the 'guest star' described by the Chinese astronomers that glowed brightly in the skies for eight months before fading from view was around 8,000 light years away – a quite colossal distance for something to shine so brightly in our skies. The ancient astronomers didn't know it at the time, of course, but they had documented the first clear evidence that the stars must all eventually die ●

STELLAR NURSERIES

BELOW: These fascinating ultraviolet images, taken by NASA's Galaxy Evolution Explorer, show a star named Mira speeding across the sky and leaving behind it an enormous trail of debris. This material is in fact 'seeds' which will be recycled to create new stars, planets and possibly even life, as it travels through our galaxy.

Above our heads a story of life and death is being told in spectacular fashion. This tale begins in the vast stellar nurseries where new stars burst into life. These fertile areas of star formation are known as nebulae and are among the most beautiful structures in the skies. One of these, the Orion Nebula (pictured far right), is perhaps the most studied astronomical object. It is usually credited as being discovered by Nicolas-Claude Fabri de Peiresc in 1610, but there is evidence from folk tales that the Mayans knew of the faint smudge beneath the stars of Orion's belt. It can be seen with the naked eye in a very dark clear sky, and it is this complex, ever-changing formation that has taught us most about how stars are born.

The Omega Nebula (the Horseshoe, or Swan, Nebula) is a vast interstellar cloud that is over fifteen light years across and illuminated by hundreds of bright young stars. These stars, depending on their masses, will burn for hundreds of millions or billions of years, sending a constant stream of light across the Universe until their voracious hunger depletes the hydrogen in their cores and forces them to expand and transform into giants.

As they near the end of their lives, the most massive stars are transformed into colossal giants – such as the red Mira, whose radius is 400 times that of our sun and only just clinging onto life. When the end finally comes for stars like these, the ensuing supernova explosion will leave only a faint trace of the star. For the largest stars, the supernova will leave a black hole behind – an object so dense that even light cannot escape its clutches. Slightly smaller stars will end their post-supernova days as neutron stars, which we detect by the lighthouse beam of radiowaves they emit as they spin every few seconds or less.

Stars much smaller than Mira won't go out with a bang. Such relatively cool stars are called red dwarfs and are the most common type of star in our galaxy. Perhaps the most famous of these we have studied is Gliese 581. Just over twenty light years away from Earth, this star has been the subject of intense observation in recent years due to the discovery of at least six exoplanets orbiting around it. Most excitingly, planet Gliese 581 g is thought to orbit within the habitable zone of the star and so is considered a prime location for the search for extraterrestrial life ◉

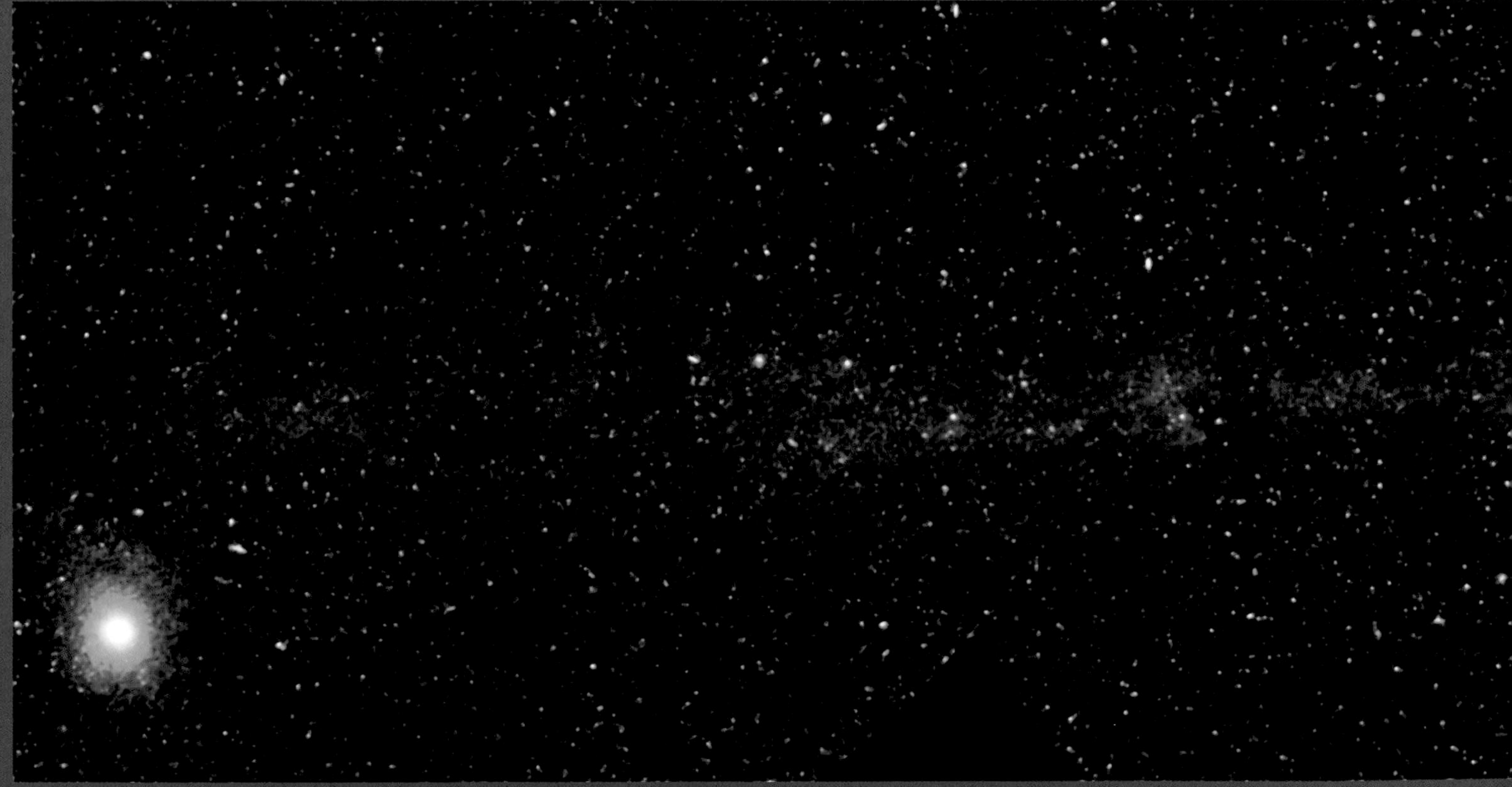

BELOW: Known as the Horseshoe, or Swan, Nebula, this molecular cloud is also often called the Omega Nebula, due to its similarity in shape to the Greek letter Omega. Ultraviolet light from a cluster of massive young stars buried within the nebula make the surrounding gas glow. This image was taken by the European Southern Observatory's 3.6-metre (11.8-foot) telescope in La Silla, Chile.

BELOW: Perhaps the most studied astronomical object, the Orion Nebula is also one of the most beautiful structures in the sky. On over 100 orbits of Earth between October 2004 and April 2005, NASA's Hubble Space Telecope captured this nebula in one of the most detailed astronomical images ever produced. On a clear, dark night sky this impressive formation – which includes more than 3,000 stars of varying sizes – can be seen with the naked eye. This complex, constantly evolving formation has provided scientists with crucial insight into how stars are formed.

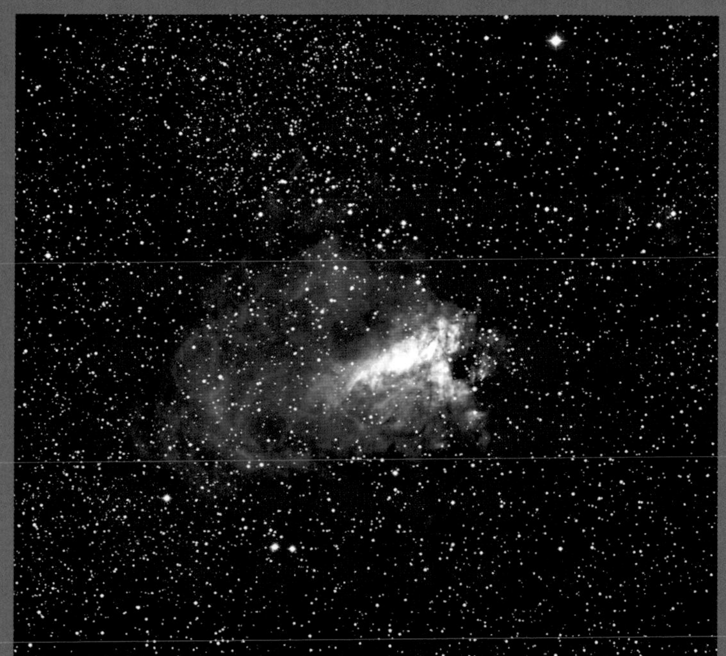

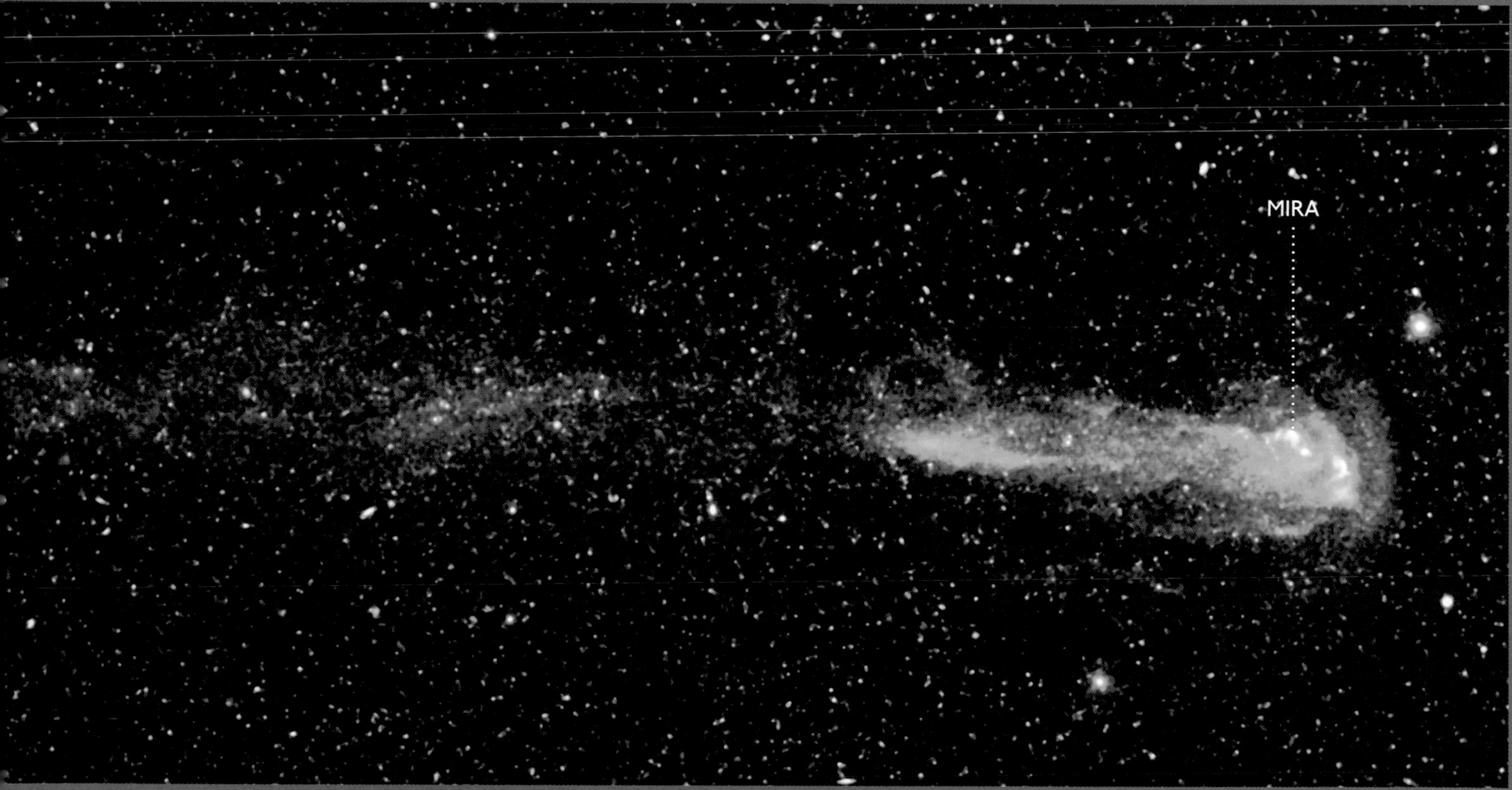

MIRA

The Venus transits of our sun are a rare occurrence, they only happen twice in eight years and won't be repeated for another 100 years. The last transit happened in 2004, with another due in 2012. We will have to wait until 2116 for the next one.

RIGHT: This is a composite image of Venus transiting the Sun on 8 June 2004. Venus can be seen from Earth as a small black disc moving across the face of the Sun.

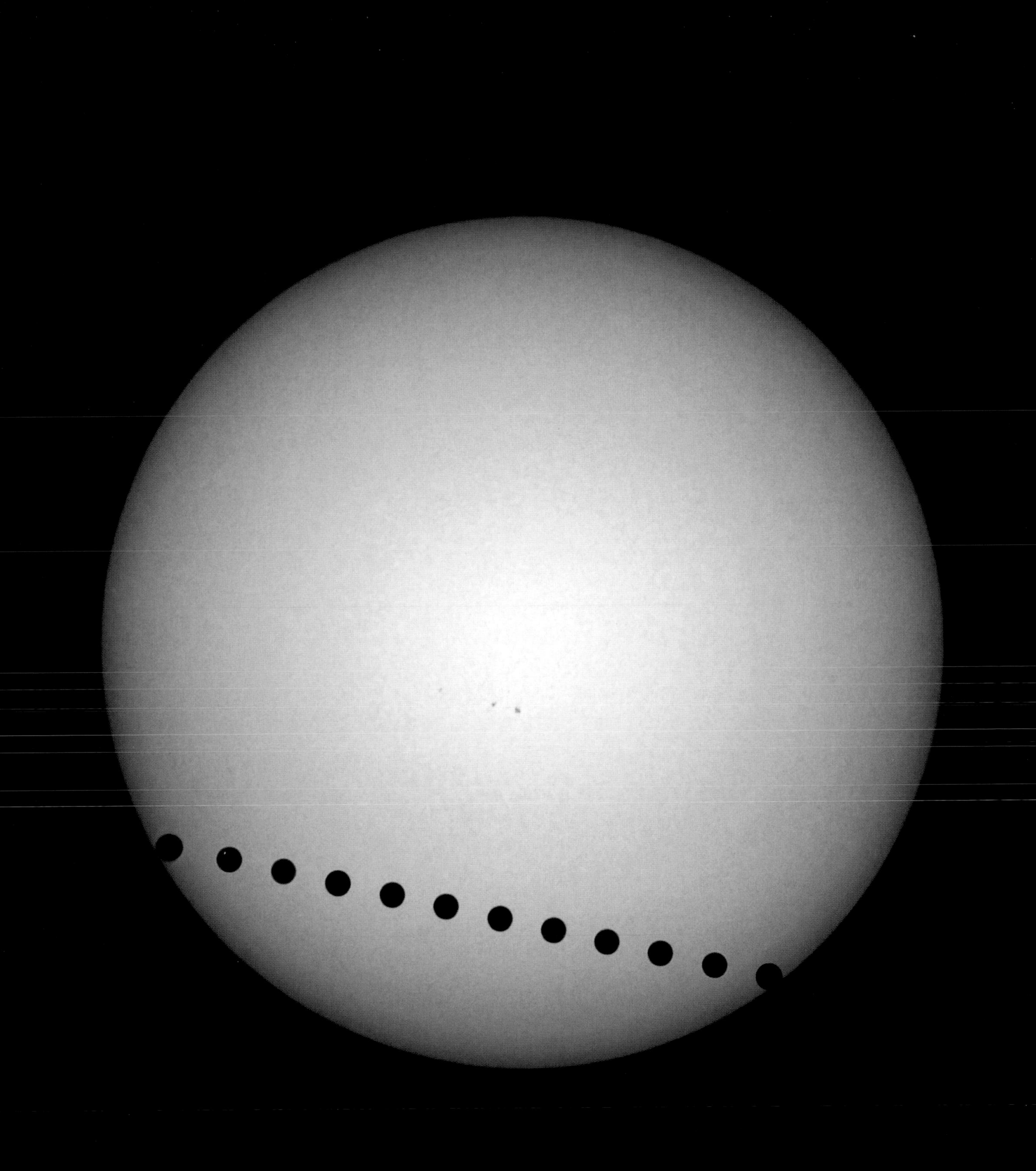

HOW TO FIND EXOPLANETS

One of the most exciting areas of current astronomical research is the hunt for planets around other stars – known simply as exoplanets – which are potential homes for extraterrestrial life. Until recently such a search would have been impossible, as planets are too faint to see over interstellar distances, however, thanks to new modern instrumentation, we are now able to detect the

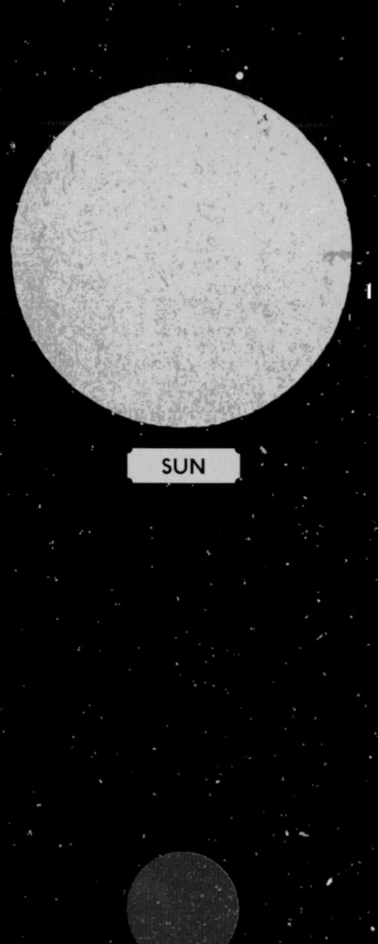

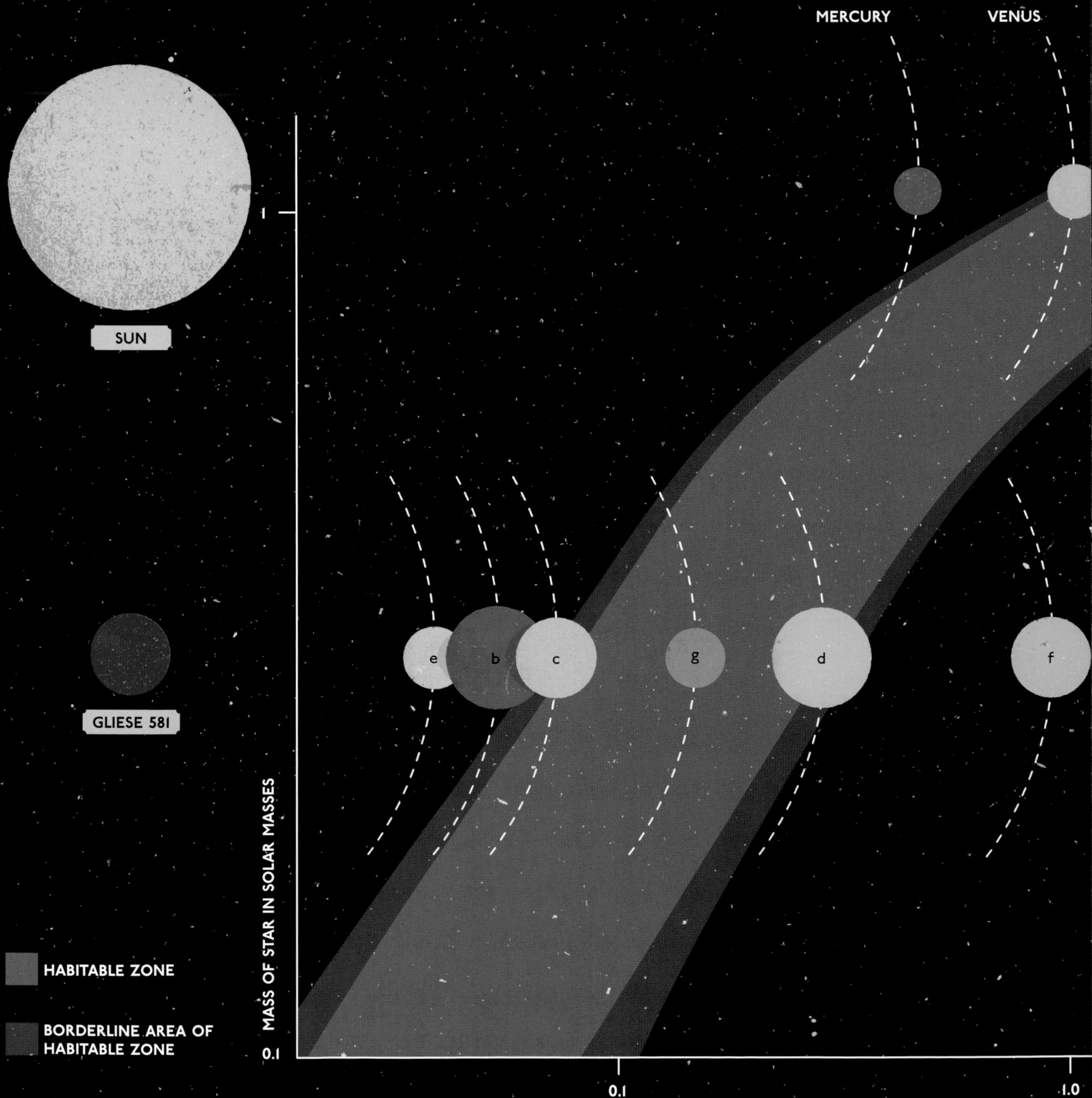

MERCURY
VENUS
SUN
GLIESE 581
e
b
c
g
d
f
1
0.1
MASS OF STAR IN SOLAR MASSES
0.1
1.0
HABITABLE ZONE
BORDERLINE AREA OF HABITABLE ZONE

telltale signals of exoplanets using two main techniques: the radial velocity method and the transit method. With these techniques, individual planets and even planetary systems have been discovered around hundreds of stars. Masses of these extrasolar planets range from a few times that of Earth, to the size of 25 Jupiters. Whether a planet could support life depends on its distance from the parent star. Around each star is a 'habitable zone', in which temperatures are suitable for water to exist as a liquid. The size of this zone depends on the energy output of the star; the faintest ones have the closest, narrowest zones. The red dwarf Gliese 581 is believed to have at least one planet within its habitable zone.

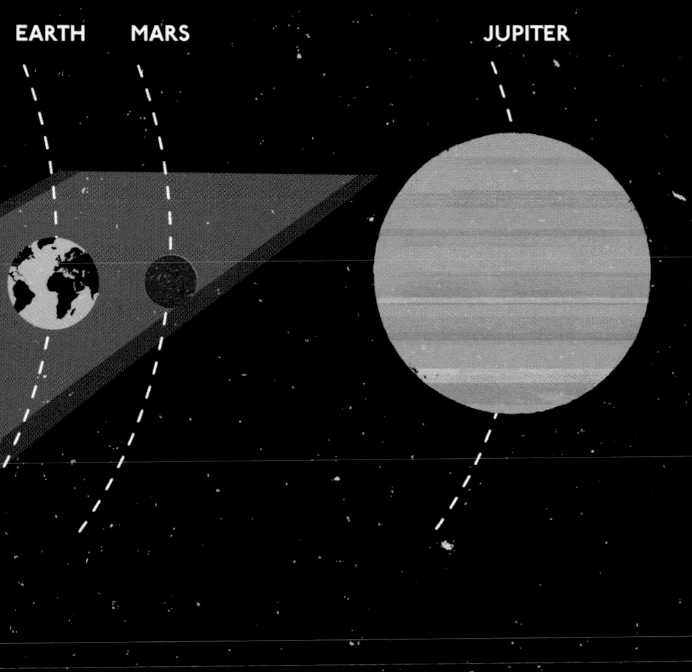

RADIAL VELOCITY METHOD

The presence of an exoplanet causes a star's orbit to wobble which can be detected by small variations in the spectrum of light reaching the Earth.

As the host star moves towards observer, blueshift occurs

Common centre of mass

As the host star moves away from observer, redshift occurs

Unseen exoplanet

TRANSIT METHOD

As the exoplanet gradually moves in front of the host star, the brightness of the host star decreases.

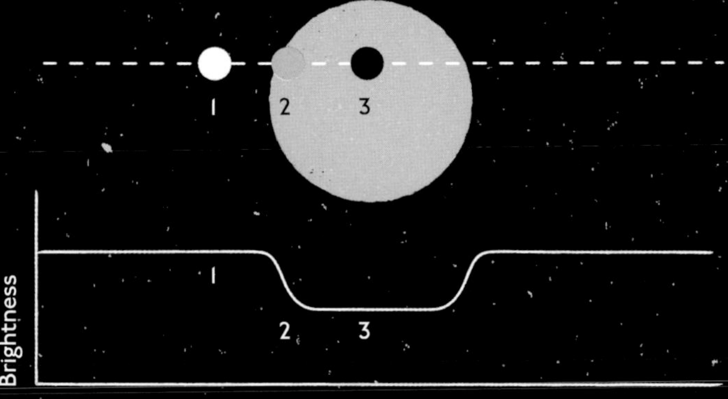

DISTANCE FROM STAR (AU) 10

As we observe all the cosmic structures around us in spectacular detail, each tells us something different about the life cycle of the stars. However, something much deeper can be learnt from understanding the existence of stars: they are the ultimate origin of all but the simplest of Leucippus' and Democritus' long-sought-after atoms, and as such are the building blocks of ourselves. To comprehend how the stars could play such a vital role in our existence, we must momentarily step back from the skies and come firmly back down to Earth.

THE ORIGINS OF LIFE

The first step in understanding how the lives of stars are precursors to our own lives is to discover exactly what we are made of. There is possibly no more beautiful, and perhaps no more instructive, place on Earth to begin this journey than in the shadow of the world's tallest mountain range. With over 100 peaks exceeding 7,200 metres (23,620 feet), the Himalayan range is truly a land of giants; nine of the ten highest mountains on Earth are part of the Himalayas. The greater Himalaya is home to forty-five of the world's top fifty highest peaks. Spectacularly beautiful, it is the sheer scale of these mountains that hides a fascinating and instructive first step on the road to understanding the building blocks of the Universe. Despite their majesty, just a few tens of millions of years ago these mountains were something very different.

As well as being the largest mountain range on the planet, the Himalayas is also one of the youngest. Just seventy million years ago (a very short time in geological terms) the Himalayas didn't exist. The relentless movement of Earth's tectonic plates shaped these mountains in a geological heartbeat. As the Indo-Australian plate collided with the Eurasian plate at the rate of about 15 centimetres (6 inches) a year, the ocean floor in between began to crumple and rise up to form the mountain range. This means that much of the rock out of which these towering peaks are made was formed at the bottom of an ocean, only to be lifted up thousands of metres into the air over a few short millions of years.

The evidence for this extraordinary journey is not difficult to find. If you look closely at any piece of Himalayan limestone you will see it has a chalky, granular structure. What you are looking at are the petrified remains of sea creatures – the bodies and shells of coral and polyps that died millions of years ago in a long-lost ocean. Given a relatively short timescale and a bit of pressure, these biological remains are quickly converted into solid rock. Limestone can also be formed by the direct precipitation of calcium carbonate from water, although the biological sedimentary form is more abundant. We know that the Himalayan limestone is predominantly biological because we have found fossils at the top of Mount Everest! There is perhaps no better example of the endless recycling of Earth's resources that has been going on since its formation almost five billion years ago.

We humans are also very much part of that system. As unsettling as it may sound, every atom in your body was once part of something else. It may have made up an ancient tree or a dinosaur, and you'll be pleased to know it was certainly part of a rock. The reason this can happen – that the rocks of Earth can become living things and that living things will eventually die and become rocks again – is simple: everything in the Universe is composed of the same basic ingredients ◉

LEFT: The largest mountain range in the world, the Himalayas is also the youngest. This panorama, taken from the top of Kala Pattar in the Sagarmatha National Park, Nepal, shows only a fraction of its scale. Understanding the creation of these impressive mountains helps us to answer many questions about the structure of all living elements in the Universe.

BELOW LEFT: When you are presented with the sheer magnitude of the Himalayas and the towering peak of Mount Everest, it is hard to believe that these huge mountains started off life at the bottom of an ocean.

BELOW RIGHT AND BOTTOM: Natural recycling at its most impressive. The Himalayan limestone has been proved to be predominantly biological, due to the quantity of fossils of sea shells and creatures that have been found at the summit of Mount Everest.

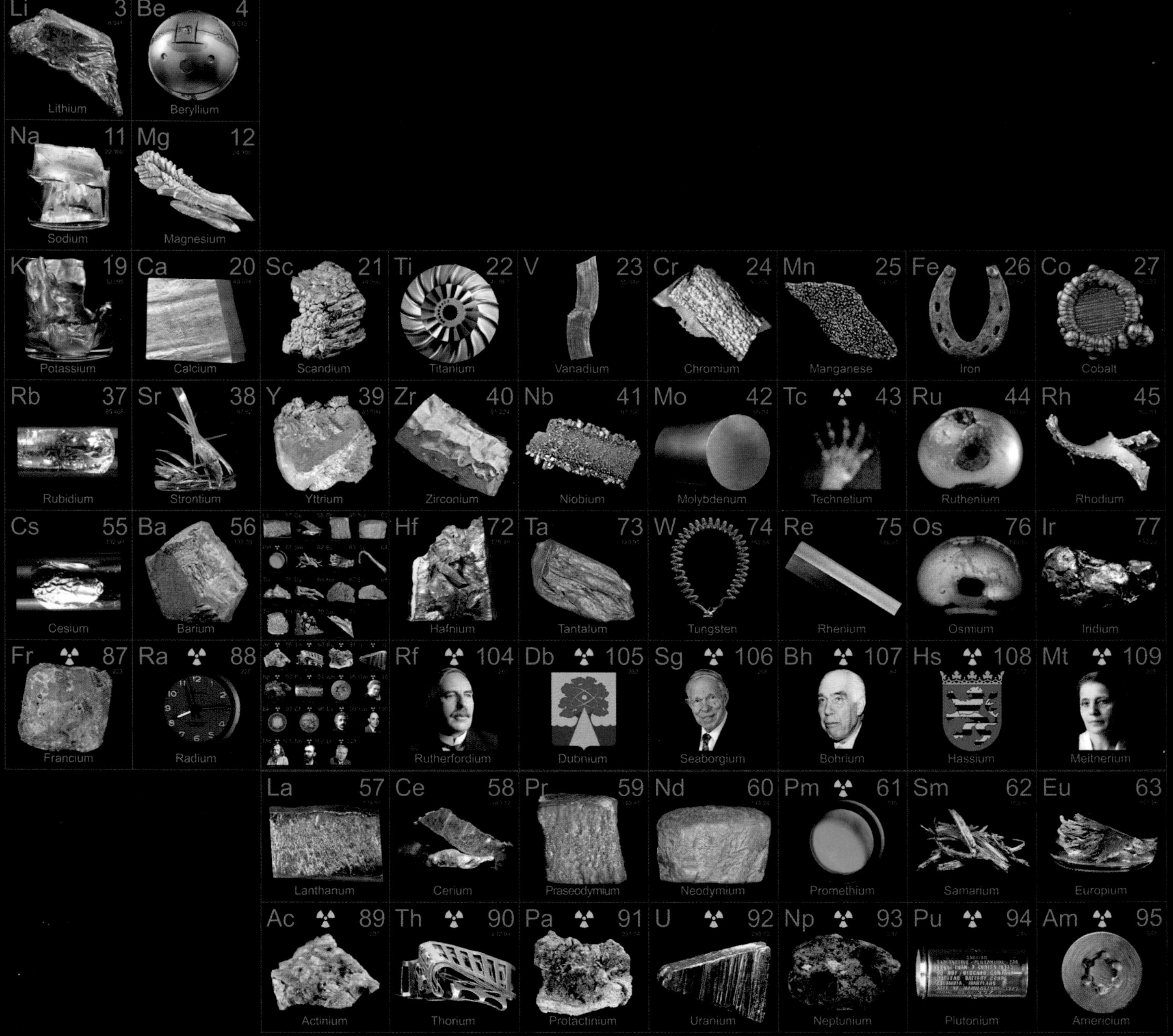

Li 3 Lithium	Be 4 Beryllium								
Na 11 Sodium	Mg 12 Magnesium								
K 19 Potassium	Ca 20 Calcium	Sc 21 Scandium	Ti 22 Titanium	V 23 Vanadium	Cr 24 Chromium	Mn 25 Manganese	Fe 26 Iron	Co 27 Cobalt	
Rb 37 Rubidium	Sr 38 Strontium	Y 39 Yttrium	Zr 40 Zirconium	Nb 41 Niobium	Mo 42 Molybdenum	Tc 43 Technetium	Ru 44 Ruthenium	Rh 45 Rhodium	
Cs 55 Cesium	Ba 56 Barium		Hf 72 Hafnium	Ta 73 Tantalum	W 74 Tungsten	Re 75 Rhenium	Os 76 Osmium	Ir 77 Iridium	
Fr 87 Francium	Ra 88 Radium		Rf 104 Rutherfordium	Db 105 Dubnium	Sg 106 Seaborgium	Bh 107 Bohrium	Hs 108 Hassium	Mt 109 Meitnerium	
		La 57 Lanthanum	Ce 58 Cerium	Pr 59 Praseodymium	Nd 60 Neodymium	Pm 61 Promethium	Sm 62 Samarium	Eu 63 Europium	
		Ac 89 Actinium	Th 90 Thorium	Pa 91 Protactinium	U 92 Uranium	Np 93 Neptunium	Pu 94 Plutonium	Am 95 Americium	

IMAGE COURTESY OF PERIODICTABLE.COM

THE PERIODIC TABLE

For many people the Periodic Table will provide a strong echo of the school science laboratory. At its simplest, this chart is a list of the chemical elements, fundamental units of matter, which were considered to be the smallest building blocks of the world. However, this table is much more than just a list. Although elemental theories of matter were first postulated in Greece, it wasn't until 6 March 1869 that the Russian chemist Dmitri Mendeleev finally tamed the ever-expanding list of the basic constituents of matter. Mendeleev's genius was to arrange the list of the sixty-six then-known elements into a table according to their chemical properties. In the process, the table not only provided a neat way of grouping the elements according to their properties, but also predicted the existence of eight elements yet to be discovered. Over the next thirty years, all eight were discovered, including gallium and germanium, and were found to have the exact properties predicted by Mendeleev's table. The number of elements continued to grow, and by 1955 the one-hundred-and-first element was discovered (named Mendelevium as a tribute to the father

of the Periodic Table) by a group of scientists at the University of California, Berkeley. To date, 118 elements have been categorised, the latest of which, ununseptium, was successfully synthesized and detected by a Russian–US team in April 2010.

Starting with hydrogen and ending with plutonium, the first ninety-four elements of the Table have been found occurring naturally on Earth. These elements are nature's building blocks; the remaining twenty-four elements, can only be created artificially and live for very short periods of time. Using these ninety-four elements you can explain all of biology and chemistry without knowing about the underlying structure of protons and neutrons, electrons and quarks. This is because you need very high energies and temperatures to break apart the elements – a condition that only exists naturally deep inside the stars.

The first step of our journey to explain where we come from is to understand the origin of these ninety-four elements. But first we must discover how we know that everything we see in the sky is made of the same stuff as us on the ground ●

THE UNIVERSAL CHEMISTRY SET

Surprising as it sounds, we know what every star, planet and moon in the observable Universe is made of, despite the fact that there is only one other place in the Universe that humans have actually visited in person.

On 21 July 1969, Neil Armstrong and Buzz Aldrin became the first humans to set foot on another world. They spent 2 hours, 36 minutes and 40 seconds walking on the surface of the Moon, but it wasn't until the last half hour that they carried out one of their most important scientific tasks. Using basic geological tools, Buzz Aldrin drove two core tubes into the lunar surface to collect the most famous rock samples taken in history. By the time they'd finished hammering and scooping up samples they had collected 22 kilogrammes (47 pounds) of lunar treasure. After using a pulley system to lift their scientifically priceless cargo on board, they closed the hatch and went to bed. As the two astronauts slept alongside the precious lunar rocks, the United States could justifiably claim to have won the greatest and arguably most glorious political victory in human history. For one rare moment, a political victory was also a triumph for all mankind.

However, it is not widely known that as the Apollo 11 lunar module rested on the Moon, a Soviet spacecraft was also in lunar orbit. The unmanned Luna 15 was the Soviets' third attempt to land on the Moon and collect lunar rock samples. Launched three days before Apollo 11, Luna 15 was a last-ditch attempt to win the scientific race to return rock samples from another world. Unfortunately, although Luna 15 successfully began its descent to the Moon's surface, it crashed into it shortly afterwards. Only Apollo 11 returned with moon rocks, which continue to be analysed to this day in the high-security labs of the lunar sample building in Houston, Texas.

Despite forty years of study, one thing has been clear pretty much from the start: these priceless examples of alien geology are remarkably similar to rocks found on Earth. In the main, they are composed of the common rock-forming elements oxygen, silicon, magnesium, iron, calcium and aluminium, but there is absolutely nothing on the Moon's surface that couldn't be found here on Earth.

Since Apollo 11's success, we have landed on Mars and Venus, parachuted into Jupiter's atmosphere, touched down on Saturn's moon Titan, and visited asteroids Eros and Itokawa and the comet Tempel 1. Each time the story is the same; the Solar System is made of the same stuff as we are. To date, eight landings on our nearest neighbour, Mars, have allowed us to explore the planet's geology in intimate detail. We now know Mars is rich in iron, which has oxidised to form its familiar rusty red colour, and that Martian soil is slightly alkaline and contains elements such as magnesium, sodium, potassium and also chloride. We also know that Venus' thick

TOP: On 21 July 1969, Neil Armstrong and Buzz Aldrin became the first humans to set foot on the Moon. This successful landing also opened up infinite possibilities for scientists to understand the formation of the lunar landscape. This photo shows Aldrin collecting some of the lunar rock samples that they took back to Earth for analysis.

ABOVE: The Apollo 11 lunar mission was launched from the Kennedy Space Center, Florida, on 16 July 1969 and safely returned to Earth on 24 July 1969, complete with its priceless cargo of samples from the Moon's surface. The first container was transferred to Ellington Air Force Base and was taken directly to the Lunar Receiving Laboratory at the Manned Spacecraft Center (MSC) in Houston, Texas.

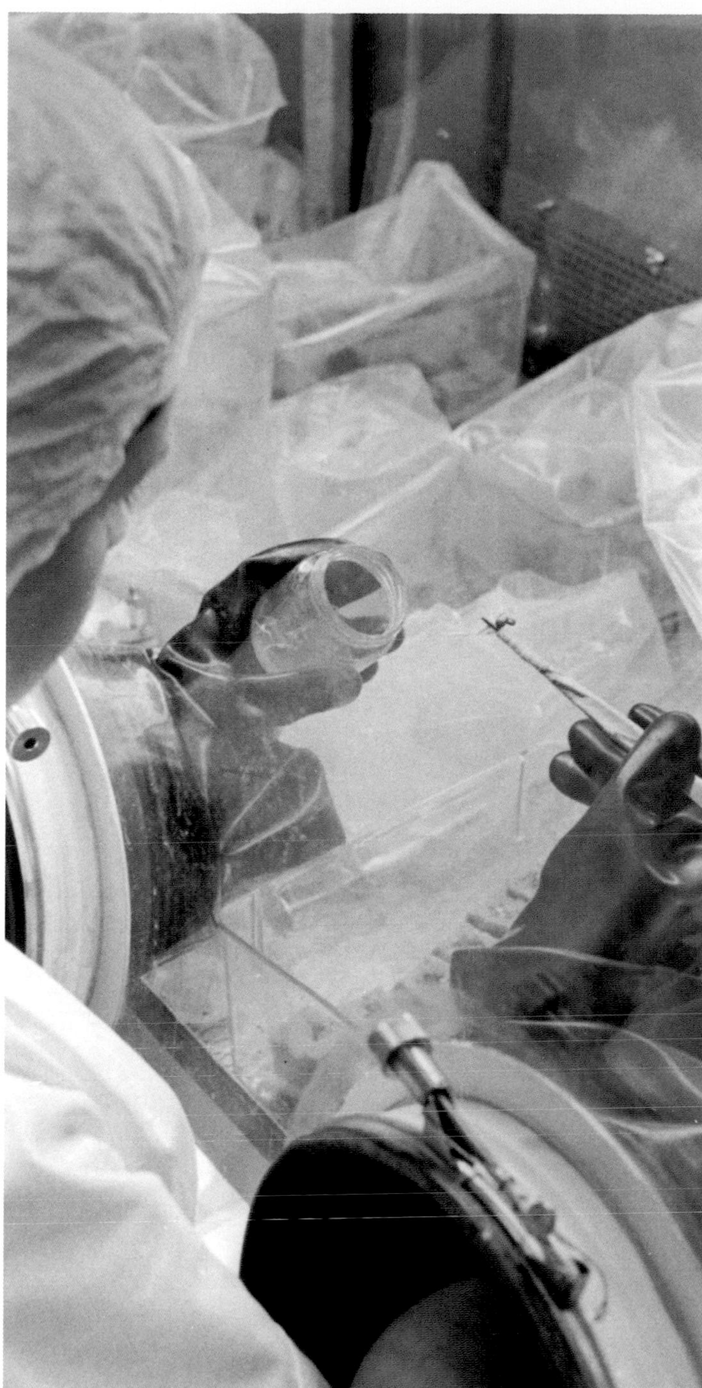

LEFT: Once safely returned to Earth, the treasures from the Moon, including rock samples, were painstakingly analysed at a high-security laboratory, and are still being used for analysis today.

BELOW: This false-colour photograph of Neptune was taken by Voyager 2. This image has enabled scientists to discover that the planet is rich in organic molecules such as methane.

Again and again we find there is much to discover in our solar system, but there are never new elements to unearth.

atmosphere is full of sulphur, and the planet Mercury is a large metal ball of iron with a thin crust comprised mostly of silicon. Even at the very edge of the Solar System, billions of miles away from Earth, we have discovered that Neptune is rich in organic molecules such as methane, a substance we find in abundance on our planet. Again and again we find there is much to discover in our solar system, but there are never new elements to unearth. From a scientific perspective this is unsurprising, because long ago Mendeleev's table revealed there isn't any room for other light elements in nature – we have discovered the full set. It would take a change in the laws of physics to discover something on the surface of another world that doesn't fit into Mendeleev's scheme, but from the explorer's perspective, seeing is believing!

So what about the rest of the Universe? How universal are these elements across the far reaches of the cosmos? Could it be that there are places in the distant Universe where the laws of physics are different? This is a legitimate question – we shouldn't simply assume that everything at the edge of the visible Universe, billions of light years away, operates exactly as it does here, no matter how persuasive the arguments from theoretical physics. Experiment and observation are the ultimate reality check. It may seem impossible to presume that we could ever answer this question directly and discover what the stars are made of, because they are so far away (they may indeed remain untouchable forever), but in fact we knew what the stars were made of long before we got our hands on that first piece of lunar rock ◉

WHAT ARE STARS MADE OF?

The Sun, the burning star at the heart of our solar system, is 150 million kilometres (93 million miles) away from Earth. Beyond that, the nearest known star, the red dwarf Proxima Centauri, requires a journey of over four light years or forty thousand billion kilometres (twenty-five thousand billion miles). We have learnt a lot about Proxima Centauri since it was discovered by Robert Innes at the Cape Observatory, in South Africa, in 1915. It is thought that Proxima Centauri is part of a triple star system with its neighbouring binary star system, Alpha Centauri A and B, and although it cannot be seen with the naked eye, we have been able to measure its mass and diameter and chart its brightness across the last 100 years. Despite the fact that our only contact with these neighbouring stars, and with any star other than our Sun, is the light that has crossed the Universe to reach us, we have been able to go much further than simply cataloguing their vital statistics. We can measure the precise constituents of any and every visible star in the sky, because encoded in the light that rains down on Earth is the key to understanding what they are made of. It is all made possible by a particularly beautiful property of the elements.

The tale of how we learnt to read the history of the stars in their light began with the work of Isaac Newton in 1670. In his 'Theory of Colour', Newton demonstrated that light is

ABOVE: Over a simple campfire I recreated the experiments of Gustav Kirchhoff and Robert Bunsen that made such a major impact in the development of quantum theory. Just as they discovered 150 years ago, when I threw the copper into the fire it burned with a spectacular blue flame.

RIGHT: In the early nineteenth century, German scientist Joseph von Fraunhofer documented the existence of 574 dark lines within the solar spectrum. This diagram is a visual representation of these Fraunhofer lines.

made up of a spectrum of colours, and that with nothing more complicated than a glass prism you can split the white light of the Sun into its colourful components. Almost 150 years later, the German scientist Joseph von Fraunhofer made a startling discovery about the solar spectrum whilst calibrating some of his state-of-the-art telescopic lenses and prisms. Lying within the solar spectrum, Fraunhofer documented the existence of 574 dark lines; there were literally hundreds of gaps – missing colours in the Sun's light. Unaware of the significance of this discovery at the time, Fraunhofer carefully mapped their positions in great detail. He went on to discover black lines in the light from the Moon and planets, and from other stars. These are now known as Fraunhofer lines.

Further work by two more of the great German scientists of the nineteenth century, Gustav Kirchhoff and Robert Bunsen (perhaps best known to schoolchildren everywhere as the inventor of the Bunsen burner), finally gave meaning to these lines. They surmised correctly that these black spectral lines were the fingerprints of the chemical elements in the atmosphere of the Sun itself. Across 150 million kilometres (93 million miles) of space, the light of our star had carried the signature of its constituents to us.

Kirchhoff and Bunsen's discovery was purely empirical – they had observed that when gases are heated on Earth they do not simply glow like a piece of hot metal, they give off light of very specific colours – and interestingly those colours depend only on the chemical composition of the gas and not on the temperature. In particular, each chemical element gives off its own unique set of colours. The element strontium, for example, burns with a beautiful red colour, sodium with a deep yellow, and copper is a haunting emerald green.

The two German scientists also noticed that the missing black lines in the solar spectrum corresponded exactly to the glowing colours of the elements. There are, for example, two black lines in the yellow part of the Sun's light that correspond exactly to the two distinct yellow emission lines of hot sodium vapour. You will be familiar with this mixture of two very slightly different yellows – it is the colour of sodium streetlights.

Interestingly, Kirchhoff and Bunsen had no idea why the elements behaved in this way, but this didn't matter if all you wanted to do was to match the signatures of elements observed on Earth with the signatures in the light from the Sun and stars. It wasn't until the turn of the twentieth century that an explanation for this strange behaviour of the elements was discovered. The answer lies in quantum mechanics, and the spectrographic work of physicists and chemists such as Kirchhoff and Bunsen was a major motivating factor in the development of the quantum theory. Elements emit and

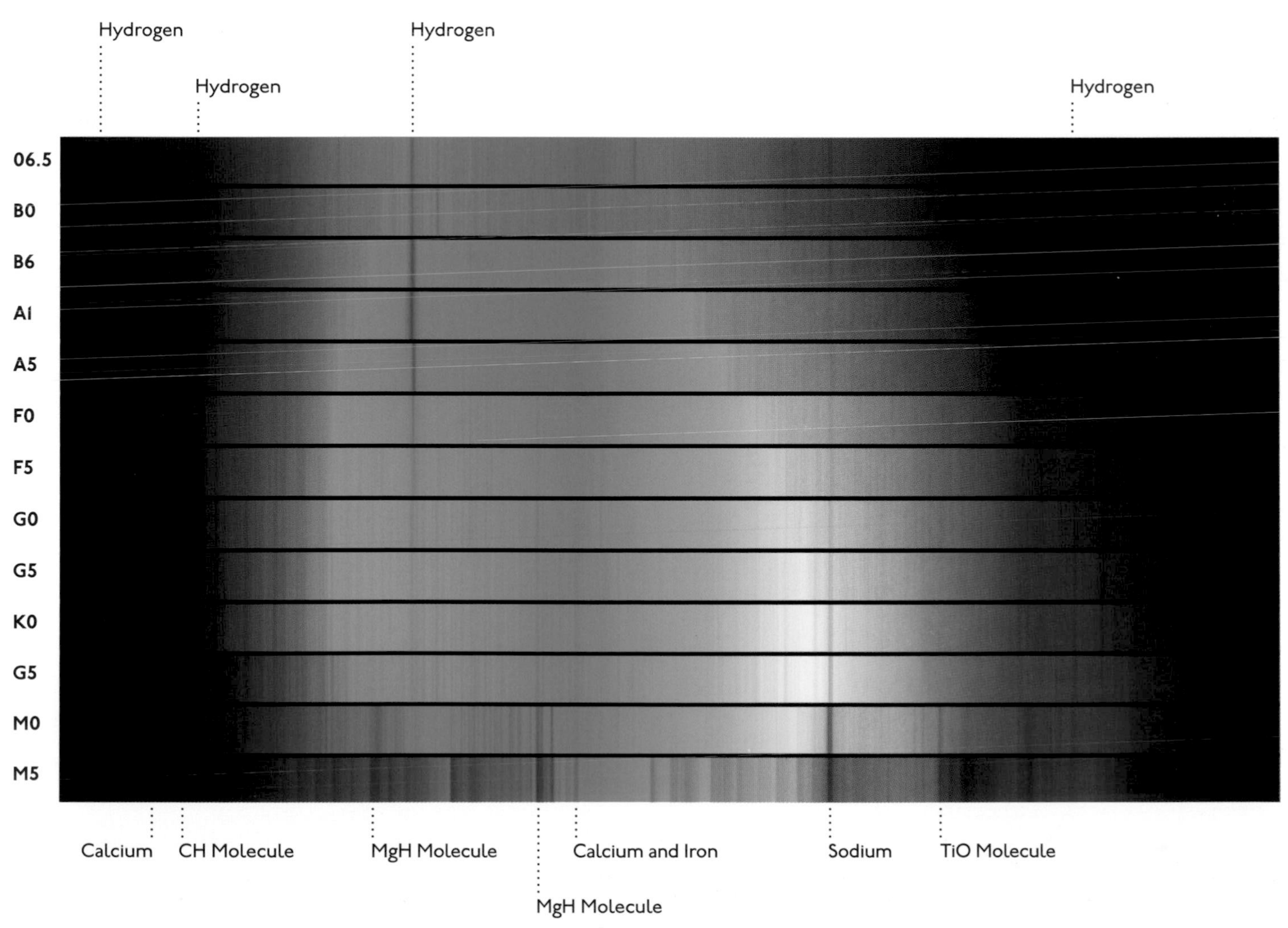

BELOW: Spectographic investigations have revealed that Sirius, the dog star, is metal-heavy, with an iron content three times that of the Sun.

RIGHT: Although Polaris, the pole star (top and middle), is 430 light years away, we know by looking that it has about the same heavy element abundance as our sun, but markedly less carbon and a lot more nitrogen. Vega (bottom), meanwhile, as the second-brightest star in the northern sky, consists of only about a third of the amount of metals as our sun.

Isn't it simply wonderful that just by looking at the light from those twinkling stars we can tell what those fiery worlds, so far away, are made of?

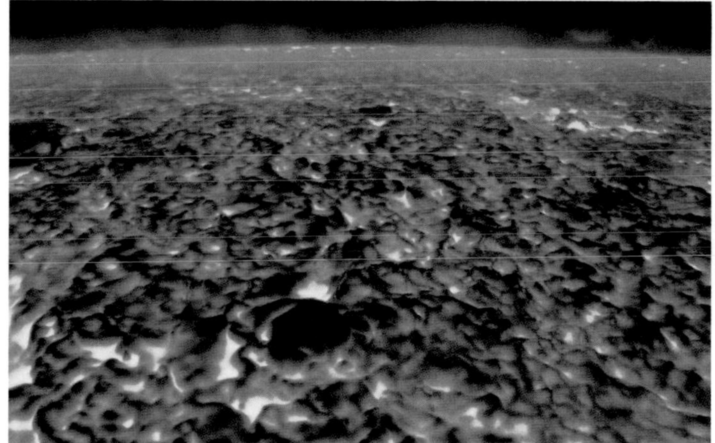

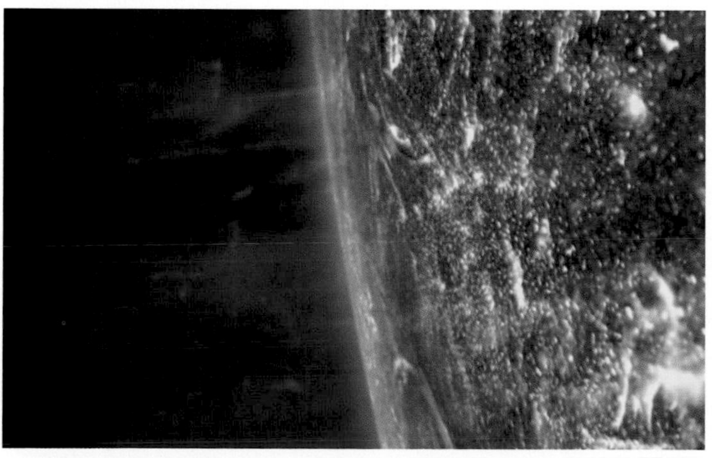

absorb light when the electrons surrounding their atomic nuclei jump around. The key insight that led to quantum theory was that electrons can't exist anywhere around a nucleus like planets around a star, but they are instead placed in specific, very restrictive 'orbits'. The deep reason for this is that electrons do not always behave as point-like particles of matter. They also exhibit wave-like properties, and this severely restricts the ways in which they can be confined around the atomic nucleus. What happens at a microscopic level when an atom absorbs some light is that an electron jumps to a different, more energetic, orbit and it emits light when the electron falls back from a higher to a lower energy orbit. The difference in energy between the lower orbit and the higher orbit must correspond exactly to the energy of the light absorbed or emitted.

However, quantum theory also stipulates that light should not always be thought of as a wave. Just like electrons, light can behave as both a wave and a stream of particles. These particles are called photons. Now, here is the key point: photons of a particular energy correspond to a particular colour of light, so red photons have a lower energy than yellow photons, which have a lower energy than blue photons. Since each element has electrons in unique orbits around the nucleus, this means that each element will only be able to absorb particular photons in order to move its electrons around into higher energy orbits. Conversely, when the electrons drop from higher to lower energy orbits, they will only emit photons of a particular energy and therefore a very particular colour. This is what we see when we observe the elements emitting or absorbing particular colours of light. We are in a very real sense seeing the structure of the atoms themselves.

When looking at a spectrum of light from our sun you can see hundreds of Fraunhofer lines, and each and every one of those corresponds to a different element in the solar atmosphere which absorbs light as it passes through. From sodium in the yellow, through iron, magnesium, and all the way across to the so-called hydrogen alpha line in the red, the signatures of each of the elements are encrypted in the solar code.

So by looking at these lines in precise detail you can work out exactly which elements are present in the Sun. This turns out to be roughly 70 per cent hydrogen, 28 per cent helium, and the remaining 2 per cent is made up of the other elements.

It is worth repeating here that you can apply this theory not only to the Sun, but for any of the stars you can see in the sky – which allows us to measure the constituents of their atmospheres with extraordinary accuracy. Isn't it simply wonderful that just by looking at the light from those twinkling stars we can tell what those fiery worlds, so far away, are made of?

These spectrographic investigations of the light from the cosmos have confirmed what our scientific intuition suggested to us: wherever we look, we only ever see the signatures of the set of ninety-four naturally occurring elements that we have collected and identified here on Earth.

So it is clear that we are connected in a very real sense to the whole of the Universe – with its hundreds of billions of stars across billions of galaxies – because we are all intrinsically made of the same stuff. And, as we will explain, there is one very simple reason for that: everything in the Universe shares the same origin ◉

THE EARLY UNIVERSE

In order to understand where we come from we have to understand events that happened in the first few seconds of the life of the Universe. When the Universe began it was unimaginably hot and dense – we literally don't have the scientific language to describe it. It was beautiful in a very real sense. There was no structure, there was certainly no matter, and it was exactly the same whichever way you looked at it. It's a difficult concept to grasp, but we can get some idea of what happened to the early Universe by looking at the behaviour of one of the most common substances on Earth: water.

RIGHT: Water is one of the most common substances on Earth, but it can produce some of the most spectacular geological wonders on our planet. The El Tatio Geysers in Chile are just one example of water's awesome activity.

BELOW: One of Earth's most incredible natural wonders, the El Tatio Geysers make up the largest geyser field in the world. As they are located at a height of 4,200 metres (13,800 feet) in the Chilean Andes, they are also the highest.

EL TATIO GEYSERS, CHILE

High in the Andes Mountains, in the far north of Chile, you will find the spectacular El Tatio Geysers. Erupting at 4,200 metres (13,800 feet) above sea level, this is one of the geological wonders of Earth's Southern Hemisphere. Not only is it one of the largest geyser fields in the world, it is also one of the highest. For those who journey here to witness the eruption of the jets of water skywards there is only one time to visit – sunrise.

In the early morning, as the Sun begins to peer over the horizon, the combination of super-heated water and freezing cold air produces a rare phenomenon. Like all geysers, the boiling water delivered to the surface by the geological plumbing bursts out and flashes into steam, forming the majestic columns. But here, because of the high altitude and bitter temperatures, the steam rapidly condenses and returns to its frozen state, covering the ground with sheets of ice. It is surely one of the most spectacular naturally occurring locations on the planet in which you can see water in all three of its phases: liquid, vapour and solid ice. It is this rapid transformation of water through its three familiar phases that provides us with a nice analogy to discuss events that happened in the very early life of the Universe.

A water molecule is made up of two chemical elements: oxygen and hydrogen. Oxygen and hydrogen atoms are symmetric when they are alone and uncombined. This particular use of the word symmetric is perhaps unfamiliar; what is meant in this context is that the atoms themselves would look the same no matter what angle you viewed them from. In the language of physics, this is called rotational symmetry. A perfect sphere has perfect rotational symmetry, because whichever way you look at it or spin it around it looks exactly the same. When an oxygen atom combines with two hydrogen atoms to form a water molecule – H_2O – this rotational symmetry disappears because the water molecules have a particular shape – there is an angle of 105 degrees

BELOW: Approximately 70 per cent of Earth's surface is covered by water. At the El Tatio Geysers you can see water in all its three forms. Walking through pools of water on the ground, I held a sheet of glass in the geysers' steam and watched ice crystals form on it.

Exactly like the journey of steam to ice, of chaos to order, this was the Universe in transition. A transition where the structure and substance of all the particles of matter emerged for the first time.

between the hydrogen and oxygen atoms. A physicist would say that the symmetry is now broken, because the water molecule has a distinct orientation. We can break the symmetry of water still further by cooling down all the molecules until they stick together and solidify into ice. Now the crystals of ice are beautiful and almost impossibly intricate; full of structure and a complexity that completely hides the perfect symmetry of the original atoms, and also the simple but different symmetry of the water molecules themselves.

The important point here is that all this complexity emerged when the symmetry was broken, but we did nothing to the water itself to break its symmetry other than cool it down. So although it looks for all the world as if a master sculptor sat down and chiselled out beautiful patterns in the ice, this intricacy and beauty emerged completely spontaneously out of building blocks that are themselves utterly symmetric.

Physicists call this process spontaneous symmetry breaking, and it is this idea that lies at the heart of our understanding of the early Universe ◉

THE BIG BANG

Thirteen billion years ago the Universe began in the event called the Big Bang. We don't know why. We also don't know why it took the initial form that it did. This is one of the unsolved mysteries that makes fundamental physics so exciting. The first milestone we can speak of in anything resembling scientific language is known as the Planck Era, a period that occurred a mind-blowing 10^{-43} seconds after the Big Bang. When written in full, that number has 42 decimal places: 0.00000000000000000000000 0000000000000000001 seconds. That's not very long at all. This number can be arrived at very simply because it is related to the strength of the gravitational force. It is so incredibly tiny ultimately because gravity is so weak – and we don't know the reason for that, either! At that time the four fundamental forces of nature that we know of today – gravity, the strong and weak nuclear forces, and electromagnetism – were one and the same force, a single 'superforce'. There was no matter at this stage, only energy and the superforce. This is what a physicist would call a very symmetric situation.

As the Universe rapidly expanded and cooled it underwent a series of symmetry-breaking events. The first, at the end of the Planck Era, saw gravity separate from the other forces of nature, and so the perfect symmetry was broken. Around 10^{-36} seconds after the Big Bang, another symmetry-breaking event occurred which marked the end of the Grand Unification Era. This saw the strong nuclear force (the force that sticks the quarks together inside protons and neutrons) split from the other forces. At this point the Universe underwent an astonishingly violent expansion known as inflation, in which the Universe expanded in size by a factor of 10^{26} (that's 100 million million million million times) in an unimaginably small space of time – it was all over in 10^{-32} seconds. This was when sub-atomic particles entered the Universe for the first time, but they weren't quite what we see today because none of them had any mass at all.

Up until this point this story is theoretically well-motivated but experimentally relatively untested. The next great symmetry-breaking event, however, which occurred 10^{-11} seconds after the Big Bang, is absolutely within our reach because this is the era we are recreating and observing at CERN's Large Hadron Collider. It is called electroweak symmetry breaking; at this point the final two forces of nature – electromagnetism and the weak nuclear force – are separated. During this process the sub-atomic building blocks of everything we see today (the quarks and electrons) acquired mass. The most popular theory for this process is known as the Higgs mechanism, and the search for the associated Higgs Particle is one of the key goals of the Large Hadron Collider project.

We are now on very firm experimental and theoretical ground. From this point on we know pretty much exactly what happened in the Universe because we can do experiments at particle accelerators to check that we understand the physics. The emergence of the familiar particles and forces we see in the Universe today happened, we believe, as a result of a series of symmetry-breaking events which began way back at the end of the Planck Era. The concept of spontaneous symmetry breaking in the early Universe is exactly the same as for the transitions from water vapour to liquid water to ice. Complex patterns emerge without prompting – just as a result of falling temperature – and these patterns obscure the underlying symmetry of the initial state. So just as the seemingly infinite complexity of snowflakes masks the simple symmetry of oxygen and hydrogen atoms, so the array of forces of nature and sub-atomic particles we see as the building blocks of the Universe today obscures the symmetry of the early Universe.

There is now one final step needed to arrive at the protons and neutrons – the building blocks of the elements – and the first elements themselves. This began around a millionth of a second after the Big Bang, when the quarks had cooled enough to become glued together by the strong nuclear force to form protons and neutrons. The simplest element, hydrogen, consists of a single proton. So after only a millionth of a second in the life of the Universe, the first chemical element had made an appearance. After three minutes, the Universe was cold enough for the protons and neutrons themselves to stick together to form helium. With two protons and one or two neutrons in its nucleus, helium is the second-simplest chemical element. There were also very, very small amounts of lithium, with three protons, and beryllium, with four protons – the third- and fourth-simplest elements. And this is pretty much where the process stopped. After three minutes the Universe had the four distinct forces we know of today – gravity, the strong and weak nuclear forces, and electromagnetism, and was composed of roughly 75 per cent hydrogen (by mass) and 25 per cent helium. This is the story of the creation of the simplest chemical elements and of successive symmetry-breaking events in the early Universe ◉

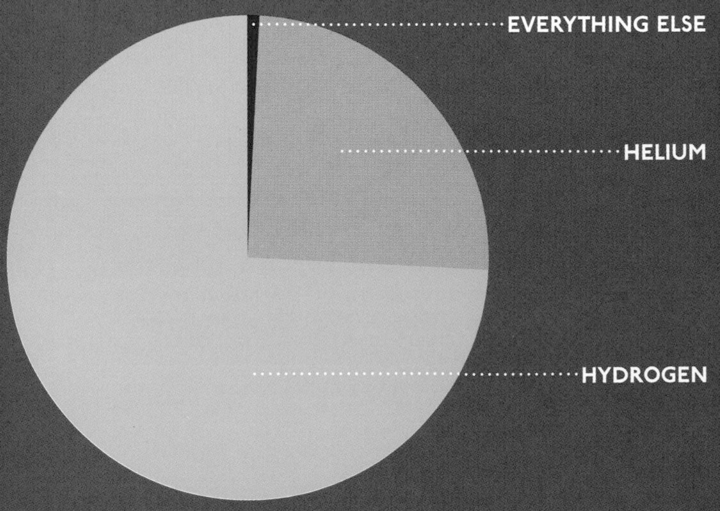

LEFT: Careful scientific study leads us to conclude that the building blocks of our Universe are fundamentally hydrogen and helium.

BELOW: A computer simulation of an event showing the decay of Higgs Bosen producing four muons (white tracks). This image shows how the Higgs Bosen might be seen in the CMS detector from the Large Hadron Collider at CERN.

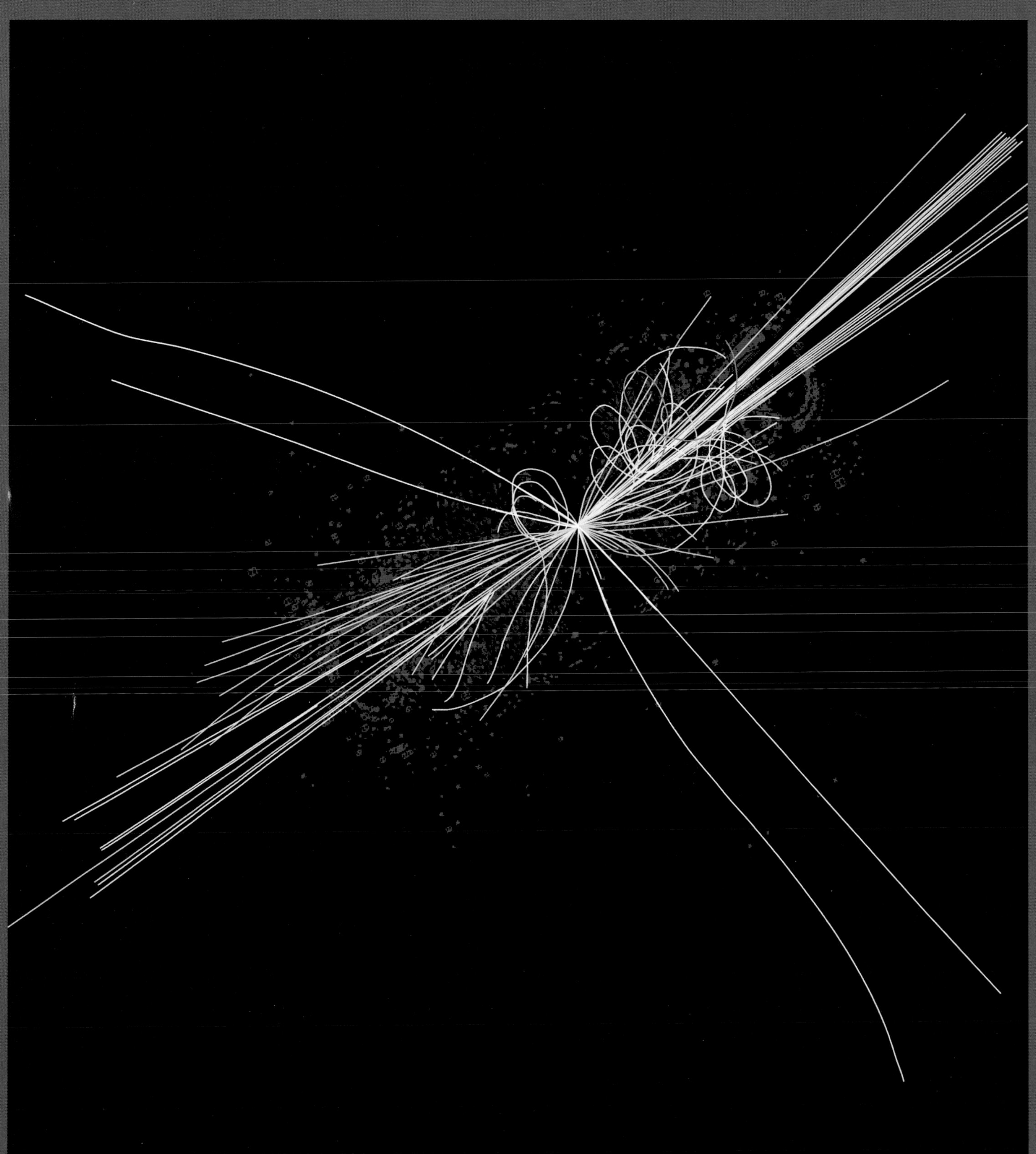

SUB-ATOMIC PARTICLES

Our understanding of the structure of matter has increased in the last century. Originally, atoms were thought to be the basic building blocks of life, but Rutherford's famous diffraction experiment proved that matter consisted mainly of space, with each atom containing a very small dense nucleus surrounded by a cloud of electrons. Further investigation showed that each nucleus was composed of protons and neutrons and that each proton was composed of up and down quarks. We have now reached what is believed to be the smallest particles possible – scientists have now discovered that all matter is composed of 9 particles and 4 forces, plus the hypothetical Higgs Boson. The search for the basic building blocks of matter has used matter colliders, which can produce the very high energies that are required to recreate the temperatures in the early Universe, when these sub-atomic particles originally existed.

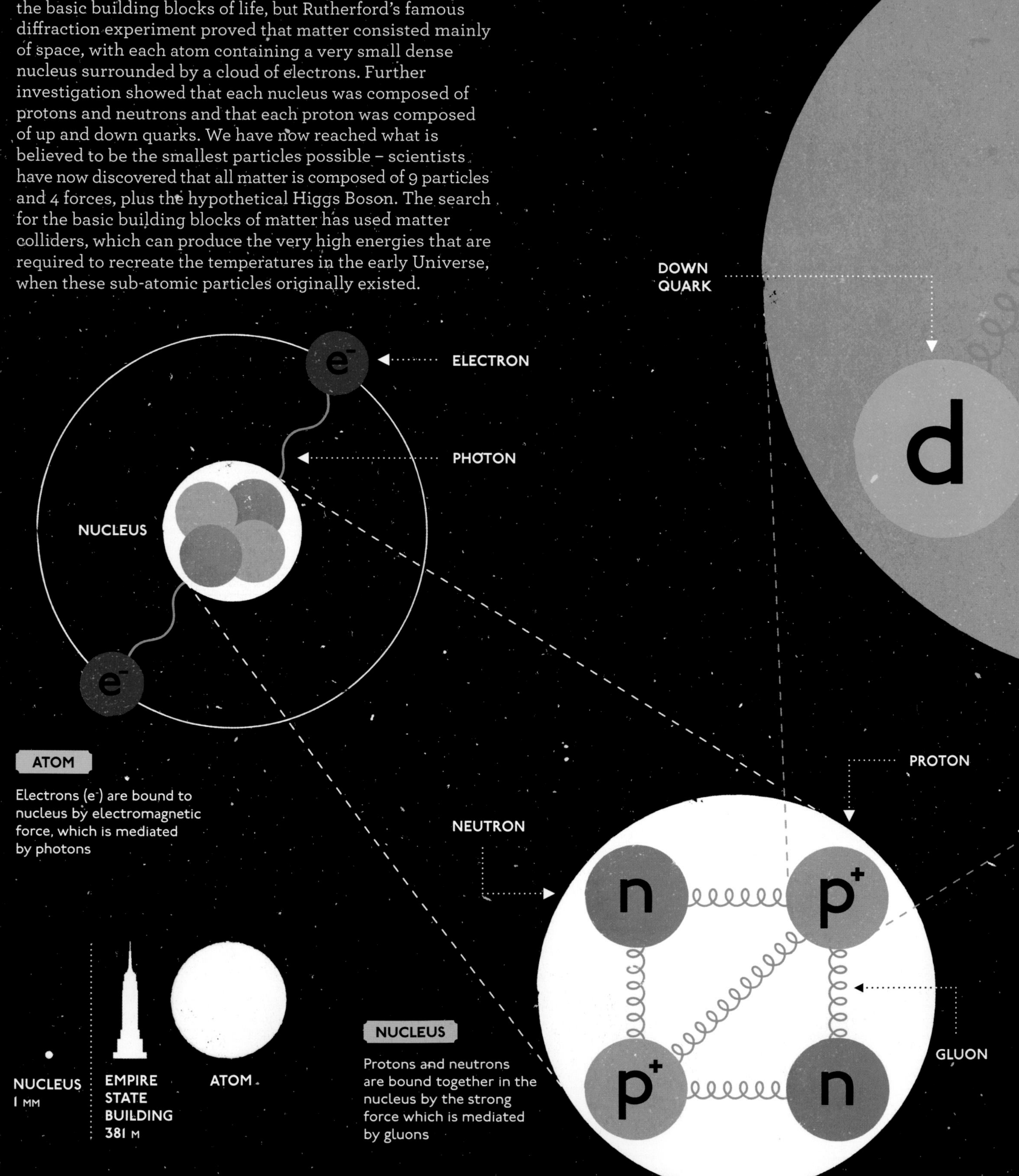

ATOM

Electrons (e^-) are bound to nucleus by electromagnetic force, which is mediated by photons

NUCLEUS

Protons and neutrons are bound together in the nucleus by the strong force which is mediated by gluons

u

u

GLUON

PARTICLE CONTENT OF THE STANDARD MODEL

QUARKS

	MASS	CHARGE	SPIN	Symbol	NAME
QUARKS	2.4 MeV	$^2/_3$	$^1/_2$	u	up
	1.27 Gev	$^2/_3$	$^1/_2$	c	charm
	171.2 Gev	$^2/_3$	$^1/_2$	t	top
	4.8 MeV	$-^1/_3$	$^1/_2$	d	down
	1.04 MeV	$-^1/_3$	$^1/_2$	s	strange
	4.2 GeV	$-^1/_3$	$^1/_2$	b	bottom
LEPTONS	< 2.2 eV	0	$^1/_2$	ν_e	electron neutrino
	< 0.17 MeV	0	$^1/_2$	ν_μ	muon neutrino
	< 15.5 MeV	0	$^1/_2$	ν_τ	tau neutrino
	0.511 MeV	-1	$^1/_2$	e	electron
	105.7 MeV	-1	$^1/_2$	μ	muon
	1.777 GeV	-1	$^1/_2$	τ	tau
BOSONS (FORCES)	0	0	1	γ	photon
	0	0	1	g	gluon
	91.2 GeV	0	1	Z^0	weak force
	80.4 GeV	±1	1	$W^\pm$	weak force

H
Higgs Boson

PROTON

The proton is made up of two 'up' quarks and one "down' quark. They are bound together inside the proton by the strong force (mediated by gluons)

WEAK FORCES

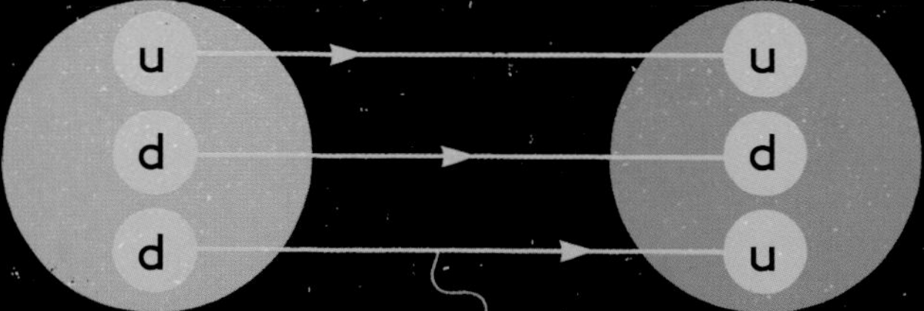

TIMELINE OF THE UNIVERSE: THE BIG BANG TO THE PRESENT

The history of the Universe can be split into several phases, according to the physical conditions that existed at the time. Things happened quickly in the first fractions of a second, when the Universe was filled with an intensely hot soup of energy and exotic particles. From this emerged the first protons and neutrons which were later to form the nuclei of the first atoms – mostly hydrogen and helium. After the emission of the cosmic microwave background, around 400,000 years after the Big Bang, the pace of events became more sedate. According to current understanding, the Universe will continue to expand forever, eventually fading into darkness in the unimaginably distant future.

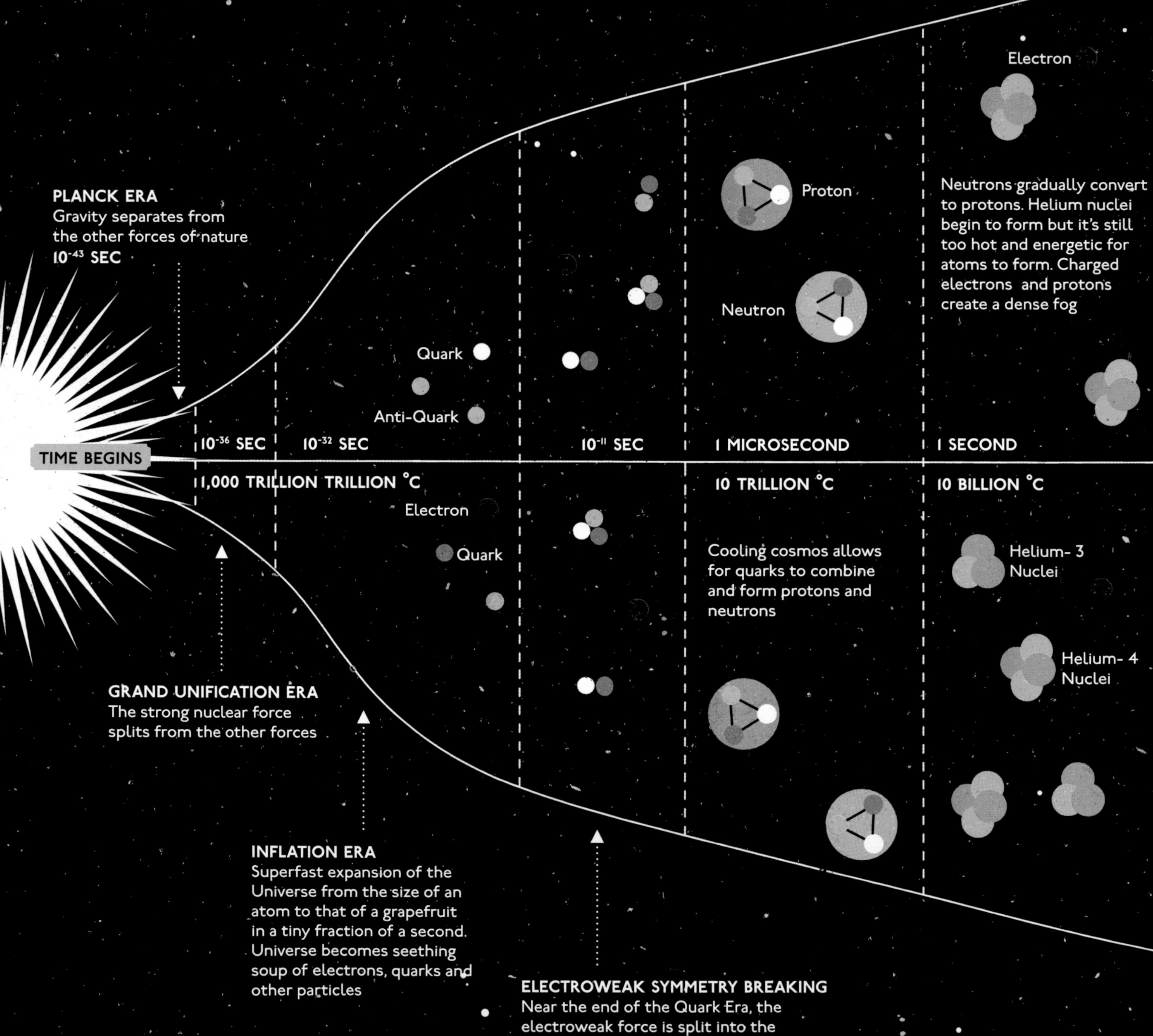

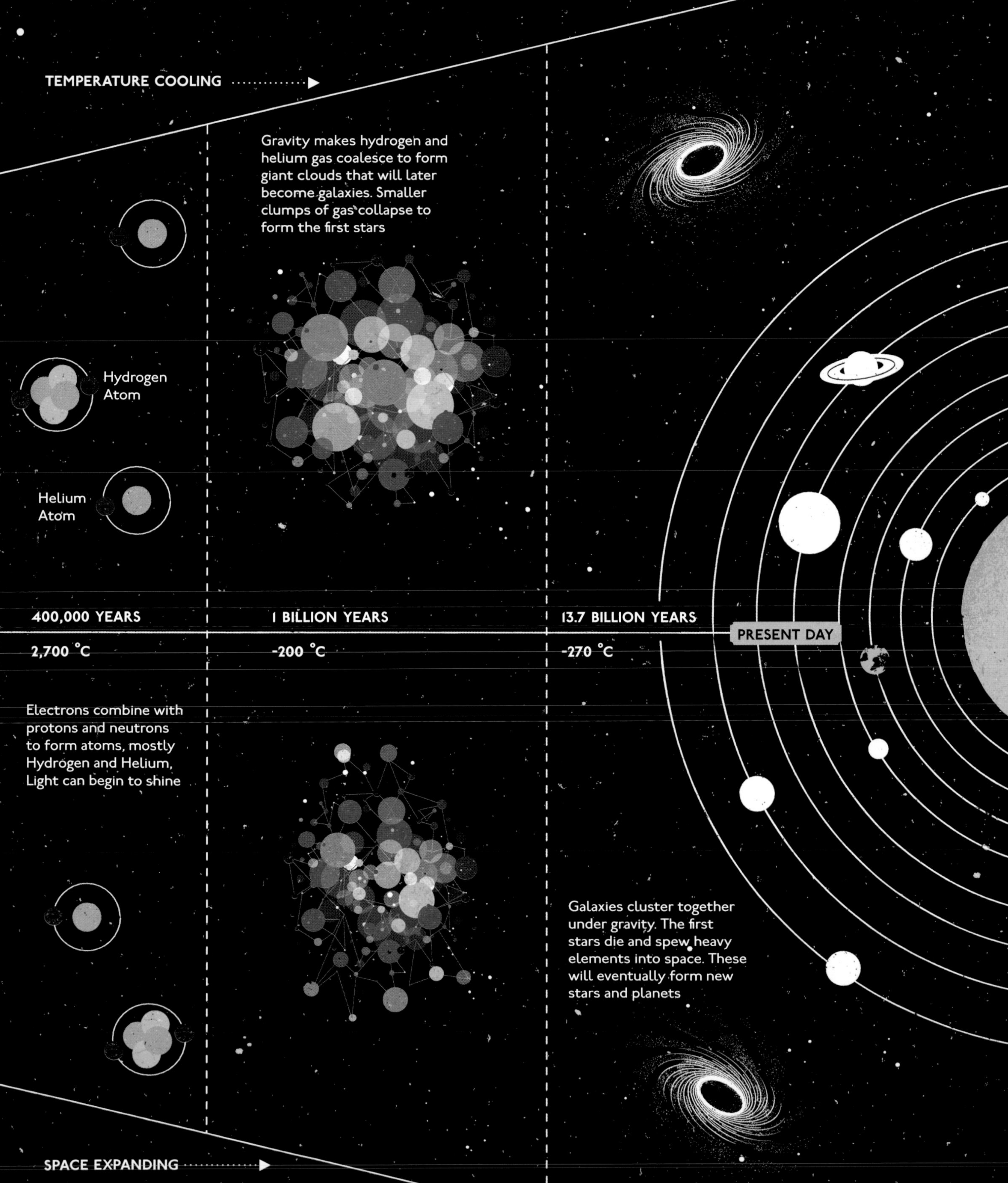
TEMPERATURE COOLING
Gravity makes hydrogen and helium gas coalesce to form giant clouds that will later become galaxies. Smaller clumps of gas collapse to form the first stars
Hydrogen Atom
Helium Atom
400,000 YEARS
1 BILLION YEARS
13.7 BILLION YEARS
PRESENT DAY
2,700 °C
-200 °C
-270 °C
Electrons combine with protons and neutrons to form atoms, mostly Hydrogen and Helium. Light can begin to shine
Galaxies cluster together under gravity. The first stars die and spew heavy elements into space. These will eventually form new stars and planets
SPACE EXPANDING

There's a mystery at the heart of science for which, as yet, we have no explanation, and that is that this universe is simple. Underlying all of the astonishing complexity appears to be a magnificent simplicity, and nowhere is that simplicity more obvious than in the construction of the elements.

LEFT: The construction of all the chemical elements in the Universe can be illustrated with the most basic demonstration – so simple, it's child's play. To understand how the structure has emerged, all you need is a pot of bubble mixture. Blow one bubble and you have returned to the beginning of time, when all that existed in the Universe was the proton.

MATTER BY NUMBERS

Throughout human history the discovery and use of specific chemical elements has been intricately linked with the rise of civilisation. It is believed that copper was first mined and crafted by humans 11,000 years ago, and the specific characteristics of this metal ushered in a new age of technology and the transition from stone tools and weapons to metal ones. Four thousand years later it happened again but with iron which, even today, when mixed with carbon to form the alloy steel is the exoskeleton of industrial civilisation.

These two elements played a role in our history because of their particular physical characteristics. Copper was almost certainly the first metal to be used by humans; as it is such an unreactive chemical that it is one of the few metals that occurs naturally in its pure state. It is also very soft and malleable and so relatively easy to work into tools and weapons. When combined with another metallic element – tin – copper forms the alloy bronze; when combined with zinc it forms brass. Iron is, perhaps surprisingly, the most abundant element on Earth, and the fourth-most abundant element in the rocks of Earth's crust. Although more difficult to extract and work with than bronze, iron is an excellent material for weapons manufacture as it is harder and lasts longer than bronze.

These two metals have had a profound influence on human history and sit just a couple of spaces apart in the periodic table. Iron (Fe) is element number 26 and copper (Cu) is at 29. The first humans to use these metals would, of course, have had no idea of the reason for the physical similarities and differences between the two elements. So what is the fundamental difference between them? The answer is remarkably simple. As described earlier, the atoms of each element are composed of three building blocks: protons, neutrons and electrons. We do not need to consider the quarks inside the protons and neutrons, because at the temperatures we encounter on Earth they stay locked away. So when discussing Earthly chemistry, we can ignore them.

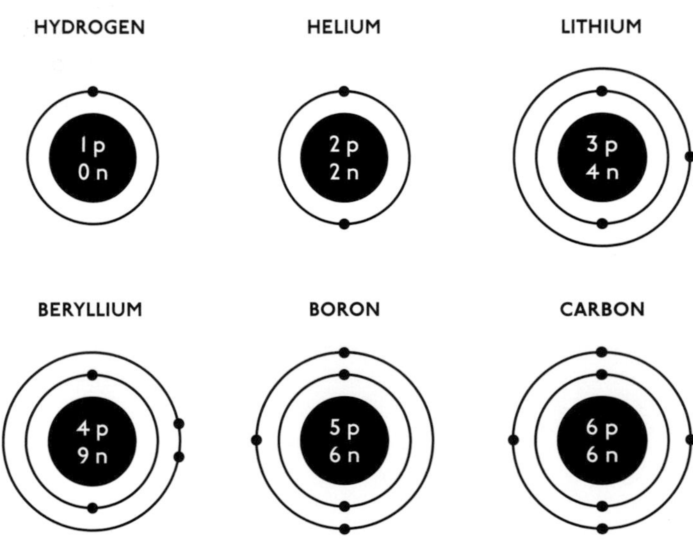

THE SIX LIGHTEST ELEMENTS IN NATURE: HYDROGEN TO CARBON
In each element the number of protons (p) in its nucleus is the same as the number of orbiting electrons, but the number of neutrons (n), which have no electric charge, can vary.

We have already encountered the first four elements; one of these, hydrogen, has an atomic nucleus consisting of a single proton. The proton has a positive electric charge, which allows it to trap an electron in orbit around it to form a hydrogen atom. The electron carries a negative electric charge, equal and opposite to that of the proton. This means that hydrogen atoms are electrically neutral. The reason why the electron has exactly the equal and opposite charge of the proton is not known. This is even more surprising when you look at the quarks that build up the proton. The proton is made up of three quarks – two up quarks and one down quark. The up quark has an electric charge of +2/3, and the down quark has a charge of -1/3. The electron has a charge of -1. So it is only when they are combined to form a proton that everything balances out properly. The neutron consists of two down quarks and an up, which means that it has no electric charge at all. This cannot be a coincidence, and it is one of the great challenges for twenty-first-century physics to explain it.

Chemical elements differ because of varying numbers of protons in their atomic nucleus, but the number of neutrons makes no difference to their chemical properties. Chemistry is down to the way the electrons behave that orbit around the nucleus, and the number of electrons is equal to the number of protons. As we know, the hydrogen atom consists of one proton and one electron, but there is another form of hydrogen called deuterium. Deuterium has a neutron attached to the proton inside its nucleus, but this doesn't change its chemical properties as there is still only one electron. Technically speaking, deuterium and hydrogen are two different isotopes of the same element. Helium atoms always have two protons and two electrons; it also has forms with one and two neutrons, known as helium-3 and helium-4 respectively. Next comes lithium, with three protons, three electrons and either three or four neutrons, sometimes more. Carbon has six protons and varying numbers of neutrons, and so on. The rule is that each successive element has one more proton in its nucleus, and at least one more neutron, although the number of neutrons varies. The neutrons help the nucleus to stick together; which is bound tightly by the strong nuclear force, and neutrons add to this, even though they have no electric charge. Electric charge is a bad thing for the nucleus; because the protons are positively charged, they repel each other and try to blow the nucleus apart. The neutrons don't suffer from this problem, which is one of the reasons why heavier nuclei tend to have more neutrons than protons.

So the construction of chemical elements is simple. If you want to turn iron into copper, add three protons and a handful of neutrons to its nucleus. That's all there is to it. This is easier said than done, of course, yet nature can do it because when the Universe was only a few minutes old the first four chemical elements existed. The building blocks were present, but the heavier elements were assembled later ◉

THE MOST POWERFUL EXPLOSION ON EARTH

BELOW: The now iconic image of a hydrogen bomb explosion. This mushroom cloud was produced by the detonation of XX-33 Romeo on 26 March 1954; it was the third-largest test ever detonated by the USA.

Years before the Manhattan project designed and delivered the most destructive weapon used in anger in the history of warfare, two of the greatest physicists of the age had already lost interest in the idea. Edward Teller and Enrico Fermi were friends and colleagues who would both go on to be members of the Manhattan team, but in 1941, before any type of nuclear bomb had been assembled, their minds were already wandering beyond the bomb that would later be dropped on Hiroshima and Nagasaki with devastating effect.

The Hiroshima and Nagasaki bombs were fission bombs, which work by splitting the nuclei of very heavy elements (uranium in the case of the Hiroshima bomb and plutonium for the Nagasaki bomb), into lighter elements such as strontium and caesium. This is the assembly of the elements in reverse. Each time a nucleus of uranium or plutonium splits, neutrons are released which trigger the splitting of other nuclei. In this way a nuclear chain reaction ensues. Each time a heavy nucleus splits, a large amount of energy is liberated – this 'nuclear binding energy' is stored in the strong nuclear force field that sticks the protons and neutrons together inside the nucleus.

However, even in the very early stages of the Manhattan project, years before the idea of a fission bomb was a physical reality, Enrico Fermi postulated that there was the very real possibility of creating a far more powerful type of bomb. Edward Teller became obsessed with his friend's idea and spent the next decade designing and building a device that would create the most powerful explosions ever made on Earth. It earned Teller the title 'father of the hydrogen bomb'.

On 1 November 1952, the fruits of Fermi's conversation with Teller were realised. Ivy Mike was the codename given to the first successful testing of a hydrogen bomb on Enewetak, an atoll in the Pacific Ocean. The explosion was estimated to be 450 times more powerful than the bomb dropped on Nagasaki, producing a fireball over five kilometres (three miles) wide, a crater two kilometres (one mile) wide and wiping the tiny atoll off the map. Teller had collaborated with another Manhattan scientist, Stanislaw Ulam, to design the bomb, but he wasn't present for the explosion. Instead he sat watching a seismometer thousands of miles away in his office in Berkeley, California. The explosion was so powerful that he was able to clearly see the shockwave from the comfort of his office. 'It's a boy!', he cryptically told his colleagues to inform them of the success.

The Ivy Mike test was the first man-made nuclear fusion reaction. Nuclear fusion is the direct opposite of fission; it is the process by which two atomic nuclei are fused to form a single heavier element. The hydrogen bomb reproduces the process that occurred in the first seconds of the evolution of the Universe – the assembly of hydrogen into helium.

The Teller–Ulam design for the hydrogen bomb that exploded on Enewetak is the basic design employed by all five of the major nuclear weapon states today. Although the fusion element of the design is only part of its explosive power, combined with the other stages contained within the bomb it creates destruction on an unparalleled scale.

Here are two completely different ways of creating new elements and releasing vast amounts of energy. The first, fission, involves taking a heavy element and splitting it. The second, fusion, involves taking lighter elements and sticking

Look up into a clear blue sky and you are bathing in the energy of nuclear explosions on an unimaginable scale.

them together. But how can both these processes result in energy being released? Isn't there a contradiction here? There isn't, of course, because this is how nature works. It's all down to the delicate balance between the electric repulsion of the protons in the nucleus and the power of the strong nuclear force to stick the protons and neutrons together. Since there are two competing forces, one trying to blow the nucleus apart and one trying to glue it together, you might think there must be some kind of balancing point – an ideal mixture of protons and neutrons that is perfectly poised between attraction and repulsion. There are in fact two elements that are very close to the mixture of optimal stability, and these are iron and nickel. Elements lighter than these can be made more stable, releasing energy in the process, by fusing them together. Elements heavier than these can be made more stable, releasing energy in the process, by breaking them apart.

To be completely accurate, we should mention that there are other factors than just the balance between the electromagnetic and nuclear forces that feed into the stability of the elements. These are to do with the shape of the nucleus itself and that the balance between protons and neutrons is favoured for quantum mechanical reasons. (If you are interested, google 'Semi-empirical mass formula' and enjoy!)

Here on Earth, fusion may seem the ultimate human technological achievement but actually it's the most natural thing in the world. It didn't only happen at the Big Bang; it's a process that can be found occurring across the Universe as we speak. In fact, it illuminates the whole Universe and happens all the time millions of miles above our heads.

Fusion is the process that powers every star in the heavens, including our sun. Look up into a clear blue sky and you are bathing in the energy of nuclear explosions on an unimaginable scale. Deep in the Sun's core, 800,000 kilometres (500,000 miles) below the surface (where temperatures reach

BELOW: The shining Sun is one of the most natural demonstrations of the effect of fusion. It, and all the other stars in the heavens, are powered by the fusing of hydrogen and helium.

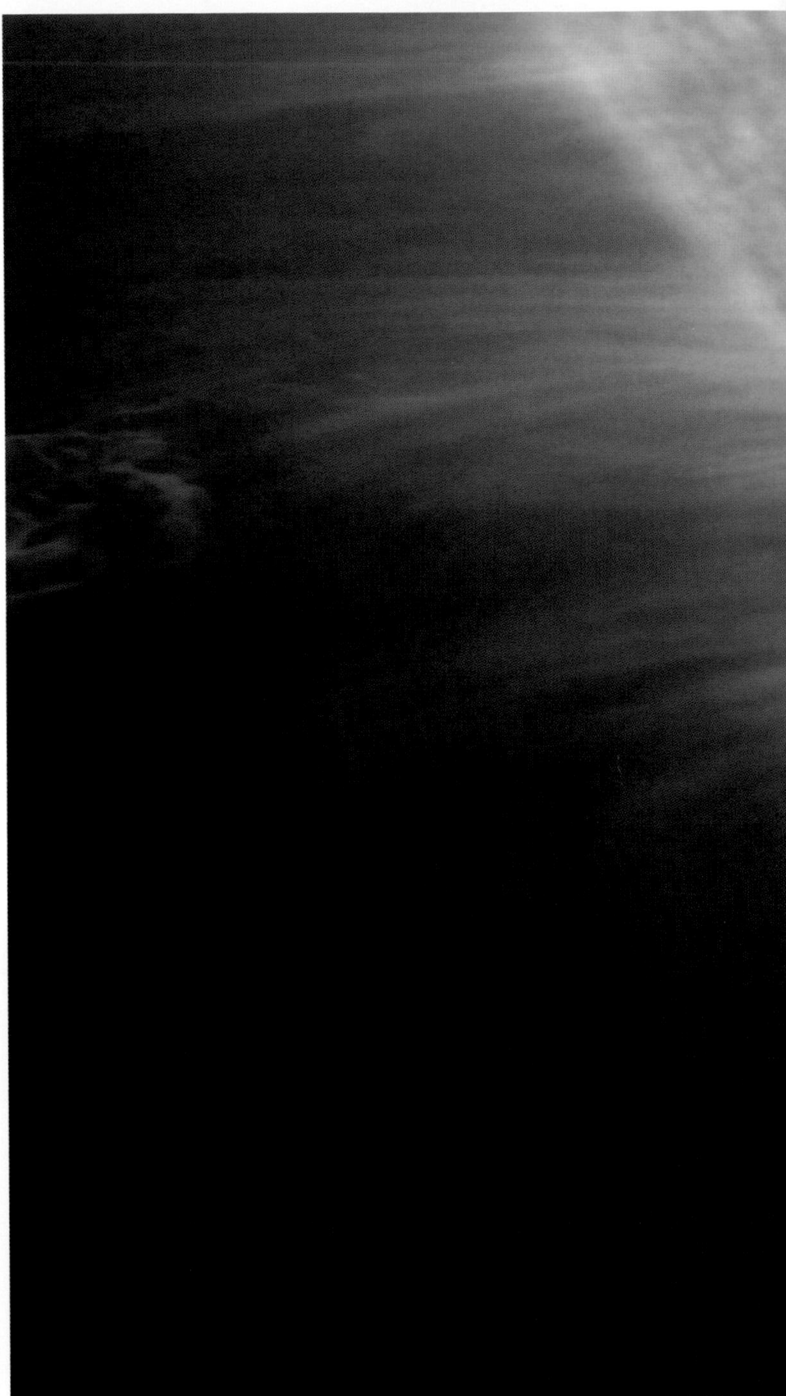

fifteen million degrees Celsius), the Sun is busy fusing hydrogen into helium at a furious rate. In just one second the Sun converts 600 million tonnes of hydrogen into helium, releasing as much energy as the human race will use in the next million years. This is the energy that makes the stars shine and fills the Solar System with heat and light.

It is the process of turning hydrogen into helium that creates the energy that allows all life on Earth to exist, but for all its power the Sun only converts hydrogen, the simplest element, into helium, the next simplest. This process is repeated across the night sky; every star in the Universe began its life fuelled by hydrogen and powered by this reaction.

So the assembly of the second-simplest element, helium, is well understood. We know the stars can do it, we know it happened in the very early Universe, and we can even do it ourselves on Earth. But this doesn't help to explain the origin of the other ninety-two naturally occurring elements. Clearly, somewhere in the Universe there must be a plentiful source of the other elements because they are everywhere, our whole planet is made from them. We are made of billions and billions of atoms; from magnesium, to zinc, to iron and, of course, the one atom that life is more dependent on than any other – carbon. Every human being on the planet is made from about a billion billion billion carbon atoms. That's an unimaginable number of carbon atoms that simply didn't exist in the early moments of the Universe. Where did they come from? The answer must be nuclear fusion, and the natural place to look is within the stars themselves◉

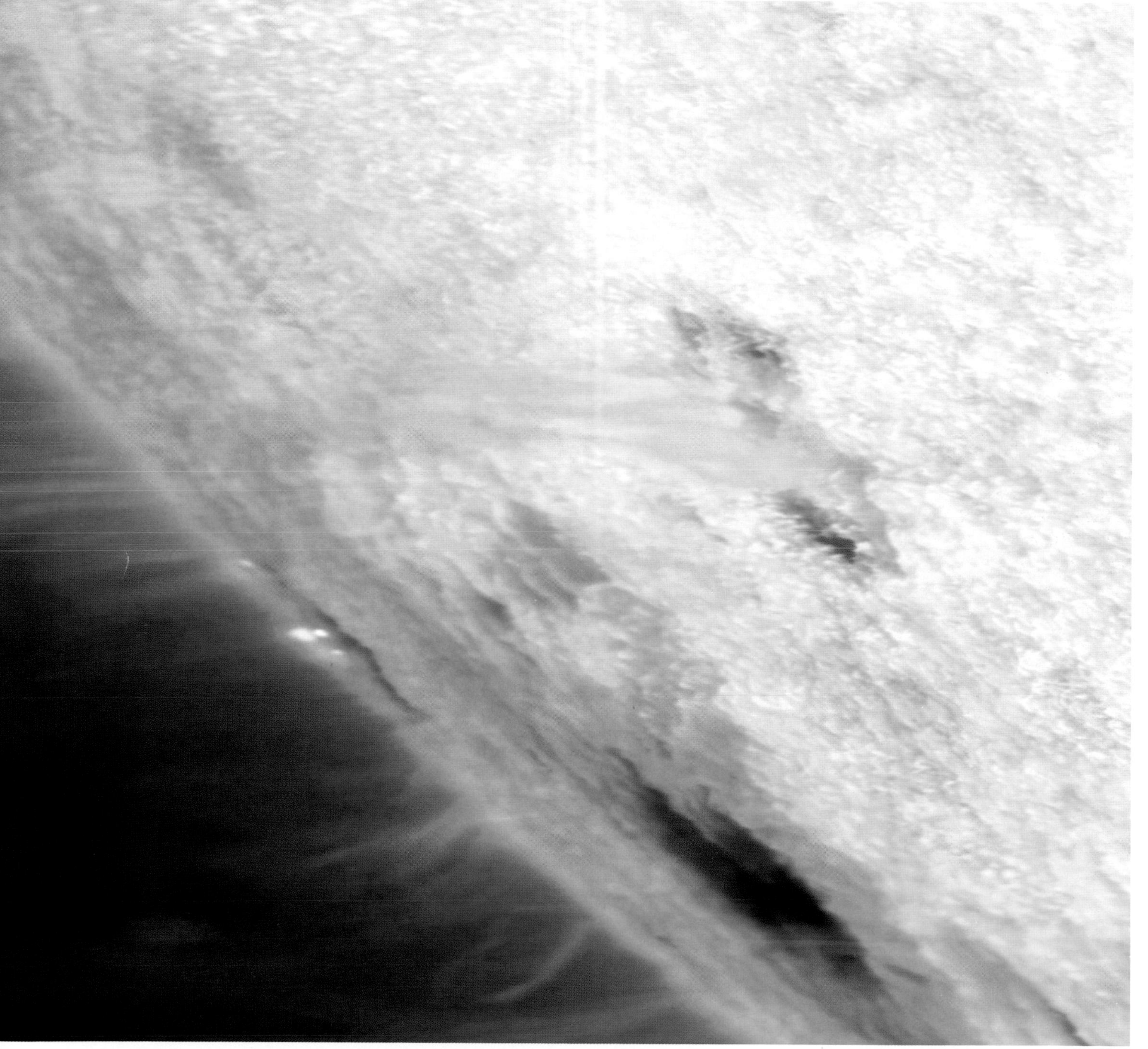

FROM BIG BANG TO SUNSHINE: THE FIRST STARS

The first stars formed around 100 million years after the Big Bang. The rate at which they burned their hydrogen fuel essentially depends on their mass. The more massive the star, the brighter it shines and the shorter its lifetime. The key to understanding how the heavier elements came into being lies in what happens to stars when they have exhausted their hydrogen fuel. For the most massive known stars, this may take only a few million years. For stars like our sun, it may take ten billion years – but the Universe has been around for plenty of time to allow generations of stars to live and die.

RIGHT: The brightly shining constellation of Orion is clearly visible as it sets in the night sky.

RED GIANT

BELOW: These images of Betelgeuse are based on pictures taken by the Very Large Telescope at the European Southern Observatory, in Chile, and show gas plumes bursting from the star's surface into space.

RIGHT: Betelgeuse is the ninth-brightest star in our galaxy and one of our nearest neighbours. It can be seen from Earth with the naked eye – easily identifiable in the night sky for its brightness and reddish tinge.

As a star exhausts its hydrogen stores you might expect it to slowly flicker away, but for stars like our sun, the opposite happens. Having spent millions or billions of years with the core as its beating heart, a star that is running out of hydrogen in fact swells up to potentially hundreds of times its original size. Such stars are known as red giants.

One of the closest red giants to Earth is the star Alpha Orionis, better known as Betelgeuse, the ninth-brightest star in our night sky and one of our nearest neighbours in cosmic terms, a mere 500 light years away. Betelgeuse has long been familiar to stargazers, notable for its brightness and reddish tinge that is clearly visible to the naked eye. Sir John Herschel studied the star intensely in the nineteenth century, recording the dramatic variations in its brightness. However, it was only when three astronomers from the Mount Wilson Observatory in California tried to measure its diameter that we realised this was no ordinary star. Albert Michelson, Francis Pease

Betelgeuse is a vast wonder that would fill our solar system with a single wispy star.

and John Anderson used a specially designed telescope to measure the scale of this red star using a technique known as interferometry. By measuring the angular diameter (the apparent size of an object from our position on Earth), they came up with a number that, although it's been refined since, revealed something profound: Betelgeuse is a true giant in every sense. This star is about twenty times the mass of our sun but its size is rather more impressive. If you put Betelgeuse at the centre of our solar system it would dwarf our sun. In fact, Betelgeuse would extend past the Earth's orbit, encompassing everything out to Jupiter. Current estimates suggest it is around 800 million kilometres (500 million miles) in diameter; a vast, ethereal wonder that would fill our solar system with a single wispy star.

Due to its immense size and relative proximity, we can study Betelgeuse in incredible detail. In 1996, the Hubble Space Telescope took a picture of Betelgeuse that was the first direct image of another star to reveal its disc and surface features. We've even imaged sunspots on its surface and been able to study its atmosphere in ever-increasing detail. However, it's not the surface of the red giant that holds the clue to where the heavy elements are made; to understand that, we need to journey deep into its dying heart ●

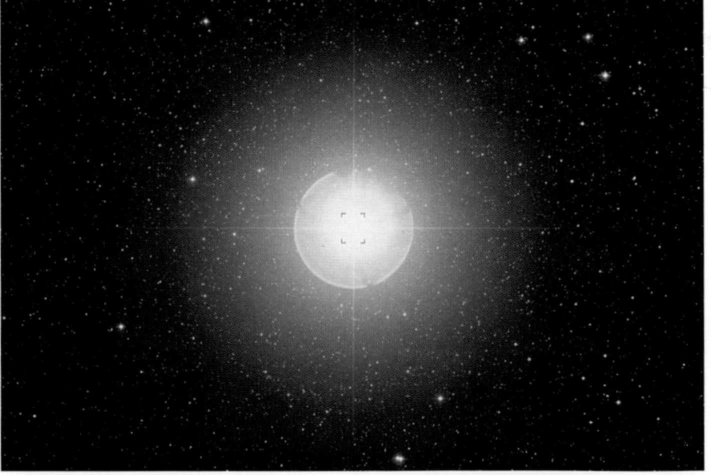

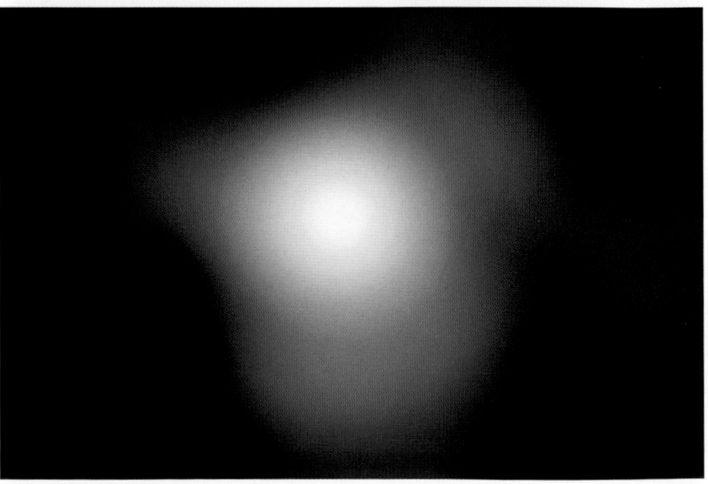

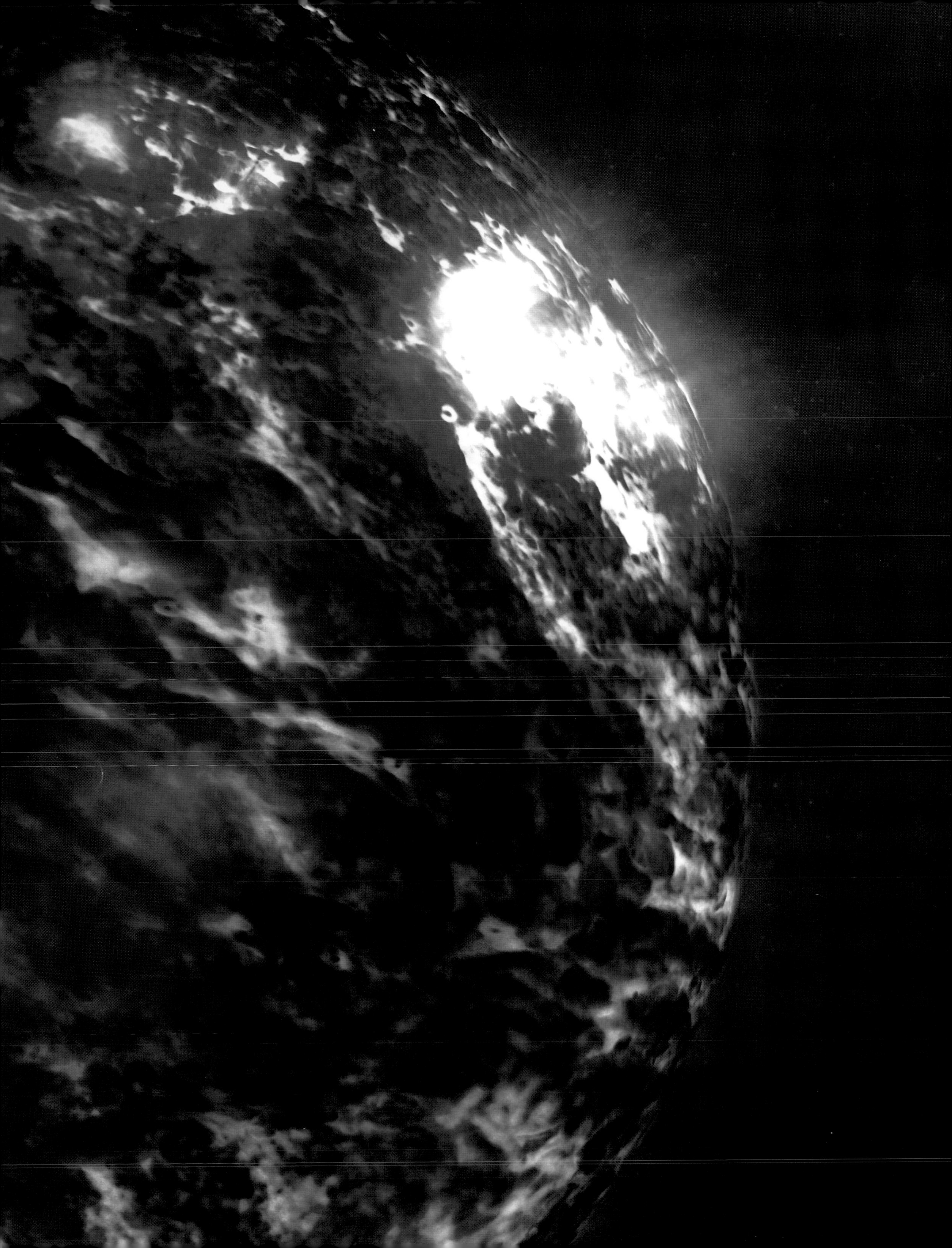

STAR DEATH

When making a television documentary, you are always looking for visual ways to tell complex stories. While filming *Wonders of the Universe*, we journeyed all over the world in search of analogies and backdrops, but for me the most successful of all was an abandoned prison in the heart of Rio de Janeiro, Brazil.

The building itself was a gutted husk, a brick skeleton; all the windows, if it ever had them, were gone. The cells were dormitories of twenty or thirty concrete bunk beds in close rows. Each had a single tiny bathroom, some with ragged pieces of cloth still draped across the entrance, paying lip service to privacy. The walls of the cells were a grotesque patchwork of ripped colour, papered with glamour girls mixed with the odd football team. I found it disturbing for two reasons. First, you can't stop wondering about incarceration there; the centre of a hot, humid city like Rio is not the place to spend years inside a steel and concrete cage. The second was less cerebral: the prison was wired with live explosives. From inside the shell the bright outside pressed and glowed like a stellar surface, impossible to view against the internal black. The light won't come in. It stays outside in the city. I could feel the analogy as I descended down holed, cement-dusted precarious stairwells into the dense heart of the dying star. It is here, inside a violent, condemned structure, far from the light of the surface, that the elements of living things are meticulously assembled. In here, the star transforms from matter consumer to matter producer.

Stars exist in an uneasy equilibrium. Their gravity acts to compress them, which heats them up until the electromagnetic repulsion between the hydrogen atoms is overcome and they fuse together to make helium. This releases energy, which keeps the star up. When the hydrogen runs out, the outward pressure disappears; gravity regains the upper hand and the structure of the star changes dramatically. The core collapses rapidly, leaving a shell of hydrogen and helium behind. Within the shrinking core the temperature rises until, at 100 million degrees Celsius, a new fusion process is triggered. At these temperatures helium nuclei can overcome their mutual electromagnetic repulsion and wander close enough together to fuse – the star begins to burn helium. This transfer from hydrogen to helium fusion has two profound effects: firstly, sufficient energy is

LEFT: Just as in a dying star, the structure of a building and the elements that keep it standing become unstable over time. This prison was given a helping hand to its destruction, but a dying star will detonate itself as it reaches the end of its life, producing spectacular planetary nebulae. It took seconds to demolish the prison block, which is the same length of time it takes for a red giant star to collapse.

released to halt the stellar collapse, so the star stabilises and rapidly swells. This is the beginning of its life as a red giant. Secondly, it fuses into existence the element vital for life. At first sight the fusion of two helium nuclei, each consisting of two protons and two neutrons, should only be able to produce the isotope beryllium-8, composed of four protons and four neutrons. This is an unstable isotope of beryllium that quickly breaks down, but in the intense temperatures of a dying star, as the core exceeds 100 million Kelvin, these nuclei live just long enough to fuse with a third helium nucleus, creating the precious element carbon-12. This is where all the carbon in the Universe comes from; every carbon atom in every living thing on the planet was produced in the heart of a dying star.

The helium-burning phase doesn't end with the alchemic synthesis of carbon, because during the same intensely hot phase in the star's life the conditions allow a nucleus of helium to latch onto a newly minted carbon nucleus to create another element vital for life. Oxygen makes up 21 per cent of the air we breathe, is a prerequisite for water, the solvent of life, and is the third-most common element in the Universe after hydrogen and helium. As you breathe in around two and a half grams of oxygen each minute, it's worth remembering that all this life-giving gas was created in an environment as far away from our understanding of what is habitable as you can get.

Compared with the lifetime of a star, this stellar production line of carbon and oxygen is over in the blink of an eye. Within about a million years the helium supply in the core is used up, and for many stars that's where fusion stops. Any average-sized star, like our sun, has by now reached the end of its productive life. When our sun reaches this stage, in about ten billion years' time, there won't be enough gravitational energy to compress the core any further and restart fusion. Instead, the star becomes more and more unstable, huge pressure points will build up, until eventually the whole stellar atmosphere explodes, hurling the precious cargo of oxygen, carbon, hydrogen, and all, on its journey into space. For at this brief moment in time, no more than a few tens of thousands of years, a dying star will create one of the most beautiful structures in our universe: a planetary nebula.

Once this brief cosmic light show is over, an average-sized star will shrink to an object no bigger than Earth. A white dwarf is the fate of such stars and billions like it, but for massive stars like Betelgeuse the action is far from over. If a star has a mass half as big again as our Sun, it will continue down the chemical production line. As helium fusion slowly comes to an end, gravity takes over and the collapse of the core restarts. The temperature rises, launching the third stage in the birth of our universe's elements, and with temperatures reaching hundreds of millions of Kelvin, carbon fuses with helium to make neon, neon fuses with more helium to make magnesium, and two carbon atoms fuse to make sodium. With more and more elemental ingredients entering the cooking pot, and temperatures rising, the heavier elements are produced one after another. The core continues to collapse, the temperature continues to rise, and the next stage of fusion begins, leaving layers of newly minted elements behind.

With the first twenty-five elements now created within the star, the runaway production line hits a block at the twenty-sixth element, iron, created from a complex cascade of fusion reactions fuelled by silicon. At this stage the temperature of the star is at least 2.5 billion Kelvin, but it has nowhere else to go. The peak of nuclear stability has been reached, and no more energy can be released by adding more protons or neutrons to iron. The final stage of iron production lasts only a couple of days, transforming the heart of the star into almost pure iron in a desperate bid to release every last gasp of nuclear binding energy and stave off gravity. This is where the fusion process stops; once the star's core has been fused into iron, it has only seconds left to live. Gravity must now win, and the star collapses under its own weight forming a planetary nebula.

As I walked away from the prison for the cameras, a button was pressed and the building fell. The demolition took seconds – the same time it takes a red giant star like Betelgeuse to collapse ◉

PLANETARY NEBULAE

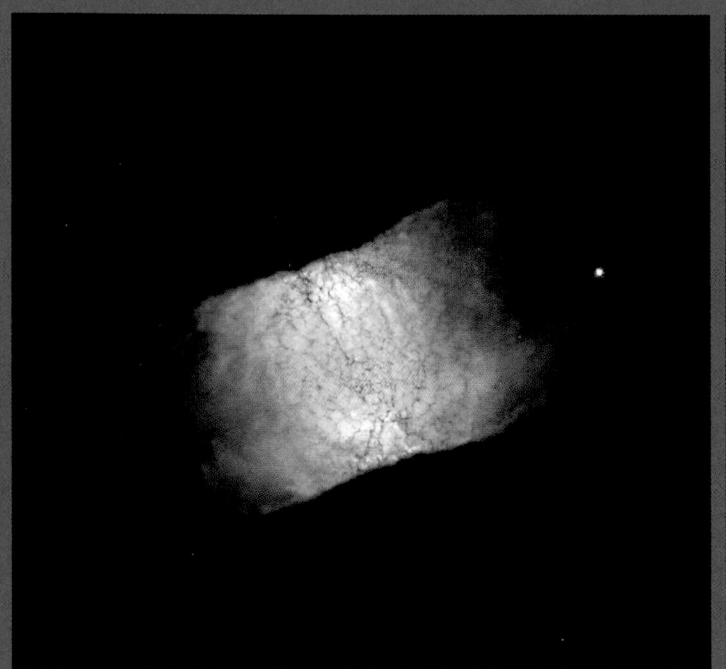

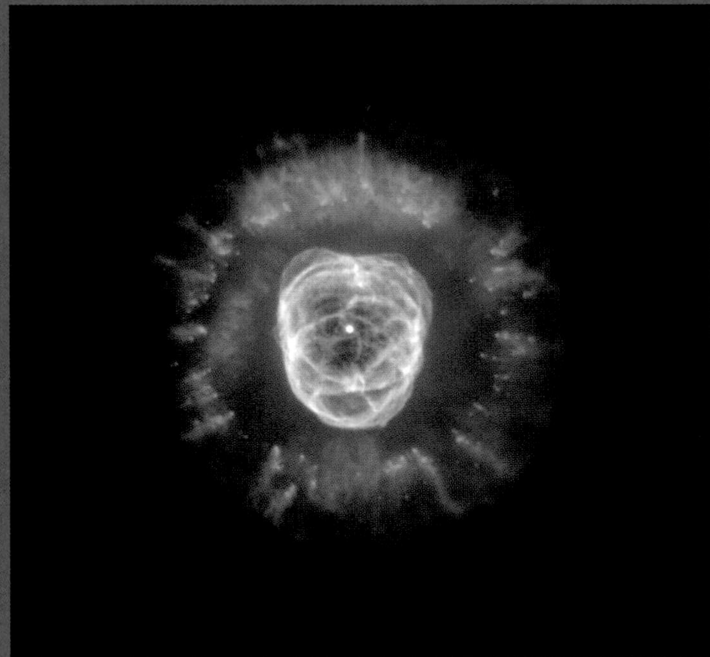

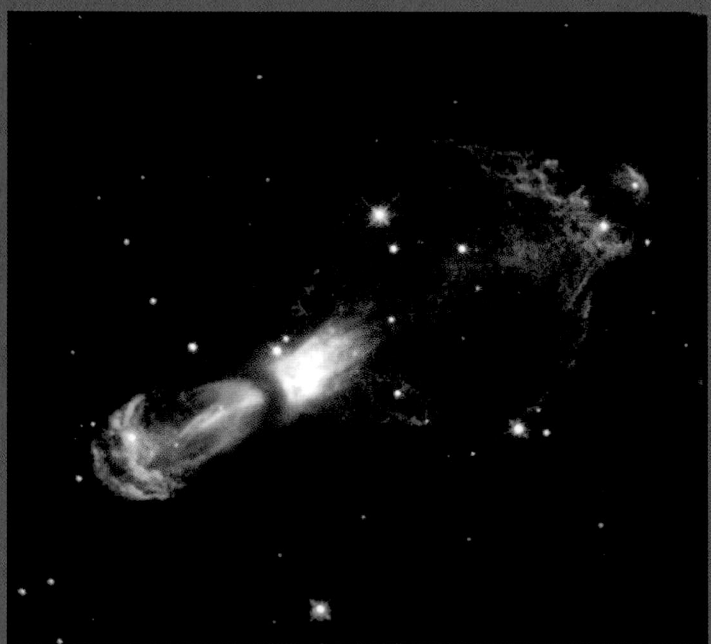

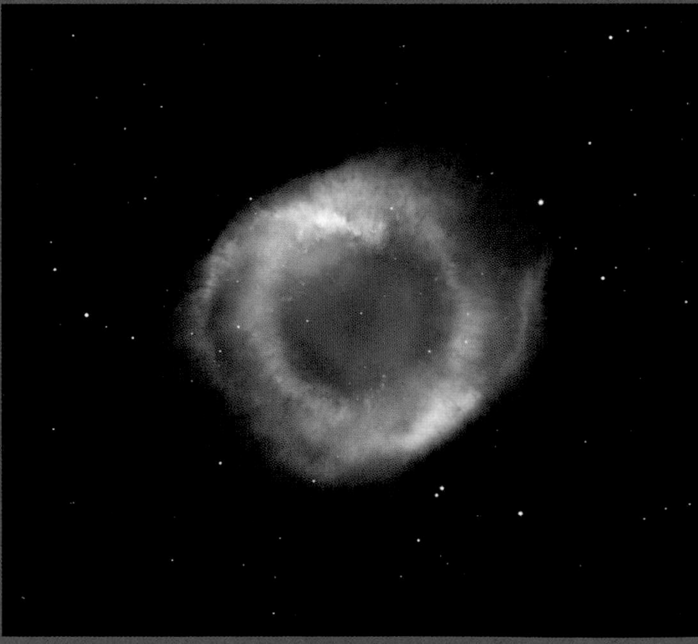

TOP:
This dying star, IC 4406, like many planetary nebulae, is highly symmetrical. It is known as the 'Retina Nebula' because the tendrils of dust emitted from it that have been compared to the eye's retina.

BOTTOM:
About 5,000 light years (4,700 trillion kilometres/2,900 trillion miles) from Earth lies the Calabash Nebula. This image, captured by the Hubble Space Telescope, shows material being ejected from the star.

TOP:
The Eskimo Nebula is so-called because of its resemblance to a head surrounded by fur-lined hood when viewed from Earth. It was discovered in 1787 by astronomer William Herschel.

BOTTOM:
This composite image depicts the Helix Nebula. This planetary nebula resembles a doughnut, as seen from Earth, but new evidence suggests that the Helix in fact consists of two gaseous discs.

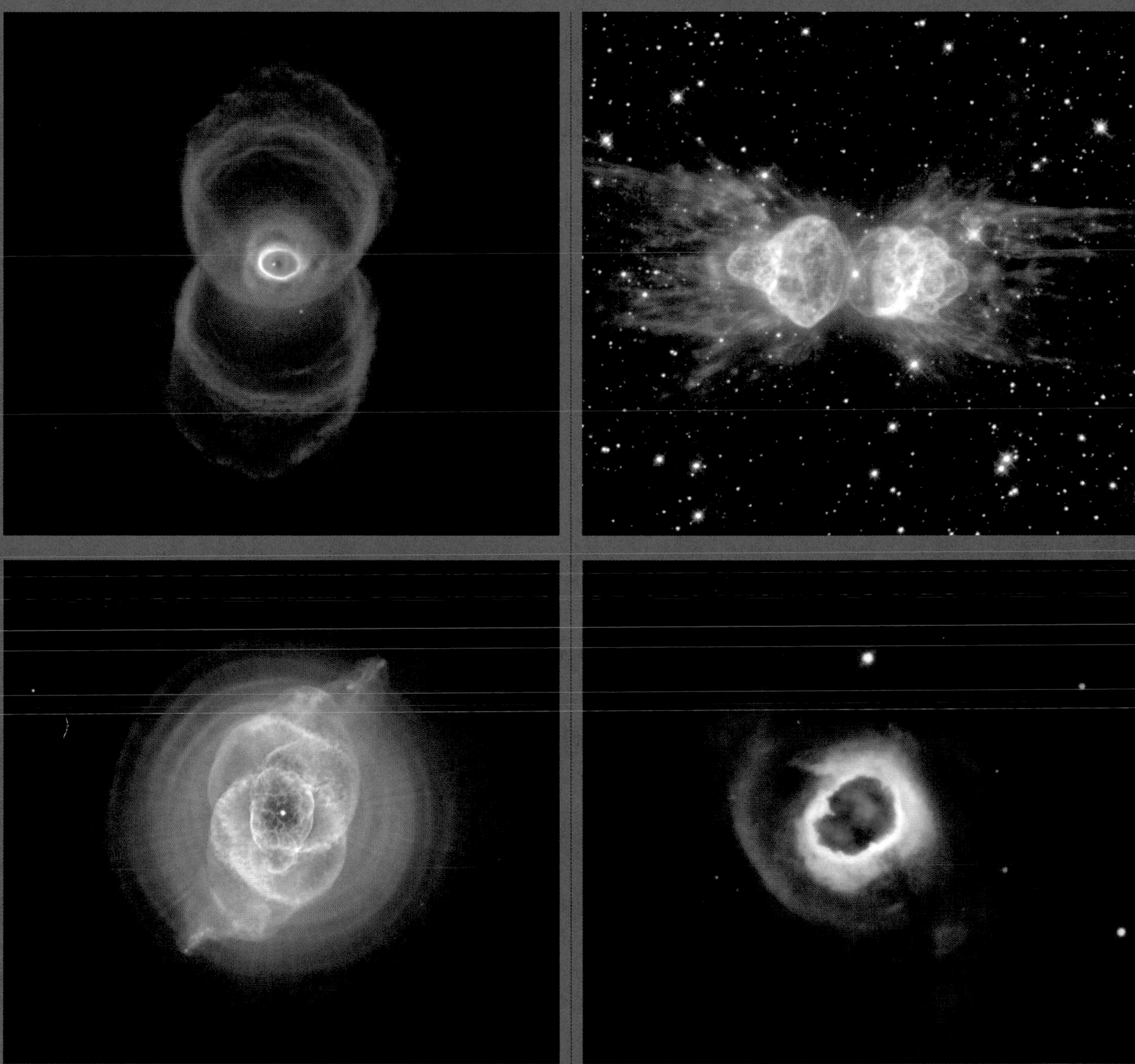

TOP:
MyCn18 is a young planetary nebula which was discovered in the early twentieth century. However, it was this Hubble Telescope image in January 1996 that revealed the nebula's hourglass shape with intricate engravings.

BOTTOM:
The aptly named Cat's Eye Nebula (officially known as NGC 6543) was one of the first planetary nebulae to be discovered (in 1786 by William Herschel). It is one of the most complex nebulae known to exist in the Universe.

TOP:
Imaged on 20 July 1997, Mz3 has been dubbed the Ant Nebula because its outline resembles the head and thorax of an ant when seen through telescopes on Earth. On close inspection, the ant's body appears to consist of two fiery lobes.

BOTTOM:
This planetary nebula is known as Kohoutek 4-55 (or K 4-55), named after its discoverer, Czech astronomer Lubos Kohoutek. It is unusual for its multi-shell structure.

THE RAREST OF ALL

BELOW AND RIGHT: Once the centre of the great American gold rush, the 16-1 mine is one of the few gold mines still operating in the state of California today. Digging for gold there with the miners was an enlightening experience. As I peered at seemingly ordinary rocks, I could see glints and glimmers of a familiar yellow colouring, revealing the stones' precious hidden cargo of gold.

The first twenty-six of the elements are forged in the cores of stars and are distributed through the Universe in their inevitable collapse. But what of the other seventy-two – some of which are vital for life, and many of which we hold most precious? If they are not formed within stellar furnaces, what could their origin possibly be?

In the remote forests of northwestern California, the mountains still hide a secret that made the quiet pine woods the ultimate destination for fortune seekers only a century ago. Although they're empty today, in the late nineteenth century this was the centre of the California gold rush. Hundreds of thousands of people arrived here, trying anything and everything to get rich, from simple panning to the most advanced mining techniques available. Gold worth billions of dollars was extracted, fuelling the rise of one of the world's great cities, San Francisco. The insatiable appetite for gold has waned today, but in the forests around Lake Tahoe, the 16–1 mine remains one of the few gold mines still operating in the state of California.

For almost 100 years, miners have been digging for gold in the 16–1, and it is still one of the richest gold deposits in the world, due to a quirk in the local geology. The unique thing about California is that it sits on the divide between the North American tectonic plate and the Pacific tectonic plate. The

whole region is one enormous fault line, with thousands of smaller faults running through the rocks of the mountains. When you travel into the mine, which is nothing more than a series of horizontal tunnels at gentle gradients hollowed out of the mountainside, you can see these fault lines everywhere; they reveal their presence as visible boundaries between rock and quartz – a maze of mini-faults. One hundred and forty million years ago, in the Jurassic period when the dinosaurs were running around above the mine, hot water bubbled up and flowed through this rock, carrying a precious cargo. Its water was laden with gold brought up from deep within the Earth, deposited through the seams of quartz. For the last 100 years all the miners have had to do is to follow quartz seams laced with shimmering gold.

The gold that runs all the way through the quartz in the 16–1 mine is unusually pure, at anything up to 85 per cent, and the thick tendrils snaking through the rock glint and glimmer that familiar yellow in the sunlight. The rest is about 14.5 per cent silver, with traces of heavier metals. The area is so rich in gold that it can even be found as simple pure nuggets that can be picked up off river beds, and at the 2010 price of around £900 per troy ounce, it's obvious why mines like this are still in operation.

If you stop to think about it though, there's something a bit odd about the value we attach to gold. Throughout history

All the gold dug out of the ground throughout all of human history would just about fill three Olympic-sized swimming pools. It is this almost vanishing scarcity that makes gold so valuable.

people have gone to extraordinary lengths to get their hands on it, which is odd because it isn't particularly useful for anything. Copper and iron will help you survive, but gold is next to useless. Most of the gold that we've struggled to extract has ended up as jewellery. The only thing that gold has going for it, other than being shiny, is that it is incredibly rare, and this is what drives up its price. All the gold dug out of the ground throughout all of human history – with all the associated tragedy and elation, hardship and riches – would just about fill three Olympic-sized swimming pools.

It is this almost vanishing scarcity (three swimming pools relative to the size of a planet) that makes gold so valuable; it is just one of many rare elements that are to be found in the most minute of traces within the Earth.

There are over sixty elements heavier than iron in the Universe, some are valuable, such as gold, silver and platinum; some are vital for life, such as copper and zinc; and some are just useful, such as uranium, tin and lead. Very massive stars can produce very tiny amounts of the heavier elements up to bismuth-209 (element number 89) in their cores by a process called neutron capture, but it is known that this makes nowhere near enough to account for the abundances we observe today. There simply haven't been enough massive stars in the Universe.

The conditions necessary to produce large amounts of the elements beyond iron are only found in the most rare of all celestial events. Blink and you'll miss them, because in a galaxy of 100 billion stars the conditions violent enough to form substantial amounts of these elements will exist on average for less than two minutes in every century ◉

SUPERNOVA: LIFE CYCLE OF A STAR

All stars are born from clouds of gas, but the length of their life and their eventual fate are governed by their mass (i.e. how much gas they contain). Stars dozens of times heavier than the Sun live for only a few million years before swelling into supergiants and exploding as supernovae (top row). However, stars like the Sun live longer and die more gently, shining steadily for billions of years before swelling into red giants and losing their outer layers as a planetary nebula (middle row). The core of the star, exposed as a white dwarf, then continues to glow for billions of years more before gradually fading out. The least massive stars, the red dwarfs (bottom), simply fade out over tens of billions of years.

HIGH-MASS STAR RED SUPERGIANT

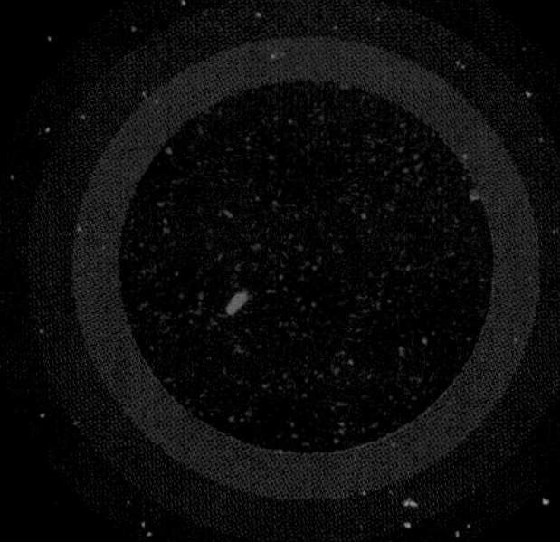

Supergiant becomes more red as it starts to cool

1,000 MILLION KM

NEBULA

Dense nebula area begins to contract

200,000 BILLION KM

PROTOSTAR

Gravitational tug will cause it to collapse and central temperature to rise to around 15 million °F

100 MILLION KM

MAIN-SEQUENCE STAR

Star emits heat and light caused by nuclear fusion

1 MILLION KM

SUN-LIKE STAR

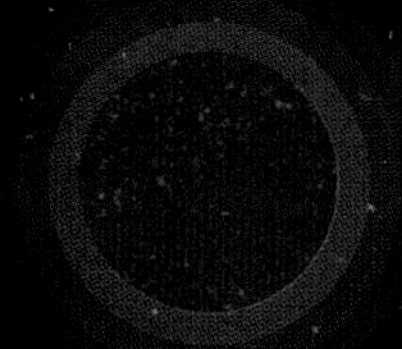

Star becomes a red giant as hydrogen-shell burning begins

LOW-MASS STAR RED DWARF

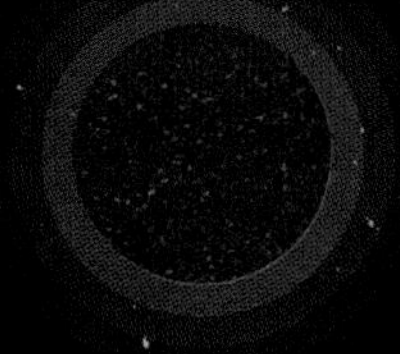

Shines for trillions of years, never becoming a red giant

100,000 KM

Star explodes as a supernova and its outer layers are blown off, producing elements heavier than iron

If star's mass is over 1.4 solar masses, it will collapse and become a neutron star. These are very dense and compact

15 KM

If the remnant is above 3 solar masses it will collapse and become a black hole. These are regions of space in which gravity is so strong that not even light can escape, surrounded by swirling discs of captured gas and dust

50 KM

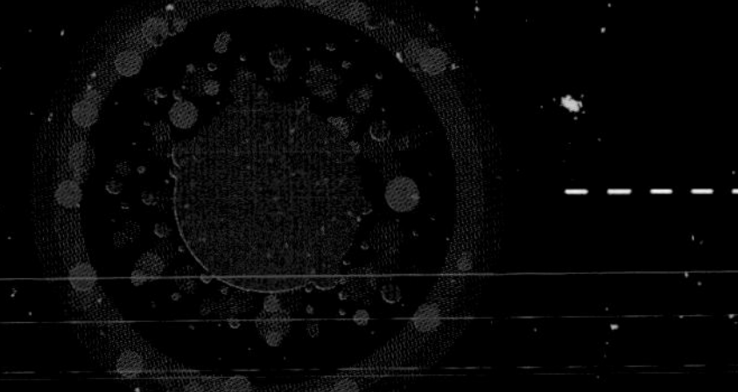

Red giant outer layers start to form planetary nebula

Star collapses after burning its helium shell to become a white dwarf

10,000 BILLION KM

This will eventually fade to become a black dwarf

10,000 KM

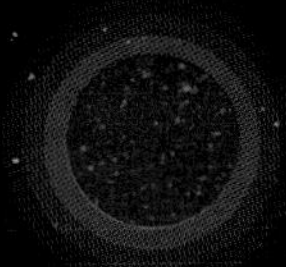

Star starts to collapse as hydrogen is used up

10,000 KM

Star becomes extremely dense with a faint core. This will eventually turn into a white dwarf

Core stops glowing

THE BEGINNING AND THE END

BELOW AND RIGHT: This computer-generated sequence of images shows what will happen when Betelgeuse goes supernova. Deep in the heart of the star, the core will succumb to gravity and fall in on itself, then rebound with colossal force. The blast wave emitted generates the highest temperatures in the Universe. Over millions of years the scattered elements of the exploded star will become a nebula, at the heart of which is a super-dense core that is Betelgeuse the neutron star.

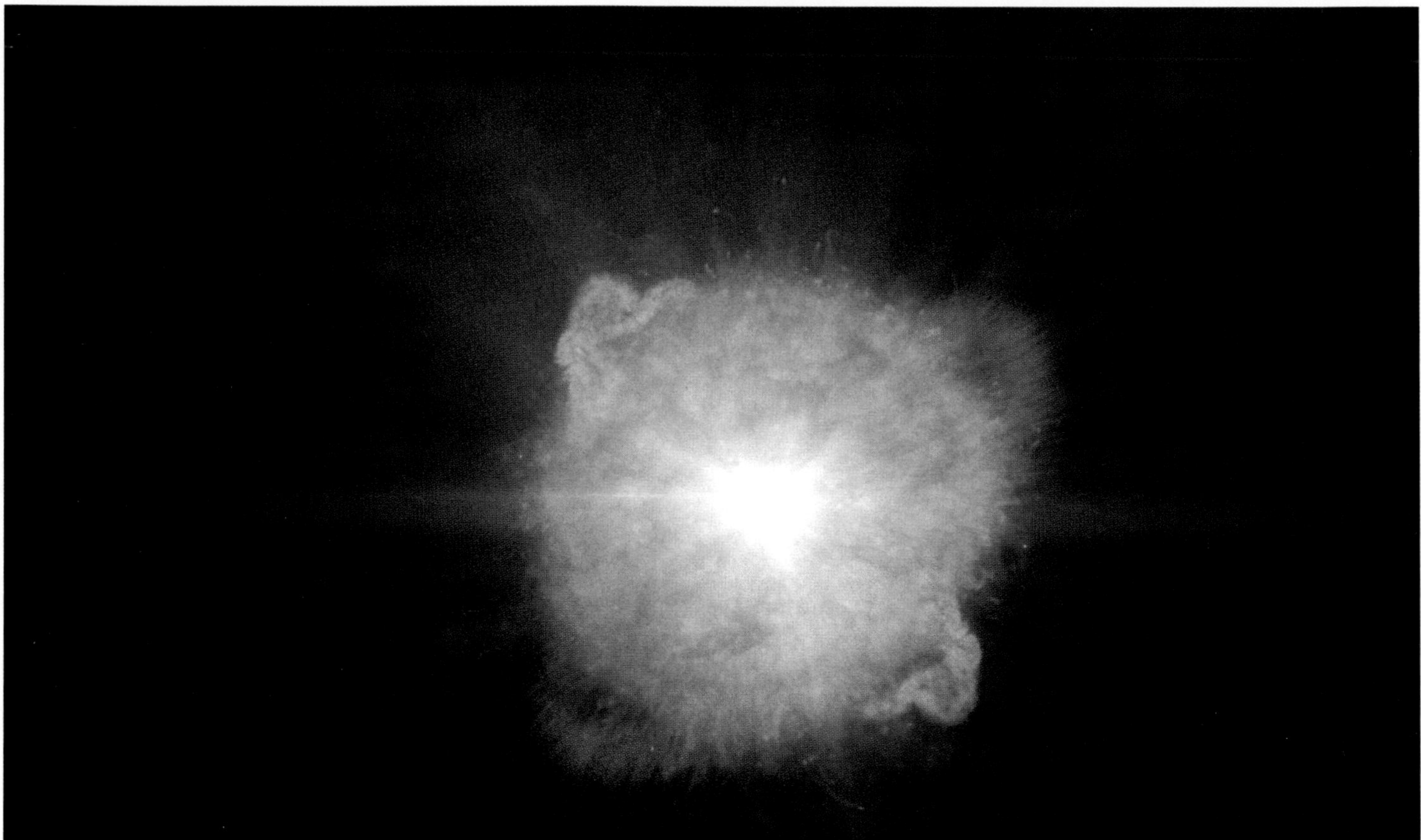

After a few million years of life, the destiny of the largest stars in our universe is a dramatic one. Having run out of hydrogen and burnt through the elements all the way to iron, giant stars teeter on the edge of collapse. Yet even in this dilapidated state these stars have one last violent act, and it is a generous one. It occurs with such intensity that it allows for the creation of the heavy elements.

If we could gaze deep into the heart of one of these dying giants, we would see the core finally succumb to gravity. As fusion grinds to a halt, this giant ball of iron falls in on itself with enormous speed, contracting at up to a quarter of the speed of light. This dramatic collapse causes a rapid increase in temperature and density as the core shrinks to a fraction of its original size. The inner core may eventually shrink to 30 kilometres (19 miles) in diameter. At this point, with temperatures nearing 100 billion Kelvin and densities comparable to those inside an atomic nucleus, quantum mechanics steps in to abruptly halt the collapse. By now most of the electrons and protons in the core have been literally forced to merge together into neutrons. Neutrons, in common with protons and electrons, obey something called the Pauli exclusion principle, which effectively prevents them from getting too close to one another (in more technical terms, no two neutrons can be in the same quantum state). This has the effect of making a ball of neutrons the most rigid material in the Universe – 100 million million million times as hard as a diamond. When the neutrons can be compressed no more, the contraction must stop and all the superheated collapsing matter rebounds with colossal force. A shockwave shoots out through the star and as this blast wave runs into the outer layers of the star it generates the highest temperatures in the Universe – 100 billion degrees. The precise mechanism for

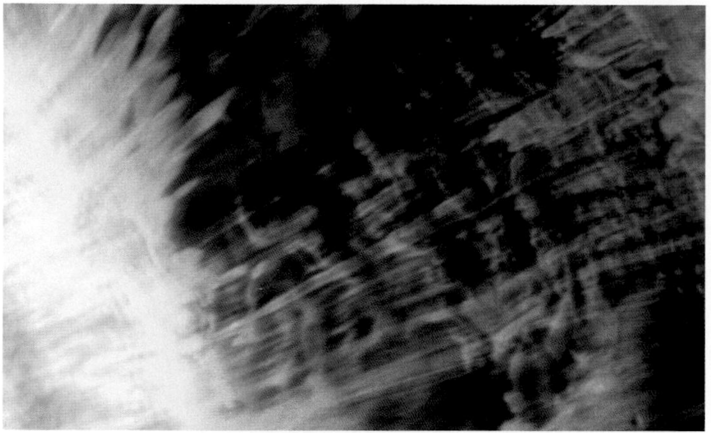

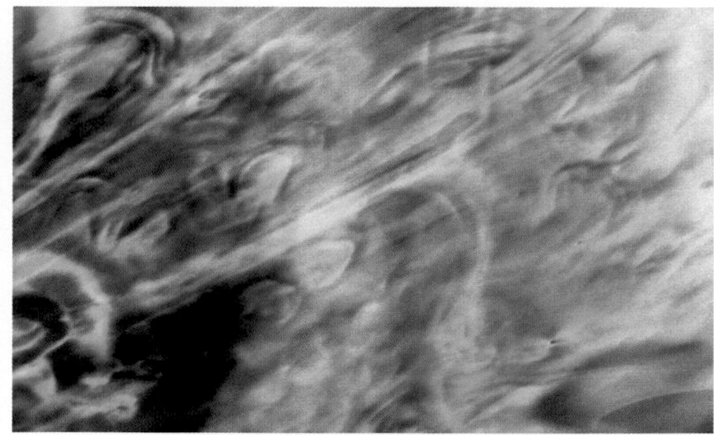

this rapid heating is not fully understood, but it is known that for a matter of seconds the conditions are intense enough to form all the heaviest elements we see in our universe, from gold to plutonium. This is a Type II supernova – the most powerful explosion we know of.

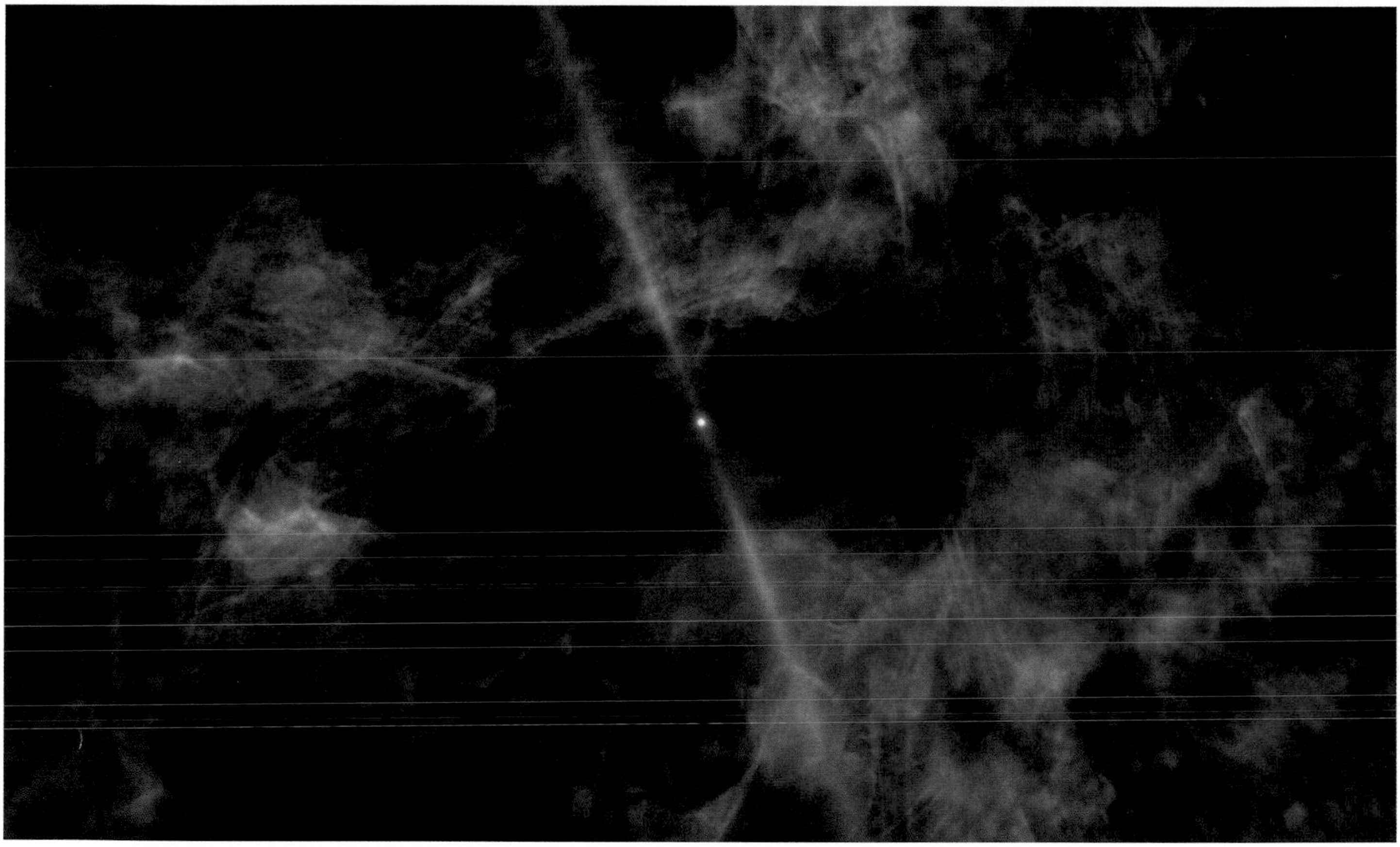

Supernovae are so rare that since the birth of modern science we have never had the chance to see one close up. The last supernova explosion seen from Earth in our galaxy was in 1604, a few years before the invention of the astronomical telescope. On average, it is expected there should be around one supernova explosion in the Milky Way per century, but for the last 400 years we've had no luck. It's long overdue and astronomers are always searching the skies for stars which they think might be the most likely candidate to go supernova.

One of the prime candidates is Orion's shining red jewel, Betelgeuse. With so many telescopes trained on this nearby star, we have been able to follow its every move for decades. Charting its brightness, we have discovered that it is extremely unstable; it has dimmed by about 15 per cent in the past decade. As supernova candidates go, Betelgeuse is top of the list. It is generally thought that Betelgeuse could go supernova at any time. It is a relatively young star, perhaps only ten million years old, and has sped through its life cycle so rapidly because it is so massive. However, when you're ten million years old, the end of your life can be quite drawn out and a phrase like 'any time soon' in stellar terms is not quite what you might expect. It means that Betelgeuse should go supernova at some point in the next million years, but equally it could explode tomorrow. What we do know is that when it does go it will provide us with quite a show. Betelgeuse is only 500 light years away, almost uncomfortably close, which means that the explosion will be incredibly bright. It will be

LEFT: The giant Orion Molecular Cloud is an extensive area of star formation about 1,500 light years from us, centred on the impressive Orion Nebula. This infrared image of it, from NASA's Spitzer Space Telescope, shows light from newborn stars within the Orion Nebula. The nebula can be seen from Earth with the naked eye as a hazy 'star' in Orion's sword.

BELOW: This computer-generated image shows just how bright scientists believe the heavens will be once Betelguese has gone supernova; it will flood the skies with light – day and night.

BOTTOM: When stars are more massive than about eight times the Sun, they end their lives in a spectacular explosion. The outer layers of the star are hurtled out into space at thousands of miles an hour, leaving a debris field of gas and dust. Where the star once was, a small, dense object called a neutron star is often found. While around only 16 kilometres (10 miles) across, the tightly packed neutrons it contains have more mass than the entire Sun. The bright blue dot in the centre of this X-ray image of RCW 103 is believed to show the neutron star that formed when the star exploded in a supernova 2,000 years ago.

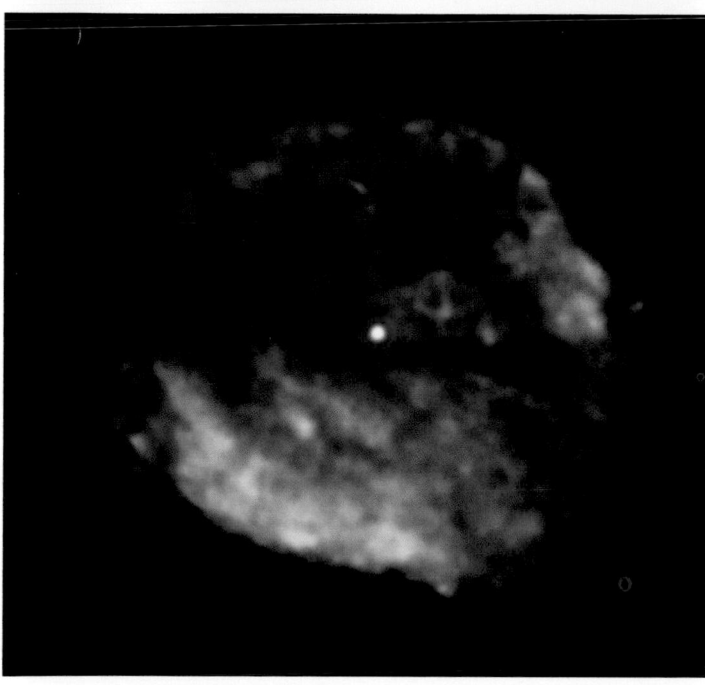

by far the brightest star in the sky and it may even shine as brightly as a full moon at night and fill the sky as a second sun during the day.

In a single instant, Betelgeuse will release more energy than our sun will produce in its entire lifetime. As the explosion tears the star apart, it will fling out into space all the elements the star has created through its life.

Over millions of years these newly minted elements will spread out to become a nebula, a rich chemical cloud drifting in space. At the heart of it, all that will remain will be the super-dense core of neutrons; the remnants of the star that was once a billion miles across will have been squashed out of all recognition by gravity. This is a neutron star, the ultimate destiny of Betelgeuse; a dense, hot ball of matter which is the same mass as our Sun but only 30 kilometres (19 miles) across.

We may not have seen neutron stars close up, but we have seen them from afar. X-ray images have been taken that give us vital information about these stars, in particular recent pictures of RCW 103, the two-thousand-year-old remnant of

When Betelgeuse explodes it will be incredibly bright. It will be by far the brightest star in the sky and it may even shine as brightly as a full moon at night and fill the sky as a second sun during the day.

a supernova explosion that occurred about 10,000 light years from Earth (see left).

This may sound like a cosmic graveyard, but it is in the deaths of old stars that new stars are born. This is the Earthly cycle of death and rebirth played out on a cosmic scale. We can see that beautiful cycle happening today in the constellation of Orion. In an area known as the sword handle lies the Orion Nebula. To the naked eye it appears to be a misty patch of light in the night sky, but through a telescope it is a majestic wonder of the Universe. Hidden in its clouds are bright points of light, new stars forming from the clouds of elements blown out by supernova explosions; the new born from the deaths of the old.

It is from such a cycle that we emerged – within a nebula just like this, five billion years ago, our sun was formed. Around that star a network of planets condensed from the ashes, and amongst them was Earth; a planet whose ingredients originated from the nebula, a cloud of elements formed in the deaths of stars, drifting through space.

But that's not quite the end of the story, because it is now thought that the chemical elements themselves are not the most complex pieces of 'us' that were assembled in the depths of space ◉

THE ORIGIN OF LIFE

BELOW: There are thousands of asteroids in our solar system, mostly within an asteroid belt that formed 4,568 million years ago, and on average one meteorite falls to Earth once a month. However, each and every one discovered is hugely important, regardless of its size, as these asteroid pieces give us a real insight into what forms the building blocks of life.

RIGHT: This seemingly ordinary piece of rock is anything but; this asteroid fragment is older than any rock on Earth and is one of the thousands of meteorites that fall onto our planet every year.

At first sight the graph opposite – depicting the spectrum of the light from the Orion Nebula (taken from the Herschel Space Observatory Telescope) – looks rather uninspiring, but the information that it contains is in fact fascinating. This illustration reveals that the Orion Nebula is not just a cloud of elements; there is complex chemistry happening out there deep in space.

Just like the black lines in the spectrum of the Sun, the peaks on this graph correspond to particular chemical elements, but some of these peaks derive from complex molecules – there is water in the nebula, and sulphur dioxide. Perhaps more surprisingly, there are also complex carbon compounds – methanol, hydrogen cyanide, formaldehyde and dimethyl ether. This is direct evidence for complex carbon chemistry occurring in deep space. This is tremendously exciting because it means that we are seeing the beginnings of the chemistry of life in a vast cloud of interstellar gas.

The connection doesn't end there; we may be connected to the chemistry out there in space even more directly. The photo opposite is of a meteorite, a piece of rock that fell to

The fundamental building blocks of life may have formed in the depths of space and been delivered to our planet by meteorites.

Earth from somewhere out in the depths of the Solar System. It is almost certainly older than any rock on Earth because it was formed from the primordial dust cloud, the nebula that collapsed to form the Sun and the planets five billion years ago. When looking inside this ancient rock we discovered something incredibly interesting: it was found to contain amino acids, the building blocks of proteins, which in turn are the building blocks of life. This strongly suggests there was very complex carbon chemistry happening out there in space, forming the building blocks of life, over four and a half billion years ago. It raises the intriguing prospect that the first amino acids on Earth may have formed in the depths of space and been delivered to our planet by meteorites.

This is one more beautiful piece of evidence that forces us to think differently about those twinkling lights and smudges of gas and dust in the sky. When we look out into space we are looking at our place of birth. We truly are children of the stars, and written into every atom and molecule of our bodies is the history of the Universe, from the Big Bang to the present day ◉

ORION'S MOLECULAR MAKE-UP: This detailed spectrum, obtained by ESA's Herschel Space Observatory, shows the fascinating chemical fingerprints of potential life-enabling organic molecules in the Orion Nebula.

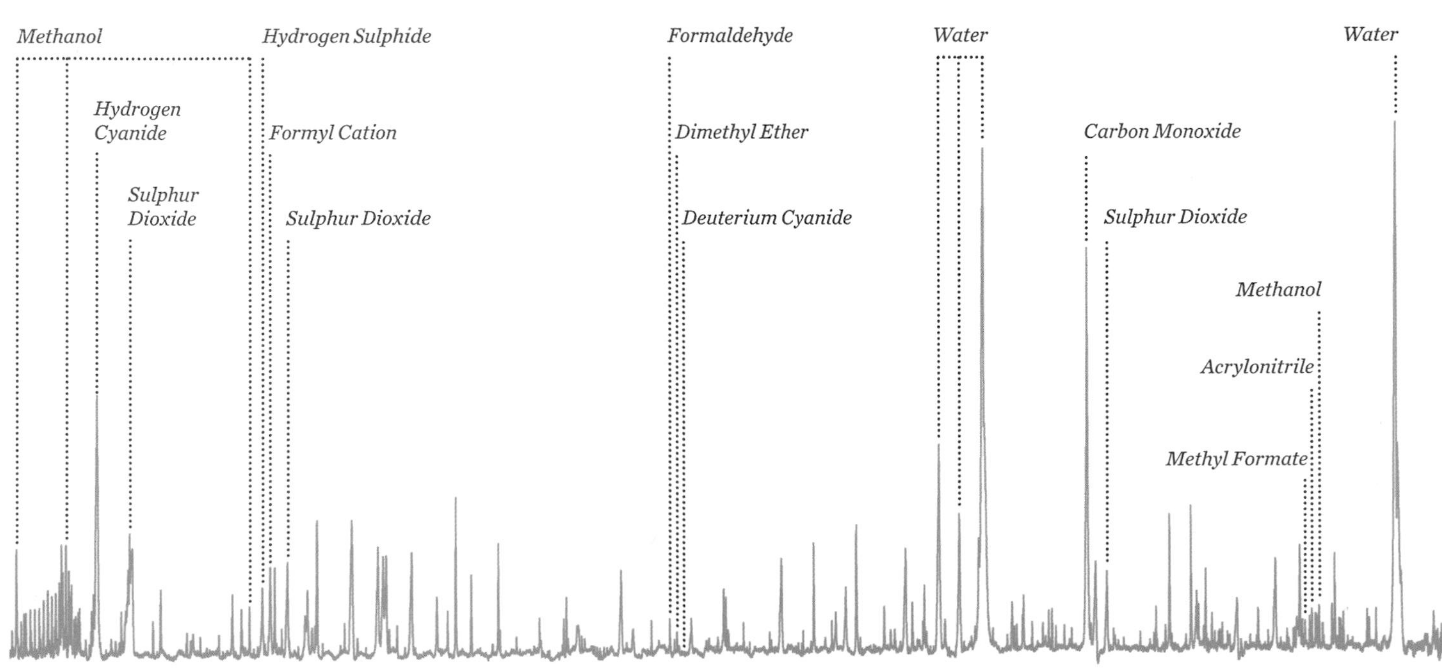

Our story is the story of the Universe. Every piece of every one and every thing you love, of every thing you hate, of every thing you hold precious, was assembled in the first few minutes of the life of the Universe, and transformed in the hearts of stars or created in their fiery deaths. When you die those pieces will be returned to the Universe in the endless cycle of death and rebirth. What a wonderful thing to be a part of that universe – and what a story. What a majestic story!

RIGHT: Supernovae are the long-awaited spectacles of the skies. It is in the death of old stars that new ones are born, and their demise plays a crucial part of the endless cycle of death and rebirth that occurs right across our universe.

NASA

CHAPTER 3

FALLING

FULL FORCE

For all its scale and grandeur, the Universe is shaped by the action of just four forces of nature. Two of these, the weak and strong nuclear forces, remain hidden from everyday experience inside the atomic nucleus. The third force, electromagnetism, is perhaps most familiar to us, as it is the one we marshal to power our lives – electric currents flow because of the action of this force. Finally, there is gravity, the great sculptor – the force that acts between the stars. Gravity shapes the cosmos on the largest distance scales. From the formless clouds of hydrogen and helium that once filled our universe, gravity forged the first stars, sculpted the first planets and arranged them into the exquisite shapes of the galaxies. Having assembled countless billions of solar systems, gravity drives their cycles and rhythms. It is the invisible string behind the revolution of every moon around every planet and every planet around every star. Gravity keeps our feet on the ground and the Universe ticking over.

BOTTOM: Before embarking on the voyage of their lives, astronauts are prepared for the flight and the sensation of weightlessness in aircrafts such as this C-131 at Wright Air Development Center, which flies at a 'zero-g' trajectory. These flight simulators are dubbed 'vomit comets' because of the nausea they often induce.

Gravity is more than a mere gentle presence; it is relentless, and for the largest agglomerations of matter in the Universe – the stars – it is both creator and destroyer. Stars shine in temporary resistance to gravitational collapse, but when they run out of nuclear fuel and the other three forces can no longer rearrange the matter in their cores in order to release energy and resist its inward pull, gravity crushes the most massive of them out of existence. In doing so, it creates the least understood objects in the Universe.

Soviet cosmonaut Gherman Titov is perhaps not the luckiest of men. In 1960 he was selected alongside Yuri Gagarin for the Soviet manned space programme. Out of the twenty men who started the programme, only these two made it through a fierce selection process that tested their physical and psychological resilience to the limit. Throughout training the two fighter pilots matched each other point for point, but someone had to be first, and Gagarin was given the ticket into the history books. On 12 April 1961, Gagarin became the first human to travel into space, completing a single orbit in 108 minutes before returning to Earth first in Vostok 1 and then by parachute. In one of those interesting bits of space trivia, Gagarin actually arrived back on Earth after his spacecraft, because he ejected at an altitude of 7,000 metres (23,000 feet) due to worries about the safety of the capsule on landing. Vostok 1 arrived safely on the ground 10 minutes before he did.

BELOW: This bus ride to the Vostok launch on 12 April 1961 was the first part of the journey that was to make Yuri Gagarin a Soviet hero and worldwide celebrity.

BELOW: Astronauts prepare for Extravehicular Activity by practising techniques on a Hubble Space Telescope mock-up in the Neutral Buoyancy Laboratory. Underwater conditions simulate the weightlessness experienced in space.

RIGHT: The race for space was on in the 1960s, as the US and Soviet nations battled to be the first to launch a human being into space.

On his return, Gagarin became a Soviet hero and a worldwide celebrity, leaving Titov to become the second man to orbit our planet. Titov's name will be unfamiliar to most, although to this day he remains the youngest man ever to make the journey into space, at just under 26 years old. He piloted Vostok 2 on 6 August 1961, completing 17 orbits of Earth. Titov also claimed a rather less glamorous place in the history books; on the 25.3-hour mission, he not only became the first man to sleep in space (snoozing for a couple of hours as his spacecraft orbited the planet), but also the first to suffer the symptoms of a condition that has affected almost half of those who have experienced weightlessness for an extended period of time. Titov was the first victim of Space Adaption Syndrome. Known more usually as space sickness, this condition includes a variety of symptoms such as nausea, vomiting, vertigo and headaches as a common reaction to the odd sensations of space travel. Although weightlessness remains one of the great thrills of being an astronaut, it is also one of the most difficult to prepare for. Since Titov introduced medics to Space Adaption Syndrome, space agencies around the world have employed the only method they can of creating weightlessness here on Earth. How is it possible to remove the effects of gravity? The answer is by doing the same thing that Gagarin and Titov did: by falling towards Earth.

The American response to the Vostok programme was Project Mercury, a series of six manned launches which included the historic flights of Alan Shephard, the first American in space, on 5 May 1961, and John Glenn, the first American to orbit Earth. The astronauts selected for the programme, known as the 'Mercury Seven', became celebrities in the United States, and all of them eventually flew into space. The final flight of the Mercury Seven was John Glenn's Space Shuttle mission in 1998, which he completed at the age of 77. The Tracy brothers in the TV series *Thunderbirds* were named after five of the Mercury Seven: Scott (Carpenter), Virgil ('Gus' Grissom), Alan (Shephard), Gordon (Cooper) and John (Glenn). Wally Schirra and Deke Slayton missed out. (I think Wally and Deke would have been great names for *Thunderbirds* pilots. The days when astronauts were bigger than rock stars are sadly missed.)

During training for Project Mercury, perhaps after hearing about the experiences of Titov, NASA developed a way of flying a regular military aircraft to take would-be astronauts on an unusual ride. Using a C-131 aircraft, weightlessness was achieved by flying an unconventional flight path. This parabolic path creates a brief period of around 25 seconds during which all the occupants of the plane experience the sensation of weightlessness. This is because they are actually weightless; it may be brief, but when repeated twenty or thirty times in succession, the physiological effects are just as intense as those felt in space. This led to the C-131 being named the 'Vomit Comet', a name that has stuck with every plane used for this task ever since.

I've known about the Vomit Comet since I was a child, because I was, and still am, passionate about the space programme. Imagine my delight when I heard we were going to ride in it for our film on gravity. Who cares if it makes you feel rough, if the Mercury Seven could face it, so could I.

The Vomit Comet is the perfect place to experience the two related aspects of the force of gravity that hold the key to

Feature Index

	Page		Page
Abby	14	Editorials	4
Amusements	6	Sports	22
Comics	25	Society	5
Crossword	28	Want Ads	26
Jumble	14	Radio-TV	26

28 PAGES TODAY

The Huntsville Times

Where Progress... Covers The Valley!

VOL. 51, NO. 21 — CHICAGO DAILY NEWS SERVICE — HUNTSVILLE, ALABAMA, WEDNESDAY, APR. 12, 1961 — ASSOCIATED PRESS — WIREPHOTO — 45c PER WEEK

Man Enters Space

'So Close, Yet So Far,' Sighs Cape

U.S. Had Hoped For Own Launch

CAPE CANAVERAL, Fla. (AP) — The Redstone rocket which the United States had hoped would boost the first man into space stands on a launching pad here. The Soviet Union beat its firing date by at least two weeks.

"So close, yet so far," commented a technician who is helping groom the Redstone to send one of America's astronauts on a short sub-orbital flight, hopefully late this month or early in May.

"If we hadn't had those troubles last fall and on the chimp and Little Joe shots this year, we might have made it," the technician said.

"But you have to give the Russian scientists credit. They've accomplished a remarkable breakthrough."

Dr. Hugh Dryden, deputy director of the National Aeronautics and Space Administration, told the House Space Committee in Washington Tuesday that the earliest possible date for the manned launching is about April 28.

Project Mercury officials had hoped to achieve a manned Redstone flight last December or January. A series of launch mishaps necessitated additional launchings to qualify the system.

On Nov. 8, a space capsule failed to separate from a Little Joe rocket fired from Wallops Island, Va., in a test of the escape system.

Two weeks later, a Redstone fizzled because of a faulty connection which caused the escape tower to fire, leaving the rocket and capsule on the pad. This test had to be repeated before Ham, the space chimpanzee, was sent up on a short trip Jan. 31.

An engine thrust regulator stuck on the chimp shot, creating excessive thrust which lofted the chimp, Ham, higher and farther than intended. Another Redstone was fired to prove out corrections made in the regulator, again delaying the manned trip.

Another setback occurred March 18 when a repeat of the Little Joe escape test fizzled. Another try is set for about April 20 and must succeed before the Redstone now on the pad hurls aloft an astronaut.

* * *

By ARTHUR J. SNIDER
Chicago Daily News Science Writer

The momentous Russian achievement has taken some of the zest out of the buildup for the first American astronaut's rocket hop down the Atlantic missile range.

There had been hope, swelling each day, that the United States might slip the first human being into space ahead of the Soviets.

For many months — ever since last fall — it had been expected that the Russians would cash in on their capability and launch a

Hobbs Admits 1944 Slaying

By BOB WARD
Of The Times Staff

Isham D. Hobbs confessed today to the brutal murder in 1944 of Mrs. Margaret Thornton Fleming, Circuit Solicitor Macon L. Weaver said.

Hobbs, now 43, is held by Air Force authorities at Eglin Air Force Base, Fla. He signed a statement there detailing his knife-slaying of the prominent 32-year-old widow, Weaver said he learned from Air Force officials.

* * *

The suspect, who has undergone psychiatric treatment by military authorities since Feb. 6, has recovered his memory in full, Weaver was told. Psychiatrists said Hobbs' apparent amnesia resulted from "hysteria" rather than from any medical cause.

Hobbs, who attempted suicide last November at Bartow, Fla., and was then exposed as a long-time fugitive, will be returned to MacDill Air Force Base, near Tampa, Fla., from Eglin AFB

Weaver plans to travel to MacDill tomorrow, he said.

Hobbs, accused also of deserting from the Army Air Corps in October, 1943, reportedly will be court-martialed, and released to civil authorities here. He was wanted for desertion and was still at large when the murder charge was brought against him in May, 1944.

* * *

Hobbs told Eglin authorities he was living in a cave in the mountainous region near Mrs. Fleming's home north of Farley when the killing occurred, Weaver said.

He stated he went to the Fleming home in an effort to get a shotgun he believed to be there. Finding Mrs. Fleming's daughter Vivian, asleep when he broke into the house before dawn, he decided to knock her unconscious and spirit her away to his cave, he stated.

The blow he struck the 21-year-old girl (now Mrs. Frederick Martin) only stunned her, and her screams attracted Mrs. Fleming and her cousin, Mrs. Vance

This is Russian Maj. Yuri Gagarin, history's first man in space. The Russians today rocketed him around the earth in an orbit taking slightly less than 90 minutes and brought him back safely to a prearranged spot in the Soviet Union. (AP Wirephoto via radio from Moscow)

Praise Is Heaped On Major Gagarin

First Man To Enter Space Is 27, Married, Father Of Two

LONDON (AP)—Moscow television presented a picture of the Soviet Union's first space man today, describing him as a man with "a good honest smile."

The portrait of Maj. Yuri A. Gagarin was shown and then came this broadcast comment, repeated by Moscow radio:

"For those who did not see this picture we should like to give a description of this splendid man.

"On the screen appears the image of a man aged about 25-28 with a kind, Russian face, eyes set well apart, fine bushy brows and high forehead.

"He wears a flying helmet, a light overall suit. He smiles a good, honest smile. And is there any need to add that this man who has been the first to dare to fly to space, to reach for the stars, to look down on our earth, is a man of a very great and very real character. This is evident in his smile, in the intelligent, fine eyes."

* * *

Gagarin was 27 just a month ago.

He is married to Valentina Gagarina, 26, who also has a scientific background. She was graduated from medical school at Orenburg.

They have two daughters, Yelena, 2, and Galya, just a month old.

* * *

The cosmonaut has an ideal So

'Worker' Stands By Story

LONDON (AP) — The Daily Worker, Communist party paper in Britain, said today it is standing by its story that the Soviet Union launched a man into space last Friday.

* * *

A spokesman for the editor said: "Our story came from good sources. All we know is what we published today. Now of course there is this one."

By "this one," he referred to the Moscow announcement that Maj. Yuri A. Gagarin made an orbital flight around the earth today in a five-ton space ship and returned safely.

* * *

The Worker said in this morning's edition that the Soviet Union sent an astronaut aloft last Friday on three trips round the world, brought him back alive, and then put him under treatment for after-effects. He was identified in the story as the test pilot son of a top-ranking Soviet air

Reds Deny Spacemen Have Died

By THE ASSOCIATED PRESS

Have some Soviet astronauts been killed in space flight experiments before Yuri A. Gagarin's sensational trip?

No, Soviet officials insist.

But some Western sources say they believe one or a few Russians did perish in unsuccessful attempts. Brig. Gen. Don Flickinger, head of the medical section of the U.S. Air Force astronaut selection and

Soviet Officer Orbits Globe In 5-Ton Ship

Maximum Height Reached Reported As 188 Miles

MOSCOW (AP)—A Soviet astronaut has orbited the globe for more than an hour and returned safely to receive the plaudits of scientists and political leaders alike. Soviet announcement of the feat brought praise from President Kennedy and U.S. space experts left behind in the contest to put the first man into successful space flight.

By the Soviet account, Maj. Yuri Alekseyvich Gargarin, rode a five-ton spaceship once around the earth in an orbit taking an hour and 20 minutes. He was in the air a total of an hour and 48 minutes.

The whole sequence of events and the announcements relating to it raised a number of questions. The Soviet announcement said the flight took place today between 9:07 and 10:55 a.m., but some persons in Moscow's Western colony were skeptical that the feat actually came off today.

There was a curious sequence of events leading up to the announcement.

Rumors had been circulating several days that the space coup had been pulled off. Two days ago, Soviet TV technicians moved into the Central Telegraph Office with the evident purpose of getting pictures of correspondents in action as they reported such a story. There were various reports, none verifiable from official sources, that the flight had been made.

* * *

Then Tuesday night the Daily Worker, London Communist newspaper with apparently sound connections in Moscow, reported that the flight took place last Friday. In splash headlines, the Daily Worker heralded "the first man in space," saying he had completed three orbits before returning to earth suffering from "after-effects of the flight."

* * *

That led up to today.

About 9:30 a.m., Western correspondents were tipped off to be listening to their radios at 10 a.m. The announcement came at 10 a.m., saying the astronaut still was in orbit. At two intervals the radio broadcast messages, reportedly from him over South America and Africa.

Then came the announcement that the spaceship had been called back to earth.

Some in the Western colony expressed wonderment that the Soviet Union, with its tight control over communications, would take such a chance—announcing the flight before a successful completion.

* * *

As these skeptics saw it, the event would have turned into perhaps the most publicized disaster in history if anything had gone wrong between 10 a.m. and the announced time of landing, 55 minutes later.

VON BRAUN'S REACTION:

'To Keep Up, U.S.A. Must Run Like Hell'

Timesfoto by William McCormick

WERNHER VON BRAUN
He Praises A Russian Achievement

By BILL AUSTIN
Of The Times Staff

A disappointed Dr. Wernher von Braun, arriving in Huntsville today, called Russia's space flight a tremendous thing and labeled it the "shot heard around the world."

"I'm disappointed because here again we came in in second place," he declared.

Von Braun arrived at the Huntsville airport from Grove City, Pa., where he had addressed a college group yesterday.

He said we had hoped all along the United States would be able to place an astronaut up first, but he said Russia has an excellent space program and they demonstrated it by this flight.

"We are going to have to run the hell to catch up," he asserted.

No Astronaut Signal Received At Ft. Monmouth

FT. MONMOUTH, N.J. (AP)—The Astro Observation Center did not receive any radio signals from the Soviet satellite containing the first space navigator, a spokesman said today.

understanding what gravity actually is. Firstly, it is possible to completely cancel out the effects of gravity by simply falling towards the ground. This sets gravity apart from all the other forces of nature; it is not possible to negate the effect of electric charge, other than by adding more electric charge of the opposite sign. The Comet achieves the removal of gravity simply by flying along the trajectory that a cannon ball would take when fired out of a gun. The plane doesn't just drop to the ground like a lift with a severed cable, of course (because then it would be impossible to control), but the acceleration of the plane towards the ground is exactly the same as the acceleration you would experience in a falling lift or a parachute jump (if you neglect air resistance). In numbers, the plane must accelerate towards the ground at 9.81 metres per second squared to cancel out the force of gravity. In order to keep the plane under control, it also flies forward at its usual flight speed. This results in the plane flying along a parabolic path. The fact that the effects of gravity are completely removed in freefall is very interesting, and the converse is also true: it is also possible to add to Earth's gravitational pull by accelerating.

Everyone knows that astronauts in space are weightless and float around inside their spacecraft, but not everybody knows why. It is not because they are a long way from Earth that gravity is absent (they are in fact only a few hundred miles above Earth's surface, and the strength of Earth's gravitational field in near-Earth orbit is not too different to the strength on the surface), it is that the effects of gravity are removed by falling, which is important point number one.

We flew in a modified Boeing 727-200, which is still used today for training shuttle astronauts. During the flight I was also able to demonstrate another strange but equally important and related aspect of gravity. Isaac Newton knew it when he wrote down his theory of gravity in 1687, as did Galileo many decades before him. The strange thing is this: all objects fall at the same rate under the force of gravity, even

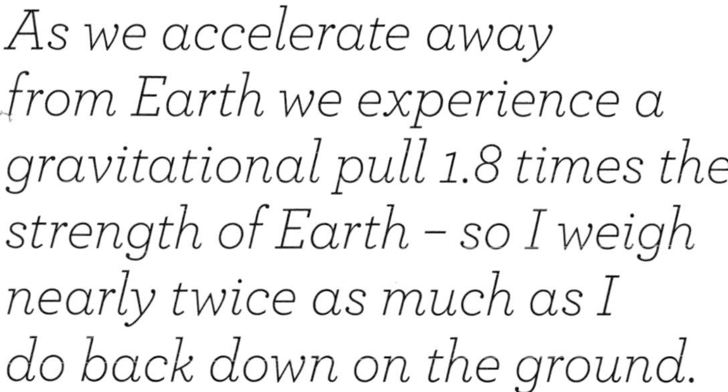

As we accelerate away from Earth we experience a gravitational pull 1.8 times the strength of Earth – so I weigh nearly twice as much as I do back down on the ground.

though gravity acts on objects in proportion to their mass. Newton and Galileo knew this to be the case because they did experiments and noticed that it was true, but they had absolutely no idea why. If you think about it for a moment, it is very odd indeed. Newton found that the gravitational force between two objects, such as Earth and you, is proportional to the product of their masses. So the force you feel due to the pull of Earth's gravity is proportional to the mass of Earth multiplied by the mass of you. If you were to double your mass, the force between you and Earth would double. But, the rate at which you accelerate towards Earth because of its gravitational pull is also proportional to your mass, and when you work everything out it turns out that your mass completely cancels out, so therefore all things fall at the same rate under gravity. This looks very strange and was famously demonstrated by Apollo 15 Commander Dave Scott on the surface of the Moon in 1971. Scott dropped a feather and a hammer to the ground and, of course, both hit the ground at the same time. The reason you can't do this on Earth is because air resistance slows the feather down, but in the high vacuum of the Lunar surface the only force acting on the falling objects is gravity. No matter how much physics you know, this is entertaining to watch because it isn't in accord with common sense! Surely a cannon ball should fall to the ground faster than a single atom? The answer is, no, it doesn't, and here is something to think about for later on: even a beam of light falls to the ground at the same rate as a cannon ball. Understanding this concept is key to understanding gravity.

I was able to demonstrate this for myself in the Vomit Comet armed with a model of Einstein. When we were weightless, I let a little plastic Albert float beside my head. One way of understanding why we floated next to each other is to simply state that we were both weightless, so we floated, but think about what this looks like from outside the plane. To someone on the ground looking up at us, the plane, myself and plastic Albert are all falling towards the ground under the action of Earth's gravity, and obviously we are falling at the same rate. If I fell faster than Einstein, he wouldn't float next to my head. Indeed, if the much more massive plane fell faster than both plastic Albert and myself, we'd both bump into the ceiling! The fact that we all floated around together is a beautiful demonstration of the fact that all objects, no matter what their mass, fall at the same rate in a gravitational field.

This simple fact inspired Albert Einstein to construct his geometric theory of gravitation, called General Relativity, which to this day is the most accurate theoretical description of gravity that we possess. We shall get to Einstein's beautiful theory later on, and in doing so we'll arrive at a very simple explanation of why everything falls at the same rate, and why gravity can be removed by the act of falling ●

Gravity holds the water in our oceans and hugs the atmosphere close to the planet. It's the reason why the rain falls and the rivers flow; it powers the ocean currents and drives the world's weather; it's why volcanoes erupt and earthquakes tear the land apart. Yet gravity also plays a role on an even grander stage. Across the Universe, from the smallest speck of dust to the most massive star, gravity is the great sculptor that created order out of chaos.

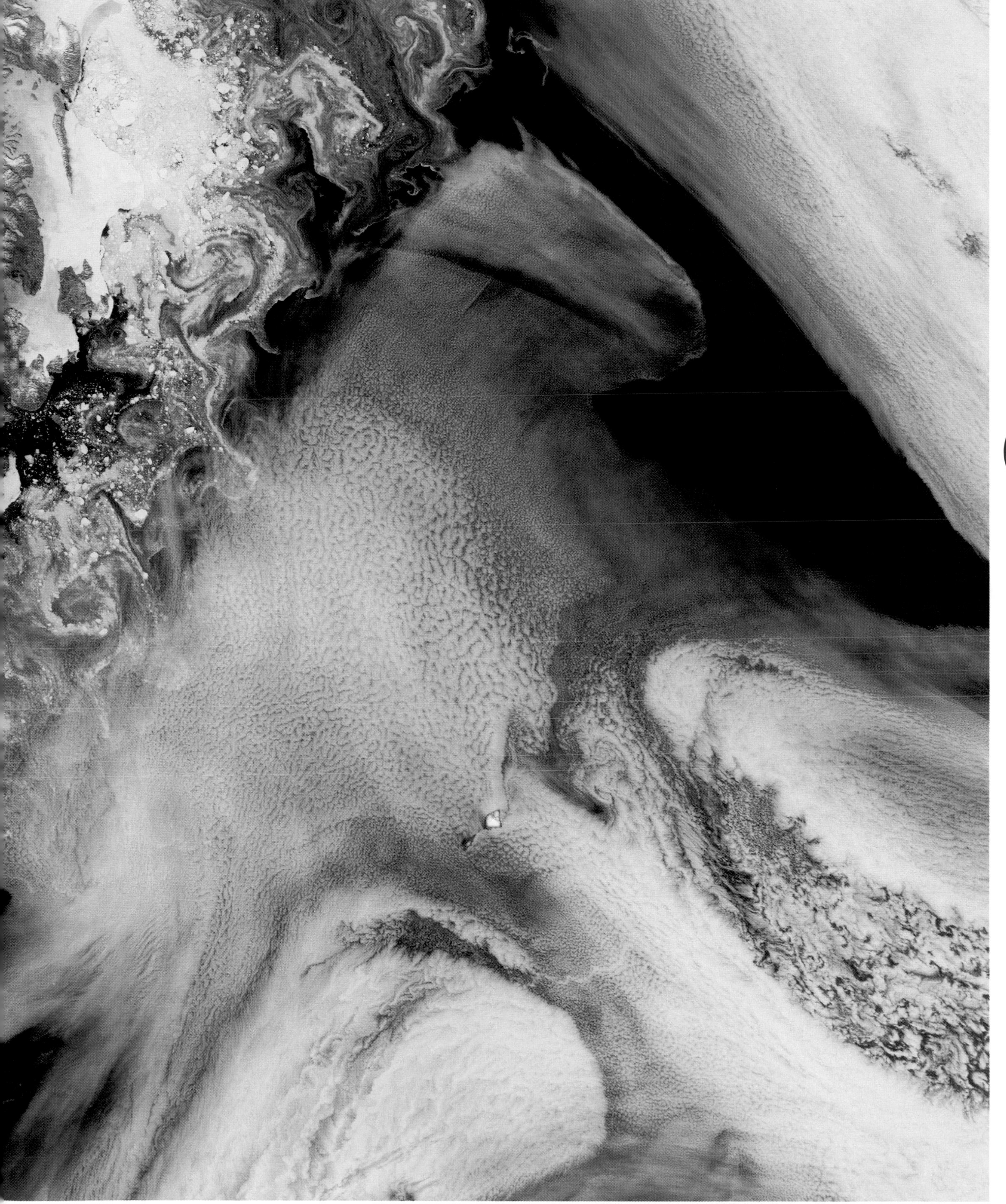

THE INVISIBLE STRING

Everything in the Cosmos is subject to the force of gravity. From the manmade satellites that rotate around our planet creating the technological infrastructure of the twenty-first century, to the orbit of our only natural satellite – the Moon – which journeys around Earth every 27.3 days, it is gravity that provides the invisible string to guide them on their path. The journey of every planet, moon, ball of rock and mote of dust in our solar system is guided by gravity; from the 365-day trip our planet takes around the Sun to each of the orbits of the seven planets and 166 known moons in our neighbourhood. Beyond our solar system, gravity continues to conduct the flow of the Universe, with everything affected by the gravitational pull of something else, no matter how tiny or how massive.

Our solar system orbits around the centre of the Milky Way Galaxy, a place dominated by a supermassive black hole, the heart of a swirling system of over 200 billion gravitationally bound stars. And even this vast, rotating structure isn't where the merry-go-round of the Universe ends, because even the galaxies are steered through the vast Universe by the action of gravity.

LEFT: The Virgo Supercluster of galaxies is a good example of how gravitational pull exerts itself. This cluster of galaxies has a gravitational pull on the Local Group of galaxies that surround our Milky Way Galaxy.

TOP: The supermassive black hole at the centre of the Milky Way Galaxy, Sagittarius A*, is the heart of a swirling system of over 200 billion stars which are gravitationally bound.

ABOVE: The elliptical galaxy M87 is located at the centre of the Virgo Cluster. This huge galaxy includes several trillion stars, a supermassive black hole, and a family of 15,000 globular star clusters which may have been graviationally pulled from nearby dwarf galaxies.

Beyond our solar system, gravity continues to conduct the flow of the Universe, with everything affected by the gravitational pull of something else, no matter how tiny or how massive.

Our galaxy is part of a collection of galaxies called the Local Group – a cluster of over 30 galaxies named by the American astronomer Edwin Hubble in 1936. Over ten million light years across, this vast dumbbell-shaped structure contains billions and billions of stars, including the trillion stars that make up our giant galactic neighbour, Andromeda. Just as the Moon orbits Earth, Earth orbits the Sun, and the Sun orbits the Milky Way, so the Local Group orbits its common centre of gravity, located somewhere in the 2.5 million light years between the two most massive galaxies in the group: our Milky Way and Andromeda. But even this giant community of galaxies isn't the largest known gravitationally bound structure. As you sit reading this book, gravity is taking you on an extraordinary ride. Not only are you spinning around as Earth rotates once a day on its axis, not only are you orbiting at just over 100,000 kilometres (62,137 miles) per hour around the Sun, not only are you rotating around the centre of our galaxy at 220 kilometres (136 miles) per second, and not only is the entire Milky Way tearing around the centre of gravity of the Local Group at 600 kilometres (372 miles) per second, but we are also part of even an grander gravitationally driven cycle.

The Local Group is part of a much larger, gravitationally bound family called the Virgo Supercluster – a collection of at least 100 galaxy clusters. Nobody is sure how long it takes our Local Group to journey around the Virgo Supercluster; vast beyond words, stretching over 110 million light years, it is, even so, only one of millions of superclusters in the observable Universe. It is now thought that even superclusters are part of far larger structures bound together by gravity, known as galaxy filaments or great walls. We are part of the Pisces-Cetus Supercluster Complex.

Gravity's scope is unlimited, its influence all-pervasive at all distance scales throughout the entire history of the Universe. Yet, perhaps surprisingly, given its colossal reach and universal importance, it is the first force that we humans understood in any detail ◉

THE APPLE THAT NEVER FELL

The history of science is littered with examples of circumstance and serendipity leading to the greatest discoveries, which is why curiosity-driven science is the foundation of our civilisation. Among the most celebrated is the convoluted story of Newton's journey to his theory of gravity – the first great universal law of physics.

The Great Plague of 1665 was the last major outbreak of bubonic plague in England, but also the most deadly. Over one hundred thousand people are thought to have died the hideous death that accompanied the rodent-borne illness. London was the epicentre of the outbreak, but even then the matrix of connections between the capital and the rest of the country caused the disease to spread rapidly across England. Extreme and often useless measures were taken to prevent its spread, from the lighting of fires to cleanse the air to the culling of innocent dogs and cats. Infected villages were quarantined and schools and colleges closed. One place affected was Trinity College Cambridge, and one of the students to take a leave of absence in the summer of 1665 was Isaac Newton.

Newton was twenty-two years old and newly graduated when he left plague-ridden Cambridge to return to his family home in Woolsthorpe, Lincolnshire. He took with him a series of books on mathematics and the geometry of Euclid and Descartes, in which he had become interested, he later wrote, through an astronomy book he purchased at a fair. Although by all accounts he was an unremarkable student, his enforced absence allowed him time to think, and his interest in the physical world and the laws underpinning it began to coalesce. Over the next two years his private studies laid the foundations for much of his later work in subjects as diverse as calculus, optics and, of course, gravity. On returning to Cambridge in 1667 he was elected as a fellow, and became the Lucasian Professor of Mathematics in October 1670 (a post recently held by Stephen Hawking and currently held by string theorist Michael Green – both of whom continue to work on the problem of the nature of gravity). Newton spent the next twenty years lecturing and working in a diverse range of scientific and pseudo-scientific endeavours, including alchemy and predictions of the date of the apocalypse. The economist John Maynard Keynes said of Newton that he was not 'the first in the age of reason, but the last of the magicians'. This is not entirely accurate, but then what can one reasonably expect from an economist? Newton lived on the cusp of pre-scientific times and the modern age and did more than most to usher in the transition. His greatest contribution to modern science was the publication in 1687 of the *Philosophiæ Naturalis Principia Mathematica*, otherwise known as the *Principia*. This book contains an equation that describes the action of gravity so precisely that it was used to guide the Apollo astronauts on their journey to the Moon. It is beautiful in its simplicity

THE EFFECT OF GRAVITY ON THE MOVEMENT OF PLANETS

PLANET

GRAVITATIONAL PULL OF SUN

PLANET'S VELOCITY

SUN

RESULTANT PATH

NEWTON'S LAW OF UNIVERSAL GRAVITATION

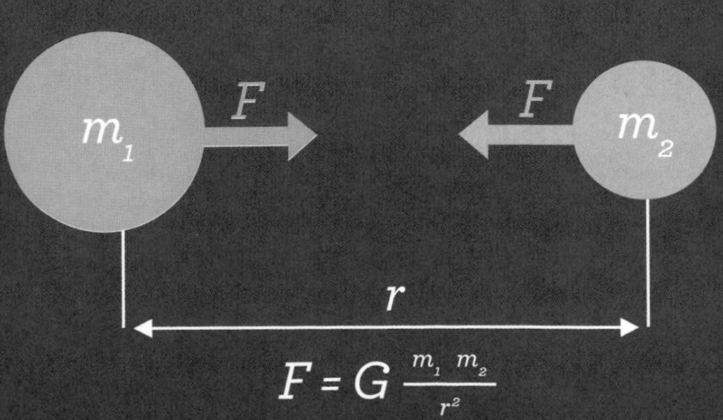

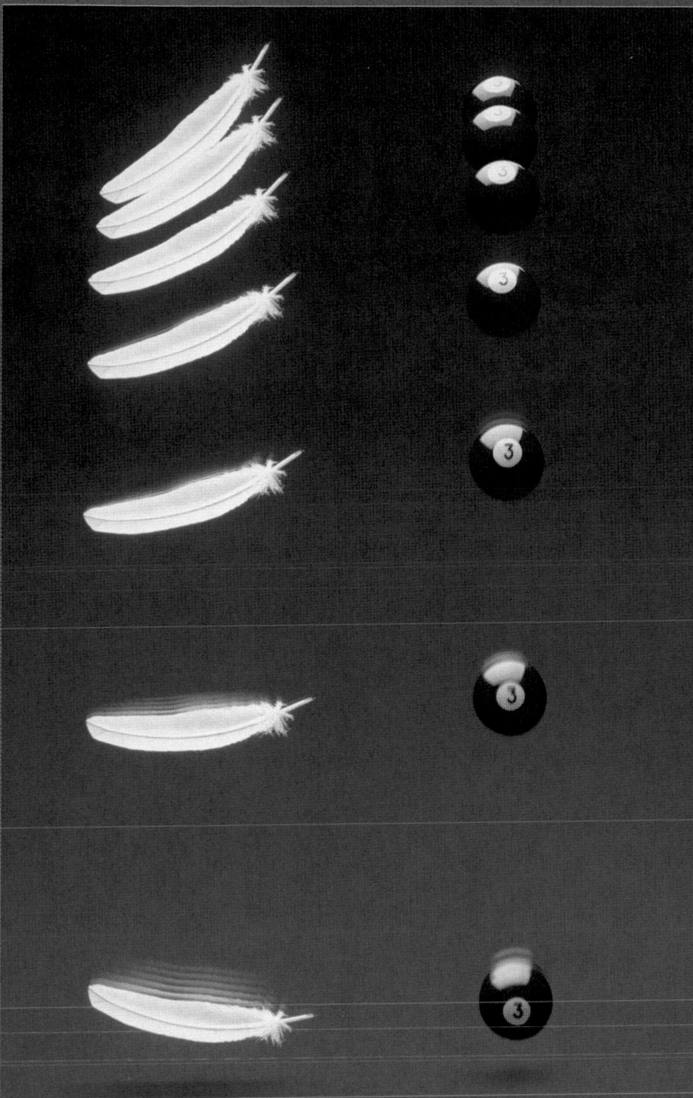

LEFT: This time-lapse image neatly illustrates the concept of gravity. The feather and ball are here seen falling at the same speed in a vacuum, proving that any two objects of different mass will accelerate at identical rates when at the same gravitational potential. The reason that this does not happen on Earth is because of the air resistance that is present, which is, of course, absent in a vacuum. This principle was also proved correct when an Apollo astronaut dropped a feather and a hammer on the Moon (which has no atmosphere) and saw them fall at the same rate.

and profound in its application and consequences for scientific thought.

$$F = G\frac{m_1 m_2}{r^2}$$

This is the mathematical expression of Newton's Law of Universal Gravitation. In words, it says that the force (F) between two objects is equal to the product of their masses (m_1 and m_2), divided by the square of the distance between them. G is a constant of proportionality known as the gravitational constant; its value encodes the strength of the gravitational force: The force between two one-kilogramme masses, 1 metre (3 feet) apart, is 6.67428 x 10^{-11} newtons – that's 0.0000000000667428 N, which is not a lot. For comparison, the force exerted on your hand by a 1kg bag of sugar is approximately 10 N. In other words, the gravitational constant G is 6.67428 x 10^{-11} N $(m/Kg)^2$. The reason why G is so tiny is unknown and one of the greatest questions in physics; the electromagnetic force is 10^{36} times stronger – that's a factor of a million million million million million million.

There are many reasons why Newton's Law of Universal Gravitation is beautiful. It is universal, which means it applies everywhere in the Universe and to everything not in the vicinity of black holes, too close to massive stars or moving close to the speed of light. In these cases, Einstein's more accurate theory of General Relativity is required. For planetary orbits around stars, orbits of stars around galaxies and the movements of the galaxies themselves, it is more than accurate enough. It has also applied at all times in the Universe's history beyond the first instants after the Big Bang. This is not to be taken for granted, because the law was derived based on the work of Johannes Kepler and the observations of Tycho Brahe, who were concerned only with the motion of the planets around the Sun. The fact that a law that governs the clockwork of our solar system is the same law that governs the motion of the galaxies is interesting and important. It is the statement that the same laws of physics govern our whole universe, and Newton's law of gravitation was the first example of such a universal law.

It is also profoundly simple. That the complex motion of everything in the cosmos can be summed up in a single mathematical formula is elegant and beautiful, and lies at the heart of modern fundamental science. You don't need to sit down with a telescope every night and use trial and error to find the positions of the planets and moons of the Solar System. You can work out where they will be at any point in the future using Newton's simple equation, and this applies not just to our solar system, but also to every solar system in the Universe. Such is the power of mathematics and physics.

Newton found that gravity is a force of attraction that exists between all objects, from the tiny immeasurable force of attraction between two rocks on the ground to the rather larger force that each and every one of us is currently experiencing between our bodies and the massive rock upon which we are stood. With a mass of almost 6 milllion million million million million kilogrammes, the force between all of us and our planet is strong enough to keep our feet on the ground. On the scale of planets, however, gravity can do much more than simply keep them in orbit and hold things on the ground; it can sculpt and shape their surfaces in profound and unexpected ways ◉

THE GRAND SCULPTURE

Fish River Canyon in the south of Namibia is one of the world's great geological features, second only in scale to the Grand Canyon in Arizona, at over 160 kilometres (99 miles) long, 26 kilometres (16 miles) wide and half a kilometre (a third of a mile) deep in places. Like the Grand Canyon, the movement of tectonic plates or volcanic action did not create this scar in Earth's crust; instead it stands testament to the erosive power of water. The Fish River is the longest river in Namibia, running for over 650 kilometres (403 miles). Despite only flowing in the summer, over millennia it has slowly but forcefully gouged the canyon out of solid rock. This takes energy, and that energy ultimately comes from the Sun as it lifts water from the oceans and deposits it upstream in the highlands to the north. Once the rain begins to fall, gravity takes over. The highlands around the source of the Fish River are at an elevation of over a thousand metres above sea level. When the rain lands on the ground at this elevation, every water droplet stores energy in the form of gravitational potential energy. There is a simple equation that says how much energy each drop has stored up:

$$U = mgh$$

U is the amount of energy that will be released if the drop falls from height (h) above sea level down to sea level, m is the mass of the drop and g is the now-familiar acceleration due to gravity – 9.81 m/s^2.

Every droplet of water raised high by the heat of the Sun has energy, due to its position in Earth's gravitational field, and this energy can be released by allowing the water to flow downwards to the sea. Some of this energy is available to cut deep into Earth's surface to form the Fish River Canyon.

The strength of Earth's gravitational field therefore has a powerful influence on its surface features. This is not only visible in the action of falling, tumbling water, but in the size of its mountains. On Earth, the tallest mountain above sea level is Mount Everest; at almost 9 kilometres (5.5 miles), it towers above the rest of the planet. But Everest is dwarfed by the tallest mountain in the Solar System which, perhaps at first sight surprisingly, sits on the surface of a much smaller planet. Around 78 million kilometres (48 million miles) from Earth, Mars is similar to our planet in many ways. Its surface is scarred by the action of water that once tumbled from the highlands to the seas, dissipating its gravitational potential energy as it fell, although today, the water has left Mars. The planet is only around 10 per cent as massive as Earth, though, so its gravitational pull is significantly weaker, and this is one of the reasons why Mars was unable to hang on to its atmosphere, despite being further away from the Sun. The possibility of liquid water flowing on the Martian surface vanished with its atmosphere, leaving the red planet to an arid and geologically dead future, but Mars's lower surface gravity has a surprising consequence for its mountains.

Towering over every other mountain in the Solar System is the extinct volcano, Olympus Mons. Rising to an altitude of around 24 kilometres (15 miles), it is almost the height of three Mount Everests stacked on top of each other. The fact that a smaller planet has higher mountains is not a coincidence; it is partly down to environmental factors such as the rate of erosion and the details of the planet's geological past, but there is also a fundamental limit to the height of mountains on any given planet: the strength of its surface gravity. Mars has a radius approximately half that of Earth's, and since it is only 10 per cent as massive, a little calculation using Newton's equation will tell you that the strength of the gravitational pull at its surface is approximately 40 per cent of that on our planet. This changes everything's weight.

Here on Earth we don't often think about the difference between mass and weight, but the distinction is very real. The mass of something is an intrinsic property of that thing – it is a measure of how much stuff the thing is made of. This doesn't change, no matter where in the Universe the thing is placed. In Einstein's Theory of Special Relativity, the rest mass of an object is an invariant quantity, which means that everyone in the Universe, no matter where they are or how they are moving, would measure the same value for the rest mass.

Weight is different. For one thing, it is not measured in kilogrammes, it is measured in the units of force – newtons. This is easy to understand if you think about how you would measure your weight. When you stand on bathroom scales, they measure the force being exerted on them by you; you can see this by pressing down on them – the harder you push, the greater the weight reading. The force you are exerting on the scales is in turn dependent on the strength of Earth's gravity. This should be obvious; if I had taken the scales up

BELOW AND PREVIOUS SPREAD: The Fish River Canyon in southern Namibia is one of the world's greatest geological sites, and a spectacular example of how the effects of climate and gravity can impact on the structure of Earth's surface.

RIGHT: The immense Olympus Mons can exist on Mars because the planet has 40 per cent of Earth's gravitational pull. However, move this extinct volcano to our planet and it would sink into the ground because of its enormous weight.

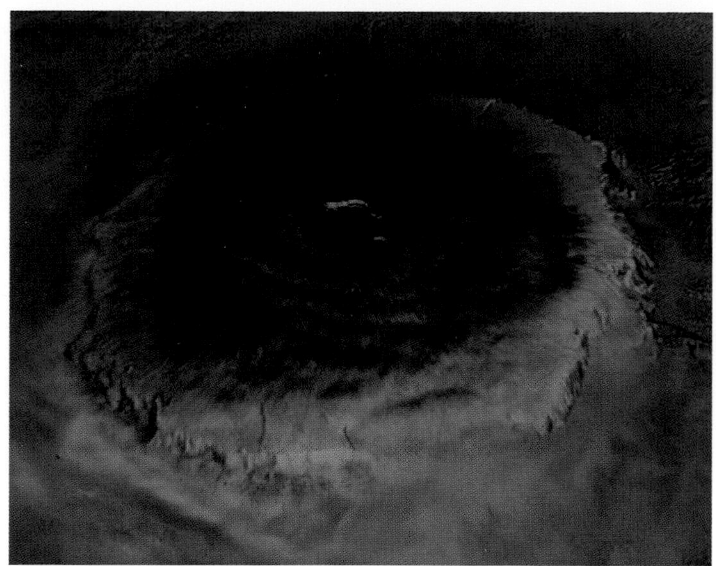

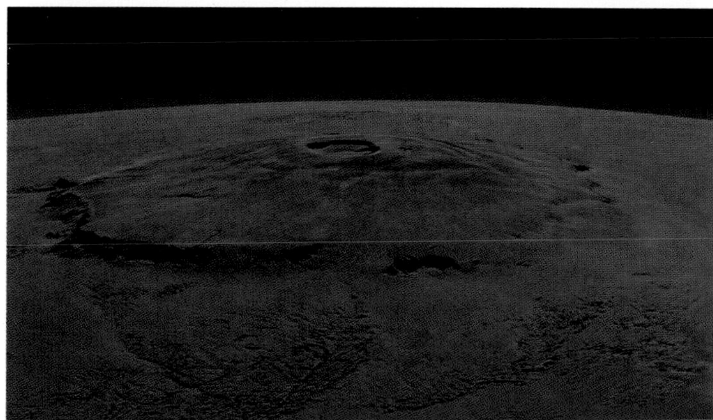

If you took Olympus Mons and stuck it on Earth ... it would weigh around two and a half times as much as it does on Mars ... A planet the size of ours cannot sustain a mountain of this size – it would weigh too much.

in the Vomit Comet and tried to stand on them, they wouldn't have read anything because I would have been floating above them – hence the word 'weightless'. In symbols, the weight of something on Earth is defined as:

$W = mg$

W is weight, m is the thing's mass, and g is the familiar measure of Earth's gravitational field strength – 9.81 m/s^2 – with a couple of caveats that we'll get to below! (For absolute accuracy, the correct definition of weight is the force that is applied on you by the scales to give you an acceleration equal to the local acceleration due to gravity – i.e. the force the scales exert on you to stop you falling through them.) So, here on Earth a human being with a mass of 80kg weighs 785 newtons; on Mars, the same 80-kg person would weigh approximately 295 newtons.

So your weight depends on a few things; one is your mass, another is the mass of the planet you are on. Your weight would also change if you were accelerating when you measured it, which is another manifestation of the equivalence principle. So, if you took Olympus Mons and stuck it on Earth, then as well as dwarfing every other mountain on the planet, it would also weigh around two and a half times as much as it does on Mars. This enormous force would put its base rock under such intense pressure that it would be unable to support the mountain, so it would sink into the ground. A planet the size of ours cannot sustain a mountain the size of Olympus Mons – it would weigh too much. The highest mountain on Earth, as measured from its base, is Mauna Kea, the vast dormant volcano on Hawaii. It is over one kilometre (half a mile) higher than Everest, and it is gradually sinking. So Mauna Kea is as high as a mountain can be on our planet, and this absolute limit is set by the strength of our gravity.

The definition of weight can get a bit convoluted, and we mentioned that there are caveats to the rule of thumb that your weight on Earth is 9.81 times your mass. One problem is that the strength of Earth's gravity varies slightly at every point on its surface. The most obvious effect is altitude; on the edge of the Fish River Canyon I would weigh slightly less than I would if I stood on the canyon floor. That's because at the top of the canyon I am further from the centre of Earth than I would be at the bottom, so the gravitational pull I feel is weaker. Earth is also not uniformly dense – some areas of Earth's surface and subsurface are made of more massive stuff than others, which also affects the local gravitational field. To complicate matters further, Earth is spinning, which means that you are accelerating when you stand on its surface, which means that the strength of gravity you feel changes in accord with the equivalence principle; this acceleration increases as you go towards the Equator, reducing the gravitational acceleration you feel there. Earth bulges out at the Equator because it is spinning, which weakens the gravitational pull there still further. The upshot of all this is that you weigh approximately 0.5 per cent less at the North and South Poles than you do at the Equator. The effects of the varying density of Earth's subsurface and the presence of surface features on Earth's gravitational field have been measured to extremely high precision and presented as a map known as the geoid ◉

Towering over every other mountain in the Solar System is the extinct volcano, Olympus Mons. It is almost the height of three Mount Everests stacked on top of each other. The fact that a smaller planet has higher mountains is not coincidence; it is partly down to environmental and geological factors, but there is also a fundamental limit to the height of mountains on any given planet; the strength of its surface gravity. Mars has a gravitational pull at its surface of approximately 40 per cent of that on our planet.

THE GEOID

BELOW: Data collected by the GOCE satellite between November and December 2009 is here used to create a map of the tiny variations in Earth's gravity field across the globe. These maps provide invaluable information for oceanographers, hydrologists and geologists in order to create accurate climate models for our planet.

RIGHT: The geoid helps us to understand unseen structures on our planet, such as here in Iceland where magma is welling upwards from Earth's mantle, affecting the gravitational field there. In this image, taken in May 2010 from a NASA satellite, the Icelandic volcano Eyjafjallajökull can be seen erupting.

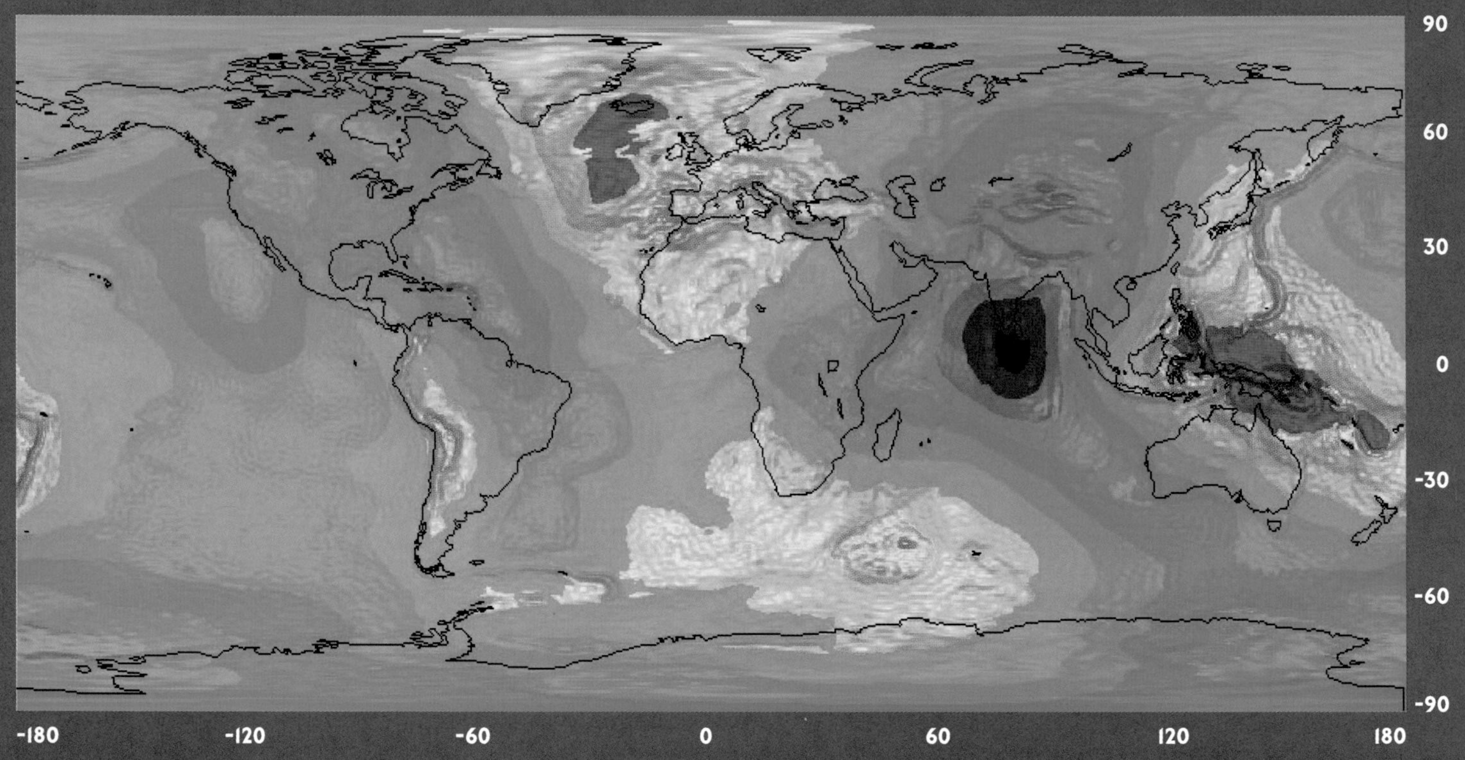

This picture of Earth's gravitational field was taken by a European Space Agency satellite, GOCE, which was launched in March 2009. GOCE is equipped with three ultra-sensitive accelerometers, arranged so that they respond to very tiny changes in the strength of Earth's gravitational field as the satellite orbits. Skimming the edge of Earth's atmosphere at an altitude of 250 kilometres (155 miles), GOCE spent two months gathering the data to create this extraordinary image. It's the first time the strength of gravity across the globe has been mapped this accurately. The blue patches indicate areas that have a weak gravitational field, the green are average and the red are places where it is stronger. The reason for these fluctuations is the density of the rocks below Earth's surface and the presence of features such as mountains or ocean trenches. More technically, the picture is presented as an equipotential surface, which means that if Earth were entirely covered in a single ocean of water, this picture would correspond to the water height at every point.

Looking at this map, it is clear that Iceland has a higher gravitational field strength than that of England. These changes are imperceptible to us, but it means that I would weigh slightly less standing at the same altitude in Manchester than I would in Reykjavik. This map was not made to show the trivial distinctions in a traveller's weight, of course; the unparalleled level of detail will enable a deeper understanding of how our planet works, because this data is a high-precision geological tool. One particular benefit will be for oceanographers; because the map defines the baseline water surface in the absence of tides, winds and currents, it is critical to understanding the factors that determine the movement of water across the oceans of our planet. This is a very important part of understanding and predicting the way energy is transferred around our planet, which is in turn an important factor in generating accurate climate models.

The geoid therefore reveals a vast amount of detailed information about the structure of our planet, just from measuring the strength of its gravity. As far as the actual height of the ocean surface is concerned, however, the most influential factor of all is not shown: the Moon ◉

THE TUG OF THE MOON

Many of the planets that exist in our solar system have families of moons; from the sixty-three satellites of Jupiter, to the thirteen moons of Neptune, and to the two tiny misshapen moons of Mars. Our planet has only a single moon; it is our constant companion, with which we have travelled through space for almost four and a half billion years.

RIGHT: The elusive far side of the Moon, which was eventually first photographed in 1959 by the Soviet Luna 3 probe.

No other planet in our solar system has a moon as large as ours in relation to its parent planet. Orbiting only 380,000 kilometres (236, 000 miles) from Earth, it is a quarter of the Earth's diameter, making it the fifth-largest moon in the Solar System after Titan, Ganymede, Callisto and Io – although of course their parent planets, Jupiter and Saturn, are significantly larger than Earth. This makes the Earth and Moon close to being a double-planet system. The current best theory for the formation of our moon is that it was created around 4.5 billion years ago when a Mars-sized planet, which has been named Theia, crashed into the newly formed Earth, blasting rock into orbit which slowly condensed into the lunar structure that we see today. The evidence for this theory is partly that the Moon has a very similar composition to that of Earth's outer crust, although it is much less dense because it has a significantly smaller iron core. This is what would be expected if the Theia/Earth collision was a glancing blow, leaving the Earth's iron core intact and so reducing the relative amount of iron in the Moon. This in turn means that the Moon's gravitational field is much weaker than ours. When Neil Armstrong took his small step onto the Moon, he weighed just 26 kilogrammes (58 pounds), despite the fact that he was wearing a space suit that had weighed 81 kilogrammes (180 pounds) on its own on Earth – this is all because the Moon's gravitational field strength is approximately one-sixth of Earth's. Despite this relatively weak gravitational pull, however, the Moon still has a profound effect on our planet.

Because of the Moon's proximity to our planet, its gravitational pull varies significantly from one side of Earth to the other. The illustration (right) shows the net gravitational force exerted at each point on Earth by the Moon, as seen by someone sitting at Earth's centre, after Earth's own gravitational field has been subtracted away. What remains is a net gravitational force pulling the side of the Earth that is facing the Moon towards the Moon, as you might expect. But there is also a net force pulling the opposite side of Earth away from the Moon. Notice also that at right angles to the position of the Moon, the lunar gravity actually adds to the Earth's gravitational pull and squashes everything! This is the origin of the tides; because water is easier to stretch than the rock that forms the ocean floor, the water in the oceans bulges outwards relative to the ground beneath the Moon and on the opposite side of Earth to the Moon. The difference in water heights is only a few metres, but can be much higher depending on the shape of the shoreline. It's worth mentioning that there are also tides in the rocks of Earth's surface; gravity doesn't just affect water! But rocks are very rigid, and so don't stretch much. The surface of Earth does, however, rise and fall by a few centimetres due to tidal effects. As Earth rotates beneath the tidal bulge raised in the oceans, the distorted water surface sweeps past the shorelines and we experience two high and low tides per day.

Next time someone starts trying to tell you that we are made of water and therefore the Moon must have an influence on us, you will now be justified in having a strange, blank and perhaps slightly pitying expression on your face for two reasons. One is that because the tides are a differential effect (that is to say they depend on the change in the strength of the Moon's gravity across the diameter of Earth), the tidal effect on you is utterly insignificant and makes no difference to you at all because the difference in the Moon's gravitational force across something the size of your body is negligible. Secondly, it has got nothing at all to do with water in any case!

Gravity is always a two-way street – just as the Moon raises tides on Earth, so Earth must cause tides to sweep across the surface of the Moon.

The relationship between the Earth and the Moon is not just a one-way street; just as the Moon's gravity has transformed our planet, so in turn Earth has transformed its neighbour.

Throughout human history, half of the Moon's surface remained hidden from view, and it wasn't until 1959, when the Soviet Luna 3 probe photographed the far side of the Moon for the first time, that we caught our first glimpse of this hidden landscape. Nine years later, the astronauts on board Apollo 8 became the first humans to leave Earth's orbit and the first human beings to directly observe the far side of the Moon with their own eyes. The reason only one side of the Moon faces Earth, appearing frozen in time and unchanging in the seemingly ever-moving night sky, is down to the tidal effects.

Billions of years ago, the view of our satellite from Earth would have been very different. In its childhood, the Moon rotated much faster, and both sides of its surface would have been visible from Earth. From the moment of its birth, the Moon felt the tug of Earth's gravity – a force that would have been even greater than it is today because the Moon was also closer to Earth.

LUNAR GRAVITY DIFFERENTIAL FIELD

The lunar gravity differential field at Earth's surface is known as the tide-generating force. This is the primary mechanism that drives tidal action and explains two equipotential tidal bulges, accounting for two daily high waters.

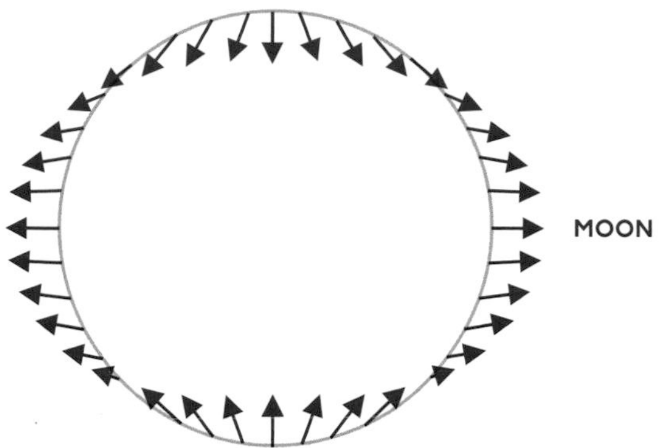

THE EFFECT OF TIDAL LOCKING ON THE EARTH AND MOON

As the Earth–Moon system moves towards being perfectly tidally locked, the Moon is gradually drifting away from Earth.

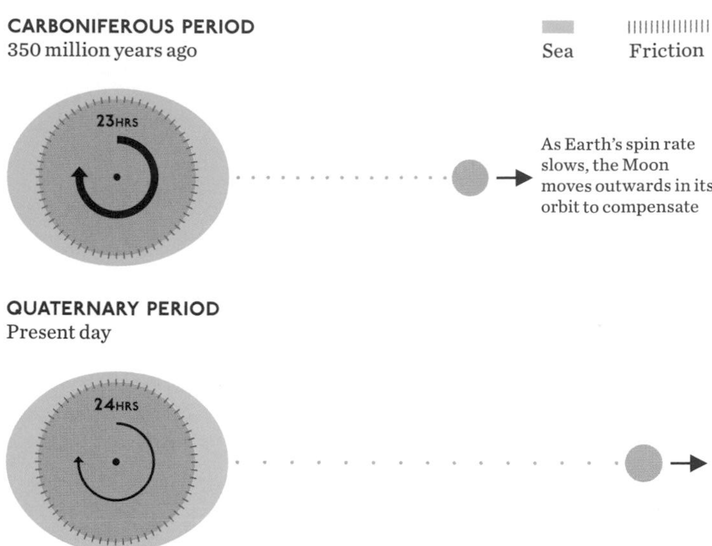

LEFT AND ABOVE: The Moon has a visible effect on our oceans. The combination of the gravitational pulls of the Moon and of Earth squashes everything , which in turn creates tides.

A glance at Newton's Law of Universal Gravitation will tell you that gravity is always a two-way street – just as the Moon raises tides on Earth, so Earth must cause tides to sweep across the surface of the Moon. These tides are not in water, of course, but in the solid rock of the lunar surface. In an amazing piece of planetary heavy lifting, the Moon's crust would have been distorted by up to 7 metres (22 feet)!

This giant tidal bulge sweeping across the Moon had an interesting effect. As the Moon turned beneath the giant parent planet hanging in the lunar sky, the rock tide was dragged across its surface, but the rising of the tide isn't instantaneous; it takes time for the surface of the Moon to respond to the pull of the Earth. During that time, the Moon will have rotated a bit, carrying the peak of the rock tide with it. The tidal bulge will therefore not be in perfect alignment with Earth, but slightly ahead of it. Earth's gravity acts on the misshapen Moon in such a way that it tries to pull it back into sync; in other words, it works like a giant brake. Over time, this effect, known as tidal locking, gradually synchronizes the rotation rate of the Moon with its orbital period, effectively meaning that the tidal bulge can remain in exactly the same place on the Moon's surface beneath Earth and doesn't have to be swept around.

The Moon is now almost, but not quite, tidally locked to Earth, which means that it takes one month to rotate around on its axis and one month to orbit Earth. So there's no dark side of the Moon – the side we can't see gets plenty of sunlight, it's just a side that perpetually faces away from Earth. The Earth–Moon system is in fact still evolving towards being perfectly tidally locked, and one interesting consequence of this is that the Moon is gradually drifting further and further away from Earth at a rate of just under 4 centimtres (1.5 inches) per year.

The power of gravity is not just in its ability to reach across the empty wastes of space and shape the surface of planets and moons; gravity also has the power to create whole new worlds, and we can see the process of that creation frozen in time in the sky, every day and every night ◉

THE FALSE DAWN

It is one of the strangest lights that appears in our night sky; a light that for centuries has puzzled those who have witnessed its glow, fooling them into thinking that a new day was arriving. The Prophet Muhammed called it the false dawn and warned the followers of Islam not to confuse it with the real dawn when setting the timing of daily prayers.

This magical glow that appears on the horizon just before sunrise and just after sunset has nothing to do with the arrival or departure of our star; instead it is a ghostly reminder of our world's origins and the power of gravity. It is the Zodiacal light; a wispy, whitish glow that appears to form a rough triangular shape rising from the horizon. The Italian astronomer Giovanni Cassini first investigated this strange phenomenon in 1683. The ethereal light perplexed many scientists of the age, and a common explanation was that the light came from the atmosphere of the Sun as it rose above the horizon before the Sun itself. It was Nicolas Fatio de Duillier, one of Cassini's students, who finally explained its origin, and in doing so he provided a first glimpse of the origin of the planets and moons in our solar system.

The story of the Zodiacal light can be traced back five billion years to the origins of our solar system. Back then, there was no Sun, nor any planets or moons; there was only a cloud of gas and dust, the building blocks of everything we now call home. Everything that makes up our solar system was contained in an enormous irregular cloud floating through space. It is thought the explosion of a nearby star sent a shockwave through the cloud, creating small fluctuations in density. It also imparted rotation. The denser regions had slightly more gravitational pull than the less dense regions, so they began to grow, and the largest one became the Sun. In its earliest days the Solar System would have been planet-less; surrounding the young Sun was a spinning disc of matter, a protoplanetary disc. Over time, the minute particles of dust in the disc collided and clumped together, and large objects the size of small asteroids, known as planetesimals, would have formed by chance. Once the larger planetesimals were big enough to have significant gravity, they began to sweep up the matter close to them and their growth accelerated. Roughly one hundred million years later, the largest planetesimals evolved into the planets and moons we see today.

However, not all this matter from the primordial cloud became a planet or moon. Out in the solar system beyond Mars there should be another planet, but a gravitational tug of war between Jupiter and the Sun stops it forming. Now, instead of a ninth planet, there is a band of dust and debris – the asteroid belt. Normally there is no way of seeing the asteroid belt from Earth with the naked eye – it's just too far away and the asteroids are too small – but collisions within the asteroid belt produce dust, and that is the secret behind the false dawn. The faint glow of the Zodiacal light after sunset and before sunrise is caused by sunlight reflecting off the debris of a failed planet; a remnant of the early Solar System and a beautiful, glimmering reminder of our origins ◉

BELOW: The wispy, whitish glow that appears on the horizon before sunrise and just after sunset was a subject of great debate among scientists for centuries. This Zodiacal light, as it is known, is in fact the debris that remains after collisions within the asteroid belt caused by a gravitational tug of war in the Solar System.

RIGHT: Theoretically, another planet should have formed from the primordial dust in the Solar System beyond Mars; however, the conflicting gravitational forces between the Sun and Jupiter prevent this happening, resulting in a band of dust and debris known as the asteroid belt.

Normally there is no way of seeing the asteroid belt from Earth with the naked eye – it's just too far away and the asteroids are too small – but collisions within the asteroid belt produce dust, and that is the secret behind the false dawn.

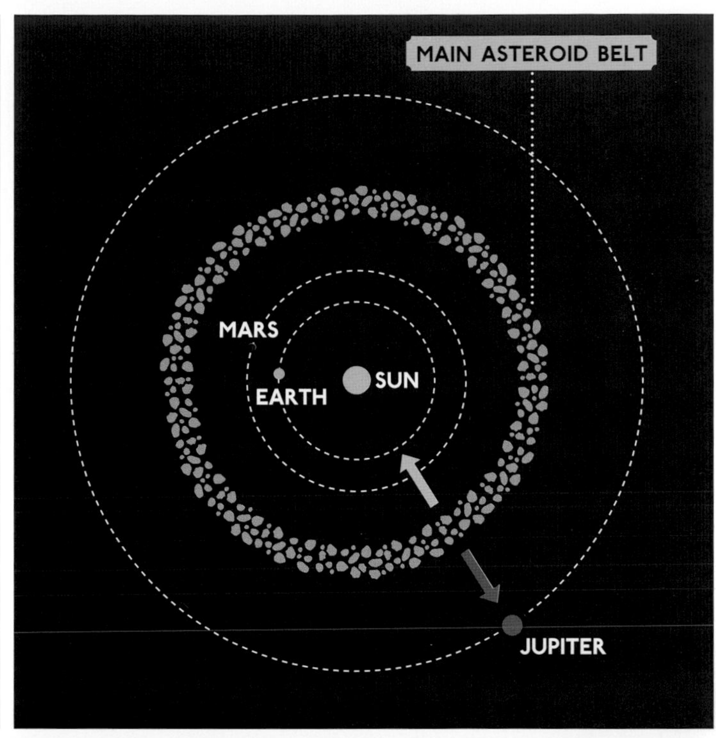

RIGHT: 'The Blue Marble' is perhaps one of the most famous photographs ever taken of Earth, and has inspired numerous images since. The photograph, taken by the Apollo 17 crew on their 1972 journey to the Moon, made history as the first true-colour image of our planet which showed Earth in unprecedented detail.

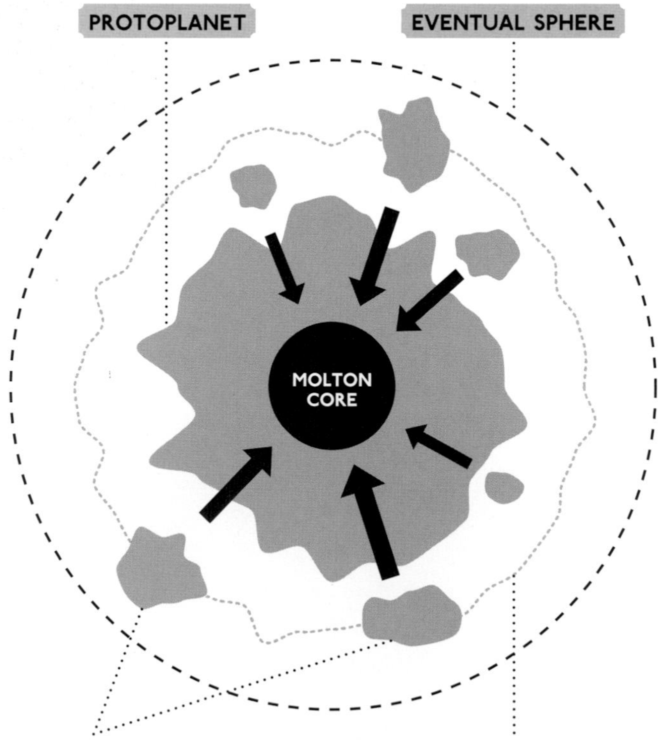

THE BLUE MARBLE

Even the most dogmatic flat-Earther would have a problem explaining away 'The Blue Marble'. This photo, taken by the astronauts on board Apollo 17 during its journey to the Moon on 7 December 1972, has caused some to speculate that this beautiful picture of our fragile world is perhaps the most distributed image in human history. But why is Earth a sphere? Actually, why are all planets and all stars spherical?

As we've discussed, we know that planets and stars are formed by the gravitational collapse of clouds of dust. You could say that the force of gravity pulls everything together,

'The Blue Marble' ... photo has caused some to speculate that this beautiful picture of our fragile world is perhaps the most distributed image in human history.

which is one way of looking at it, but another way of saying the same thing is that all the little particles in the primordial cloud of dust had gravitational potential energy, because they were all floating around in each other's tiny gravitational fields. Just like the water droplets that fell as rain high up in the mountains above the Fish River Canyon, these particles would all try to fall 'downhill' to minimise their gravitational potential energy. This leads us to a very general and very deep principle in physics, and you can pretty much explain everything that happens in the Universe by applying it: things will minimise their potential energy if they can find a way of doing so. So, you could answer the question 'why does a ball roll down a hill?' by saying that the ball would have lower gravitational potential energy at the bottom of the hill than the top, so it rolls down. You could also, of course, say that there is a force pulling the ball down the hill. Physicists often work with energies rather than forces, and the two languages are interchangeable.

With a collapsing cloud of dust, the shape that ultimately forms will therefore be the shape that minimises the gravitational potential energy. The shape must be the one that allows everything within the cloud to get as close to the centre of it as it possibly can, because anything that is located further away from the centre will have more gravitational potential energy! So, the shape that ensures that everything is as close to the centre as possible is, naturally, a sphere, which is why stars and planets are spherical ◉

PROTOPLANET

EVENTUAL SPHERE

MOLTON CORE

accretion of smaller objects

threshold of mass beyond which sphere is formed

VERY LARGE ARRAY

BELOW: A very large array indeed – the 27 dishes on the Plains of San Augustin are an impressive sight, stretching into the horizon. Through these, the radio astronomy observatory can take some even more impressive images.

In the US state of New Mexico, on the Plains of San Augustin between the towns of Magdalena and Datil, lies one of the most spectacular and iconic observatories on the planet. The Very Large Array (VLA) is a radio astronomy observatory consisting of 27 identical dishes, each 25 metres (82 feet) in diameter, arranged in a gigantic Y shape across the landscape. Although each dish works independently, they can be combined together to create a single antenna with an effective diameter of over 36 kilometres (22 miles). This allows this vast virtual telescope to achieve very high-resolution images of the sky at radio wavelengths.

Radio astronomy has a history dating back to the 1930s, when the astronomer Karl Jansky discovered that the Universe could be explored not just through the visible part of the electromagnetic spectrum, but also through the detection of radio waves. Over a period of several months, Jansky used an antenna that looked more like a Meccano set than the VLA to record the radio waves from the sky. He initially identified two types of signal: radio waves generated by nearby thunderstorms, and radio waves generated by distant thunderstorms. He also found a third type, a form of what he thought was static. The interesting thing about the static was that it seemed to rise and fall once a day, which suggested to Jansky that it consisted of radio waves being generated from the Sun, but then over a period of weeks the rise and fall of the static deviated from a 24-hour cycle. Jansky could rotate his antennae on a set of Ford Model T tyres to follow the mysterious signal, and he soon realised the brightest point was not coming from the direction of the Sun, but from the centre of the Milky Way Galaxy in the direction of the constellation of Sagittarius.

Coinciding with the economic impact of the Great Depression, Jansky's pioneering work did not immediately lead to an expansion in the new science of radio astronomy, but ultimately exploring the radio sky has become one of the most powerful techniques used in understanding the Universe beyond our solar system ◉

COLLISION COURSE

BELOW: The Andromeda Galaxy is shown here in its full glory through an infrared composite image from NASA's Spitzer Space Telescope, which shows the galaxy's older stars (left) and dust (right) separately. Spiral galaxies such as this one tend to form new stars in their dusty, clumpy arms.

Of the six thousand or so stars we can see from Earth with the naked eye, only one object lies beyond the gravitational pull of our galaxy. The picture below is of Andromeda, which is the nearest spiral galaxy to the Milky Way Galaxy and the most distant object visible to anyone who looks up into the night sky with just the naked eye. It may appear as nothing more than a smudge in the heavens, but recent observations by NASA's Spitzer Space Telescope suggest that it is home to a trillion suns.

Andromeda is just one of a hundred billion galaxies in the observable Universe, but there is one thing that singles it out, other than its proximity. While most galaxies are rushing away from each other as the Universe expands, Andromeda is in fact moving directly towards us, getting closer at a rate of around half a million kilometres (310,000 miles) every hour. It seems the two galaxies are destined to meet, guided by the force of gravity.

A galactic collision sounds like a rare and catastrophic event – the meeting of a trillion suns – but in fact such collisions and the resultant mergers of galaxies are not unusual occurrences in the history of the Universe; both the galaxies of Andromeda and the Milky Way have absorbed other galaxies into their structures over the billions of years of their existence.

The sequence of images on the next page has been created as a computer simulation of what would happen during a galactic collision between our neighbour Andromeda and our own Milky Way. The Milky Way Galaxy is shown face-on and you can see it moving from the bottom, up to the left of Andromeda, and then finally to the upper right. From this perspective Andromeda appears tilted.

These images are 1 million light years across, and the timescale between each frame of the sequence is 90 million years. After the initial collision, an open spiral pattern is excited in both the Milky Way and Andromeda, and long tidal tails and the formation of a connecting bridge of stars are apparent. Initially the galaxies move apart one from another, but then they fall back together to meet in a second collision.

As more stars are thrown off in complex ripple patterns, they settle into one huge elliptical galaxy. Spiral galaxies such as Andromeda and the Milky Way are the pinnacle of complexity, order and beauty, but elliptical galaxies are sterile worlds where few stars form. If we humans, and indeed Earth itself, are still here in roughly 3 billion years, this collision will be a spectacular event. Just before we collide, the night sky will be filled by our giant neighbour. When the two galaxies clash there will be so much energy pumped into the system that vast amounts of stars will form, lighting up the whole sky ◉

WHEN GALAXIES COLLIDE

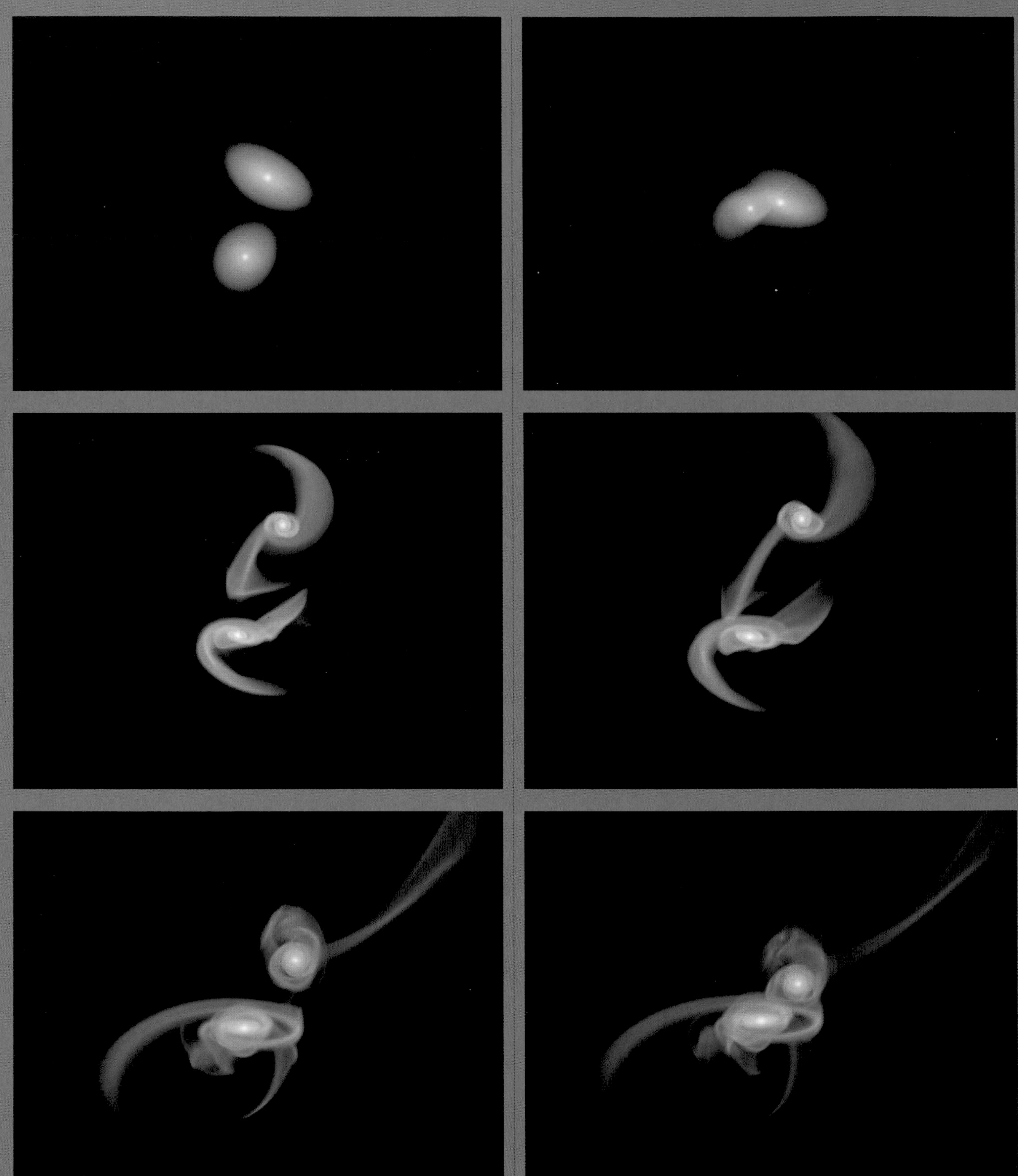

BELOW: This supercomputer animated sequence shows the merger of the Milky Way and Andromeda Galaxies. The sequence begins just before the collision and follows the dynamics of the galaxies until they merge. There are about 90 million years between each frame shown in this sequence.

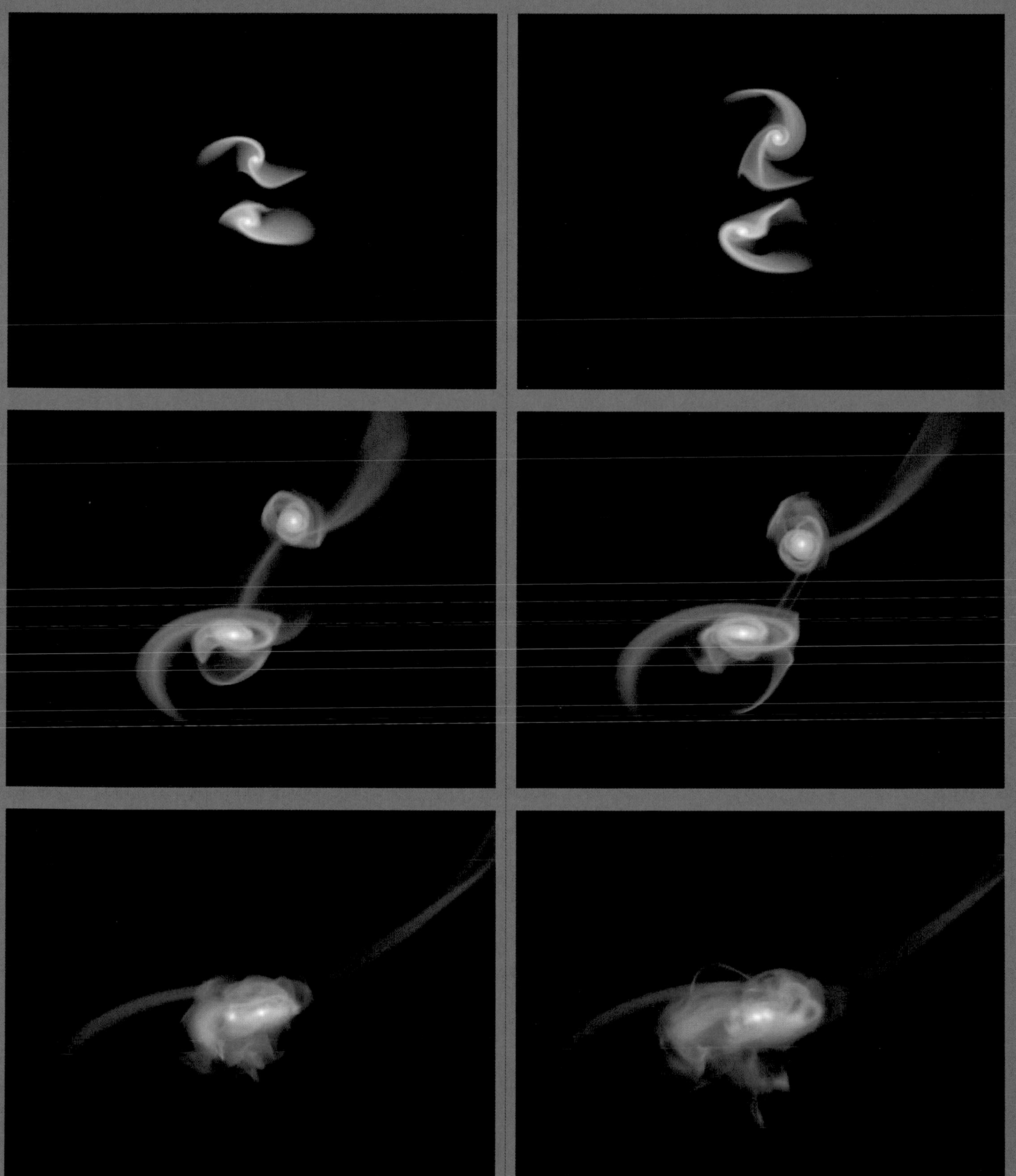

FEELING THE FORCE

Gravity certainly feels like a powerful force. It built our planet, our solar system, and all the billions of star systems in the Universe, diligently assembling clouds of dust and gas into neatly ordered spheres. Matter curves the fabric of the Universe, and in doing so the spheres are bound together and marshalled into orbits, generating the cyclical cosmos we witness from Earth – from our journey through the yearly seasons to the daily ebb and flow of the tides. Gravity reaches far across the space between the star systems, forming galaxies, clusters and superclusters which all beat out orbital rhythms on longer and longer timescales. Gravity is the creator of order and rhythm in our dynamic and turbulent universe.

RIGHT: Galaxy clusters like this one, MS0735.6+7421, are all subject to the power and force of gravity.

THE GRAVITY PARADOX

Despite its reach and influence, there is a mystery surrounding nature's great organisational force; although it is an all-pervasive influence, it is in fact an incredibly weak force – by far the weakest force in the Universe. It is so weak that we overcome it every day in the most mundane of actions. Lift up a teacup and you are resisting the force of gravity exerted on the cup by an entire planet – Earth is trying to stop you, but it is no match for the power of your arm. The reason for this weakness is not known, and the puzzle is brought into stark relief by considering what happens when you lift up the cup. The force that operates your muscles and holds the atoms of your body together is electromagnetism. It is a million million million million million million times stronger than gravity, which is why you will always win in a battle against Earth. Even so, we have evolved to live on the surface of a planet with a particular gravitational field strength, and evolution doesn't produce animals with muscles and skeletons that are stronger than they need to be. Biology rarely wastes precious resources! To demonstrate this, someone at the BBC thought that it would be amusing to see how a human body – mine – would respond if it were transported to a more massive planet.

MY FACE ON A MORE MASSIVE PLANET

The centrifuge at the Royal Netherlands Air Force physiology department was one of the first devices built to spin humans around at speed. Its purpose is to subject fighter pilots to the high G-forces they experience in combat, both for research and to teach them not to black out. As we have discussed, acceleration is indistinguishable from gravity, and spinning around is a good way to achieve high accelerations in a small space. In the case of the human centrifuge, the acceleration is directed towards the centre of the spinning arm, and is caused by the force (known as centripetal force) that acts on your body through the seat to keep you flying in a circle.

My first destination was the gas giant Neptune. Just over seventeen times more massive than Earth, you might expect that the force of gravity would be seventeen times stronger at its surface. However, Neptune's radius is 3.89 times that of Earth at its Equator, so by using Newton's law of gravitation, you'll find that the surface gravity on Neptune is only around 14 per cent greater than Earth's (written as 1.14G). Even with such a small change, I could feel a difference as I lifted up my arms, because they were 14 per cent heavier than normal.

Next up was Jupiter, which is 318 times more massive than Earth. With an equatorial radius 11.2 times greater, the surface gravity would be just over 2.5 times that of our planet. At 2.5G, my arms were 2.5 times heavier than normal, which made them difficult to lift. Apart from this, though, I wasn't in too much discomfort. This all changed when my director decided to send me to exoplanet OGLE2 TR L9b in the constellation of Carina. Over four times the mass of Jupiter, but with a radius only 50 per cent bigger, OGLE2 TR L9b has a surface gravity four times that of Earth. At 4G, things got

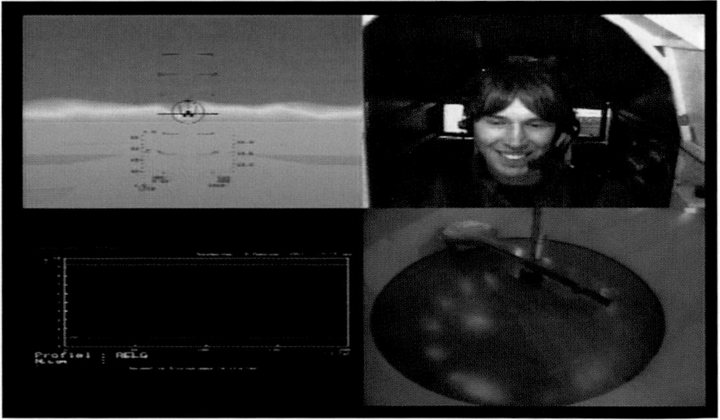

TOP: It may look like a diabolical machine designed to assassinate James Bond and test his escapolgy skills, but this centrifuge at Cologne, Germany, is used to prepare astronauts and fighter pilots for very high G-forces.

quite uncomfortable. I could still speak, but I couldn't lift my arms. It was also quite difficult to breathe because my ribcage and everything else in my body was four times its normal weight, and my muscles aren't used to working that hard.

We then decided to journey beyond OGLE and see how far I could go. As the G-force increased, things got uncomfortable. After a minute or so at 5G, the blood begins to drain from the head, because the heart finds it difficult to pump it up into the brain. This causes faintness and is accompanied by a slight but noticeable narrowing of vision. I had had enough just below 6G, when I was told that my face had been contorted into a funny enough shape to be amusing to the viewers. My job was done. Slowing down was probably more unpleasant than the high-G bit, because the senses are so confused that you feel as if you are tumbling forwards. Gus Grissom described this sensation in the post-flight report of the second manned Mercury mission on Liberty Bell 7, noting that when the main engines shut down after launch, reducing the G-force rapidly, he had to glance at his instruments to reassure himself that his spacecraft was not tumbling.

After my ride I chatted with an F16 pilot who had been subjected to a very fast acceleration and deceleration to 9G. (NATO requires all fighter pilots to be able to deal with this violent ride without passing out.) He told me the centrifuge is far worse than anything you feel in a fighter jet, and having flown in a Lightning and a Hunter, I concur. It's the sustained nature of the G-force in the centrifuge that makes you feel odd; our bodies have not evolved to cope with the weak force of gravity at strengths much greater than those on Earth.

The body with the highest surface gravitational force in the Solar System is the Sun; with a mass 333,000 times that of our planet, it has a surface gravity over 28 times more powerful. The centrifuge cannot go that fast, because this would be a completely unsurvivable G-load.

To find still stronger gravitational fields we have to travel beyond our solar system and look for objects more exotic than mere stars. Our next stop is on one of the strangest worlds in the Universe – one once thought to be populated by aliens ◉

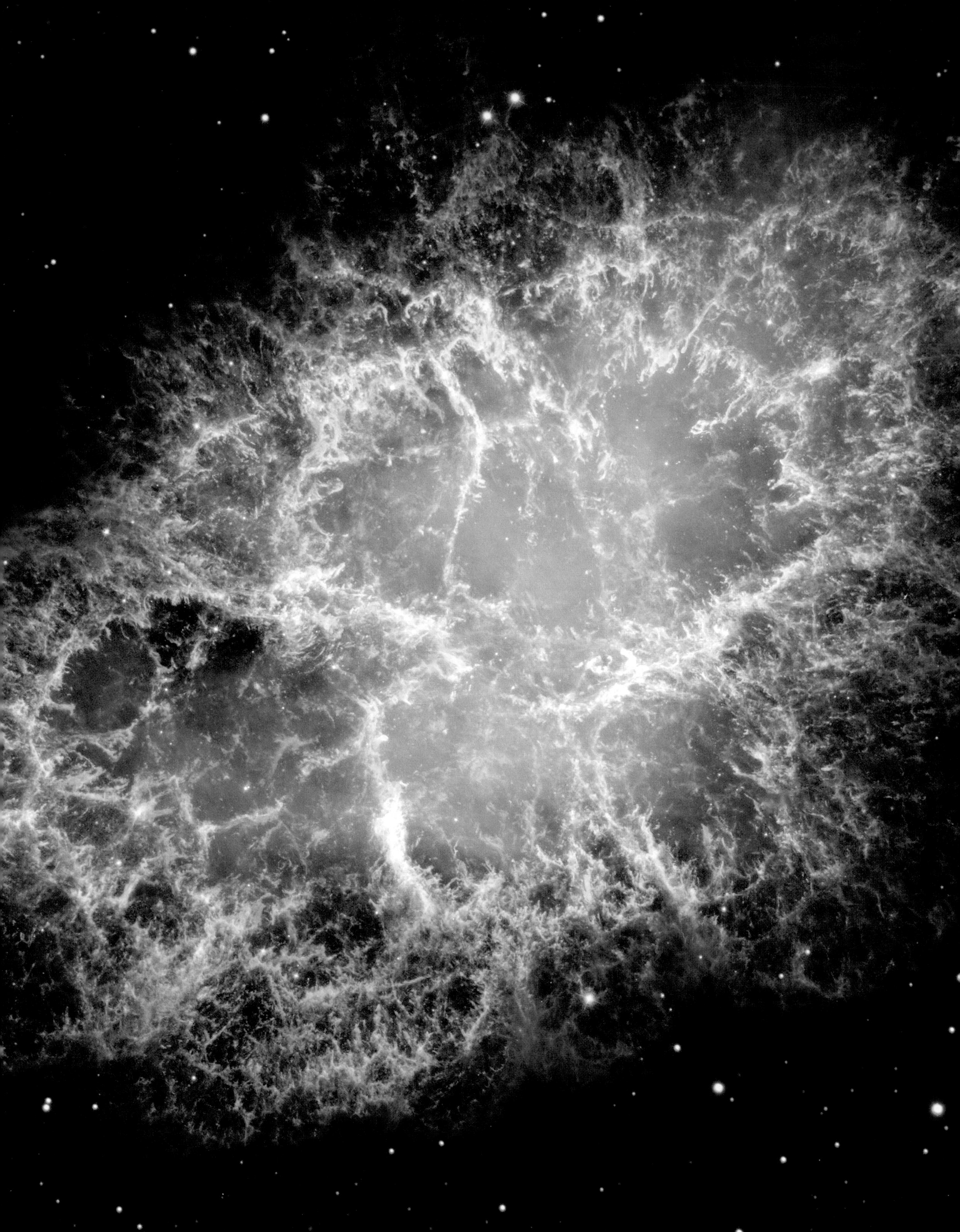

THE LAND OF LITTLE GREEN MEN

In 1967 postgraduate student Jocelyn Bell and her supervisor Anthony Hewish were using a newly completed radio telescope at Cambridge to search for quasars, the most luminous, powerful and energetic objects in the Universe. Quasars, or quasi-stellar radio sources, are now widely believed to be the small, compact regions around supermassive black holes at the centre of very young galaxies. A vast amount of radiation (in excess of the output of an entire galaxy of a trillion suns), is emitted as gas and dust spiral into the black hole.

As Bell and Hewish searched the data for these highly active, ancient galactic centres, they stumbled upon a very strange signal; a pulse that repeated every 1.3373 seconds precisely. It seemed to the Cambridge team to be almost impossible to believe that such a fast regular pulse could come from a natural source, so they named it LGM-1, which stands for Little Green Men.

LEFT: This mosaic image, taken by NASA's Hubble Space Telescope, shows the Crab Nebula, an expanding remnant of a star's supernova explosion. Chinese astronomers recorded this violent event in July 1054, and so too did the people of the Chaco Canyon in New Mexico.

ABOVE: At Chaco Canyon a small, unremarkable-looking painting has been discovered amongst the rocks which probably depicts the explosion of the star that created the Crab Nebula.

If they had discovered a radio beacon from an alien civilisation, you'd have heard about it. The source was entirely natural, as astronomer Sir Fred Hoyle realised immediately on hearing the announcement. However, they had made a new discovery, for which Hewish and fellow astronomer Martin Ryle (though inexplicably and controversially not Bell) received the Nobel Prize in Physics in 1974. Interestingly, though, Bell and Hewish were certainly not the first humans to see one of these wonders – they were beaten to it by an ancient civilisation that witnessed the birth of one almost a thousand years earlier.

CHACO CANYON

A thousand years ago, between AD 900 and 1150, a great civilisation built a series of vast stone structures, known as the Great Houses, along the floor of the arid Chaco Canyon in New Mexico. These buildings remained the largest manmade structures in North America until the nineteenth century. The largest contains more than 700 rooms, many of which are still intact. It is known that these buildings, bizarrely, were not used as permanent residences, because they contain no traces of fires, cooking implements or animal bones. Instead, they seem to have been largely ceremonial; some archaeologists believe that the architecture of the canyon, including its precisely aligned and complex road system, were designed to symbolise and re-enforce the canyon's position not only as the centre of local culture, commerce and religion, but also as the centre of the Universe. The roads and buildings in the canyon and surrounding areas certainly appear to be aligned with the compass points and, it has been suggested, with important moments in the yearly cycle of the Sun – such as the summer and winter solstices. It is difficult to know for sure whether all of the claimed alignments were intentional, but it is known that the Chacoan peoples were keen observers of the skies and possessed a very intricate and advanced cosmology, along with stories of the creation of the constellations and the Universe itself.

One particular site, hidden a mile or so from the main ruins, is the reason for our visit. I have known about it and wanted to come here since I was a little boy; I had no idea where Chaco Canyon was, but I knew about the existence of a small, unremarkable-looking painting on the underside of a rocky overhang next to a dry riverbed half a world away. It was Carl Sagan's *Cosmos,* the book and television series, that introduced me to the wonders of the Universe. In the chapter 'The Lives of the Stars', there is a small black and white photo of the painting, showing three symbols: a handprint, a crescent moon and a bright star. It is known that the painting was made some time around AD 1054, and this was the year of one of the most spectacular astronomical events in recorded history. On 4 July AD 1054, a nearby star exploded. Chinese astronomers recorded the precise date, and the Chacoans would certainly have seen it too because the explosion was visible even in daylight for three weeks, and the fading new star remained visible to the naked eye at night for two years. It would have dominated the skies; a strange and magical sight, perhaps celebrated, perhaps feared; we will never know. We do know precisely where the explosion happened in the sky because its remnant is today one of the most famous and beautiful sights in the heavens: the Crab Nebula.

Apart from the date of the painting, which is not precisely known, the best evidence that this does indeed chronicle the event that the Chinese astronomers recorded is the alignment of the painting. Every 18.5 years, the Moon and Earth will return to the same positions they were in on the nights around 4 July AD 1054. If on one of those rare evenings you go to Chaco Canyon and position yourself beside the painting, the Moon will pass by the position in the sky indicated by the hand print. At that moment, to the left of the Moon, exactly as depicted in the painting, you will see the Crab Nebula.

LEFT: Every 18.5 years, the ruins of the Great Houses of Chaco Canyon and the beautiful rock faces that line the floor of this arid valley are the perfect place from which to see the Crab Nebula in all its glory.

The explosion of 4 July 1054 was a supernova, the violent death of a massive star. It is expected that, on average, there should be around one supernova in our galaxy every century, and this one was almost uncomfortably close, at only 6,000 light years away. The Crab Nebula is the rapidly expanding remains of a star that was once around ten times the mass of our sun; after only a thousand years, the cloud of glowing gas is 11 light years across and expanding at 1,500 kilometres per second. At the heart of the glowing cloud sits the exposed stellar core, which is all that remains of a once-massive sun. It might not look like much when viewed with an optical telescope, but point a radio telescope at it and you will detect a radio signal, pulsing at a rate of precisely 30.2 times a second. It was an object like this that Jocelyn Bell and her colleagues observed in 1967. The Cambridge team weren't listening to little green men, they were listening to the extraordinary sound of a rapidly rotating neutron star – called a pulsar.

Neutron stars are truly amongst the strangest worlds in the Universe; they are matter's last stand against the relentless force of gravity. For most of a star's life, the inward pull of gravity is balanced by the outward pressure caused by the energy released from the nuclear fusion reactions within its core. When the fuel runs out, the star explodes, leaving the core behind. But what prevents this stellar remnant from collapsing further under its own weight? The answer lies not in the physics of stars, but in the world of sub-atomic particles.

The answer to the question of what stops normal matter collapsing in on itself, surprisingly, was not proven until 1967, when physicists Freeman Dyson and Andrew Lenard showed that the stability of matter is down to a quantum mechanical

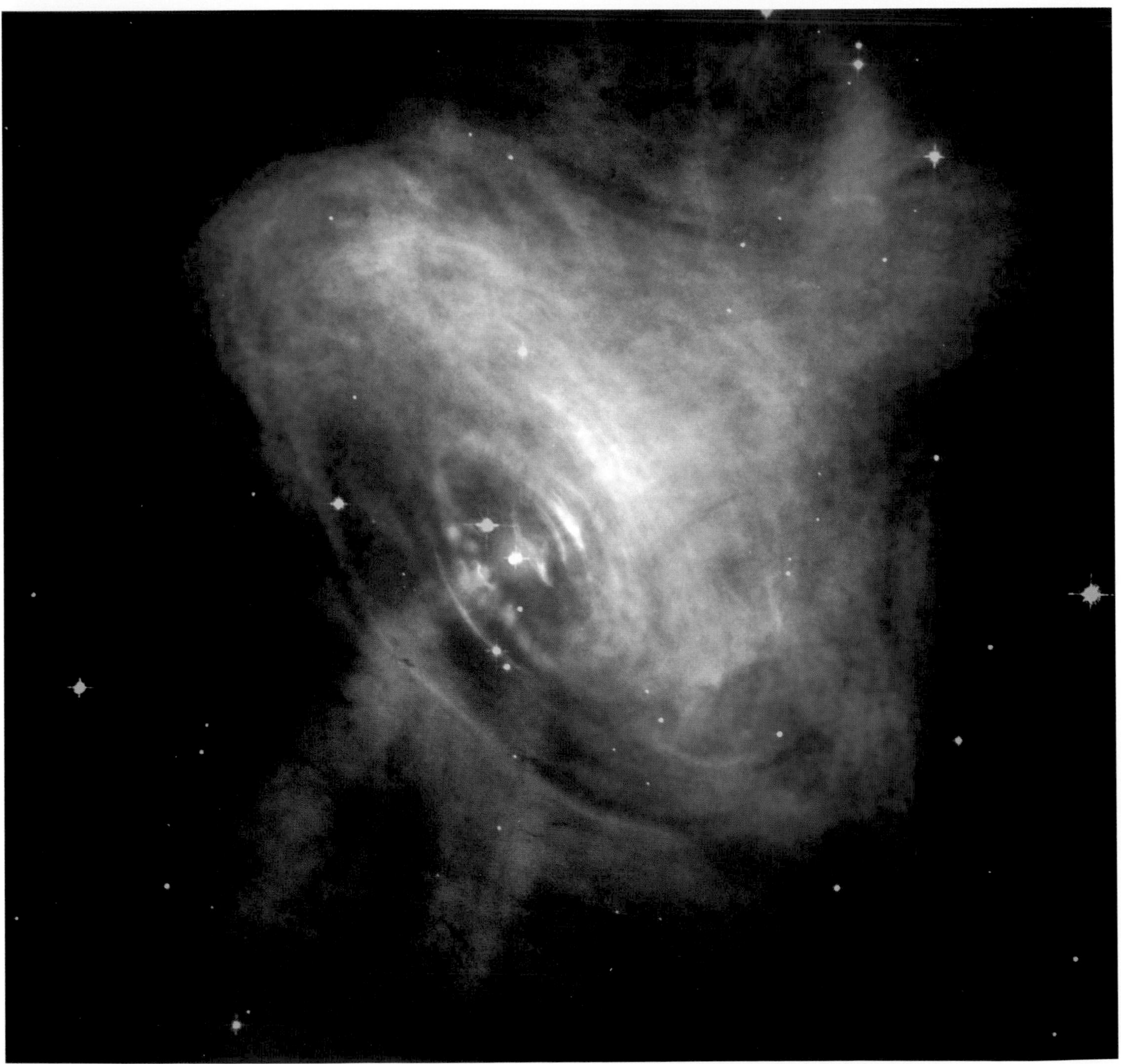

LEFT: Located around 6,000 light-years from Earth, the Crab Nebula is the remnant of a star that exploded as a supernova in AD 1054. This image, taken by NASA's Hubble Space Telescope, shows the centre of the nebula in unprecedented detail.

RIGHT: This composite image of the Crab Nebula has X-ray (blue), and optical (red) images superimposed on it. It is an ever-expanding cloud of gas, and is perhaps the most famous and conspicuous of its kind.

The Crab Nebula is the rapidly expanding remains of a star that was once around ten times the mass of our sun; after only a thousand years, the cloud of glowing gas is 11 light years across and expanding at 1,500 kilometres per second.

effect called the Pauli exclusion principle. There are two types of particles in nature, which are distinguished by a property known as spin. The fundamental matter particles, such as electrons and quarks, and composite particles, such as protons and neutrons, have half-integer spin; these are known collectively as fermions. The fundamental force carrying particles such as photons have integer spin; these are known as bosons. Fermions have the important property that no two of them can occupy the same quantum state. Put more simply, but slightly less accurately, this means you can't pile lots and lots of them into the same place. This is the reason why atoms are stable and chemistry happens. Electrons occupy distinct shells around the atomic nucleus, and as you add more and more electrons, they go into orbits further and further away from the nucleus. It is only the behaviour of the outermost electrons that determine the chemical properties of an element. Without the exclusion principle, all the electrons would crowd into the lowest possible orbit and there would be no complex chemical reactions and therefore no people.

If you try to press atoms together you force their electron clouds together until at some point you are asking all the electrons to occupy the same place (it is more correct to say the same quantum state). This is forbidden, and leads to an effective force that prevents you squashing the atoms together any further. This force is called electron degeneracy pressure, and it is very powerful. In Chapter 4, we will discuss white dwarf stars, the fading embers of suns left to slowly cool after nuclear fusion in their cores ceased. How did they continue to defy the crushing force of gravity? The answer is by electron degeneracy pressure, the dogged reluctance of electrons to being forced too closely together.

But what happens if you keep building more massive white dwarfs, increasing the gravitational force still further? The great Indian astrophysicist Subrahmanyan Chandrasekhar found the answer in one of the landmark calculations of the early years of quantum theory. In 1930, Chandrasekhar showed that electron degeneracy pressure can prevent the collapse of white dwarfs with masses up to 1.38 times the mass

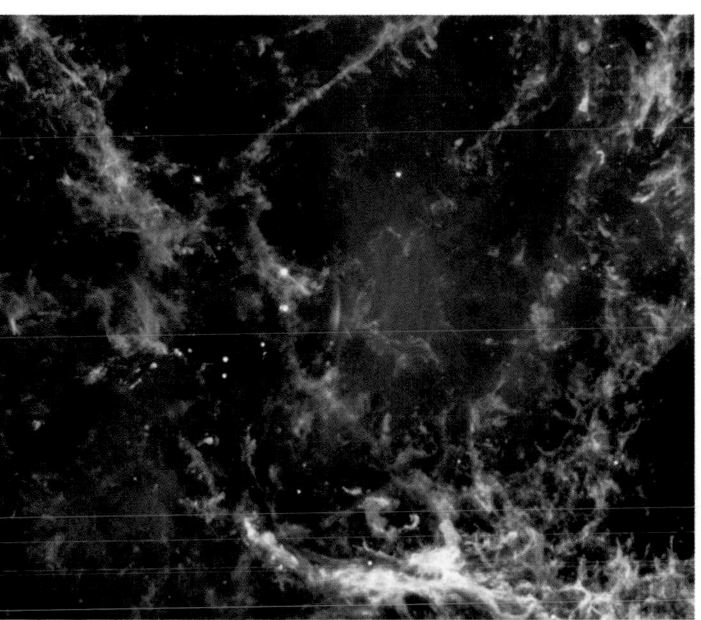

of our sun. For masses greater than this, the electrons won't give in to gravity and move closer together, because they can't. Instead, they give up and disappear.

They don't, of course, vanish into thin air, because they carry properties such as electric charge which cannot be created or destroyed. Instead, the intense force of gravity makes it favourable for them to merge with the protons in the nuclei of the atoms to form neutrons. This is possible through the action of the weak nuclear force in the reverse of the process that turns protons into neutrons in the heart of our sun, allowing hydrogen to fuse into helium. For dying stars with masses above the Chandrasekhar limit, this is the only option, and the entire core turns into a dense ball of neutrons.

Most of the matter that makes up the world around us is empty space. A typical nucleus of a neutron star, which contains virtually all the mass, is around a hundred thousand times smaller in diameter than its atom; the rest is made up of the fizzing clouds of electrons, kept well away from each other by the exclusion principle. If the nucleus were the size of a pea, the atom would be a vast sphere around a hundred metres across, and this is all empty space. With the electrons gone, matter collapses to the density of the nucleus itself; all the space is squashed out of it by gravity, leaving an impossibly

BELOW: This computer simulation of a pulsar shows the beams of radiation emitting from a spinning neutron star. First observed in 1967, the actual mechanism is still the subject of intense theoretical and experimental study.

RIGHT: The Lovell Telescope at Jodrell Bank Centre for Astrophysics aided the exciting discovery of a double pulsar system, announced in January 2004.

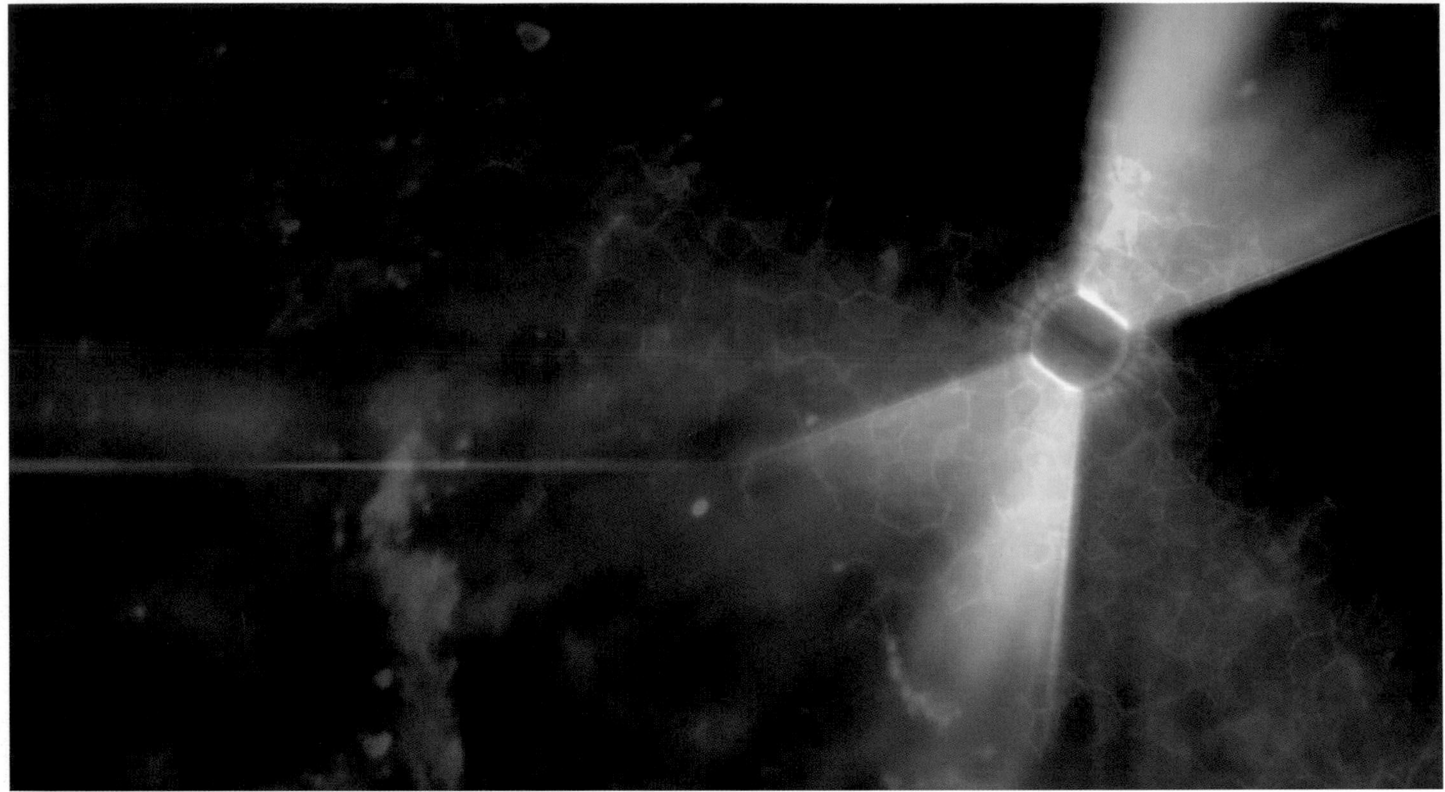

dense nuclear ball. A typical neutron star is around 1.4 times as massive as the Sun, just around the Chandrasekhar limit, crushed into a perfect sphere 20 kilometres (12 miles) across. Neutron star matter is so dense that just one sugar cube of it would weigh more than Mount Everest here on Earth.

The anatomy of neutron stars is still being intensely researched, but they are certainly far more complex than just a ball of neutrons. The surface gravity is of the order of 100,000,000,000G, which is little more than I experienced in the centrifuge. The surface is probably made up of a thin crust of iron and some lighter elements, but the density of neutrons increases as you burrow inwards, for the reasons explained above. Deep in the core, temperatures may be so great that more exotic forms of matter may exist; perhaps quark-gluon plasma, the exotic form of pre-nuclear matter that existed in the Universe a few millionths of a second after the Big Bang.

The unimaginable density and exotic structure aren't the only fantastical feature of neutron stars; many of these worlds, including LGM1 and the neutron star at the heart of the Crab Nebula, have intense magnetic fields and spin very fast. The magnetic field lines, which resemble those of a bar magnet, get dragged around with the stars' rotation, and if the magnetic axis is tilted with respect to the spin axis, this results in two high-energy beams of radiation sweeping around like lighthouse beams. The details of this mechanism are the subject of intense theoretical and experimental study. These are the pulses Bell and Hewitt observed in 1967; the stars are known as pulsars. The fastest known pulsars – millisecond pulsars – rotate over a thousand times every second. Imagine the violence of such a thing; a star the size of a city, a single atomic nucleus, spinning on its axis a thousand times every second.

In January 2004, astronomers using the Lovell Telescope at the Jodrell Bank Centre for Astrophysics, near Manchester, and the Parkes Radio Telescope, in Australia, announced the discovery of a double pulsar system, surely one of the most incredible of all the wonders of the Universe. The system is made up of two pulsars; one with a rotational period of 23 thousandths of a second, the other with a period of 2.8 seconds, orbiting around each other every 2.4 hours. The diameter of the orbit is so small that the whole system would comfortably fit inside our sun. Pulsars are incredibly accurate clocks, allowing astronomers to use the system to test Einstein's theory of gravity in the most extreme conditions known. Imagine the intense warping and bending of space and time close to these two massive, spinning neutron stars. Remarkably, in perhaps the most powerful and beautiful test of any physical theory I know, the predictions of Einstein's Theory of General Relativity, our best current theory of gravity, in the double pulsar system have been confirmed to an accuracy of better than 0.05 per cent. How majestic, how powerful, how wonderful is the human intellect that a man living at the turn of the twentieth century could devise a theory of gravity, inspired by thinking carefully about falling rocks and elevators, that is able to account so precisely for the motion of the most alien objects in the Universe in the most extreme known conditions. That is why I love physics ●

WHAT IS GRAVITY?

BELOW: Mercury's unpredictable orbit has caused real problems for scientists researching Newton's theory of gravity within the Solar System.

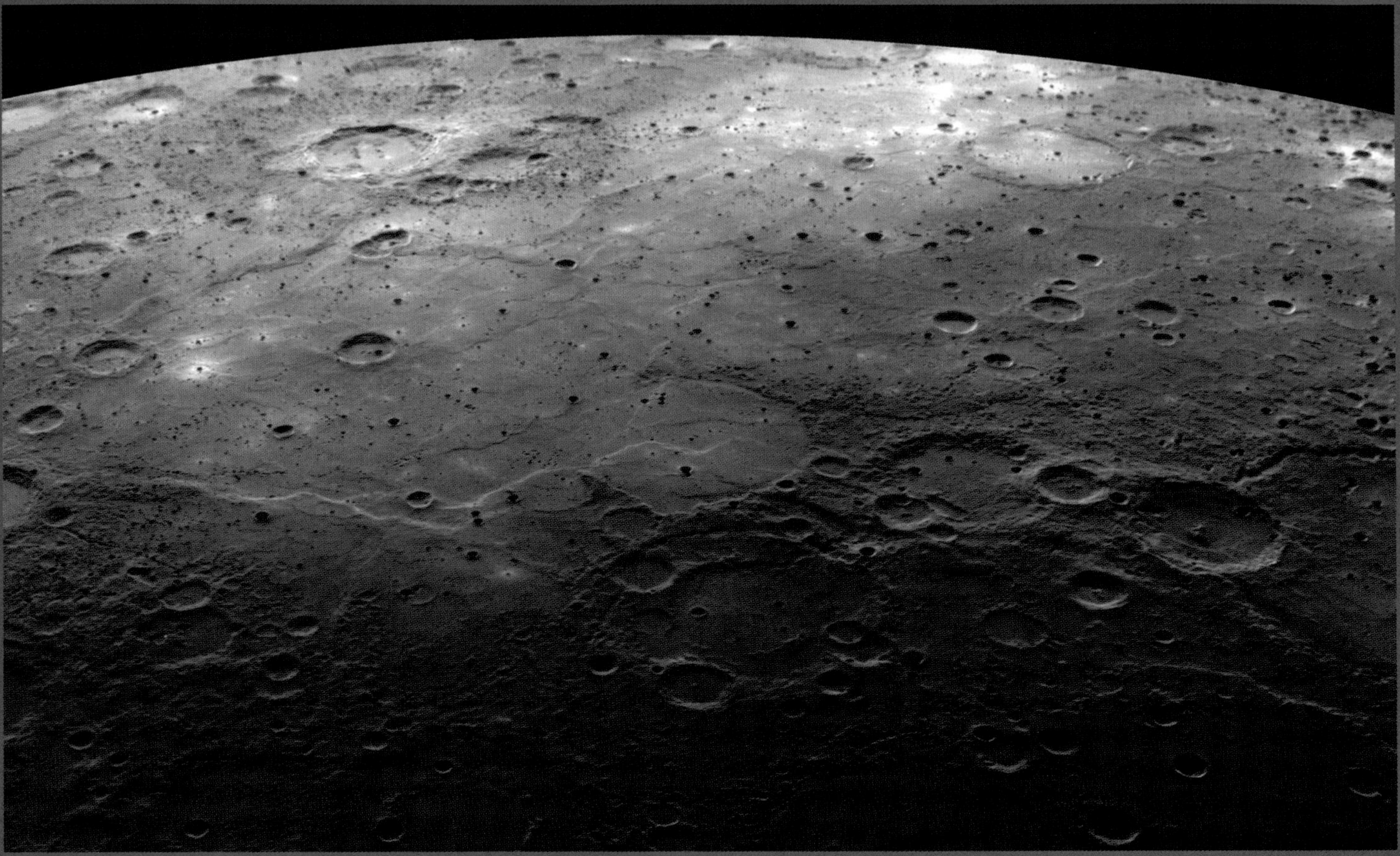

When Newton first published his Law of Universal Gravitation in 1687 he transformed our understanding of the Universe. As we have seen, his simple mathematical formula is able to describe with unerring precision the motion of moons around planets, planets around the Sun, solar systems around galaxies, and galaxies around galaxies. Newton's law is, however, only a model of gravity; it has nothing at all to say about how gravity actually is, and it certainly has nothing to say about a central mystery: why do all objects fall at the same rate in gravitational fields? This question can be posed in a different way by looking again at Newton's famous equation:

$$F = G\frac{m_1 m_2}{r^2}$$

This states that the gravitational force between two objects is proportional to the product of their masses – let's say that m_1 is the mass of Earth and m_2 is the mass of a stone falling towards Earth. Now look at another of Newton's equations: $F = ma$, which can be written with a bit of mathematical rearrangement as $a = F/m$. This is Newton's Second Law of Motion, which describes how the stone accelerates if a force is applied to it. It says that the acceleration (a) of the stone is equal to the force you

WHY DO OBJECTS FALL AT THE SAME RATE?

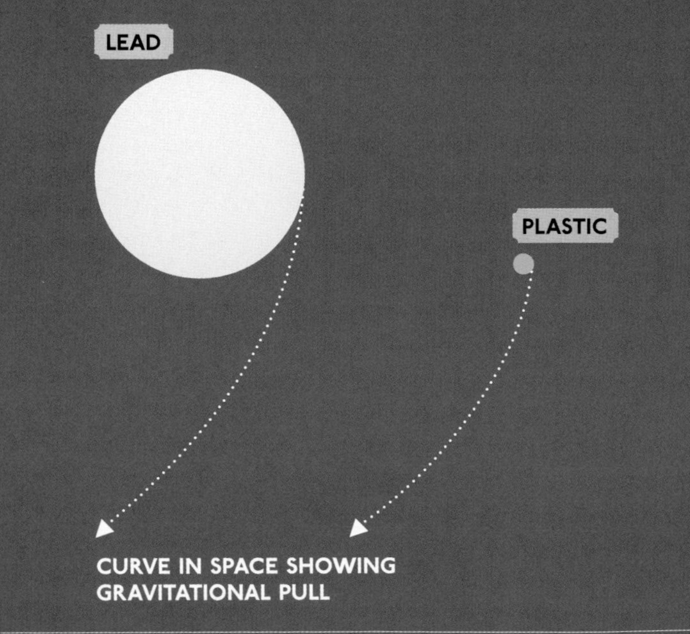

apply to it (F) divided by its mass (m). The reason why things fall at the same rate in a gravitational field, irrespective of their mass, is that the mass of the stone in these two equations (labelled m_2 in the first equation and m in the second), are equal to each other. This means that when you work out the acceleration, the mass of the stone cancels out and you get an answer which only depends on the mass of Earth – the famous 9.81 m/s^2. We said this earlier in the chapter in words: if you double the mass of something falling towards Earth, the gravitational force on it doubles, but so does the force needed to accelerate it. But there is a very important assumption here that has no justification at all, other than the fact that it works: why should these two masses be the same? Why should the so-called inertial mass – which appears in $F = ma$ and tells you how difficult it is to accelerate something – have anything to do with the gravitational mass, which tells you how gravity acts on something? This is a very important question, and Newton had no answer to it.

Newton, then, provided a beautiful model for calculating how things move around under the action of the force of gravity, without actually saying what gravity is. He knew this, of course, and he famously said that gravity is the work of God.

If a theory is able to account for every piece of observational evidence, however, it is very difficult to work out how to replace it with a better one. This didn't stop Albert Einstein, who thought very deeply about the equivalence of gravitational and inertial mass and the related equivalence between acceleration and the force of gravity. At the turn of the twentieth century, following his great success with the Special Theory of Relativity in 1905 (which included his famous equation $E=mc^2$), Einstein began to search for a new theory of gravitation that might offer a deeper explanation for these profoundly interesting assumptions.

Although not specifically motivated by it, Einstein would certainly have known that there were problems with Newton's theory, beyond the philosophical. The most unsettling of these was the distinctly problematic behaviour of a ball of rock that was located over 77 million kilometres (48 million miles) from Earth.

The planet Mercury has been a source of fascination for thousands of years. It is the nearest planet to the Sun and is tortured by the most extreme temperature variations in the Solar System. Due to its proximity to our star, Mercury is a difficult planet to observe from Earth, but occasionally the planets align such that Mercury passes directly across the face of the Sun as seen from Earth. These transits of Mercury are one of the great astronomical spectacles, occurring only 13 or 14 times every century. Mercury has the most eccentric orbit of any planet in the Solar System. At its closest, Mercury passes just 46 million kilometres (28 million miles) from the Sun; at its most distant it is over 69 million kilometres (42 million miles) away. This highly elliptical orbit means that the speed of the movement of this planet varies a lot during its orbit, which means in turn that very high-precision measurements were necessary to map its orbit and make predictions of its future transits. Throughout the seventeenth and eighteenth centuries, scientists would gather across the globe to watch the rare transits of Mercury. These scientists used Newton's Law of Gravity to predict exactly when and where they could view the spectacle, but it became a source of scientific fascination and no little embarrassment when, time after time, Mercury didn't appear on cue. The planet regularly crossed the Sun's disc later than expected, sometimes by as much as several hours.

Mercury's unusual orbit was a real problem, but because of the observational uncertainties it wasn't until 1859 that the French astronomer Urbain Le Verrier proved that the details of Mercury's orbit could not be completely explained by Newtonian gravity. To solve the problem, many astronomers reasoned there must be another planet orbiting between the Sun and Mercury. This planet had to be invisible to our telescopes, but it must also exert a gravitational force large enough to disturb Mercury's orbit. Encouraged by the recent discovery of the planet Neptune, based on a similar anomaly in the orbit of Uranus, they named the ghost planet Vulcan ◉

MERCURY'S ORBIT AROUND THE SUN

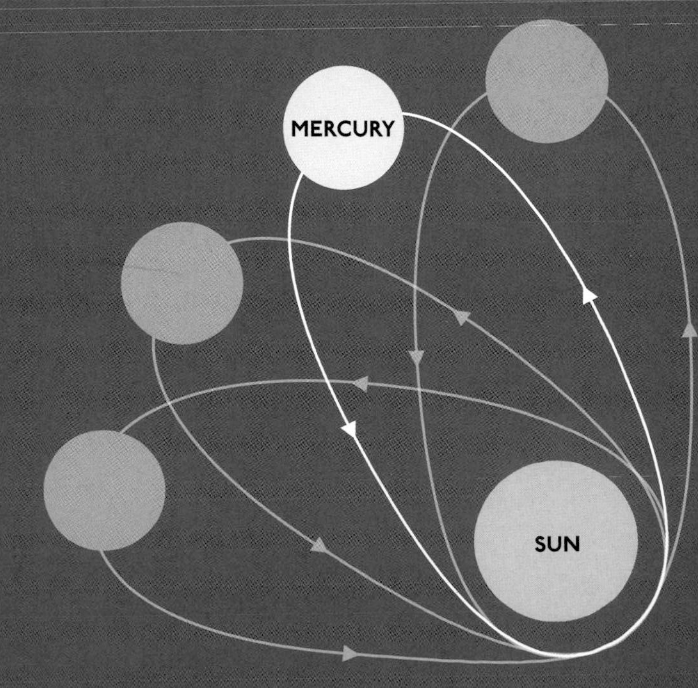

For decades astronomers searched and searched for Vulcan, but they never found it. The reason for this is that Vulcan doesn't exist. The errors in the predictions in fact signalled something far more profound: Newton's Theory of Universal Gravitation is not correct.

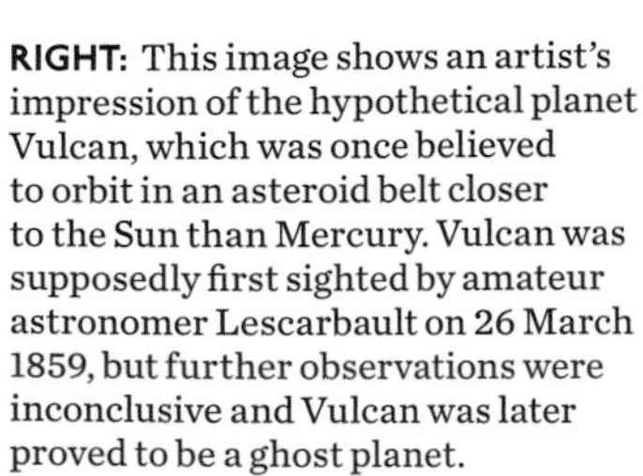

RIGHT: This image shows an artist's impression of the hypothetical planet Vulcan, which was once believed to orbit in an asteroid belt closer to the Sun than Mercury. Vulcan was supposedly first sighted by amateur astronomer Lescarbault on 26 March 1859, but further observations were inconclusive and Vulcan was later proved to be a ghost planet.

EINSTEIN'S THEORY OF GENERAL RELATIVITY

LEFT: German-born physicist Albert Einstein (left) created the famous Theory of General Relativity. British astrophysicist Sir Arthur Eddington (right), later put this theory to the test and confirmed its accuracy.

Einstein would have loved the Vomit Comet. The fact that the effects of gravity can be completely removed by falling freely in a gravitational field was, for him, the thought experiment that led to his theory of General Relativity. How wonderful it would have been for him to experience it as I did! The reason I say this is that, as I floated next to my little plastic Albert in the Vomit Comet, I understood very deeply why Einstein was so interested in freefall. The point is this; inside the plane, falling towards Earth, it is absolutely impossible to tell that you are moving. It is impossible to tell that you are near a planet. It is impossible to tell that, according to someone stood on the ground, you are accelerating at 9.81 m/s^2 towards the ground. You are simply floating, along with everything else in the plane. I let some little drops of water out of a bottle and they floated in front of my face; the cameraman and director floated next to the water droplets, little plastic Albert and me. There was self-evidently no force acting on anything at all, otherwise things would have moved around.

And yet, from the point of view of someone on the ground, we were flying in a parabolic arc, moving forwards through the air at hundreds of miles an hour and accelerating violently towards the ground. The force of gravity is very much present in this description. Einstein's theory takes the view that the two ways of looking at the Vomit Comet – from inside and outside – should be treated as equivalent. No one inside the plane or out has the right to claim that they are right and the other is wrong! If, inside the plane, there is no experiment you can do to prove that you are accelerating towards the ground, you are well within your rights to claim that you are not. Acceleration has cancelled out gravity. Of course, you could look out of the windows, but even then you could claim that Earth is accelerating up towards you and that you are simply floating. From this perspective, everyone on Earth feels a gravitational force pulling them onto the ground because they are being accelerated upwards at a rate of 9.81 m/s^2. Acceleration is therefore equivalent to gravity; this is known as the equivalence principle, and it was very important to Einstein.

So what, then, is gravity? The explanation in Einstein's theory is beautifully simple: gravity is the curvature of spacetime.

In technical language, Einstein would have defined the Vomit Comet, during its time in freefall, as an inertial frame of reference – which is to say that it can be legitimately considered to be at rest, with no forces acting on it.

The assertion that sitting in a falling aircraft should be considered as being absolutely equivalent to floating around in space, far beyond the gravitational pull of any planet or moon, can be used to explain why all objects fall at the same rate.

Why? Simply because there are two equally valid ways of looking at what is happening. From the point of view inside the plane, nothing at all is happening; everything is simply floating, untouched by any forces of any kind. If no forces are acting, then everything naturally stays where it is put. Shift outside the plane, however, and things appear different; everything is falling towards Earth, accelerating under the action of the force of gravity. But, very importantly, the reality of the situation cannot change depending on which point of view we adopt – everything has to behave in the same way in reality, irrespective of how you look at it. If plastic Albert and the globules of water float in front of my face when viewed from my vantage point inside the plane, then plastic Albert and the globules of water had better float in front of my face when viewed from a vantage point outside the plane. In other words, we had all better be accelerating towards the ground at exactly the same rate! Notice that we've made no assumptions about the equivalence between gravitational and inertial masses here; we've just said that a freely falling box in Earth's gravitational field is indistinguishable from a freely falling box in space, or indeed any freely falling box anywhere in the Universe, around any planet, any star, or any moon.

So what, then, is gravity? The explanation in Einstein's theory is beautifully simple: gravity is the curvature of spacetime. What is spacetime? Spacetime is the fabric of the Universe itself.

A good way to picture spacetime, and what it means to curve it, is to think about a simpler surface; the surface of Earth. Our planet has a two-dimensional surface, which is to say that you only need two numbers to identify any point on it: latitude and longitude. Earth's surface is curved into a sphere, but you don't need to know that to move around on it and navigate from place to place. The reason we can picture the curvature is that we are happy to think in three dimensions, so we can actually see that Earth's surface is curved. But imagine that we were two-dimensional beings, confined to move on the surface of Earth with absolutely no concept of a third dimension. We would know nothing about up and down, only about latitude and longitude. It would be very difficult indeed for us to picture in our mind's eye the curvature of our planet's surface.

RIGHT: As light has no mass, Newton's theory states that it is not affected by gravity, although observation does infact show that it is.

Now let's extend our analogy to see how the curvature of something can give rise to a force. Imagine that a pair of two-dimensional friends are standing on the Equator and decide to take a journey due north. They decide to walk parallel to each other, with the intention of never bumping into each other. If they both keep walking, they will walk up parallel lines of longitude, and they will find that as they get closer and closer to the North Pole they will get closer and closer together. Eventually, when they reach the North Pole, they will bump into each other! As three-dimensional beings, we can see what happened; Earth's surface is curved, so all the lines of longitude meet at the poles. However, from the perspective of our two-dimensional friends, even though they kept assiduously to their parallel lines they still were mysteriously drawn together. They may well conclude from this that a force was acting between them, attracting them towards one another. In Einstein's theory, that force is gravity.

The complicated bit about Einstein's Theory of General Relativity is that the surface we need to think about, spacetime, is not two-dimensional but four-dimensional. It is a mixture of the familiar three dimensions of space, plus an additional dimension of time mixed in. It will take us too far from our story to explore spacetime in detail, but it was found to be necessary by Einstein and others at the turn of the twentieth century to explain, in particular, the behaviour of light and the form of Maxwell's equations that we met in Chapter 1. Suffice to say that the surface of our universe, on which we all live our lives, is four-dimensional. What Einstein showed is that the presence of matter and energy – in the form of stars, planets and moons– curves the surface of spacetime, distorting it into hills and valleys. His equations describe exactly what shape spacetime should be around any particular object, such as the Sun, for example, and they also describe how things move over the curved surface. And here is the key point: just like our two-dimensional friends, things move in straight lines; but just like our two-dimensional friends, this isn't what it looks like if you don't know that spacetime is curved. When you're moving across the curved surface, it appears that a force is acting on you, distorting your path. One of the first things Einstein did with his new, geometric theory of gravity was to calculate what Mercury's straight-line path through the curved spacetime around the Sun would look like to us, trapped on the surface of spacetime. To his delight, he found that Mercury would orbit the Sun, and in precisely the way that had been observed over the centuries of transit observations. Where Newton failed, Einstein succeeded.

Einstein had found a completely geometrical way of describing the force of gravity, and it is quite wonderfully elegant. Not only does it predict the orbit of Mercury, but it also provides a very appealing explanation for the equivalence principle. Why do all objects fall at the same rate in a gravitational field, irrespective of their mass or composition? Because the path they take has nothing to do with them at all – they are simply following straight-line paths through the curved spacetime.

Perhaps the most startling demonstration of this is the bending of light by gravity. Light has no mass, and so in Newton's theory it shouldn't be affected by gravity at all. However, according to Einstein's theory, it doesn't matter that it has no mass, it will still be following a straight line through the curved spacetime, so it will appear to follow exactly the same path as everything else. Let's do a thought experiment to see how strange this is. Stand on the ground (on a very, very big planet – I'll explain why I said this in a moment!) with a rock in one hand and a laser beam in the other. Point the laser beam horizontally, drop the rock and fire the laser. Which one hits the ground first? The answer is that they both hit the ground at the same time, because they both move through the same curved space. Light falls at the same rate in a gravitational field as everything else. Now, there is a caveat here. Why did I say a very very big planet? Because light travels at almost 300,000 kilometres per second, so if the rock takes a second to hit the ground, so will the light. But it will

THE GRAVITY CONUNDRUM

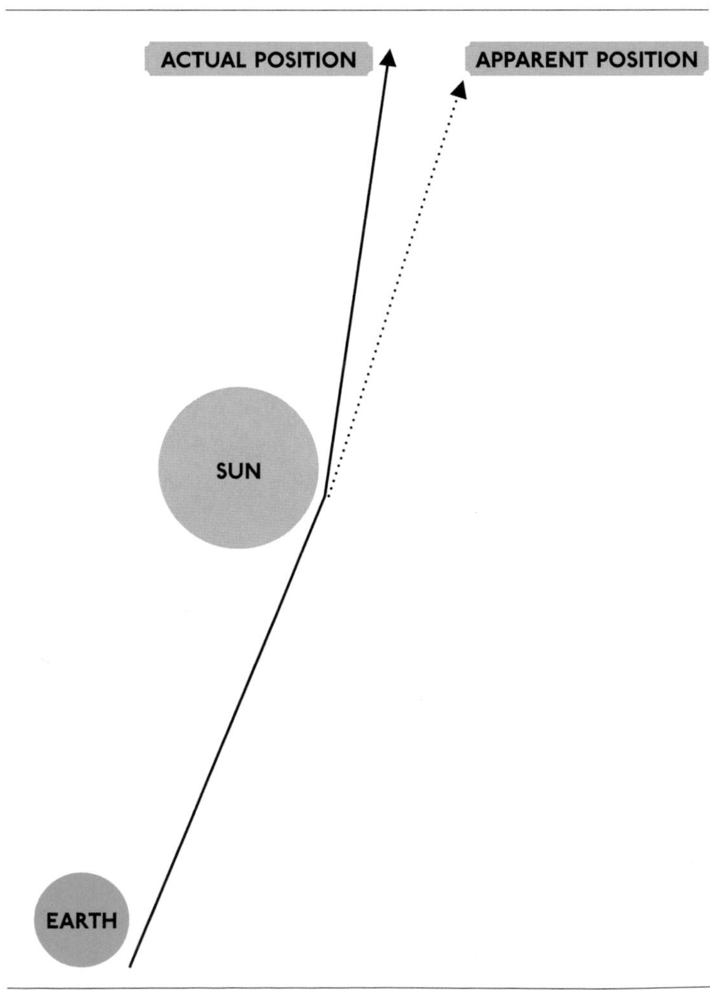

have flown 300,000 kilometres in the horizontal direction by the time it reaches the ground, and on Earth that would mean the surface of the planet had long since curved away! However, the principle still holds.

As an interesting aside, what would happen if you fired the laser beam directly at the ground? Light must always travel at the same speed, it can't speed up, so it will travel towards the ground at exactly 299,792,458 metres per second. But shouldn't it accelerate at 9.81 m/s^2 as it drops? No, it can't, because it always travels at exactly 299,792,458 metres per second. So what happens? Well, the energy of the light can change, although the speed cannot, so the light gets shifted towards the blue end of the spectrum as it flies towards the ground and gains energy from its fall. That is to say that its wavelength gets shorter and its frequency increases. This is very interesting because the second is defined as the length of time it takes a fixed number of wavelengths of a particular colour of light to pass by an observer. Let's say that you use the frequency of the laser beam held in your hand to synchronize a clock, then you fire the laser at the ground; when the light hits the ground, its frequency will have increased. This means that the peaks and troughs of the laser light beam are arriving more frequently than they did when they set off. So, from the point of view of someone on the ground, the clock above the ground will be running

In the language of General Relativity, we might say that the presence of Earth bends spacetime near it such that time passes more slowly than it does far away.

slightly fast. Is this true? Yes, it is. The effect is known as gravitational time dilation; gravity slows down time, so clocks close to the ground run slower than those in orbit. In the language of General Relativity, we might say that the presence of Earth bends spacetime near it such that time passes more slowly than it does far away. This is a very real effect and is one that has to be taken into account in the GPS satellite navigation system, which relies on precise timekeeping to measure distances. The GPS satellites orbit at an altitude of 20,000 kilometres (12,500 miles), which means that their clocks run faster than they do on the ground by 45 microseconds per day, because they are in a weaker gravitational field. The fact that they are moving relative to the ground also affects the rate of their clocks, and when everything is taken into account the timeshift reduces to 38 microseconds per day. This would be equivalent to a distance error of over 10 kilometres (6 miles) per day, which would make the system useless. So, every time we get into our cars and use satellite navigation, we are using Einstein's theory of gravity in order to correctly ascertain our position on the surface of Earth.

To summarise, then, had Einstein experienced the Vomit Comet, he would have described it, during its time in freefall, as following a straight-line path through spacetime. As long as it continues on this path, the plane and its passengers will not feel the force of gravity at all; it is only when something stops the plane following its straight-line path through spacetime that a force is felt. If the plane didn't stop itself falling, this obstacle would be the ground!

It is worth making a final brief aside here, which also serves to underline what we've just learnt. The experimental fact that triggered all this discussion is that the gravitational and inertial masses of objects are the same. Einstein provides a natural explanation for this: gravity is simply a result of the fact that there is such a thing as spacetime, and that it is curved, and that things move in straight lines through this curved spacetime. It is also possible to take a different view; there could be some deep reason why the gravitational and inertial masses of things are equal – a reason that we have yet to discover. The fact that they are equal allows us to build a geometric theory of gravity. In that case, Einstein's theory might more properly be considered to be a model, in the same way that Newton's theory is a model. At the moment we have no way of deciding between these two possibilities, but it's worth being aware that they are both valid ways of looking at the situation.

Einstein's Theory of General Relativity is rightly considered to be one of the great intellectual achievements of all time. It is conceptually elegant and probably the theory that physicists most often attach the word 'beautiful' to. Ultimately, though, it doesn't matter how beautiful a theory is, the only thing that matters is that its predictions are in accord with our observations of the natural world. The orbit of Mercury is one such observation; the slowing down of time in gravitational fields is another; but to really test Einstein's theory to the limit, we have to journey far out into space and visit the most exotic and massive objects in the known Universe – places where the force of gravity becomes exceptionally strong ●

INTO THE DARKNESS

The success of Einstein's Theory of General Relativity is one of the greatest of human achievements, and in my view it will be remembered as such for as long as there is anything worth calling a civilisation. But there is a final twist to the story of gravitation, because Einstein's remarkable theory predicts its own demise.

The collapse of a neutron star is prevented by neutron degeneracy pressure. Neutrons are fermions, as are electrons, but because they are more massive than electrons, they can be packed much more tightly together before the Pauli exclusion principle steps in once more and forbids further contraction. Another stable staging post against gravity should be provided by quark degeneracy pressure, because quarks too are fermions, but ultimately, if the star is too massive gravity will overwhelm even these fantastically dense objects. It is believed that the limit above which no known law of physics can intervene to stop gravity is around three times the mass of the Sun. This is known as the Tolman-Oppenheimer-Volkoff limit. For the remnants of stars with masses beyond this limit, gravity will win.

In 1915, only one month after Einstein published the Theory of General Relativity, the physicist Karl Schwarzschild found a solution to Einstein's equations which is now known as the Schwarzschild metric. The Schwarzschild metric describes the structure of spacetime around a perfectly spherical object. There are two interesting features of Schwarzschild's spacetime: one occurs at a particular distance from the object, known as the Schwarzschild radius, but for distances less than the Schwarzschild radius, space and time are distorted in such a way that the entire future of anything that falls in will point inwards. This sounds weird,

LEFT: This coloured X-ray image shows the area around the supermassive black hole, known as Sagittarius A*, which sits at the centre of the Milky Way Galaxy.

BELOW: This artist's impression helps us to visualise the mysterious objects in space that are black holes.

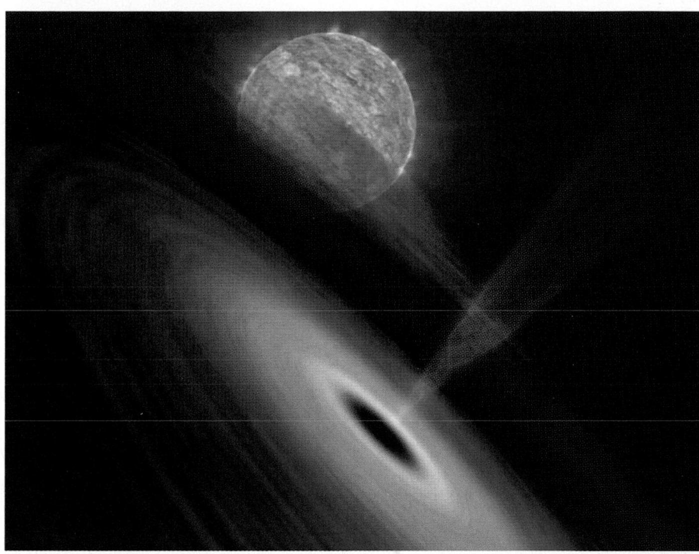

but remember that space and time are mixed up together in Einstein's theory. In more technical language, we say that the future light cones inside the Schwarzschild radius all point towards the centre. This means that, as inexorably as we here on Earth march into the future, if you were to cross the line defined by the Schwarzschild radius, you would inexorably march inwards towards the object that is bending spacetime. There would be no escape, not even for light itself, in the same way that you cannot escape your future. This surface, defined by the Schwarzschild radius surrounding the object, is known as the event horizon. But what has happened to the object itself? This is the second interesting feature of the Schwarzschild metric. Let's first think about the Sun. If you asked what the Schwarszchild radius for a star with the mass of the Sun is, it would be 3 kilometres (1 mile). This is inside the Sun! So there is no problem here, because you can't get that close to the Sun without actually being inside it, at which point all the mass outside you doesn't count any more.

But what about an object like a collapsing neutron star, getting smaller and smaller and denser and denser? What if you could have an object that was dense enough to have the mass of the Sun and yet be physically smaller than the Schwarszchild radius? It seems that there are such objects in the Universe; the stars for which even neutron degeneracy

Black holes are fascinating objects; we don't understand them, and yet we know they exist. They are of immense importance ... the physics that lies inside the event horizon is undoubtedly fundamental.

pressure will not suffice to resist the force of gravity. These objects are called black holes. At the very centre of the black hole, at $r=0$, the Schwarzschild metric has another surprise in store; the spacetime curvature becomes infinite. In other words, the gravitational field becomes infinite. This is known as a singularity. In physical theories, the existence of singularities signals the edge of the applicability of the theory; in simple language, there must be more to it! This has led many physicists to search for a new theory of gravity. Quantum theories of gravity such as string theory may be able to avoid the appearance of singularities, by effectively setting a minimum distance scale below which spacetime does not behave in the manner described by Einstein's equations.

As yet, we do not know whether any of these current theories are correct, or even if they are on the road to being correct, but what we do know is that black holes exist. At the centre of our galaxy, and possibly every galaxy in the Universe, there is believed to be a supermassive black hole. Astronomers believe this because of precise measurements of the orbit of a star known as S2. This star orbits around the intense source of radio waves known as Sagittarius A* that sits at the galactic centre. S2's orbital period is just over 15 years, which makes it the fastest-known orbiting object, reaching speeds of up to 2 per cent of the speed of light. If the precise orbital path of an object is known, the mass of the thing it is orbiting can be calculated, and the mass of Sagittarius A* is enormous – 4.1 million times the mass of our Sun. Since the star S2 has a closest approach to the object of only 17 light hours, it is known that Saggitarus A* must be smaller than this, otherwise S2 would literally bump into it. The only known way of cramming 4.1 million times the mass of the Sun into a space less than 17 light hours across is as a black hole, which is why astronomers are so confident that a giant black hole sits at the centre of the Milky Way. These observations have recently been confirmed and refined by studying a further 27 stars, known as the S-stars, all with orbits taking them very close to Sagittarius A*.

Black holes are fascinating objects; we don't understand them, and yet we know they exist. They are of immense importance, because despite the fact that we will never encounter one directly, the physics that lies inside the event horizon is undoubtedly fundamental. These are objects that will require a new theory of gravity, indeed a new theory of space and time, to describe. One of the holy grails of observational astronomy is to find a pulsar orbiting around a black hole. Such a system surely exists somewhere, and to be able to observe the behaviour of one of these massive cosmic clocks in the intensely curved spacetime close to a black hole would surely test Einstein's Theory of General Relativity to its limit. It may even, if we are lucky, reveal flaws that point us towards a new theory ◉

THE ANATOMY OF A BLACK HOLE

For all their mystery, we do know that black holes exist. The idea of a body so massive that even light could not escape its grip was first suggested in the eighteenth century, and today we now know that there is not only a black hole at the centre of our galaxy, but also possibly in the centre of every galaxy. We may never directly see one, but the secrets they contain may one day help us answer some of the most fundamental questions in the Universe.

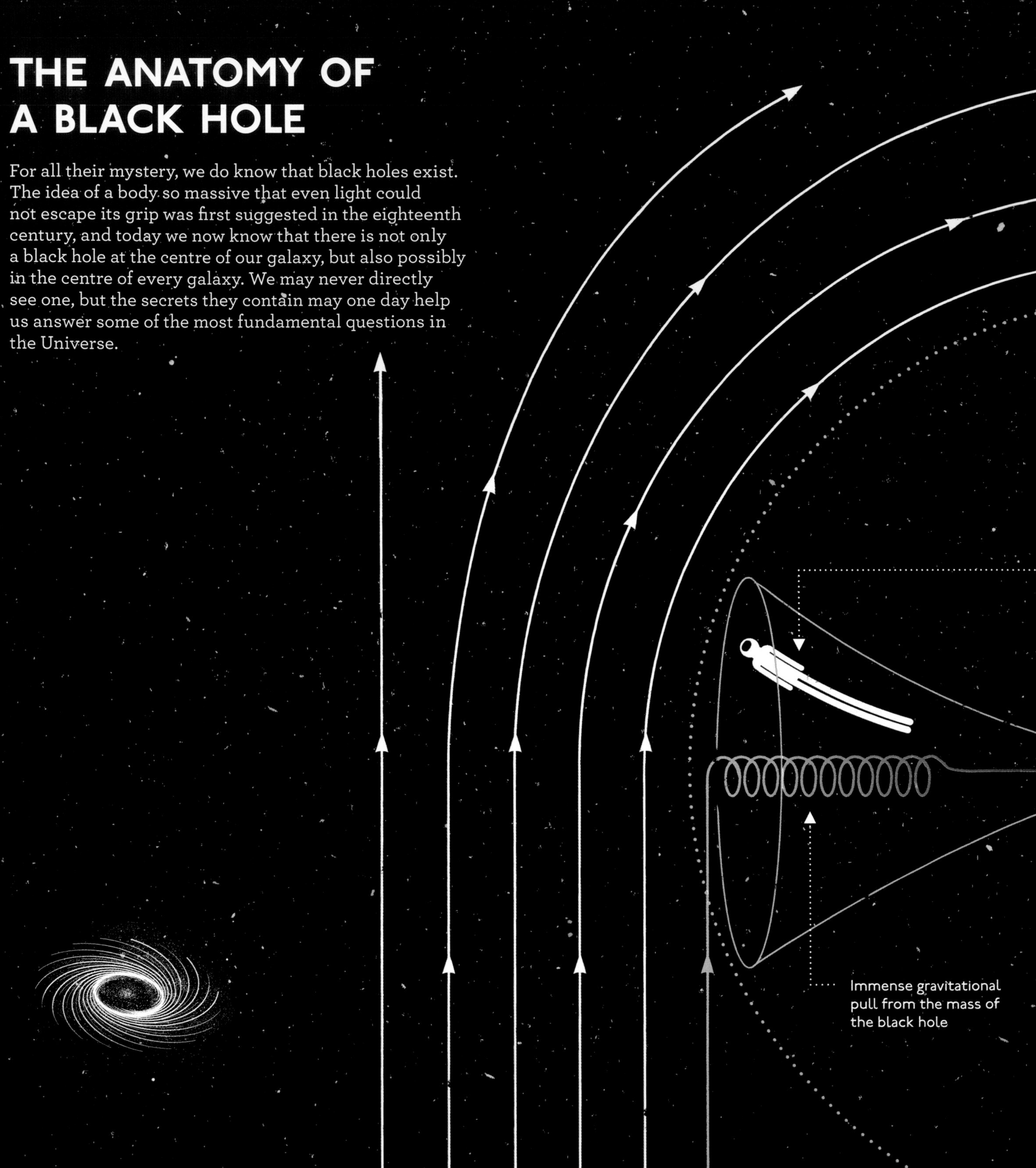

LIGHT RAYS

Light rays become bent as they get closer to the black hole

SPAGHETTIFICATION

This is the vertical stretching and horizontal compression of objects into long thin shapes in a very strong gravitational field. The stretching is so powerful that no object can withstand it, no matter how strong its components

EVENT HORIZON

This is the point at which the gravitational pull from its centre becomes so great as to make escape impossible. Light emitted from within the event horizon can never reach the observer, and things that fall in can never escape. The more massive the black hole, the larger the event horizon. So black holes grow as gas falls in

SINGULARITY

This is the centre of the black hole and is a point of infinitely small size and infinite density. All the original mass of the star that formed the black hole, and all the other matter it has sucked in, is still there, but it is crushed out of normal existence

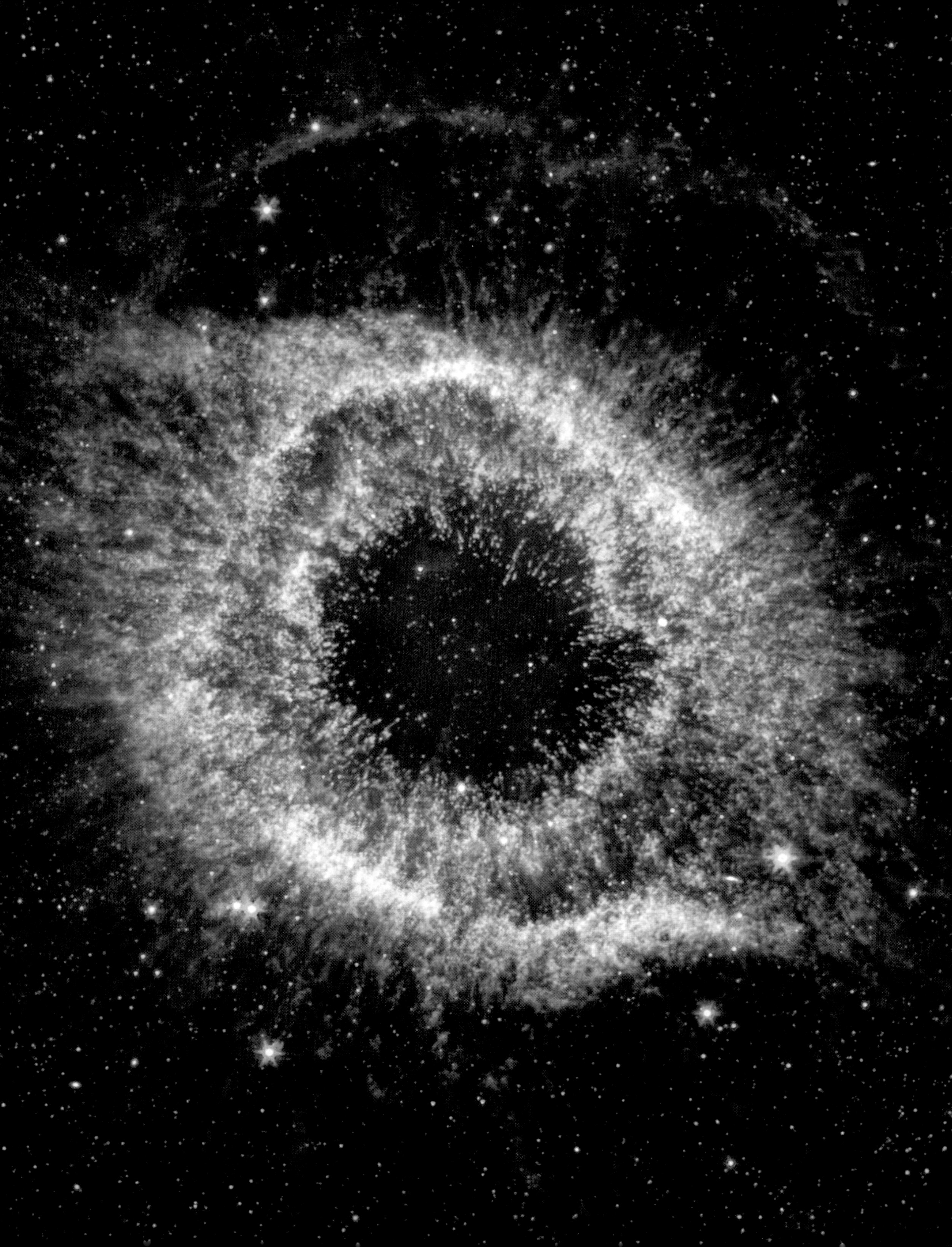

CHAPTER 4

DESTINY

THE PASSAGE OF TIME

This is the story of something so fundamental that it's impossible to imagine a universe without it, yet it is a property of the Universe that modern science still struggles to explain. Time is something that feels very human; it regulates our days and its relentless and unavoidable passing drives our lives forward. It is why each one of us has a beginning and an end. But time isn't a human creation; we evolve with its passing, but so does the rest of the Universe. Time is woven into the very fabric of the cosmos. Even with our incomplete understanding, our exploration of time has allowed us to do something remarkable: just by investigating the nature of time and the natural world as we find it here on Earth, we've been able to not only glimpse the beginning of the Universe, but to imagine how it might end.

BELOW: The towers of the ruined temple of the ancient hilltop fortress at Chankillo are a remarkable sight, standing tall through the sand-laden skies of the Peruvian desert.

OVERLEAF: The Thirteen Towers of the temple at Chankillo are believed to serve a dual purpose: they are also an ancient calendar. The towers are carefully placed to use sunrise to mark the passing of the days.

On the arid coastal plain of northwestern Peru lies one of South America's greatest astronomical secrets. Few people know about the hilltop fortress at Chankillo, and even fewer visit it, but for archaeologist and astronomer alike it is both evocative and fascinating. Two and a half thousand years ago, a civilisation we know almost nothing about built a city in this inhospitable place. The grandest of the structures was a fortified temple with walls of brilliant white covered with red-painted figures. Commanding a sweeping view across the desert, the temple would have dominated the sand-laden skies, however, today all but the smallest fragments of the decorations are gone, dulled by passing centuries. The building's location has puzzled archaeologists for many years because, while it is commanding, the hilltop site is not the best defensive position in the area, and it is unimaginable that the residents of Chankillo made a mistake when siting their fortress. Recent research has suggested that the key to understanding this place may lie not on the hilltop, but on the desert plain below.

Away from the ruined fortress and aligned north to south along the ridge of a nearby hill are thirteen towers. Recent excavations have uncovered further buildings to the east and west of the towers which archaeologists now believe to be intimately connected to this reptilian structure's true purpose. To see why, you must stand at the western observation point at the end of a night, facing the brightening eastern horizon through the towers. I have seen many sunrises, but nothing as dramatic and evocative as a Chankillo dawn. The edge of the solar disc, reddened and distorted by air heavy with sand, suddenly flares between two of the towers on the hill, and for the briefest of moments the Sun emerges as a single sparkling diamond in the desert sky. Within seconds, the normally imperceptible rotation of our planet drags the star into full view, and you must avert your gaze as if to avoid staring into the face of a god.

The Thirteen Towers of Chankillo are more than a temple, however. It is thought that they are an ancient calendar, diligent timekeepers that have measured the passing of the days for thousands of years, outliving their creators by millennia. There is no clockwork here, no pendulums or cogs to keep the timepiece ticking; instead, time is measured using the most reliable pulse that the ancients had at their disposal – the Sun. In a beautiful piece of grand astronomical engineering, the thirteen towers are placed to mark the passing of time using the position of the sunrise on the eastern

The Thirteen Towers of Chankillo ... stand testament to our ancestor's instinct and desire to quantify and understand the ticking of the cosmic clock.

horizon. On 21 December, which in the Southern Hemisphere is the summer solstice – the longest day – the Sun rises just to the right of the most southerly tower, marking the beginning of a journey that will take it across the horizon as Earth orbits the Sun. As the year passes, the sunrise moves along the towers until, on 21 June – the shortest day – it rises just to the left of the northerly tower. So at any time of year, watching the sunrise at Chankillo would have allowed its inhabitants to determine the date within an accuracy of two or three days. I stood at the western observing point on 15 September, aware that the Sun has risen between the fifth and the sixth towers on this morning for the past two thousand years. Chankillo still works as a calendar because the Sun still rises and sets in very nearly the same places on the horizon today as it did when these stones were first set down.

Even though I understand the true nature of the Sun, when confronted with such a magnificent sunrise in such a dramatic and quiet place, I understand why these people would have almost certainly deified it. The high status of this place is clear, in that the scale of Chankillo is far grander than is necessary simply for a calendar. It is part-clock, part-temple, part-observatory; a place where on sacred days the people of Chankillo would have been able to greet the appearance of their god, the rising Sun, in the most spectacular of settings.

Today, the Thirteen Towers of Chankillo continue to tell the time, having long outlived their creators; they stand testament to our ancestors' instinct and desire to quantify and understand the ticking of the cosmic clock ◉

THE COSMIC CLOCK

Each day we awake to the rhythm of our planet as it spins at over 1,500 kilometres (932 miles) an hour, relentlessly rolling us in and out of the Sun's glare. Earth's ceaseless motion beats out the tempo of our lives with unerring repetition. A day is the twenty-four hours it takes Earth to rotate once on its axis; the 86,400 seconds it takes for anyone standing on the Equator to be whipped around the 40,074-kilometre (24,901-mile) circumference of our planet. This is the most obvious rhythm of the Earth, which comes about because of the spin rate of our rocky, iron-cored ball that was laid down somewhere in Earth's formation and 4.5-billion-year history.

Travelling at 108,000 kilometres (67,108 miles) an hour, we move through space in orbit around our star. Racing around the Sun at an average distance of 150 million kilometres (93 million miles), we complete one lap of our 970-million-kilometre (600-million-mile) journey in 365 days, five hours, 48 minutes and 46 seconds, returning regularly to an arbitrarily defined starting point. As we sweep through this place in space relative to the Sun, we mark the beginning and end of what we call a year.

Everywhere we look in the heavens we see celestial clocks marking the passage of time in rhythms. Our moon rotates around Earth every 27 days, seven hours and 43 minutes, and because it is tidally locked to Earth it also takes almost exactly the same amount of time to rotate on its own axis: 27 Earth days. This means that the Moon always presents the same face to Earth. Further out in the Solar System, a Martian day is very similar to our own, lasting one Earth day and an additional 37 minutes. But because Mars is further from the Sun, a Martian year lasts longer, with the red planet taking 687 Earth days

BELOW: Here on Earth our calendar is determined by the clockwork rhythm and movement of our planet as it rotates on its axis, working its way through space and along its annual orbit around the Sun.

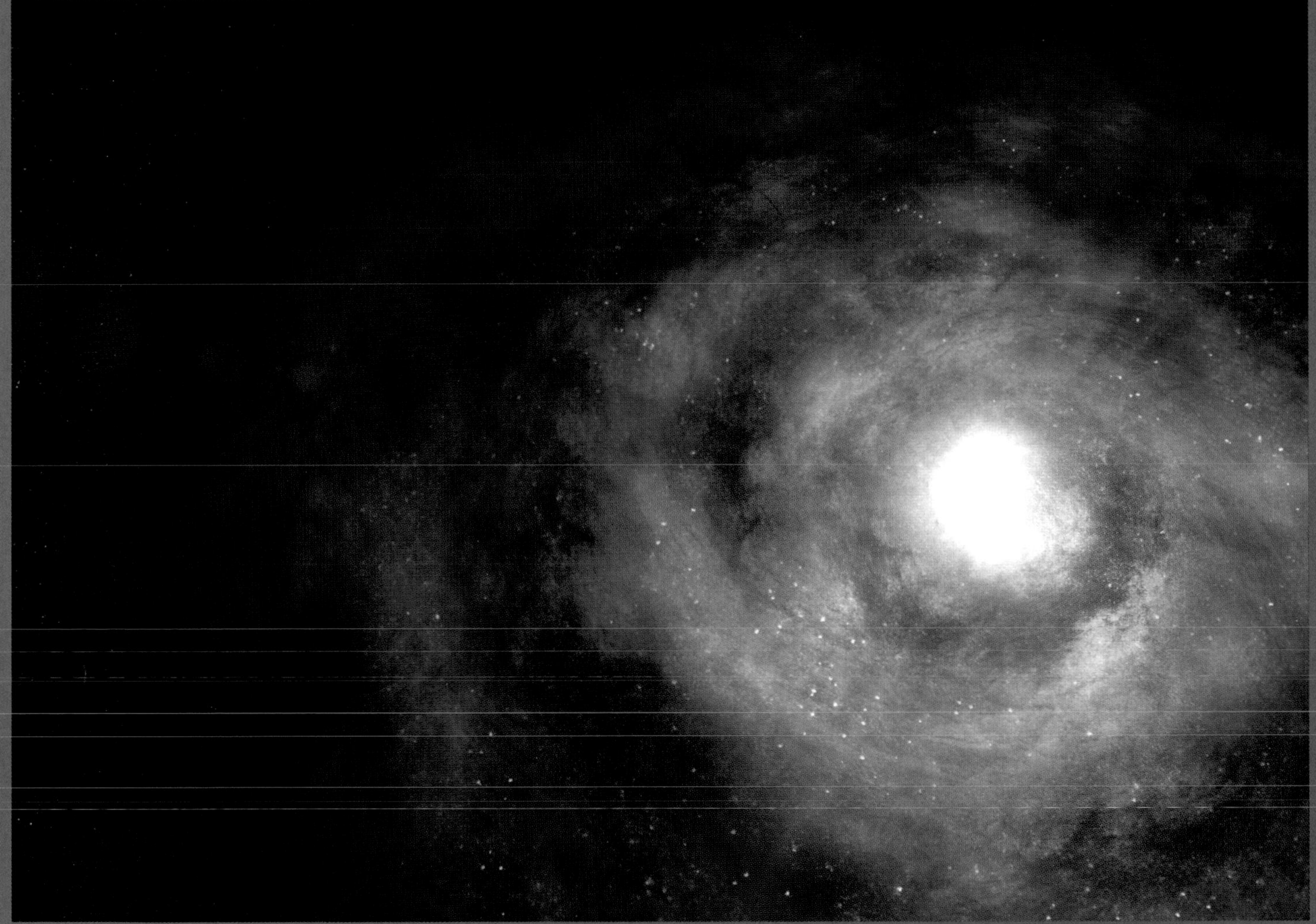

to complete an orbit. In the farthest reaches of the Solar System, the length of a year gets progressively greater, with distant Neptune taking over 60,000 Earth days or 165 Earth years to make its way around its parent star. In September 2011, Neptune will have completed its first full orbit of the Sun since it was discovered in 1846.

As we look deep into space, the clockwork of the cosmos continues unabated, but as the distances extend, the cycles become grander, repeating on truly humbling timescales. Just as Earth and other planets mark out the passing of the years as they orbit the Sun, so our entire solar system traces out its own vast orbit. We are just one star system amongst at least 200 billion in our galaxy, and all these star systems are making their own individual journeys around the galactic centre. We are all in orbit around the super-massive black hole that lies at the heart of the Milky Way. It is estimated that it takes us about 225 million years, travelling at 792,000 kilometres (492, 125 miles) per hour to complete one circuit, a period of time known as a galactic year. Since Earth was formed four and a half billion years ago, our planet has made 20 trips around the galaxy, so Earth is 20 galactic years old. Since humans appeared on Earth a quarter of a million years ago, less than one-thousandth of a galactic year has slipped by. In Earth terms, that is the length of a summer's afternoon.

This is an immense amount of time; difficult to comprehend when we speak of the entire history of our species as the blink of a galactic eye. We live our lives in minutes, days, months and years, and to extend our feel for history across a galactic year is almost impossible. Yet here on Earth there are creatures that have existed for lengths of time that span these grandest of rhythms ◉

THE GALACTIC CLOCK

Nothing stays still in the Universe, our galactic clock is forever ticking, moving everything on to a new chapter in the story of the Universe, marking out the days, weeks, months and years in each and every planet in our galaxy. Everywhere in the heavens, time moves on using its own rhythms; as you journey to the farthest reaches of the Solar System the length of a year gets progressively greater and the cycles become grander. Every solar system among the 200 billion that exist in our galaxy makes its own unique journey around the galactic centre, as we all orbit the supermassive black hole that lies at the heart of the Milky Way Galaxy.

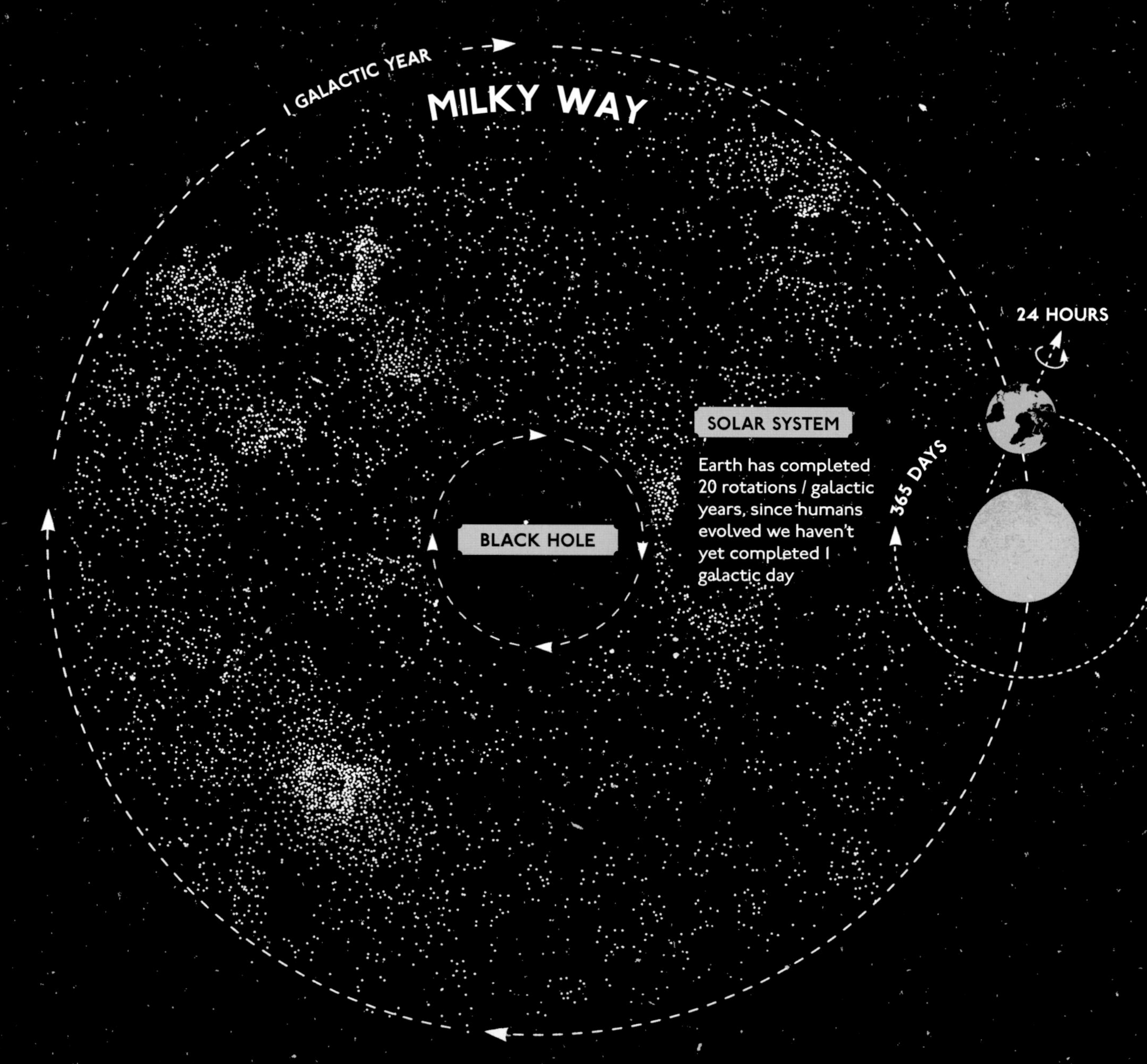

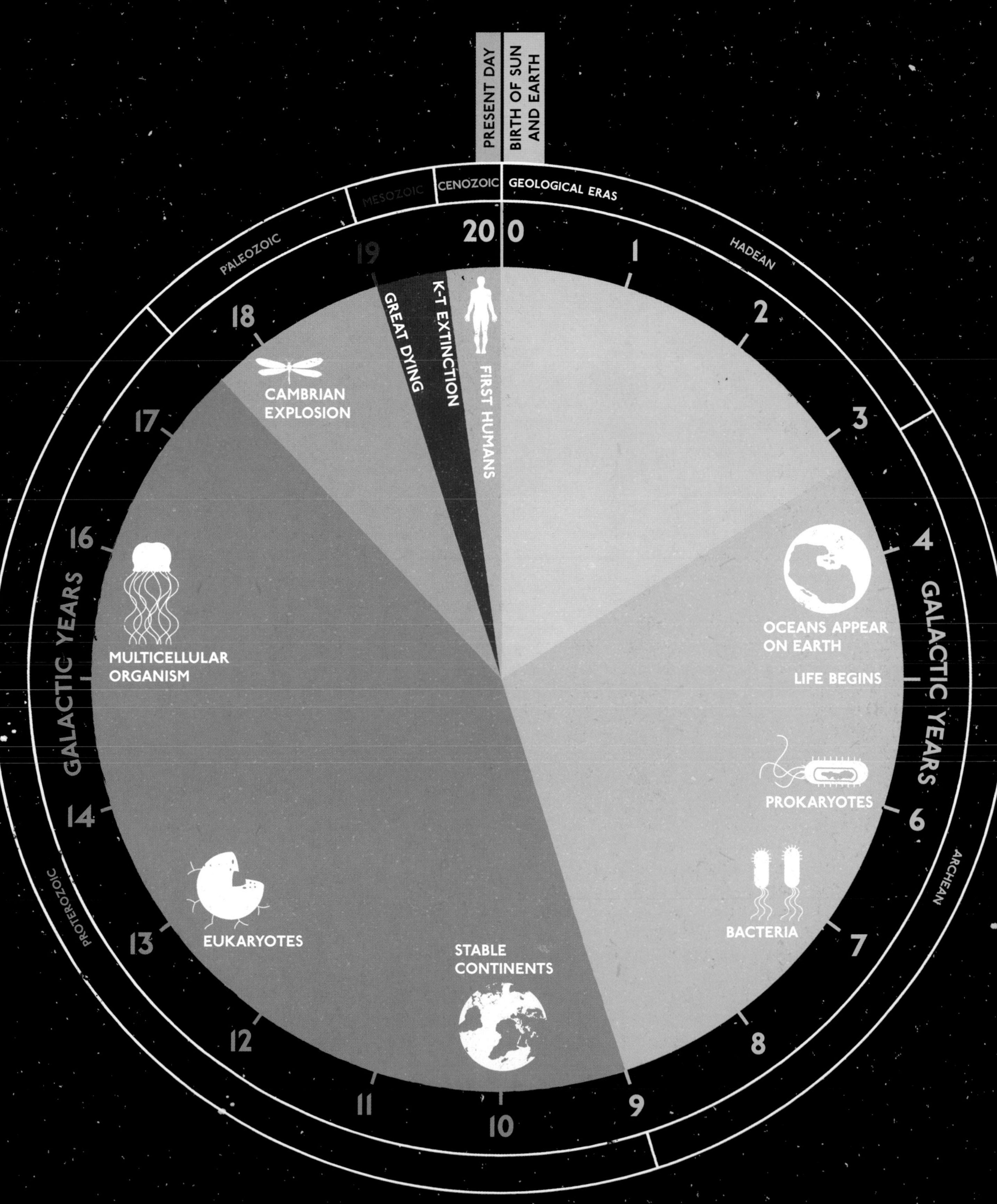

PRESENT DAY
BIRTH OF SUN AND EARTH
GEOLOGICAL ERAS
CENOZOIC
MESOZOIC
PALEOZOIC
PROTEROZOIC
ARCHEAN
HADEAN
GALACTIC YEARS
GALACTIC YEARS
0
1
2
3
4
6
7
8
9
10
11
12
13
14
16
17
18
19
20
FIRST HUMANS
K-T EXTINCTION
GREAT DYING
CAMBRIAN EXPLOSION
MULTICELLULAR ORGANISM
EUKARYOTES
STABLE CONTINENTS
BACTERIA
PROKARYOTES
LIFE BEGINS
OCEANS APPEAR ON EARTH

BELOW: Pregnant sea turtles return to the sands on the Pacific coast year after year in one of the oldest life cycles on Earth.

RIGHT: Galileo first investigated the physics of a swinging pendulum and how it could be used effectively for keeping time.

The Ostional wildlife refuge on the Pacific coast of Costa Rica is home to one of nature's most spectacular sights. On many nights of the year, a small number of tropical beaches along this thin land bridge between North and South America are visited by prehistoric creatures. They emerge from the ocean to lay their eggs in the sand. We filmed on Playa Ostional, a tiny strip of sand which is adjacent to a friendly village clustered around a makeshift football pitch. It is one of the few beaches in the world where large numbers of sea turtles make their nests, and the events that occur here form part of one of the oldest life cycles on Earth.

We are here to film the turtles hauling themselves from the ocean as they have done year on year without interruption for over 120 million years – half a galactic year. As we wait for them with our night-vision camera equipment, it is hard not to reflect on the sheer size of the mismatch in the histories of these ancient creatures and the species that built the football pitch by the sea. We humans know our planet well. We know there is a landmass called Europe, separated from Africa by a thin strip of ocean. We know that if you journey east from northern Europe you cross the vast expanses of Siberia and arrive eventually in Japan. Carry on, and you'll cross the Pacific Ocean and meet the Californian coast in the United States. The shape of our countries and continents is familiar and seemingly eternal, but the ancestors of the turtles I can see bobbing offshore were waiting for the right moment to crawl out onto the land when the shape of our continents was very different; they were waiting one hundred million years ago in the same ocean, but in those days the beaches marked out shorelines of continents that would be totally unrecognisable to our eyes. As the turtles patiently waited for their moment to give birth in the sand, the continents of Earth were slowly on the move. North America was close to Europe, South America was connected to Africa and Australia was joined with the Antarctic. It is moving to see the care with which these ancient creatures dig deep into the sand to protect their precious eggs, but equally powerful to reflect on the temporal mismatch between us and them. Collectively, they have witnessed the reshaping of our planet and the heavens above; the patterns of the stars must look very different from the other side of the Galaxy. I watch as one after another of these beautiful creatures covers its eggs and silently return to the ocean.

MEASURING TIME

Humans have long been measuring time, and we've developed our skills from the bluntest of temporal measurements to the extreme accuracy with which we can measure time today. The first attempts in chronometry may have begun thirty thousand years ago, when Stone Age humans used the lunar cycle to mark time. To early humans, the Moon would have marked out the clearest rhythm in the night sky, and by following it through its phases they were able to create the first calendars. Giving structure to the year beyond the day–night cycle allowed them to name periods of time, and so our classification and division of the cycles of the cosmos began.

Beyond the naming of the morning, afternoon and evening, the fine division of the day required the invention of one of our most enduring pieces of technology, the influence of which has been incalculable.

The first clocks were simple pieces of technology employed throughout the ancient world. Using nothing more complicated than a stick known as a 'gnomon' to cast a shadow, many civilisations were able to use sundials to track the passing of time during the day by measuring the movement of the shadow across a calibrated surface. Sundials are surprisingly accurate, but they have limited use as timekeepers, not least because they are difficult to use on a cloudy day and impossible to use at night!

Ancient Egypt was the first civilisation we know of that took measuring time beyond the sundial. The technique of using the flow of water to measure time may date as far back as 6000 BC, but the oldest physical evidence of a water clock can be found in the reign of Pharaoh Amenhotep III in 1400 BC. These elegant devices were simply stone vessels that allowed water to escape at a near-constant rate from a hole in the base. Inside the clock were twelve markings by which time could be measured as the water level dropped. These primitive clocks gave accurate measurements both night and day so that priests could perform their rituals at the appointed hour.

Water clocks continued to be refined and used by cultures across the globe for many centuries, and hourglasses employing the flow of sand to measure time were also used extensively. The Portuguese explorer Ferdinand Magellan used 18 hourglasses as a navigation tool on his ship when he circumnavigated the globe in 1522.

Time keeping was elevated to a completely new level of accuracy with the invention of pendulum clocks. Galileo was the first scientist to investigate the physics of a swinging pendulum. The key property of the pendulum, which makes it useful as a timekeeping device, is that the period of the swing – the familiar tick-tock of the clock – depends only on the length of the pendulum and Earth's gravitational pull. Perhaps counterintuitively, the period doesn't depend on how high you lift the pendulum to start the swing, as long as it's not too high. Physics students have the formula for the time period of a pendulum permanently etched in their minds. It is:

Christiaan Huygens invented the first pendulum clock in 1656, and it remained the most accurate way of telling the time until the 1930s.

$$T \approx 2\pi\sqrt{\frac{L}{g}}$$

where T is the period, L is the length and g is the acceleration due to gravity – in other words, a measure of the strength of Earth's gravitational field, which is almost the same wherever you are on Earth; approximately 9.81 metres (300 feet) per second squared. This means that all you need to do to make a clock that ticks accurately is get the length of the pendulum right. Most grandfather clocks have a pendulum that swings with a period of two seconds, which a little simple mathematics will tell you requires a pendulum approximately one metre long. The Dutch astronomer Christiaan Huygens invented the first pendulum clock in 1656, and it remained the most accurate way of telling the time until the 1930s.

Today we rely on atomic clocks to measure time with extraordinary accuracy. Atomic clocks use the frequency of light emitted when electrons jump around in atoms (usually caesium) as the 'pendulum'. This is highly accurate because the structure of atoms is unchanging, and therefore the light emitted from them always has the same frequency. This light can be used, with some clever engineering, to keep an oscillator ticking at a precise rate, allowing atomic clocks to tell the time with an accuracy of one-thousand-millionth of a second per day. The second itself has been defined since 1967 using the theory behind atomic clocks; one second is defined as the duration of 9,192,631,770 periods of the radiation corresponding to the transition between the two hyperfine levels of the ground state of the caesium 133 atom. In English, this means a second is the time it takes for 9,192,631,770 peaks in a wave of light, emitted when an electron makes a specific jump in an atom of caesium, to fly past you.

Atomic clocks allow us to measure incredibly small periods of time. Until now, the shortest period we have been able to measure is 12 attoseconds, or 12 quadrillionths of a second. This is how long it takes light to travel past 36 hydrogen atoms lined up together. That's not far at all ◉

For all the accuracy and precision we have achieved in keeping time, we have never managed to do anything more than observe it. From the very earliest solar calendars to the electrons jumping around in caesium atoms, one thing about the nature of time is clear: we can measure its passing, but we cannot control it. It moves inexorably forward; it cannot be stopped. This tells us something profound about our universe.

RIGHT: The Perito Moreno glacier in Patagonia, Southern Argentina, is a stark but beautiful place where the passage of time moves progressively forward but so slowly that it almost goes unnoticed.

Few places on our planet are as spectacular as the Perito Moreno glacier in Patagonia, southern Argentina. This dense blue wall of frozen water in the Los Glaciares National Park is part of a system of hundreds of glaciers that sweep down the continent from the southern Patagonian ice fields. Together they form the third-largest icecap on our planet. The Perito Moreno glacier alone covers an area of 250 square kilometres (96 square miles) and in places it is 170 metres (560 feet) deep. The ice ends where solid meets liquid at Lake Argentino; a great wall of ice towers over the surface of the lake, and the few who make it to this bleak but utterly beautiful place have the chance to sail along its edge across one of the most dramatic expanses of water in the world.

At first sight the glacier appears static and unmoving; standing on the lake shore, this seems like a place where the passage of time goes as unnoticed as the laws of physics will allow. Yet there is a reason why boats don't venture too close to the edge of the ice cliff. As we approached I didn't only see the passage of time; I felt it. This glacier is in constant motion; relentlessly carving its way down from the Andes as it has done for tens of thousands of years. At the glacier's edge, the wall of ice is 70 metres (230 feet) high, and the whole face of the glacier is sliding into the lake at around 50 centimetres (20 inches) per day. That means that well over a quarter of a billion tonnes of ice cascades into the lake every year. You don't often see it, but you can hear it; every now and then there is a tremendous cracking sound, followed by a deep rumbling. The surface of the lake comes alive as a turbulent wave powers beneath your boat. The pace of change in this place is anything but glacial. It is so vast and complex that you perceive it to be alive; an unpredictable, overwhelmingly powerful organism clawing the land in vain as it inevitably slides into the waters.

This is all part of a highly ordered sequence. As time passes, snow falls, ice forms, the glacier gradually inches down the valley, and when the ice meets the water, pieces break off and fall into the lake creating waves. In many ways

We expect to see ice fall from the glacier, splash into the water and create waves. If it happened in any other way we'd immediately know there was something wrong.

LEFT AND BELOW: A great wall of ice towers over the surface of Lake Argentino, where this vast, seemingly immovable glacier is slowly and relentlessly sliding down into the icy waters below.

this ordering of events into a sequence is the simplest way to think about time. The fact that sequences of events always happen in order is a fundamental part of our experience of the world. We expect to see ice fall from the glacier, splash into the water and create waves. If it happened in any other way we'd immediately know there was something wrong. Yet there is a legitimate question here about what we mean by events happening 'in order'. However long we might stand on the edge of this beautiful lake we would never expect to see this dramatic sequence of events happen in reverse, even though there is nothing in the laws of nature that prevents this happening. There is no physical reason why all the water molecules moving around in the lake shouldn't gather together on the surface, reduce their collective temperature such that they bind together to form ice, jump out of the water and glue themselves onto the surface of the glacier. We do, however, have a scientific explanation for why such a dramatic reversal never happens; we call it the 'arrow of time'.

This phrase was first used by the British physicist Sir Arthur Eddington in the early twentieth century to describe this deceptively simple and yet profound quality of our universe: it always seems to run in a particular direction. Eddington was instrumental in bringing Einstein's theory of relativity to the English-speaking world during the First World War, and also one of the first scientists to directly confirm the findings of relativity when he led an expedition to observe the total solar eclipse on 29 May 1919. In 1928 he published *The Nature of the Physical World,* in which he introduced two great ideas that have endured in popular scientific culture to this day. The first was the image of the infinite monkey theorem, which states that given an infinite amount of time, anything consistent with the laws of physics will happen: 'If an army of monkeys were strumming on typewriters, they might write all the books in the British Museum'. This is related in a deep way to the arrow of time, which Eddington described as follows:

'Let us draw an arrow arbitrarily. If as we follow the arrow we find more and more of the random element in the state of the world, then the arrow is pointing towards the future; if the random element decreases the arrow points towards the past. That is the only distinction known to physics. This follows at once if our fundamental contention is admitted that the introduction of randomness is the only thing that cannot be undone. I shall use the phase "time's arrow" to express this one-way property of time which has no analogue in space.'

Eddington's arrow vividly and economically expresses a key property of time; it only goes in one direction. But what does he mean by randomness? It seems obvious that the Universe is constantly evolving, but what drives this evolution? How should we quantify how random something is? Why is the past different from the future? Why is there an arrow of time? Time is something we all understand, and yet a plausible scientific reason as to why time marches inexorably forward wasn't offered until the late nineteenth century, coming about as the solution to a practical problem on Earth ◉

THE ORDER OF DISORDER

BELOW: In a series of simple experiments, Joule demonstrated that mechanical work could be converted into heat. Using a paddle wheel turned by falling weights, he stirred water in an insulated barrel and observed how the temperature of the water rose by the amount that depended on how far the weights fell.

In 1712 the English inventor Sir Thomas Newcomen created the first commercially successful steam engine, paving the way for the Industrial Revolution. This accolade is more usually awarded to the Scottish inventor James Watt. In 1763 Watt was asked to repair a Newcomen engine by the University of Glasgow, and in doing so he developed a new steam engine which, it is appropriate to say without hyperbole, transformed the landscape of modern life. Watt's steam engine was more efficient and more flexible than its predecessor; it used far less coal than the Newcomen for a given power output, and was therefore much cheaper to run. More importantly still, Watt's engine could do more than pump water out of the wet mines, it could also generate the rotary motion that was needed to power the machines on the factory floor. No longer did a factory have to be situated by a river to turn its equipment; with the help of Watt's engine a factory could be sited anywhere, catalysing the emergence of the modern industrial landscape. Steam-powered machines changed the course of history, and yet despite their importance, the nineteenth-century engineers who followed Watt struggled to improve them. There seemed to be fundamental principles that restricted their efficiency, but with profit margins to maximise, even a small increase in their effectiveness would be highly valuable. So understanding how hot the fire should be or what substance should be boiled in the engine were problems that were not only interesting from a scientific perspective but were also critical for businesses. It was out of these questions of engineering design that the science of thermodynamics arose, and with it the concepts of heat, temperature and energy entered the scientific vocabulary in a precise way for the first time.

One of the scientists working on these problems was the German mathematician Rudolf Clausius. Clausius was interested in heat, which until the first half of the nineteenth century was thought to be a fluid that flowed from hot things to cold things. Clausius and others realised that this description was not able to explain the cycle of a steam engine. The foundation for Clausius's theoretical advances was laid by one of his contemporaries, the English physicist and brewer James Joule, who was working to improve the efficiency of the steam engines in his brewery. What finer motivation for the advance of fundamental physics? The quest for cheaper beer motivated him to investigate the relationship between the work his steam engines could do, and heat. In doing so he managed to reduce the costs of beer production and lay one of the cornerstones of the science of thermodynamics.

Using a series of beautifully simple experiments, Joule was able to demonstrate that mechanical work could be converted into heat. One such experiment used a falling weight to spin a paddle within an insulated barrel of water. Joule knew how much work was done by the falling weight and so could measure the temperature rise of the water. He conducted similar experiments on compressed gases and flowing water, and each time he found that it took the same amount of work to raise the temperature of a fixed amount of water by one degree Fahrenheit. Inscribed on his tombstone in Brooklands cemetery near Manchester is the number 772.55 – his measurement of the amount of work done in foot-pounds force that is required to raise the temperature of one pound of water by one degree Fahrenheit.

The reason that Joule's work was important is that it demonstrated that heat is not a thing that can be created or destroyed. It doesn't literally flow between things or move around, it is in fact a measure of something else. Even today, this is perhaps not obvious because we still speak of the flow of heat from hot to cold things. Heat, we now understand, is simply a form of energy. Just as a ball resting on a table has energy which can be released by dropping it (known as gravitational potential energy), so a

$$C\Delta T = Mgh$$

- M is the mass of the falling weight
- g is the acceleration due to gravity
- h is the distance through which the weight falls
- C is 'the specific heat capacity of water' (the amount of heat required to heat one kilogramme of water by 1°)
- ΔT is the actual rise in temperature caused by the stirring

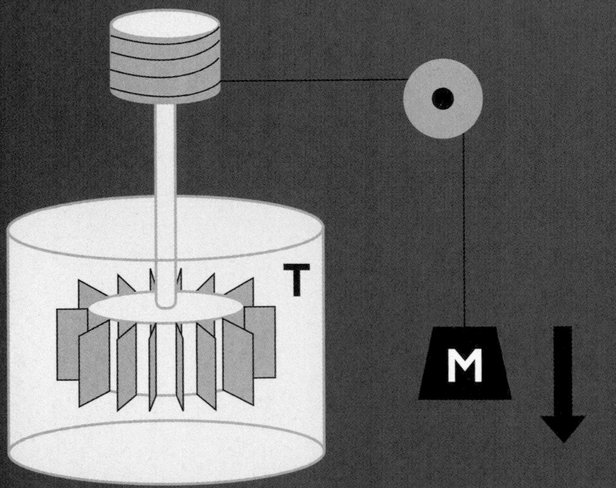

BELOW: Newcomen's engine, created in 1712, was the first commercially successful steam engine and laid the foundations for the work of other inventors, such as James Watt, which would power forward the Industrial Revolution in Britain. The Newcomen atmospheric engine was used to pump water out of coal mines, using a pivoted arm (top) to transfer power between the piston and the rod. The piston was driven down by the pressure of a partial vacuum in the cylinder, which drew the rod upwards. As steam in the cylinder condensed, the piston was forced up, and the rod down.

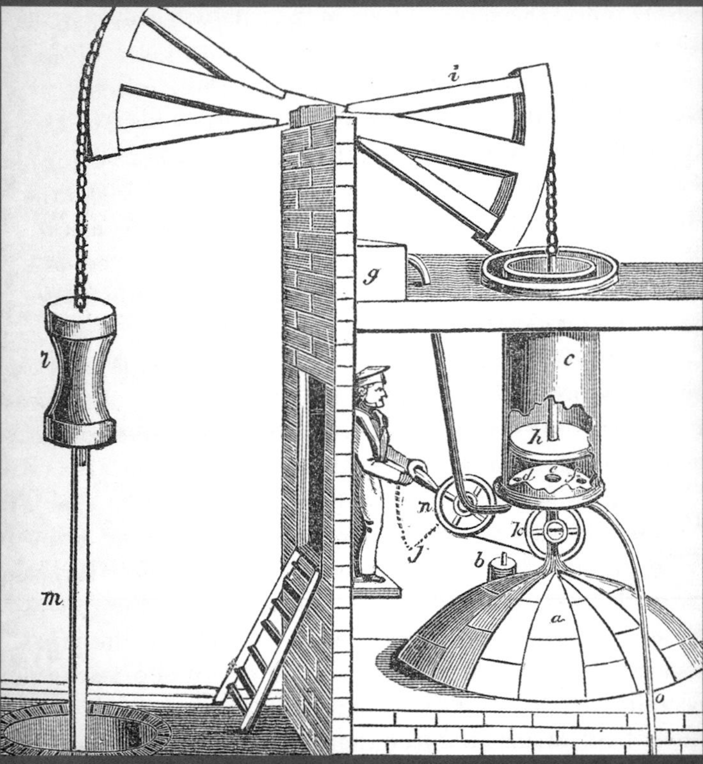

hot thing has energy that can be released, at least in part, by putting it next to a cold thing. To heat something up, you simply have to transfer energy to it by doing work on it, as Joule found by using a falling weight, and it doesn't matter how that work is done. It can be a falling weight, a shining light or an electric current, but as long as you do the same amount of work, the temperature increase will be the same. This was all quantified, as a result of Joule's work, into the First Law of Thermodynamics, which is a statement of the fact that energy cannot be created or destroyed; it can only be changed from one form into another. Rudolf Clausius made the first explicit statement of the law, and laid down the foundations of the science of thermodynamics, in his landmark 1850 publication 'On the mechanical theory of heat'.

The first law can be written down mathematically as

$$\Delta U = Q - W$$

which in words says that the increase in the internal energy of something (ΔU) is equal to the heat flow into it (Q) minus the work performed by it (W). If you performed work on it, the W would have a plus sign, and if you took heat out of it, the Q would have a minus sign.

Fifteen years after writing down the first law of thermodynamics, and far more importantly for our understanding of the arrow of time, Clausius introduced a new concept known as entropy, which lies at the heart of the Second Law of Thermodynamics. Clausius's statement of the second law does not at first sight sound as if it has profound implications for the future of our universe. He simply stated that 'No process is possible whose sole result is the transfer of heat from a body of lower temperature to a body of higher temperature'. This simple proposition occupies such a profound position in modern science that Arthur Eddington said of the second law:

'If someone points out to you that your pet theory of the Universe is in disagreement with Maxwell's equations, then so much the worse for Maxwell's equations. If it is found to be contradicted by observation, well, these experimentalists do bungle things sometimes. But if your theory is found to be against the Second Law of Thermodynamics I can give you no hope; there is nothing for it but to collapse in deepest humiliation.'

The concept of entropy enters when the second law is written down in quantitative form. The change in entropy of a system, such as a tank of water, is simply the amount of heat added to it at a fixed temperature. In symbols,

$$\Delta S = \frac{\Delta Q}{T}$$

where ΔS is the change in the entropy as a result of adding a small amount of heat, ΔQ, at a fixed temperature T. It may still be unclear what this has to do with the Universe, but here is the profound point discovered by Clausius. In any physical process at all, you find that entropy either stays the same or increases. It *never* decreases. Here is the thermodynamic arrow of time. Clausius had discovered a physical quantity that can be measured and quantified which only ever increases in practice, and never decreases even in theory, no matter how cleverly you design your experiment or piece of machinery. This is extremely useful information if you are designing a steam engine, because it puts a fundamental limit on the efficiency. It also prevents the construction of the so-called 'perpetual motion machines' so beloved of crackpot inventors to this day. You could say that the second law tells you that you can't get something for nothing, but the second law is more profound than this, because it introduces a difference between the past and the future. In the future, entropy will be higher than it is in the present because it always increases. In the past, entropy was lower than it is now because it always increases.

Clausius introduced the concept of entropy because he found it useful, but what exactly is entropy, and what is the deep reason that it always increases? And what was the meaning of Eddington's cryptic quote about randomness and the arrow of time? He seemed to be equating entropy with the amount of randomness in the world, and indeed he was. Understanding this will make it clear why the Second Law of Thermodynamics mandates that our entire universe must, one day, die ●

ENTROPY IN ACTION

In 1908 in the small town of Kolmanskop in southern Namibia, a railway worker by the name of Zacharias Lewala found a single diamond lying in the sand. He showed the precious stone to his manager – railway inspector August Stauch – who immediately realised its significance and set in motion a train of events that turned this desolate place into one of the most valuable diamond mines in the world. The colonial German government closed the entire area to outsiders; only German entrepreneurs were allowed to make their fortunes here. For 40 years, Kolmanskop was home to a thriving community as over a thousand people gathered, seeking to become millionaires by picking diamonds out of the desert. As the money rolled in, the residents built a town in the finest German tradition; grand houses stood beside a casino, a ballroom and the first X-ray station in the Southern Hemisphere. They led a champagne lifestyle in the desert, and created a little piece of opulent German architecture in the sand. Eventually, though, as with all cash cows, the diamonds could no longer be found and the town gradually lost its sparkle until it was abandoned in 1954. For half a century it has fallen into disrepair as the buildings are slowly reclaimed by the sands.

Today Kolmanskop is a ghost town, a place where our efforts to replace the geological grandeur of the desert with architectural grandeur of our own have been thwarted by the power of the winds.

Kolmanskop lies just outside the modern port town of Lüderitz, which sits in spectacular isolation on the southern Namibian coast. One of our guides told us that it takes a special kind of Namibian to set up home in Lüderitz – you have to really want to live there. The reason this place has a reputation for being particularly harsh, even by the standards of this part of the world, is the wind. This strip of the southern African

BELOW: The opulent buildings of the once-glorious town of Kolmanskop are a shadow of their former selves as the desert sands blow across them and reclaim the landscape.

coast is permanently assaulted by the untamed winds of the South Atlantic that whip up the fine-grained sands of the Namib Desert and hurl them unrelentingly into machinery, houses, camera equipment and eyes. I have never experienced anything like it. While filming, I found myself walking through the wind at Kolmanskop with my hands completely shielding my face. I didn't do this for dramatic effect, I genuinely couldn't look into the lacerating sand-laden wind. We also shot a scene showing a little sandcastle gradually blowing away; the camera we left in the desert for hours to film that had its lens sandblasted – the high-precision optics felt like sandpaper after a single spring afternoon in the vicinity of Lüderitz. If it wasn't for the fact that it never rains here, and nothing rots, the ghost town of Kolmanskop would surely already have disappeared back into the desert.

The little sandcastle slowly decaying in the desert wind vividly demonstrates the connection between decay, randomness and entropy. To understand why this is so, we'll need a different and much more intuitive definition of entropy than that given by Clausius. Known as the statistical definition of entropy, it was developed by Ludwig Boltzmann in the 1870s.

A sandcastle is made of lots of little grains of sand, arranged into a distinctive shape – a castle. Let's say there are a million sand grains in our little castle. We could take those million grains and, instead of carefully ordering them into a castle, we could just drop them onto the ground. They would then form a pile of sand. We would be surprised, to say the least, if we dropped our sand grains onto the floor and they assembled themselves into a castle, but why does this not happen? What is the difference between a pile of sand and a sandcastle? They both have the same number of sand grains, and both shapes are obviously possible arrangements of the grains. Boltzmann's definition of entropy is essentially a mathematical description of the difference between a sandcastle and a sand pile. It says that the entropy of something is the number of ways in which you can rearrange its constituent parts and not notice that you've done so. For a sandcastle, the number of ways in which you can arrange the grains and still keep the highly-ordered shape of the castle is quite low, so it therefore has low entropy. For a sand pile, on the other hand, pretty much anything you do to it will still result in there being a pile of sand in the desert, indistinguishable from any other pile of sand. The sand pile therefore has a higher entropy than the sandcastle, simply because there are many more ways of arranging the grains of sand such that they form a pile of sand than arranging them into a castle. Boltzmann wrote this down in a simple equation, which is written on his gravestone:

$$S = k_B \ln W$$

S is the entropy, W is the number of ways in which you can arrange the component bits of something such that it is not changed, and k_B is a number known as Boltzmann's constant. For the more mathematically adventurous, ln stands for 'natural logarithm'. If you don't know what that means, don't worry; the equation simply relates to the number of ways in which you can arrange things to the entropy.

As long as each particular arrangement of the sand grains is equally likely, then if you start moving sand grains around at random they are overwhelmingly more likely to form a shapeless pile of sand than a sandcastle.

That may seem a bit complicated, and not entirely illuminating yet, but here is the key point: as long as each particular arrangement of the sand grains is equally likely, then if you start moving sand grains around at random they are overwhelmingly more likely to form a shapeless pile of sand than a sandcastle. This is because most of the arrangements you create at random look like a formless pile, and very few look like a sandcastle.

This is common sense, of course, but now think about what this looks like at a microscopic level – the level of individual sand grains. There is nothing at all in the laws of nature to stop the wind blowing a grain of sand off one of the turrets of our castle and then picking up another grain from the desert and blowing it back onto the turret again, leaving our castle perfectly unchanged. Nothing at all, that is, other than pure chance. It is much more likely that the grains of sand blown off the castle are not replaced with others from the desert, and so our castle gradually disintegrates, which is to say it gradually changes into a formless sand pile. In Boltzmann's language, this is simply the statement that the entropy of the castle will increase over time; the castle will become more and more like a sand pile. Why? Because there are many more ways of arranging the grains of sand into a pile than there are into a castle, so if you just randomly blow grains around they will tend to form piles more often than castles. Here is the deep reason that entropy always increases: it's simply more likely that it will! Notice that there is nothing in the laws of nature that prevent it from decreasing; it's possible that the wind will build a sandcastle, but the chances are akin to tossing a coin billions of times and each one coming up heads. It's simply not going to happen.

LEFT AND BELOW: Watching my carefully constructed sandcastle gradually disintegrate in the strong desert winds perfectly demonstrates how entropy increases, and the idea that the past is always more ordered than the future.

DISORDER IS MORE PROBABLE THAN ORDER

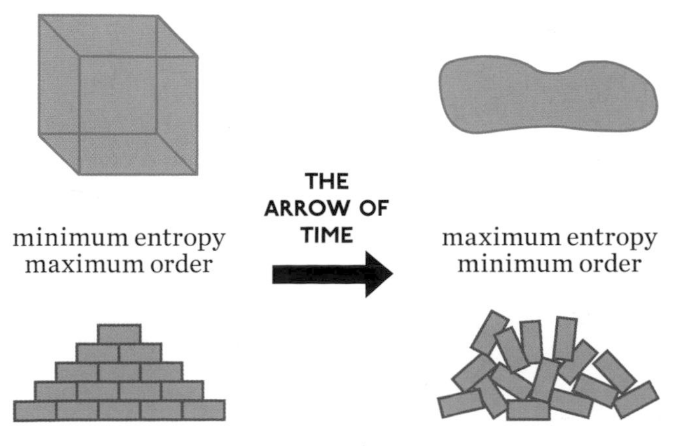

Boltzmann's statistical definition of entropy is the key to understanding Eddington's arrow of time. This is such a key concept with such profound consequences that it is worth repeating it once more in a slightly different way. If there are a million different ways of arranging a handful of sand grains, with 999,999 of the ways producing disordered sand piles but only 1 producing a beautifully ordered castle, then if you keep throwing the sand grains up in the air they will usually land in the form of a disordered pile. So, over time, if there is a force like the wind that acts to rearrange things, things will get more messy or disordered simply because there are more ways of being disordered than ordered. This means that there is a difference between the past and the future: the past was more ordered and the future will be less ordered, because this is the most likely way for things to play out. This is what Eddington meant by his statement that the future is more random than the past, and his description of the arrow of time as the thing that points in the direction of increasing randomness. And this is why entropy always increases.

For the purposes of our story, this is sufficient; if you take a university physics degree, this is what you will learn about entropy and the arrow of time. But there is still a great deal of debate and research surrounding entropy, and it centres on something we have dodged slightly. We have only spoken about entropy differences; the past had a lower entropy than the future; ordered things become disordered as time ticks by, but one might legitimately ask where all the order in the Universe came from in the first place. In the case of our sandcastle, it's obvious – I made it – but how did I get here? I'm very ordered. How did Earth get here? It's very ordered too. And how did the Milky Way appear if it is composed of billions of ordered worlds orbiting around billions of ordered stars? There must have been some reason why the Universe began in such a highly ordered state, such that it can gradually fall to bits. The answer is that we don't know why the Universe began with sufficient order in the bank to allow planets, stars and galaxies to appear. We understand how gravity can create local order in the form of solar systems and stars, but this must be at the expense of creating more disorder somewhere else. So there must have been a lot of order to begin with. In other words, the Universe was born in a highly ordered state, and there should be a reason for that. It is unlikely to have been chance, because by definition a highly ordered state is less likely to pop into existence than a less ordered one; a sandcastle is less likely to be formed by the desert winds than a pile of sand. Since the Universe is far less ordered today than it was 13.75 billion years ago, this means it is far more likely that our universe popped into existence a billionth of a second ago, fully formed with planets, stars, galaxies and people, than it is that the Universe popped into existence at the Big Bang in a highly ordered state. There is clearly something fascinating about the entropy of the early Universe that we have yet to understand ●

The arrow of time has been playing out dramatically in Kolmanskop since the mining facility was abandoned in 1954. In every building you can see the gradual transition from order to disorder; every room that was once full of structure is slowly being returned to a less-ordered state. This is the march of the arrow of time on Earth, but it is nothing compared to the grand journey that time's arrow forces our universe to make.

LEFT: The sands of time are slowly and literally overrunning Kolmanskop, dismantling the highly crafted town and returning it to dust once more.

THE LIFE CYCLE OF THE UNIVERSE

Our Universe follows the law of any living thing: it develops in stages from birth through life and ultimately to death. We understand the early stages of its life because observations by scientists have provided valuable information as to how the Universe was created, and also fill in the crucial facts about the history of the Universe thus far. We are living in an early phase of our universe, the Stelliferous Era, with many more stages of life and change still to come, and yet we can confidently make predictions about our Universe's future. By observing the life cycles of the stars above us we can map out the remaining years of our universe's life.

Electron

Quark

Hydrogen Atom

Brown Dwarf

White Dwarf

Black Hole

Photon

Electron

1. PRIMORDIAL

$0 - 10^5$

Big Bang, inflation, and nucleosynthesis take place. Towards end of this era the Universe becomes transparent for the first time

2. STELLIFEROUS

$10^6 - 10^{14}$

Our current era. Matter is arranged in stars, galaxies, and galaxy clusters

3. DEGENERATE

$10^{15} - 10^{35}$

Galaxies no longer exist. This is the era of brown dwarfs, white dwarfs, and black holes. The Sun becomes a black dwarf. White dwarfs will assimilate dark matter and continue with minimal energy output

4. BLACK HOLE ERA

$10^{40} - 10^{100}$

Organized matter will remain only in the form of black holes. Black holes slowly 'evaporate' away the matter contained in them. By the end of this era, only extremely low-energy photons, electrons, positrons, and neutrinos will remain

ULTIMATE FATE OF THE UNIVERSE: THE THEORIES

Positron

5. DARK ERA

$10^{101} - \infty$

The Universe will be nearly empty. Photons, neutrinos, electrons, and positrons will fly from place to place. Electrons and positrons will occasionally form positronium atoms. These structures are unstable, however, and their constituent element will eventually annihilate each other

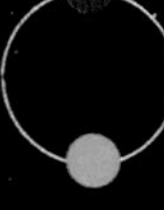

Neutrino

6. HEAT DEATH

Considered to be the most likely fate of the Universe. It will occur if the Universe continues expanding as it has been. The continued expansion will result in a universe that approaches absolute zero temperature

6. BIG BOUNCE

This is a cyclical repetition interpretation of the Big Bang whereby the first cosmological event was the result of the collapse of a previous universe

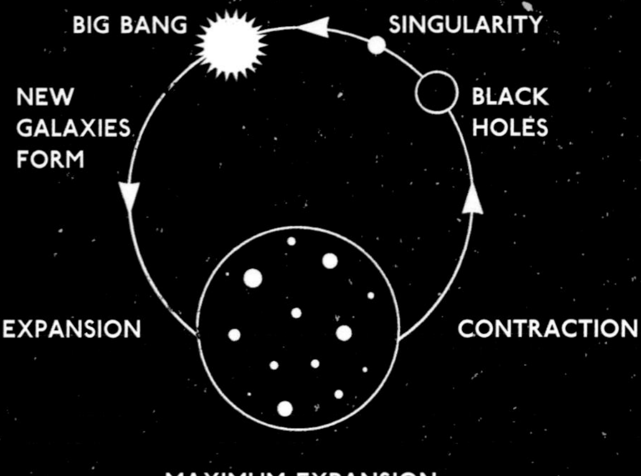

6. BIG CRUNCH

The expansion of space will reverse and the Universe will re-collapse, ultimately ending as a black hole singularity

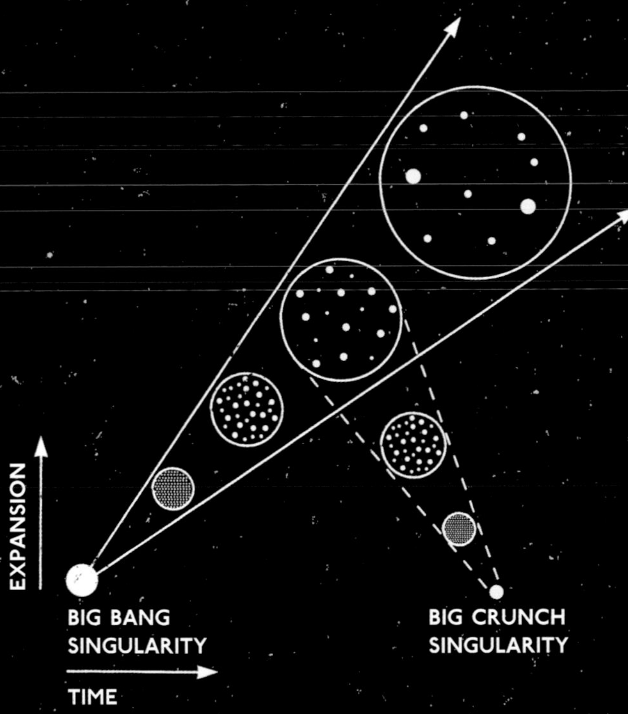

6. MULTIVERSE

Our universe is merely one Big Bang among an infinite number of simultaneously expanding Big Bangs that are spread out over endless distances

THE LIFE OF THE UNIVERSE

BELOW: The Sun is one of at least two hundred billion stars in our galaxy, and it, along with countless others, shine brightly over Earth, night and day, in an ever-changing, ever-evolving cosmos.

RIGHT: In our age of stars, the Milky Way Galaxy is filled with stars igniting and scattering their light across the night sky.

Just as human beings, planets and stars are born, live their lives and die, so the Universe also lives its life in distinct stages. It began 13.75 billion years ago with the Big Bang, and in this embryonic period, known as the Primordial Era, the Universe was a place without the light from the stars, although in its early years the swirling hot matter would have glowed as brightly as a sun. For the first 100 million years, the conditions were far too violent for stars to form. This changed when the Universe had expanded and cooled sufficiently for the weak force of gravity to begin to clump the primordial dust, gas and dark matter into galaxies. With this came the dawning of the second great epoch in the life of our universe: the Stelliferous Era, the age of stars.

The moment the first stars were born is one of the most evocative milestones in the evolution of the cosmos. It signals the end of an alien time when the Universe was without structure – a formless void. The beginning of the Stelliferous Era marks the beginning of the age of light, the moment when the Universe would have become recognisable to us. The sky would have become black, punctuated with the glowing mist of the galaxies and the sharp silver of the stars. This is our universe today – a place where starlight decorates our nights and illuminates our days.

Our sun is one of at least two hundred billion stars in our galaxy; one of a hundred billion galaxies in the observable universe. We live in a cosmos of countless islands of countless stars which bathe the Universe in light. Yet despite the fact that the Universe is over 13 billion years old, we are still just at the beginning. Although the cosmos is awash with stars, is populated with vast nebulae and systems of planets and countless billions of worlds that we've yet to explore, we are living close to the beginning of the Stelliferous Era, an era of astonishing beauty and complexity. But the cosmos isn't static and unchanging; it won't always be this way because as the arrow of time plays out, it produces a cosmos that is as dynamic as it is beautiful.

The moment the first stars were born is one of the most evocative milestones in the evolution of the cosmos ... it marks the beginning of the age of light, the moment when the Universe would have become recognisable to us.

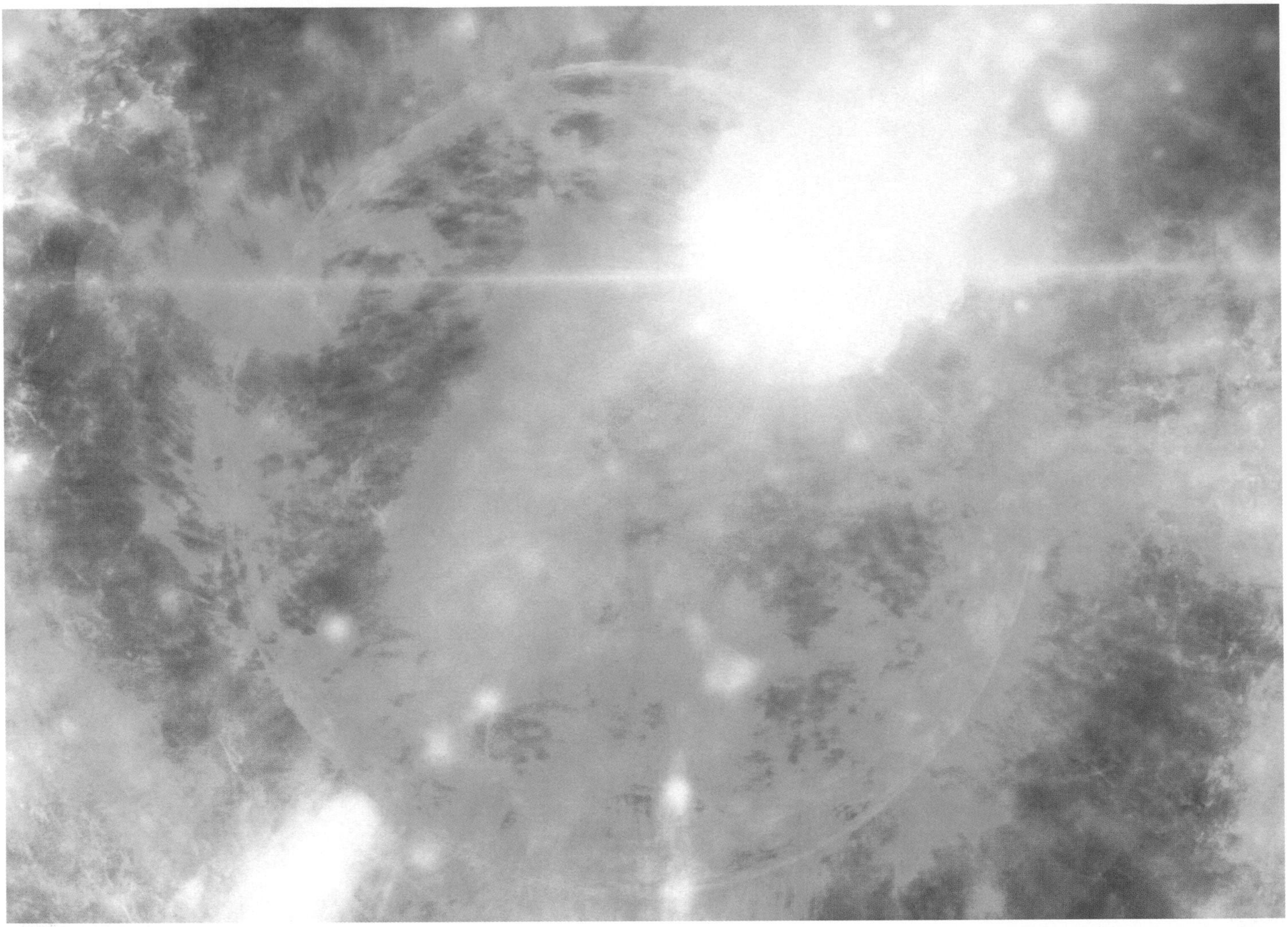

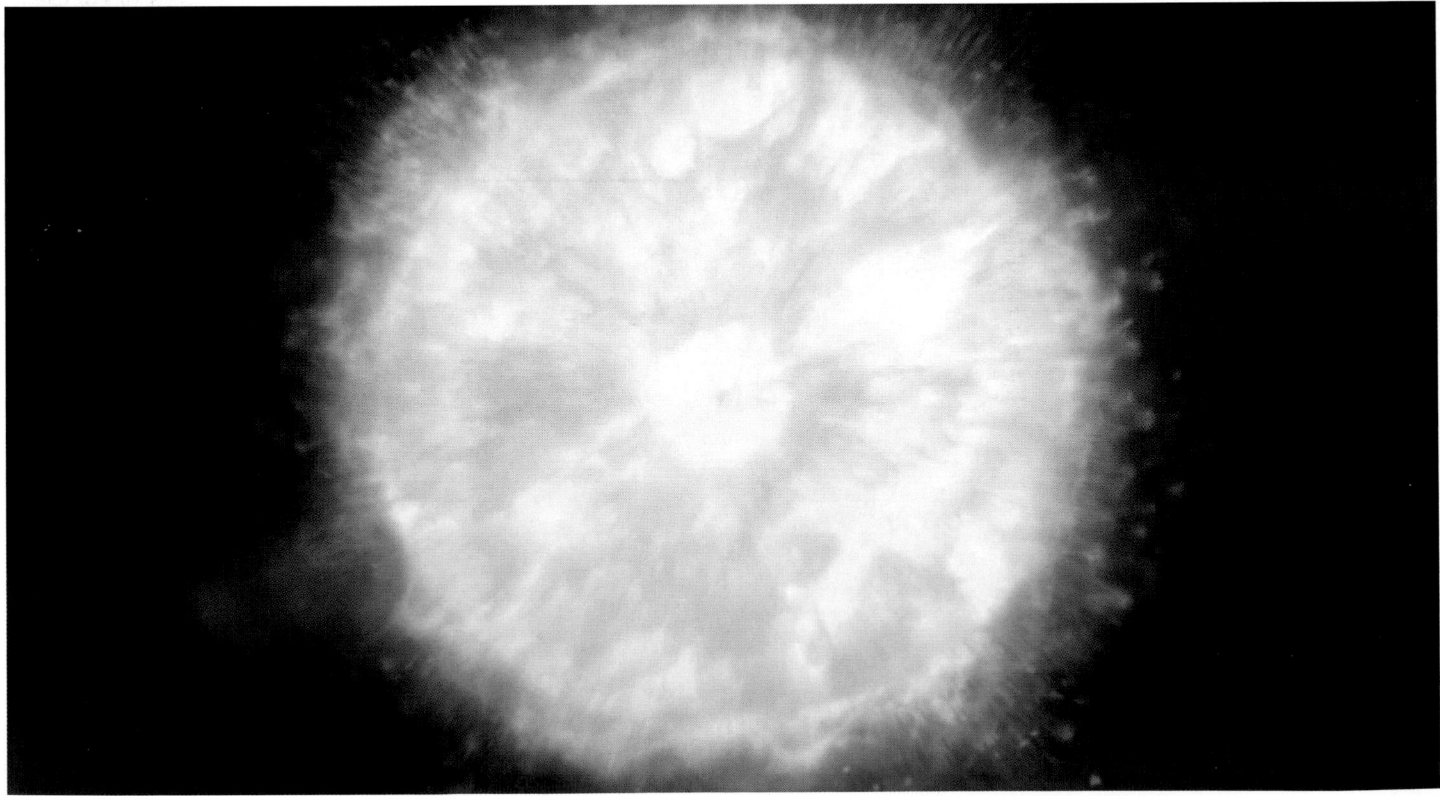

LEFT: A gamma-ray burst is one of the Universe's most spectacular and luminous explosions. As the core of a dying star collapses into a black hole, gas jets blast out from it into space.

BELOW: This dramatic image shows the gamma-ray burst from GRB 090423, combining data from the Ultraviolet/Optical (blue, green) and X-ray (orange, red) telescopes of NASA's Swift satellite.

When these stars run out of nuclear fuel ... they die in a dramatic fashion, collapsing in an instant and releasing more energy in one second than our sun will produce in its entire 10-billion-year lifetime.

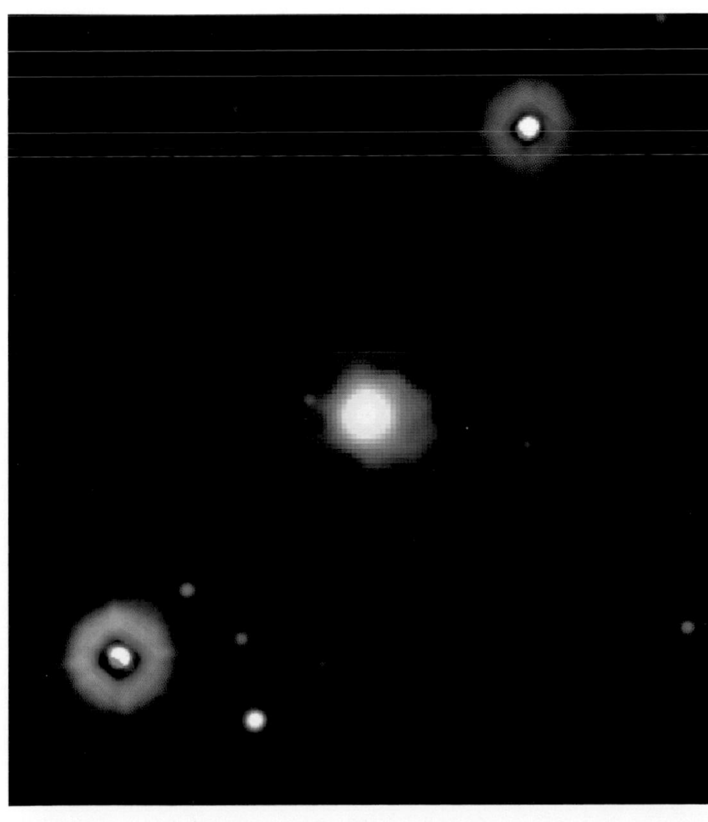

THE FIRST STAR

On 23 April 2009 at 07.55 GMT, NASA's Swift detected one of the most distant cosmic explosions ever seen – a gamma-ray burst that lasted ten seconds. The Swift satellite was designed and built with the intention that it would aid the study of a rare type of event known as a gamma-ray burst. These events, which last only a few seconds, are the most energetic and powerful emitters of radiation in the known universe. It is thought that gamma-ray bursts occur in supernova explosions – as the dying act of the most massive stars as they collapse to form black holes. By 08.16 GMT, minutes after the burst had faded away, the UK's Infrared Telescope (UKIRT) in Hawaii saw the glowing ember of the explosion. As the day wore on, the largest telescopes across the world focused on the event as it appeared above their horizon. The afterglow was observed for several hours, but by 28 April the event had faded completely from view.

The picture shown here merges data from two of Swift's telescopes, and the important feature of this composite image is the rather unremarkable-looking red blob at the centre. This blob is the fading remains of GRB 090423 – once one of the brightest stars in the Universe. The poetically named GRB 090423 was once a Wolf-Rayet star. Named after the two French astronomers who discovered the first one in 1867, Wolf-Rayet stars are massive – over twenty times the mass of our sun – and because they are so massive, and burn so brightly, they are also extremely short-lived. When these stars run out of nuclear fuel after only a few hundred thousand years, they die in a dramatic fashion, collapsing in an instant and releasing more energy in one second than our sun will produce in its entire 10-billion-year lifetime.

GRB 090423 was a big Wolf-Rayet star – perhaps 40 or 50 times the mass of the Sun – however, this is not the only thing that is interesting about it. It's not just the story of the death of this star, revealed by the brief appearance of the pale red dot, that has captivated astronomers, it's the age of it. The light from this dot has travelled a very long way across the Universe to reach us, and has taken a very long time to do it. When we look at the afterglow of this explosion, we are looking at an event that happened a long time ago, in a galaxy far, far away. In fact, this light has been travelling towards us for almost the entire history of the Universe. GRB 090423 died over thirteen billion years ago, just over 600 million years after the Universe began. This is incredibly early in the Universe's history. At the time of filming *Wonders of the Universe*, in autumn 2010, GRB 090423 was the oldest single object ever seen, although just after filming a galaxy was discovered in the Hubble Space Telescope's Ultra Deep Field Image (see pages 54–55) that is slightly older than GRB 090423. Even more poetically named UDFy-38135539, this galaxy currently holds the distance and age record with a light travel time of slightly over 13 billion years. Allowing for the expansion of the Universe, the (so-called co-moving) distance of UDFy-38135539 is currently 30 billion light years away from Earth.

However, it is the discovery of GRB 090423, this ghostly pale red dot, and the sight of the explosive death of one of the first stars in the Universe, that gives us a glimpse of the grandest timescale of them all ◉

THE DESTINY OF STARS

The arrow of time has been playing out in every corner of the Universe since the beginning of time. It dictates the destiny of everything; our civilisation, our planet, the Solar System, and all that lies beyond. The entropic march is inevitable and relentless. Nothing can resist the arrow of time, nothing can last forever, no star can shine without end and no planet can continue to turn. The Universe, bound by the laws of nature, must decay towards a radically different tomorrow.

BELOW: We take for granted the sight of the Sun rising and setting on our horizon, but we now know its presence is not eternal.

BOTTOM: The computer-generated image shows how dramatically different the Sun will look in our heavens as it dies and dims.

Today, 13.7 billion years after the Universe began, we are living through the most productive era that our universe will ever know. The Stelliferous Era is a time of life and death, with the constant dance between gravity and nuclear fusion creating a dynamic, ever-changing landscape in the heavens. For a human being, for whom a century is a lifetime, the changes may appear slow, but be in no doubt that you are part of the Universe at its most vibrant. As we've watched the stories of stars like GRB 090423 play themselves out in the night sky, we have seen at first hand that no star can last forever. Every one of those brightly burning lights has a destiny as defined and as certain as our own, and this of course includes the star at the centre of our solar system.

The Sun was formed 4.57 billion years ago from a collapsing cloud of hydrogen and helium and a sprinkling of heavier elements. For the tiniest fraction of this time, humans have marked the passing of the days as it rose and set, and surely considered it to be an eternal presence. It was only during the twentieth century that we discovered the Sun's fires must one day dim ◉

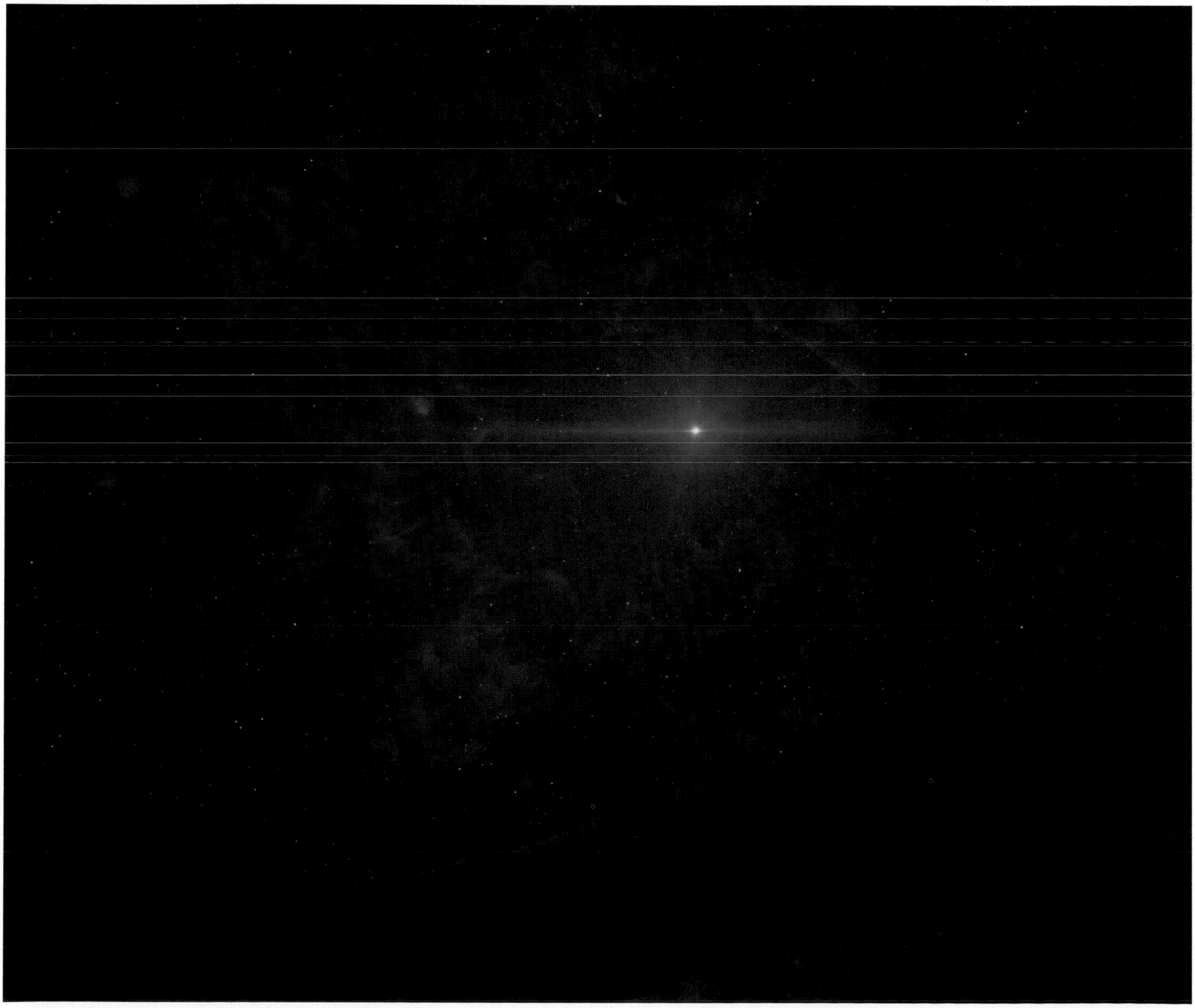

THE DEMISE OF OUR UNIVERSE

RIGHT, TOP: An artist's impression of Sirius A and its diminutive companion Sirius B in close-up. They are overlain on a real image of the night sky containing the three stars of the Summer Triangle: Vega, Deneb and Altair. As seen from Sirius, our sun would appear as a moderately bright star in this same area of sky. It is shown here just below right of Sirius A.

RIGHT, BOTTOM LEFT: This image from NASA's Hubble Space Telescope shows the Boomerang Nebula in early 2005 and the two lobes of matter that are being ejected from the star as it dies. The rapid expansion of the planetary nebula around this dying star has made it one of the coldest places found in the Universe so far.

RIGHT, BOTTOM RIGHT: A Hubble Space Telescope image of the dazzling Sirius A with the faint speck of Sirius B to its lower left. Sirius B is 10,000 times fainter than Sirius itself.

At the moment the Sun is in the middle of its life, fusing hydrogen into helium at a rate of around 600 million tonnes every second. It will continue to do this for another five billion years; but eventually, perhaps fittingly given the grandeur and beauty it has nurtured in its empire, it won't simply fade away. As the stores of hydrogen run dry, the Sun's core will collapse and momentarily, as helium begins to fuse into oxygen and carbon, a last release of energy will cause its outer layers to expand. Imperceptibly at first, the extra heat of the Sun will extend towards us as its diameter increases by around 250 times. The fiery surface of our star will move beyond Mercury, towards Venus and onwards to our fragile world.

The effects on our planet will be as catastrophic as they are certain. Gradually, the Earth will become hotter. In the distant future, if any of our descendants still remain, someone will experience the last perfect day on Earth. As the surface of the Sun encroaches, our oceans will boil away, the molecules in our atmosphere will be agitated off into space, and the memory of life on Earth will fade into someone's history; or perhaps no one's history if we have steadfastly remained at home.

Long after life has disappeared, the Sun will fill the horizon; it may extend beyond Earth itself. This swollen stage in a star's life is known as the Red Giant phase, marked by the final release of energy and the beginning of a long, long decline. In six billion years' time, in a most beautiful display of light and colour, our sun will shed its outer layers into space to form a planetary nebula. We know this because we have seen this sequence of events unfold in the final breath of distant stars – on someone else's sun? Written across the night sky in filamentary patches of colour are the echoes of our future.

If in the far future, somewhere in the Universe, astronomers on a world not yet formed gaze through a telescope at our planetary nebula and reflect on its beauty, they may glimpse at its heart a faintly glowing ember; all that remains of a star we once thought of as magnificent. She will be smaller than the size of Earth, less than a millionth of her current volume and a fraction of her brightness. Our sun will have become a white dwarf – the destiny of almost all the stars in our galaxy – a fading, dense remnant, momentarily masked by a colourful cloud.

If our planet survives, little more than a scorched and barren rock will remain, silhouetted darkly against the fading embers of a star.

Sirius, the brightest star in our sky, sits at just over eight light years away, which makes it one of our nearest neighbours. It is so bright that on occasion it can be observed during bright twilight, partly because of its proximity but also because it is twice as big as our sun and twenty-five times as bright. It is therefore not surprising that observations of Sirius have been recorded in the oldest of astronomical records.

For thousands of years we looked up at this beacon and assumed it was a single star, but in 1862 American astronomer Alvan Graham Clark observed a sister star hidden in the glare of Sirius's light. It took so long to notice Sirius's companion because, as the photograph taken by the Hubble Space Telescope (bottom right) reveals, it is so much dimmer than its sibling. Shining faintly in the lower left-hand corner, the small dot of light is an image of the white dwarf star Sirius B. This is one of the larger white dwarf stars discovered by astronomers, with a mass similar to our sun that is packed into a sphere the size of Earth. With no fuel left to burn, white dwarfs like Sirius B glow faintly with the residual heat of their extinguished furnaces. Like most white dwarfs, Sirius B is made primarily of oxygen and carbon (the remnants of helium fusion) packed tightly with a density a million times that of a younger, living star. This is the future of our star; a vision of the Sun's death. Slowly cooling in the freezing temperatures of deep space, it is estimated that our sun will reach this phase in around 6 billion years' time. From Earth, if indeed there is an Earth at that time, our sun will shine no brighter than a full moon on a clear night.

Death must come to all stars. One day every light in the night sky will fade and the cosmos will be plunged into eternal night. This is the most profound consequence of the arrow of time; this structured Universe that we inhabit alongside all its wonders – the stars, the planets and the galaxies – cannot last forever. As we move through the age of stars, through the aeons ahead, countless billions of stars will live and die. Eventually, though, there will be only one type of star that will remain to illuminate the Universe in its old age ◉

SIRIUS A
The brightest star in our night sky. Only 8.6 light years away, it is one of the closest stars to the Sun

SIRIUS B
The faint, hot companion to Sirius A, this is the closest white dwarf to us. It orbits Sirius A every 50 years

ALTAIR
Part of the Summer Triangle

THE SUN
As seen from Sirius, this is where our sun would appear to lie – near the stars of the Summer Triangle

DENEB
Part of the Summer Triangle

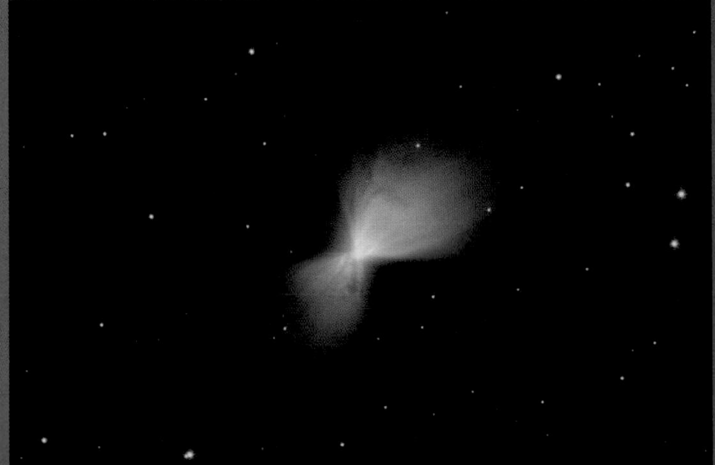

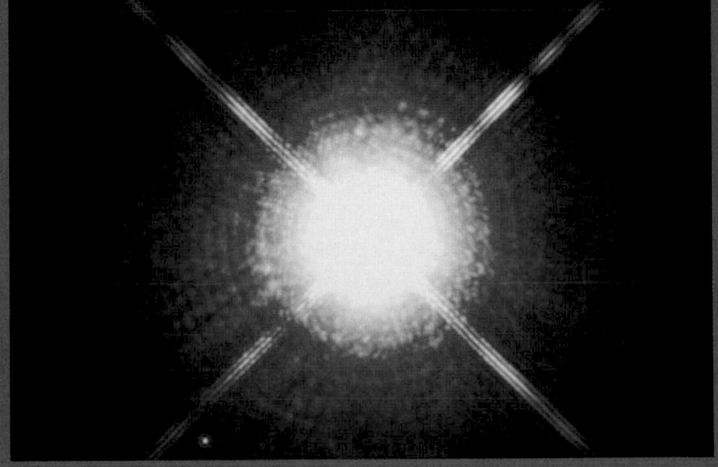

THE DEATH OF THE SUN

Although relatively young now, the Sun, like every other star in the Universe, must one day die. In around five billion years' time, the Sun's stores of hydrogen will run dry and the star will begin its long, dramatic swansong. During this lengthy goodbye, the last dying bursts of extra heat will extend towards us, passing Mercury and Venus on the way and leaving a trail of destruction in its wake. Long after life has disappeared on Earth, the Sun will continue to fill the horizon as it swells in the Red Giant phase until, in about six billion years' time, our Sun will shed its outer layers of gas and dust into space, exposing its core which will fade into a white dwarf, living on in the heavens as a shadow of its former self.

MERCURY

VENUS

EARTH

STAGE 1
MAIN SEQUENCE STAR

STAGE 2
RED GIANT

The Sun becomes a red giant as its stores of hydrogen run dry. Its core collapses and the extra heat this generates will cause its outer layers to expand

Outer layers of the Sun expand, cool and become redder. Its radius will increase around 250 times, taking it past Mercury, Venus and towards Earth

Earth will become increasingly hot until oceans boil away, the atmosphere escapes into space and it is left as a charred, lifeless cinder

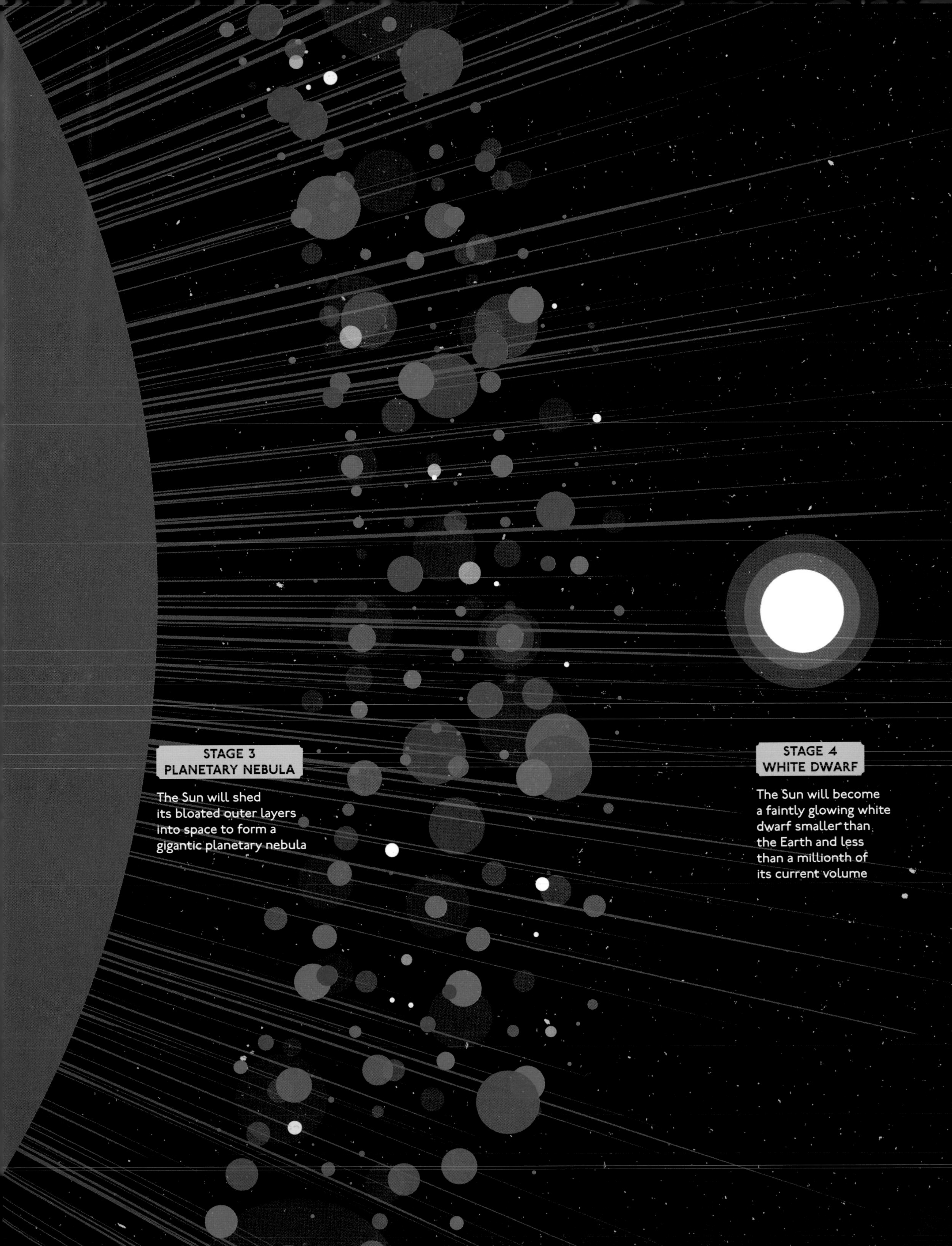
STAGE 3
PLANETARY NEBULA
The Sun will shed
its bloated outer layers
into space to form a
gigantic planetary nebula
STAGE 4
WHITE DWARF
The Sun will become
a faintly glowing white
dwarf smaller than
the Earth and less
than a millionth of
its current volume

THE LAST STARS

The nearest star to our solar system is Proxima Centauri. Although only a mere 4.2 light years away, Proxima Centauri is not visible to the naked eye from Earth and doesn't even stand out against more distant stars in many of the photographs that have been taken of it. The reason for this is that Proxima Centauri is small, very small when compared to our sun – having just 12 per cent of the Sun's mass – so to our eyes this star would appear to shine 18,000 times less brightly than our sun.

Proxima Centauri is a red dwarf star – the most common type of star in our universe. Red dwarfs are diminutive and cold, with surface temperatures in the region of 4,000K, but they do have one advantage over their more luminous and magnificent stellar brethren: because they're so small, they burn their nuclear fuel extremely slowly, and consequently they have life spans of trillions of years. This means that stars like Proxima Centauri will be the last living stars in the Universe.

If we do in fact survive into the far future of the Universe, it is possible to imagine our distant descendants building their civilisations around red dwarfs in order to capture the energy of those last fading embers of stars. Just as our ancestors crowded around campfires for warmth on cold winter nights, so some time long in the future humans may take their warmth from a red dwarf as the last available energy in the Universe.

The rate of the fusion reactions in the cores of these red dwarfs that is needed to provide the thermal pressure to resist the inward pull of their weak gravity is very low, which enables them to live longer. Even so, these are still active stars, and their surfaces are whipped up into turmoil by the turbulent convective currents that constantly churn their interiors. Amongst all this activity, explosive solar flares occur almost continually, blasting bursts of light and X-rays out into space.

Ultimately, though, the frugality of these stars is no defence against the arrow of time. Four trillion years from now, at 300 times the current age of the Universe, Proxima Centauri's fuel reserves will finally run out and the star will slowly collapse into a white dwarf. After trillions of years of stellar life and death, only white dwarfs and black holes will remain in the Universe, and then, in around 100 trillion years' time, this age of the stars will draw to a close and the cosmos will enter its next phase: The Degenerate Era. And yet, even after 100 trillion years of light, the vast majority of the Universe's history still lies ahead. Bleak, lifeless and desolate, our universe will go on, as it enters the dark ●

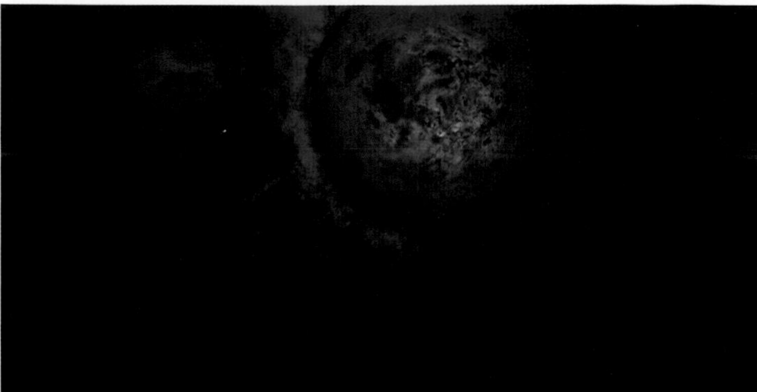

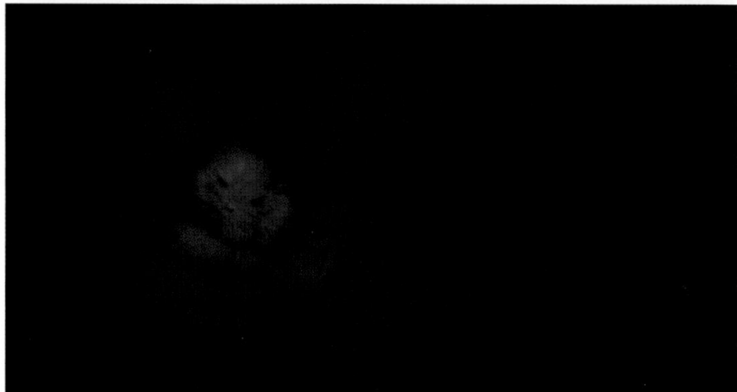

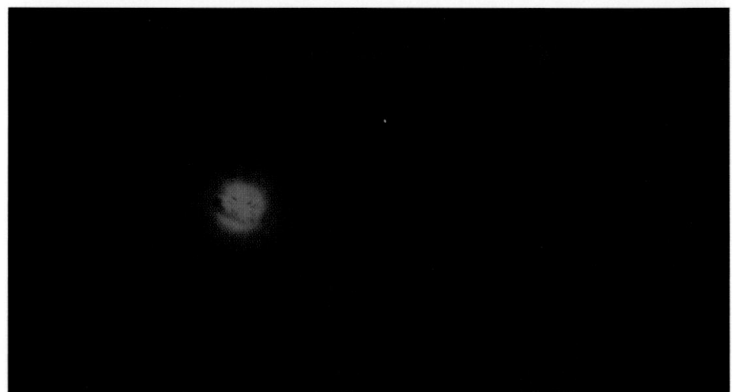

ABOVE: These computer-generated images reveal how Proxima Centauri will meet its end. Over the next four trillion years, this red dwarf will gradually collapse into a much dimmer white dwarf.

RIGHT: A white dwarf is visible amongst brighter, living stars in this enhanced image, taken by NASA's Galaxy Evolution Explorer, of Z Camelopardalis, a binary star system.

After trillions of years of stellar life and death, only white dwarfs and black holes will remain in the Universe, and then, in around 100 trillion years' time, this age of the stars will draw to a close and the cosmos will enter its next phase: The Degenerate Era.

THE BEGINNING OF THE END

On the northern coast of Namibia, where the cold waters of the South Atlantic meet the Namib Desert, lies one of the most inhospitable places on Earth. The Skeleton Coast has been feared for as long as sailors have travelled near its shores; seventeenth-century Portuguese mariners used to call this place 'the gates to hell', and the native Namib Bushmen named it 'the land God made anger in'. Today, you can just about make it to the coast in a sturdy 4x4, or effortlessly cruise in from the port city of Walvis Bay in a helicopter. But even so, when you stand on the sands beside the South Atlantic, the gods still have anger left. Each morning a dense ocean fog rolls along the coastline, fed by the upwelling of the cold Benguela current. Coupled with the constantly shifting shape of the sandbanks in the intense Atlantic winds, this toxic navigational conspiracy has meant that over the years thousands of ships have been wrecked along the Skeleton Coast. The decaying carcasses of the rusting ships and the bleached bones of marine life swept ashore by the currents all add to the coast's gothic feel. The name Skeleton Coast also reflects the large number of human lives lost here over the centuries; even if you made it ashore after a shipwreck, the onshore currents are so strong that there is no way of rowing back out to sea, and the only route to safety is through hundreds of miles of inhospitable desert. This genuinely was a place of no return: if you were shipwrecked here, this was the end of your universe.

One of the ships to end her days here was the Eduard Bohlen, a 91-metre (300-foot), 2,272-tonne steamship that ran aground here on the 5 September 1909 on a journey from Germany to West Africa. A century's shifting sands have carried her hundreds of metres inland and the Atlantic winds have attacked her carcass, leaving her rusting and skeletal. When we arrive she is guarded by a phalanx of jackals who are less wary of us than I expected. She forms an abstract

Just as the ship's iron will eventually rust and be carried away by the desert winds, so we think the last matter in the Universe will eventually be carried off into the void.

BELOW: The Skeleton Coast: one of the most inhospitable places on Earth, where humans have perished for centuries, and where only jackals and the strongest life forms remain.

backdrop to our story; the symbolism is immediate, brutal even, and for me surprisingly powerful. These wrecks, complex structures dismantled by the passage of time, are like our last stars.

In the far future of the cosmos, the last remaining beacons of light will no more be permitted to evade the second law of thermodynamics than the Eduard Bohlen. Even the white dwarfs must fade as the laws of physics methodically dismantle the Universe. Slowly, as the glowing embers of the last stars lose their warmth to space, they will cease to emit visible light. After trillions of years, the final beacons burning in the cosmic sky will turn cold and dark – their remnants are known as black dwarfs.

Black dwarfs are dark, dense, decaying balls of degenerate matter. Nothing more than the ashes of stars, they take so long to form that after almost 14 billion years, the Universe is currently too young to contain any at all. Yet despite never seeing one, our understanding of fundamental physics allows us to make concrete predictions about how they will end their days. Just as the iron that makes up the ships of the Skeleton

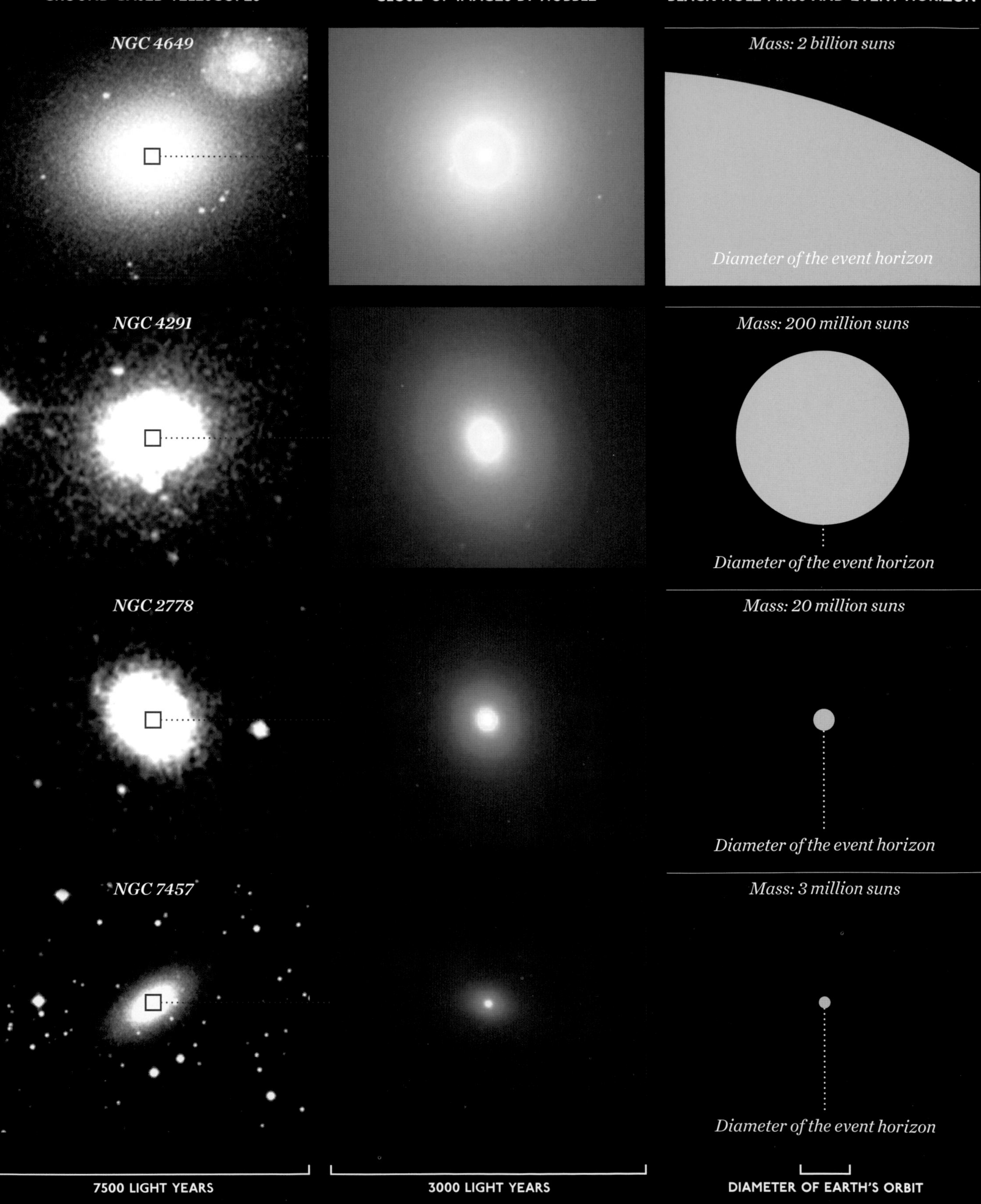
BLACK HOLE MASS SCALES WITH GALAXY SIZE
GROUND-BASED TELESCOPES
CLOSE-UP IMAGES BY HUBBLE
BLACK HOLE MASS AND EVENT HORIZON
NGC 4649
Mass: 2 billion suns
Diameter of the event horizon
NGC 4291
Mass: 200 million suns
Diameter of the event horizon
NGC 2778
Mass: 20 million suns
Diameter of the event horizon
NGC 7457
Mass: 3 million suns
Diameter of the event horizon
7500 LIGHT YEARS
3000 LIGHT YEARS
DIAMETER OF EARTH'S ORBIT

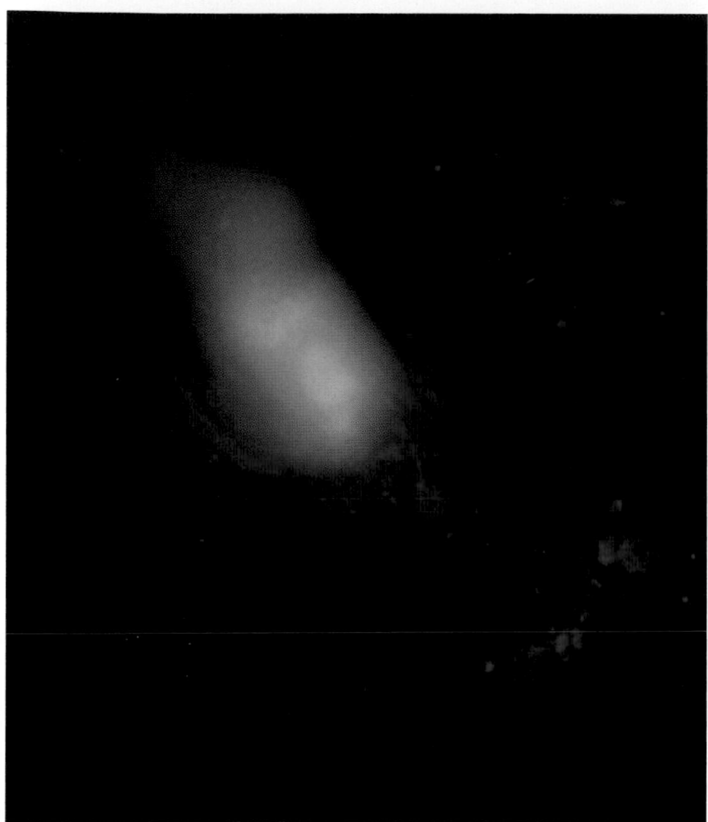

LEFT: This composite X-ray image from the Chandra X-ray Observatory shows gas blowing away from a central supermassive black hole in the active galaxy NGC 1068.

BELOW: In trillions of years, our universe will be littered with black dwarfs. From the ashes of stars, dark, dense and decaying balls of degenerate matter will form.

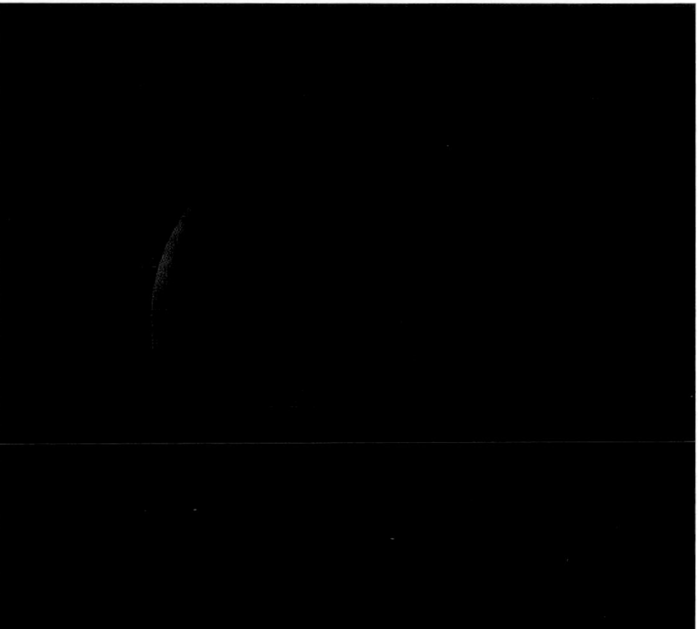

Once the last remnants of the last stars have decayed away to nothing . . . the story of our universe will finally come to an end.

Coast will eventually be carried away by the desert winds, so it is thought that the matter inside black dwarfs, the last matter in the Universe, will eventually evaporate away and be carried off into the void as radiation, leaving nothing behind. The processes by which matter might, given enough time, decay, are not understood. Physicists need a more advanced theory of the forces of nature, known as a Grand Unified Theory, to speak with certainty about the behaviour of protons, neutrons and electrons over trillion-year timescales. There are reasons to expect that such a theory may exist, and that a mechanism for even the most stable sub-atomic particles to decay into radiation might be present in nature. For this reason, experiments to measure the lifetime of protons are ongoing in laboratories around the world, but as yet nobody has observed proton decay, and we are therefore now in the realm of speculation. But here is one possible, and given our understanding of physics today, probable, story of how our universe will end.

With the black dwarfs gone, there will not be a single atom of matter left in the Universe. All that will remain of our once-rich cosmos will be particles of light and black holes. After an unimaginable expanse of time, it is thought that even the black holes will evaporate away, and the Universe will consist of a sea of light; photons all tending to the same temperature as the expansion of the Universe cools them towards absolute zero. When I say unimaginable period of time, I really mean it: ten thousand trillion trillion trillion trillion trillion trillion trillion trillion years. In scientific notation, that's 10^{100} years. That is a very big number indeed; if I were to start counting with a single atom representing one year, there wouldn't be enough atoms in all the stars and planets in all the galaxies in the entire observable universe to get anywhere near that number.

Once the last remnants of the last stars have decayed away to nothing and everything reaches the same temperature, the story of our universe will finally come to an end. For the first time in its life the Universe will be permanent and unchanging. Entropy finally stops increasing because the cosmos cannot get any more disorganised. Nothing happens, and it keeps not happening forever.

This is known as the heat death of the Universe, an era when the cosmos will remain vast, cold, desolate and unchanging for the rest of time. There's no way of measuring the passing of time, because nothing in the cosmos changes. Nothing changes because there are no temperature differences, and therefore no way of moving energy around to make anything happen. The arrow of time has simply ceased to exist. This is an inescapable fact, written into the fundamental laws of physics. The cosmos will die; every single one of the hundreds of billions of stars in the hundreds of billions of galaxies in the Universe will expire, and with them any possibility of life in the Universe will be extinguished ◉

A VERY PRECIOUS TIME

The fact that the Sun will die, incinerating Earth and obliterating all life on our planet, and that eventually the rest of the stars in the Universe will follow suit to leave a vast, formless cosmos with no possibility of supporting any life or retaining any record of the living things that brought meaning to its past, might sound a bit depressing to you. You might legitimately ask questions about the way our universe is put together. Surely you could build a universe in a different way? Surely you build a universe such that it didn't have to descend from order into chaos? Well, the answer is 'no', you couldn't, if you wanted life to exist in it.

The arrow of time, the sequence of changes that will slowly but inexorably lead the Universe to its death, is the very thing that created the conditions for life in the first place. It took time for the Universe to cool sufficiently after the Big Bang and for matter to form; it took time for gravity to clump the matter together to form galaxies, stars and planets, and it took time for the matter on our planet to form the complex patterns that we call life. Each of these steps took place in perfect accord with the Second Law of Thermodynamics; each is a step on the long road from order to disorder.

The arrow of time has created a bright window in the Universe's adolescence during which life is possible, but it's a window that won't stay open for long. As a fraction of the lifespan of the Universe, as measured from its beginning to the evaporation of the last black hole, life as we know it is only possible for one-thousandth of a billion billion billionth, billion billion billionth, billion billion billionth of a per cent.

And that's why, for me, the most astonishing wonder of the Universe isn't a star or a planet or a galaxy; it isn't a thing at all – it's a moment in time. And that time is now.

Around 3.8 billion years ago life first emerged on Earth; two hundred thousand years ago the first humans walked the plains of Africa; two and a half thousand years ago humans believed the Sun was a god and measured its orbit with stone towers built on the top of a hill. Today, our curiosity manifests itself not as sun gods but as science, and we have observatories – almost infinitely more sophisticated than the Thirteen Towers – that can gaze deep into the Universe. We have witnessed its past and now understand a significant amount about its present. Even more remarkably, using the twin disciplines of theoretical physics and mathematics, we can

ABOVE: This colour image of the Earth, named the 'Pale Blue Dot', is a part of the first-ever portrait of the Solar System taken by NASA's Voyager 1. The spacecraft took 60 frames which could be used to create a mosaic image of the Solar System from a distance of over four billion miles from Earth.

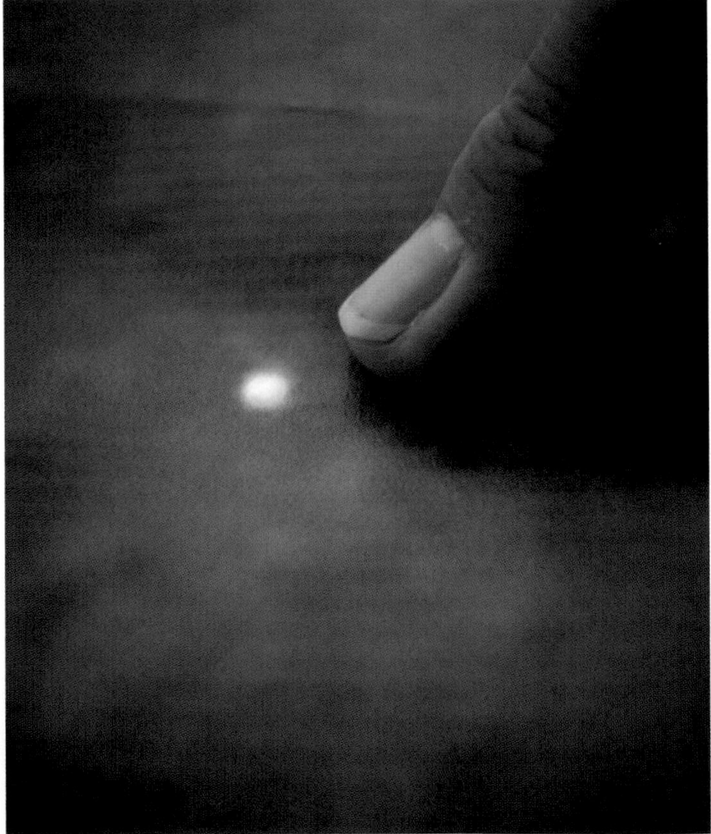

ABOVE: This seemingly insignificant image of a pale blue dot is in fact one of the most important and beautiful images ever taken, revealing our planet at a distance of over six billion kilometres away.

RIGHT: Our time on Earth is precious and fleeting. The most important use of this time that we can make is to ask questions about our wonderful universe, so that perhaps one day one of our descendants will truly understand the natural laws that govern our cosmos.

calculate what the Universe will look like in the distant future and make concrete predictions about its end.

I believe it is only by looking out to the heavens, by continuing our exploration of the cosmos and the rules that govern it, and by allowing our curiosity free reign to wander the limitless natural world, that we can understand ourselves and our true significance within this Universe of wonders.

In 1977, a space probe called Voyager 1 was launched on a 'grand tour' of the Solar System. It visited the great gas giant planets Jupiter and Saturn and made wonderful discoveries before heading off into interstellar space. Thirteen years later, after its mission was almost over, Voyager turned its cameras around and took one last picture of its home. This picture (left) is known as the Pale Blue Dot. The beautiful thing, perhaps the most beautiful thing ever photographed, is the single pixel of light at its centre; because that pixel, that point, is our planet, Earth. At a distance of over six billion kilometres (3.7 billion miles) away, this is the most distant picture of our planet that has ever been taken.

The powerful and moving thing about this tiny, tiny point of light is that every living thing that we know of that has ever existed in the history of the Universe has lived out its life on that pixel, on a pale blue dot hanging against the blackness of space.

As the great astronomer Carl Sagan wrote:

'It has been said that astronomy is a humbling and character-building experience. There is perhaps no better demonstration of the folly of human conceits than this distant image of our tiny world. To me, it underscores our responsibility to deal more kindly with one another, and to preserve and cherish the pale blue dot, the only home we've ever known.'

Just as we, and all life on Earth, stand on this tiny speck adrift in infinite space, so life in the Universe will only exist for a fleeting, dazzling instant in infinite time, because life, just like the stars, is a temporary structure on the long road from order to disorder.

But that doesn't make us insignificant, because life is the means by which the Universe can understand itself, if only for an instant. This is what we've done in our brief moments on Earth: we have sent space probes to the edge of our solar system and beyond; we have built telescopes that can glimpse the oldest and most distant stars, and we have discovered and understood at least some of the natural laws that govern the cosmos. This, ultimately, is why I believe we are important. Our true significance lies in our continuing desire to understand and explore this beautiful Universe – our magnificent, beautiful, fleeting home ◉

'Somewhere, something incredible is waiting to be known'

– Carl Sagan, 1934–1996

INDEX

Entries in *italics* indicate photographs and images

B

D

E

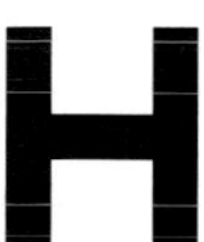

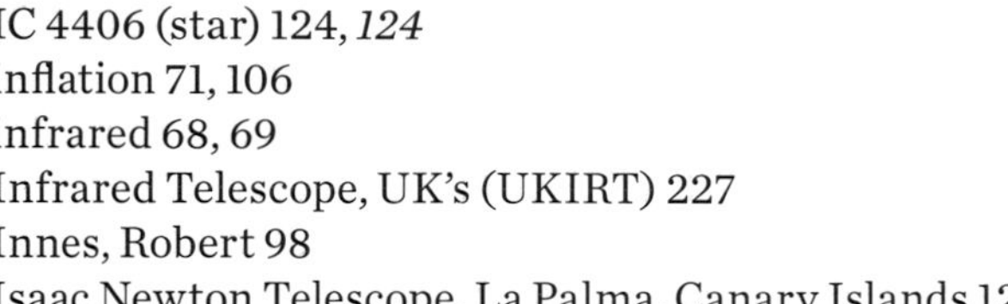

N

P

S

T

U

V

W

Z

PICTURE CREDITS

The authors and publisher would like to thank Burrell Durrant Hifle for all the CGI images and for their help with the project as well as Jon Murray at UNIT for his help.

All pictures are copyright of the BBC except:

22–23, 62–63, 88–89, 108–109, 110–111, 128–129, 196–197, 206–207, 222–223, 232–233 Nathalie Lees © HarperCollins; 24, 25, 26, 27, 29 (bottom), 30, 37, 41, 49, 51, 52, 53, 54, 61, 67, 69 (bottom), 70, 74–75, 76, 83, 84, 85, 96, 97, 120, 124, 125, 132, 133 (bottom), 138, 141, 142, 143, 149 (top), 155 (bottom), 161, 167, 169, 176, 180, 181, 184, 191, 198, 227, 231, 235, 238, 239 (left), 240 (left) NASA; 34 GIPHOTOSTOCK / SCIENCE PHOTO LIBRARY; 39 © Scott Smith/Corbis; 45 © JASON REED/Reuters/CORBIS; 48 (left) PASCAL GOETGHELUCK / SCIENCE PHOTO LIBRARY; 48 (right) AlltheSky.com; 79 DAVID PARKER / SCIENCE PHOTO LIBRARY; 87 ECKHARD SLAWIK / SCIENCE PHOTO LIBRARY; 93 (bottom) DIRK WIERSMA / SCIENCE PHOTO LIBRARY; 94–95 © 2010 Theodore Gray; 103 © Charles O'Rear/ CORBIS; 107 CERN / SCIENCE PHOTO LIBRARY; 115 US DEPARTMENT OF ENERGY / SCIENCE PHOTO LIBRARY; 119 © Tony Hallas/Science Faction/Corbis; 146– 147 © NASA/Corbis; 148 NASA / SCIENCE PHOTO LIBRARY; 149 (bottom) Caltech; 151 ERICH SCHREMPP / SCIENCE PHOTO LIBRARY; 156–157 ESA / DLR / FU BERLIN (G.NEUKUM) / SCIENCE PHOTO LIBRARY; 164–165 © Tony Hallas/Science Faction/Corbis; 170–171 John Dubinski; 173 B. MCNAMARA (UNIVERSITY OF WATERLOO) / NASA / ESA/ STScI / SCIENCE PHOTO LIBRARY; 174–175 © Roger Ressmeyer/CORBIS; 183 MARTIN BOND / SCIENCE PHOTO LIBRARY; 186–187 SCIENCE PHOTO LIBRARY; 188 ROYAL ASTRONOMICAL SOCIETY / SCIENCE PHOTO LIBRARY; 194 NASA / SCIENCE PHOTO LIBRARY; 209 SCIENCE PHOTO LIBRARY; 215 SCIENCE, INDUSTRY & BUSINESS LIBRARY / NEW YORK PUBLIC LIBRARY / SCIENCE PHOTO LIBRARY; 242-243 © CORBIS.

ACKNOWLEDGEMENTS

In writing this book we'd like to thank all of those who were involved in the BBC television production of *Wonders of the Universe*. We'd especially like to thank Jonathan Renouf and James van der Pool for their commitment and dedication to the series and Stephen Cooter, Michael Lachmann and Chris Holt for transforming such complex content into beautiful television.

We'd like to thank, Rebecca Edwards, Diana Ellis-Hill, Laura Mulholland, Ben Wilson, Kevin White, George McMillan, Chris Openshaw, Darren Jonusas, Peter Norrey, Simon Sykes, Suzie Brand, Louise Salkow, Laura Davey, Paul Appleton, Sheridan Tongue, Julie Wilkinson, Laetitia Ducom , Lydia Delmonte, Daisy Newman, Jane Rundle, Nicola Kingham and the team at BDH and Unit post production.

We'd like to thank Sue Ryder, Professor Jeff Forshaw, Myles Archibald and all the team at Harper Collins for their help and guidance.

We'd like to thank Kevin White for his outstanding photography on location.

Brian would like to thank The University of Manchester and The Royal Society for allowing him the time to make *Wonders*.

Andrew would like to thank Anna for her endless support in the writing of this book.

William Collins
An imprint of HarperCollins*Publishers*
1 London Bridge Street
London SE1 9GF
WilliamCollinsBooks.com

This combined edition first published in Great Britain by
William Collins in 2015

As an exclusive edition for W H Smith

This combined edition previously published in two separate volumes as:

Wonders of the Solar System and *Wonders of the Universe*

Wonders of the Solar System first published by Collins, an imprint of
HarperCollins*Publishers*, in 2010.

Wonders of the Universe first published by Collins, an imprint of
HarperCollins*Publishers*, in 2011.

By arrangement with the BBC.

21 20 19 18 17 16
10 9 8 7 6 5 4 3 2

A catalogue record for this book is
available from the British Library.

ISBN 978-0-00-795006-5

Colour reproduction by FMG
Printed and bound in China.